3/04

The Auditory Culture Reader

SENSORY FORMATIONS

· ·

Series Editor: David Howes

- ■ What is the world like to cultures that privilege touch or smell over sight or hearing?
- ■ Do men's and women's sensory experiences differ?
- ■ What lies beyond the aesthetic gaze?
- ■ Who says money has no smell?
- ■ How has the proliferation of 'taste cultures' resulted in new forms of social discrimination?
- ■ How is the sixth sense to be defined?
- ■ What is the future of the senses in cyberspace?

From the Ancient Greeks to medieval mystics and eighteenth-century empiricists, Karl Marx to Marshall McLuhan, the senses have been the subject of dramatic proclamations. Senses are sources of pleasure and pain, knowledge and power. Sites of intense personal experience, they are also fields of extensive cultural elaboration. Yet surprisingly, it is only recently that scholars in the humanities and social sciences have turned their full attention to sensory experience and expression as a subject for enquiry.

This path-breaking series aims to show how the 'sensual revolution' has supplanted both the linguistic and the pictorial turns in the human sciences to generate a new field – *sensual culture*, where all manner of disciplines converge. Its objective is to enhance our understanding of the role of the senses in history, culture and aesthetics, by redressing an imbalance: the hegemony of vision and privileging of discourse in contemporary theory and cultural studies must be overthrown in order to reveal the role all senses play in mediating cultural experience. The extraordinary richness and diversity of the social and material worlds, as constituted through touch, taste, smell, hearing, sight and, pro-vocatively, the sixth sense, are addressed in the volumes of this series as follows:*

Empire of the Senses: The Sensual Culture Reader (Ed. David Howes) documents the sensual revolution in the humanities and social sciences, and reclaims sensation as a domain for cultural inquiry.

The Auditory Culture Reader (Eds Michael Bull & Les Back) articulates a strategy of 'deep listening' – a powerful new methodology for making sense of the social.

The Smell Culture Reader (Ed. Jim Drobnick) foregrounds the most marginalized, and potentially subversive, sense of modernity, in addition to sampling how diverse cultures scent the universe.

The Book of Touch (Ed. Constance Classen) maps the tactile contours of culture, exploring the powerful and often inarticulate world of touch, the most basic of our senses.

The Taste Culture Reader (Ed. Carolyn Korsmeyer) serves up a savoury stew of cultural analysis, blending together the multiple senses of the term 'taste'.

The Alternative Visual Culture Reader (Eds Elizabeth Edwards & Kaushik Bhaumik) explores and interrogates the multiplicity of scopic regimes within and without the Western tradition.

The Sixth Sense Reader (Ed. David Howes) asks: What lies beyond the bounds of sense? Is the sixth sense ESP, electromagnetic sensitivity, intuition, revelation, gut instinct or simply unfathomable?

* Full publication details are available from the publishers, Berg, 1st Floor, Angel Court, 81 St Clements Street, Oxford OX4 1AW, UK; or consult http://www.bergpublishers.com

The Auditory Culture Reader

Edited by

MICHAEL BULL AND LES BACK

Sensory Formations Series   Oxford • New York

First published in 2003 by
Berg
Editorial offices:
1st Floor, Angel Court, 81 St Clements Road, Oxford OX4 1AW, UK
838 Broadway, Third Floor, New York, NY 10003-4812, USA

Berg is the imprint of Oxford International Publishers Ltd.

Library of Congress Cataloging-in-Publication Data

The auditory culture reader / edited by Michael Bull and Les Back.
        p. cm. — (Sensory formations series)
Includes bibliographical references and index.
     ISBN 1-85973-613-0 (cloth) — ISBN 1-85973-618-1 (pbk.)
    1. Hearing. 2. Listening. 3. Audiology. 4. Senses and sensation.
I. Bull, Michael, 1952– II. Back, Les, 1962– III. Series.
GN275.A83 2003
306.4—dc22

                                                            2003022159

British Library Cataloguing-in-Publication Data

A catalogue record for this book is available from the British Library.

ISBN 1 85973 613 0 (Cloth)
        1 85973 618 1 (Paper)

Typeset by JS Typesetting Ltd, Wellingborough, Northants.
Printed in the United Kingdom by Biddles Ltd, Kings Lynn.

www.bergpublishers.com

To my son, Theo, who was born in the final
stages of preparing this volume and whose
sounds bring light into my day. M.B.

For my dear friend Ron Warshow, a great
musician and listener – the best tuned
ears I know. L.B.

Contents

Notes on Contributors   xi

Acknowledgements   xvii

Introduction: Into Sound
Michael Bull and Les Back   1

Part I: Thinking about Sound

1   Open Ears
         Murray Schafer   25

2   Hearing Loss
         Leigh Eric Schmidt   41

3   Auditory Imagination
         Don Ihde   61

4   The Help of Your Good Hands: Reports on Clapping
         Steven Connor   67

5   The Sound of Music
         Douglas Kahn   77

6   Songtime: Sound Culture, Rhythm and Sociality
         Paul Filmer   91

Part II: Histories of Sound

7   The Auditory Markers of the Village
Alain Corbin   117

8   Tuning into London c.1600
Bruce R. Smith   127

9   Listening to the Heard Worlds of Antebellum America
Mark M. Smith   137

10 The Diabolical Symphony of the Mechanical Age:
Technology and Symbolism of Sound in European
and North American Noise Abatement Campaigns,
1900–40
Karin Bijsterveld   165

11 Medicine's Acoustic Culture: Mediate Auscultation, the
Stethoscope and the 'Autopsy of the Living'
Jonathan Sterne   191

Part III: Anthropologies of Sound

12 A Rainforest Acoustemology
Steven Feld   223

13 Performing Patriotism in Native North America: Ojibwa
Powwow-sounds and the Paradoxes of Identity
Cora Bender   241

14 Sectarian Sound and Cultural Identity in Northern
Ireland
Paul Moore   265

15 Nostalgia and Radio Sound
Jo Tacchi   281

Part IV: Sounds in the City

16 Aural Postcards: Sound, Memory and the City
Fran Tonkiss   303

17 Sounds in the Crowd
Les Back   311

18 The Sonic Composition of the City
Jean-Paul Thibaud   329

19 How Many Movements?
Caroline Bassett   343

20 Soundscapes of the Car: A Critical Study of Automobile
Habitation
Michael Bull   357

Part V: Living and Thinking with Music

21 Between the Blues and the Blues Dance: Some Soundscapes
of the Black Atlantic
Paul Gilroy   381

22 Diasporic Sounds: Dis/Located Sounds
Vic Seidler   397

23 The Sounds of Alterity
Sanjay Sharma   409

24 Calypso Kings
Stuart Hall   419

25 Bessie Smith: 'Thinking Blues'
Susan McClary   427

26 'Chatting' for Change!: Interview with William
(Lez) Henry   435

27 Sonic Dominance and the Reggae Sound System Session
Julian Henriques   451

28 Resistance
Richard Sennett   481

Afterword

The Indefensible Ear: A History
Hillel Schwartz   487

Index   503

Contributors

Les Back teaches sociology and urban studies at Goldsmiths College, London. His recent books include *Out of Whiteness: Colour, Politics and Culture* (Chicago: University of Chicago Press, 2002) and *The Changing Face of Football: Racism and Multiculture in the English Game* (Oxford: Berg, 2001).

Caroline Bassett works in the Department of Media and Cultural Studies at the University of Sussex. She is currently writing on narrative and new media, and is also working on cybernetics.

Cora Bender, a social/cultural anthropologist, is a member of the Special Research College 'Knowledge Cultures and Change in Society' at the J. W. Goethe University, Frankfurt am Main, Germany, where she is completing an ethnographic research project about contemporary Native American media. She is also co-editing an essay collection about Aby Warburg's *Snake Dance* (with E. Schuettpelz and T. Hensel).

Karin Bijsterveld is historian and associate professor at the Technology and Society Studies Department, University of Maastricht, Netherlands. She has published on the history of old age in the *Journal of Family History* and elsewhere. With Wiebe Bijker she is author of 'Woman Walking Through Plans' in *Technology and Culture* (July 2000, awarded the Usher Prize in 2002). Her current research focuses on the history of noise and on technology and music, the key topics of her publications in *Social Studies of Science* (February 2001), *Technology and Music in the 20th Century* (ed. Hans-Joachim Braun, Baltimore: John Hopkins University Press, 2002), *Technology and Culture* (with Trevor Pinch, July 2003, forthcoming), and *Osiris* (July 2003, forthcoming).

Michael Bull teaches in the School of Social and Cultural Sciences at the University of Sussex. He is the author of *Sounding Out the City. Personal Stereos and the Management of Everyday Life* (Oxford: Berg, 2000) as well as many articles on sound technologies and their use. He is currently writing *Mobilising the Social: Sound, Technology and the City* for Routledge.

Steven Connor is Professor of Modern Literature and Theory at Birkbeck College, London. He is a writer and broadcaster for radio as well as the author of books on Dickens, Beckett, Joyce and postwar British fiction, as well as *Postmodern Culture* (Oxford: Blackwell, 1989, second edition 1996), *Theory and Cultural Value* (Oxford: Blackwell, 1992) and *Dumstruck: A Cultural History of Ventriloquism* (Oxford: Oxford University Press, 2000). *The Book of Skin* will appear from Reaktion Books in 2003. Many other unpublished papers, broadcasts and lectures are to be found on his Web site at www.bbk.ac.uk/eh.skc/.

Alain Corbin is Professor of Contemporary History at the Sorbonne. He is the author of numerous books including *The Foul and the Fragrant* (Cambridge MA: Harvard University Press, 1988); *The Lure of the Sea* (Cambridge MA: Harvard University Press, 1996); *Village Cannibals: Rage and Murder in France, 1870* (Cambridge MA: Harvard University Press, 1993); *Women for Hire: Prostitution and Sexuality in France after 1850* (Harmondsworth: Penguin, 1995); and *Village Bells: Sound and Meaning in the 19th-Century French Countryside* (New York: Columbia University Press, 1998).

Steven Feld is Professor of Music and Anthropology at the University of Columbia. He is the author of *Sound and Sentiment* (Philadelphia: University of Pennsylvania Press, second edition 1990) and *Music Grooves* (with Charles Keil, Chicago: University of Chicago Press, 1994).

Paul Filmer is Senior Lecturer of Sociology at Goldsmiths College. He has recently contributed to *Researching Society and Culture* edited by Clive Seale (London: Sage, 2003) and to *Core Sociological Dichotomies* edited by Chris Jenks (London: Sage, 2003).

Paul Gilroy is Professor of Sociology and African-American studies at Yale University. He is the author of *There Ain't No Black in the Union Jack* (Chicago: University of Chicago Press, 1991); *The Black Atlantic* (Cambridge MA: Harvard University Press, 1995); *Small Acts: Thoughts on the*

Politics of Black Cultures (London: Serpent's Tail, 1994) and *Between Camps* (Harmondsworth: Penguin, 2000). Paul Gilroy is widely recognized for his critical commentaries on black music and vernacular culture. His work has been translated into ten languages.

Stuart Hall was for a decade Director of the Centre for Cultural Studies, Birmingham, where he edited and co-authored such volumes as *Resistance through Ritual* (London: Routledge 1989), *Policing the Crises* (London: Routledge 1981) and *Culture, Media, Language* (Routledge 1980). He was until recently Professor of Sociology at the Open University; among his recent publications are *The Hard Road to Renewal: Thatcherism and the Crises of the Left* (London, Verso 1988) and the co-edited volumes *New Times* (London: Lawrence and Wishart, 1989), *Modernity and its Futures* (Cambridge: Polity Press, 1992), *Representation: Cultural Representations and Signifying Practices* (London: Sage, 1997) and *Visual Culture: The Reader* (London: Sage, 1999).

Julian Henriques has made documentaries for London Weekend Television, the BBC and Channel 4 Television. *We the Ragamuffin* was his first short film and *Babymother* his first feature film as writer and director. He was Senior Lecturer in film and television at the University of the West Indies, Kingston, Jamaica and is currently convenor of the MA script writing programme at Goldsmiths College. With others he authored *Changing the Subject: Psychology, Social Regulation and Subject-ivity* (New York: Routledge, 1998) and was a founding editor of the journal *Ideology and Consciousness*.

Les Henry is both a sociologist and dancehall DJ.

Don Ihde is Distinguished Professor of Philosophy at Stony Brook University in New York. He is the author of thirteen books, including *Listening and Voice: A Phenomenology of Sound* (Athens OH: Ohio University Press, 1974). His phenomenological work has focused upon perception with auditory and visual analysis, samples of which may be found in *Consequences of Phenomenology* (New York: State University of New York, 1986), *Experimental Phenomenology* (New York: State University of New York, 1986), and *Expanding Hermeneutics: Visualism in Science* (Chicago: Northwestern University, 1999). His most recent book is *Bodies in Technology* (Minneapolis: University of Minnesota Press, 2001), which examines the role of embodiment and technologies.

Douglas Kahn is the inaugural director of the Program in Techno-cultural Studies and Professor of Art History at the University of California at Davis. He writes on the history and theory of sound in the arts from modernism to the present, auditory culture, art and technology, and contemporary media arts. He is the author of *Noise, Water, Meat: A History of Sound in the Arts* (Cambridge MA: MIT Press, 1999) and co-editor of *Wireless Imagination: Sound, Radio and the Avant-garde* (Cambridge MA: MIT Press, 1992).

Susan McClary is Professor of Musicology at the University of California, Los Angeles, and author of *Feminine Endings: Music, Gender and Sexuality* (Minneapolis: University of Minnesota Press, 1991), *Georges Bizet: Carmen* (Cambridge: Cambridge University Press, 1992) and *Conventional Wisdom: The Content of Musical Form* (Berkeley and Los Angeles: University of California Press, 2000).

Paul Moore teaches media studies at the University of Ulster.

R. Murray Schafer is an internationally renowned composer and writer of many books including *The Tuning of the World* (London: Random House, 1977).

Leigh E. Schmidt is Professor of Religion at Princeton University. His books include *Hearing Things* (Harvard: Harvard University Press, 2000); *Consumer Rites* (Princeton: Princeton University Press, 1995), and *Holy Fairs* (Princeton: Princeton University Press, 1989). He is currently working on a project on the cultural history of American spirituality, which takes account of the history of solitude and silence, among other things. It is forthcoming from Harper, San Francisco.

Hillel Schwartz is a cultural historian at work on a cultural history of noise. He was, until recently, Director of the core curriculum for a new college at University College San Diego, Sixth College: Culture, Art, and Technology. Among his publications as poet, playwright and historian is *The Culture of the Copy: Striking Likeness, Unreasonable Facsimiles* (New York: Zone/MIT, 1996).

Vic Seidler is Professor of Sociology at Goldsmiths College, University of London. He is the author of *Shadows of the Shoah* (Oxford: Berg, 2000); *Man Enough, Embodying Masculinity* (London: Routledge, 1997) and *Recovering the Self: Morality and Social Theory* (London: Routledge, 1995).

Richard Sennett is Professor of Sociology at New York University and the London School of Economics. He is President of the American Council of Work and is the internationally acclaimed author of *The Fall of Public Man* (New York: Norton, 1992), *The Conscience of the Eye* (New York: Norton, 1992), *Flesh and Stone* (New York: Norton, 1996), *The Corrosion of Character* (New York: Norton, 2000) and most recently *Respect in a World of Inequality* (New York: Norton, 2003).

Sanjay Sharma teaches in the School of Cultural and Innovative Studies, University of East London. He is a co-editor *of Dis-Orienting Rhythms: The Politics of New Asian Dance Music* (London: Zed Books, 1996) and current research interests include multicultural praxis, critical pedagogy and the politics of alterity.

Bruce R. Smith is Professor of English at Georgetown University. He is author of *Homosexual Desire in Shakespeare's England: A Cultural Poetics* (Chicago: University of Chicago Press, 1991) and *The Acoustic World of Early Modern Britain* (Chicago: University of Chicago Press, 1999).

Mark M. Smith is Professor of History at the University of South Carolina. He is author of *Mastered by the Clock: Time, Slavery, and Freedom in the American South* (Chapel Hill NC: University of North Carolina Press, 1997), *Debating Slavery: Economy and Society in the Antebellum American South* (Cambridge: Cambridge University Press, 1998) and, most recently, *Listening to Nineteenth-Century America* (Chapel Hill NC: University of North Carolina Press, 2001). He is currently working on a book tentatively entitled *Sensing Race: From Slavery to Integration in the American South*.

Jonathan Sterne teaches in the Department of Communication and the Program for Cultural Studies at the University of Pittsburgh. He is the author of *The Audible Past: Cultural Origins of Sound Reproduction* (Durham NC: Duke University Press, 2003) and has written widely on sound, media, culture and politics. He is also an editor of the online 'zine, *Bad Subjects: Political Education for Everyday Life* (www.badsubjects.org).

Jo Tacchi is a social anthropologist specializing in the anthropology of the media. Jo is a Research Fellow in the Creative Industries Research and Applications Centre (CIRAC) at Queensland University of Technology (QUT) and a Visiting Fellow at the Oxford Internet Institute. Jo has conducted research on radio and new technologies in the UK,

Australia, South Asia and South Africa. She has established a Creative Industries Streaming Studio within CIRAC for the development of online research and applications, including Internet radio sites (see emit.qut. com).

Jean-Paul Thibaud is a sociologist who is currently a researcher at the CNRS (Centre National de la Recherche Scientific – National Centre of Scientific Research) in the Cresson Laboratory (Centre de Recherche Sonore et l'Environment Urbain – Centre for Sonic Space and Urban Environment). The laboratory is located at the School of Architecture in Grenoble. His main research areas concern 'sociability in public spaces', 'theories of action and situated perception' and most recently 'urban ambiences'.

Fran Tonkiss teaches in the Department of Sociology at Goldsmiths College, University of London. She works in the fields of urban and economic sociology and her publications in these areas include *Trust and Civil Society* (Basingstoke: Macmillan, 2000); *Market Society* (with Don Slater, Cambridge: Polity, 2001), and *Space, the City and Social Theory* (London: Sage, 2002).

Acknowledgements

We would like to thank Kathryn Earle of Berg Publishers for her patience and faith in the project. Compiling this book has been a long task and the truth is we've had more fun thinking, talking and planning it than is probably allowed. The fact that many of these discussions took place by the sea in assorted tea shops on the Brighton seafront didn't help matters. We hope that some of the excitement of those discussions comes through in the pages that follow. We would also like to thank the contributors for their commitment and enthusiasm. The quality of the writing speaks for itself but we are very grateful to them for allowing us to include their work in this reader. Our families have been patient and Michael would like to thank Ros for her enduring and endearing support whilst pregnant and beyond and Les sends his love and thanks to Debbie and Stevie, Sophie and Charlie. There are a number of people we would like to name individually for help and/or inspiration. Our deepest thanks to Ron Warshow, Tom Rice, Michael Keith, Paul Moody, Pete Merchant, Ben Gidley, Paul Halliday, John Welch, Hiroki Ogasawara, Michael E. Stone and Douglas Kahn.

Introduction: Into Sound

Michael Bull and Les Back

> For twenty-five centuries Western knowledge has tried to look upon the
> world. It has failed to understand that the world is not for beholding. It
> is for hearing . . . Now we must learn to judge a society by its noise.
>
> (Jacques Attali)

What are the senses of sense? Jacques Attali points out that the dominant mode of apprehending and understanding society has been through
staring at its spectacle. Scopic metaphors are routinely invoked when
thinking about how and what it is we know. In these terms knowledge
is a quest for 'enlightenment' or 'illumination' and understanding is
identified with *seeing*. Yet the experience of everyday life is increasingly
mediated by a multitude of mechanically reproduced sounds. Waking,
walking, driving, working and even falling asleep are all done to music,
or some other acoustic accompaniment. In parallel to this, cities are
noisier than they ever were in the past and more people complain about
levels of noise than ever before. Noise tests our sense of the social to
the limit. Sound thus has both utopian and dystopian associations: it
enables individuals to create intimate, manageable and aestheticized
spaces to inhabit but it can also become an unwanted and deafening
roar threatening the body politic of the subject.

In the hierarchy of the senses, the epistemological status of hearing
has come a poor second to that of vision. In this volume Bruce Smith
argues that 'knowing the world through sound is fundamentally
different from knowing the world through vision'. The dominance of
the visual has often meant that the experience of the other senses –

touch, taste, smell and listening – has been filtered through a visualist framework. The reduction of knowledge to the visual has placed serious limitations on our ability to grasp the meanings attached to much social behaviour, be it contemporary, historical or comparative. Joachim-Ernst Berendt in his extraordinary book, *The Third Ear,* argues that the dominance of 'The Eye' limits our imagination and he suggests that human experience can only be accounted for through what he calls a 'a democracy of the senses' (Berendt 1985: 32). This volume is dedicated to a similar aspiration – toward broadening the senses of sense. Thinking with our ears offers an opportunity to augment our critical imaginations, to comprehend our world and our encounters with it according to multiple registers of feeling.

Thinking within a 'democracy of the senses' means that no sense is privileged in relation to its counterparts. Indeed, the kind of sensory democracy that we are proposing enables traces of the past to be registered in the present beyond what might be thought on first sight. The attack on the World Trade Centre on 11 September 2001 was experienced as a global event in real time. What is significant is that the attacks were witnessed visually and endlessly replayed on camera via television and in cyberspace. It was something that was *seen.* Now the date itself has come to signify the quality of what happened on that bright New York morning as well as signalling the start of an epoch. Clifford Geertz wrote:

> It is always very difficult to determine just when it was that 'now' began. Virginia Woolf thought it was 'on or about December 1, 1910,' for W. H. Auden it was 'September 1, 1939,' for many of us who worried our way through the balance of terror, it was 1989 and the Fall of the Wall. And now, having survived all that, there is September 11, 2001. (Geertz 2002: 13)

The mediated forms of visual witness facilitated through Sky and CNN filtered the human cost and devastation: TV screens acted like a sensory prophylactic.

Pilgrimages to the wreckage at ground zero invariably involved the taking of photographs, snapped like souvenirs reminiscent of the plucking of pieces of the Berlin Wall after its fall. The vulgar exhibitionism of Ground Zero tourism reached such proportions that, a month after the attacks, photography was prohibited at the site. Darryl Pinckney wrote 'So many were bearing witness on camera. . . But we couldn't know the smell. People downtown were still saying weeks later

that the dogs made it impossible to forget the dead were a presence,
that the waste remained' (Pinckney 2001: 12). This is a solemn reminder
of the limits of visual, and for that matter, auditory forms of representation.

This book is primarily concerned with sound but we do not want to
supplant one 'primary sense' with another. Rather, our book is about
moving into sound and the opportunities provided by thinking with
our ears. As Richard Sennett points out in this volume, it is difficult to
separate out our senses, so the sounds produced through the musician's
art are products of his or her sense of touch and feel – 'lips applied to
reed, fingers pushing down on keys or strings'. The volume presents
twenty-nine different takes on what it is to know the world through
sound.

We have taken the disparate threads of an ever-expanding field of
writing on the social nature and meaning of sound and brought them
together to produce this *Auditory Culture Reader*. Contributors come from
the fields of sociology, cultural studies, media studies, anthropology,
cultural history, philosophy, urban geography and musicology. The aim
of the volume is to put the study of the auditory soundly on the agenda
of these academic disciplines and at the same time provide an integrated
picture of what sound studies should 'look' like; just as sound is no
respecter of space, so sound studies transgress academic divisions.
Furthermore, the volume aims to counter the assumed supremacy of
the 'visual' in accounts of the social. In doing so we do not try to displace the visual but rather point to the equally crucial role that sound
plays in our experience and understanding of the world. In short, we
claim that a visually based epistemology is both insufficient and often
erroneous in its description, analysis and thus understanding of the
social world.

The volume provides a comparative template for, in Steven Feld's
words, the production of an acoustemology by investigating 'the
primacy of sound as a modality of knowing and being in the world'.
In this introduction we propose a set of concerns through which to filter
'sound' studies. This is neither a literature review in the conventional
sense nor a manifesto. Rather, we would like the following to be read
as a series of provocations towards *deep listening*. The kind of listening
we envision is not straightforward, not self-evident – it is not easy
listening. Rather, we have to work toward what might be called agile
listening and this involves attuning our ears to listen again to the
multiple layers of meaning potentially embedded in the same sound.
More than this, deep listening involves practices of dialogue and

procedures for investigation, transposition and interpretation. Echoing these methodological concerns, the ensuing account of the contours of 'sound' studies is presented in the form of a series of aphoristic reflections on how the world presents itself when we listen to rather than look upon it.

What is at Stake in Deep Listening?

- Sound makes us re-think the meaning, nature and significance of our social experience.
- Sound makes us re-think our relation to community.
- Sound makes us re-think our relational experiences, how we relate to others, ourselves and the spaces and places we inhabit.
- Sound makes us re-think our relationship to power.

Unsound Objectivity

The philosopher Thomas Nagel (1986) defined objectivity as 'the view from nowhere'. Pure objectivity forgets the subjective mechanisms through which we experience the world. For Nagel this implied that the 'looker' takes no account of the eyes through which the look operated. To adopt an objective point of view is to look upon the world as if one wasn't there. The effort to clear away the subjective in the pursuit of pure, disembodied knowledge has a long heritage in visually based epistemologies ranging from Plato through Descartes down to the present. Bourdieu was thinking of the dangers leading from this objectivist illusion when commenting:

> How can one avoid succumbing to this dream of omnipotence? I think it important above all to reflect not only on the limits of thought and of the powers of thought, but also on the conditions in which it is exercised, which lead so many thinkers to overstep the limits of a social experience that is necessarily partial and local, both geographically and socially. (Bourdieu 2000: 2)

Bourdieu is not merely criticizing the proclivity of academics to universalize from particular experiences; he is talking about the failure to recognize the particular in social investigation. Both the impetuses to objectify and to universalize appear to be rooted in the historical ascendancy of visual epistemologies in Western culture. Of the five senses, vision is the most 'distancing' one. In vision, subject and object 'appear' as transparent. Implied in the objectification of the world through sight is the control of that world. Yet if, as Bishop Berkeley notes, 'sounds are as close to us as our thoughts' then by listening we may be able to perceive the relationship between subject and object, inside and outside, and the public and private altogether differently. In its engulfing multi-directionality sound blurs the above distinctions and enables us to re-think our relationship to them.

Walls have Ears

Accounts of surveillance often begin with Foucault's description of Bentham's panopticon. Bentham designed his perfect prison as one in which the inmates were always visible to the guardians of the institution. The panopticon becomes a metaphor for the transparency of vision. However, Foucault's description presents only part of the picture, the uncritical embracing of which represents the reading of the past through the epistemological lens of the present. We tend to see what we want to see! Bentham's prison was also a listening prison in which, through a series of tubes, the inmates could be heard at all times. Just as God is supposed to hear our prayers (Schafer, in this volume), so the state may now hear our mobile phone calls. Indeed, there is an element of everyday surveillance associated with both domestic and business use of the mobile phone. The history of surveillance is as much a sound history as a history of vision.

Just as we need a sound history of surveillance, so we need to recognize that the senses cannot be 'looked' at in abstraction or isolation. Parents invariably felt more secure in observing the wellbeing of their children without the intrusion of their 'spontaneous' noises of pleasure. The noise of children playing might well destroy the illusion of parental supremacy: who's in charge anyway? Yet the notion that 'children should be seen and not heard' has now been largely super-seded by the ever-attentive 'child monitor' left as closely to the child as possible whilst the parent is free to roam the house at will. Parents now wish to hear their child at all times – the sound of breathing ensuring their security. So today it might be more accurate to say that 'children shall be heard and not seen!'

Sound Structures

We regulate space and time through our use of sound. In this volume Corbin describes the daily regulation of life through the ringing of the village bell in French communes in the nineteenth century. Moore investigates the structuring of the year through the seasonal marching of Protestants in Northern Ireland. Tacchi describes the privatized 'affective rhythms of the home' through radio listening in Britain. Thibauld describes the stepping out to music through Walkman use in urban France. The polyphony of sounds increasingly regulates and is regulated by us as we move through daily life. The historical and comparative significance of this structuring process has yet to be adequately investigated.

Sound connects us in ways that vision does not. Music has been described as a 'mutual tuning in relationship' (Schutz in Filmer in this volume). Paul Gilroy in this volume cites Bloch's observation that 'a note of music comes with us and is "we" unlike the visual, which is primarily, an "I" divorced from the "other"'. Elsewhere in this volume Susan McClary quotes John Coltrane as saying, 'the audience heard "we" even if the singer said "I"'.

This we-ness in music is also central in Adorno's analysis of the reception of music in the twentieth century. For Adorno, states of 'we-ness' or 'being with', refer to the eclipse of direct experience by technologically mediated forms of experience in the twentieth century. For Adorno, we are alone together through sound reception. The nature and meaning of being tuned in needs further investigation in cultures that possess mobile phones, Walkmans, radios and the ubiquitous sound system of the automobile.

Passive Ears

Historically the ears have often been portrayed as helpless, they let every noise in indiscriminately, but Schwartz in this volume makes a good case for the intentionality of listening and forms of auditory discrimination. Recently technology has come to the aid of the ears. Walkman users can now filter out the random sounds of the street to be replaced by the chosen sounds of the user. Power to the ear?

What do we listen to? Schafer argues in this volume that we increasingly fail to listen to the natural sounds of the world and that this inattention could have dire consequences. The assumed decline in listening has a long intellectual history. Sometimes it is taken to mean that we don't know how to listen, as in Adorno's prognosis of music reception in the twentieth century. Alternatively, notions of decline fit in with assumptions about the rise of the visual in culture. In essence it means, as we look more, we hear less. Schmidt, in this volume, traces the development of visually based theories deriving from the European

Enlightenment and furthered in the work of Walter Ong and Marshall McLuhan. Within this schema, orally based cultures were progressively supplanted by print-based cultures, and the world became increasingly 'silent' as sight (reading) replaced speech. Yet Hillel Schwartz argues persuasively that the aural rather than the visual was most significant between 1870–1914 with the invention and development of loud artillery, telephone, gramophone, the radio, loudspeaker, subway, elevator and so forth. Beware of listening to the past through contemporary eyes.

Dangerous Sounds

> The allurement of the Sirens remains superior; no one who hears their song can escape.
>
> (Max Horkheimer and Theodor Adorno)

Sound and its reception are infused with cultural values. Just as sight is understood in terms of scopophilia, so sound has its own narrative of desire. In the *Dialectic of Enlightenment,* Horkheimer and Adorno analyse the passage from Homer's Odyssey in which Odysseus pits his wits against the Sirens whose song evokes 'the recent past, with the irresistible promise of pleasure as which their song is heard'. Even though the Sirens know all that has happened, they demand the future as the price of that knowledge (Horkheimer and Adorno 1972). All who hear the song perish. Odysseus' aim is to outwit the Sirens by having himself tied to the mast of his ship thereby enabling him to listen to the enticements of the Sirens' song without being destroyed on the rocks as all others had who sought to have their desires fulfilled. For his strategy to succeed the oarsmen of his ship have their ears blocked with wax, rendering them deaf. The oarsmen are unable to hear both the Sirens' song and Odysseus' increasingly desperate orders to steer the ship onto the rocks. Horkheimer and Adorno discuss this passage in terms of a dialectic in which myth, domination and work are intertwined. Odysseus' desire for pleasure is sublimated into aesthetic experience; he can hear but do nothing about it. If Odysseus experiences the Sirens' song, he gains knowledge of all that can be known. The Sirens' song literally enters Odysseus. As Odysseus listens, tied safely to the mast of his ship, the Sirens' song transforms the distance between his ship and the rocks from which they sing their beguiling song. Their song colonizes him whilst he uses this experience to fulfil his own desires. Aesthetic reflection is a price worth paying for gaining the seductive experience of song. Only Odysseus hears, the oarsmen continue to row in silence. It is the Sirens who construct Odysseus' soundscape. Yet through his cunning he transforms the nature of this soundscape by having the oarsmen's ears blocked with wax. The soundscape now encompasses only Odysseus and the Sirens; it exists only between him and them. Socially speaking, Odysseus is in his very own soundworld. This passage from Homer becomes the first description of the privatization of experience through sound.

Odysseus is also a traveller who makes himself through his journey. He outwits the Sirens and in doing so furthers his self-development. Odysseus becomes an early tourist of experience whose experience becomes aestheticized. The Sirens form an aesthetic presence in his biography, representing, in part, the draw of the 'exotic' and the forbidden as encountered in his travels and mastered through his intellect. Odysseus becomes an early 'tourist' of experiences (Todorov 1993). Western narratives of sound are associated with dominance, exoticism and Orientalism.

Sound Progress

New technologies of sound give us as much sound as we want. Sound consumerables of the home permit us to recreate the cinema in our living rooms with the advent of digital wrap-around sound for our television sets. Home hi-fi units had already achieved this for our favourite sounds. Privatization and individualism have increasingly divided the home into multiple listening (and watching) nodules. We sit contentedly in our pulsating homes as sound becomes more like the 'real thing'. Domestic architecture has not yet caught up with this acoustic explosion. As our living spaces become smaller and flimsier so we make more noise! Over 80 per cent of complaints in Britain concerning noise are about neighbours' music. Sound is no respecter of space!

Schafer points out that no natural sound is deafening. In the past the loudest thing most people heard was the sound of thunder. People used to go out of their way to hear more noise – noise was an event! Yet industrialized sounds were always ambivalently received. Bijsterveld's fascinating study of early responses to the sounds of industrialization point to the fact that sound 'progress' is always a contested field. Ironically, she points to the fact that the noisiest people often complain about the noise of others. The upper classes' response to the automobile was invariably negative in the early years of the twentieth century, yet they were the only people who could afford to drive. Paradoxically, it was the driver, not the machine, which took the blame, thus consigning sound to class values. Not in my backyard!

Sound Values and Sonic Bridges

Sensitivity to noise is often class and culturally based. Cultures with strong notions of 'private space' as a form of entitlement are more prone to complaints about noise. The production of noise is often perceived as 'uncivilized' within a bourgeois ethic (Mark Smith in this volume) in which silence was truly 'golden' – yet this begs the question as to who defines the nature of noise, sound and music (Julian Henriques in this volume). Smith points to the positive reception of the noise of the crowd in the north of antebellum America as symbolizing democracy whilst Kahn points to the debate concerning the distinction between noise and music in avant-garde musical circles in the twentieth century. Your noise, my music!

Walkmans are the iconic urban technology of privatization, permitting users to construct their own individualized sound world wherever they go. Experience is aestheticized and the world becomes what the user wants it to be. Sound manages the user's mood, feelings and sense of time and place. Public space is transformed as users move through city spaces. Tonkiss, in this volume, discusses the forms of 'social deafness' that arise when individuals become lost in their own personal sonic universe. These individuals are not like Walter Benjamin or Joseph Roth – urban flaneurs – but rather preoccupied, narcissus-like, with the management of their own experience. Similarly, automobile users engage in multiple sound-technology use. The car becomes a perfectible mobile acoustic chamber in which individuals invariable prefer to listen in solitude (Putnam 2000). Thibaud uses the term 'sonic bridge' to describe the way in which music links the insides and outsides of social experience into a seamless web. Meanwhile mobile phone use provides the sounds of intimacy wherever the user may be. Sound transforms public space into private property. Home is where my sounds are!

Sounds of the Wind and Silence

Sounds are embedded with both cultural and personal meanings; sounds do not come at us merely raw. Adorno makes this point when he says:

> We can tell whether we are happy by the sound of the wind. It warns the unhappy man of the fragility of his house, hounding him from

shallow sleep and violent dreams. To the happy man it is the song of his protectedness: its furious howling concedes that it has power over him no longer. (Adorno 1974: 49)

Adorno wrote the above whilst living in exile in Hollywood during World War Two. Adorno's lament is of one who senses the fragility of home. The wind is a variable upon which cultural specificity is written. One senses that Adorno felt the roof was falling in on him many times. Moore in his piece on Northern Ireland describes the sound of Chinook helicopters hovering over North Belfast: for Protestants this was security, for Catholics a threat. For the rest of us it is *Apocalypse Now.*

John Cage commented: 'There is no such thing as an empty space or an empty time. There is always something to see something to hear. In fact, try as we may to make a silence, we cannot.' Our notions of peaceful silence are mediated through culture. Rousseau describes in his journals escaping from the city to walk in the countryside so that he could be alone with his thoughts. The sounds of nature were no hindrance to him, only the sounds of people and technology. Gustav Mahler, whilst writing in the sounds of nature to his Third Symphony on the shores of Lake Geneva, found the sounds of birds singing intolerable. Glenn Gould, the eccentric Canadian pianist, found the sound of the vacuum cleaner an aid to his memorizing and playing the music of Bach. Mark Smith, in this volume, describes how southern slaveholder families in antebellum America feared the silence of slaves whilst today in urban culture many of us switch on the television set as soon as we enter home and many of us put music on to lull ourselves to sleep at night. Silence becomes something to banish. Silence is illusive. Fran Tonkiss writes in this volume on the difficulty of finding silence in urban life. It is precarious and full of a silent presence – 'Empty space that doesn't talk back is as evocative as the hush that falls over the crowd, the telephone that doesn't ring, the dog that doesn't bark.'

Living with Music and Keeping Time

Ralph Ellison, the renowned African American writer and one-time musician, stated the choice starkly. In his early days as a writer he lived in a black neighbourhood surrounded by a cacophony of sounds from assorted drunks in the street to the flat melodies of an aspiring singer who lived in the apartment above. The streets of sound unsettled him and he struggled in vain to write sentences that would sing, or even to find his own voice. One day he turned on the radio to hear Kathleen

Ferrier singing Handel's *Rodelinda*. She reached out to him from the speaker: *Art thou troubled? Music will calm thee* . . . From then on Ellison resolved to block out the metropolitan clamour. He acquired and assembled audio equipment and filled his room with the melodies of Mozart and Duke Ellington and waged war with noisy neighbours through the Hi-Fi volume control. Remembering this hostile aural terrain and the refuge he found in music, he wrote in 1955: 'In those days it was either live with music or die with noise, and we chose rather desperately to live' (Ellison 1972: 187).

Ralph Ellison's parable alerts us to think about one's neighbourhood as an acoustic landscape. In this sense he anticipated what Murray Shafer calls a *soundscape*, or the auditory terrain in its entirety of over-lapping noises, sounds and human melodies (Shafer 1977). Susan J. Smith has pointed out the usefulness of examining cultures of sound and music as a means to move beyond geography's concern with visible worlds (Smith 1994; 1997; 2000). Indeed, if we listen to it the landscape is not so much a static topography that can be mapped and drawn, as a fluid and changing surface that is transformed as it is enveloped by different sounds. Fran Tonkiss in this volume comments that the modern city it is not just spectacular but sonic – 'the heat of July is there in the murmur of electric fans'. Indeed, thinking with our ears directs us to the temporal aspect of social life. Ellison reached the same conclusion close to half a century ago: 'Perhaps in the swift change of American society in which the meanings of one's origin are so quickly lost, one of the chief values of living with music lies in its power to give us an orientation in time' (Ellison 1972: 198).

The history of marching songs is also the history of keeping in time, in step. Music regulates where bodies meet sound. The history of dancing is also the history of keeping in time. To keep in time manifests itself in Cora Bender's analysis of 'pow wow' drumming ceremonies and equally in Paul Filmer's discussion of amateur choral singers. Together we move in time to sound. It can involve moving outside the time signatures of dominant social forces. Yet, sound regulation can also be coercive, the enforced marching of the prisoner, the enforced singing of the southern slave described by Mark Smith in this volume.

Vibrant Melody to Lifeless Corpse?

Roland Barthes pointed out the written language is the only semiotic system capable of interpreting another semiotic system. He asked, 'How, then, does language manage when it has to interpret music? Alas, it seems very badly' (Barthes 1977: 179). Confronted with music there is a poverty of language; we simply don't have the words to transpose the alchemy of sound. Barthes concluded that in describing music we have to rely on 'the poorest of linguistic categories: the adjective' (Barthes 1977: 179). The best one can hope for in writing about music is better kinds of failure: the least that should be insisted on is to avoid prose that strangles the life in music.

The types of deep listening proposed here involve adopting forms of representations – including musical notation – that are beyond The Word. This, in many respects, is the territory of musicologists and there are dangers inherent within this approach, such as viewing musical form as a closed system. As Sebastian Chan warns, 'Musicological analysis [can] reduce vibrant musics to lifeless corpses fit for autopsy' (Chan 1998: 93). The dangers identified by Chan are important but, equally, it is important to reach for a way of representing the qualities of sound without merely resorting to adjectives following Roland Barthes' warning. David Brackett's analysis of the music of James Brown is the kind of 'brilliant failure' to be recommended (Brackett 1995). In this study Brackett develops aural inventory of Brown's tune *Superbad* identifying its 'double voiced' quality and notating meticulously the singer's screams and vocal timbre. In the end, he fails but the result is a better kind of failure because Brackett takes the form of the music seriously and offers a way to name some of its elements and structures.

Sounding Places and Acoustic Maps

Paul Gilroy has written extensively about the relationship between music, place and time. His book *There Ain't No Black in the Union Jack*, published in 1987, included an extended discussion of black music as containing opposition frameworks, a critique of capitalism and registers of memory. The traces of the past and present of the African diaspora are rendered and recovered through the analysis of music ranging from Bobby Womack to Jah Shaka. The relationship between the aesthetics and form of the music and the contexts of its consumption and where it is enjoyed is central to Gilroy's analysis. His contribution to this volume situates the music of Jimi Hendrix at the crossroads between a kind of 'non tradition' and futuristic modernist experimentation.

Particularly important, here, is the role that the technology of sound reproduction plays in giving the music a unique quality in the dance hall. Henriques' and Henry's contributions in different ways point to the transformation of space and time achieved through the massive purpose-built reggae sound systems that endow the music with a new sonic quality. The bass registers of the sound systems also transform the inhospitable concrete metropolitan architecture in which they find an itinerant home:

> The town halls and municipal buildings of the inner-city in which dances are sometimes held are transformed by the power of these musics to disperse and suspend the temporal and spatial order of the dominant culture. As the sound system wires are strung up and the lights go down, dancers could be transported anywhere in the diaspora without altering the quality of their pleasures. (Gilroy 2002: 284)

Through this process, *outernational* forms of culture, music and expression flourish despite the inhospitalities of racism.

Comparable conclusions might be drawn about the way in which the urban (and sometimes suburban and rural) landscapes are transformed albeit in different ways by a host of dance music cultures from soul and funk warehouse parties to the unofficial raves of the 1980s and including the kaleidoscopic cultures of dance found in contemporary club culture. In each case a subterranean cartography is drawn through sound and the night-time consumption of music. More than this, each of these scenes – be it R&B or Techno – have deeper connections with cognate scenes elsewhere in New York or Berlin than they do with the next club night and the music that brings local space and its physical structure to life in a new way (Straw 1997).

David Hesmondhalgh and Keith Negus suggest that within the studies of popular music there has been:

> a move from the nation as the prime focus for understanding the relationship of popular music to places, and a growing emphasis on the minutiae of locality, and on international musical movements. This has been accompanied by a growing realization that popular music forms are no longer integrally tied to specific ethnic groups (assumptions that link white American males to rock music, Latin identities to salsa and African-Americans to rhythm and blues). Instead, musical forms are increasingly being theorized as the result of a series of transforming stylistic practices and transnational human musical interactions. (Hesmondhalgh and Negus 2002: 8)

Listening to music offers new opportunities to address issues of globalization, place, identity, belonging, history and memory. Think about the way in which hearing a particular piece of music can invoke a vivid memory, or how a record collection can act as a kind of jukebox of remembrance, each piece of music associated with a particular time and place.

The kind of listening we want to argue for in approaching musical cultures consists of three main elements. First, a commitment to taking musical form seriously, to search for ways to represent and transpose sound and music. Second, engaging in dialogue with the people who produce and create music as well as those who consume it. This is not a matter of just listening to people tell of how it 'really is'; rather, it involves engaging in a critical and reflective dialogue that examines the status of each account as well as the terms and frameworks of interpretation. Finally, deep listening also involves participation in the spaces where music is made, felt and enjoyed.

Natural Voices, Sound Identities

Racism is a discourse of power that thinks with its eyes. The idea of race, itself a product of history rather than nature, is a categorical mode of thinking that anchors human difference in The Visible. Variegations in humankind are organized into colour-coded containers of identity. The power of racial thinking lay in its capacity to shroud its social construction in a seeming 'matter of fact' natural authority. It would be impossible to think about the history of racism without its scopic component. You can't hear race in the same way that you see it or recognize its mirage. Sound may offer many confusions. A young woman who learned to speak within multi-racial peer groups in London is constantly told 'you don't sound white on the telephone?' as her clients walk through the door of the Citizen's Advice Bureau. A racist employer is appalled to see a black person turn up for a job interview – 'he sounded white on the phone'. The violence exacted by racism is that it places the life world of people into what Imre Kertese called 'identity enclosures' wrapped in systems of 'collective labelling' (Kertese 2002: 34).

This is also true for whole genres of music. In the MTV age, music is something to be seen animated through visual presentation in music videos. The effects of this has been to code genres of music racially. In America this means consigning R&B and hip-hop to ghetto blackness and rock and country-and-western to the vanilla suburbs and white rural interiors respectively. But, the music sings another song for those who listen to it with respect. African American singer Charley Pride learned to love country music through listening to the Grand Ole Opry that his father tuned into on an old Philco radio. Even in the segregated world of his youth in Sledge, Mississippi, sounds escaped. But Pride's career illustrates how profoundly a world coloured by racism listens with its eyes.

In his autobiography he recounts the story of how he came to Nashville and auditioned for Jack Johnson the man who would eventually manage him. 'Well, they tell me you sing country music,' said Johnson. 'So sing some country music for me.' Pride ran through a couple of songs finishing with a Hank Williams's number. He remembered:

> When I finished, Johnson said, 'Pretty good. Pretty good. Now sing one in your natural voice.'
> 'What do you mean' I said. 'This is my natural voice.'
> He shrugged. 'Sing another one'. (Pride and Henderson 1994: 135)

Racialized logic confines some sounds to particular colour-coded bodies but music offers what Berendt calls a kind of 'crossing place'. Put simply, you can't segregate the airwaves – sounds move, they escape, they carry. The sound proofing around culture is always incomplete even in the face of those who forbid it to be so.

'Auditory space has no point of favored focus', wrote D. C. Williams in 1955. It is a space in which multiple registers can co-exist simultaneously – the hum of the computer, the rattle of the keypad, the sound of the television in the next room, a child laughing in the street. There is no focus all are there at the same time with definition and clarity. Thinking with sound and music may offer the opportunity for thinking through issues of inclusion, coexistence and multicultural in a more humane way and allow us to think through what a multicultural landscape might sound like in the age of information and global interdependency. But there are no guarantees.

Sanjay Sharma writes in this volume about the ways in which exoticism and Orientalism may process the sounds of alterity. Through this cultural hybridity may 'enter into the smorgasbord of contemporary urban culture'. Following others, he argues that there may be things within the sounds that remain untranslatable within the regimes of hegemonic representation. He concludes: 'A subaltern musical politics of transfiguration isn't an unrealizable utopia, but a register for concrete, site-specific minitorian becomings. Untranslatable Asian sounds operate on a sonic plane which evade capture and yet their alterity is at work all around us.'

It is the fact that sound provides a place in which these traces can be present and sometimes latent that makes it so important. It may be that within the registers of aural culture that memories are carried regardless of whether the bearers of such embodied traditions are aware of them. Vic Seidler concludes his contribution on diaspora sounds with the reflection that certain sounds call us at different moments in our lives: 'In my twenties I never thought that a time might come when I would need to explore my Jewish identities and that music and sound might be an important part of these explorations.' It is this sense that sound and music can call us by turns toward the past and the future. With a different but not unrelated emphasis Ralph Ellison concluded in 1955:

> Those who know their native culture and love it unchauvinistically are never lost when encountering the unfamiliar. Living with music today we find Mozart and Ellington, Kirsten Flagstad and Chippie Hill, William L. Dawson and Carl Orff all forming part of our regular fare; all add to its significance . . . In so doing, it gives significance to all those indefinable aspects of experience which nevertheless help to make us what we are. In the swift whirl of time music is a constant, reminding us of what we were and of that toward which we aspired. Are thou troubled? Music will not only calm, it will ennoble thee. (Ellison 1972: 198)

It is not only a matter of choosing to 'live with music' but also embracing the invitation to listen to the social world actively with depth and humility. Moving away from these opening comments we want to briefly introduce the extraordinary writing contained in the pages that follow. We have collected here a combination of specially commissions new writing and previously published articles. All of them address the project of thinking with and through sound.

The Auditory Cultures Reader is divided into five major sections each prefaced with a short introduction. Here we have tried to group literatures thematically while featuring writers from a wide range of traditions and academic disciplines. The book's main thematic threads include theoretical and epistemological questions (thinking about sound); historical studies (histories of sound), cross cultural examples (anthropologies of sound), accounts of urban life and popular culture (sounds in the city: arenas, rituals, pathways) and finally an account of the place and significance of music (narratives of sound: music, voice and identity). We hope the invitation to move *into sound* will open up new ways of thinking about the 'senses of sense' and the rich insights offered by the writers represented in this book will invite fresh appreciation of the quality of social experience, memory, time and place.

References

Adorno, T. (1974), *Minima Moralia: Reflections on a Damaged Life*, London: New Left Books.

Barthes, Roland (1977), 'The Grain of the Voice', in *Image Music Text*, London: Fontana.

Berendt, Joachim-Ernst (1985), *The Third Ear: On Listening to the World*, New York: Henry Holt.

Bourdieu, Pierre (2000), *Pascalian Meditations*, Cambridge: Polity Press.

Brackett, David (1995), *Interpreting Popular Music*, Cambridge: Cambridge University Press.

Chan, Sebastian (1998), 'Music(ology) Needs Context – Reinterpreting Goa Trance', *Perfect Beat*, 3(4): 93–7.

Ellison, Ralph (1972), 'Living with Music', in *Shadow and Act*, New York: Random House, pp. 187–98.

Geertz, Clifford (2002), 'An Inconsistent Profession: The Anthropological Life in Interesting Times', *Annual Review of Anthropology*, 31: 1–19.

Gilroy, Paul (1993), *The Black Atlantic: Modernity and Double Consciousness*, London and New York: Verso.

— (2000), *Between camps: Nations, Cultures and the Allure of Race*, London: Allen Lane Penguin.

— (2002), *There Ain't No Black in the Union Jack: The Cultural Politics of race and Nation*, London and New York: Routledge.

Hesmondhalgh, D. and Negus, K. (2002), *Popular Music Studies*, London: Edward Arnold.

Horkheimer, M. and Adorno, T. (1972), *The Dialectic of Enlightenment*, London: Penguin.

Kertesz, Imre (2002), 'The Freedom of Self-definition', in Horace Engdahl (ed.), *Witness Literature: Proceeding of the Nobel Sentennial Symposium*, New Jersey, London, Singapore and Hong Kong: World Scientific.

Pinckney, D. (2001) 'Diary', *Guardian Saturday Review*, 27 October, p. 12.

Pride, C. and Henderson, J. (1994), *Pride: The Charley Pride Story*, New York: Quill.

Putnam, R. (2000), *Bowling Alone. The Collapse and Revival of American Community*, New York: Simon & Schuster.

Shafer, R. Murray (1977), *Tuning the World*, New York: Alfred A Knopf.

Smith, S. J. (1994), 'Soundscape', *Arena*, 26(3): 232–40.

— (1997), 'Beyond Geography's Visible Worlds: A Cultural Politics of Music', *Progress in Human Geography*, 21: 502–29.

—   (2000), 'Performing the (Sound)world', *Environment and Planning D: Society and Space*, 18: 615–37.

Straw, W. (1997), 'Communities and Scenes in Popular Music', in Ken Gelder and Sarah Thornton (eds) *The Subcultures Reader*, London and New York: Routledge.

Part I

Thinking about Sound

The entries in this section are both eclectic and interdisciplinary. Fittingly, we begin with the work of Murray Schafer, a name mentioned in many of the following entries (along with Alain Corbin and Steven Feld) as having influenced their own work on sound. Murray Schafer, the Canadian composer and influential founder of the 'soundscape' movement coined the term 'soundscape' in his *The Tuning of the World* in 1977. His work has spawned a host of soundscape projects around the world in subsequent years. Schafer's concerns have been pedagogical, in as much as his writings demonstrate how one is to 'listen' to the world, and prescriptive in their rejection of the 'noise' of much urban sound. In *Open Ears* Schafer asks whose ears are open and whose are closed. He provides a cultural history of those who have listened and those who have not. Listening, for Schafer, is not merely descriptive, but cognitive, value laden and hierarchical. The silencing of sound in academic discourse is indicative of a broader based 'silencing' in the fields of politics and in everyday life. Schafer's message is that we no longer 'hear' the sounds of the natural world and that our leaders no longer 'listen' to us. Both trends augur badly for both the natural world and the democratic process. Whilst many in the soundscape movement broadly reject the sounds of the modern urban world, we believe that Schafer's work can still provide many of the necessary tools for reaching a deeper understanding of contemporary soundscapes, urban or otherwise.

Leigh Schmidt also takes on the history of listening in terms of the supposition of the 'decline in listening' and the attendant 'dwindling of hearing as a spiritual sense'. However Schmidt argues that we have read the Enlightenment as overly occularcentric and have gone on, because of this, to presume the dominance of visuality within modernity. This presumption has led to a familiar tale of the ascendancy of vision through which all things 'heard' are filtered. In discussing the work of Walter Ong and Marshall McLuhan he argues they produce the familiar (and often counter factual) narrative of the eclipse of the ear. In the world of the telegraph, telephone, phonograph, radio and television they dwell on the importance of print, reading sound as if it were merely a script. This bias is replicated in much work in media and cultural studies in which one would be mistaken in believing that we watch the television in silence, with the sound turned off! Schmidt also points to the incipient orientalism involved in the romanticising of pre-print cultures in the work of McLuhan in which the 'we look, they listen' dichotomy is unreflectively asserted. Schmidt goes on to paint a more complex picture of Enlightenment thought, one which also had room for the other senses, and especially sound. In doing so Schmidt's work demonstrates the need to re-interpret the past through the filter of an auditory or rather multi-sensory lens.

Don Ihde, one of the few contemporary philosophers to engage with sound, addresses a largely ignored philosophical issue, that is also central to much everyday experience; the auditory imagination. Ihde provides a fascinating phenomenology of what it means to imagine in 'sound' in discussing how we operationalise our auditory imagination. Sound and volition are discussed in terms of sound disruptions and sound intensities. In doing so Ihde situates the auditory imagination firmly in the social. What indeed interrupts our imagination, what triggers it and what circumstances enhance it. (The intensity of sound and its effects on the body and thought are also discussed by Julian Henriques later in this volume.) Ihde also offers an original account of the penetration of sound into the 'thinking self' in terms of notions of 'inner speech'. Analysis and understanding of the auditory nature of forms of 'inner speech' have been neglected in philosophical thought despite the fact that, as Ihde claims, 'inner speech is an almost *continuous* aspect of self presence'. Finally, Ihde discusses the bodily nature of sound, we hear through our bodies as well as our ears. Even the deaf feel the vibrations of sound as well documented in the piano playing of the deaf Beethoven.

The bodily nature of sound is also taken up in Steven Connor's piece on the nature and social meaning of 'clapping'. Connor takes us on a fascinating journey through biblical, religious and cross-cultural accounts of clapping, before ending up with the contemporary activities of western audiences in the act of clapping. Connor describes the multi-faceted way in which acts of clapping regulates time and shapes place; witness the effects of a slow handclap on a performer or politician! Connor points to the simultaneity of subject and object in the act of clapping, 'a doer and a done to'. Clapping is both a sound act and a touching act, his work thus points to the need to see the relational qualities of our various senses together with a call to carry out more work into the nature and historical meanings of the noise of audiences in the West and elsewhere.

Implied in the above is how we distinguish and evaluate sound, noise and music.

Douglas Kahn in his chapter asks how musical sounds were distinguished from 'sound' in Western avant-garde music of the 20th century. Surprisingly he finds much resistance to 'worldly sounds' in the music of the avant-garde. He argues that notions of musical integrity created a conservatism, even in avant-garde circles, that was not so apparent in the modernism of the art movement at the same time. In part he locates this situation as a form of resistance to the advent of mechanical reproduction in the form of the gramophone, in part to the assumed 'unmediated' communicative function of music. Thus the musical avant-garde was paradoxically conservative when it came down to distinguishing 'musical sounds' from 'noise'. Kahn charts the movement into 'noise' through the work of John Cage, the post-war champion of musique *concrete* in relation to intellectual responses, which defined noise in terms of 'primitivism'. Thus Kahn's work points us in the direction, not just of in-house music debates, but to the underlying cultural assumptions concerning the nature and meaning of musical sounds.

Paul Filmer, from a largely sociological perspective, discusses the intellectual meanings attached to rhythm and time through musical performance through the work of Schutz, Barthes, McNeill and Putnam. He finds their work too ready to consign to the flames the activities of 'musica practica', the local activities of music making, often amongst amateurs, within a broadly conceived culture of mechanical reproduction. Filmer points to the British tradition of choral singing to demonstrate the persistence of forms of collective amateur music activity, pointing to the way in which performance practice can often transcend other distinctive social categories of class or ethnicity.

1

Open Ears

Murray Schafer

We have no ear lids. We are condemned to listen. But this does not mean our ears are always open. 'The violent and the righteous are hard of hearing', said Gunter Grass (1973). In every society it is possible to detect individuals or classes of people whose ears are open and those whose ears are closed. Open to change? Open to obey? Open to criticism? Open to new ideas? Open to the voices of God? Or closed to them.

So far as I know, no historian has ever listened to history, that is, listened to those who were listening, in contradistinction to those who were not, in an attempt to deduce what might have been happening or about to happen as a result of the claireaudience of some and the deafness of others. This is not to imply that listeners have always had an upper hand over non-listeners. Often the situation is reversed, as it seems to be at the present time, when the deaf increasingly rules us. The three questions to ask are these:

- Who's listening?
- What are they listening to?
- What are they ignoring or refusing to listen to?

Countless dictators have fallen because they failed to detect the sounds of revolution soon enough. And probably an equal number have been hurled into power by bawling multitudes who couldn't even hear their own voices. The deaf can lead the deaf just as the blind can lead the blind.

But there are also real flash points in history where something revolutionary was heard for the first time. Big noises like cannons, church bells, steam engines and jets have changed history as much as bold proclamations. So have small sounds, pronounced in whispers at clandestine meetings. In every case someone is listening and others not. What follows are a few examples of significant social changes attributable to sound events.

The Ear of God

The notion of God as an omniscient microphone, hearing or overhearing everything, is at least implicitly present in many religions. When I was a child going to church with my parents, I always felt awkward when the minister said 'let us offer up a silent prayer to the Lord'. Then all heads would bow and all eyes would close. The church was silent until the minister would break the stillness to inform us that God had heard our prayers. He was confident about that. God always heard the prayers of earthly sinners. It amazed me to think that at any moment, millions of people all over the world were speaking to God, and that God could understand all the languages, unscramble all the confessions, and even decipher the silent thoughts of the praying multitudes. Of course, Christianity functioned, and stills functions, on the supposition that nothing can be concealed from God, neither in darkness nor in silence.

But if the ears of God are always open, why do we have to signal when we want to make contact? Why the rattling of the bones, the blowing of the ram's horn or the ringing of the church bells to announce our readiness for communication? Certain tribal societies could explain this simply: the gods were often sleeping and needed to be awakened. Any ritual object has a complex function. The church bell, for instance, is an apotrapaic instrument, intended to sanctify a holy place or holy time. It is centrifugal in the sense that it frightens off evil spirits, and centripetal in the sense that it draws people together for collective religious observance. I have shown how authoritative the bell became in the convent of Bernardines of the Obedience of Martin Verga (1815) from a description given by Victor Hugo in *Les Miserables* (Schafer 1993) Not only did bells announce prayers, but also all activities were directed by their ringing; and this was true wherever there were churches and monasteries.

Quebec City, 1857, Order of St. Augustine

4:00 a.m.	*Reveil*. Bell sounded for the duration of one Pater and Ave.
4:30 a.m.	Thirty tolls on the church bell.
5:15 a.m.	*Les Petites Heures*. Bell sounded for the duration of one Pater and Ave.
5:45 a.m.	Mass, announced by thirty tolls on the church bell. Housekeeping signalled on the monastery bell for the duration of the two Ave Marias.
9:00 a.m.	General lecture signalled by the monastery bell and the hand bell for the duration of the De Profundis.
10:45 a.m.	First announcement of the *Diner des Pauvres* on the monastery bell for the duration of two Ave Marias.
11:00 a.m.	*Diner des Pauvres* signalled by hand bell and monastery bell sounding two Ave Marias, separated by a pause lasting one Sancta Maria.
11:15 a.m.	Examination. Thirty strokes on the monastery bell.
11:30 a.m.	*Diner des Religieuses* announced by hand bell and monastery bell sounding two Ave Marias, separated by a pause lasting one Sancta Maria.
Noon	Angelus. Three times three strokes leaving the duration of a Sancta Maria between each group.
1:25 p.m.	*Chapelet*. Monastery bell and hand bell sounded for the duration of one De Profundis.
2:25 p.m.	Catechism. Thirty tolls on the monastery bell.
2:45 p.m.	*Lecture particulaire*. Announced by the monastery bell and the hand bell for the duration of one De Profundis.
3:10 p.m.	Vespers. Hand bell and church bell sounded for the duration of one De Profundis.
4:45 p.m.	First announcement of the *Souper des Pauvres*. The monastery bell sounded for the duration of two Ave Marias.
5:00 p.m.	*Souper des Pauvres*. The hand bell and monastery bell sounded for two Ave Marias separated by one Sancta Maria.
5:30 p.m.	*Matins*. Hand bell and church bell sounded for the duration of one Pater and one Ave.
6:00 p.m.	Supper for the monks announced on the monastery bell for the duration of two Ave Marias separated by a pause of one Sancta Maria.
6:30 p.m.	Second refectory. The monastery bell sounded for two Ave Marias without pause.

| 7:45 p.m. | *Examen.* Seven or eight strokes on the monastery bell, then thirty strokes on the church bell after having rung the hand bell. |
| 8:45 p.m. | Bedtime. The monastery bell is sounded for the duration of one De Profundis. (Source: Sonnerie. Ordre des Observ-ances, *Reglements des Religieuses hospitalieres de la Misericorde, de l'ordre de St Augustin.* Manuscript in the Archives du Monastere de l'Hotal-dieu de Quebec.) |

In one sense all this bell tolling was intended for God's ears, because the durations were determined by prayers recited aloud or silently by the monks who tolled them. But the more obvious intention was to maintain the regimen of the monastery and, in a broader sense, to regulate the behaviour of everyone living within Christian society. When the authority of Christianity weakened, church bells grew fewer. Perhaps God was no longer listening, or at least wasn't speaking. The many sounds once regarded as divine voices – the storms, the thunder, and the mysterious voices of nature and of dreams – were rationalized differently. God became silent. With God's silence, human vocabulary changed. No more Pater Nostas or Ave Marias. Other ears opened to listen to the human predicament.

The Ear of Dionysius

Dionysius of Syracuse (circa 430–367 BC) was known as a brutal tyrant, although he made Syracuse the most powerful city west of the main-land. His name, or rather his ear, survives eponymously in the famous S-shaped grotto that resembles the cochlea of the human ear in enormous proportions. The cave is about 210 feet long and over 70 feet high with a narrow, uniform channel a few feet wide at the top. The unique sound properties of the cave were studied by the acoustician Wallace Clement Sabine:

> When being shown the grotto from below, one's attention is called to its remarkable reverberation. When above, one's attention is called to the ability to hear what is said at any point on the ground. It is related that Tyrant Dionysius ... [who] so designed his prisons that at certain concealed points of observation he could not only see everything that was done, but through remarkable acoustic design, could hear every word that was spoken, even when whispered only. (Sabine 1964)

Whether or not the grotto was a prison is not substantiated.

Nevertheless, the Ear of Dionysius is the prototype for all subsequent developments in acoustic surveillance by the state, passing through centuries of architectural curiosities intended to detect treachery through listening tubes (the seventeenth-century versions of which are preserved with faulty acoustics in the vivid illustrations of Athansius Kircher's *Phonurgia Nova*) (Kircher 1966) down to the reality of hidden microphones and wire-tapping in the twentieth century.

The ears of the state have never been more curious and open. Everyone has a voiceprint and somewhere everyone's voice print is on file. The setting of Solzhenitsyn's novel *First Circle* is a top-secret laboratory, committed to research on voice scramblers, simulators and decoders.

'Eavesdropping, censorship, recording, and surveillance are weapons of power', writes Jacques Attali.

> The technology of listening in on, ordering, transmitting, and recording noise is at the heart of this apparatus . . . Who among us is free of the feeling that this process, taken to an extreme, is turning the modern state into a gigantic, monopolising noise emitter, and at the same time, a generalised eavesdropping device. (Attali 1985)

A remarkable example of this is recorded by Milan Kundera in *The Unbearable Lightness of Being*: during the communist era, Prague police evidently broadcast tapes from bugged apartments over the state radio as a public incrimination of the inhabitants.

Not all of this listening is carried on in secret. This is no longer necessary once mechanisms are created for society to express itself openly on every possible issue. Then all that's necessary is to monitor the radio phone-in shows and opinion polls to know where to release and apply pressure. Music is probably more informative. I refer, of course, to pop music, which is really the only kind permitted in the free world. (Any other kind of music might be, and on occasion has been, considered conspiratorial.) Listen closely to its tempo, its beat, its vocal machinations and song texts and it tells you all you need to know about the mood of the people.

> The music of a well-ruled state is peaceful and joyous and its government is orderly; that of a country in confusion is full of resentment and anger and its government is disordered; and that of a dying country is mournful and pensive and its people are in distress. (De Bary et al. 1960)

Compare today's song literature with any collection of folk songs from the past – the ballads, the romances, the laments and the marches – and ask yourself, which kind of government is reflected in each style? History is a songbook for anyone who would listen to it. Songs for war, songs for peace, and a heteroclite of forms between them. The downgrading of the marching band. Patriotic ballads giving way to crooners. Spirituals giving way to Afro drumming. The disappearance of Christian hymns. The emergence of Latin rhythms as Latin America bulges north. Petatonic music as the Far East spreads everywhere. Rap music by bitter young men. Doodle music for doodlers. Drug music for the smashed up. Techno music for flesh machines. The world sings itself to death and back to life.

'Where you want to have slaves, there you should have as much music as possible', Tolstoy once said to Gorki. A society too drunk with music is incapable of other operational achievements, and the ruler who wishes to stay in power knows how to stimulate music and when to withhold it, as the church did in the Middle Ages or as Stalin did when he slapped the wrists of Shostakovich and Prokofiev and strangled American jazz.

The Ear of the Confessor

Confessions rarely go unheard. There is always someone willing or required to hear the confession of misdeeds, apologies and repentance, someone to whom these confessions are of interest and value, perhaps to provide a catharsis for the sufferer, perhaps to scrutinize incipient disorders that might upset the frictionless functioning of society.

The Latin word *audire* (to hear) has many derivations. One may have an 'audience' with the king – that is, a chance to have him hear your petitions. One's financial affairs are 'audited' by an accountant, because originally accounts were read aloud for clarity (cf. Ong 1982). An accused person is given a 'hearing', that is, a chance for the accused and witnesses to offer aural testimony in the courtroom. Of course, rooms are often constructed or appointed to favour the transmission of some voices over others, and the courtroom, like the royal court, is no exception, with the judge as the king occupying the most elevated position, reminding us that the Latin word *obaudire* meant 'hearing from below' – obeying. Similar relationships have been noticed in other languages, for instance in German, where *horen* (to hear) is also the root of *gehoren* (to belong to) and *gehorchen* (to obey). We hear sound. We belong to sound. We obey sound.

In his *History of Sexuality* Michel Foucault has shown how the sexual freedom in both action and vocabulary that existed in Europe in the seventeenth century was gradually repressed during the eighteenth and nineteenth centuries. The task of introducing and maintaining this repression was assigned to churches and schools, and the reason, he claimed, was because the pleasures of sex were incompatible with the work ethic:

> At a time when labour capacity was being systematically exploited, how could this capacity be allowed to dissipate itself in pleasurable pursuits, except in those-reduced to a minimum-that enabled it to reproduce itself? (Rabinow 1984)

And 'if sex is repressed, that is, condemned to prohibition, non-existence, and silence, then the mere fact that one is speaking about it has the appearance of a deliberate transgression.' Sexual discussion needed to be controlled, and the channel through which this was accomplished was the confessional, not the bedroom or the brothel, where the discourse of sex most regularly took place, where the confessor's secret lusts and weaknesses achieved their most intensified expression, and where the whole subject was given its most vivid coloration of iniquity. To a modern 'liberated' person it seems outrageous that a celibate should have been empowered to deal with all the confessions of our sexual desires and appetites – doubly outrageous in respect to recent disclosures about the behaviour of some priests and clergy; but the point Foucault wishes us to realize is that, despite all attempts to invalidate sex during the nineteenth century, all that really happened was that it was spoken about in a different context, that the ear open to our confessions was less frequently that of the beloved than of a third party, inquisitive, seemingly neutral, but at root intolerant.

Freud's revelations did much to dispel this, although the technique of enquiry remained remarkably similar. One of Freud's most celebrated patients, the Russian aristocrat known only by the pseudonym 'Wolf-man', tells us, in his 'Recollections of Sigmund Freud', how the 'psycho-analytic situation' came about.

> This situation, as is well known, is that of the patient lying on the couch with the analyst sitting near the couch in a position where the analysand cannot see him. Freud told me that he had originally sat at the opposite end of the couch, so that the analyst and analysand could look at each other. One female patient, exploiting this situation, made all possible –

or rather all impossible – attempts to seduce him. To rule out anything similar, once and for all, Freud moved from his earlier position to the opposite end of the couch. (Gardiner 1971: 142)

The darkened room and invisible analyst perpetuate the confessional booth and the hidden priest, but the couch put the analysand in a more comfortable position to encourage free disclosure. It is well known that Freud spoke little during sessions with patients, but he listened intently, almost the way a music teacher listens to a pupil's performance; and, like a music teacher, he saw Freud attached great significance to slips of the tongue (Freudian slips) and to other spontaneous or inadvertent sounds such as harsh breathing and the tapping of foot or fingers, sounds that he believed recalled the 'primal scene' of coitus between parents heard during infancy, and a frequent cause of later neuroses (the best study of Freud's listening habits is Lecourt 1992). That spontaneous or uncontrollable sound-making had important implications and could be deciphered like a secret language was a revelation. It was as if the human being was signalling in one way through controlled grammatical speech and in another way in the accents and accidents that surrounded conscious communication. Yet Freud, and later Jung, failed to realize the implications of the acoustics of the unconscious, both in dreams as well as in music. Neither Freud nor Jung seems to have been particularly musical. There are a few references to music in Freud's letters but none in his theoretical writings. Nor are there in the writings of Jung. This made them particularly unsuited to deal with patients who had obsessions with sounds, musical or otherwise. A tune, for them, could only be analysed through the words that accompanied it. I have elsewhere mentioned the unsatisfactory manner in which Jung dealt with the acoustic contents of his patient's dreams (Schafer 1993). Freud once denied the auditory dimension of dreams altogether, 'for, in dreams we see images but we hear nothing' (Freud 1950). At other times he admitted that we might hear voices in dreams, which he quite dogmatically considered memories of conversations from the previous day. The only accommodation he made to sounds was to acknowledge that occasionally an external sound, overheard by a dreamer, might signal a change in a dream – that church bells, for instance, might take a dream in a religious direction.

The indifference of early psychiatrists to sounds in dreams is unusual, and rather sets them apart from other interpreters of psychic experiences. Most of the big dreams of the Old Testament were aural or had important aural elements. Among the North-American Indians, the prophet's song comes out of a dream and is sung immediately on waking. Even in nineteenth-century Europe, aural dreams seemed significant, at least in the lives of musicians, as E.T.A. Hoffmann's Tales indicate.

> As I was in the realm of dreams a thousand fears and pains tormented me. It was night and I was terrified of the leering masks of the monsters who dragged me one moment into the abyss of the sea and the next raised me on high. Rays of light came through the night, and the rays of light were tones which surrounded me with their serene purity. I awoke from my pains and saw a great, clear eye, which stared into an organ; and as it stared, tones arose and wound themselves into more shimmering and majestical chords than I had ever thought possible. Melodies poured up and down and I swam their current and wanted to drown. (Schafer 1975)

Vivid acoustic dreams recounted by Nietzsche, Thomas Mann and other German authors rather fly in the face of Freud's assertion that we dream deafly. Freud evidently did not benefit from Novalis's suggestion that medicine is a musical art, even though passages like the following were quite well known during Freud's day: 'Every disease is a musical problem – the healing a musical solution. The shorter and more successful the solution – the greater the musical talent of the doctor.'

Novalis believed that the rhythms of the body move in harmonic order, and disease can be detected as a dissonance in the harmonic ordering. Paracelsus would have understood that, as would practitioners of holistic medicine today, but not the tone-deaf psychiatrist. In her study of Freud's listening habits, Edith Lacourt makes the case that Freud was actually envious of the musical talent of others (for instance of Mahler, who briefly consulted him), talents he would gladly have developed had he possessed them. But, as I said at the beginning, history has been as dramatically shaped by closed or impaired ears as by open ears. Twentieth-century practice has concentrated on the visual content of dreams leaving the aural territory for others to explore.

The Ear Within

The ear of the dreamer, the ear of the shaman, the ear of the prophet and the ear of the schizophrenic have this in common: messages are heard, but no matter how clear or compelling they may be, there is no evidence of a verifiable external source. The transmission seems intra-cranial, from an interior sound source to an ear within the brain. Julian

Jaynes (1976) attempted to explain how we hear voices that are heard by no one but ourselves. Jaynes tried to demonstrate that, while speech is normally a function of the left hemisphere of the brain, the right hemisphere may, at one time, also have had a speech-producing function, a freer, more hallucinatory activity, vocalizing that he called 'the language of the gods' – messages that were passed from the right hemisphere to the left by means of an 'anterior commissure', to be heard as audible voices.

The whole of the *Iliad* is directed this way. Apollo speaks to Hector; Athena speaks to Achilles. As Jaynes explains it, 'the Trojan War was directed by hallucinations'. The formula 'Yahweh said to Moses', repeated throughout Exodus and again in Leviticus, where the laws are dictated, might be interpreted in this way, although some believers might prefer a god who shouts from on high to one who inhabits the head. What cannot be denied is that exclusively Moses heard the voice of Yahweh. 'Speak to us yourself', they said to Moses, 'and we will listen; but do not let God speak to us or we shall die' (Exodus 20: 19). There is a parallel here with Zaroastrianism, where Srosh, 'the genius of hearing', interprets the message of Ahura Mazda for the faithful.

At some point (Jaynes dates it at about 3,000 years ago) the commissure connecting the brain hemispheres was weakened, and the voices began to be stilled. Jayne's theory has been criticized, although it has not been replaced by any more convincing explanation of why voices were heard with such astonishing force in ancient times, or that their presence has diminished today and is only found among people society regards as mad. The steady development of consciousness and rational thought has transformed the inner voice into a symptom of psychic disorder. A person might ask: have they really disappeared or were they merely suppressed because they are too frightening or irrational for the modern mind? Even in the time of Joan of Arc one could be punished for the arrogance of claiming to hear them. 'During her trial, worn out with questions and scholastic subtleties, she is asked whether she still hears her voices. "Take me to the woods", she says, "and I shall hear them clearly".'

Ear Muffs

Rationalism extinguished the rich treasury of imaginary voices that once existed in Europe and still exist in many less civilized parts of the world. The empirical Greeks often referred to sound in their writings. Pythagoras created a musical system based on harmonics derived from listening to the heavenly spheres in motion. Socrates took counsel from his 'demon', an interior psychic voice that warned him about danger and evil. In his *Problemata,* Aristotle asked many questions about sounds and attempted to answer them. In *De Rerum Natura* (*On the Nature of Things*) the Latin poet-philosopher Lucretius has a vigorous discussion on vocal sound and acoustics in general. But by the time we reach St Augustine, philosophy was beginning to settle into a quieter mode, for, as he said, 'It might be contended that, though we utter no sound, we nevertheless use words in thinking and therefore use speech within our minds' (St Augustine, 'The Teacher', in Shapiro 1964). Logic, ethics and aesthetics became silent disciplines and remained so for centuries until Schopenhauer proclaimed music and noise as indispensable ingredients of philosophical speculation – noise because it can 'instantly shatter the power of thought', and music because the 'combined, rational, numerical relations set the brain fibres themselves vibrating in a similar way' (Schopenhauer 1966). Still, a reader of Western philosophy might conclude that everything worth serious discussion exists in a silent vacuum: war, revolution, all social enterprise, and even the universe. This repudiation of sound passed over into science as well where major theories (the space-time continuum, the atomic structure of matter, and the wave-corpuscular theory of light) were construed as silent, as were the instruments used in their measurement (the telescope, the micro-scope, equations, graphs, statistics and numbers). It is almost as if the great achievements of Western philosophy and science were produced in a huge anechoic chamber. Myriads of books written in silent rooms and read in silent libraries. But has the world become more quiet and peaceful for it?

A person suffering from acousmata is taken to a psychiatrist. A person found mumbling in a public place is considered dotty. But we all hear voices in the mind and may converse with them out loud when alone, just to fill the solitude. A musician may also hear musical sounds, and while unmusical people often express astonishment that a composer could hold the contents of a whole symphony in the head, playing it all through at will while shaping and reshaping details, there is no doubt that this skill can be learned, and has been learned by countless musicians. A legend says that Mozart wrote the overture to *Don Giovanni* only hours before the premiere. In reality, he had accumulated it in his mind throughout the writing of the opera and needed only a few hours to write it down. (Closer to home, Glenn Gould spent fewer hours practising than most pianists, but he spent many more hours studying scores and silently memorizing them.)

The Ear of the Imagination

Everyone has the power to imagine sounds; and fairy tales, literature and radio once developed this skill in ways that television cannot. Try this experiment. Imagine the following sounds, taking time to let each resonate in the mind before cross fading to the next:

- a baby laughing;
- a woman weeping;
- a bowling alley;
- Niagara Falls;
- a fish jumping out of water;
- an iceberg slowly melting;
- a giraffe with hiccups.

The technique of imagining sounds was developed with great subtlety by the Japanese haiku poets. Basho's celebrated poem about the frog is a good example.

> Furuiki ya
> Kawazu tobikomu
> Mizu no oto

> An old pond
> A frog leaps in
> With a splash

It could be translated more vividly with three words: frog, pond, splash. The diminutive sound of birds inhabiting vast spaces was a favourite of the haiku poets:

> Hark! The voice of the pheasant
> Has swallowed up the wide field
> at a gulp. (Yamei)

> The voice of the cuckoo
> Dropped to the lake
> Where it lay floating
> On the surface. (Basho)

The movement of sound was another speciality:

> The sound of an acorn
> Falling down a shingled roof.
> Cold of the night. (Gyotai)

> Cricket!
> Although it was next door you sang
> I hear you there. (Issa)

One of the fundamental paradoxes of the listening experience is revealed in this poem. Is sound where it originates or where it is detected? Is it in the soundscape or is it in the ear? The reply 'both' is not satisfactory because we do not hear sound in two places, but only in one. Issa recognizes this and opts for the subjective sensation of sound in the ear as more authentic.

At times an aural phenomenon may merge synaesthetically with the visual:

> The sea darkens
> And a wild duck's call
> Is faintly white. (Basho)

The Japanese also cultivated the suspense of waiting for sound to happen:

> The butterfly rests on the temple bell, asleep.

Of course, the Japanese were not alone in hearing vibrating worlds beyond visual appearances. A striking example by a Western writer comes from August Strindberg, who heard a cricket singing in his pillow:

> Now, assuming that these creatures once sang in a field of flax, do you not believe that Nature or the creator could use the vegetable fibre (of linen) as a phonograph, so that it plays to my inner ear which through suffering, deprivation and prayer has become willing to hear further than before?

Attending to the immanence of sound in silent objects is stimulated by meditation, especially the unfocused meditation of Zen Buddhism.

The composer Toru Takemitsu explains the difference between the oriental and the occidental listener in this way:

> The bells of Westminster Abbey speak in terms of first person singular: they have an individual motive with a distinctive statement. The Japanese temple going, however, speaks without personal identification: its sound seems to melt into the world beyond persons, static and sensual. (Takemitsu 1995)

Sound objects in the oriental landscape encourage peripheral listening, while sounds in the West compete for focused attention – can this be true?

Most of the sounds busy people listen to are signals of activity. This explains their immunity to the sounds of nature. One of the essential differences between the natural environment and the engineered environments in which most people now live is that nature can't be shut off with a button. Things that can't be generated or shut off with buttons or switches attract little attention in the modern world.

The failure of the twentieth century to protect the natural habitats of birds and animals is largely due to the fact that we no longer hear nature or can put names to its voices. If you can't name the birds, if you don't know how to recognize the leaves of the trees by the sounds they make, or hear a cataract down the river, or recognize when a winter wind is bringing in a storm, nature is anaesthetized, and its survival will depend on forces other than human.

The power of technology really comes down to a fascination with buttons and switches in an attempt to modulate information intake. As the twentieth century progressed there were fewer 'off' switches; media-massaged society remained in a perpetual state of 'red alert'.

The cellular phone, which the Germans appropriately called the 'Handy', is the latest instalment in this drama. Answer when you're master calls. Life without secrets, without privacy, without freedom. The latest shackle for the technological prisoner to carry about.

In the 1790s Jeremy Bentham designed his 'panopticon', a circular prison with cells in tiers facing a central rotunda where guards were able to observe all moves of the isolated prisoners twenty-four hours a day. At the time it was considered outrageous; but isn't this what today are tyrants want to achieve: a transparency of the population in which nothing remains secret? The Ear of Dionysius has never ceased to haunt the imaginations of those seeking power in the world. And accordingly we find that power seekers are never very far from microphones.

But no one can hear everything – unless God can. Beyond what fascinates your ear today is something else, incessantly and obdurately present, although you cannot or do not hear it yet – but whoever hears it first has a good chance of inheriting the future.

References

Attali, J. (1985) *Noise*, Minneapolis: University of Minnesota Press, p. 7.

De Bary, W. T. et al. (1960) 'Book of Rites (Li Chi or Li Ki)', in *Sources of Chinese Tradition*, New York, p. 184.

Freud, S. (1950), *Aus den Anfangen der Psychoanalyse, 1887–1902*, London, p. 175.

Grass, G. (1973), *From the Diary of a Snail*, New York: Harvest Books.

Gardiner, M. (ed.) (1971), *The Wolf-Man*, New York: Basic Books.

Jaynes, J. (1976), *On the Origin of Consciousness in the Breakdown of the Bicameral Mind*, Boston.

Kircher, A. (1966), *Phonurgia Nova*, facsimile of the 1673 Kempton Edition, New York.

Lecourt, E. (1992), *Freud at la sonore: le tic-tac du desir*, Paris: L'Harmattan.

Ong, W. (1982), *Orality and Literacy*, New York: Routledge, p. 119.

Rabinow, P. (ed.) (1984), *Foucault Reader*, New York, Random House, p. 294.

Sabine, W. C. (1964), *Collected Papers on Acoustics*, New York: Peninsula Publications, pp. 274–5.

Schafer, R. M. (1975), *E.T.A. Hoffmanm and Music*, Toronto, p. 35.

— (1993), *Voices of Tyranny: Temples of Silence*, Indian River: Arcane Editions.

Schopenhauer, A. (1966), *The World as will and Representation*, New York: Dover Publications, vol. 2, ch. 3.

Shapiro, H. (ed.) (1964), *Medieval Philosophy*, New York, p. 6.

Takemitsu, T. (1995), *Confronting Silence*, Berkeley CA: Fallen Leaf Press, pp. 10–11.

2

Hearing Loss*

Leigh Eric Schmidt

The voices of the past are especially lost to us. The world of unrecorded sound is irreclaimable, so the disjunction that separates our ears from what people heard in the past are doubly profound. I can see evangelist George Whitefield's crossed eyes in a portrait; I can still see some of the pulpits from which he preached; I can pore over his sermons; I can read his journals. But I can never lend him my ears or eavesdrop on his prayers. Almost all of history is eerily silent and so, to evoke those stilled and faded voices, the historian must act as a kind of necromancer. The historian's ventriloquy, like that of the Witch of Endor, allows the living to hear the dead. And that is the inevitable direction of travel: historians bring the past into the present, a conversation that when necessary rings with contemporary questions.

With the sense of hearing, the presence of the contemporary at the historian's table has created not only resonance but also an excess of clarity about the past. This is especially evident in two sprawling discourses about hearing's modern diminution, twin narrative structures of loss and absence that have taken on the aura of the universal. The first involves the eye's clear eclipse of the ear, the decline of listening in the face of the ascendant power of vision in modern culture. The second concerns the dwindling of hearing as a spiritual sense and the lost presence of divine speech – that is, the peculiar acoustics of modern forms of alienation, disillusionment, and secularism. Recognizing how

* This piece was first published in Schmidt, L. E. (2000), *Hearing Things. Religion, Illusion, and the American Enlightenment,* Cambridge MA: Harvard University Press, pp. 15–28. Reproduced with permission of the publisher.

the sense of hearing has been framed within the metanarratives of modernity is a prerequisite for a more intricate historical narrative. It allows for acknowledgement of the universalized philosophical and religious inscriptions with which modern ears have been marked. The prisoners in Plato's cave, it is easily forgotten, were troubled not only by the flickering images but also by the echoes. What historians hear reflected back at them often proves to be little more than the sounds of their own tongues, but this particular treachery of knowledge is a reality to face, not efface.

More than Meets the Eye

The hearing impairments of modernity are so often presented as extensive and profound that one is sometimes tempted to scramble for a hearing-aid, or perhaps the early modern equivalent – an ear trumpet. As much of the writing on the modern sensorium has argued or presumed, vision is the dominant sense of modernity, the other senses being comparably repressed (such as smell) or vestigial (such as hearing's former centrality in oral cultures). In the very long view, the shift from orality to literacy – according, most famously, to Walter Ong and Marshall McLuhan – gradually transformed people from engaged speakers and listeners into silent scanners of written words, isolated readers in the linear world of texts. The print revolution of the early modern period sharply accelerated this bending toward visuality, this hearing loss, as books, newspapers, tracts, broadsides, charts, and Bibles flooded the cultural marketplace. Words became printed objects more than breathed speech, things to be seen rather than voices to be heard.

With its clear-eyed pursuit of detached observation, imperial sweep, and visual instrumentation, the Enlightenment was the keystone in the arch of the eye's ascendancy. 'The ocular obsession of Enlightenment thought', as historian of the senses Constance Classen has recently labelled it, served to clinch the gaze's domination of the modern sensorium. So the favoured story goes. From this critical perspective, the consumer society of spectacle, with its mediated and cinematic pleasures, becomes little more than the froth on the Enlightenment's visual wave, the bedazzled eyes of the shopper and the spectator only redoubling vision's power. With Chance the gardener, in the film *Being There*, we moderns like to watch. In a culture of science, spectacle, surveillance, sexism, shopping, and simulacra (to conflate the views of many cultural critics into one), voyeurism is often the least of the eye's transgressions (Classen 1993a).

That ocularcentrism is peculiarly modern may seem at first glance surprising, especially given the deep-rootedness of such visuality in classical orderings of the senses. For both knowledge and delight, the sense of sight was, according to Aristotle, 'above all others'; it was the most developed sense, the clearest and most discerning, the one most able to bring 'to light many differences between things'. Hearing was a close second, superior for its conduciveness to learning. Taste and touch, associated with animality, had the 'least honour'. Smell fell as a mediator in the middle. Despite Christian reservations about the dangers of the eye and its seductions, this hierarchic view of the senses was widely replicated in theological terms from Augustine onward, including Aquinas's repetition of sight's crowning perfection in the *Summa Theologica* (followed still by hearing and smell, then by taste and touch). In commentary on the senses, this has been one of most deep-seated philosophical formulas – to follow the ancients in establishing a hierarchy of perception, a system of nobility. Though hearing has had its apologists, from Lactantius in the fourth century to Charles de Bovelles in the sixteenth to Walter Ong in the twentieth, sight has commonly stood at the apex for more than two millennia. Even after the time-worn suppositions have largely passed that made such rankings seem so sensible – ordered relationships of honour and nobility are not how one would think modern citizens would imagine the senses – the Aristotelian forms of appraisal have continued, often with a vengeance.[1]

If the supreme nobility of sight is thus deeply ingrained in Western religious and philosophical traditions, many nonetheless argue that this privileging of visuality reached its apogee only during the Enlightenment and its aftermath. Modernity is seen as distinctly ocularcentric, even hypervisual; it is marked, as philosopher Jaques Ellul puts it, by 'the unconditional victory of the visual and images'. Historian Martin Jay, in his monumental account of modern ocularcentrism, has surveyed the dominance of the eyes and the ambivalences that power has generated, especially since the ascent of what he calls Cartesian perspectivalism. It is evident, Jay concludes

> that the dawn of the modern era was accompanied by the vigorous privileging of vision. From the curious, observant scientist to the exhibitionist, self-displaying courtier, from the private reader of printed books to the painter of perspectival landscapes, from the map-making colonizer of foreign lands to the quantifying businessman guided by instrumental rationality, modern men and women opened their eyes and beheld a world unveiled to their eager gaze.

While acknowledging some Enlightenment dissenters from the visual paradigm, Jay nonetheless builds on and replicates the hierarchy of the senses in which sight is the noblest and most powerful. Whether in Francis Bacon's aphorism, 'I admit nothing but on the faith of the eyes', or in Thomas Reid's, 'Of all the faculties called the five senses, sight is without doubt the noblest', Jay lifts up vision as 'the dominant sense in the modern world'. He also presents the technologies of vision – from the microscope to the panopticon – as the quintessential instruments of the modern 'scopic regime'. Sight, 'the most comprehensive of all our senses', as John Locke concluded in his *Essay Concerning Human Understanding*, reigns with unquestioned supremacy over the Enlightenment enterprise.[2]

The counterpart to the history of increasing ocularcentrism has been the history of diminished hearing. As an aspect of cultural history, this account of the senses was pioneered by the *Annales* school, especially Lucien Febvre and Robert Mandrou. In an evocative section entitled 'Smells, Tastes, and Sounds' in *The Problem of Unbelief in the Sixteenth Century*, Febvre commented of Rabelais and his contemporaries: 'They were open-air men, seeing nature but also feeling, sniffing, touching, breathing her through all their senses.' Smell and hearing for pre-Cartesians, Febvre argued, 'were exercised much more and were more highly developed (or less atrophied) than ours'. 'The sixteenth century did not see first', he concluded; 'it heard and smelled, it sniffed the air and caught sound' (*pace* the considerable evidence that Aristotelian privileges were still widely accorded to sight). Only in the seventeenth century was this experiential hierarchy reordered, Febvre hypothesized; only then was '*vision* unleashed in the world of science as it was in the world of physical sensations, and the world of beauty as well'. Mandrou followed Febvre in detailing a history of hearing loss in his inventory of the senses in early modern France: sight, 'dominant today, stood in third position', he calculated, 'a long way behind hearing and touch. The eye, which organises, classifies and orders, was not the favourite organ of a period which preferred to listen.' The quotidian evidences for such claims were slim – a touch of poetry here, a smuggling of Luther there – but the conclusions were certainly enticing, especially because they meshed so well with wider cultural criticism of the modern emergence of a society of cold observation and spectacular consumption.[3]

If there was thinness to these early attempts to incorporate perceptual modalities into the history of *mentalités*, subsequent efforts in French historiography to offer a historical anthropology of the senses have been richer and more nuanced. This is especially evident in the work of Alain

Corbin who, in *The Foul and the Fragrent, Village Bells, and Time, Desire and Horror*, has plotted 'the organisation and balance of the senses' in the late eighteenth and nineteenth centuries, notably the shifting thresholds of the tolerable and the intolerable, the sensory gauges of the pure and the polluted. Smell, in particular, became the dangerous (and hence alluring) sense of the period, used repeatedly to imagine social difference – that is, to distinguish the refined and the reasonable from the uncivilized, the erotic, the diseased, the animal, and the unclean. Thresholds around sound were similarly reworked. Corbin has argued, and the construction of the category of noise also reverberated off the cavernous walls of the social imagination. By analysing fragrances and odours as well as tolling bells, Corbin has broken out of the vision-dominated storyline and has brilliantly connected the pursuit of these sensory modes to social representations. With an evocative subtlety, Corbin shows the limits of the eye's modern ascendancy by tracking the powerful emanations of sound and odour, both of which were so ambiguously intertwined with fear, desire, memory, and difference.[4]

The history of the senses has hardly been left to the French alone. On the North American side, Father Walter Ong – historian, literary critic, cultural commentator, and Jesuit – has been the most sustained interpreter of hearing's modern diminution, again offering a historical account that is intended simultaneously as a critique of modern visuality and its disenchantments. Ong's view is ironically panoramic as he moves from ancient 'oral-aural' cultures through literacy and prints to the visualism of modern science to the 'secondary orality' of the electronic media (this last ascendancy still fails to reverse the prevailing epistemic regime of detached observation and silent reading). With a deeply Pauline conviction guiding him – faith comes through hearing – Ong offers his own metaphysics of sound, his own homily on the immediate face-to-face encounters of speakers and listeners in oral cultures, on the human and divine presences in spoken words. For Ong, the ear, or what T. S. Elliot called 'the auditory imagination', stands as the other to modernity's fractioning eye, the embodiment of the bardic and the inspired, and the now muted vehicle of both community and God's revelation. To understand the richness of oral traditions is, at some level, restorationist: it is, for Ong, a way to reconnect to the auditory modes that underpin scripture itself and that make possible Christian redemption.[5]

Ong's development of the sensorium as a domain for religious and cultural history, more than his metaphysics or his sweeping history from orality to literacy to visuality, remains a generative contribution.

Like Jay's focus on ocularcentrism, Ong's picture of 'visualist man' as the presiding power over modernity left the auditory without much of a history after the Enlightenment – after the Lockean assimilation of 'the entire sensorium to sight', after the early modern 'watershed dividing residually oral culture from typographical culture', after the learned quest for 'total written control over the spoken word', after 'the devocalisation of the universe' through the visual objectification of the physical world. How could listening have a hearing in the face of such a lofty mythology about the eye's dominion? Ong, one of the ear's great apologists, ironically helped sever it from the history of the Enlightenment and the modern aftermath.[6]

Dismay in the 1950s and 1960s about shifting patterns in communications, about human senses vastly extended and overwhelmed by technological change, gave Ong's grand historical narrative a propitious timing. But it was Ong's mentor, Marshall McLuhan, who made it chic. As technological guide and probing analyst, McLuhan was the epigrammatic therapist to those who felt the 'collective sanity' of contemporary society was fraying under the influence of the new media. In offering up a comprehensive myth of Western history timed to the revolutions in media, McLuhan saw modernity as built on the inexorable rise of a Newtonian sight, a 'cool visual detachment' again made concrete via the vast extension of typography in the early modern world. Even as successive waves of media innovations – the telegraph, telephone, phonograph, radio, and television – were unravelling this print culture, the visuality at the heart of the Gutenberg revolution remained in McLuhan's account a defining matrix for the making of modern knowledge.[7]

Crucial to McLuhan's construction of his mythology of modern Western visuality were common rhetorical strategies of alterity. The other to this Western technology and epistemology was for McLuhan the 'ear culture' of tribal, non-literate peoples in which spoken words had 'magical resonance'. With an unreflective colonialist lens, McLuhan made Africa his imaginary for constructing through black-and-white contrast a sense of which modern Europeans and North Americans were at their epistemic core. 'The African' lived in 'the magical world of the ear', while modern Western 'typographic man' lived in 'the neutral visual world' of the eye. The one was a world of vision, objectification, and progress; the other a world of sound, magic and timelessness. The animated intensity of the auditory was something that the lettered had been forced to set aside but that oral peoples all experienced – tribal worlds, which were characterised by an 'overwhelming tyranny of the ear over the eye'.[8] If McLuhan, as a Catholic convert, shared Ong's anti-modern yearning for the living presence of Christianity's revivified Word, He was also far more fearful than his Jesuit companion about the return of the repressed (evident in his imagining of the 'tribal drum of radio' and his condescension toward Romantic 'irrationalists' like Mircea Eliade). At best ambivalent about the revival of a 'primitive' aurality through the new electronic media, McLuhan wanted to engineer a new synthesis, an orderly transformation in this momentous sensory struggle: 'There can be no greater contradiction or clash in human cultures than that between those representing the eye and the ear', he exhorted with typical excess. He wanted to move people through the entrancing effects of the new media and to awaken them from the hypnotic modern drugs of television and advertising. He hoped to stay 'the return to the Africa within' (McLuhan 1961, 1964, 1969).

McLuhan's cultural juxtapositions make all too apparent how the discourse of modern Western visuality has often rested on a larger racialized frame of comparison: 'the inability of oral and intuitive oriental culture', as McLuhan phrased it in *Understanding Media*, 'to meet with the rational, visual European patterns of experience'. Given such a grand story of modern ocularcentrism, a history of modern aurality is hardly possible – especially a history of religious modes of hearing, because, in this myth, the very origin of modern culture is grounded in the exclusion of the 'primitive' or 'ancient' ecstasies of listening. The otherness, blackness, or primalness of the auditory keeps it from having a history within modern Western culture (at least, on McLuhan's terms, in between the Gutenburg revolution and the twentieth-century proliferation of electronic media). Accounts of bardic songs, narratives of oracular voices, encounters with oral scriptures, and stories of mystical auditions are plots that work for 'other' cultures – societies that are all ears – not modern ones that are all eyes. 'With them the binding power of the oral tradition is so strong', anthropologist Edmund Carpenter wrote of Eskimo perception, 'as to make the eye subservient to the ear . . . In our society, to be real, a thing must be visible . . . We trust the eye, not the ear.' In a word, we look, they listen. If McLuhan's badinage and Carpenter's ethnographic adaptations now seem exotic themselves, this discursive polarity nonetheless lingers. In a necessarily more subtle form, the storyline continues to structure descriptions of 'a Western sensory model' of visuality in contrast to the complex orality of 'premodern' cultures – that is, to divide the world between us and them.[9]

These, then, are two of the larger twentieth-century motifs around which the story of modern vision and hearing has been plotted:

- a hierarchy of the senses, with sight vastly ennobled and hearing sharply diminished; and
- a marked dichotomy between eye and ear cultures that has commonly drawn on racialized constructions of Western rationality and ecstatic primitivism.

What such narratives demand is not a carnivalesque reversal – not a dethroning of the eye and a raising up of the ear; that would only perpetuate the hierarchic, oppositional convention.

As Ong's own theology of listening suggests, to romanticize hearing at the expense of vision is an all-too-common counter-Enlightenment move already; it hardly needs reamplification. Instead, as in the work of Alain Corbin, the multisensory complexity of the social, religious, aesthetic, and erotic imaginations of the culture of the Enlightenment and its successors warrants further attention.[10] The modern sensorium remains more intricate and uneven, its perceptual disciplines and experiential modes more diffuse and heterogeneous, than the discourses of Western visuality and ocularcentrism allow. This is true of the religious dimensions of the sensorium, but it is also true of its Enlightenment valences, even that notorious source of scopic domination, seventeenth- and eighteenth-century natural philosophy.

The learned from Bacon and Mersenne onward were intent on advancing not only optics, but also acoustics – a field of enquiry that was broadly extended in the seventeenth and eighteenth centuries. Bringing together physics, anatomy, and music, the newly demarcated science of sound throve as part of the expanding experimental philosophy. Bacon, for example, was as intent on listening as on viewing, any self-profession about singular reliance on the eye to the contrary. In the *New Atlantis* (1627), his blueprint for a model college to advance learning, Bacon envisioned 'perspective-houses' for the study of light, colour, and vision, but he also had 'sound-houses' and 'perfume-houses' without noticeable difference in endowments (Speeding et al. 1963: 13), following both classical and Renaissance arguments about the considerable effects of music on body and soul, he presented hearing as the most powerful sense in its operation upon human 'manners'. What 'men' listened to had the power 'to make them warlike' or 'to make them soft and effeminate' or 'to make them gentle and inclined to pity'. Such hidden powers in sound required penetration, and Bacon lifted up 'visibles' and 'audibles' together as central to his experimental programme. 'The sight of the eye', he concluded, 'is like a crystal, or glass, or water; so is the ear a sinuous cave.' Bacon never shied away from that labyrinthine complexity, and it is the sinuous cave of the ear, more than the crystalline glass of the eye, that stands as the better similitude for the modern sensorium's twistings (Speeding et al. 1963).

'The enquiry about sounds is worthy of philosophers', Robert Boyle wrote in a letter in 1665, and his appraisal ended up widely shared among the learned. In 1684, when natural philosopher and churchman Narcissus Marsh outlined for both the Royal Society in London and its inchoate equivalent in Dublin a programme of research on acoustics, he started with a revealing 'comparison 'twixt the Senses of *Seeing* and *Hearing* as to their improvements':

> I mean, by shewing, that this lat [t] er of *Hearing*, is capable of all those improvements which the sense of *Seeing* has received from Art; besides many more advantages, that the *Ear* may enjoy, by the help of our Doctrine, above the *Eye*; all which moreover will be of as great benefit to mankind, as any thing that *Opticks* has yet discovered, if not of greater; which, with some other preeminences that it has upon another Score, will happily render *Acousticks* the nobler Science of the two.

Marsh dwelled especially on the technological potential in acoustic instrumentation, particularly '*Microphones* or . . . *Magnifying Ear Instruments*' for rendering 'the most minute Sound in nature distinctly *Audible*, by *Magnifying* it to an inconceivable loudness'. Otacousticks, implements that could act as reliable hearing-aids for those in old age, Marsh thought were even more important than eye-spectacles, 'forasmuch as the Hearing of what's spoken is of more daily use and concern to such men, th [a] n to be able to *Read Books* or to *View Pictures*'. A notably auditory hierarchy, Marsh's – one that suggests clearly how the ear could rival the eye for experimental attention (Boyle 1966; Marsh 1685).

The learned enquiry into acoustics only accelerated in the eighteenth and early nineteenth centuries. A summary sense of the perceived revolution in the science of sound and its prominent place in the Enlightenment can be garnered from the *Edinburgh Encyclopaedia* (1832), an eighteen-volume landmark that had both British and American incarnations. Surveying 'the exquisite refinements in modern mathematics' and 'the spirit of experimental philosophy, which has diffused itself over Europe since the time of Bacon', the encyclopaedia lifted up the achievements in acoustics as one of the great fruits of these modern enquiries:

By the labours of these philosophers. Acoustics has been brought to a state of great perfection. The science now presents a very different aspect from what it exhibited in the time of the ancients. The properties by which bodies act in producing sound, are now known; and their mode of operation has, in general, been successfully investigated; - the laws which sound obeys in its transmission to the organ of hearing, have been reduced to the common principles of mechanics; – the essential differences between various sounds have been detected; and their mode of action upon the ear pretty well understood: thus affording us a more complete knowledge concerning sound, and the sense of hearing, than we possess with respect to any other of our senses or their objects.

The fact that the *Edinburgh Encyclopaedia* was compiled by the eminent Scottish natural philosopher David Brewster, who was renowned for his work in optics and was hence never one to slight the eye, makes this estimation all the more telling. Light was hardly an unrivalled emblem of mastery and progress.

In at least one crucial way, the expanding inquiry into acoustics did demonstrate the ocular biases of knowledge-making in the experimental philosophy, for it was one of the central ambitions of early modern students of acoustics to visualize sound. The very invisibility of sonorous vibrations was recognized as an impediment to understanding them, so the goal was to render them 'more sensible to the eye by a little artifice' – namely, through observing the vibratory patterns reproduced in water, sand, or flames of light. Already in the 1670s Robert Hooke conducted acoustic experiments in which patterns of vibrations were displayed through the use of flour, and by the end of the eighteenth century E. F. F. Chladni had performed widely recognized demonstrations of sound's motion through the changing patterns of sand on brass plating. Arising with the Enlightenment was a new visual culture of sound, a spectacle of the auditory, that became all the more marked on the lecture circuit in the nineteenth century, with popular demonstrations that featured a whole panoply of devices for showing off acoustic principles. Also, with the growing anatomical attentiveness of the seventeenth and eighteenth centuries, the ear itself was increasingly visualized through dissection as the body was broken down graphically into ever more precise parts. The new experimental philosophy sought at a number of levels to make sound intelligible by rendering it manifest to the eye.[11]

It would be wrong simply to turn this visualizing impulse into further evidence for the singular power of vision – that the ear was made intelligible only on the eye's terms. Visualizing sound was indicative also of the sensorial play of the natural philosophers, the concern with the movement between and among the senses. For example, since sound vibrations could be felt as well as seen, tactility was crucial to acoustic study. The touch of vibrations provided, indeed, a peculiar corporeality to the notion of 'sound bites'. As Galileo observed in his dialogues on music, sound produces 'a Titillation upon the Cartilage of the *Timpanum*'; certain tones seem 'at one and the same Time to kiss and bite'. Also with an expanding set of auditory technologies – from the speaking trumpet in the 1670s to the stethoscope in the 1810s – sound was given a new material culture, a hands-on tangibility that the phrase 'hearing things' is intended to evoke alongside its psychological and illusory connotations (Galileo Galilei, *Mathematical Discourse Concerning Two New Sciences*, excerpted in Lindsay 1973: 59).

The philosophical exchange among the senses was evident in another endeavour of the late seventeenth and eighteenth centuries: that is, the effort to remake the spectrum of colours into a scale of music, a mathematical system of correspondences between light and tone. Hence, the play between sound and sight worked also in the other direction – as in Newton's speculations on vibration theory in which he suggested that 'vision is very conformable to the sense of hearing which is made by like vibrations'. The model drawn from acoustic vibrations became such a forceful analogy for how sensation worked that some Enlightenment theorists, such as David Hartley and John Elliot, were ready to incorporate all of sensory experience into an acoustic paradigm. 'Since the discovery of the analogy between colours and sounds', Elliot explained in his *Philosophical Observations on the Senses of Vision and Hearing* in 1780, 'the various kinds of tastes and smells have been considered as so many different tones or notes of these sensations'. Under this model, even the very fragrances of a garden were joined to musical experience. As Benjamin Rush, one of Hartley's American disciples, explained: 'The rose and the pink resemble tenor; and the jonquil, the minionet and the wall flower are striking analogies of the softness and delicacy of treble tones.'[12]

The crucial counterpoint to the growing visualization of knowledge among Enlightenment natural philosophers was the inductive concern with the senses as a whole. The very sensationalism of the Lockean epistemology ultimately made each of the senses the source of intense study, vigilance, commentary, and pleasure. Take, for example, Edmund Burke's 'erotic empiricism', in which all the senses were explored for their powers to produce the sublime and the beautiful. Or take Etienne Bonnet de Condillac's intent examination of all modes of sensation as sources of knowledge, with primacy accorded to touch, part of what historian Elisabeth de Fontenay identifies as 'a carnival of the senses' in the French Enlightenment. Or even take Thomas Reid's *Inquiry into the Human Mind*, the flagship of common-sense thought, a tome that grew out of a series of discourses presented before the Aberdeen Philosophical Society and dedicated to the discrete analysis of the senses. While there is little room for mistaking Reid as anything but a privilegist of the eye, he accorded such honour only after giving distinct scrutiny to smell, taste, hearing, and touch as well. In the nuances that the literati discovered through all their sensory comparisons, inspections, meditations, and delights, sight often ended up toppled from its lofty perch. This was evident, for example, in David Hartley's observation in 1749 that 'the ear is of much more importance to us, considered as spiritual beings, than the eye'.[13]

Benjamin Rush, sharing in Hartley's view of the harmonies of Christianity and vibrational mechanisms, directly echoed this estimation of the ear's spiritual supremacy in his lectures on the senses to his students in Philadelphia. This did not make Rush the patron of any one sense, however. Sometimes touch was on top, at other point's vision or hearing, and all of them were the source of intense pleasure and unbridled possibility. 'Our bodies may be compared to a violin: the senses are the strings', and the fleshly concert that results are one of 'nearly constant pleasure', Rush told his pupils. What mattered most to this American *philosophe* was the cultivation and relishing of all the senses, the perfecting of their exercise through education: 'The more acute and extensive we render the senses in their capacity of receiving impressions, the more we shall be able to increase our knowledge.' As he told his medical students, 'In a sick room, we should endeavour to be all touch, all taste, all smell, all eye, and all ear, in order that we may be all mind; for our minds, as I shall say presently, are the products of impressions upon our senses.' Enlightenment understandings of the senses were inevitably much more fluid and sophisticated than any emphasis on vision's hegemony suggests (Carlson, Wollock and Noel 1981).

None of this insistence on sensuous complexity is intended to make the Enlightenment ways of knowing seem innocent – that is, to put aside the substance of critical concerns over the objectifying gaze of manly autonomy or the watchful eye of state surveillance through an emphasis on a free play of sensual pleasures. Many of the counter-Enlightenment concerns about the detached imperiousness of the philosophical observer or the omnipresent, interiorized eye of modernity's various wardens have their counterpart in similarly sinister modes of

listening. Jeremy Bentham, for example, imagined a vast system of eaves-
dropping through speaking tubes as a crucial part of the panopticon,
and Benjamin Rush illustrated how the sense of hearing works by
alluding to the Ear of Dionysius, part of a legendary prison of antiquity
in which 'spiral windings' were supposedly used to hear 'the smallest
whisper' uttered by the inmates.[14] In their cultivation of acoustics and
their training of the ear, the literati also imagined a mastery of eaves-
dropping, an invasive mode of hearing that found embodiment in the
desire to turn the new technologies of the auditory into tools of surveillance. *Walls have ears* – the saying was given new meaning during the
Enlightenment.

One thing that all these acoustic ambitions make plain is that
printing had plenty of company in the technological transformation
of listening in the early modern world. Walter Ong imagined a long-
term disincarnation of the voice – the body that makes the words – and
connected that loss of presence, including the participatory encounter
with divine speech, to the spread of typographical models of knowledge.
Certainly, developments in communications had profound effects on
the way the literati thought about the auditory qualities of revealed
words. Illustrative is deist Tom Paine's sharp depreciation of speaking
as compared to printing: 'A man's voice can be heard but a few yards
of distance; and his person can be but in one place . . . But the art of
printing changes all the cases, and opens a scene as vast as the world.
It gives to man a sort of divine attribute . . . He can be everywhere and
at the same instant.' Paine actually made this technological observation
about simultaneity in the context of deriding Christ's 'pretended
mission', since Jesus had relied exclusively on verbal expressions in
delivering his message: God's *real* son, Paine suggested snidely, would
have arrived with a command of printing. Finding all of Christian
revelation a bundle of 'hearsay upon hearsay', Paine gave such unre-
liable voices all the less credit in comparison to the Promethean medium
of print. On top of these word-of-mouth vulnerabilities, the mastered
art of printing, Paine reasoned, only multiplied the instabilities of the
scripture as text: 'That book says (Genesis 1: 27), "*So God created man
in His own image*"; but the printer can make it say, "*So man created God
in his own image.*" To Paine, print was subversive of a speaking God,
calling into question the value of an oral gospel and pointing up the
contingencies of its textualization (Paine 1945: 1: 466, 505; 2: 786–7,
793).

Pain's use of printing to discredit the auditory qualities of Christian
revelation was embedded in a larger mechanistic critique of the oracular

voice. By the time Paine's *Age of Reason* appeared in the 1790s, natural philosophers had long been trying to detach the voice from the presence of the speaker through a series of artificial mediations. Speaking trumpets, acoustic tubes, ventriloquism, voice-producing statues, and talking machines all suggested the disembodiment of the human voice, the transmission of sound from an absent, hidden, detached, or simulated speaker. Printing, in other words, had performative accompaniments in the disincarnation of spoken words, counterparts that have very much continued to thrive – from the mediated voices of the radio to computer simulations. (Today 'electronic impersonators' not only reproduce but also even generate a person's voice, turning particular pieces of speech into a 'voice font' completely independent of the speaking body) (Andrew Pollack 1997: D1, D8). The growing fascination among natural philosophers with the ventriloquizing of human voices, with the machineries of reproduction and illusion, also fed their critique of the suspicious immateriality of heavenly voices. God's voice, too, seemed increasingly hard to place: was not that voices an illusory presence as well? The sinuous cave of the ear beckoned philosophers into complex entanglements with the auditory, with hearing and voices, and those imbrications need to become a fuller part of historical narratives about modernity. There is so much more to the Enlightenment than meets the eye.

Notes

1. See Synnott (1991: 63–4; 1993: 128-155); Vinge (1975: 15–21); Smith (1997). In the Aristotelian corpus, the critical works for the ordering of the senses are *On the Soul* and *Sense and Sensibilia* — see Barnes (1984). For Christian interactions with these classical discourses, see Chidester (1992). Chidester points to a prevailing Christian preference for the eye over the ear, from Augustine to Bonaventure, though noting some auditory dissenters, including Meister Eckhart and then, predictably, Protestants such as Luther and Melancthon. For other advocates of the minority position of elevating the ear over the eye, see Frangenberg (1991) and Vinge (1975: 36–7, 58–9).

2. See Ellul (1985: 2); Martin Jay (1993: 45, 64, 69, 85); Locke (1975: 146). Jay's care in qualifying these conclusions should be emphasized – as, for example, in his recognition of 'the complexity of the modern scopic regime,

both in theoretical and practical terms, even at its moment of apparent triumph in the Enlightenment'; but such qualifications are finally peripheral to his larger argument about ocularcentrism (p. 105). For additional samplings of this extensive literature on modern visuality, see Levin (1993); Crary (1990); Brennan and Jay (1996). For a strong, if rare, 'auditory' challenge to these visualist constructions, see Connor (1997: 203–23).

3. See Febvre (1982: 423–42); Mandrou (1976: 49–50). On the philosophical uses and contexts for the French history of the senses, see Jay (1993).

4. Corbin (1986, 1995: 181–92, 1998: esp. 298–308). For a work that helpfully broadens interpretation of the senses of smell both temporally and culturally, see Classen et al. (1994)

5. Eliot quoted in Willmott (1996: 225); Ong (1992–5: 1: 218, 2: 162, 3: 73). For an analysis of the impact that the modern print culture had on the aurality of sacred texts, see Graham (1987: 19–44).

6. See Ong (1967: 9, 14, 64–73, 174). Ong laid the foundation for his larger history through his study of sixteenth-century Ramist logic in which diagrammatic, spatialized printed knowledge displaces dialogic ways of knowing. That Ramist reorientation of the intellectual world ends in 'the elimination of sound and voice from man's understanding of the intellectual world' and in 'the silences of a spatialized universe'. See also Ong (1958, 1977, 1982). Penelope Gouk has also recently underlined the shortcomings of Ong's linear model of visualist ascendancy – see Gouk (1999).

7. McLuhan, M. (1961, 1962). The historian who has done the most to give grounding and nuance to these mythic assessments of the print revolution is Elizabeth Eisenstein. For a summary volume of her research, see Eisenstein (1983).

8. McLuhan (1964, 1969: 27–39, 45–8). McLuhan was heavily influenced in these oppositional constructions of ear and eye cultures by Carothers (1959: 307–20).

9. McLuhan (1964: 15, 298; 1969: 68); Carpenter (1973: 33–4). For a recent example of how these sensory distinctions continue to structure cultural differentiation, see Classen (1993b: 5–7). On the use of primitivism in McLuhan's thought and his visual-acoustic dichotomies, see Neill (1993: 67–71); Willmott (1996: 119–34).

10. Also available is the work of Constance Classen, although, unlike Corbin, she reiterates as much as complicates the ocularcentric narrative about the Enlightenment and modernity: 'Modern Western culture is a culture of the eye'. See Classen (1998: 1).

11. See *Encyclopaedia Americana* vol. 1: 35. On the Hooke experiments as a precedent for Chadni's, see Gouk (1980). On anatomy see, for example, Stafford (1991) and Hillman and Mazzio (1997). For the pictorialization of sound, see Schafer (1977: 127–8) and Hankins and Silverman (1995: 130–3).

12. Newton cited in Dostrovsky (1969: 236–7); Hartley (1834: 121–4); Elliot (1780: 11–15, 42); Carlson, Wollock and Noel (1981: 574). Hartley and Elliot pursue music-colour, sound-sight correspondences from their reading of Newton, whose Pythagorean and acoustic sources are outlined in Gouk (1988: 102–25); Gouk (1999: 224–57). For those colour-tone debates, see Hankins and Silverman (1995: 74–7). Within its visualist focus, Barbara Stafford's *Body Criticism* contains various reminders of the sensorial complexity of the Enlightenment. See, for example, her reflections on smell on pp. 428–430.

13. Phillips (1990); Condillac (1930); Fontenay (1982); Hartley (1834: 147). Hartley's upending of the eye came in the context of a discussion of music and the passions it stimulated; Hartley emphasized 'religious contemplations' as one of music's primary associations (p. 267).

14. Carlson, Wollock and Noel (1981: 336). For Foucault's elision of eaves-dropping in his emphasis on the interiorized gaze of surveillance, see Jay (1993: 411n) and Foucault, (1980: 154–5). For critical analysis of such auditory forms of surveillance from one of Foucault's poststructuralist compatriots, see Attali (1985: esp. 5–8).

References

Attali, J. (1985), *Noise: The Political Economy of Music*, trans. Brian Massumi, Minneapolis: University of Minnesota Press.

Barnes, J. (ed.) (1984), *The Complete Works of Aristotle*, 2 vols, Princeton: Princeton University Press.

Brennan, T. and Jay, M. (eds) (1996), *Vision in Context: Historical and Contemporary Perspectives on Sight*, London: Routledge.

Carlson, E., Wollock, J. and Noel, P. S. (eds) (1981), *Benjamin Rush's Lectures on the Mind*, Philadelphia: American Philosophical Society.

Carothers, J. C. (1959), 'Culture, Psychiatry, and the Written Word', *Psychiatry*, 22: 307–20.

Carpenter, E. (1973), *Eskimo Realities*, New York: Holt, Rineheart & Winston.

Chidester, D. (1992), *Word and Light: Seeing, Hearing, and Religious Discourse*, Urbana IL: University of Illinois Press.

Classen, C. (1993a), *Worlds of Sense: Exploring the Senses in History and Across Cultures*, London: Routledge, p. 28.

—— (1993b) *Inca Cosmology and the Human Body*, Salt Lake City: University of Utah Press.

—— (1998), *The Color of Angels: Cosmology, Gender and the Aesthetic Imagination*, London: Routledge.

Classen, C., David Howes and Anthony Synnott (1994), *Aroma: The Cultural History of Smell*, London: Routledge.

Condillac, E. B. de (1982), *Condillac's Treatise on the Sensations*, trans. Geraldine Carr, London: Favil.

Connor, S. (1997), 'The Modern Auditory I', in Roy Porter (ed.), *Rewriting the Self: Histories from the Renaissance to the Present*, London: Routledge, pp. 203–23.

Corbin, A. (1986), *The Foul and the Fragrant: Odor and the French Social Imagination*, trans. Miriam L. Kochan, Cambridge MA: Harvard University Press.

—— (1995), *Time, Desire and Horror: Towards a History of the Senses*, trans. Jean Birrell, Cambridge: Polity Press: 181–92

—— (1998), *Village Bells: Sound and Meaning in the Nineteenth Century French Countryside*, trans. Martin Thom, New York: Columbia University Press, pp. 298–308.

Crary, J. (1990), *Techniques of the Observer: On Vision and Modernity in the Nineteenth Century*, Cambridge MA: MIT Press.

Dostrovsky, S. (1969), 'The Origins of Vibration Theory: The Scientific Revolution and the Nature of Music', Ph.D. dissertation, Princeton University.

Eisenstein, E. L. (1983), *The Printing Revolution in Early Modern Europe*, Cambridge: Cambridge University Press.

Elliot, J. (1780), *Philosophical Observations on the Senses of Vision and Hearing*, London: Murray.

Ellul, J. (1985), *The Humiliation of the Word*, trans. Joyce Main Hanks, Grand Rapids, MI: Eerdmans, p. 2.

Febvre, L. (1982), *The Problem of Unbelief in the Sixteenth century: The Religion of Rabelais*, trans. Beatrice Gottlieb, Cambridge MA: Harvard University Press.

Fontenay, E. de (1982), *Diderot: Reason and Resonance*, trans. Jeffrey Mehlman, New York: Braziller.

Foucault, M. (1980), *Power and Knowledge: Selected Interviews and Other Writings, 1972–1977*, in Colin Gordon (ed.), New York: Pantheon.

Frangenberg, T. (1991), '*Auditus visu prestantior*: Comparisons of Hearing and Vision in Charles de Bovelles's *Liber de sensibus*', in Charles Burnett, Michael Fend, and Penelope Gouk (eds), *The Second Sense: Studies in Hearing and Musical Judgement from Antiquity to the Seventeenth Century*, London: Warburg Institute, pp. 71–89.

Gouk, P. (1980), 'The Role of Acoustics and Music Theory in the Scientific Work of Robert Hooke', *Annals of Science*, 37 (September): 581–2.

— (1988), 'The Harmonic Roots of Newtonian Science', in John Fauvel, Raymond Flood, Michael Shortland, and Robin Williams (eds), *Let Newton Be!*, Oxford: Oxford University Press.

— (1999), *Music, Science and Natural Magic in Seventeenth Century England*, New Haven: Yale University Press.

Graham, W. A. (1987), *Beyond the Written Word: Oral Aspects of Scripture in the History of Religion*, Cambridge: Cambridge University Press, especially pp. 19–44.

Hankins, T. L. and Silverman, R. J. (1995), *Instruments and the Imagination*, Princeton: Princeton University Press.

Hartley, D. (1834), *Observations on Man, His Frame, His Duty, and His Expectations*, 6th edition, London: Thomas Tegg & Son.

Hillman, D. and Mazzio, C. (eds) (1997), *The Body in Parts: Fantasies of Corporeality in Early Modern Europe*, New York: Routledge.

Jay, M. (1993), *Downcast Eyes: The Denigration of Vision in Twentieth Century French Thought*, Berkeley: University of California Press.

Levin, D. M. (ed.) (1993), *Modernity and the Hegemony of Vision*, Berkeley: University of California Press.

Lindsay, R. B. (ed.) (1973), *Acoustics: Historical and Philosophical Development*, Stroudberg PA: Dowden, Hutchinson & Ross.

Locke, J. (1975), *An Essay Concerning Human Understanding*, Peter H. Nidditch (ed.), Oxford: Clarendon.

Mandrou, R. (1976), *Introduction to Modern France, 1500–1640: An Essay in Historical Psychology*, trans. R.E. Hallmark, New York: Holmes & Meier.

McLuhan, M. (1961), 'Inside the Five Sense Sensorium', *Canadian Architect*, 6 (June): 54

— (1964), *Understanding Media: The Extensions of Man*, New York: McGraw-Hill.

— (1969), *The Gutenberg Galaxy: The Making of Typographic Man*, Toronto, 1962; New York: Signet, 1969: 39.

Neill, S. D. (1993), *Clarifying McLuhan: An Assessment of Process and Product*, Westport CT: Greenwood.

Ong, W. J. (1958), *Ramus, Method, and the Decay of Dialogue*, Cambridge MA: Harvard University Press.

— (1967), *The Presence of the Word: Some Prolegomena for Cultural and Religious History*, New Haven: Yale University Press.

— (1977), *Interfaces of the Word: Studies in the Evolution of Consciousness and Culture*, Ithaca: Cornell University Press.

— (1982), *Orality and Literacy: The Technologizing of the Word*, London: Routledge.

— (ed.) (1992–5), *Faith and Contexts*, Thomas J. Farrell and Paul A. Soukup (eds), 3 vols, Atlanta: Scholars Press.

Paine, T. (1945), *The Complete Writings of Thomas Paine*, ed. Philip S. Foner, 2 vols, New York: Citadel.

Phillips, A. (1990), 'Introduction', in Edmund Burke, *A Philosophical Enquiry into the Origin of Our Ideas of the Sublime and the Beautiful*, Oxford: Oxford University Press.

Pollack, A. (1997), 'Sound Bites and Then Some', *New York Times*, 21 April, D1, D8.

Schafer, R. M. (1977), *The Tuning of the World*, New York: Knopf, 1977.

Smith, P. C. (1997), 'From Acoustics to Optics: The Rise of the Metaphysical and the Demise of the Melodic in Aristotle's *Poetics*', in David Michael Levin (ed.), *Sites of Vision: The Discursive Construction of Sight in the History of Philosophy*, Cambridge MA: MIT Press, pp. 68–91.

James Speeding, Robert Leslie Ellis, and Douglas Denim Heath (eds) (1963), *The Works of Francis Bacon*, 14 vols, Stuttgart: Forman.

Stafford, B. M. (1991), *Body Criticism: Imagining the Unseen in Enlightenment Art and Medicine*, Cambridge MA: MIT Press.

Synnott, A. (1991), 'Puzzling over the Senses from Plato to Marx', in David Howes (ed.) *The Varieties of Sensory Experience: A Sourcebook in the Anthropology of the Senses*, Toronto: University of Toronto Press, pp. 61–76.

— (1993), *The Body Social: Symbolism, Self and Society*, London: Routledge, pp. 128–55.

Vinge, L. (1975), *The Five Sense: Studies in a Literary Tradition*, Lund: Gleerup.

Willmott, G. (1996), *McLuhan, or Modernism in Reverse*, Toronto: University of Toronto Press.

3

Auditory Imagination*

Don Ihde

Not all auditory imagination assumes the form of inner speech. There are also the varied possibilities that surround thinking in a language, and which, without investigation, could hopelessly confuse the issue. In the most general terms, auditory imagination as a whole displays the same generic possibilities as the full imaginative mode of experience. Within the active imaginative mode of experience lies the full range from sedimented memories to wildest fantasy.

In memory I can recall the voice of my grandmother's quaint Germanic 'oncets' and my grandfather's mumbled dinner grace beginning with, 'Komm'n Sie Jesu'. In fantasy I can presentify and represent the sounds of the world. I can imaginatively hear the strains of a flute or a 'cello or both, or I can fantasize a debate between two of my colleagues who are not on speaking terms.

Within the realm of the imaginative, auditory imagination may accompany other dimensional presentifications. I recall looking at a *National Geographic* map of the Middle East, and it presents itself irreally in the imaginative mode. But to it I 'add', while recalling the myriad faces of the peoples, the strains of a Near-Eastern wailing melody I once heard.

Both of these presentifications may then be 'released', and they disappear. But I seek out the peculiarities of the auditory dimensional characteristics. I notice that there are distances and resistances between

* From Ihde, D. (1976), *Listening and Voice. A Phenomenology of Sound*, Athens OH: Ohio University Press, pp. 133–9. Reproduced with permission.

the imaginative and perceptual modes of experience regarding co-presence. There is a ratio of focus to fringe in the dual polyphony of perceived and imagined sound. Perceived sound, as in the case of 'white sound', or programmed background music, floats lazily around me, and I find I can easily retire into my 'thinking self' and allow the perceptual presence to recede from focal awareness. But a series of variations illustrate that there are also distances and resistances in the polyphony of perceived and imagined sound.

If suddenly the sounds of the environment increase in intensity and volume, particularly if not constant, I begin to find a resistance to the maintenance of 'inner' focus to 'outer' sound. The perceived sound in its penetrating capacity disturbs my train of thought. Auditory interruptions of 'thinking' are particularly noticeable. A sudden noise, the annual engine trial of someone's hydroplane on the harbour, poses a serious distraction. I recall when living in another town, the intrusions of the attempts of a nascent rock drummer whose practice sessions at an open window across my backyard made the truth of the statement *it's so loud I can't hear myself think* apparent. The intrusive presence of sound may penetrate into even my 'thinking' self-presence.

A second variation of the 'disruptive' quality of sound on the occurrences of auditory imagination and the continuities of 'thinking' comes more pleasantly in the enchantment of music, which can also overwhelm inner self-presence. In its sometimes orgiastic auditory presence the body-auditory motion enticed in the midst of music may lead to a temporary sense of the 'dissolution' of self-presence. Music takes me 'out of myself' in such occurrences.

Each of these variations revolves around the penetration of sound into the very region of the 'thinking self'. But while sound poses a threat of seduction in some of its occurrences, which intrude 'inwardly', there are also possibilities of co-present polyphony of auditory experiences of the perceptual and imaginative modalities. Here the variations begin, however, to leave the realm of strictly ordinary experiences and move toward more extreme variations. However, many of the following experiences are better known, and some are quite familiar to the musician whose auditory imagination is often better tuned than that of the non-musician.

There is, in auditory imagination, the possibility of a synthesis of imagined and perceived sound as noted previously in a visual example. But in this case the auditory 'hallucination' is not a matter of hearing one thing as something else but a matter of a doubled sound, a synthesized harmonic *echo*. I listen to a record of Vivaldi's *Four Seasons*. In my new intensified listening I pay particular attention to the trailing off of sounds, following them in Husserlian fashion in their reverberations which meet the horizon of retentiveness. I 'hold on' to these notes as deliberately as possible as they trail off. After some attempts at 'stretching' attention in this fashion, suddenly and spontaneously there occurs a fully 'doubled' passage in the form of a harmonically synthesized gestalt. That is, the notes that were 'trailing off' return, doubled as co-present with the next phrase as if suddenly *two* orchestras are playing, one slightly out of time with the other. But the momentary co-presence of a 'now-point' with the 'just-past' sound occurs as a full harmonic echo. Later I find that musicians following this period of composition have actually written such effects into their music.

Less dramatically, a variation of the above possibility is more easily detected not as a harmonic synthesis but as a fading reverberational echo of tones just passing off being vividly retained and 'added' to tones coming into presence with a definite sense of 'distance' such that the echo reverberation is distinguished from the oncoming sounds but also remains as a fringe effect. In exercises of extremely intense listening the doubling effect can produce dissonances as well as harmonies. However, in both the above-noted examples it is unclear what other roles an imaginative modality plays, if any, because the situation described above is close to being an auditory equivalent to the doubled sight which occurs when one crosses his eyes.

In all of the variations upon auditory polyphony cited above, forms of co-presence show themselves as variations upon harmonies or dissonances, upon musical sound. But if I try to imagine and perceive the same sounds at the same time, I find the same *resistance* previously noted. Again the sense of rapid alterations shows itself as the closest approximation to this lack of distance within auditory experience. In this there is an essential isomorphism of the structure of intentionality within perceptual and imaginative listenings.

Further variations begin to show related polyphonies, which double perceptual and imaginative possibilities in different ways. I attend a concert, and while it is playing I begin, in fancy, to 'embroider' the perceived piece of music with co-present imaginative tonalities. With some practice it soon becomes possible to create quasi-synthetic dissonances, adumbrations, variations upon the actual themes being played. There is some evidence that this 'distracted', although intense, listening may have been practised by Mozart, who was always accused of never listening to anyone else's music but was busy creating his own version of it even in the presence of another's music. In this form of co-presence there remains a slight sense of distance between the modalities either in the sense of one being an 'echo' of the other in a version of foreground and background attentiveness or in the form of alternating bursts of perceptual and imaginative sounds.

In all of the above-noted examples of auditory polyphony the forms of co-presence maintain at least a minimal distance. The perceived sound is in harmony with or in dissonance with the imagined sound. A much stronger resistance is found in trying to perceive and imagine the same sound simultaneously. Here, if any success is achieved at all, close reflection shows a series of rapid alternations between focally perceived and imagined modes of experience. Here a clue is offered regarding an essential isomorphism of intentional structures in the perceptual and imaginative modes.

In spite of what historically has been a massive lack of philosophical attention to the phenomena of auditory imagination, the development of its possibilities, particularly in music, is worthy of investigation. For example, auditory temporal significance may be exceedingly accurate. In the case of Toscanini, tapes of original cuts of symphonies which had been recorded twelve years apart showed that his sense of time was accurate enough for the tempo of one symphony to be within microseconds of the other.

If philosophy has largely ignored the musical ear in both its perceptual and imaginative modes, it *has* attended to the problem of the 'linguistic'. Although there has been a vast amount of work done on philosophical problems of language, little has been done concerning the examination of concrete forms of thinking as inner speech considered as a type of auditory imagination. In part, this phenomenon as a phenomenon of a special type of auditory imaginative activity may have been overlooked because of the long tradition of interpretation that maintains a 'metaphysical' and 'Cartesian' stance toward thought. This tradition takes for granted that thought is disembodied. Thus in spite of discussion of 'mental word', the persistence of a dualism of 'acoustic tokens' and disembodied 'meanings' continues.

But there are phenomenologically locatable reasons for the failure to locate 'linguistic thinking' in inner speech as part of the auditory dimension. These reasons lie within the fragility and structure of the phenomenon itself. Inner speech as a form of auditory imagination *hides* itself. Yet in this hidden, fragile, and difficult to locate phenomenon are deeper existential significances for the understanding of human *beings as language*.

Thinking in a language, inner speech, although hidden, is also familiar. And as in the case of all familiar phenomena the familiarity itself is a bar to thematizing the phenomena. Inner speech is an almost *continuous* aspect of self-presence. Within the 'contingency' of human language it is focally embodied in thought as an imaginative modality of spoken and heard language. As an *accompaniment* to the rest of experience it is a most 'inward' continuity of self-presence and the hidden familiar presence of an experiential polyphony.

The first proximate variations within the auditory dimension displayed the intrusive capacity of sound to disrupt patterns and trains of 'thought'. And the first indications of distances and resistances begin to foster a more positive suspicion regarding the location and role of inner speech as a special type of auditory imagination. However, further variations are needed to make this phenomenon stand out more clearly.

I return to variations upon musical imaginative presence. When involved in presentifying the 'embroidery' of an imaginative musical 'addition' to the perceived music, I note that my inner speech ceases. I am 'in' the music. I discover here a resistance to simultaneously 'thinking in a language' and imaginatively presenting music. On the other hand, when, focused totally upon the multiplicity of imaginative phenomena, I find that I can easily imagine the philosopher's centaur while continuing to 'think' in inner speech. Such considerations are not conclusive, although as indirect indexes of the isolation of inner speech as auditory imagination they begin to narrow further the region of location.

Each of the above continues to be a variation in the midst of an often confusing wealth of experiential polymorphy. A reverse set of variations in the form of a detour into pathology of listening serves to isolate indirectly and inversely the embodiment of language in inner speech. Defects of hearing and, most extremely, deafness symptomatically point to both the 'contingency' of what is focally the role of inner speech and to the existential importance of the auditory in the human community. Helen Keller confessed that 'the problems of deafness are deeper and more complex, if not more important, than those of blindness. Deafness is a much worse misfortune. For it means the loss of the most vital stimulus – the sound of the voice that brings language, sets thoughts astir, and keeps us in the intellectual company of man' (Stevens and Warshofsky 1966).

Language 'contingently' focally embodied in sound forms the intersubjective 'opening' to the world in terms of the linguistic core of language. Two qualifications concerning this assertion should be noted on a preliminary basis: first, the claim is not to be taken to mean that a loss of the auditory dimension makes 'thinking' impossible – this is clearly false – but that the loss of the focal capacities of the auditory dimension displaces the 'contingent' focus on thought, although thought continues to be embodied in different ways. Empirically, it has long been recognized that the problems of deafness are essentially tied to the problems of language, and that such a relation poses the most serious problem for those afflicted. Secondly, there is at least a weak sense in which, unlike blindness, there is never a case of total deafness. The gradations of hearing shade off into a larger sense of one's body in listening. The ears may be focal 'organs' of hearing, but one listens with one's whole body. The folk music fan 'hears' the bass in his belly and through his feet, and the deaf child learns to 'hear' music through his hands and fingers. There is, usually, some extremely vestigial hearing in the deaf that can also be partly extended through intensive amplification. But the deaf person continues to 'hear' in an essentially different way from the ordinary listener in that what to the ordinary listener remains a fringe effect – sounds felt and experienced in the body – is sometimes the entirety of the deaf person's auditory 'focus': he 'hears' from *only* the fringe.

Not only does this close off the 'contingent' *focal* intersubjective language of humankind; it also affects the way in which it 'hears' itself. When I speak, I also listen to myself. I feel and take for granted the sounds that I hear returning from my voice. This also gives me a sense of how correctly I may be projecting or enunciating.

But it may be that I fail to notice, until provided with the auditory mirror of a tape recorder, that I do not hear myself as others hear me nor do they hear me as I hear myself. When I speak, if I attend to the entire bodily sense of speaking, I feel my voice resonate throughout at least the upper part of my body. I feel my whole head 'sounding' in what I take to be sonoric resonance. This self-resonance, which I take for granted, does not appear on the tape, and I am initially surprised at the 'thinness' and the 'higher tone' my voice has on the recording. Physically, of course, not only can these effects be measured indicating the effect of my voice on my skeletal and muscular framework. I hear through bone conduction as well as through the acoustical properties of the air, but the two 'media' of self-hearing are essentially separate. There is an essential sense in which *my hearing of myself is distinct from all other forms of hearing*. The same is the case in the presence of my 'inner voice' that 'thinks' in a language.

Reference

Stevens, S. S. and Warshofsky, F. (1966), 'Sound and Hearing', *Time Life International*, p. 144.

4

The Help of Your Good Hands

Reports on Clapping

Steven Connor

Adversity

It is to be supposed that clapping among humans may have evolved from the action of slapping and cuffing the body, often accompanied by jumping and stamping, which is characteristic of primates in states of excitement. It is sometimes suggested that clapping and stamping may have provided the first systematic music produced by human beings. Clapping the hands together has several advantages over slapping the body. First of all, it produces a much more emphatic, consistent and easily controllable sound. In clapping, one aims to do more than merely sound skin against skin: think of the flat, insulting patter of applause delivered with gloved hands. Clapping is actually a complex action to perform: the truly effective or vital clap aims to compress and explode a little bubble or bomb of air, compressing and accelerating the air momentarily trapped between the palms, just at the sonorous 'sweet spot' so relished by tennis players. Despite the association of handclapping with childish glee, children take a long time to learn how to do it properly, although they seem to learn – or are taught – very early on to want to.

Clapping can be understood as a specialization of the action of manual striking that is a distinctive accomplishment of primates. Most animals employ an action of tearing to attack or defend themselves: lions and sharks with teeth, owls and eagles with beaks, crabs and stag-beetles with claws. Some quadrupeds (mostly those whose real speciality is in fact running away) rely upon kicking, of which the action of hitting with the fist, particular to primates, is a specialization. Given the import-ance to primates of the actions of pushing, prodding, shoving, rapping, knocking, thumping, slapping, slamming, buffeting, punching, and the other actions proper to the hand, it is not surprising that we should have evolved such an interest in the actions of concussion or violent conjuncture in nature. *Ad-vers-ity*, the impacting of things, things that come up violently against each other: many other kinds of contact or encounter occur in nature, but the attention of human beings continues to be drawn irresistibly to such processes. The work of war continues to enlarge and develop the typologies of impact, through the club, the knife, the arrow, the bullet, the bomb, the missile. It is surprising that other ways of defeating or exterminating one's opponent – through radiation, poison gas or biological agents, and other forms of infiltrating assault – should have taken so long to develop. Many of the words em-ployed to designate enemies – the opponent, the adversary – suggest this meeting, collision or coming together of what stands face to face. This notion of adversity – the agon of the blow or smiting – has predom-inated in definitions of sound.

Not that adversity is always adverse. The word 'smack', which can refer to the sharp sound of an impact with the open hand, usually on another expanse of skin, to the sound of the lips coming together and parting, and to a taste (as also in German *schmecken*), seems to suggest the compacting of sound, touch and taste in the primary action of feed-ing from the breast. Is not the birth cry itself traditionally elicited by the midwife's smack, as though to start the infant's clock of skin? William James (1890: 481) refers to the suggestion (apparently first advanced in F. G. J. Henle's *Anthropologische Vorträge* of 1876–80) that the action of clapping is a 'symbolic abridgement of an embrace'.

Triumph

Clapping is a neutralization and diversification of these actions. In its primary meaning, clapping retains its associations with violence, functioning as an emblematic display on the body of the aggressor of what may be in the offing for his victim. Clapping of hands retains its association with anger, triumph and insulting contempt through the Old Testament. When Balaam has failed to curse the tribes of Israel as he had been commanded, 'Balak's anger was kindled against Balaam, and he smote his hands together' (Numbers 24:10). It is said of the despised Job that 'Men shall clap their hands at him, And shall hiss him out of his place' (Job 27: 23), and Job is said to return the insult: 'he addeth rebellion unto his sin. He clappeth his hands among us, And multiplieth his words against God' (Job 34:37). In fact, the expression 'clapping hands' in English translations of the Old Testament collapses together a number of expressions from different semantic fields (Fox 1995; Rogland 2001).

Similarly, clapping the hands is also associated with the accomplishment of magical actions and transformations in many cultures, presumably because it enacts a sudden, paroxysmic concentration and release of vital force. Many cultures share a notion of the annunciatory role of the thunderclap. Clapping can summon spirits, and also drive them away. I am told by Santanu Das that, in rural parts of India, hermaphrodites or sexually indeterminate persons signify their approach by clapping.

Compulsive hand clapping is a common behaviour among autistic children, and can also be therapeutically employed among victims of burns suffering the intense solitude of sensory deprivation, perhaps because it provides definition and structure in an otherwise chaotic and insufficiently differentiated flux of experience (Christenberry 1979). There is some evidence (Van der Meij 1997) that clapping can induce pleasurable epileptiform episodes in the brain.

There are important distinctions to be made between the individual clap – the Caliph calling for his dancers, the magician dismissing or summoning his spirits, the clapping which inaugurates and completes the action of Shinto prayer – and collective clapping. A single clap is convulsive and climactic. It marks a precipitate change of state, a coming to completion, or a new beginning, or a reversal: in all cases, a sudden, sharp interruption to the steady unrolling of time. Clapping draws a line in time, as in the 'clapperboard' that divides up scenes in film-making. Clapping belongs with the instinctive ejaculations of the body – coughing, sneezing, vomiting, ejaculation of sperm, all of those actions of violent exteriorization that have been thought of as the overtaking of the body by some outside agency, but which can be brought under voluntary control in the single or separated clap. During the 1990s, Krishan Chander Bajaj began a clapping cult in Delhi, claiming that clapping for about 20 minutes a day had reversed his glaucoma and could cure many other diseases by increasing circulation and dispersing blockages in the blood (http://www.sholay.com/stories/2000/june/10062000.htm).

Collective clapping, by contrast, is convergent and conjunctive. Rather than intensifying time, it thickens and spreads it. One might say that the single clap temporalizes time, takes a featureless space of time and exposes it to temporality by concentrating it into an instantly diffused instant, while collective clapping slows or arrests the passage of time, forming it into a mass, or durative volume. The clap enacts instantaneity; applause enacts extension. At the same time, extended passages of formless applause themselves mark transitions. It has been suggested (Needham 1967) that the principal role of percussion in some cultures is to mark contacts between the human and supernatural worlds, and ritual transitions between them, and clapping may be a specialized form of this general use of percussion to produce amorphous masses of sound.

Clapping mediates two primary aspects of sound, namely its power to penetrate boundaries and, by a reparative action, its power to form protective milieus. Put simply, sound can be both an intolerable wound, and an armour or cataplasm against the injurious effects of sound itself. Sound pervades, but also surrounds. Clapping turns the puncturing, penetrating sound of the individual clap into a diffuse, knitted multiplicity.

Claptrap

In my book *Dumbstruck* (Connor 2000), I suggested that the voice formed itself into characteristic profiles and postures that could be thought of as imaginary 'voice-bodies', bodies shaped performatively out of the implied or enacted relations of the voice to the substance of its sound – self-caressing, self-assaulting, self-inflating. Perhaps clapping, by contrast, is a body-voice, noise made quasi-vocal. Clapping is a spilling over of feeling into formless expression: that nevertheless gives expression a form (a sharp, rapidly declining, rapidly renewed, spike of sound). The clap is one of a number of profane (because indeterminate) sounds that humans make. If the distinctive sound of the human is the sound of language, then the quasi-language of non-articulate sound produced from other places than the mouth always has the taint of the gratuitous, the excessive, or the proscribed. Clapping is the benign superflux of the body, the diarrhoea of sound. Clapping is the absence of speech: clapping is a reduction of sound to primary elements. Early usages of the word clapping reflect discredit on the tongue, which, in empty speech, is reduced to a percussion instrument, knocking vacantly against the mouth.

What is wrong with desultory applause, the kind rendered so effectively in the 'Sirens' episode of *Ulysses*, to mark the end of a song sung
in a bar – 'Clapclap. Clipclap. Clappyclap'? It is applause that is tattered
by gaps. There are few actions as acidly derisive as the slow handclap,
especially when conducted by a single individual. Instead of an excited
crackle of sound, there is an ominous series of empty clacks, leaving
gaping silences between them. The warmly lapping or engulfing
garment of sound produced by applause is thereby rent and emaciated.
The analogies between clapping and the idea of an ideal garment are
dramatized in W. B. Yeats's question at the beginning of *Sailing to
Byzantium:*

> An aged man is but a paltry thing,
> A tattered coat upon a stick, unless
> Soul clap its hands and sing, and louder sing
> For every tatter in its mortal dress

Clapping is made up of gaps, but it aims to obliterate them. Clapping
is like the fiercest, most effacing sort of scribbling. Why can no audience
sustain a slow handclap? It always disintegrates, or speeds up. It is as
though we crave the merging of the separate rhythms, the white noise,
the drip painting, the blizzard, the palimpsest. Clapping is the attempt
to knit a continuum of sound, a surface, a volume, a body of sound.
Applause forms a warmly lapping garment, a comfortable engulfment
formed of many skins. When teams leave the savage exposure of the
field of play, the passage into the safety of the dressing room through
the birth canal of the player's tunnel is often mediated by the practice
of 'clapping one's opponents in'. In this one team forms two lines of
applauding players through which the other team funnels in single file.
Usually the applauded team will then form themselves into a tunnel
through which the applauders can pass, recalling the threading exchanges
of inside and outside employed in many forms of country dancing,
which are themselves sometimes accompanied by clapping. In both
contexts, clapping participates in an interweaving topology of sound
and movement that converts adversary standoffs into inversive interrelations.

Overlapping

Clapping has silent correlatives in actions of self-touching, in prayer,
crossing oneself, or in bringing a finger to the lips, or scratching a nose

or ear, which often accompany actions of thought. If clapping is a form of bodily overflow into sound, we might also say that clapping belongs to a bodily system of overlapping. Perhaps the closest correlative to the use of the hands to produce sharp sounds is the conventional action of Christian prayer, which seems to act to close and double the body in on itself, as a way of turning it outwards towards some other centre of concern.

Clapping makes you aware of yourself and of the other in yourself. In clapping, as in many other activities, you lay the two surfaces of yourself one against another. Children clap by bringing both hands together – the symmetry looks very awkward. Most adults in the West clap by clapping one hand on another; percussion of the self on self, usually the right on the left, or of the I-hand on the it-hand, the me-skin on the world skin. Clapping is ecstatic: it puts us beside ourselves; singular clapping is as inadequate and paradoxical as the idea of one hand clapping. This makes the Zen koan of the one-hand clapping poignantly appropriate to contexts such as the experience of stroke in which there may be the agonizing sensation of the loss of part of the self (Veith 1988). Clapping one hand on another dramatizes the fact that you are a subject and an object simultaneously, a doer and a done to; you fold yourself over yourself, you form an interface with yourself, which joins to the interface you form with others. This, after all, is the condition of all sound. John Cage was mistaken in his dream of an art that would liberate the voices buried within things, letting things sing out their individual songs. For there is no sound that is not collateral, the sound of at least two things coming together. The voice is the abstract dream that an entity could have its own sound, although this is as impossible as the sound of a one-handed clap. Clapping lets copulation thrive and itself prospers on it. Clapulation. Collapulation. Collabatteration.

You cannot clap alone. Clapping is not applause (the word that has so much of the spattering plosiveness of clapping in it). Applause is a kind of infection, inflammation, conflagration, cloudburst. The impulse to clap runs as fast as an electric shock, and certainly faster than thought. This makes applause both unstable and subject to manipulation. The growth of organized 'claques' and 'claqueurs' in early nineteenth-century French theatre stimulated outrage on the part of those who sought to restore to manipulated audiences their powers of independent judgement. But when the author of the 1849 pamphlet *A bas le claque!* sought to characterize the authentically attentive audience it was in terms of a quivering, sensitive organism, whose corporeal judgement goes too fast to be overseen by rational evaluation. This is not free and unswayed judgement, but a different kind of automatism:

Observe this attentive face, these dilated nostrils, these quivering lips, this taut neck, these hands ready to come together . . . What fire! What heat! What impetuosity! The pleasure experienced and the emotion felt in common run like an electric current through the whole crowd. There is no touch of the dead hand in this public! (Segaud 1849: 9)

Applause has sometimes suggested itself as belonging to the sphere of the irrational or the incalculable in human life. For example, the impulse to applause provided William MacDougall with one of his arguments against behaviourism in his 1928 debate with one of its leading exponents, J. B. Watson:

I come into this hall and see a man on this platform scraping the guts of a cat with hairs from the tail of a horse; and, sitting silently in attitudes of rapt attention, are a thousand persons, who presently break out into wild applause. How will the Behaviorist explain these strange incidents? How explain the fact that the vibrations emitted by the catgut stimulate all the thousand into absolute silence and quiescence; and the further fact that the cessation of the stimulus seems to be a stimulus to the most frantic activity? (Watson and Macdougall 1928: 62–3)

Presumably we speak of a 'round of applause' because of a sense of the circulation of energies within it, a transmission, a passage. It is for this reason, surely, that the size of an audience is proportional to the duration of its applause: why does it take an arena full of people much longer to deliver even a perfunctory round of applause than a small concert hall? Presumably because the clapping has to go around more people. Applause and the desire to applaud feeds on itself. Individuals certainly feel the need to clap hands in pleasure and exaltation, but rarely feel the impulse to applaud out of a crowd. Individual clapping is always slow and deliberate when one might expect it to be fast and furious, as though to fill all the available gaps. Clapping creates a space, a shape in time and space. A group of people define themselves as a group, rather than merely an aggregate; they enter into an exchange with the one being applauded, who is at once placed in front of the applause, and centred in its midst. Applause performs the same merging together of particularities as occurs in what it names, because applause is a collective name for 'plaudits'.

Clapping involves listening as well as the creation of sound, in an agitated, energetic feedback loop; one is adjusting oneself all the time to what one hears, and what one hears is nothing more than the ongoing aggregation of all these minuscule adjustments. I know of no integrated history of the act, as well as the fact, of audience in human history, of the specific material ways in which listening has occurred, in different material circumstances, theatres, concert-halls, churches, classrooms, barracks. All the histories of audience response I have encountered (but I am still looking) seem to concern themselves with more cognitive or moral functions – with the ways in which audiences identify, understand, approve, and so on – rather than with their verifiable actions. The noisy action of clapping, along with all its accompaniments and variants – cheering, stamping, whistling, booing, hissing, catcalling – would form a central part of such a history. In its absence, it is surprisingly hard to know how and how much audiences have clapped in different places, circumstances and times. Although the word 'applause' derives from the Latin *plaudere*, which means to beat or strike (the hands) together, the uses of the English word 'applause' that I have been able to chart up to the twentieth century may include handclapping but need not refer exclusively to it. It is clear that, in the age in which recorded and transmitted performances are more commonly experienced than 'live' performance, the transmission of applause is a way of making audiences and the fact and act of audience audible. All orators and actors learn the art of manipulating the subtle, hairtrigger mechanisms of applause, but the increased audibility of applause makes the sound of this answering response enter into the performance itself, in something of the way in which sound entered into the silent film image, not supplementing or colouring or rounding out the image, but penetrating and renaturing it. Applause is present as a field phenomenological possibility at every moment of the performance.

Applause can only really succeed in relatively formal situations, in which time is formally segmented or strophed. Under certain circumstances, a speaker taking the podium after having been introduced, the failure, or suppression of the urge to applaud can be as poignant as an absconded sneeze. Time, which is broken up by action and response, is also blended into itself – the gaps between the claps are suffused with the incipience of the applause, the applause itself is mingled with silence and its own dying fall.

Clapped Out

Clapping is a pure multiplicity, which is neither decomposable into its separate elements nor wholly totalizable. It belongs to the order of swarms, storms, floods, epidemics and nature's semi-random specklings, frecklings and maculations, of 'crowds, packs, hordes on the move, and filling with their clamor, space' (Serres 1995: 2). Clapping is a quasi-organism, a quasi-animate substance. The landscape of clapping has its very distinctive and individual contours, as well as its own tones and colours, loops, undulations and fault-lines. It has its moods, weathers, textures, consistencies, rhythms, intensities. Clapping is somewhere between an energy and a substance; an energy trying to solidify itself as a substance, a substance coagulated from events and energies. Clapping is solidity forming out of rupture. The clapperboard marks the place of the cut, but also the place of the synchronizing join. Clapping derives its shape and sound from interference patterns, from the intersections and knittings-together of these interruptions. It is the background noise of things brought into the foreground, noise become signal. The function of clapping is to interrupt, but it becomes interruption interrupted, as it forms a kind of shape and syntax out of interruption. Clapping involves the filling and the emptying of time. It occupies time by suspending it. The telling of a joke, the action of a play, must be held back while applause breaks out; but the holding back prepares another impulse to applaud, even while the first is dying away, like an under-wave or cross-wave pushing through the ebb.

There are precise gradations of duration in clapping, and clapping is a way of projecting duration into bodily form and taking duration into the body. Under certain circumstances, only clapping for *too long* can be enough. The operators of the house lights in theatres know that they must be brought up at a precise moment before the applause starts to flag, becomes conscious of its own fatigue. Clapping conjures life: At the end of J.M. Barrie's *Peter Pan*, children are enjoined to clap to signify their belief in fairies and to bring the expiring Tinkerbell to life. But clapping is itself subject to ageing and decomposition. Clapping gathers and loses intensity, in a cycle of increase and diminishment: clapping is associated both with the propagation of energy – 'going like the clappers' – and with its depletion – becoming 'clapped out'.

References

Christenberry, E. (1979), 'The Use of Music Therapy With Burn Patients', *Journal of Music Therapy*, 16, 138–48.

Connor, S. (2000), *Dumbstruck: A Cultural History of Ventriloquism*, Oxford: Oxford University Press.

Fox, N. (1995), 'Clapping Hands as a Gesture of Anguish and Anger in Mesopotamia and in Israel', *Journal of the Ancient Near Eastern Society of Columbia University*, 23, 49–60.

James, W. (1890), *The Principles of Psychology*, 2 vols, New York: Henry Holt.

Needham, R. (1967), 'Percussion and Transition', *Man*, NS 2, 606–14.

Rogland, M. (2001), '"Striking a Hand" (*tq' kp*) in Biblical Hebrew', *Vetus Testamentum*, 51: 107–9.

Segaud, E. (1849), *A bas le claque!* Paris.

Serres, M. (1995), *Genesis*, trans. Geneviève James and James Nielson, Ann Arbor: University of Michigan Press.

Van der Meij, W., Franssen, H., Van Nieuwenhuizen, O., Van Huffelen, A.C. (1997), 'Tactile Self-Induction of Epileptiform EEG Phenomena in the Context of Extreme Somatosensory Evoked Potentials', *Journal of Epilepsy*, 10, 242–6.

Veith, I. (1988), *Can You Hear the Clapping of One Hand? Learning to Live With a Stroke*, Berkeley and Los Angeles: University of California Press.

Watson, J. B. and Macdougall, W. (1928), *The Battle of Behaviourism: An Exposition and An Exposure*, London: Kegan Paul & Co.

5

The Sound of Music*

Douglas Kahn

There has been a line drawn between sound and musical sound, describing disciplinary demarcation and maintaining musical integrity at an historical juncture in which there were the means to do otherwise. In the absence of any practical challenge from the other arts, music was considered the *sine qua non* of the arts of sound, and what appeared to be a challenge mounted by *avant garde* music was instead primarily a recuperation of sound into musical preoccupations. What little pressure was put on musical practices to change was largely discursive and had little positive effect in actual sonic practice. During the heyday of the *avant garde,* some of the most provocative artistic instances of sound came from literature and other writings, and were distant from the development of the arts or aurality of the time. In the latter half of the 1920s, with the increased technological sophistication of film sound, radio, amplification and microphony, and phonography, as well as a changed aurality shaped by mass-mediated culture, the questioning of musical integrity started to become more pronounced. Soon, however, economic collapse, consolidation and expansion of authoritarian regimes, exile and repression against artists and intellectuals, military activities, would remove what conditions had existed for major artistic revision and elaboration. Nevertheless, although the sporadic activities during the late-1920s and early-1930s failed to assume the broader continuities of an artistic practice, they did indicate a qualitatively different artistic approach toward significant sound.[1]

* This chapter is excerpted, with minor modifications, from Kahn, D. (1999), *Noise, Water, Meat: A History of Sound in the Arts*, Cambridge MA: MIT Press. Reproduced with permission.

The tradition of what is called *avant garde,* modernist and experimental music during this century is usually understood as the radical edge of the larger practice of Western art music, a small minority of composers and other practitioners important for the evolution or assertion of different philosophies, poetics, politics, techniques, technologies, styles, and so forth within the larger realm of composition, a way to keep pace with the present. It can also be understood as an adaptive manoeuvre by which arts in the West confronted larger transformations in the social conditions of aurality and kept the full extent of their social, political and poetic provocation at bay by recuperating significant sound into musical materiality. While the first understanding is regularly rehearsed and the second seldom so, they are in many instances functionally interdependent.

Despite the concentration of the bulk of Western art music activity upon the music of past centuries, played on vintage classes of instruments couched within equally vintage rites, the actions of venturesome contemporary *avant garde* composers grappling with changing conditions of aurality have given rise to an impression that Western art music as a whole has the capacity to respond to the world in which people presently live. Whether they responded admirably in musical terms is not up to question here, merely whether, through the discursive dint of associating musical sound with sound in general, or other aspects on an historical scale quite apart from the personal integrity or the value of the music of this or that composer, they responded as well they could to the changing conditions of sound and aurality. Likewise, the process of musicalization not only acts on one front to rejuvenate Western art music practice, expanding the material and technical base while maintaining the autonomy of musical practice – more significantly it casts musical premises far afield of their natural habitat, where music is further situated and supported through its incorporation into other practices and discourses of culture and aurality. Thus, from the timbral tactics of Russolo's art of noises, through the homegrown legitimation of resident noise, through John Cage's musicalization of aurality itself, Western art music has developed a number of means through its *avant garde* to maintain its integrity and expand its resources in the changing auditive environments of this century.

One thing that remained tenaciously extramusical, however, was what was usually called imitation. However it may have been invoked past or present – noise, sound, reproduction, representation, meaning, semiotics, and so forth – the primarily sonic has been recuperated into music with relative ease while significant sound has met with great resistance. Only the briefest and most infrequent instances of worldly sound were allowed into Western art musical practice, while its broader applications of imitation, such as programme music, were commonly considered to be lower life forms. Contraptual sounds produced by non-instrumental objects were banished to the circus, variety theatre, novelty music, vaudeville, theatrical sound effects and folk traditions, and even quotation from musics outside one's own tradition could be an exercise in extramusicality.

It was more difficult to keep 'imitative' sounds at bay after the advent of viable phonographic techniques. Unlike the effect that photographic verisimilitude had upon painting and drawing, music was not relieved of any tradition or aspiration toward phonographic realism. Phonography did, nevertheless, promise an alternative to musical notation as a means to store sonic time and, in the process, deliver *all sound* into artistic materiality, and musical discourse responded by trivializing the complexity of significant sounds and their settings. Indeed, after a certain historical point, it was not so much the potential for musical practices of imitation that were debased, as it was the concept of imitation within musical discourse. Only by distancing itself from attempts at a comprehension of the conditions of aurality within a particular time and place, including the operations of music itself within those conditions, could music protect itself from sound.

How could this be the case within the radical transformations that occurred during the vigorous days of modernism and the *avant garde*? How could Western art music be so successful in protecting its own domain when, at the very same time, so many other arts inverted their representational modes. If painting could jettison the recognizable for the non-objective, how could Western art music not follow suit and jettison the non-objective for the recognizable? What was the source of this sensorial asymmetry in modernism? Perhaps the most obvious reason why music was not compelled to radicalize its representational means relative to the other arts was the privileged position that music itself was placed among those same arts. Music was valued as a model for modernist ambitions toward self-containment, self-reflexivity and unmediated communication. Its abstracted character was thought to have already achieved what the other arts were attempting. Gabrielle Buffet-Picabia, a musician in a world of visual artists, was in a good position to make a statement very typical of the time:

> I had been initiated into the organization of sounds into music, into the strict discipline of harmony and counterpoint, which make up its complex

and artificial structure, the problems of musical composition became for
me a constant source of amazement and reflection. Consequently, I was
well prepared to hear Picabia speak of revolutionary transformations in
pictorial vision, and to accept the hypothesis of a painting endowed with
a life of its own, exploiting the visual field solely for the sake of an arbitrary
and poetic organization of forms and colours, free from the contingent
need to represent or transpose the forms of nature as we are accustomed
to see them. (Buffet-Picabia 1949: 256)

Music ceases being mere legitimization and becomes even more
central to the work of numerous modernist painters, Wassily Kandinsky
and Piet Mondrian being two of the more notable.

Another reason has to do with the conservatism of Western art music
itself, against which a relatively modest departure would appear to be
transgressive. Dissonance comes immediately to mind, but for our
purposes a better case in point would be the reaction that *avant garde*
music incurred through its use of percussion, a reaction based upon the
failure to reproduce a certain set of instruments, artistic conventions
and sounds. That percussion fell within the bounds of a musical
materiality meant that it only had (decreasing) strength as a sign for
extramusical sounds. In this way, modernist conflicts over representation could be reproduced internally, without appealing to an external
sense of representation. This was played out in terms of noise, resident
noise, figures of worldliness such as the glissando, and eventually in
the sphere of sound recording.

And then there are institutional and societal factors. The early *avant
garde* had relatively little to do with music; in fact, prior to the middle
of the twentieth century the term *avant garde* music was nearly oxymor-
onic. Relatively few composers frequented the bohemian haunts of
artists and writers, breeding grounds for radicalism of all types because
their attendance could be better spent elsewhere. Unlike the relatively
affordable technologies needed by writers or painters to complete their
art (pen and paper, brush, paints, canvas, and the like), composers were
more closely linked to string quartets or symphony orchestras to hear
common forms of their practice realized. The artistic and literary avant-
garde looked like a cottage industry when compared to the big factory
of musical modernism. To gain access to their technologies, composers
were required to circulate in the upper reaches of society, participate
within the formal rites of high musical culture, and to speak through
the discourses attending these scenes. Edgar Varèse, one of the few composers to intersect with the ranks of bohemia, described in 1924 the

stifling effects operating within a generational and class logic. 'There is little hope for the bourgeoisie. The education of this class is almost entirely a matter of memory, and at twenty-five they cease to learn, and they live the remainder of their lives within the limitations of conceptions at least a generation behind the times' (Varése 1924). The surrealist Philippe Soupault put it more succinctly: 'The area of music, a colonial possession inhabited by snobs.' He continues, 'Surrealism was unable to exercise any influence: and this helps explain the decadence of the French school of music before Messiaen' (Soupault 1964). John Cage understood it less as a class phenomenon and more a difference arising between individual and institutional modes of support:

> The people who control taste and who give funds to buy things in the field of art are individuals. I think institutions in the case of art follow the lead of those individuals and individual collectors. Whereas in music, institutions get in the way in the very beginning and they close the doors to what they would consider to be rabid experimentation. (Cage 1982: 169)

According to Félix Guattari, the institutions and practices of music worked against music itself:

> One has here to contrast the abstract machines of music (perhaps the most non-signifying and de-territorializing of all!) with the whole musical caste system – its conservatories, its educational traditions, its rules for correct composition, its stress on the impresario and so on. It becomes clear that the collectivity of musical production is so organized as to hamper and delay the force of de-territorialization inherent in music as such. (Guattari 1984: 106–7)

If music has the de-territorializing capacities that Guattari attributes to it then its inability to challenge basic premises regarding its artistic materiality can be traced in part to these conventions, and economic and institutional conditions. As we shall see below, however, Guattari would have disagreed because moves toward signification would de-territorialize the de-territorializing capacities he found inherent in music as such.

Demarcative procedures were widely practised throughout philosophies, theories and commentary on music, or anywhere music was used as a rhetorical entity. Although different composers or musics served as signposts for different thinkers, who themselves may have been composers, there was surprisingly little variation among different schools of thought in recourse to the line. If an historical census could be taken mapping the meandering of this line negotiating the difference between sound and musical sound, it would show the line was more adamantly inscribed the greater the proximity to phonography, noise and other signs of the world. For a conservative philosopher like Roger Scruton extra-musical sounds posed a specific threat to music. 'When music attempts the direct "representation" of sounds it has a tendency to become transparent, as it were, to its subject. Representation gives way to reproduction, and the musical medium drops out of consideration altogether as superfluous' (Scruton 1983: 72). It may come as a surprise to discover that superfluousness, for Scruton, begins with musical quotation, with its emblematic composer being Charles Ives whose

> evocation of sounds of Central Park [demonstrates] a constant tendency on the part of the musical medium to collapse into the sound represented . . . All that we are left with is a succession of brass-bands, jazz groups, cries and murmurs, which stand out in the music as isolated particulars bearing no musical relation one to another, just like the sounds in Central Park. (Scruton 1983: 72)

If quotation could prove so vexatious, what then of the pressures brought upon music by phonography? One measure can be found in the lamentations of Pierre Schaeffer, founder in 1948 of *musique concrète*. Using phonographic recording equipment to make his early compositions (only later moving to tape recorders), he rejected his very first composition *Étude aux chemins de fer* (1948) soon after completion because the train station sounds remained too recognizable. He thereafter employed a variety of manipulation techniques that would more assuredly diminish or entirely eradicate any associative properties a sound might have. Once such severance had taken place music was inevitable: 'From the moment you accumulate sounds and noises, deprived of their dramatic connotations, you cannot help but make music' (Diliberto 1986: 56). Yet, over the course of time, even this formulation was not immune to rejection:

> You have two sources for sounds: noises, which always tell you something – a door cracking, a dog barking, the thunder, the storm; and then you have instruments. An instrument tells you, la-la-la-la [sings a scale]. Music has to find a passage between noises and instruments. It has to escape. It has to find a compromise and an evasion at the same time; something

that would not be dramatic because that has no interest to us, but something that would be more interesting than sounds like Do-Re-Mi-Fa . . . (Diliberto 1986: 56)

The intrinsic despair of 'compromise and evasion' finally developed into Schaeffer's remarkable dismissal of his entire career: 'Musique Concrète in its work of assembling sound, produces sound-works, sound-structures, but not music' (Schaeffer 1987: 8). He returned to the notion that no music was possible outside of conventional musical sounds. 'It took me forty years to conclude that nothing is possible outside DoReMi . . . In other words, I wasted my life' (Schaeffer 1987: 8).

In 1988 I had occasion to describe Schaeffer's lament to John Cage over the dinner table. He quickly responded, 'He should have kept going up the scale!'[2]

To rationalize his new found conservatism Schaeffer sought recourse in the structural anthropology of Claude Lévi-Strauss: 'I'll bring in Lévi-Strauss, who has said again and again that it's only things that change; the structures, the structures of humanity, stay the same – and the uses we make of these things' (Schaefer 1987: 7). For Schaeffer to invoke Lévi-Strauss to account for the failure of *musique concrète* was an act of insult upon injury bordering on masochism, because Lévi-Strauss had already criticized *musique concrète* in his best known book, *The Raw and the Cooked*. Given the architectonics of his thought and the central role music played, it was inevitable that Lévi-Strauss would draw the line at what was and what was not music, and he found it in *musique concrète*, which, it seems, had abdicated the significance of sound but failed to find significance in music.

It is precisely in the hierarchical structure of the scale that the first level of articulation of music is to be found. It follows that there is a striking parallel between the ambitions of that variety of music which has been paradoxically dubbed concrete and those of what is more properly called abstract painting. By rejecting musical sounds and restricting itself exclusively to noises, *musique concrète* puts itself into a situation that is comparable, from the formal point of view, to that of painting of whatever kind: it is in immediate communion with the given phenomena of nature. And like abstract painting, its first concern is to disrupt the system of actual or potential meanings of which these phenomena are the elements. Before using the noises it has collected, *musique concrète* takes care to make them unrecognizable, so that the listener cannot yield to the natural tendency to relate them to sense images: the breaking of china, a train whistle, a fit of coughing, or the snapping off of a tree branch. It thus wipes out a first level of articulation, whose usefulness would in any case be very limited, since man is poor at perceiving and distinguishing noises, perhaps because of the overriding importance for him of a privileged category of noises: those of articulate speech.

The existence of *musique concrète* therefore involves a curious paradox. If such music used noises while retaining their representative value, it would have at its disposal a first articulation which would allow it to set up a system of signs through the bringing into operation of a second articulation. But this system would allow almost nothing to be said. To be convinced of this, one has only to imagine what kind of stories could be told by means of noises, with reasonable assurance that such stories would be both intelligible and moving. Hence the solution that has been adopted – the alteration of noises to turn them into pseudo-sounds; but it is then impossible to define simple relations among the latter, such as would form an already significant system on another level and would be capable of providing the basis for a second articulation. *Musique concrète* may be intoxicated with the illusion that it is saying something; in fact, it is floundering in non-significance. (Lévi-Strauss 1969: 22–3)

As Stanley Diamond has written, 'Lévi-Strauss' central metaphor is music, which he considers the most basic of all art forms precisely because it is wordless, hardly cognitive, a pristine syntax of sounds, of harmonic and rhythmic contradictions and progressions – structuralism incarnate' (Diamond 1981: 298). Lévi-Strauss' musical tastes for sonatas, symphonies, cantatas, fugues and for musicians the likes of Stravinsky and especially Wagner (Lévi-Strauss 1969: 14) lead him to elitist and ethnocentric positions, endemic to many practices of anthropology. He fixes upon the Western forms emanating from the lone mind of the composer, circumvents collectivist musics both within and outside Western culture, and adopts the 'hierarchical structure of the scale' as a means toward his own thought. The latter in particular belies a neo-Pythagorean and Leibnizian association of mathematics and music.

The supreme mystery essentialized in music is the ultimate, inescapable anthropological problem. Lévi-Strauss is obviously referring to a final principle of order underlying all cognition and communication, a principle, one would add, that he believes may one day be reducible to mathematical formulation. (Diamond 1981: 300)

Karlheinz Stockhausen, in an electronic music laboratory competing with Schaeffer's studio, also had *musique concrète* in mind when he valorized electronic sounds over 'all instrumental or other auditive associations; such associations divert the listener's comprehension from the self-evidence of the sound-world presented to him because he thinks of bells, organs, birds or faucets' (Stockhausen 1961: 59–67). So too Pierre Boulez:

> Sound which has too evident an affinity with the noises of everyday life . . . any sound of this kind, with its anecdotal connotations, becomes completely isolated from its context; it could be integrated. . . . Any allusive element breaks up the dialectic of form and morphology and its unyielding incompatibility makes the relating of partial to global struct- ures a problematical task. (cited in Wishart 1985: 70)

And as Dmitri Shostakovich stated, or stated with a censor in the wings:

> 'Concrete music' is extremely primitive. By the way, a collection of the sound-imitating and noise effects of this form of 'art' can be used for certain episodes of radio-telefilm with an appropriate subject, or in certain instances for sound effects on the stage: for example, shipwreck, fire, railway accident, earthquake, etc. . . . We cannot be too emphatic in stressing the fact that all these anti-humanistic trends are entirely alien to socialistic realism, as well as to the requirements of Soviet people in general and creative artists in particular. (Shostakovich 1962: 21)

Along with *musique concrète* the other dominant sound/musical sound signpost in the postwar years was John Cage. He earned this role for his championing of noise, use of recorded and transmitted sound, his idea that all sounds can be music, his championing of sound and listening *per se*, and so forth. His attitude about *musique concrète* itself was somewhat conflicted. After years of musing and theorizing about the use of recorded sound for musical purposes, he became moved to action, but only after meeting Pierre Schaeffer in Paris, the person who had beaten him out of this particular artistic gate. Cage's first audiotape work, *Williams Mix* (1952), part of the Music for Magnetic Tape project, consisted of minutely and obliquely cut pieces of magnetic audiotape, chosen and spliced together through chance operations from a stock of 500 to 600 recorded sounds in six categories – city sounds, country sounds, electronic sounds, manually produced sounds (including the literature of music), wind-produced sounds (including songs), and small sounds requiring amplification to be heard with the others. It required an incredible effort on the part of several people to construct and still only lasted about four-and-one-half minutes (at 15 inches-per-second), when played back on eight tracks deployed spatially with speakers encircling the audience. Although both *Williams Mix* and works of *musique concrète* are premised on the musicalization of sound, the former made sure that not only imitation would be banished, but also any subjective factors attendant upon composition.

People familiar with *Williams Mix* will know that whatever associative properties the recorded sounds might have once possessed are almost entirely obliterated, except for what sounds like crickets (intense, high-pitched sounds identify themselves quickly). Familiarity with *Williams Mix* usually derives from its inclusion on the *25-Year Retrospective* album. In the album's notes Cage writes, 'Since the pioneer work of Pierre Schaeffer at the Radio Diffusion of Paris in 1948, the making of tape music has become international. (The different approaches of the various world centres – Paris, Cologne, Milan, New York are excellently set forth in an article by Roger Maren in *The Reporter*, issue of Oct. 6, 1955, pages 38–42.)' Looking at the Maren article that Cage so enthusiastically recommended, we find an interesting tripartite categorization. One category pertains to work where tape is used but nothing radical is attempted, for example Luening and Ussachevsky. More interesting is the categorical wedge Maren drives between Schaeffer's *musique concrète* and Cage's work. Because 'the strong referential significance attached to certain noises' have not been sufficiently eradicated, Schaeffer's musique concrète is, according to Maren, therefore, 'closer to cubist poetry than to music . . . This does not necessarily nullify the value of the work. It simply places the work outside the domain of pure music.' In the third category, Maren distinguishes Cage's work, as well as the tape work of Messiaen, Boulez and Varèse, as pure music because recorded sounds are 'manipulated to the point where they lose all referential significance. The composer's interest is in the sound itself and the patterns into which it can be formed.' In other words, the quality of general organization of recorded sounds – the formidable compositional means of Cage, Messiaen, Boulez and Varèse versus the relatively simplistic arrangements of Schaeffer and company – signalled the extent to which referentiality persisted, despite the attempts to eradicate it. By referring people to the Maren article, in other words, on the occasion of a major retrospective release of his work, Cage conforms to a view that *musique concrète* is not really musical. In many other instances, of course, Cage not only understands *musique concrète* as musical but too conventionally musical, indicting Schaeffer later on for, among other things, simulating solfeggio by imposing a twelve-tiered taxonomy upon the expanse of sound.

A demarcative use of Cage's own music comes from an unlikely source – that of Gilles Deleuze and Félix Guattari. One would suspect they might share Cage's musical radicalism, yet they thought Cage went too far and, more surprisingly, the offending works were not among his most raucous but were instead the fairly benign prepared piano pieces. They begin with a paean:

> Varèse's procedure, at the dawn of this age, is exemplary: a musical machine of consistency, a sound machine (not a machine for reproducing sounds), which molecularizes and atomizes, ionizes sound matter, and harnesses a cosmic energy. If this machine must have an assemblage, it is the synthesizer. (Deleuze and Guattari 1987: 343)

The reference is to Varèse's statement, 'Personally, for my conceptions, I need an entirely new medium of expression: a sound-*producing* machine (not a sound-*reproducing* one)' (Varèse 1939). Deleuze and Guattari's synthesizer will not be entirely recognizable to electronic music buffs, because it would be philosophical, 'like a thought synthesizer functioning to make thought travel, make it mobile, make it a force of the Cosmos (in the same way as one makes sound travel)' (Deleuze and Guattari 1987: 343). That sound could not travel too far across the never-ending vacuum of the cosmos would not prevent it from travelling back in time in order to dust off a few stellar pages from Schopenhauer. Letting actual sound travel freely where it might cross the terrestrial spaces through which it travels best would be 'opening music to all events', which might rupture the type of 'machine of consistency' by coming too close to that most-feared phenomenon of all space travel: the black hole of Cage's prepared piano pieces.

> Sometimes one overdoes it, puts too much in, works with a jumble of lines and sounds; then instead of producing a cosmic machine capable of 'rendering sonorous,' one lapses back to a machine of reproduction that ends up reproducing nothing but a scribble effacing all lines, a scramble effacing all sounds. The claim that one is opening music to all events, all irruptions, but one ends up reproducing a scrambling that prevents any event from happening. All one has left is a resonance chamber well on the way to forming a black hole. A material is too rich remains too *territorialized*: on noise sources, on the nature of the objects . . . (this even applies to Cage's prepared piano). (Deleuze and Guattari 1987: 344)

This will surely be difficult to understand among people who think that Cage's prepared piano music alone could be called music. What terrestrial and territorial hazards drove Deleuze and Guattari away from Cage's music? Their portrayal of Varèse's music as a synthesizer would be appropriate to his percussion-laden music but not, say, *Poème Électronique* (1958), which used new technologies to both produce and reproduce sound. The prepared piano was an act of melding a percussion ensemble with the piano (itself an instrument already equipped with percussive functions) following Varèse's own formidable forays into percussion. The specific occasion for its development was a dance by Syvilla Fort at the Cornish Institute in Seattle. Fort, an African-American choreographer and dancer, wanted music with an African feel to it, but the stage was too small for a percussion ensemble, thus its miniaturization under the lid of a piano. In this way, Deleuze and Guattari's complaint does not synthesize thought but reproduces the tradition of Europeans hearing non-European music, especially percussion music in a modernist response to primitivism as noise. Why was it, then, that their interpretation of musical events so easily sailed skyward to the unpopulated vacuum of the Cosmos, and not south?

The urge to demarcate in favour of a sanctity of music survives to more recent times as well. After reviewing an article on the history of live electronic music, the British musician Chris Cutler, in his capacity as editor of *ReRecords Quarterly Magazine*, felt compelled to 'resist the unquestioning inclusion of a randomly derived, aleatory and raw environmental sound in what we understand when we use the work *music*.' Pitted specifically against the threat posed by Cage, he argued:

> If, suddenly, *all sound* is 'music,' then by definition, there can be no such thing as sound that is *not* music. The word music becomes meaningless, or rather it means 'sound.' But 'sound' already means that. And when the word 'music' has been long minted and nurtured to refer to a *particular* activity in respect to sound – namely its conscious and deliberate organization within a definite aesthetic and tradition – I can see no convincing argument at this late stage for throwing these useful limitations into the dustbin. (Cutler 1988: 46–7)

The irony is that Cutler's attempt to fend off the totalizing effects of Cagean thought occurred at a time when so many of Cage's ideas had been benignly internalized by many other musicians in both artistic and popular contexts. Thus, such an appeal would find Cage himself in the ranks of that same tradition called music. Instead of appealing to either a pre-Cagean or Cagean throwback of what music is or is not in order to re-establish inviolable ground, it would make more sense to experience artistic works in their own right, not how they might conform to gross categorical distinctions, and imagine the fruitful possibilities attending the convoluted and elaborate moments where sound and music fuse, intermingle, and pull apart.

Many of these problems could be credited to a general lack of understanding about sound; there is, after all, little discourse on sound. Moreover, if we leave it to the type of candour expressed by Jean Baudrillard in acknowledging his lack of understanding about sound, then the situation may not improve very soon. When asked about the theoretical implications of sound he said, 'I have some difficulty replying to this question because sound, the sphere of sound, the acoustic sphere, audio, is really more alien to me than the visual. It is true there is a *feeling* [spoken in English] about the visual, or rather for the image and the concept itself, whereas sound is less familiar to me. I have less perception, less analytic perception, of this aspect.' Yet he could not refrain from saying in the very next sentence: 'That is not to say that I would not make a distinction between noise and sound' (Baudrillard 1995).

Notes

1. I use the term *significant sound* not to differentiate such a sound from insignificant or meaningless ones but to counter long-standing habits of imagining that sounds completely transcend or escape meaning or that sounds elude sociality despite the fact they are made, heard, imagined, and thought by humans.

2. This took place at the home of Alvin Lucier, when Cage was in town for the Cage at Wesleyan Symposium, Middletown, Connecticut (February 1988).

References

Baudrillard, J. (1995), 'Vivisecting the 90s, An Interview with Jean Baudrillard, Part 1', interviewed by Caroline Bayard and Graham Knight, *CTHEORY*, 18(1–2), article a024: www.ctheory.net.

Buffet-Picabia, G. (1949), 'Some Memories of Pre-Dada: Picabia and Duchamp', in Robert Motherwell (ed.) (1981), *The Dada Painters and Poets: An Anthology*, New York: G. K. Hall.

Cage, J. (1982), 'After Antiquity, in Conversation with Peter Gena', *A John Cage Reader*, Peter Gena and Jonathan Brent (eds), New York: C. F. Peters Corporation.

Cutler, C. (1988), 'Editorial Afterword', *ReRecords Quarterly Magazine*, 2(3): 46–7.

Deleuze, G. and Guattari, F. (1987), *A Thousand Plateaus: Capitalism and Schizophrenia*, translated by Brian Massumi, Minneapolis: University of Minnesota Press.

Diamond, S. (1981), 'The Inauthenticity of Anthropology', *In Search of the Primitive: A Critique of Civilization*, New Brunswick: Transaction Books.

Diliberto, J. (1986), 'Pierre Schaeffer and Pierre Henry: Pioneers in Sampling', *Electronic Musician* (December): 54–9, 72.

Guattari, F. (1984), 'Towards a Micro-Politics of Desire', in *Molecular Revolution: Psychiatry and Politics*, London: Penguin Books.

Kahn, D. (1999), *Noise, Water, Meat: A History of Sound in the Arts*, Cambridge: MIT Press.

Lévi-Strauss, C. (1969), *The Raw and the Cooked*, trans. J. and D. Weightman, New York: Harper & Row.

Schaeffer, P. (1987), interviewed by Tim Hodgkinson, *Re Records Quarterly Magazine*, 2, (1): 5, 7, 8.

Scruton, R. (1983), *The Aesthetic Understanding*, New York: Methuen & Co.

Shostakovich, D. (1962), 'Art Must Reflect Reality', *Music Journal*, 20 (September): 20–1, 77, 83.

Soupault, P. (1964), 'Traces Which Last', *Yale French Studies*, 31 (May).

Stockhausen, K. (1961), 'Electronic and Instrumental Music', *Die Reihe*, 5: 59–67.

Varèse, E. (1924), '"The Music of To-morrow," *The Evening News* (New York), (14 June)', reproduced in Timothy Day (1984), 'The Organized Sound of Edgard Varèse', *Recorded Sound: The Journal of the British Library National Sound Archive*, 85 (January): 77.

—— (1939), 'Music as an Art-Science', in Elliott Schwartz and Barney Childs (eds) (1967), *Contemporary Composers on Contemporary Music*, New York: Holt, Rinehart & Winston.

Wishart, T. (1985), *On Sonic Art*, York: Imagineering Press.

6

Songtime
Sound Culture, Rhythm and Sociality

Paul Filmer

Introduction: Sounding Time

Mediated by rhythm, time and culture are structurally interrelated and interdependent. The concept of time itself is socially constructed. The particular forms that it takes differ between cultures and they change historically. These latter phenomena – change and history – are themselves so fundamentally contingent upon time that they represent versions of its recurrent process, implying different versions of the measured passing of time, from the present to the past, from the past through the present to a predicable future. Their invocation as part of such an elementary formulation of the sociological character of time demonstrates its essentially reflexive character: it is invariably necessary to invoke normative conceptualizations of time whenever it is introduced as a topic for analysis. The reasons for this can be found in what Elias (1995: 18) has noted as 'the extent to which self-regulation to social time becomes second nature to people in the more advanced countries'. This practice of timing, which Elias (1992: 43) has elsewhere referred to as 'the reifying character of the substantival form "time"', disguises its instrumental function 'of relating to each other the positions of events on the successive order of two or more change continua'. These change continua can be interpretatively constructed as both natural and sociocultural. The patterned, recurrent and thus predictable cycles of physical environmental change, because of their relative invariance, are treated as natural and provide, in turn, a resource for metaphoricizing more consciously reflexive constructions of time as a social and cultural phenomenon. The reflexivity of time can be seen in such terms as a structuring of social interaction which is accomplished through ordering the relation between practices of self-regulation along change continua – one way of formulating what Elias terms the civilizing process itself. The social construction of time is thus a necessary condition of culture, since it enables individuals and groups to sustain shared concepts of changes in meanings and values, and thus differentiations between them.

This sense of social time is related primarily, as Elias' formulation of it proposes, to developed societies. For less-developed, pre-literate societies, time, whilst being always clearly a social construction, has a markedly different character indicated by a conception of change as continual and gradual, rather than episodic and radical. Shepherd (1991: 22–4) describes the sense of time in such societies as a constitutive feature of a 'hermetic and revelationary world of oral-aural people . . . a revelationary circumjacence of concretely recurring events, which is constantly in flux, and over which, *in western terms*, there is relatively little control' (Shepherd 1991: 22–4).

In such an oral-aural world, sound takes on a much greater significance for time than in a social world in which visual culture – and thus literacy – predominate.

> Sound is more symptomatic of the flow of time than any other phenomena . . . Although all other phenomena occur within a stream of time, the fact that they may be generally isolated and examined at leisure demonstrates that, *as far as their influence on the arrangement of people's sensoria is concerned*, they are not so inexorably tied to that stream as sound is. Pre-literate people seem to sense themselves as being at the centre of a sound universe, which is dynamic and bounding with energy. Furthermore, since the paradigm of sound for people is the human voice, they seem to impute power and influence to the physical phenomena that surround their existence as they would impute it to the human voice. (Shepherd 1991: 20–1)

It follows from this that the active, conscious use of the voice as a central feature of concerted human action can be considered an important initial step in asserting the differentiated character and identity of human collectivity within such a sound universe. Moreover, the coordination of sustained, collective vocal action is thus an important feature of the social structuring of time which is further reinforced when it is integrated with other forms of social action. These can be both functional and ritual collective actions, such as instrumental work and celebratory dance, all of which involve concerted movement. Thus, notwithstanding the apparent predominance of visuality and literacy amongst developed societies, all societies, at every stage of structural differentiation and in every form of institutional development, nevertheless appear to integrate the concerted social movements of song and dance with some or all other significant social activities (Lomax 1968; Merriam 1964; Van Leeuwen 1999; Sachs 1965).

The manner in which social time structures interaction is accomplished by making it 'second nature' to the initial human experiential sense of process – that of the physiological time which regulates the body as an organism and according to which it functions normally and homeostatically. The interface between these two senses of time – physiological and social – is mediated by rhythm and explored through various forms of movement socialization, which have been characterized by McNeill (1995: 2–3) as the process of learning how to keep together in time. This visceral experience, he proposes, is

> far older than language and critically important in human history, because the emotion it arouses constitutes an indefinitely expansible basis for social cohesion among any and every group that keeps together in time, moving big muscles together and chanting, singing, or shouting rhythmically. 'Muscular bonding' is ... the euphoric fellow feeling that prolonged and rhythmic muscular movement arouses among nearly all participants in such exercises.

Whilst there is no originary empirical historical basis for invoking rhythmic muscular bonding as an originary cause of social cohesion, which is invariably manifested through the developed and institutionalised pattern of social relations that constitute a social structure, it seems clear that it is an essential feature of the social bonding that is a necessary condition of social cohesion. McNeill argues for it as an essentially human and social characteristic on a number of grounds:

> First, throughout recorded history, moving and singing together made collective tasks far more efficient ... Second, ... before written records allowed us to know anything precise about human behavior, keeping together in time became important for human evolution, allowing early human groups to increase their size, enhance their cohesion, and assure survival by improving their success in guarding territory, securing food, and nurturing the young. (McNeill 1995: 4)

Thirdly, McNeill (1995: 6) refers to neurophysiological evidence that locates 'bodily response to rhythmic movement . . . in the sympathetic and para-sympathetic nervous systems . . . (which) are involved in all emotions.' Although the exact paths of emotional excitation are not understood, organically excreted hormones are involved in the restoration of homeostasis, which follows it, as are the parts of the central nervous system least involved with the production of verbal expression. Similarly, Robinson and Winold (1976: 4) note that the choral experience is

> a physiological and sociological phenomenon. Obvious physical changes manifest emotional events of any depth, and choral singing is no exception: changes in pulse rate, respiration, adrenalin flow, and similar symptoms are present, as well as a feeling . . . of satisfying physical exhaustion.

In this sense, 'the excitation derived from rhythmic muscular movement and voicing' is paralinguistic. As Finnegan (1989: 340) observes:

> Music . . . is not essentially a *cognitive* code, and extends beyond the 'mind' to the 'body'. It is associated . . . primarily with . . . rhythm, movement, and overt physical enactment, a context in which it is perhaps scarcely surprising that participants experience a particular sense of active control and of personal creativity . . . a different and unique modality of human action *sui generis*.

McNeill (1995: 7) suggests that 'rhythmic input from muscles and voice, after gradually suffusing through the entire nervous system, may provoke echoes of the fetal condition when a major and perhaps principal external stimulus to the developing brain was the mother's heartbeat . . . prolonged and insistent rhythmic stimuli may restore a simulacrum of fetal emotions to consciousness.' This speculation is reinforced by Van Leeuwen's (1999: 6) account of measured time, in both music and speech, which

> divides the flow of time into measures which are of equal duration and which are marked off by a regularly occurring explicit pulse ('accent', 'stress', 'beat') which comes on the first syllable or note or other sound of each measure and is made more prominent than the surrounding sounds by means of increased loudness, pitch or duration, or some combination of some or all of these . . . Tempo results from the duration

of the measures. On metronomes the slowest tempo is 40 pulses per minute, the fastest 208 pulses per minute. An average speed would therefore be about 90 pulses per minute. This range corresponds closely to that of the heartbeat, which ranges from 50 beats per minute to just over 200 beats per minute. Ninety beats per minute is the pulse rate of an average male adult walking at an easy pace.

On these grounds, van Leeuwen concludes, following Tagg (1984: 22), that tempo in music may be a determinant of the physiological aspect of an affective relationship to time, providing a further link between physiological time, through musical rhythm, and the social timing through which social activities in general are ordered. As Ballantine (1984: 5) notes: 'social structures crystallize in musical structures . . . in various ways and with varying degrees of critical awareness, the musical microcosm replicates the social macrocosm'.

The musically grounded, rhythmically concerted social practice of choral performance, which is the focus of this discussion, is thus an embodiment of an essential sociality that articulates the role of time in the relations between musical and social structures. Music is central to rhythmic muscular movement: as McNeill points out, voicing is one of the forms that such movement takes and, in the concerted voicing that becomes choral song, it provides a more elaborated rhythmic structure for more complex sequences of concerted movement involved, for example, in work and dance. McNeill's thesis also embraces military drill as a means of establishing group cohesion among armed forces, for whom keeping together in time, as well as being a condition of functional effectiveness, can be also a prerequisite for survival in military engagements. Indeed, Lomax (1968: 170) describes as 'one of the most fascinating and sometimes disturbing of all social phenomena . . . the concerted activity of the mob, the army, or the choir that seems to feel and act as one person'. All these activities invariably involve music as a way of structuring the rhythmic tempo of concerted move-ment over measured time intervals and it is perhaps for this reason that such large claims are routinely made for the functional necessity of music to social life. Mellers (1984: ix), for example, claims that it is as vital to human existence 'as bread: perhaps more so, since whereas an individual would die without food, without music a whole society, perhaps even the cosmos itself, might disintegrate'. In more restrained terms, Chanan (1994: 23) makes a similar point by identifyng music as a performance art which is, thus 'a form of social communication; musical performance is a site of social intercourse and a form of social dialogue' and Finnegan (1989: 340) proposes that music, as a form of social action, is 'a universally shared propensity of human beings to realise themselves and their culture'. Small (1998: 9) terms these practices *musicking*, the gerund of the arcane verb *to music*, that is 'to take part, in any capacity, in a musical performance, whether by performing, by listening, by rehearsing or practicing, by providing material for performance (what is called composing) or by dancing'. Music's propensity to social and cultural realization (Storr 1992: 123) elaborates the homology between the musical microcosm and the social macrocosm into a basis for considering choral singing as an originary and essentially social activity. Yet it is an activity that, in some of its traditional forms, is clearly in decline and is undergoing significant change in the cultural conditions of late industrial societies. McNeill (1995: 156–7) warns that contemporary disregard of what he terms the 'primitive' level of the muscular, rhythmic dimension of human sociality is 'unwise and probably unsustainable' because of its significance for the emergence of human beings as such a dominant species, and because of its power to create and sustain stable human communities.

Making Music and Song: The Rhythmic Dimensions of Interactional Time

An indication of how such claims might be grounded is offered by Schutz (1964: 159), who proposes that 'music is a meaningful context which is not bound to a conceptual scheme. Yet this meaningful context can be communicated'. He proposes (1964: 161–2) that music is an instance of what he terms 'the "mutual tuning-in relationship" upon which all communication is founded . . . by which the "I" and "Thou" are experienced by both participants as a "We" in vivid presence".' This communicative relationship comes to the foreground in such well-known social practices as 'marching together, dancing together, making love together, or making music together' because the mutual tuning-in relationship 'originates in the possibility of living together simultaneously in specific dimensions of time'. Schutz (1964: 164) disagrees with the proposition that music derives from rhythm, which he attributes to Halbwachs (1939), on the grounds that no evidence exists for such an argument. This is a claim both odd and quite inaccurate. Sachs (1965: 111–31), in a detailed discussion of the relation between rhythm and form in music, states unequivocally that 'rhythm in its beginnings is extra-musical' and cites Plato, who allotted rhythm 'to the artful motion of bodies'. Sachs (1965: 112) draws on anthropological evidence

to conclude that rhythm is 'a slowly developing psycho-physiological
urge . . . the impulse to equalize continuous, regular movements . . . the
awareness of greater ease and gusto through constant evenness in
motion'. McNeill's (1995: 6–7, 13–35, 37–66, 159–73) historical account
reviews some relevant neurophysiological, evolutionary and anthropological evidence, as does Chanan's (1994: 85–9) discussion of the
neurophysiological basis of the different schemes of sonic articulation
possessed by verbal language and music.

Schutz (1964: 170), however, formulates 'the very form of existence
of music' rather as

> a meaningful arrangement of tones in inner time . . . The flux of tones
> unrolling in inner time . . . evokes in the stream of consciousness
> participating in it an interplay of recollections, retentions, protentions,
> and anticipations which interrelate the successive elements.

Those participating in the process of making music, whether individually or together, are involved in the fundamentally social process
of human being itself. They are

> tuned-in to one another, are living together in the same flux, are growing
> older together while the musical process lasts . . . not only . . . the . . .
> measurable outer time required for the performance . . . but the coperf-
> ormance in simultaneity of the polythetic steps by which the musical
> content articulates itself in inner time. (Schutz 1964: 174–5)

Schutz terms this relation between inner and outer time 'pluridimens-
ional time', which is simultaneously lived through when two or more
individuals are making music together. The process is as complex to
explicate as is the phenomenology of any social interaction and follows
the model outlined as Schutz's (1971: 11–13) general thesis of the reciprocity of perspectives in his discussion of the intersubjective character
of common-sense knowledge and its implications. Performers have to
take into account what they will have to execute simultaneously with
others, interpreting their own parts whilst anticipating the others' interpretations of their own parts, as well as the others' interpretations of
each other performer's part. All share both the inner time in which the
music actualizes itself in performance and, simultaneously, the immediacy of the streams of consciousness of the others in the vivid present
of the outer time of the duration of the performance. Schutz (1964: 176–
8) notes that 'making music together occurs in a true face-to-face

relationship – inasmuch as the participants are sharing not only a section of time but also a sector of space'. This is the key to its character as essential social bonding. The tuning-in relationship depends upon reciprocal sharing, and living through together in a vivid present as 'We', the flux of interaction partners' experiences in inner time. 'Only within this experience', Schutz concludes, 'does the Other's conduct become meaningful to the partner tuned in on him – that is, the Other's body and its movements can be and are interpreted as a field of expression of events within his inner life'. In effect, thus, the interaction of individuals making music together becomes meaningful as concerted movement structured by the 'meaningful arrangement of tones in inner time which is the very form of existence of music'. And this, as Martin (1995: 200) has noted, is a special, important and illuminating case of what must occur for any kind of human communication to take place and any intersubjective, social lifeworld to be sustained. In effect, the very form of existence of music is a microcosm of the very conditions of existence of the social macrocosm.

Musical Practice and the Aura of Performance

Although the initial excitations produced by concerted movement in time may be seen as paralinguistic and, in terms of Schutz's argument, may be sustained in the non-verbal language of instrumental music, the movements themselves can also quickly become involved reflexively with vocal language as song. Barthes (1977: 182–8) offers one account of how this occurs through his concept of the 'grain' of the singing voice, which

> is . . . the materiality of the body speaking its mother tongue; perhaps the letter, almost certainly *signifiance* . . . (it) is not – or is not merely – its timbre: the *signifiance* it opens cannot better be defined, indeed, than by the very friction between the music and something else, which . . . is the particular language . . .

The grain of the voice articulates what Barthes terms *geno-song*, which he contrasts with *pheno-song*. *Pheno-song* 'covers all the phenomena, all the features which belong to the structure of the language being sung, the rules of the genre . . . everything in the performance which is in the service of communication, representation, expression'. By contrast, *geno-song*, as the term suggests, is, in effect, the generative sense of singing itself which is beneath *pheno-song* and which makes it possible; it is the ontic condition of vocal music which

is the volume of the singing and speaking voice, the space where signif-
ications germinate 'from within language and in its very materiality'; it
forms a signifiying play having nothing to do with communication,
representation (of feelings), expression; it is that apex (or that depth) of
production where the melody really works at the language – not at what
it says, but the voluptuousness of its sounds-signifiers, of its letters – where
melody explores how the language works and identifies with that work.
It is . . . the *diction* of the language.

This sense of vocal song, Barthes (1977: 185–8) points out, is a reflexive
engagement and re-engagement for speakers and singers with an
embodied sense of language itself as ontology:

The 'grain' is the body in the voice as it sings, the hand as it writes, the
limb as it performs. If I perceive the 'grain' in a piece of music and accord
this 'grain' a theoretical value . . . I am determined to listen to my relation
with the body of the man or woman singing or playing and that relation
is erotic – but in no way 'subjective' . . . there is a progressive movement
from the language to the poem, from the poem to the song and from
the song to its performance. The song must speak, must *write* – for what
is produced at the level of the geno-song is finally writing . . .

Barthes' sense of ontic vocal music is located in a wider sense of what
he refers to as *musica practica* (Barthes 1977: 149), a term that he takes
from the mediaeval concept of *ars mecanica* which consisted of 'the
practical aspects of music making, whether composing, tuning instruments or actually performing' (Chanan 1994: 31). Barthes (1977: 149)
applies the term to

The music one plays [that] comes from an activity that is very little auditory, being above all manual (and thus in a way much more sensual). It is
the music which you or I can play, alone or among friends, with no other
audience than its participants (that is, with all risk of theatre, all
temptation of hysteria removed); a muscular music in which the part
taken by the sense of hearing is one only of ratification as though the
body were hearing – and not 'the soul'; a music which is not played 'by
heart': seated at the keyboard or the music stand, the body controls,
conducts, coordinates, having itself to transcribe what it reads, making
sound and meaning, the body as inscriber and not just transmitter, simple
receiver.

This formulates, in different terms, the reflexive, essentially social character of Schutz's mutual tuning-in relationship. It produces, and is reinforced by, a diverse and informed musical culture characteristic of nineteenth-century Europe when, Chanan (1994: 27) notes

> the spread of musical education also produced distinctively musical effects. As long as an audience is made up of listeners who themselves play and sing, their listening also becomes, in crucial respects, an active process. Such listeners are able to adopt an attitude which bases its musical judgement neither on subjective emotion, nor on detached intellect, but on a third matrix: the practical knowledge of the instrument or the voice, which guides both intellect and emotion in the moment of performance.

Apparently, however, this self-sustaining musical culture and its social structure have not survived into late modernity. Barthes (1977: 149–50) announces that

> This music has disappeared; . . . musical activity is no longer manual, muscular, kneadingly physical, but merely liquid, effusive . . . So too has the performer changed. The amateur, a role defined much more by a style than by a technical imperfection, is no longer anywhere to be found.

Such a demise of the tradition of *musica practica*, should it have occurred, could be expected to have manifested as a crisis precipitated by the lack of the social functions it performed, and may well be both a manifestation of, and a consequence attributable to, the compression of the space-time continuum identified by Harvey (1990: 284–307) as a central characteristic of the social and cultural condition of late modernity. Barthes (1977: 153–4) indicates this possibility by remarking that the collective sociality inherent in the performance of *musica practica* has become supplanted, finally, by the more private act of composition:

> To compose . . . is *to give to do*, not to give to hear but to give to write. The modern location for music is not the concert hall but the stage on which the musicians pass . . . from one source of sound to another. It is we who are playing . . . one can imagine the concert . . . as exclusively a workshop, from which nothing spills over - no dream, no imaginary, in short, no 'soul' and where all the musical art is absorbed in a praxis *with no remainder*. (Barthes 1977: 154)

What has been lost, if Barthes is correct about the disappearance of *musica practica*, is what Chanan (1994: 28–30) refers to as 'the musical equivalent of the way the baby learns to talk ... an authentic object of popular pleasure, an embodiment of the human need for community'. Such a loss would fundamentally damage the possibility of sustaining human sociality altogether and endorse Mellers' (1984: ix) dire warning of societal and cosmic disintegration.

There has been no such loss. What Barthes is implicitly mourning is a consequence of changes in patterns of popular social relations to music and engagements with music-making which, with an opinion-ation that Chanan (1991: 28) generously characterizes merely as singularly unfair, he attributes monocausally to the widespread avail-ability of the piano as the instrument of choice for amateur, domestic music-making. What Barthes seems to have failed to understand, according to Chanan (1991: 28), is that *musica practica* is

> an ever-present form of musical knowledge which takes on different historical and class aspects, appears in different periods in altered social and historical guises, but still remains the essential feature of the way music is transmitted from generation to generation.

Barthes' pessimistic confusion is common. Finnegan (1989: 333) notes that 'any perceived changes in musical practice ... can be feared as entailing almost cosmic results ... until new groups or new practices are redefined as after all acceptable ones'. In relation to vocal music, Banfield (1995: 402) points out that the loss of an intimate relation between speech inflection and musical gesture in vocal art music during the twentieth century has been countered by a rise in its direct expression:

> in folk, jazz, pop, commercial and ethnic musics ... most twentieth century popular music is vocal, its communicative partnership – not just between voice and audience but between voice and microphone, voice and guitar, voice and saxophone or voice and voice – as intimate, direct and rhetorical as one could wish.

Singing the Changes: Continuity and Change in Contemporary Musical Practice

The manner of intergenerational, social transmission of music has changed during the twentieth century in a number of ways, of which two are of particular significance: first, the forms of communication and transmission themselves have become dominated by electronic technology – particularly the broadcasting of both live and recorded music (Putnam 2000: 216–17). Secondly, amateur musical practices have become less ubiquitous and have taken on what Finnegan (1989) refers to as a 'hidden' character (Russell 1995: 160–3).

The effects of electronic broadcast reproduction and transmission of music have been twofold: they have deprived musical life of the auratic quality of live performance and have changed considerably the amateur traditions of *musica practica* for both musicians and their audiences, by making less necessary, and thus limiting their opportunities for participation in the social practices of making music together. As Putnam (1995: 216) notes: 'with my hi-fi Walkman CD, wherever I live I can listen to precisely what I want when I want and where I want'. The piano has lost its domestic social cachet in favour of other status symbols, and its absence from most homes inevitably affects the potential for collective domestic music making. It has been replaced by other instruments – the guitar, electronic keyboards – but these are designed precisely to minimize wider domestic involvement with, or disruption by the player (Russell 1995: 160–1).

These changes mark a break in a long tradition of amateur musical practices. Chanan (1999: 7–22) dates its rise from the second half of the seventeenth century, reaching its high point initially in the Baroque music of the first half of the eighteenth century when it was sustained by the brilliance and productivity of Handel and Bach. The intense musicality that this produced in Britain and throughout Europe was sustained into the beginning of the twentieth century, when recorded music rapidly became widely available. By the early eighteenth century, musical performance had become, with art, literature and the development of published critical discussion of all three sets of aesthetic social practice, part of the cultural dimension of the emerging public sphere that had come to define the public and political life of the bourgeois society then developing throughout Europe (McVeigh 2000). Collective music making in the performance of the work of individual composers, especially those whose work was created within the formal rhythmic conventions of the baroque, demonstrates a model synthesis of the new sense of subjectivity, which accompanied the political individualism of the public sphere, with the social necessity of its regulation in the interests of social order and interactional decorum. In the salons of bourgeois private homes, as well as at concerts in public halls and, later, even in the collective participation of performers and audience in the music hall, musical performance becomes a site for the self-preoccupation of the private individual. Here, precisely because of its profound subjectivity, music becomes a medium of negotiation of the often confused feelings which accompany, at the deepest level, the new conceptual framework of individual identity. (Chanan 1999: 33)

This is what may be construed as giving musical performance its auratic quality, what Benjamin (1969: 220) terms the key element of a work of art that is lacking in even the most perfect reproduction of it: 'its presence in time and space, its unique existence at the place where it happens to be'. Engagement with auratic performance art, both high and popular, requires an immersion of both performers and audience to accomplish it. The absence of aura is both a consequence and a condition of engaging with performance in a state of distraction rather than immersion (Lash 1990: 162). Performance is consumed, in its reproduced form, in the course of undertaking other activities and thus engages the audience less than fully and the performers no longer at all, becoming muzak rather than music. Yet the engagement, to whatever degree less than full, is nevertheless at some level a structuring of time through its rhythmic organization. Even the discordant character of atonal notated orchestral or electronically synthesized music, or of punk, dub and related forms of mainstream popular music, are at the very least different, more or less contemporary forms of the expressive capacities of music which change historically. Chanan (1994: 44–51; 1999: 40–6) adapts Bakhtin's literary critical concept of the chronotope in order to analyse this aspect of musical genres in their historical and cultural contexts to show how 'all music gives structure to time and creates its own sense of space and volume' (Chanan 1994: 48). The chronotope, which Bakhtin 'borrows' from Einstein's theory of relativity, is the spatio-temporal character of music, 'a formal matrix which is present in music of all kinds . . . all types of music give structure to time'. Chanan (1999: 41) cites Langer's (1953: 109) formulation of the duration of musical time as

an image of what might be termed 'lived' or 'experienced' time . . . measurable only in terms of sensibilities, tensions, and emotions; and it has not merely a different measure, but an altogether different structure from practical or scientific time.

This structure is complex. Chanan (1999: 42) explicates it as an unfolding stream of notes [that] is constantly infused with subtle differences and interactions between rhythm, beat and pulse, music always comprises different time spans that overlay each other in the passing moment: the phrase, the passage to which the phrase belongs, the section in which the passage is embedded, the movement in which the section occurs, and the time span of the whole work.

These are the formal properties of all musical chronotopes and the means by which they structure time in and for the social and cultural structures in which they are located. This structuring of lived or experienced time functions as a way of placing the subject's sense of self in changing social and cultural contexts, because 'music is always . . . an expression of actual or ideal social relations . . . as part of the lifeworld of musical society, these relations . . . evoked an intuitive response in every musician and every listener' (Chanan 1999: 47). This was accomplished in part by the spatial conditions under which live musical performance was generated before its dissemination in recorded form through electronic broadcast media.

The virtual space of music and the physical space of performance and audition is not one of indifference, it is complementary, and music has always directly exploited the acoustic space of performance in order to render the virtual space of the music in a particularly plastic form. The virtual space of music, however, is always physically embodied (until the invention of the gramophone), represented in the figure and role of the performing musician engaged in a social activity. (Chanan 1999: 47)

Thus the de-auraticization of musical performance follows from its disembodiment from real space into the synthesized uniformity of the commercial gramophone recording, which becomes a ubiquitous feature of what Chanan (1999: 51–2) describes as the inescapably heterogeneous, heteroglot, acousmatic cultural polyphony that is the contemporary musical lifeworld. Yet a multiplicity of musical genres is characteristic of the cultural dimension of the public sphere, which in Habermas's (1989) formulation, is itself a comprehensive subsuming and integration of a diversity of sectors of unavoidably interrelating political, social and cultural practices. Thus, as Chanan notes, the musical chronotopes of the late seventeenth, eighteenth and nineteenth centuries throughout Europe all show a diversity which is homologous with the structural heterogeneity of the public sphere as it is developed and consolidated. Finnegan (1989: 336) suggests, indeed, that the pervasive and influential enjoyment of music as leisure which was typical of nineteenth and early twentieth England is equally characteristic of late twentieth-century English culture. The issue is, first, whether there has been a qualitative change in the structural homology between music and society in the twentieth century, as a consequence of the de-auraticization and disembodiment of musical performance, and secondly, whether this has affected the social integration founded on the concerted muscular bonding involved in the rhythmic coordination of making music together.

If passive listening to recorded music had actually supplanted the active engagement of *musica practica*, then clearly there would be grounds for such a conclusion. But what appears to have occurred is a decline in the social activities of amateur music making that is difficult to measure (Russell 1995). There are a number of causes of this decline, which stretch back through the history of modernity itself. The representation of many of them is tinged with a more general nostalgia for a way of life that is being unavoidably if indirectly changed through such large-scale struct-ural and ecological social processes as industrialization and metropolit-anization. Thomas Hardy conjures such an experience in writing recurrently in his Wessex novels of the 'sound and powerful musicians, and strong-winded men' of the Mellstock Quire and parish players:

> they were very much in demand Christmas week for little reels and dancing parties; for they could turn a jig or a hornpipe out of hand as well as ever they could turn out a psalm, and perhaps better, not to speak irreverent. In short, one half-hour they could be playing a Christmas carol in the squire's hall to the ladies and gentlemen, and drinking tay and coffee with 'em as modest as saints; and the next, at The Tinker's Arms, blazing away like wild horses with the 'Dashing White Sergeant' to nine couple of dancers and more, and swallowing rum and cider hot as flame. (Hardy 1998: 170–2)

The Quire's presence is ubiquitous at all the major seasonal and social occasions of the agrarian year in Mellstock and its environs, and in this sense is quite characteristic of the increasing significance of parish choirs in England, and the growth in prominence and autonomy of their performers, since the Reformation (Potter 1998: 78–9). But the begin-ning of the end of their central involvement is marked by the squire's introduction into the church of 'a barrel organ that would play two-and-twenty new psalm-tunes, so exact and particular . . . and the old players played no more'. As with Barthes' attribution of the decline in *musica practica* to the introduction of the piano, so the barrel organ represents for Hardy the consequences of technological innovation for traditional cultural and artistic practices.

Other causes can clearly be attributed directly, in part, to a decline in musical education and training – a part itself of a wider restructuring of education which is still in process of transition, and which has affected arts education generally (Banfield 1995: 403–5; Russell 1995: 167–71). The direction of secondary and tertiary education has been towards an increasingly instrumental form of both academic and occupational training and has, inevitably, produced a sense of professional rather than amateur identity for practitioners in all the arts. This has meant that the essentially amateur engagement with *musica practica* is less prominent as a contemporary cultural practice. Russell (1995: 145–67) has detailed the patterns of 'overall steady decline' during the twentieth century of the 'vigorous network of amateur musical societies in Britain' which had become firmly established by the mid-1920s and were notable particularly among the larger, mixed-voice choral societies. Yet Banfield (1995: 402) suggests that this may also be a consequence of a significant change in underlying cultural politics manifest as

> the modern reluctance towards, or plain suspicion of, massed exhortatory expression, perhaps a paradoxical inhibition in democratic societies but a pervasive one nonetheless, particularly after the Second World War, when popular and choral expression in working-class music went their separate ways.

Banfield (1995: 410) goes still further in conjecturing that 'British confidence in choral expression has never been entirely regained since the First World War'. A specific instance of such change is developed in detail in Herbert's (2000: 255–74) discussion of the Welsh choral tradition, the generic mythopoetic resource for Wales as a 'land of song', its significance for Welsh cultural nationhood during the mid-nineteenth to mid-centuries centuries and its subsequent decline outside the traditional eisteddfods. Putnam's (2000) influential study of change in the structure and processes of community in contemporary America, like McNeill, links such changes to a problematic decline in communal social integration. Whereas contemporary Americans maintain high levels of 'consumption' of culture, such as listening to music, what Putnam (2000: 114–15) terms 'doing' culture has been declining. The significance of this, he argues (2000: 344–7), can be seen, by comparison, in the continuing maintenance of high levels of traditional civic engagement through participation in cultural activities in some northern Italian towns. Such participation and engagment generates what he terms (2000: 411) 'bridging social capital' that enhances social and democratic political integration by enabling people to transcend their social, political and professional activities to connect with others unlike themselves, thus convening diverse groups of fellow citizens: 'Singing together (like bowling together) does not require shared ideology or shared social or ethnic provenance.'

However, Finnegan's (1989) study of music making in an English town (Milton Keynes) suggests that the tradition of *musica practica* continues to thrive in the overlapping memberships of a range of amateur orchestras, bands and choirs who regularly give public performances throughout the year and at an annual festival in which some 3,000 musicians participate, as well as semi-professional instrumental groups who perform at various social functions and entertainment venues. The practical work of bringing off amateur musical performances is fundamentally social, and directly homologous with the socially structured, functionally interdependent character of work in complex, bureaucratically administered societies. It requires

> a constant input of organised co-ordinated effort from those who . . . participate in them . . . the organisational processes of effective work, decision-making, communication, choice between alternative methods of achieving objectives, delegation of responsibilities, and, above all, co-operation in the attaining of more or less agreed ends. (Finnegan 1989: 254)

Yet to the amateur orchestral players and choristers, drawn from 'great heterogeneity of background, education and occupation', making music together in rehearsals and performances also means

> something over and above the time and work they put into them or the incidental results (sociability or friendship or status) that certainly also flowed from them. The rewards for those committed to the classical music world . . . included a sense of beauty and fundamental value, of intense and profoundly felt artistic experience which could reach the depths of one's nature . . . somehow implicating the deep core of people's being. (Finnegan 1989: 41)

At all levels of involvement in bringing off musical performance, but most intensely in the active performance modes, people are *practising* music, not just passively 'consuming' or 'theorising' about it; they are engaged in the actively realised and purposeful enacting of a widely recognised form of human experience and action. (Finnegan 1989: 336)

There is no reason to suppose, even allowing for regional variation, that the extent of continuing 'hidden' musical practice uncovered by Finnegan a decade ago in a single town is untypical of contemporary Britain, nor uncharacteristic of structurally and demographically similar societies, and that the rhythmic structuring of shared time involved in making music together still functions to reinforce social integration. The active, embodied engagement required by collective musical performance is a clear challenge to contentions that *musica practica* no longer exists, and that the demise of the aura of live performance 'entails the obliteration of the distinction between the cultural and the social' (Lash 1990: 159).

Conclusion: Shifting Homologies between the Musical Microcosm and the Social Macrocosm

All musical practices and performance depend upon style and technique. Changes in the former both require and are precipitated by changes in the latter, and this is especially the case with singing because of the considerable range and flexibility of the human voice as an instrument of musical expression. The production of voiced sounds involves complex interrelations between the respiratory system, the vocal and ventricular folds, including the larynx and laryngeal ventricle, and the vocal tract, the cavity formed by the pharynx and the mouth, complemented by the nasal cavity (Sundberg 2000; Sutherland 1995: 1–27). How the muscular actions of the respiratory system and the vocal tract are exercised in rhythmic combination to generate the voice source has varied widely over historical time both within and between cultures, and continues to do so (Potter 1998). A dominant hegemony of traditional art music and song practices and related techniques, however, coexists in what Potter (2000: 2) terms 'a peculiarly awkward, shifting relationship with economics, art and status' as a result of the impact on art music funding of institutional judgements about artistic value. Thus, jazz attracts a fraction of the institutional funding of opera, despite the similar size of the concert-going audiences for each form, and despite the vibrant state of the former in comparison with the recurrent crises of funding and relevance of the latter. Both training for and performance of opera and notated orchestral music continue to be protected by public and private subsidy from routine market economic pressures. This is scarcely surprising: the traditional repertoire of art music is that which emerged and developed in a legitimating socio-cultural reciprocity with the political and economic dominance of the bourgeoisie in Europe. It was reinforced recurrently during the nineteenth century by the introduction of forms of discipline into musical educ-ation and performance and choral training (Potter 1998: 80–6, 178–86) which go well beyond those required for the development and perfection of technique alone. One legacy of this remains the continuing fondness of choral conductors for remarking during rehearsals, not wholly iron-ically, that a choir is not a democracy, that it might be appropriate for the choir to sing the score, in their voice parts, as written by the composer – especially in the specified time signature! – rather than entering or interpreting it as if soloists. The authority implied by such remarks is necessary, in part, to accomplishing a coherent interpretation of the work for performance from the separate and disparate skills and levels of competence of the singers themselves (Martin 1995: 203–4). But the conventions of both professional and amateur performances of tradit-ional art music and song are also quite rigid and have changed little since the second half of the nineteenth century, and these remain pre-dominantly middle-class in character (Potter 1998: 182–6). The venues of the performances, the demeanour and dress of the performers, the comportment and responses of the audiences, are all characterized by a formal sobriety that reinforces the respect in which the traditional repertoire is held – almost as if it needs the reinforcement that such rigidity gives it.

This, indeed, may be the case, since alongside this declining dominant homology there have emerged, since the late nineteenth century, parallel homologies across a range of popular musics that have increased in number and diversified in range considerably during the twentieth century. Popular music and song in music hall and musical theatre, jazz, film musicals, rhythm and blues, folk, skiffle, rock and country music, gospel, disco, rap, dub and legion other forms, have all been recorded, broadcast and consumed as the expression of diverse ethnic, gender and generational subcultural identities (Potter 1998: 87–112, 133–57). These are the voices and musics of the constitutive groups of contemporary multicultural societies, articulating the complexities of identity in late modernity through their textual contents and the vocal techniques required to perform them. They form a counterpoint to the established sociomusical practices of the traditional bourgeois hegemony, but with which they are also increasingly engaged in creative explorations of differences (Potter 1998: 186–9). The performance of popular song, whatever the extent to which it may depend upon vocal training, is less a product of the conventions of trained singing than of the application of the voice to the implication and expression of a variety of subtextual meanings of the songs. Middleton (2000: 29) notes, for example, that 'the "naturalistic" tendency (of rock vocals) is such that a para-linguistic dimension is often as important as direct verbal meanings' – a ubiquitous feature of virtually all popular song. The words of popular song can be deliberately simple – even simplistic, but it is precisely this informality, which is invariably characteristic of its various genres, which marks the breakdown of existing conventions, and the subversion of established traditions of singing, providing for changes in the musical microcosm expressive of the structural reconfigurations of social relations in the changing societal macrocosm. Even the popularity of recordings of the recurrent pseudo-genre of 'novelty' songs, Potter (1998: 143) suggests, are important indicators of such changes – 'a case of the new waiting to be born while the old dies'. Such homologies constitute what Williams (1977:128–35) has termed 'structures of feeling', the interpretative textures of which are made still more dense by the crossovers between popular musical genres which have occurred increasingly during the twentieth century.

With the emergence of the long-term social and cultural processes of globalization, a further sociomusical homology has begun to develop, of world music, an emergent genre that consists in its entirety of crossovers between existing genres in different cultures. McNeill (1995: 154–5) points out the need for far-ranging adjustments to human behaviour in adaptating to 'an urban-based global economy and commercialised cosmopolitan society . . . in which keeping together in time is sure to play a part'. The vocal elements of world music have already begun to make a significant contribution to this process of adaptation. Schaefer (2000: 28) notes that 'even a casual look at song traditions around the world reveals an intricate web of songlines between apparently disparate cultures . . . (which) suggest that something fundamental and universal, something that affects people regardless of their specific place and time, lies at the heart of all musical impulse'. The time for song, it seems, is always and already present as a continuing rhythmic impulse for the articulation and enactment of human sociality . . .

References

Ballantine, C. (1984), *Music and its Social Meanings*, London: Gordon & Breach.

Banfield, S. (1995), 'Vocal Music' in Banfield, S. (ed.) (1995) *The Blackwell History of Music in Britain: The Twentieth Century*, Oxford: Blackwell.

Barthes, R. (1977), *Image-Music-Text: Essays Selected and Translated by Stephen Heath*, London: Fontana/Collins.

Benjamin, W. (1969), *Illuminations*, Hannah Arendt (ed.), New York: Schocken Books.

Chanan, M. (1994), *Musica Practica: The Social Practice of Western Music from Gregorian Chant to Postmodernism*, London and New York: Verso.

—— (1999), *From Handel to Hendrix: The Composer in the Public Sphere*, London and New York: Verso.

Elias, N. (1992), *Time: An Essay*, Oxford: Blackwell.

—— (1995), Technization and Civilization, *Theory, Culture and Society*, 12(3).

Finnegan, R. (1989), *The Hidden Musicians: Music-Making in an English Town*, Cambridge: Cambridge University Press.

Habermas, J. (1989), *The Structural Transformation of the Public Sphere*, Cambridge: Polity Press.

Halbwachs, M. (1939), 'La memoire collective chez musiciens', *Revue Philosophique*, (March-April).

Hardy, T. (1998 – first published 1872), *Under the Greenwood Tree: A Rural Painting of the Dutch School*, edited and introduced by Tim Dolin, London: Penguin Books.

Harvey, D. (1990), *The Condition of Postmodernity*, Oxford: Blackwell.

Herbert, T. (2000), 'Caradog' and the Welsh Choral Tradition, in Bashford, C. and Langley, L. (eds) (2000), *Music and British Culture, 1785-1913: Essays in Honour of Cyril Ehrlich*, Oxford: OUP.

Langer, S. (1953), *Feeling and Form*, London: Routledge & Kegan Paul.

Lash, S. (1990), *Sociology of Postmodernism*, London: Routledge.

Lomax, A. (1968), *Folk Song Style and Culture*, New Brunswick NJ: Transaction Books.

Martin, P. (1995), *Sounds and Society: Themes in the Sociology of Music*, Manchester and New York, Manchester University Press.

McNeill, W. (1995), *Keeping Together in Time: Dance and Drill in Human History*, Cambridge MA, Harvard University Press.

McVeigh, S. (2000), 'The Society of British Musicians (1834–65) and the Campaign for Native Talent', in Bashford, C. and Langley, L. (2000), *Music and British Culture, 1785–1914*, Oxford: OUP.

Mellers, W. (1984), 'Introduction', in Ballantine, C., *Music and its Social Meanings*, London: Gordon & Breach.

Merriam, A. (1964), *The Anthropology of Music*, Evanston IL: Northwestern University Press.

Potter, J. (1998), *Vocal Authority: Singing Style and Ideology*, Cambridge: CUP.

— (ed.) (2000), *The Cambridge Companion to Singing*, Cambridge: CUP.

Putnam, R. (2000), *Bowling Alone: The Collapse and Revival of American Community*, New York: Simon & Schuster.

Radcliffe-Brown, A. (1922), *The Andaman Islanders*, Cambridge: CUP.

Robinson, R. and Winold, A. (1976), *The Choral Experience: Literature, Materials, and Methods*, New York: Harper & Row.

Russell, D. (1995), Amateur Musicians and their Repertoire, in Banfield, S. (ed.) (1995), *The Blackwell History of Music in Britain: The Twentieth Century*, Oxford: Blackwell.

Sachs, C. (1965), *The Wellsprings of Music*, edited by Jaap Kunst, New York and Toronto: McGraw Hill.

Schaefer, J. (2000), '"Songlines": Vocal Traditions in World Music', in Potter, J. (ed.) (2000): *The Cambridge Companion to Singing*, Cambridge: CUP.

Schutz, A. (1964), *Making Music Together, Collected Papers II: Studies in Social Theory*, edited and introduced by Arvid Brodersen, The Hague: Martinus Nijhoff.

— (1971), *Common Sense and Scientific Interpretation of Human Action, Collected Papers I: The Problem of Social Reality*, The Hague: Martinus Nijhoff.

Shepherd, J. (1991), *Music as Social Text*, Cambridge: Polity Press.

Small, C. (1998), *Musicking: The Meanings of Performing and Listening*, Hanover NH: Wesleyan University Press.

Storr, A. (1992), *Music and the Mind*, London: HarperCollins.

Sundberg, J. (2000), 'Where Does the Sound Come From', in Potter, J. (ed.) (2000), *The Cambridge Companion to Singing*, Cambridge: CUP.

Sutherland, S. (1995), *Teach Yourself Singing*, London: Hodder Headline.

Tagg, P. (1984), 'Understanding Musical "Time Sense" – Concepts, Sketches and Consequences', *Tvarspel-Festskrift for Jan Ling (50 Ar)*, Goteborg: Skrifter fran Musidvetenskapliga Institutionen.

Van Leeuwen, T. (1999), *Speech, Music, Sound*, London: Macmillan.

Williams, R. (1977), *Marxism and Literature*, Oxford: OUP.

Part II

Histories of Sound

The soundworlds of history produce their own problems of interpretation and study. Yet the following entries demonstrate the riches to be found in understanding the soundworlds of the past. Corbin sets out to define the landscape of 19th century France through the sound of the village bell. Corbin argues that "bells provided a sort of auditory certification, transmitted information about the major events of private life, and solemnized rites of passage . . . (they) imparted a rhythm to the ordinary functioning of a community...(producing) a subtle auditory rhetoric." (Corbin 1998 p.x-xi) Corbin's work has provided a model for both subsequent researches into the role of sound in history and into our understanding of the historical role and place of the senses in general.

Bruce Smith in *Tuning to London* investigates the soundscape of London in 1600 and in doing so provides an instructive methodology of how to listen to the silent voices of the past. In this case through the written commentaries of visitors to London coupled with imaginative aural re-creations of the remaining 16th century sites of habitation in London. Historically, sound studies have to confront the problematic nature of the absence of sounds in history prior to the end of the 19th century, before the age of mechanical reproduction. Smith thus provides important markers for future research into the past.

Mark Smith takes us into the fascinating and conflicting soundworlds of antebellum America providing detailed political, economic and social accounts of the perceived and ideologically articulated sounds of the industrialised North and the slave dominated south. Smith provides us with an invaluable account of the power relations surrounding the generation of 'sound' in antebellum America, in terms of both social class and slavery. Smith analyses both the generation of sound and silence, providing an insightful analysis of the dynamics of 'silence' within the soundscape of slavery.

Bijsterfeld provides an alternative response to the sounds of industrialism and urbanism in both America and Europe in the early part of the 20th century through a comparative analysis of Noise Abatement Campaigns during the early part of the 20th century. Bijsterfeld points to the class element involved in definitions of noise and noise pollution in cities and highlights the debates concerning the relationship of technology and human volition within the period. She notes that the problems associated with noise were often framed in terms of human volition and habits rather than in the noise making machines themselves. Thus car owners were blamed rather than the automobiles themselves for making noise in the city. Bijsterfeld thus provides us with a fascinating analysis of how the machinery of industrialism becomes invisible within a rhetoric of individual responsibility and civility.

Jonathan Sterne casts his eyes over the hidden role of sound in the history and philosophy of medicine through an investigation of the development of listening technologies, primarily the stethoscope. Sterne argues that the use of the stethoscope to ascertain disease is paralleled by both industrialisation and the professionalisation of medicine. Sterne investigates the writings of Laennec, the inventor of the stethoscope, in order to analyse the nature of this technological distancing instrument with which doctors could simultaneously create sound proximity whilst remaining physically distant. Sterne argues that this physical distance mirrored the social distance that the medical profession sought over its patients. Equally Sterne analyses the ambitious but failed attempt at objectivity in 'sound' prognoses of disease sought by the medical profession in its use of the stethoscope in the 19th century. Sterne's work provides an analytically rich account of the auditory history of medicine that opens our eyes to possible alternative narratives of historical experience in general.

7

The Auditory Markers of the Village*

Alain Corbin

Bell, Space and Territory: Centre and Boundary[1]

The emotional impact of a bell helped to create a territorial identity for individuals living in range of its sound. When they heard it ringing, villagers, townsfolk, and those 'in the trades' in the centres of ancient towns experienced a sense of being rooted in space that the nascent urban proletariat lacked. Bell ringing was one of a range of markers obviating the quest for an identity of the sort that defined the very being of the proletarian[2] who, as a migrant, was isolated in a condition that all too often resembled exile.

The bell tower prescribed an auditory space that corresponded to a particular notion of territoriality, one obsessed with mutual acquaintance. The bell reinforced divisions between an inside and an outside, as one might infer from the pejorative use of terms such as *l'esprit du clocher*. Marcel Maget has identified a set of concentric circles containing a zone of mutual alliances, a zone of leisure activities, and a *zone of hearsay* that defined social acquaintance in rural societies.[3] The range of a bell should be analysed in very much the same terms.[4]

This auditory space is not much affected by the acceleration that swept the nineteenth century along, and entails no tendency toward mobility

* From: Corbin, A. (1998), *Village Bells. Sound and Meaning in the Nineteenth Century French Countryside*, New York: Columbia University Press, pp. 95–101. Reproduced with permission.

and speed. Listening to a bell conjures up a space that is, by its nature, slow, prone to conserve what lies within it and redolent of a world in which walking was the chief mode of locomotion.[5] Such a sound is attuned to the quiet tread of a peasant.

The territory circumscribed by the sound of a bell obeyed the classical code of the beautiful – the schema of cradle, nest, and cell. It was an enclosed space structured by the sound emanating from its centre. The bell tower was supposed to be situated in the middle of its auditory territory. Received wisdom has long rested on the assumption that such bounded spaces, inasmuch as they served to perpetuate the notion of walking distance, were in stark contrast to the coherent space of the nation and republican citizenship,[6] and that the advent of democratic regimes presupposed the construction of a new kind of territoriality. We are obliged, however, to qualify such claims once we scrutinize the imaginary attributes of the space upon which the triumph of republic-anism was based. The landscape enshrined in the official ideology of turn-of-the-century France was construed in terms of classical harmony; it consisted of village cells, each permeated by the sound of bells. The Third Republic succeeded in rebuilding this reassuring notion of territory in its own image. It might be truer to the terms of the debate staged in those years to speak of the construction of a space, the basic structure of which was preserved while an attempt was made to desacralize its key markers, namely, bell tower, public square, crossroads and all the sites where public announcements might be made or the inhabitants might assemble.

The range of a bell, inscribed in a classical perspective of harmony, served to define a territory that was haunted by the notion of limits as well as the threat of those limits being transgressed. The crucial functions of the bell tower were to raise the alarm and ensure the preservation of the community. A sort of correlation was established between bell and boundary and between bell ringing and processions. Both served to define a space with readily perceptible limits.[7] Another correlation arose between the loudness of a bell and the extent of a parish or commune's territory. It was important to ensure that no part of that territory remained obdurately deaf to public announcements, alarms, or commands, and that there were no fragments of isolated space in which the auditory identity was ill defined and threatened to impede rapid assembly.

Bells shaped the habitués of a community or, if you will, its culture of the senses. They served to anchor localism,[8] imparting depth to the desire for rootedness and offering the peace of near, well-defined horizons. This is borne out by the correspondence between the historical literature on bells and the structuring of the space across which their sound carried. The histories were invariably the work of local antiquaries obsessed with their *petit pays,* and they took the form of fragments or tiny essays cut to fit the episodic nature of everyday life. Such research, of which there is a huge amount,[9] represents a history of the minuscule; the narrowness of its scope and its scattered state precludes its ever being raised to the level of a more prestigious, all embracing history.[10]

In the nineteenth century, at least in the countryside, bell ringing defined a space within which only fragmented, discontinuous noises were heard, none of which could really vie with the bell tower.[11] After all there were as yet no aeroplanes, which nowadays are capable of competing with, overwhelming and, above all, *neutralizing* the sound of bells. Aerial sounds have been desacralized. Since the dawn of the twentieth century, bell and cannon have ceased to be the sole rivals of the almighty thunderbolt.

The continuous noise of the internal combustion engine, electric motor, or amplifier was also unknown. People liked, therefore, being sporadically deafened, primarily by the ringing of bells, but also by the sound of cannon being fired or the explosion of 'firecrackers', all of which were regarded as indispensable complements to public rejoicing. The charivari, or 'rough music' we tend to regard as unwelcome disturbance, was all the more appreciated for its breaching of a habitual silence and for its links with the structure of the auditory landscape. Let me reiterate, however, that nothing in a milieu of this kind could vie with the bell.

Owing to the regularity with which they were rung, bells played a part in the periodic 'sacral recharging of the surrounding space' (Dupront, as cited in Corbin 1998). Whatever the degree of religious fervour of the local population, the church served to define a small place at the very heart of the village that was generally respected. From this centre of padded silence emanated the sound waves that extended their 'sacralizing' hold over an aerial space undisturbed by any other din.

Since the dawn of the Catholic Reformation, the Church has aspired to such a mastery of airborne sound. It has tried, although not entirely successfully, to heirarchize bell ringing. According to norms laid down by Carlo Borromeo in the sixteenth century (cf. Blavignac 1877), a cathedral was supposed to have between five and seven bells while a collegiate church might have three, and a parish church two, or at the most three. Monastery bells were not supposed to drown out those of a parish church. Ringers were expected to respect the 'rules of deference' that reflected the hierarchy of edifices. The Council of Toulouse (1590) prohibited the 'ringing of bells in any church before those of the Cathedral or of the mother church [sic] had given the signal.'[12] Such refinements had been unknown during the Middle Ages but equivalent norms nonetheless existed. When a church was first founded its filial status was emphasized by its being permitted just one bell.[13]

In truth, there was such a quantity of bells and such a love of peals in modern France that it was very hard to maintain any control over the messages they emitted. Doctor Billon, the man responsible for inaugurating the campanarian survey in 1853, found that in the eighteenth century it was the custom to accord pre-eminence to cathedrals. In the following century this principle of deference in the sphere of bell ringing seems to have been observed in the episcopal towns. A romantic traveller perched on a hill could readily make out the aerial music that emanated from such places that used to be known as 'ringing' towns.

A bell was supposed to be audible everywhere within the bounds of a specified territory.[14] As we have seen earlier, this implied adjusting the loudness of a ring of bells so that it could cover the surface area of the parish or commune and surmount any obstacles in the terrain. 'We have found', Remi Carre noted in 1757, 'that bells may be heard further on the plains than in the mountains, and that bells in the valleys may be heard still further than those on the plains' (Carre 1757: 7) A mountainous terrain called for both a loud bell and early announcements. The 1837 regulation stipulated that in the valleys of the Pyrenees the offices might be rung a full hour before the service was due to start (ANF 4373 and ANF 4377, as cited in Corbin 1998). The 1885 regulation deemed even this advance notice insufficient in the Haute-Savoie.

The archives are full to bursting with complaints that a ring of bells did not cover a given territory. Consider the department of Finistere. On 19 June 1808 the inhabitants of Ouessant unsuccessfully petitioned the prefect, requesting a bell 'whose sound could be heard in every corner' of the island (A D. Finistere, IV9, as cited in Corbin 1998). Three years later the Mayor of Plouider reminded the same magistrate that his commune had given four bells during the Revolution, among them 'the loveliest in the land', which 'could be heard from a great way off' (A. D. Finistere, IV 276). Plouider, however, now only had one very soft bell that could not cover portions of 'mountain' and sea supposedly lying within its range. Once again, in 1892, the inhabitants of Plouneour-Lanvern complained that they could not hear their only bell more than a kilometre away from the town, and that it rang a *sol* though 'the wish of the local population' was to hear a *fa* (A. D. Finistere, IV 276).

A large number of complaints about the failure of the bells to carry concerned ringing in secular contexts. The clergy reserved the loudest and most solemn bells for announcing religious services, leaving only the small bell used for low masses for other kinds of ringing. Sometimes a community would therefore claim the right to use the largest bell under all circumstances.

In 1880 the priest in charge at Ceffonds (Haute-Marne) refused to ring the curfew with the great bell although this was what the town council had requested. In his view, custom decreed that it should be rung by 'the second'. The dispute divided the commune for several years. At first, opposition to the priest led the council to withhold the bell ringer's fee to stop the ringing of the curfew. In November 1884, however, emboldened by the new political circumstances, the municipality began reinstating the practice, this time 'with the largest bell'. The mayor appointed a bell ringer and the municipality decided to offer him remuneration for this task alone. The parish priest complained to the authorities and the dispute then led to a heated exchange between the sub-prefect and the bishop of Langres. When challenged by the Ministre des Cultes, who had been alerted by the bishop, the prefect sought to justify the mayor's point of view. He stressed that the 'second' bell was 'none too loud', and that the affair had erupted five years ago when the hamlets far from the centre of Ceffonds repeatedly complained. Today, he said, the great bell was in use 'to the general satisfaction of all'. In his opinion the size of the commune fully justified the innovation. The dispute ended in May 1886 with victory for the municipality (A. D. Haute-Marne, 48V2 as cited in Corbin 1998). In 1900 the commune of Lagrave (Tarn) was divided by a dispute of this kind.

According to the mayor, a number of day labourers and landowners asked that 'the great bell' be rung at six in the evening to mark the end of the working day. The bishop endorsed the parish priest's refusal to ring with that instrument. The commune had a clock whose bell chimed every hour and the two clerics deemed this perfectly adequate. The dispute was becoming bitter, the bishop stressed, and was being exploited by anticlericals. The mayor asked the Ministre des Cultes for permission to mark the end of the working day with the great bell. A refusal would be bound, he said, to undermine his position, that of the municipal council, and therefore that of the republicans at the next election (ANF 4377, Tarn cited in Corbin 1998. The shape of this affair is reminiscent of the conflict in Lonlay-L'Abbaye in 1958).

One of the functions of a bell was to orient travellers or navigators within the space covered by its sound. Local customs bear traces of the protection offered by such instruments, as much in the mountains as in coastal areas, but also in hilly regions, on the fringes of forests, and sometimes even in flat country. The monks of Grand-Saint-Bernard used a bell located forty minutes from the monastery that rang to orient straying travellers (Dergny 2: 18, as cited in Corbin 1998). In the mountains of the Auvergne 'it is the custom to ring the bells from five to six o' clock in the evening, and until eleven o' clock at night whenever the countryside is covered in snow' (Dergny 2: 18–21, as cited in Corbin 1998). The bell in Aubrac rang every night for the same reason (Dergny 2: 18–21, as cited in Corbin 1998, for the examples that follow). In some communes of the Puy-de-Dome, 'the Angelus is rung at eight in the evening, for a long time'. In the canton of Saint-Beat (Haut-Garonne), the bell began ringing at 10 p.m. in winter for the same reason. This practice was also followed at Haudricourt (Sainte-Inferieure), a wooded, very hilly commune. Likewise the mayors of the Meuse, who had refused the prefect's request made in 1852 to ring at 10 p.m. on summer evenings (cf. A. D. Meuse 37V1 as cited in Corbin 1998) acknowledged that it was useful in winter to let the bell be heard at nine o' clock to reorientate travellers who had lost their way in the forest.[15]

Along the coast where there was no lighthouse, and everywhere when the fog came down, it was bell ringing that served to guide – and sometimes, it was said, to lead astray – disorientated sailors. In Dieppe (Saint-Valery-en-Caux) and Bourg-d'Ault (Sainte-Inferieure), the bells were rung in bad weather. In 1864 Treport municipal council had a bell installed on the jetty (for all these examples, see Dergny Les Cloches 2: 21, as cited in Corbin 1998). In Sables-d'Olonne there was a rescue bell. It was placed 'high on the bell tower dome' and 'it rang in time of storm'. In 1881 the parish of Ile-Tudy (Finistere) requested a second bell 'to [be] better able to signal to sailors the precise location of the coastline in times of thick fog, which obscured the lighthouses' (Dergny, Les Cloches, 2: 21, as cited in Corbin 1998). The minister granted the sum required.

The Path of the Good Angels

Bells were supposed to preserve the space of a community from all conceivable threats. This prophylactic virtue was perhaps one that aroused the fiercest passions; alone it justified the deep attachment to bells until the symbolic tie between ringing and communities began to unravel.

There was a perfectly respectable theological justification for this function, as expounded by the abbot Jean-Baptiste Thiers in the *Traite des cloches*, one of his posthumously published works. Invoking the church fathers, John Chrystosom in particular, as well as the key texts in the Catholic Reformation, Thiers distinguished faith in the preservation of bells from the cluster of superstitions that he set out to denounce in order to purify beliefs. As far as he was concerned the formulas used in the benediction justified belief in the preservative value of the sacred bronze.

Demons dwelt in the air and were responsible for the spread of plagues and epizootic diseases. They precipitated swarms of insects, unleashed storms, provoked floods, and produced frosts. Above all, their aerial presence prevented prayer.

The point is that the demons were horrified by the sound of bells; they had only to hear them and they would let witches fall on the roads to the sabbath, and take flight. Bells were credited with the power to drive away thunder, thunderstorms, and tempests, and cleanse the air of every infernal presence. 'Such effects are not achieved naturally', Jean-Baptiste Thiers elaborated, 'but through the divine virtue impressed upon them when one blesses them, or when one rings them against these meteors'(Thiers: 136, cited in Corbin 1998). Bells also possessed the crucial power to summon angels. Bells had the power to break up the maleficent clouds that impeded the perpetual movement of angels and prevented contact between heaven and earth.

Notes

1. This is the constant refrain of those who deplore the loss of territorial frameworks through which the memory of individuals or groups was built up, and the representations of society delineated. Cf. the already fairly old study by Halbwachs (1925). On the perceptual structuration of space, 'the territorial sentiment', and the distinction between territoriality and rootedness, see Roncayola (1983), and in particular, his observation on Marcel Maus's contribution to the debate.

2. Cf. the works of Jacques Ranciere.

3. Maget (1955). On the marking of territories and the indication of boundaries, see also Jacques Boutier's observations in Territoires, pp. 42ff (cited in Corbin 1998).

4. Marcel Maget also studied the ways in which each group was emblazoned, a process in which the bell was clearly involved.

5. See Studeny (1990) and Leonard 1986: 18–20

6. In this regard, see Ihl (1992) and Ihl (forthcoming).

7. 'In towns with several parishes', we read in the regulation for peals agreed upon between the archbishop of Rennes and the prefect of the Ille-et-Vilaine in 1885, 'the bells shall be rung when the procession passes across the territory of one of the parishes, and in the church of that parish' (ANF 4375, Ille-et-Valaine, cited in Corbin 1998).

8. On the meaning of localism and on the existence of particular discourses and territories, local memory, and the culture of local space, see Gasnier (1992: 463–25)

9. As is borne out by reading the volumes of the Bibliographie *annuelle de l'Histoire de France.*

10. Which is why it was something of a gamble even to embark upon the writing of the present study, because it aspires to impose some order on this proliferating history of the minuscule.

11. For an inventory of such sounds, see Thuillier (1977: 230–44).

12. A ruling confirmed by the congregation of Rites on 21 March 1606 and 9 February 1608.

13. Before 1240 the Franscicans were not permitted bells. Subsequently, as a token of humility, their monasteries very often possessed one of them.

14. Conversely, according to ancient law (cf. Blavignac 1877: 256), the extent of a given jurisdiction was sometimes defined in terms of the range of its bell.

15. In Normandy, it is claimed that William the Conqueror was saved in 1044 while in the neighbourhood of Bayeux, by the peal from an evening bell. He thereafter gave the order for the curfew to be rung in every town and village in the Duchy to put lost travellers back on the right road.

References

Blavignac, J. D. (1877), *La Cloche: étude sur son histoire ET sur SES rapports avec la societé aux differents âges,* Geneva, pp. 22ff.

Carre, R. (1757), *Recueil curieux et édifiant,* cited in Corbin, A. (1998), *Village Bells. Sound and Meaning in the Nineteenth Century French Countryside,* New York: Columbia University Press, pp. 95–101.

Corbin, A. (1998), *Village Bells. Sound and Meaning in the Nineteenth Century French Countryside,* New York: Columbia University Press, pp. 95–101.

Dergny, *Les Cloches,* cited in Corbin, A. (1998), *Village Bells. Sound and Meaning in the Nineteenth Century French Countryside,* New York: Columbia University Press, pp. 95–101.

Dupront, *Du sacre*, p. 447, cited in Corbin, A. (1998), *Village Bells. Sound and Meaning in the Nineteenth Century French Countryside*, New York: Columbia University Press, pp. 95–101.

Gasnier, T. (1992), 'Le local: une et indivisible', in Nora (ed.), *Les Lieux de Mémoire*, Paris: Traditions, vol. 3, pt. 2, pp. 463–525.

Halbwachs, M. (1925), *Les Cadre's sociaux de la mémoire*, Paris: Alcan.

Ihl, O. (1992), *La Citoyennete en fête: Célébrations nationales et integration politique dans la France republicaine (1870–1914)*, thesis.

Ihl, O. (forthcoming), 'Du politique au sacre: Les fetes republicaines dans les campagnes de la Creuse (1870–1914)', in *Mémoires de la Societé des sciences naturelles et archéologiques de la Creuse* (forthcoming).

Leonard, J. (1986), *Archives du corp: La santé au XIXe siècle*, Renne: University of Rennes.

Maget, M. (1955), 'Remarques sur le village comme cadre des récherches anthropologiques', *Bulletin de Psychologie*, 8 (special issue no. 7–8): 376–82.

Roncayola, M. (1983), in Territoires, ENS, no. 1: 4–21, cited in Corbin, A. (1998), *Village Bells. Sound and Meaning in the Nineteenth Century French Countryside*, New York: Columbia University Press, pp. 95–101.

Studeny, C. (1990), *Le Vertige de la vitesse: L'acceleration de la France (1830–1940)* (thesis in 5 vols). EHESS.

Thiers, J. *Traite des Cloches*, cited in Corbin, A. (1998), *Village Bells. Sound and Meaning in the Nineteenth Century French Countryside*, New York: Columbia University Press, pp. 95–101.

Thuillier, G. (1977), 'Les bruits', in *Pour une histoire de quotidien au XIXe siècle en Nivernais*, Paris and The Hague: EHESS-Moutin.

8

Tuning into London c. 1600

Bruce R. Smith

The *chkty-chkty-chkty-chkty* spilling out of someone else's headphones, the *yeow-yeow* clearing the way for ambulances and police cars, the *bllliiiiii* heralding the banalities of a stranger's one-sided conversation on a mobile phone – these serve as keen reminders that most of us live immersed in a world of sound. Why, then, don't we think very much about sound except when it calls attention to itself as noise or music? About vision we are much more (telling word) *reflective*. Two books of the 1990s, Martin Jay's *Downcast Eyes: The Denigration of Vision in Twentieth-Century French Thought* and David M. Levin's *Modernity and the Hegemony of Vision,* chart the persistent visual bias in Western culture – a bias that goes back to the Greeks. It is by light, not by echo, that Plato's thinker finds his way out of the cave. Not every culture depends so exclusively on vision. Steven Feld's experience among the Kaluli people of Papua New Guinea suggests that these dwellers in dense rainforests use sound as much as visual cues to locate themselves in space and time (Feld 1982, 1996). In a recent CD ('Voices of the Rainforest', Rykodisc 10173) Feld records the emergence of the Kaluli people's music and speech patterns out of the ambient sounds of their forest home. What sort of relationship could be traced between ambient sounds and the music and speech patterns of the Londoniensis people of WC1? Over the past century technology has dislocated sounds from their sources and made them infinitely repeatable, producing a 'schizophonia' that is arguably greater than any sense of alienation we are likely to experience in visual terms.

127

Sound is at once the most forceful stimulus that human beings experience, and the most evanescent. Periodic waves of air molecules strike against the listener's eardrums and set up vibrations inside the body. If the waves are strong enough (as, for example, when a large drum is being struck), the vibrations can be felt in the viscera of the gut as well as in the ears. At the same time, sounds rapidly dissipate into nothing. For an historian interested in the sounds of the past, there would seem to be nothing *there* to study, at least until the advent of electromagnetic recording devices early in the twentieth century. It was the thought (I can no longer recall where I first encountered it) that all the sounds that have ever occurred still reverberate, however faintly, somewhere in the wild blue yonder that originally set me onto the project of historical recovery that became my book *The Acoustic World of Early Modern England* (1999). However dubious as a scientifically demonstrable proposition, the *findableness* of sounds that occurred in the historical past excited my imagination – and challenged my skills as a scholar who was trained to deal with tangible physical objects in the form of literary texts. Guideposts in my quest had been set in place by R. Murray Schafer's *The Tuning of the World* (1977), the foundational text of acoustic ecology, as well as by the work of Feld and other anthropologists. The study of sound as an historical phenomenon is not quite the same thing, however. Schafer, a composer noted for combining 'found sounds' with orchestral music, is focused on the here-and-now realities of sound in cities, towns, industrial parks, and so-called 'open' spaces. Feld could journey to Papua New Guinea, switch on his tape recorder, and ask his subjects questions. What happens when the sounds in question are no longer there to be heard? When the informants are no longer living? When the analyst and the subjects cannot interact? Alain Corbin confronted just such logistical challenges in writing *Village Bells: Sound and Meaning in the Nineteenth-Century French Countryside* (French text 1994, English translation 1998). Drawing on the methodology of his earlier study of smell, Corbin has reconstructed what church bells meant to ordinary people in the course of their daily lives and has suggested how the bells connected them to events far beyond their fields. More recently, Mark M. Smith has traced the role of sounds in defining political sectionalism in *Listening to Nineteenth-Century America* (2001). Smith is able to draw on taped interviews with former slaves made in the 1930s, but for the most part the sounds that he studies have had to be reconstructed from written sources. All these projects converge on three principles:

- that sound has been a neglected object of study;
- that knowing the world through sound is fundamentally different from knowing the world through vision, and
- that most academic disciplines are vision-based, not only in the materials they study, but in the theoretical models they deploy to interpret those materials.

How to listen to history? Two challenges face anyone who wants to tune into London c. 1600: cataloguing sounds and finding a syntax.

Cataloguing Sounds

Just as a more conventional archaeologist first unearths the objects to be studied and then ranges them into categories, so an acoustical archaeologist must 'un-air' sounds that have faded into the air's atmosphere and catalogue them. What kinds of sounds did Shakespeare and his contemporaries hear? What kinds of sounds occurred in the world around them? What kinds of sounds did they make themselves? Where were those sounds located? In a few cases we have direct physical evidence. For example, musical instruments from the period survive and can still be played (Munrow 1976). Some of the same church bells still hang in some of the same belfries and can still be rung. Some of the same interior spaces still exist, and their acoustic properties can still be experienced. Although put to other uses today, Westminster Hall was one of the largest interior public spaces in early modern London. The law courts and merchants' stalls that occupied the vast space under the hammer-beam roof made Westminster Hall one of the loudest places in London – a fact that more than one contemporary Londoner noted (Smith 1999: 60–2).

The best source of information turned out to be, not the inhabitants of England themselves, but foreign visitors like Paul Hentzner (1598), Thomas Platter (1599), Philip Gerschow (1602), and Orazio Busino (1617–18). About sound, as about everything else, they often noticed things that natives took for granted. Gerschow, for example, records among his first impressions of London the fact that church bells were loudly bonging as he arrived in the city. When he inquired what was going on, he was told that the youths of London rang the bells every afternoon, competing with one another as to who could ring the loudest and longest. Hentzner, who noted the same custom, commented that English people are 'vastly fond of great noises that fill the ear, such as the firing of cannon and the ringing of bells' (quoted in B. Smith 1999: 52–3).

Another place in which the sounds of early modern England lie imbedded is imaginative fiction. Ben Jonson's play *Epicene, or The Silent Woman* is among the richest of these texts in its representations of sound. The play's protagonist, Morose, is so hyper-sensitive to noise that he lives all the way at the bottom of a cul-de-sac too narrow for carts and coaches, and he never comes out on Sundays and holidays, when the ringing of church bells fills the air. In the course of his complaints about noise, Morose provides the acoustic archaeologist with a list of London's loudest places. If he were to marry, Morose worries, his wife might turn out not to be the model of silence that women are supposed to be. To get rid of such a wife, he would be willing to do penance 'in a belfry, at Westminster Hall, in the cock pit at the fall of a stag, the Tower Wharf – what place is there else? – London Bridge, Paris Garden, Billingsgate, when the noises are at the height and loudest. Nay, I would sit out a play that were nothing but fights at sea, drum, trumpet, and target!' (quoted in Smith 1999: 60).

More allusive are the physical sounds *implied* by fictional texts if not *represented* in those texts. Play scripts, after all, were designed to be performed, not read. A chapter in *The Acoustic World of Early Modern England* is devoted to acoustic reconstructions of the 1599 *Globe* theatre and the indoor *Blackfriars* theatre where Shakespeare's company also performed after 1609. My method in reconstructing the *Globe* involved correlating several different kinds of evidence: the resonance of building materials like oak beams and plaster over lathing; the disposition of the building's main features as specified in the builder's contract for the Fortune Theatre, set up to be closely modelled on the *Globe*; the dimensions implied by archaeological remains of the *Globe* uncovered in the early 1990s in Southwark; indications of special sound effects in scripts; and the calculations of modern acoustical engineering with respect to the reflectivity of the *Globe*'s building materials, the directional properties of the building's shape, and the reverberation delays to be expected in its volume. Also important to the project were the findings of modern linguistic research with respect to the mathematical modes of pitches of adult male voices reading aloud, as compared with the pitches of women and adolescent boys. By comparing these linguistic data on pitch with psycho-acoustic research on the perceived loudness and locatablity of sounds at various pitches I was able to place men's voices in the space of the Globe *vis-à-vis* boys' voices. Putting together all these various pieces of information – from architectural acoustics, linguistics, and psycho-acoustics – I concluded that scripts written by Shakespeare and other writers for the outdoor amphitheatres are designed to capitalize on those

spaces' distinctive sound qualities: a broad, side-to-side sound in which
percussion and brass instruments provided the predominant keynotes
in a matrix of sound that featured mostly adult male voices. Scripts for
these outdoor theatres contrast with scripts for the indoor *Blackfriars*
theatre, which offered a more rounded sound and featured a wider range
of musical instruments in a matrix that gave some prominence to boys'
voices. In the 1590s the Blackfriars Theatre had been home to several
all-boy troupes of actors, and interludes provided by musical consorts
had been a regular feature of performances in that space. Play scripts
provide the most obvious instance of sound as implied by written texts,
but early modern culture offers plenty of other examples: ballads,
sermons, even letters and poems written out by hand.

Finding a Syntax

Once the sounds of early modern England had been found and catal-
ogued, I faced an even greater challenge: to find a 'syntax' for making
sense of the sounds. How did Shakespeare and his contemporaries order
the sounds that they heard and made? How did they use those sounds
to position themselves in the world? In my bafflement I found myself
in the position of Geoffrey Streamer, a fictional character in William
Baldwin's satire *Beware the Cat* (1584). Sitting in a friend's house near
Aldersgate in London, Streamer cooked up a magic potion that, applied
to his ears, allowed him to hear all the sounds within a hundred miles:
'barking of dogs, grunting of hogs, wailing of cats, rambling of rats,
gaggling of geese, humming of bees . . . flittering of fowls, routing of
knaves, snorting of slaves, farting of churls, fizzling of girls . . . ringing
of bells, counting of coins, mounting of groins, whispering of lovers'
. . . and a great deal more (quoted in Smith 1999: 30–1). As an English
professor, I knew all about the function of syntax in ordering the sounds
of speech. But how could I make sense of all that Geoffrey Streamer
heard?

It was at this confused juncture that I turned to the discipline of
acoustic ecology, in particular to the work of Murray Schafer and Barry
Truax. In *Acoustic Communication* Truax challenges listeners to free
themselves from the narrow confines of speech and to listen to all the
sounds around them. He orders these sounds along a continuum of
syntax that is temporally more and more extended:

primal cries – speech – music – ambient sound

Discussing this model in the course of a seminar I convened at the
Folger Shakespeare Library in Washington in 1996, a professional voice
coach suggested that what we have here is not a linear continuum but
a circle that begins and ends in primal cries. Human exclamations of
'oh', 'ah', 'mmm', and the like take their place in the ambient world of
animal sounds, wind, and rushing water. The resulting model inscribes
an O, which is, in two dimensions at least, a representation of the shape
of sound, i.e.

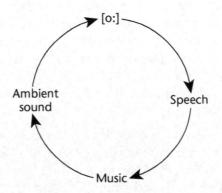

Most historians of early modern England have focused their attention
on a very narrow range of sounds – those involved in speech. My goal
in *The Acoustic World* was to attend to the full range of sounds that made
England in the late sixteenth and early seventeenth centuries a place
distinct from other places. That project occupied me particularly in a
chapter on three representative soundscapes: city, country, and court.
In each case, I singled out one specific place – the Aldersgate quarter
where Geoffrey Streamer lodged in the City of London, Kenilworth in
Warwickshire, and Whitehall Palace in Westminster – and attempted
to provide what anthropologists would call 'thick description'. Maps,
site plans, legal documents, travellers' accounts, literary allusions, and
surviving structures and landscape features gave me the evidence I
sought. I turned also to the findings of modern acoustics with respect
to decibel measurements, the effects of wind direction, greater and lesser
degrees of humidity according to the seasons of the year, and so forth.
    The soundscape of Kenilworth can stand as an example of my project.
An estate map of 1628, housed in the Public Record Office, and an
engraved view of Kenilworth Castle by Wenceslas Hollar (1656) allowed
me to locate just which parts of the land had been forested, which had
been used as open meadows for grazing, which had been farmed under
the open field system, and which had been farmed or grazed as enclosed

lands. Accounts of Queen Elizabeth's visit to the site in 1575 filled the woods with the sounds of hunting: horn blasts, halloing humans, yelping hounds. The research of agricultural historians like Joan Thirsk described the communal conditions under which work was carried out in open fields, suggesting that continuous talk and perhaps singing accompanied the rasps, swishes, cuts, and thumps of the workers' tools as they laboured in close proximity to one another, all focused on the same tasks at the same time. Travellers' accounts added barking dogs to the soundscape. Gerschow observed that as a relatively underpopulated country in 1602 England provided enough food for even the humblest farmer to keep dogs as pets and for farm use. Packing up all this evidence, I paid a visit to the site and was able to overlay the soundscape of today's Kenilworth with the sounds heard there 400 years ago. My findings in the chapter on the soundscapes of early modern England became the basis for a series of four programs broadcast in spring and autumn 2000 over BBC Radio 4.

For all that, I have become increasingly sceptical about the idea of a universal syntax of sound, even one so inclusive as a circle of sound beginning and ending in [o:]. The witnesses whose written accounts I consulted suggested, at the minimum, three quite distinct syntaxes for country, court, and city. At least as these literate witnesses heard it, the countryside not only contained many more non-verbal sounds than the court and the city but recognized more ways in which those non-verbal sounds were meaningful. Take, for example, sounds made by birds. Temporary refugees from urban life like Thomas Dekker in his pamphlet *The Bellman of London* (1616) are apt to hear bird sounds as abstract music: 'The melody which the birds made . . . put me in mind of that garden whereof our great grandsire [Adam] was the keeper' (quoted in Smith 1999: 75). To a full-time denizen of the country, however, bird sounds took on meaning in a seasonal syntax, as Thomas Tusser in his versified farming manual *A Hundred Good Points of Husbandry* (1557) explains with respect to the ploughman in spring: 'A whole flight of crows follow him for their food, and when they fly away they give him ill language' (quoted in Smith 1999: 75). By contrast, the court, attendant on the monarch's every word, employed a syntax of sound that was extremely logocentric. The city's syntax was somewhere in between. Certainly there were places in the city – the Royal Exchange, the law courts, St Paul's Cathedral – where words held sway. But the varieties of trade, still associated with specific wards of the city of London, ordered sounds in their own distinctive ways. Tailors, blacksmiths, weavers, and tinkers were associated not only with the specific sounds of their crafts (snipping, pounding, thrustling, banging) but with specific catches or rounds that they sang while they worked (Fox 2000: 29). Street vendors, too, had their distinctive quasi-musical cries (Smith 1999: 64–70).

If geography was one determinant of the syntax of sound, social class was another. Adam Fox has studied the pressures toward standardization in diction and pronunciation that rapid economic development brought to England's speech communities in the late sixteenth and early seventeenth centuries, particularly along lines of social hierarchy (Fox 2000: 100–10). Over the course of this time period 'hey nonny nonny' and 'hey troly loly' increasingly became the preserve of the lower orders (Fox 2000: 27). The most significant factor of all seems to be book-based education. Among educated listeners in early modern England there was a pronounced distrust of non-verbal sounds. The whoops and hollers of countryfolk and lower-class craftsmen might be amusing in a pageant or a masque but such sounds marked the boundary between civility and barbarity. That became ever more apparent as colonial expansion and voyages of conquest placed the strategic boundary between civility and barbarity ever farther away in geographical space – and made the people on the other side of the boundary ever more remote. The Irish 'hubbub' in times of mourning, argument, or celebration struck horror and contempt in English ears (Smith 1999: 305–6). So, too, did the music and speeches of Native Americans. John Smith in *A Map of Virginia* (1612) describes the chanting of the Powhatan Indians as 'a terrible noise as would rather affright than delight any man' (quoted in Smith 1999: 324). (One notes here the unquestioned universal criterion of judgement implied by 'any man'.) The distrust of non-verbal sound extended even to music. The musical contest between Apollo and Marsyas, recounted in Ovid's *Metamorphoses*, Book 6, and elsewhere, provides the paradigmatic myth for understanding this distrust. Marsyas, man from the waist up, goat from the waist down, chanced to find a pipe that had been cast off by Pallas. The satyr became so proud of his playing that he challenged Apollo, whose instrument was the lyre. Apollo's victory, according to Renaissance commentators, had to do not only with cosmic resonance between the lengths of the lyre's strings and the distances between the planets but with Apollo's ability to sing words while he played. As the Greek statesman Alcibiades is quoted to have said, 'Let the Thebans play on the flute, who know not how to speak: but for us Athenians, we have Pallas and Apollo for the patrons of our country' (Sandys 1632: 225). The ultimate authority for such a prejudice is Plato, who refers sound, like all other sensible experience, to the jurisdiction of Ideas. Sound without *logos* is, to Plato's mind, noise. For sound without *logos* there can *be* no syntax. Our own culture's anxiety in the presence of non-verbal sounds has a very long history.

References

Corbin, A. (1998), *Village Bells: Sound and Meaning in the Nineteenth-Century French Countryside*, translated by Martin Thom, New York: Columbia University Press.

Feld, Stephen (1982), *Sound and Sentiment: Birds, Weeping, Poetics, and Song in Kaluli Expression*, Philadelphia: University of Pennsylvania Press.

—— (1996), 'Waterfalls of Sound: An Acoustemology of Place Resounding in Bosavi, Papua New Guinea', in Stephen Feld and Keith H. Basso (eds), *Senses of Place*, Santa Fe: School of American Research.

Fox, A. (2000), *Oral and Literature Culture in England 1500–1700*, Oxford: Clarendon Press.

Jay, M. (1993), *Downcast Eyes: The Denigration of Vision in Twentieth-Century French Thought*, Berkeley: University of California Press.

Levin, D. M. (1993), *Modernity and the Hegemony of Vision*, Berkeley: University of California Press.

Munrow, D. (1976), *Instruments of the Middle Ages and Renaissance*, Oxford: Oxford University Press.

Sandys, G. (1632), *Ovid's Metamorphosis Englished, Mythologized, and Represented in Figures*, Oxford: J. Lichfield.

Schafer, R. M. (1977), *The Tuning of the World*, New York: Knopf.

Smith, B. R. (1999), *The Acoustic World of Early Modern England: Attending to the O Factor*. Chicago: University of Chicago Press.

Smith, M. M. (2001), *Listening to Nineteenth-Century America*, Chapel Hill: University of North Carolina Press.

Truax, B. (1984), *Acoustic Communication*, Norwood NJ: Ablex.

9

Listening to the Heard Worlds of Antebellum America*

Mark M. Smith

Despite calls by linguists and theorists to end the privilege that sight enjoys over hearing, historians have only just begun to overcome their deafness to the aural worlds of the past. Recent and forthcoming work on acoustic pasts notwithstanding, the study of American sound and noises is still in its infancy. This chapter attempts to sensitize our ears to heard pasts. It will explore the historical construction and meaning of aurality, noise, and sound in antebellum America to reveal how regional soundscapes became something contemporaries called 'modern' and to show how these constructions both impinged on and helped to define social relations in general and class and sectional identities in particular. My concern is not so much to frame heard pasts exclusively within the co-ordinates of cultural history as to listen to how contemporaries heard the articulated and intimately related principal political, economic, and social developments of antebellum America, in particular class formation, the market revolution, and, ultimately, sectionalism and the coming of the Civil War. The aural perceptions of American elites, accustomed to hearing the health and pulse of their own societies, began to hear ominous discordance during the final decades before the Civil War.[1] These new strains fostered warped perceptions, including

* First appeared in *Journal of the Historical Society*, 1(1) (Spring 2000). Reproduced with permission.

an inclination to minimize objective sectional similarities, and ultimately contributed to the violent disintegration of the Union.

There are several ways of inaugurating a history of sounds made by particular people and objects. One could examine sound in the objective, as in the proposition that history becomes louder as society modernizes and industrializes. Thanks to exhaustive work by the World Soundscape Project, it is theoretically possible to demonstrate that the US became louder as it modernized by measuring increases in decibel levels (levels in sound pressure) over time (Truax 1978: 126). But such an emphasis deafens us to the social and historical implications of the heard world. Instead, to follow the lead of acoustic theorists, I turn primarily to subjective or cognitive understandings of sound and the heard world to historicize and contextualize them. If the study of acoustics exclusively concerns the physical behaviour of sound, then historical soundscape studies should bridge the gap between physical, measurable sound and the perception of what is heard. Subjective appreciations of sound and noise – their constructions and imagined projections – are necessarily related to their acoustic environment. Metaphors, analogies, and similes are not invented in a vacuum; for example, tornadoes cannot sound like trains until trains exist and listeners are accustomed to them. Conversely, very small actual differences in sound (decibels) or timbre (acoustic and, hence, social texture) can be amplified through the filters of social and economic relations and modes of production. Sound operates as reality and as a construction, sometimes simultaneously, and because historical soundscapes may be both actual environments and abstract constructions, we must treat them as both. (see, for example, Handel 1989; Kryter 1970).

Elite Ears

Although nineteenth-century Anglo-American elites came to define their economic, political, and cultural authority by emphasizing what James Joyce called 'the ineluctable modality of the visual', the heard world still retained considerable currency among ruling classes. As proxies for progress and refinement, sounds in particular were 'as much a mark of their nationality as their class', to follow Peter Bailey's observation of the Victorian English bourgeoisie (Bailey 1998). Antebellum elites appealed to the heard world when defining and reaffirming some of the core values of their class. Most obviously, elites from North and South applauded and encouraged the association of sound with notions of 'progress', broadly conceived. For example, revolutions in markets

and transport both manifested an aural dimension. As Americans pushed
westward, the rhythmic, ordered sound of progress quashed the sporadic,
unpredictable noise of the frontier before then. Hezekiah Niles cooed
in 1815: 'Everywhere the sound of the axe is heard opening the forest
to the sun . . . The busy hum of ten thousand wheels fills our seaports,
and the sound of the spindle and loom succeeds the yell of the savage
or the screech of the night owl in the late wilderness of the interior.'
Defined by nascent capitalists and boosters, sound heralded progress
and, as such, it was sound, not noise. Rhythmic and predictable, it regulated, controlled, and silenced the visceral and undisciplined 'yell of the
savage'. Moreover, each push westward was an aural victory over howling wilderness. Noisy, 'ungovernable' rivers, opined Benjamin Franklin
in a fit of wishful thinking, would be tamed by coming of 'quiet and
very manageable' canals. Industry echoed in the blasting of rock, and
the 'ceaseless music' of man's expanding mastery of nature was sufficient
to convince antebellum expansionists, North and South, that canals
were indeed a soundmark of industry (quoted in Sellers 1991: 71).

All good (sound) men, it was maintained, should promote the modernization of their country regardless of their region, and they quoted
approvingly one another's views on how that process should be heard.
In 1811, for example, New York's *Independent Mechanic* reprinted an
article from the Richmond Enquirer that related sound to progress. The
author recounting a trip to Switzerland in 1772, commented: 'If I entered
a town . . . I heard, on every hand, the rattling of the hammer, and the
clinking of the trowel', which, in his estimation, bore 'witness to the
progress of wealth and population'. These essentially pre-industrial
sounds of progress were heard elsewhere: 'If I sauntered into the
country, I heard the rosy daughters of industry, singing aloud in their
spinning wheels.' The rattling of urban hammers and the sounds of
rural trowels, songs, and spinning wheels were not in tension because
they were fundamentally pre-industrial. Still, they offered aural testimony to 'the effect of industry . . . virtue and health'; in a word,
activity. So, too, it was in the early national North and South, where a
man's character was measured by sonance of his pre-industrial industriousness. 'My neighbour, Samuel Steady', commented one writer in
1811, is 'an industrious man'. How did he know? 'His hammer is heard
at the cock's crowing.'[2]

Association of progress with cadence meant that economic depression
was ominously silent both to southern planters and northern indus-
trialists. Recession meant an aural interregnum in the sound of progress,
and antebellum elites dreaded the silence of the looms. The editor of a

New York City newspaper couched the matter in verse and, perhaps unwittingly, foretold of the silence that would result from the War of 1812. Via their eyes, he told readers' ears:

> Let saw and hammer still resound;
> Ne'er let the shuttle still be found,
> Throughout the western clime.

War threatened fledgling industry, and silence testified to the threat. Southern elites agreed and similarly fretted about the absence of the sound of economic activity and industriousness during periods of recession.

On other matters, northern elites nodded agreement with their southern brethren on what constituted sound and noise. All concurred that particular constituencies were prone to noisiness. At base, what was deemed noise – and who was noisy – was very much shaped by class relations, which were they influenced by considerations of race and gender. Gentlemen North and south blasted putative ladies for their 'love of little tittle-tattle' and 'gossiping tales', but remained convinced that 'doubtless, there are very many ladies . . . who do not come under the denomination of gossips, which prefer silence to scandal'.[3] Class dimensions were also at work here. Poor women who joined male relatives in revolutionary military encampments, for example, offended military leaders' sensibilities about women's place, and so these women were heard 'yelling in sluttish shrills' (quoted in Wilson 1976: 422). By contrast, the middle-class woman of the antebellum period, although given to emotional, noisy outbursts, was woman not least because she was quiet and submissive. Entrusted to raise sons of a 'sound and virtuous character', woman 'was to work in silence' in this endeavour, to bear indignation 'quietly', 'suffer and be silent', and so help cultivate a 'quiet life' for the antebellum family in the North and South. Poets described women who supported men's work as reassuringly domestic and silent. John Greenleaf Whittier used the quiet industry of wives as an aural counterpoint to celebrate the public, masculine, and republican world of 'The Drovers' in 1850: 'quiet wives [were] knitting' while loud men worked. Some observers considered women who publicly flouted this aural etiquette with loud sounds to be more than merely noisy – they were unsexed.[4]

'Otherness' in different guises was also constructed aurally. Native Americans, for example, occupied an ambiguous place in the ear of the antebellum elites. Nineteenth-century historians of Indian pasts depicted 'the murmur of voices' and their 'peals of laughter' that echoed in primordial forests. Native American 'old women who were forever whispering like the forest leaves' were peaceful creatures. But quiet preceded storms. With cultivated stealth, Indians paralysed white settlers with 'the terrible war-whoop'. Only white victory ensured that all 'was hushed and still as though the voice of pain or discord had never echoed through the wilderness'. The aural slate of former Indian lands was now clean for the cadence of white industriousness. Yet Native Americans were not beyond bourgeois redemption. 'Settling them in a quiet home', it was believed, was a 'wise policy' (Monro 1850; 'Reports of the Secretary of War' 1847).

Class relations were the keys. Elites listened for and heard the putative lack of disciplined and supposed excesses of passion of the lower orders with impressive precision. Attempts to control or discipline this 'canting and shrieking, very wretched generation of ours' required firm self-restraint. Should individuals prove unable or unwilling to control themselves, then patricians would gladly assume the responsibility. The basis for the criminalization of noise, especially for alcohol-induced and wilful breaches of the peace, was well established by the middle decades of the antebellum period. 'For making a noise while in his cell', one Massachusetts prisoner in 1845 was given a day in solitary confinement. The control of inmates' minds and bodies via the 'silent system' was an important component of discipline in antebellum northern penitentiaries and on southern plantations (Thomas 1965).

If lower orders distinguished themselves by producing noise, elites delimited their own aesthetic superiority through the consumption of sound. When attempts by the elite to listen to good music were disrupted by those they considered too uncouth to appreciate it, conflict was likely. In a particularly snotty letter to *Harper's Weekly*, one self-styled aesthete complained in 1858 that, following a recent concert

> I am going to complain, as loud as you will let me, that people who do like music . . . and who came far to hear it, were not allowed to hear it by those who do not like it, and who lounged in from some neighbouring street. We sat in the balcony; and such scuffling, talking, rustling, tapping, beating time inanely with the feet, and general indifference and indecorous riot, I have never before encountered.

What was 'every real lover of music' to do? Consequently, antebellum elites mandated quiet when they could. They believed in 'a sort of Sabbath quiet', the aural sanctity of the night, and they accordingly legislated against disruption (Rus 1858).

The heard world, then, served as an index of identity. Inflection, timbre, and the timing and situatedness of sound cemented class identities and demarcated difference. Quietude was tied to gentility and godliness. 'The Gentleman at Church', reported New York's *Colored American* in 1838, 'Comes in good season, so as neither to interrupt the pastor nor the congregation by a late arrival . . . Opens and shuts the door gently, and walks lightly . . . and gets his seat quietly . . . Does not cargo in conversation . . . Does not whisper, or laugh', and 'Does not rush out of the church like a trampling horse, the moment the benediction is pronounced, but retires slowly, in a noiseless, quiet manner.' Bodily sounds, especially when heard in the public realm, were similarly vulgar and, hence, noisy to elites. *Harper's Weekly* printed a letter from a man in New Orleans in 1859 on the aurality of public kissing. 'I have often been very much shocked', he wrote, 'by the manner in which some people kiss each other; that is, in giving one of those unearthly smacks that sound like the explosion of a . . . gun.'[5]

Quietude was only part of the constructed aural order. The social fabric was indebted to sound and, especially, to bells. Good bells, after all, had the same qualities as sound social order. The best makers produced bells with a 'homogenous character' deemed 'essential for producing evenness of tone, freedom of vibration, and strength of cohesion'.[6] Tintinnabulations infused northern and southern landscapes with predictable, familiar, and assuring aural signatures. Peals signalling Christmas and national holidays were important for sacred and secular reasons. They ensured that God heard pious devotions and, simultaneously, marked the civil soundscape with social, historical and national meaning. Their distinctive tone of bells also anchored people in place and time. One man remarked that, throughout his travels, he always remembered the timbre of his village chimes. 'He had heard grander bells, louder bells, more famous bells, but none so dear and touching as his own.'[7]

The elite classes in both North and South observed careful distinctions between the ordered sounds they created and the chaotic noisiness of lower orders, women, and evangelical Christians. Southern masters and northern patricians alike shared in the use of sound to identify and re-affirm their presumed cultural authenticity and political authority, although social and economic changes made the southern landscape steadily less distinctive. Thus, function and conglomeration assured the southern cities sounded like any other. Southern towns used 'systems of fire bells' and passed noise ordinances similar to those in the North.[8] And, as nervous southern commentators never tired of remarking, the southern urban environment was becoming dangerously northern in its cadence. The sound of the market revolution did not spare the Old South, as evidenced by market bells and, increasingly, railroad bells. But because they connected plantations and southern markets, railroads and the sounds, they made were considered functional, although some upcountry Georgia farmers complained that noisy railroad engines tended to spook livestock. Railroads and other aural accoutrements associated with the market revolution were integral to the South's market economy, so even such sibilant sounds were considered necessary noise (Hahn 1983: 37). The slavocracy, in short, applauded the sound of industriousness and sometimes that meant the region's limited industry was accepted as necessary or, indeed, sound.

Heard Worlds, North and South

Important similarities notwithstanding, differences divided north and south from the early national period and grew from the 1830s onwards. Whatever else antebellum southern masters coveted, they cherished what South Carolina slaveholder Alfred Huger called 'the quiet and retirement of Plantation life'. Sounds perceived to threaten this invented pastoralism they defined as socially disruptive, wholly unnecessary noise. Masters wanted the quiet life, a set of social and economic relations that, while modernist in some respects, militated against the noise of liberal capitalism and was facilitated by their non-industrial slave mode of production. The noise of southern urban centres to be sure, sometimes intruded into their imagined and actual aural gardens. But as long as planters could retreat to the tranquillity of country life, they put up with the bustle of city as a necessary evil. As John Basil Lamar wrote to his sister from his Georgia country retreat in 1835: 'I took your letter from the office in Macon yesterday, & should have answer'd it forthwith, but preferring the calm of Swift Creek to the boisterous crowd of the Central Hotel, for that purpose, I deffer'd it until now.'[9] In this sense, then, planters turned quietude into a commodity they could buy.

Plantation soundscapes were the model for the slaveholder's acoustic and social environment. The quiet of the plantation acted as a counterpoint to the noise of urbanism and industrialism. William Gilmore Simms, for one, had no ears for the 'crowd and noise of city life'. He preferred the melancholy but spiritually pure quietude of nature. What he wrote in the *Southern Literary Gazette* in 1829 would have sent shivers up the spines of northern boosters for industrial urban life:

> I think there is more sublimity in barrenness, in ruin, in decay and desolation, than any other collection of objects in nature . . . The gloom of silence tends perhaps as much as anything else to invest such objects with

that kind of sublimity we speak of. We feel a sense of awe for which there is no accounting, whilst listening to and hearing only the sullen and continuous murmurings of ocean, or the swelling mutterings of the wind among the treetops of the forest. The hum of men and cities is puerile and childish to this great and solemn voicing of nature. We feel the contrast immediately, and by our own silence and awe, we seem to acknowledge ourselves in the presence of God.[10]

The slaveholders' embrace of a constructed and actual soundscape was not so much an attempt to regain a putative quieter past as it was an effort to promote a particular vision of social order in the face of an emerging bourgeois northern alternative. Masters trained their ears northward and heard, literally and figuratively, industrialism, democratic capitalism, and the unmistakable keynote of reckless modernity. Unable to close their ears to the hum of northern progress, slaveholders countered with the construction of an acoustic environment that celebrated the sounds of industriousness, not industrialism, and the cadence of organic social and economic relations, not the clamour of mobocracy or din of withering wage labour. Elite slaveholders did not reject all modern innovations. Indeed, they actively embraced sounds that bolstered their social order and helped keep the slaves in check. But they refused to countenance alien noises that threatened to disrupt their organic, hierarchic society.[11]

Challenges to the slaveholders' vision of quietude and to the social decorum it implied came from the various quarters within their own society. Rowdy poor whites threatened to disrupt the Southern peace, in particular by fighting. Patrician planters contrasted the quiet duels of the elite with the boisterous noise of the South's white rabble. And yet, in slaveholders' society dependent on the support of non-slave-holding whites for its continued longevity, this noise, while unpalatable, was considered necessary (see Gorn 1985).

Masters had a better chance of quieting slaves. Certainly, they went to some lengths to regulate the sounds of slaves in an effort to establish plantation harmony, literally and metaphorically. Slaves, however, did not invariably comply. Slaveholders' efforts to impose safety and order on their plantations never wholly succeeded because slaves manipulated plantation soundscapes to survive and, at times, escape. Slaves' resistance to the realities of plantation life drew on the heard world in a variety of ways. Sometimes, bondpeople invented alternative definitions of sound and noise. For them, plantations were not quiet, serene places: 'Everything was in a bustle – always there was slashing and whipping . . .

It was awful to hear the cracking of that whip . . . so loud and sharp
was the noise' (Hughes 1897). Although they did not endorse the
slaveholders' quiet soundscape, slaves used the art and skill of silence
as an effective tool for resistance. Slaves turned the masters' ideal of
quietude against them.

Much has been made of slaves' production of sound (singing in particular) on plantations. Most historians rightly applaud the spiritual and
functional value of slave songs and music. Yet the heavy emphasis on
song is misleading, first because it slights the other sounds produced
by slaves, and second because it tacitly undervalues the importance of
silence and quietude to the continued viability of the slave community
and the achievement of individual freedom.[12] Masters exercised
immense influence over how plantations sounded, and they regulated
the times at which slave songs were permitted. As Charles Dickens
observed of a Virginia tobacco factory: 'Many of the workmen appeared
to be strong men, and it is hardly necessary to add that they were all
labouring quietly, then. After two o'clock in the day, they are allowed
to sing, a certain number at a certain time.' By the same token, songs
could be coerced with masters threatening to whip if the slaves would
not 'sing and dance some mo''. Tight temporal strictures, which were
heard rather than seen, were placed on slaves' actions. As one former
slave recalled: 'Den we sang all de songs dat we could think of, till nine
o' clock, when Mass rang de bell, for all de noise to be cut out, soas all
de white folks could go to sleep. Den we had to go to bed, or be awful
quiet.' Easter Jones, an ex-slave from Georgia, echoed the sentiment:
'No'm, aint sing nothin', too tired when dey git in fum wuk. We warn't
lowed to make no noise nohow' (Dickens 1914: 80; Radwick 1972–9:
10). Other masters went much further to control slave sound. Charles
Johnson, a former slave from Alabama, offered chilling testimony to
slaveholders' desire to preserve the preferred cadence of plantation
slavery by controlling slaves' bodies: 'En de on reliable ones, dey'd
bell'um – Tempie en Snip wore a bell – en make um work in de fiel's so
they couldn't run away en de overseer could keep up wid where dey
was sat. Dey'd de a iron band roun' de waist, en another iron bandd
roun'd de neck, en a thing stick up de back, way up, wid de bell on hit
what dey could'nt git hit off – warn't no way reach hit' (Brown and
Taylor 1997: 80–1). Slaves, always alert to the aural betrayal of their
physical acts, muted the bell's clapper with mud. But slaveholders pre-
empted this too by encasing the bells.

Effective resistance to bondage lay in slaves' learning to control their
own sounds and being attentive to the heard world. By contributing

to and, in effect, shaping the plantation soundscape, slaves managed at least to protect themselves. As rawhide dug flesh, loud screams reminded masters of slaves' humanity and perhaps shortened the beating. Hence, slaves referred to a 'whooping' not least because they whooped their pain into the ears of masters. They reminded whip-happy slaveholders that whereas inanimate objects were dumb and silent, slaves were neither. Slaves also employed aural devices to communicate. To contact his wife, for example, an escaped slave ran to her cabin 'and gave his peculiar whistle under her window'. Slave women developed strategies similar to those of whiter women, North and South, to avoid the wrath of men by limiting the noise of children. Laura Clark recalled that, when she was a slave child on an Alabama plantation, slave women gave the children candy 'to keep us quiet' (Brown and Taylor 1997: 23-33; Channing 1843).

Aural techniques for survival and resistance were taught early among slaves. The young were trained in the use and abuse of sound, and parables were particularly useful in instructing slave children. When former slave Josh Horn lost his dog, a voice in his head 'say to me, jes' lak dis: Josh, blow your horn!' Josh did so: 'Well I give three loud, long blows.' Too late, the trick had been played, for another voice intervened, 'whispering: Josh, you out here in dese woods by yo'self. You blowed dat horn and your enemy heard you. You's a fool, you is.' Josh barely managed to escape a patrol that arrived soon thereafter. Slaves understood that aural betrayal of their minor infractions was everywhere. 'Our boss didn' keep no parrot to tell on d'niggers', remembered Horatio Williams, 'but some did' (Brown and Taylor 1997: 64). Betrayal, though, could be pre-empted by hard listening. 'De slaves', recalled Andy Williams, 'ud lie on de groun' an' put dier ear on de groun' ter lis'en an' see effen er pattyroller er comin.' The world of the slaves, then, was often and deliberately onomatopoeic. They spoke of 'paddlerollers' when the patrol beat them with paddles, and they stressed the patter of the 'patterrollers' because that was precisely what they meant. It was a point seemingly lost on those who interviewed former slaves in the 1930s.

The religious practices of the slaves were also characterized by controlled volume rather than by unfettered, shouted passion or, as one historian has put it, 'the riot of sound'. That slave religion had a silent quality to it did not detract from the depth of conviction of their spiritual beliefs. Indeed, they believed God's voice was naturally silent. As a frequent co-conspirator against slaveholders, it had to be. Slaves deliberately used 'a voice silent to sense, but audible to spirit and God'.

This aural intimacy manifested itself in a quiet, barely audible religious worship facilitated, perhaps, by singing or praying into upturned pots (Raboteau 1978: 22). According to former slave William Lee: 'we couldn't serve God unless we stole to de cabins or woods. In our meetings we turn de pot down wid a stick on one side to drown singing to keep de patterrollers from catching us' (William Lee in Purdue et al. 1976: 196). Wholly upturned pots served no acoustic muffling function because they were 'closed off', so some were upturned only in part, often propped up against a wall or up by sticks, as William Lee noted. Some ex-slaves recalled that a number of large empty vessels were scattered around during worship services with open ends up, which probably enhanced the reverberation properties of the pots' or vessels' space, especially in the bass frequency range. As a result of excitation by the sound of each new voice, the vessels stored the sound and released it slowly, thereby giving rise to an upward masking effect. While this did not reduce the level of sound that reached the remote listener, it did reduce the intelligibility of the speech.[13] This was resistance *sotto voce*.

Slaves also exploited the acoustic properties of other plantation materials. Given the fairly high sabine or absorbency coefficient levels of wood, it is likely that slave cabins, at least those of pine construction, absorbed middle- and upper frequency sounds, to muffle what plantation authorities could hear emanating from slave quarters. The sabine levels of some slave cabins made of 'rough logs, and daubed with red clay or mud of the region' and 'only a dirt floor', was probably high. Some slaves appreciated the absorptive capacity of dirt floors. 'Sometimes us slip off an' have a little prayer meetin' by use'ves in a ole house wid a dirt flo'', recalled George Young. 'Dey'd git happy an' shout an' couldn't nobody hyar 'em 'caze dey didn't make no fuss on de dirt flo'.' Just in case, though, 'on Stan' in de do' an' watch' and 'Some folks put dey head in de wash pot, an' pray easy' (Hughes 1897: 25; Brown 1997: 108).

Slaves' ability to quash sound, to impose silence, was itself an act of resistance against the will of the master. Slaves learned how to control sound to maintain their dignity, and their understanding of the aural world allowed them to commit resonant acts of resistance. Indeed, it was of immeasurable importance for slaves to listen to the world, because the plantation South was typical of a 'hi-fi soundscape [where] even the slightest disturbance can communicate vital or interesting information.' Its rural nature and absence of louder, competing sounds from large-scale urban and industrial pursuits meant that sounds were heard discretely and at some distance. Slaves, therefore, had to master quietness if they were to go on nocturnal ramblings, trade goods on the side, or escape. Slaves used their knowledge of the aural landscape to their benefit. Harriet Tubman learned from her father 'how to walk soundlessly through the woods', a skill that served her well, as posterity testifies (Davis 1983: 23). Other runaway slaves used what they had learnt about the aural world under slavery during their escapes. J. W. Loguen, for example, correctly recognized that the Ohio 'river was quiet in the embrace of Winter' and that horses' hooves on ice could generate dangerous noise. To escape the plantation demanded that slaves move as 'swiftly and noiselessly as possible'. Often, this involved 'a gentle whisper'. Unnecessarily loud voices or potentially dangerous statements elicited a 'Hush!' from worried conspirators, followed by this advice: '"Hallo, friend!" – a little too loud. There are things a colored man may think, but not speak above his breath, until his eyes and ears assure him that he is alone' (Loguen 1968).

Charles Ball, an escaped slave, understood the necessity of aural sensitivity in his environment. With his homemade (and noiseless) Moccasins on foot, Ball prepared to leave his plantation (Ball 1859). He understood that successful escape depended on his ability to control sound. He left behind his beloved dog because 'I knew the success of my undertaking depended on secrecy and silence', and the dog could not be trusted to keep quiet. And so, with feline stealth, he left his plantation, 'seeking refuge in the deepest solitudes of the forest'. Acoustic sleuthing began in earnest with his 'listening attentively to every noise that I heard in the trees or amongst the canebrakes.' Ball had been enslaved long enough to know the sounds of danger. When he caught 'the voices of people in loud conversation' and 'the cry of hounds', he recognized that he would have to adjust his tactics. 'The first resolution that I took was, that I would travel no more in the day-time.' Knowledge of seasonal southern soundscapes informed his decision: 'This was the season of hunting deer, and knowing that the hunters were under the necessity of being as silent as possible in the woods, I saw at a glance that they would be at least as likely to discover me in the forest, before I could see them, as I should be to see them.' This was an aural skirmish with real stakes (Ball 1859). In short, although it is critical to recognize the sustenance that songs provided for slaves, such an emphasis should not deafen us to their ability to cultivate silence and physically manipulate the heard environment to resist bondage.

Certainly, planters recognized the slaves' use of sound to resist. The silence of slaves, like Native Americans' prowling stealth, was feared by slaveholders, even as they insisted on quietude. Mary Boykin Chesnut certainly feared slaves' silence. 'If they want to kill us', she muttered, 'they can do it when they please, they are noiseless as panthers' (Chesnut 1949: 43). The slaveholders' world was a skittish one in which slight sounds and curious rustles rubbed already raw nerves, even as they re-affirmed the quietude of plantation life. Abolitionists, too, were aware of southern skittishness about slave insurrections. Some captured the aural dimensions of such fear with wonderful clarity. The 'appalling terror of a slave revolt', opined the *Liberty Bell* in 1848, 'pervades the community' in the South to the point where conversations were 'whispered along the streets'. The silence of the slaves themselves added to the tension. Slaveholders found slaves keeping mum, and they worried. 'They were as silent as the grave', fretted one master, who con-cluded, 'Even "Momma," privileged to say and do what she pleased, and who would be heard amid the laughter and tongue-clatter of the rest' was ominously quiet. 'A silent slave', remarked Frederick Douglass, 'is not liked by masters or overseers'.[14]

Northern elites, like their southern counterparts, cultivated social quietude, but instead of the cadence of industriousness, they actively encouraged the throb of liberal capitalism, at least rhetorically. It was a source of pride for northern boosters that bustling cities replaced silent farms, that the boom of urban, industrial capitalism drowned quiet, sober pre-industrialism. 'Louder and louder, on each succeeding day, waxes the tumultuous hum of this bustling Babel', said a listener to modernization in New York City in 1850. 'In all directions', he continued, 'the great city of the New World is stretching forth her restless hands, converting silent fields into crowded streets, and invading all the old peaceful retreats with thousands of her fast-growing population.' This aural assessment was not ambivalent. The westward expansion of the sound of the modern that enveloped the silence of the old with the rhythm of the new was cause for celebration, not lamentation, in the minds of northern capitalists. Listen to how New York City sounded to men of capital in 1948:

> all along the noble rivers which embrace the city in their loving arms, how rapidly swells the great tide of life and industry! Miles and miles of ships . . . propelled by steam; and what a ceaseless chorus of human voices, and rattling of vehicles, and clanking of machinery, and ringing of bells, broken in upon, ever and anon, by the far-resounding echoes of ponderous hammers, fashioning into shape the iron skeleton of some new monster of the deep.

All this was to the good, for it betokened 'more and more of a metropolitan air', and 'civilization, refinement, and wealth'. Progress was
heard as much seen, and its meaning was invested with the future of a
country.[15]

And what of the cadence of the northern factory and free wage
labour? To the antebellum bourgeoisie, factory bells, because they were
associated with liberty and God, could be pleasing. A 'New bell at the
Cotton mill' for someone who did not work there could have a 'Very
clear musical sound' in 1849.[16] Moreover, a few in the first generation
of factory workers constructed the sound of progress very much like
their managers. They testified, often eloquently, to the association of
industrial sound with progress. Lowell workers, for example, appear to
have been converted to the sound of progress, even though their labour
was increasingly hedged by it. One recalled:

> At first the hours seemed very long, but I was so interested in learning
> that I endured it very well; and when I went out at night the sound of
> the mill was in my ears, as of crickets, frogs, and jewharps, all mingled
> together in strange discord. After that it seemed as though cotton-wool
> was in my ears, but now I do not mind at all.

Lucy Larcom agreed. She maintained that she came to miss the
sibilance of progress even as it polluted her soundscape and organized
her work. 'When I returned', she mused, 'I found that I enjoyed even
the familiar, unremitting clatter of the mill, because it indicated that
something was going on' (Woloch 1992: 246–7; Cott 1972: 129).

For other factory operatives the tocsin became toxic, and the aim was
to be 'far from the factory's deaf'ning sound, From all its noise and
strife.' Workers and slaves resisted their exploitation in similar ways.
Their rejection of the din of the looms led factory hands to develop
strategies of silence such as 'a hymn to sing to herself, unheard within
the deep solitude of unceasing sound' (Foner 1977: 114). Religious
silence and prayerful quietude also offered refuge from the racket of
progress, and therefore factory workers took their spiritual duties
seriously. Owners often required the women to attend public worship,
but workers also chose to do so at inopportune moments when the
noise of progress and work disrupted the solemnity of God's divine
silence. They asked:

> Will those who are obliged to hear the noise and confusion caused by
> some fifty or more men, with teams of oxen, and all the noise consequent

on such occasions, together with the splitting and blasting of rocks, to their great annoyance while in their places of worship – will these be deceived by such hypocritical pretensions of piety, and love to the moral interests of the community in which they live?

The religious instruction of the working class, and the silence appropriate to such occasions, were compromised by the sound of progress, as workers knew (Foner 1977: 132). The northern working class, though, had a tool that slaves did not: their collective voice, which was best heard in strikes, rowdy meetings, and sometimes-violent protest. The throat of the crowd wrapped worker's voices in the shroud of democracy, which enabled them to critique their exploitation and remind managers that the sound of progress was also the noise of exploitation.

Democratic capitalism was at times, then, discordant to elite northern ears. Some lamented the noise of the mob, although even this was tolerable provided property was not threatened. The howl of the mob could be reconfigured as the happy hum of democracy. Moreover, acoustic refuges existed for the elite. Nature's sounds could ease the necessary noise of modern urban life. 'The tradesman, the attorney, comes out of the din and craft of the street, and sees the sky and the woods, and is man again', wrote Ralph Waldo Emerson. Indeed, holidays from the buzz of liberal modernity were often sought and found in Nature's soothing cadence. 'At least I have escaped from the dust and turmoil, the thronging crowds, the ceaseless din . . . and ten thousand annoyances of the great city of New York!' cheered one New Yorker in 1847. He had found the countryside. Tuckerton, New Jersey, 'about fifty-two miles from Philadelphia', was a 'delightful refuge . . . from a noisy world. You get rid of hubbub and humbug the moment you leave Camden. No locomotive shakes you to a jelly; no turnpike keeps up an incessant din in your ears.'[17] But such refuges were mere escapes for northerners, islands of rural serenity to be consumed for brief periods before they returned to their progressive, bustling society. For slaveholders, such islands were continents, a way of life to be preserved.

Aural Sectionalism: When Soundscapes Collide

Despite widespread agreement on what constituted sound and noise, the Northern bourgeoisie and the Southern master class construed one another as threatening the integrity of their respective acoustic environments and, by close association, their preferred set of social and economic relations. Sounds that Northern elites considered progressive, Southern masters qualified. To be sure, the sounds of railroads, the market, and pre-industrial activity especially were testimony to progress in the South. The mobocratic tendencies of wage labour, though, were nothing but noise to the Southern master class. Northern elites also construed the mob as noisy, but given the nature of their democratic and pro-gressively industrializing society, the northern bourgeoisie reluctantly deemed such noise as necessary and entirely appropriate to a pulsating democracy. To Southern masters' ears, Northern cities (and, indeed, many of their own) were distinctly noisy places filled with the caco-phony of the mob and the unpalatable cadence of industrialism. Conversely, where Southerners found comfort in the sound of discipline on their plantations and revelled in the quiet industry of the Southern pastoral, Northerners heard only the chilling silence and deafening noise of immoral slavery, a politically tyrannous institution that retarded the industrial capitalist progress of the region.

In the 1840s, the abolitionist Ebenezer Davies contrasted the industry of the North with the backwardness of the South in aural terms. As he made his way up the Ohio, Davies observed:

> Upon the left bank of the stream the population is rare; from time to time one descries a troop of slaves loitering in the half-desert fields; society seems to be asleep, man to be idle . . . From the right bank, on the contrary, a confused hum is heard, which proclaims the presence of industry; . . . and man appears to be in the enjoyment of that wealth and contentment which are the reward of labour. (Davies 1849: 177)

Abolitionists often heard the rapid urbanization and industrialization of the North in stark contrast to the stagnation of the South. One anti-slavery writer from Kentucky said in 1849:

> As a free State, she would resound from her centre to her extremities with the busy sounds of enterprise . . . school-houses and churches would be greatly multiplied – and the hum of industry would rise to heaven from every hill-side and smiling valley, like an anthem of praise from a happy and thriving people.[18]

Verse – even when it is wretched – says much about social value and cultural authority. The following excerpt from Toronto's *Provincial Freeman* of 1854 struck chords deep in the ears of northern republican boosters and abolitionists as the author mingled pre-industrial and industrial sounds to reinforce the legitimate, inexorable movement towards the modern:

I love the clanging hammer,
The whirling of the plane,
The crushing of the busy saw,
The creaking of the crane,
The ringing of the anvil,
The grating of the drill,
The clattering of the turning lathe,
The whirling of the mill;
The buzzing of the spindles,
The rattling of the loom,
The clipping of the tailor's shears,
The driving of the awl,
The sounds of busy labor,
I love, I love them all.

Slaveholders agreed that these sounds connoted activity. But it was how these sounds were generated, the social and economic context of this aurality, that differentiated North from South. For, as the verse continued, these strains of industry were 'Not the toil and strife that groaneth, Beneath the tyrant's sway', but, rather, the sounds produced by 'willing heart'.[19]

Because sound and noise were linked to individual virtue, and since virtue was patently political, it is hardly a surprise to hear sectional wrangles begin to evolve in the early national period. As early as 1811, abolitionists cast slavery in negative aural terms and used the printed word to evoke sound in an effort to help readers imagine the horror of slavery. To describe bondage in the West Indies for New York's *Independent Mechanic*, for example, one writer listened to slavery and crafted the morally defunct institution in aural terms: 'the groans of slavery are heard among you, which sound more painful and horrible to the ears of humanity and justice, than the dying shrieks of an infant to its mother or the deep-toned thunder of hell's dark abyss to a damned spirit.'[20] From the early claims of noisy slavery, anti-slavery men and women of the 1830s narrowed their critique not to slavery per se but to slavery, Southern style. The sound of the slave market was especially offensive to abolitionists of all stripes and persuasions, whose moral and economic assessment of slave sales was imagined acoustically as much as visually. Of the St Louis market, one free-soiler remarked: 'The clock was striking twelve; and, before it had finished, the vast dome reverberated with the noise of half-a-dozen man-sellers brawling at once, disposing of God's images to the highest bidders. It was a terrible din' (Davies 1849: 59). Markets for labour, after all, were supposed to be regulated not simply by an invisible hand, but by one that was silent.

Slavery's noise and silence, though, were two sides of the same loathed coin for northerners – abolitionists and Republicans alike. Tyranny everywhere was silent, they believed. For Republicans, the threat slavery posed to the successful westward expansion of industrial capitalism was decidedly aural and reminiscent of the eerie silence of economic stagnation. In 1854 Republican John P. Hale asked a New York audience whether slavery's expansion westward would jeopardize wage labour's progress. 'Shall the hum of busy industry be heard on [the West's] hills and in its valleys?' he asked. Not if slaveholders had anything to do with it, he concluded (quoted in Foner 1970: 56).

However much Northern patricians complained about the noise of their lower orders, no matter how many ordinances they passed, how many thick walls they built, and how many floors they carpeted to transform private tranquillity into a commodity, they saw the rural activities of the Northern working class as testimony to the efficacy and appropriateness of Northern freedom and democracy. The North, then, was free to make noise. Conversely, in certain public contexts excessive quietness was to be feared, as with conspiracies of labour, and shunned. It was, in short, too familiar to slavery. Hubbub, provided it occurred within a politically delimited context, was testimony to the health of northern democracy. 'The various speeches', delivered at the Free Soil Convention in 1848, chortled the *National Era*, 'were received with loud cheers, and excited great enthusiasm among the vast assemblage'. Then, 'Mr Chase mounted the box and called the meeting to order, amid such a din as was never heard.' All this betokened the sound, not the noise, of democracy. And so resolutions were proposed in support of free soil in the West, and the 'response was a deafening "Aye," which burst forth with entire unanimity from the throats of twenty thousand men, and which resembled a terrific clap of thunder', or, more presciently, 'the roar of a park of artillery.' That the 'entire mass of men . . . yelled and howled like tigers in a fray' was simple, aural eloquence.[21]

If abolitionists sounded liberty, the enslaved had to learn to hear its call. Do not 'Bow down in silence to what tyrants bid', advised the *Colored American* in 1841. Instead, listen carefully to the strains emanating from the North:

> Come! Rouse ye brothers, rouse! A peal now breaks
> From the lowest island to our gallant lakes:
> 'Tis summoning you, who long in bonds have lain,

And then, the warning to the master class:

> The captive in his hut, with watchful ear,
> Awaits, the sweet, triumphant song to hear,
> That shall proclaim the glorious jubilee.
> When crippled thousands shall in truth is free.

Slaves, fancied abolitionists, strained their ears to hear the North speak.[22]

Shall 'we ourselves be free?' was the question of the day, which led to the real issue – how shall we know freedom? One common test was what the silent lands to the west would sound like. In 'An Appeal to the Women of the United States', in 1848, anti-slavery women answered and identified the political crux of the sectional crises:

> shall the air of our mountains and our prairies, that hitherto has borne only the songs of the wild bird, ring and echo of the pioneer's axe, and the busy hum of free labour, be burdened with the groan of the slave, the crack of the lash falling on women's back, the mother's wail as her infant is torn from her embrace, the husband's muttered curse as he sees with fettered limb the wife of his bosom made the victim of lust?

The answer, predictably, was no. 'But what, it may be asked, can women do?' She should 'raise her voice in eloquent appeal', and, presumably, be heard by virtue of her customary quietude without desexing herself. The aural novelty created by the voices of ordinarily silent women would cause them to be heard more readily. And so the chorus of free labour and political liberty would grow louder, loud enough, perhaps, to be heard south of the Mason-Dixie line; loud enough to be heard in the cabins of the unfree. The stakes were high and heard.[23]

Southern sounds must not be allowed to pollute free lands to the West, went the free labour argument. Rather, new lands should echo with northern sounds. The crack of the whip, which could be heard clearly in the slave South, no longer resounded in the liberal North, and it should not be allowed to sound in the West. As Michael Meranze explains: 'Both penitential punishments and free labour aimed ultimately to create a productive and prudent work force. And they did so by denying that they acted on the body, insisting instead that they reformed and empowered the will.' This is why Northerners excoriated the sound of the whip, for it was the sound of the old, the corrupt, the cruel, the unenlightened, the pre-modern (Meranze 1996: 299).

The real fear, though, was that slavery's tyrannical silence would creep northward. When Northerners – even those hostile to abolitionism – anticipated the possibility that the Slave Power might map the silent regime of the plantation onto the national body politic via the Gag Acts (1836 and 1840) and the efforts to silence congressional debate on slavery, they interpreted such inscriptions as palpable threats to their freedom to make sound in the name of national progress. Some northern politicians felt that planter's insistence on plantation silence was being extended to the floor of the House of Representatives. One Ohio representative made the point in 1848 in the course of congressional debate. 'The [southern] gentlemen charges me with uttering sentiments on this floor, and out of this House, which have tended "to excite the slaves to rebellion,"' he frothed. Lest 'Southern gentlemen suppose they can bring into this body the practices which they pursue on their plantations', he reminded Southern representatives that although freedom of speech 'was for years trampled under foot by the slave power' and that he 'sat here . . . in degrading and humiliating silence', a new day had dawned. 'Gentlemen may play the tyrant on their plantations', he declared, 'but they shall not impose silence upon northern men, nor dictate the language we shall use on this floor.' Frederick Douglass chimed in, for he had heard the ring of the slave whip, the 'clank' of slaves' chains. 'The wails of bondmen', he declared in 1848, 'are on my ear' still. Such things would not be heard in the North, and neither would Northerners be slaves to Southern silence.[24]

Elizabeth Fox-Genovese and Eugene D. Genovese argue, 'Order depended upon freedom, to which it was logically subordinated. Defenders of slavery reversed the priorities. Freedom could be understood only as a function of order.' Here, we encounter the fundamental difference in the heard worlds of North and South. The radical individualism of antebellum northern society, closed and regulated although it was in many respects, nevertheless embraced a more elastic definition of necessary noise and acceptable sound. Freedom allowed citizens the right to speak their minds. Even when the sounds generated by such activities proved unpalatable to northern elites, they tended to construct them as necessary noises. There were limits, to be sure, and patricians sometimes issued scathing condemnations of the labouring classes, just as slaveholders did of slaves. There were also contradictions. Again, as Meranze has shown, 'northern society proclaimed that limits to individual liberty existed only at its margin'. His work on penitentiary reform in Philadelphia, however, suggests another possibility. The system of enforced silence in Philadelphia's prisons 'presumed that citizens could be produced by reducing individuals to silent labour. But the alleged source of liberal citizenship, or liberal manhood at least, was exercising one's voice.' In truth, northern elites treated their most refractory populations the same way that masters treated theirs – they attempted to reduce them to silence. On the whole, though, democratic capitalism gave rise to a more boisterous social order that tolerated the cadence and enormous productive capacity of a more liberal approach. Slaveholders heard things differently. Noise was created by any activity that posed a threat to the harmony of their world, and they dealt harshly with those who jeopardized the day-to-day as well as the abstract functioning of their social order (Fox-Genovese and Genovese 1987: 213; Meranze 1996: 327–8).

Southern elites, then, resented what they heard as the cacophony of fanaticism and, like abolitionists, wrote essays to persuade readers of their point of view. They drew on acoustic metaphors, which were in turn communicated through the printed and spoken word. One southern states' rightist claimed that northern agitation over the expansion of slavery 'remind [s] one of the struggles of Chance and Tumult in the reign of ancient Night, when Chaos sat as umpire . . .' Abolitionists he charged 'as being common disturbers of the public peace', whose noisy behaviour served as a distinct aural counterpoint to the 'great body of Southern people' who, of course, were known for 'being quiet and silent' folk. The Charleston *Mercury* jousted during the secession crisis that northern noise in protest of South Carolina's actions was no more than 'frogs in chorus'. The Palmetto State, by contrast, exhibited 'a deep, calm feeling, very different from the excitement of the mob'. Northerners should nonetheless fear Dixie's quietude, just as master shuddered at excessive silence in slave society. The South's actions and protests were 'the quiet tread of Caesar's forces crossing the Rubicon'.[25]

Southern editors dichotomized the aural essence of sectionalism, perhaps none more so than the editor of Jackson's *Mississippian*, who heard the difference in characters and social relations of North and South in the debate on the Kansas-Nebraska bill. Southerners, he maintained, demonstrated 'calm, deliberate judgement' during the debate, 'which characterize the action of the people . . . Look to the North, and what do we realize?' Harsh words from the New York *Tribune*, 'the insane ranting of Fessenden . . . the sickly cant of Sumner . . . and the disgraceful orgies of tumultuous assemblages of all colors, conditions, who make night hideous with their frantic howlings.' But what of the South? 'In the South, scarce a ripple seems to agitate the surface

of society', he wrote. 'All is calmness . . . We hear of no burnings in effigy
. . . we listen to no furious declamation . . . we show that we are
controlled by reason – not by passion . . . we prefer leaving such
weapons to the blusterers, fools, and fanatics, to whom they appropriately belong'. Abolitionism, claimed Richmond's *Enquirer* in 1857,
'always clamored loudly for liberty and equality . . . its designing
demagogues have been wont to shriek and wail . . . as they impose upon
the popular mind of the North . . . their perverted portraiture of
Southern slavery.' The worry was that the movement would engulf all
northern men so that 'all the insane asylums in Yankeedom will be
inadequate for the accommodation of its victims.' The 'abolitionists',
after all, 'are leaping and weeping, kneeling and swearing . . . fuming,
yelling and gesticulating, like so many bedlamites.'[26]

Metaphors and analogies of aural sectionalism exerted a powerful
influence on elites in the North and the South and acquired authenticity
by virtue of their insertion into local and national political discourse.
The acoustic construction of otherness enabled many slaveholders who
had never seen democratic capitalism, and abolitionists who had never
witnessed slavery, to become increasingly exercised about the 'other'.
Modal metaphors, in particular those that play on the heard world,
have, as Bernard Hibbitts points out, in their 'very specificity, familiarity,
and tangibility' the power to 'obscure and distort'. In effect, the metaphor becomes real and 'so compelling that it is . . . no longer recognized
as a metaphor, it redefines the truth on its own limited terms (Hibbitts
1994). Northern and southern elites hear each other through increasingly diverse modal metaphors, which allowed passions to flare for war.

Soundscapes at War

If we listen to antebellum America, we hear that modernity, capitalism,
freedom, and construction of gender, class and otherness had distinct
and meaningful aural components. It also suggests that workers, black
and white, understood the power of silence and the control of sound
as tools of effective resistance to their enslavement and exploitation.
None of this was lost on the ruling classes, North or South. Elites heard
social order at the everyday level of interaction and, simultaneously,
as an abstraction, often with the former reinforcing the latter. What
they heard either reassured or frightened them. Metaphors and analogies are clumsy devices, because when actual sounds gain metaphorical
status they lose some of their precision. Southerners heard most
Northerners to be noisy, and Northerners heard most Southerners –

slave and free – to be disturbingly silent or cacophonous. Obviously, these metaphors did not accurately reflect the entire scope and range of sounds in the sections, but that is precisely the point. By the middle decades of the antebellum period, few were interested in the accuracy of these clumsy aural metaphors, which proved to be eminently digestible and communicable. Sound-sensitive elites, their ears pricked by the day-to-day shape and defence of their worlds, used these aural metaphors that described the ideological differences between North and South to augment an increasingly pronounced sectionalism. Aural constructions of 'the North' and 'the South' gained wide currency, so that soon Northerners and Southerners heard one another in divisive ways, although in reality some sectional differences were not pronounced. The heard world, imagined and distorted though it was in part, was real to those who did the selective listening; real enough, in fact, to prompt men to palpable, destructive action.

Essentially, then, we are talking about what soundscape theorist R. Murray Schafer has termed 'keynote' sounds. Schafer maintains that the 'keynote sounds of a landscape are those created by its geography and climate: water, wind, forests, plains, birds, insects, and animals.' True enough, but keynote sounds – sounds that imprint 'themselves so deeply on the people hearing them that life without them would be sensed as a distinct impoverishment' – may also be produced by specific configurations of social and economic relations and modes of production. These sounds, because they are both assumed and cultivated deliberately, may be termed either keynotes or soundmarks. Slavery as a mode of production had a particular and meaningful keynote to antebellum slaveholders, for Northern elites, the sound of democratic capitalism and industry had its own soundmark. Schafer argues that, 'once a soundmark has been identified, it deserves to be protected, for soundmarks make the acoustic life of the community unique.' Sounds, then, serve as anchors to regions, as acoustic identifiers of community. As a result, if those soundmarks are threatened by other strains and rhythms, communities interpret these alien sounds as noise, as palpable and metaphorical threats to their identities and ways of life. Cadences of war, noises of loss, shrieks of death, chortles of success, and sounds of victory can follow – and they did, beginning in 1861, with unprecedented volume and terrible irony. The noises associated with the Civil War, the boom of battlefields, and the increasing volume of dissatisfied labourers on the northern home front, only encouraged northern elites to turn eagerly to a quiet, tamed South once the thunder of cannon and tumult of war had ended (Schafer 1980).

Notes

1. There is no compelling reason for historians to treat the history of sound as a cultural, political, or economic history project. The subject is best served by examining historical soundscapes' cultural, economic, and political meanings, complexities, and interrelatedness – what Hobsbawm (1997) has called a genuine social history.

2. From the New York *Independent Mechanic*, 29 June 1811, p. 1; New York *Independent Mechanic*, 30 November 1811, p. 2.

3. 'Censor, No.V1', New York *Independent Mechanic*, 6 July 1811, p. 1.

4. From the 1832 publication *Prospectus of the Young Ladies' Seminary in Keene*, New Hampshire: n.p., p. 20.

5. From *Colored America*, 13 October 1838; *Harper's Weekly*, 26 February 1859, p. 131.

6. 'Chime of Church-Bells', *Harper's Weekly*, 26 May 1860, p. 324; 'Amalgam Bells', *Harper's Weekly*, 25 April 1863, p. 272.

7. *Harper's Weekly*, 30 October 1858, p. 691.

8. Charleston *Mercury*, 4 February 1863.

9. John Basil Lamar, Swift Creek, to 'My Dear Sister', 27 January 1835, Howell Cobb Papers, Hargrett Rare Book and Manuscript Library, University of Georgia, Athens, GA.

10. Walterboro [Simms], 'Angling', *Southern Literary Gazette*, new series, 1(11), 15 October 1829, p. 257; 'The Cypress Swamp', *Southern Literary Gazette*, new series, 1(9), 15 September 1829, p. 211.

11. On Southern visitors to the North and their hearing of Northern liberal capitalism, see Calhoun (1990).

12. See, for example, Levine (1977: 54–5), and Cruz (1999: 43–66).

13. I am indebted to Frank Fahy, Professor Emeritus of Engineering Acoustics of Southampton University's Institute of sound and vibration Research for suggesting this possibility. Personal communication to the author, 11 March 1999.

14. 'Selections', reprinted in *North Star*, 11 February 1848; Douglas cited in Cruz (1999: 43).

15. 'Rambling Epistles from New York, by John Smith the Younger, No. 1, the City of New York', *National Era*, 2(93) 12 October 1848.

16. Anon., Diary, Lancaster Co., 1849, July 3, box 2, folder 10, Eleanor Fulton/ Presbyterian Collection, MG-50, Mass. Coll., Lancaster Historical Society, Lancaster PA.

17. Emerson, R. W. 'Nature', *Northern Star*, 25 February 1848; John Smith the Younger, 'Bon Sejour', *National Era* 1(33): 19 August 1847.

18. 'Contrasts of Slavery and Freedom', *National Era*, 111(120) 19 April 1949.

19. 'The Sound of Industry', *Provincial Freeman*, 20 January 1854.

20. 'From the Northern Budget, Negro Slavery, No. VIII', New York, *Independent Mechanic*, 29 June 1811, p. 1.

21. 'Free Soil Convention', *National Era*, 2(85), 17 August 1848.

22. C.L.R., 'The Spirit Voice, or Liberty Call to the Disfranchised', *Colored American*, 7 August 1841.

23. 'An Appeal', *National Era*, 2(86), 24 August 1848.

24. 'Extract', *North Star*, 26 May 848; 'Frederick Douglass' Address', *North Star*, 4 August 1848.

25. 'Speech of Mr. Clingman, of North Carolina, On the Question of Slavery', *National Era*, 2(55), 20 January 1848; 'The Hullaballoo about the Forts', Charleston *Mercury*, 19 December 1860.

26. Jackson *Mississipian*, 31 March 1854; Richmond, *Enquirer*, 13 March 1857.

References

Bailey, P.(1998), *Popular Culture and Performance in the Victorian City*, Cambridge: Cambridge University Press, pp. 205–6.

Ball, C. (1859), *Fifty Years in Chains: Or, the Life of an American Slave*, New York: H. Dayton.

Brown, A. and Taylor, D. (eds) (1997), *Gabr'l Blow Sof: Sumter County, Alabama, Slave Narratives*, Livingstone AL: Livingstone Press.

Calhoun, R. J. (ed.) (1990), *Witness to Sorrow: The Antebellum Autobiography of William J. Grayson*, Columbia: University of South Carolina Press.

Channing, W. H. (1843), 'A Day in Kentucky', *Liberty Bell*, p. 63.

Chesnut, M. B. (1949), *A Diary from Dixie*, Boston: Houghton Mifflin.

Cott, N. F. (ed.) (1972), *Root of Bitterness: Documents of the Social History of American Women*, New York: Dutton.

Cruz, J. (1999), *Culture on the Margins: The Black Spiritual and the Rise of American Cultural Interpretation*, Princeton NJ: Princeton University Press.

Davies, E. (1849), *American Scenes and Christian Slavery: A Recent Tour of Four Thousand Miles in the United States*, London: John Snow.

Davis, A. Y. (1983), *Women, Race and Class*, New York: Vintage Books.

Dickens, C. (1914), *American Notes for General Circulation, and Pictures from Italy*, London: Chapman & Hall.

Foner, E. (1970), *Free Soil, Free Labor, Free Men: The Ideology of the Republican Party Before the Civil War*, New York: Oxford University Press.

Foner, P. (ed.) (1985), *The Factory Girls: A Collection of Writings on Life and Strugglers in the New England Factories of the 1840s*, Urbana: University of Illinois Press.

Fox-Genovese, E. and Genovese, E. D. (1987), 'Divine Sanction of Social Order: Religious Foundations of the Southern Slaveholders' World View', *Journal of the American Academy of Religion* LV (Summer): 190–223.

Gorn, E. J. (1985), 'Gouge and Bite, Pull Hair and Scratch: The Social Significance of Fighting in the Southern Backcountry', *American Historical Review* 90 (February): 1–35.

Hahn, D. (1983), *The Roots of Southern Populism: Yeomen Farmers and the Transformation of the Georgia Upcountry, 1850–1890*, New York: Oxford University Press.

Handel, S. (1989), *Listening: An Introduction to the Perception of Auditory Events*, Cambridge MA: MIT Press.

Hibbitts, B (1994), 'Making Sense of Metaphors: Visuality, Aurality and the Reconfiguration of American Legal Discourse', 16 *Cardozo Law Review* 229. (This article is available online at www.law.pitt.edu/hibbitts/meta_int.html.)

Hobsbawm, E. (1997), *On History*, New York: The New Press.

Hughes, L. (1897), *Thirty Years a Slave. From Bondage to Freedom: The Institution of Slavery as Seen on the Plantation and in the Home of the Planter*, Milwaukee. South Side Printing Company. Electronic Edition, University of North Carolina at Chapel Hill digitalization project, 1998, pp. 23–4.

Kryter, K. D. (1970), *The Effects of Noise on Man*, New York: Academic Press.

Levine, L. W. (1977), *Black Culture and Black Consciousness: Afro-American Folk Thought From Slavery to Freedom*, New York: Oxford University Press.

Loguen, J. W. (1968), *The Rev. J. W. Loguen, as a Slave and as a Freeman. A Narrative of Real Life*, New York: Negro University Press.

Meranze, M. (1996), *Laboratories of Virtue, Revolution, and Authority in Philadelphia, 1760–1835*, Chapel Hill: University of North Carolina Press.

Monro, G. C. (1850), 'The Life Ransom', *North Star*, 3 October.

Purdue, C. L. Jr., Barden, T. E. and Phillips, R. K. (eds) (1976), *Weevils in the Wheat: Interviews with Virginia Ex-Slaves*, Charlottesville VA: University Press of Virginia.

Raboteau, A. J. (1978), *Slave Religion: The Invisible Institution in the Antebellum South*, New York: Oxford University Press.

Radwick, G. P. (ed.) (1972–9), *The American Slave: A Composite Auto-biography,* Westport CT: Greenwood Press, supp. ser. 1, vol. 11.

'Reports of the Secretary of War' (1847), *National Era,* 1(50).

Rus, U. (1858), 'Casting Pearls Before-', *Harpers Weekly,* 8 May: 291.

Schafer, R. M. (1980), *Tuning of the World: Toward a Theory of Soundscape Design,* Philadelphia PA: University of Pennsylvania Press.

Sellers, C. (1991), *The Market Revolution: Jacksonian America 1815–1846,* New York: Oxford University Press.

Thomas, J. (1965), 'Romantic Reform in America, 1815–1865', *American Quarterly* 17 (October): 672.

Truax, B. (1978), *The World Soundscape Project's Handbook for Acoustic Ecology,* Vancouver BC: ARC Publications.

Wilson, J. H. (1976) 'The Illusion of Change: Women and the American Revolution', in Alfred F. Young (ed.), *The American Revolution: Explorations in the History of American Radicalism,* Dekalb IL: Northern Illinois Press.

Woloch, N. (ed.) (1992), *Early American Women: A Documentary History, 1600–1900,* Belmont CA: Wadsworth.

10

The Diabolical Symphony of the Mechanical Age

Technology and Symbolism of Sound in
European and North American Noise
Abatement Campaigns, 1900–40*

Karin Bijsterveld

Introduction

This chapter aims to show that the sound of technology is a key aspect of technological culture, because sound has been highly controversial and deeply invested with symbolic significance. This will be illustrated by analysing the history of noise abatement in European and North American cities in the first half of the twentieth century. If we are to understand the genesis of the problem, definitions regarding noise, the proposed solutions and the extent to which the proposals came to be accepted, we must invoke the cultural meaning of sound. By doing so, research into sound and its symbols will enhance our understanding of responses to technology-related changes in early twentieth-century city life.

* This chapter is an abridged part of a larger paper published in *Social Studies of Science*, 31(1): 37–70. A section reviewing the literature on the history and anthropology of sound has been left out to prevent overlap with other contributions to this reader. Reproduced with permission from Sage Publications.

The City Noise Problem: Civilization versus Barbarism

Complaints about noise seem to be a part of all recorded history.[1] In the second half of the nineteenth and at the start of the twentieth century, many such complaints, at least the European and the public ones, came from intellectuals. They generally considered noise to be a brute assault on their mental refinement. The lamentation of Arthur Schopenhauer, published in 1851, is the most famous of their charges – an ever recurring *leitmotiv* in the noise literature. Schopenhauer regarded the cracking of whips as a hideous sound, distracting him from his philosophical work:

> [Whip-cracking makes] a peaceful life impossible; it puts an end to all quiet thought . . . No one with anything like an idea in his head can avoid a feeling of actual pain at this sudden, sharp crack, which paralyzes the brain, rends the thread of reflection, and murders thought. (Schopenhauer 1974: 157)[2]

According to Schopenhauer, many people showed no sensitivity to noise. However, such people were likewise insensible to 'arguments, ideas, poetry and art – in sum, to mental impressions of all kinds, due to the tough and rude texture of their brains' (Schopenhauer 1974: 156).

Phrasing his complaints in a similar way, the mathematician Charles Babbage successfully campaigned against the 'nuisance' of London street music in 1864. 'The great encouragers of street music', Babbage wrote, 'belong chiefly to the lower classes of society', such as tavern-keepers, servants, visitors from the country and 'Ladies of doubtful virtue' (Babbage 1989: 254). The instruments of 'torture', which they seemed to love, destroyed 'the time and the energies of all the intellectual classes of society' (Babbage 1989: 253). Although Babbage knew that the invalid and the musical man were also annoyed, his pamphlet mainly focused on 'the tyranny of the lowest mob' upon 'intellectual workers' (Babbage 1989: 259).[3] The Austrian anthropologist Michael Haberlandt simply claimed that the more noise a culture could bear, the more 'barbarian' it was; in contrast, tranquillity was 'the womb of all higher intellectuality' (Haberlandt 1900: 177–8).

Neither Schopenhauer, Babbage nor Haberlandt mentioned the roar of machines or motorized traffic. Succeeding intellectuals, however, increasingly transferred the élitist convictions of their predecessors to such new sounds and spoke, as Bailey (1996) has shown, about the struggle for silence in terms of civilization versus barbarism. The psychologist

James Sully, for instance, published an essay entitled *Civilisation and Noise* in 1878, in which he argued that:

> If a man wanted to illustrate the glorious gains of civilisation he could hardly do better, perhaps, than contrast the rude and monotonous sounds which serve the savage as music and the rich and complex world of tones which invite the ear of a cultivated European to ever new and prolonged enjoyment . . . Yet flattering as this contrast may be to our cultivated vanity, it has another side which is by no means fitted to feed our self-complacency. If the savage is incapable of experiencing the varied and refined delight which is known to our more highly developed ear, he is on the other hand secure from the many torments to which our delicate organs are exposed. (Sully 1878: 704)[4]

Such a torment was the 'piercing noise of a train, when brought to a standstill by a break', he explained. Another was the 'diabolical hooter' reminding railway workers of 'their hour of work'. The loudness and harshness of these and comparable sounds of traffic and factories were the 'proverbial plague' of the student. Concentration, the 'counteractive force' of civilized man, was not enough to neutralize the effects of the increased sensibility and the irritating impressions amid the dense, and often indifferent, population of the cities (Sully 1878: 706, 720, 707, 709).

In 1908, the German cultural philosopher and physician Theodor Lessing was even more outspoken in his essay *Der Lärm. Eine Kampf-schrift gegen die Geräusche unseres Lebens*. Lessing declared himself to be annoyed by both traditional noise, such as the din of church bells and carpet beating, and the more recent nuisance of rattling machines, shrilling gramophones, ringing telephones, and roaring automobiles, autobuses, trams and trains. The latter type of noise, however, was 'incomparably worse' than the former and made present-day life 'nerve-racking' (Lessing 1908a: 45).[5] For Lessing, as for Sully, noise was profoundly anti-intellectual. Noise, he asserted, raised and exaggerated deeply-rooted human instincts and emotions – the 'subjective' functions of man's soul – and narrowed and dimmed the intellectual and rational – 'objective' – functions of the soul. Noise was the most primitive and most widely applied means to deafen consciousness. In fact, noise was the *'vengeance'* of the labourer working with his hands against the brainworker who laid down the law to the former. Silence, on the other hand, was the sign of wisdom and justice. 'Culture', Lessing stressed, 'embodied the genesis of keeping silent' (Lessing 1908a: 11, 20).

Dan McKenzie, an English surgeon and author of *The City of Din. A Tirade Against Noise* (1916) claimed roughly the same. If his crusade would be successful, he wrote, one of the consequences would be that 'the raucous tones of the raucous-minded would give place to the gently-voiced opinions of the mild and tolerant. So that this particular crusade is only one small part of a grand effort at the refinement of the human spirit . . .' (McKenzie 1916). 'In the long run', the English accounting expert Stanley Rowland stated in 1923, the difference between the noisy and the not-noisy was that 'between self-possession and self-assertion – or, more generally, self-diffusion'. One could encounter such self-diffusion at the theatre, where people kept up 'a running commentary on the action', in the 'abominable shrieks' of newsboys distributing newspapers, as well as in the 'brutal objurgative-ness' of the motor-horn, the 'outrageous noisiness of the motor cycle', and the 'semi-barbarious emotional music' of jazz (Rowland 1923: 315, 317, 318, 319, 314).

In short, pamphlets and essays as those of Sully, Lessing, McKenzie and Rowland displayed a deep concern about the disrupting effects of noise on societies' intellectual strength and cultural maturity. The higher classes, the refined mind and cultivated self-control were now thought to be threatened by the mechanical and non-mechanical sounds of the lower classes, the lowest emotions and brutal self-diffusion. With respect to some technologies, this transference of a traditional sound symbolism to new sounds seems illogical. The early automobile, for instance, was the privilege of the rich rather than of the masses: to assoc-iate the noise of cars with the lower classes seems strange. Yet this only underlines the significance of the cultural symbolism of sound. Further-more, it is important to note that the sounds of individually owned cars and gramophones were less impersonal than those of trains and factories, enabling direct attacks on identifiable groups of people.

Even the machine itself came to be invoked as a metaphor of mind in order to underline the latter's refined and vulnerable character. According to Rowland, 'the avoidance of friction of the human senses is as important for the equable functioning of the mind as is the elim-ination of mechanical friction for the proper working of a dynamic machine' (Rowland 1923: 313); and for McKenzie, the modern mind was

a delicate instrument, the needle-indicator of which trembles and oscil-lates to the finest currents of thought and feeling. By culture and education we have acquired the sensibility of the artist or poet. And yet we continue

to expose this poised and fragile instrument to the buffeting of a steam-
hammer, to the shriek of a locomotive! (McKenzie 1916: 52)

This situation was felt to be most acute in the cities. In the years
between 1900 and 1914, the motorization of cities such as Hanover,
Lessing's home base, was still moderate. In 1907, Hanover itself had
1,472 motorcars – Germany as a whole had over 27,000 motorcars versus
about 2 million horses used for transport (Birkefeld and Jung 1994: 45).
Still, the density of traffic – the many horse-drawn vehicles, electric trams
and motor-vehicles taken together – rapidly increased. Along a busy spot
in Hanover in 1900, trams came by 850 times every twenty-hour day,
resulting in the production of sounds of brakes and metallic creaks of
wheels in the curves of rails every 90 seconds (Birkefeld and Jung 1994:
39). Articles on noise in the popular press became common, and were
part of a more general concern about an increase of nervousness as a
consequence of the new urban sensory experiences enabled by motorized
traffic (Birkefeld and Jung 1994: 48).[6] And although the quality of the
sound in the streets of London had improved by 1916, McKenzie claimed,
being 'less clattering, less jarring, less varied' as a result of smoothly
surfaced roads such as asphalt, wood and pitch, of rubber tires instead
of iron-girt wheels, and of electric instead of steam engines, the noise
had increased in quantity (McKenzie 1916: 32, 105).

> The roar of the traffic of motor-buses, taxi-cabs, and motor-cars is of a
> deeper, more thunderous, and more overpowering nature than in former
> days, principally because vehicles are heavier and are driven at a much
> greater speed. (McKenzie 1916: 33)

The irregular and unexpected sound of the motor horn, the sounds
of change-speed levers of buses, and the sounds of trains such as 'the
clank of the wheel at the end of each length of rail', all contributed to
this din (McKenzie 1916: 69).

Fleeing the city and seeking silence in rural life was not promoted as
a solution, however. Nature, in contrast to the human-made environment, was considered to be without unpleasant sound, and rural as well
as urban life was once thought to have been silent once (Haberlandt
1900: 178; McKenzie 1916: 1, 25–8). Yet noise was now felt to be ubiquitous, even in the country. Lessing, for instance, tried to find tranquility
in villages, but felt haunted by sounds like that of the carrousel, the
steam-plough, threshing-floors, boilermakers and all kinds of animal.
Even in the most far-away valley of the Alps, he lamented, one would

encounter a gramophone (Lessing 1908a: 15). But technology itself was not seen as the bad genius. Of course, it had been 'left to scientific civilisation to fill the world with stridency' (McKenzie 1916: 28). Yet no one asked society to refrain from technological progress. Even Lessing, socialist in political perspective, yet culturally conservative in many of his expectations with respect to modernization, had nothing against technology *per se*. He really believed that automobiles, motorcycles and airplanes were the vehicles of the future. Society *itself* had to be re-organized.

In line with their characterization that making noise was disruptive behaviour, and that noise indicated a degeneration of societal order and mental life, the noise abating intellectuals saw education of the public as the most fundamental solution to the noise problem. Although the intellectuals considered all kinds of practical measures to be of help, they stressed that teaching the public how to behave was the best strategy to attain lasting results. In every school, Haberlandt wrote, an eleventh command should be taught: 'Thou shalt not make noise' (Haberlandt 1900: 182). '[T]he only hope of ultimate reform', Rowland thought, 'would seem to lie with our schools, where the subject of general social deportment might well occupy a more important place' (Rowland 1923: 316). Much could be done, McKenzie claimed. 'But the victory will come all the sooner if public opinion can be educated . . .' (McKenzie 1916: 111). And Lessing's campaign focused on fostering 'societal conscience' (Birkefeld and Jung 1994: 48).

Such an education could be sustained by law. Sully pointed out that, as the ear, unlike the eye, had no natural defence, the law should recognize and more precisely protect the right to silence in one's own dwelling – by transforming certain noises into penal offences. More specifically, McKenzie wanted to prohibit the use of the motor-horn at night. Prohibitions of that kind were far from new. Municipal laws that restrcted the shouting and crying of sellers in the streets and the barking of dogs date back to the seventeenth century, and laws against the blacksmith's hammer even to the thirteenth century (Schafer 1994: 190).[7] Yet, as Lessing made clear for Germany, law was still inadequate for the abatement of most noises. Since noise could only be punished in cases where it was 'generally disturbing', 'unnecessary' and 'intentional', judgement was quite arbitrary. Moreover, the noise of machines could hardly be sentenced, since the noise of trains, trams and factories was supposed to arise from the 'nature' of things and 'harm' only mattered in case of damage to 'possessions', thus not to one's fortitude, health and sleep (Lessing 1908a: 73–91).

Other proposed solutions focused on a spatial reorganization and visualization of city life, with help of new technologies. According to the German social psychologist and nerve specialist Willy Hellpach, the railway station of his day, anno 1902, was far less noisy than it had been before. This could be attributed, he argued, to 'visualization'. Many 'toxicating' aural signals – horns, whistles, shouts, jingles – announcing and accompanying the arrival of trains had been replaced by 'sober and non-obtrusive' inscriptions (Hellpach 1902: 32). Furthermore, he welcomed the increasing separation of the home and the workplace, as the noises of manual workers such as the locksmith, cabinet-maker and cobbler were more disturbing to neighbours than the dimmed, continuous noise of a factory. The real causes of noise, he made clear, could be found in the things that had remained as they were: the narrow, dark streets through which the traffic squirmed. In the future city, the centre should only be accessible to silent and slow traffic aiming for business. New, broad roads should be planned at the periphery, and factories at the remote corners of the city. 'Today', Hellpach concluded, 'the best assistant of the nerve specialist is the *engineer*' (Hellpach 1902: 38, my italics).

Lessing also suggested changes that implied reform of public space. For car racing, he stressed, one should construct private roads instead of public ones. In contrast, the many awful noises of housekeeping in each separate apartment, could be diminished by centralizing housekeeping in new enterprises. Moreover, he considered the ringing of churchbells at every private event of life to be the non-functional remainder of an age in which the individual had really been part of the community (Lessing 1908a).[8] Corbin has also noted such resistance against collective bell ringing, especially in the early morning, in late nineteenth- and early twentieth-century France. He attributes this to a de-standardization of the rhythm of life, a consequence of the genesis of an active nocturnal life of parts of the urban population, another important context for the rise of anti-noise essays and noise abatement campaigns (Corbin 1999: 302–5).

Public space was also the topic of a treatise on city noise that Berlin's town-planning inspector produced as early as 1903. In complete contrast with Hellpach, it was precisely the separation of work and home, although rational in itself, which the inspector considered to be the cause of noise, since it was the by-product of the resulting increased transportation. He took this ultimate cause for granted, so his solutions focused on diminishing the noise of the transportation facilities by proposing new materials and constructions for pavements, cars, wagons, trams, tires, rails and rail-road crossings. According to the Berlin inspector, the noise produced by man himself – shouting or the use of bicycle-bells and car-horns – was the most difficult to control. One could not give every citizen a personal policeman to check his behaviour, nor objectively judge the noise of their vehicles. Even worse, most people did not recognize the health hazard of noise, although noise damaged their nerves and shortened their sleep (Pinkenburg 1903).

Yet trying to control people's behaviour, especially on the road, became precisely the rhetorical heart of the campaigns that followed the first essays on noise, a result of the enduring conceptualization of city noise as a problem caused by disruptive and uncivilized behaviour. Even the introduction of noise measurement did not change the special place of public education among the proposed solutions. Again, practical improvements were on the agenda. Public education, however, remained to be seen as the crown of noise abatement, as well as the straw at which to clutch in case success failed to come. How that education was modelled, and how the extent of its success relates to the symbolism of sound, will be the focus of the next section.

Noise Abatement Campaigns: The Need for a Noise Etiquette

A few months after the publication of Lessing's Der Lärm, the 'German Association for Protection from Noise' (Deutscher Lärmschutzverband) was founded – by Lessing himself. The Association became generally known as the Anti-Noise Society (Antilärmverein) and published a journal entitled Antirowdy: Right to Silence. In New York, The Society for the Suppression of Unnecessary Noise started in 1906, whereas the London Street-Noise-Abatement-Committee started two years later (Lentz 1994: 85).[9] France had a Society for the Suppression of Noise as early as in 1928. The German Society of Mechanical Engineers (Verein Deutscher Ingenieure) raised a Noise Abatement Committee (Fachausschuss für Lärmminderung) in 1930. In the UK, the (national) Anti-Noise League was founded in 1933, followed by the Austrian 'Anti-Noise League' (Antilärm-Liga Oesterreichs) and the Dutch 'Sound Foundation' (Geluidstichting) in 1934, as well as the Dutch 'Anti-Noise League' (Anti-Lawaaibond) in 1937. The British named their journal Quiet, which the Dutch imitated with Stilte, a journal first published in 1938 (Davis 1937: 132; Meyer and Potman 1987: 10–12; Dubois 1938; Noise 1935: 39–43).[10]

By that time, most anti-noise campaigns had already been completed, both in Europe and beyond. The first wave of campaigns occurred between 1906 and 1914, the second wave presented itself in the first half of the 1930s. The societies and committees behind the campaigns did not become mass movements. As the British Anti-Noise League admitted in 1936: 'The interest taken by the public in the cause of the League has been disproportionately greater than the growth of its membership roll' (Horder 1936: 3). The press coverage of their activities was, however, substantial, especially in the 1930, when hundreds of newspaper and magazine articles accompanied the campaigns.

The rate of success of the early campaigns differed. Lessing's Anti-Noise Society had over a thousand members, primarily scholars, physicians and lawyers, and really hit the headlines. Yet, although the society attained some local successes, such as the introduction of new pavements in specific streets and new ordinances for controlling the ways in which wood, iron, copper and the like were transported, it did not achieve any changes in national law, and was disbanded in 1914.[11] According to several historians, this was due to the society's élitist point of view. 'Tranquillity is distinguished' (Ruhe ist Vornehm) was its slogan. Such an approach did little to foster alliances between the Anti-Noise Society and, for instance, labour unions. Moreover, Lessing's society had far less to say about industrial noise than about the noise of traffic, which again reflected its élitist approach. Furthermore, Lessing's conviction that refined people were the most likely to suffer from loud sounds was ridiculed by the press. Members of the Anti-Noise Society were portrayed as non-masculine hysterics. What's more, no sufficient measuring equipment was available to lend force to noise control measures, and World War I made noise abatement seem quite unimportant (Birkefeld and Jung 1994: 57; Lentz 1994: 93; Saul 1996a; Saul 1996b).[12]

As can be inferred from the work of the environmental historian Raymond Smilor, the early noise abatement campaings in the United States were more successful. Just as in Europe, noise abators in the United States associated silence with 'civilization'.[13] However, noise was not merely seen as 'primitive', but also as 'inefficient'. Dembe (1996) has shown that noise referred to waste such as loss of productive power and detoriation of machines. What's more, noise in industry and offices threatened the powers of concentration of employees, and city noise in general undermined public health – a theme typical for the Progressive Era, in which urban reform was an important issue.[14] Public health became the focus of the New York City Society for the Suppression of Unnecessary Noise, raised by Julia Barnett Rice. Instead of lightening the burden of noise mainly on behalf of intellectuals, the New York Society first and foremost all aimed at reducing noise for the sake of children and the sick, so as to promote processes of learning and recovery. It successfully campaigned for the creation of silence zones around hospitals and schools, for a law against unneccessary horn signals in shipping, and for the reduction of fireworks, both noisy and unsafe, on the Fourth of July. Such a focus on the protection of children and the sick facilitated obtaining support from the press and industry, because – apart from those of the fireworks industry – no vested interests were at stake. The same went for the focus on unnecessary noise, that is to say, noise that was not associated with technological progress. Yet the 'unrestricted use' of automobile signals and muffler cut-outs, the Society made clear, remained to be tackled (*Report* (n.d.): 20, my page numbering; Smilor 1971; Smilor 1980; Schwartz 1998).

In the late 1920s and early 1930s, these early noise-abatement campaigns were followed by big campaigns of noise-abatement societies all over Europe and the US. Now, the definition of noise as a costly threat to the health and efficiency of *all* citizens was common. Henry J. Spooner, of the London Polytechnic School of Engineering, said that future generations would look back on an

> age of folly vulgarized by an absence of quietude and repose, and notorious for uncontrolled devastating din that tortured the thinkers, deprived countless invalids and workers of recuperative sleep, impoverished owners of traffic route properties, increased the overhead costs in modern business and shortened the lives of countless sufferers. (Spooner cited in 'The World's' 1928: 18)

Besides, the focus on traffic noise became even more predominant than it had been before World War I. Street noise already had a bad reputation, so it was an obvious topic to focus the first noise measurements on. Such measurements brought the loudness of traffic noise into the limelight, and the first noise surveys did the same to the annoyance traffic noise evoked. What's more, the topic of traffic noise allowed noise abatement societies to enter into alliances with traffic societies, as will be illustrated below. Yet even with respect to traffic noise, public education remained on top of the list of solutions. After all, noise was still thought of as being 'vulgar'.

Let me first elaborate on the changes concerning the measurement of noise. According to Birkefeld and Jung, the definition of noise as 'unwanted sound' goes back as far as to the early Middle Ages, at least in general dictionaries (Birkefeld and Jung 1994: 40). Yet within acoustics, 'noise' was initially thought of as non-periodic, irregular vibrations, in contrast to the periodic soundwaves of musical tones. Not until the 1920s and 1930s did the definition of noise as 'unwanted sound' become common among acoustical engineers. This happened, Ronald Beyer claims, because engineers dealing with telephone reception 'found that the presence of other sounds interfered with such reception and began calling these extraneous sound noise', as well (Beyer 1999: 206).[15]

At about the same time the measurement of sound drastically changed. The intensity of sound had been very difficult to measure because of the extreme low energy levels emitted. Only after the development of telephone technology, which enabled the separation of different frequencies, and of the radio valve, which made it possible to intensify small energy levels, did sound intensity become easier to measure (Dubois 1937: 26). Subsequently, both telephone technology and experimental psychology contributed to the establishment, in 1925, of the 'decibel' (deci-Bell) as unit of loudness. Telephone technology contributed because of its search for a unit for measuring the transmission efficiency of telephone circuits, and experimental psychology because it showed the dependence of the sensation level of sound on the logarithm of the sound's intensity, at least for those frequencies for which the ear is relatively sensitive (Beyer 1999: 219–22). The threshold limit of a tone of 1,000 Hz became established as the zero-point of 0 decibel (dB), and two powers were said 'to differ by n dB where $n = 10 \log P1/P2$. An increase of 1 dB corresponds to a 26 percent increment in power or intensity, 10 dB to a tenfold increase, 20 dB to a hundredfold increase and so on' (Serle 1936: 20).[16]

The first surveys of city noise were published between 1926 and 1930, and had been executed in London, Chicago and New York with help of audiometers (or subjective noise meters) and, shortly afterwards, of acousti-meters (or objective noise meters). In case of an audiometer, the loudness of a tone was measured by changing the intensity of a reference tone until it was felt to be masked by the tone to be measured. The objective noise meters were basically made up of a microphone, an amplifier and an indicating meter, which made the measurement of loudness a purely physical issue. A next step was the development of noise meters for complex tones. Although there were still significant difficulties – for instance, noise meters could not exactly follow noises that fluctuated rapidly – the first noise surveys, of which the ones of 1929–30 in New York were the most extensive, were reviewed by Rogers Galt in 1930 in the *Journal of the Acoustical Society of America*. Galt's figures, graphs and tables became widely known, and showed up in popular as well as scientific publications on noise all over the Western world (Galt 1930). Galt underlined that noise was not the same as annoyance, since circumstances such as the frequency of occurrence of a specific noise, its component frequencies, the noise being steady or intermittent, being regarded as necessary or not, were also significant. In other early publications, remarks of the same kind can be found. Along with such remarks, however, loudness levels increasingly became the sign of 'how bad' the situation was.

In 1929, complaints from citizens urged the New York Commissioner of Health to appoint a commission to study city noise and the means of abating 'the diabolical symphony' of 'our present mechanical age' (Wynne 1930: 13). Its members represented the worlds of engineering, medicine, acoustics, the police and city administration, the automobile and telephone industries. The commission produced two reports and started a huge anti-noise campaign in which the first report, and the press responses it evoked, were considered to be important steps in creating public consciousness of noise. According to the first report, the noise nuisance varied from the use of loudspeakers outside shops, the screeching of brakes and the abuse of automobile klaxons, to the use of muffler cutouts on motor boats, the noises of milk and ash cans, of pneumatic drills, of the turnstiles in subways and of elevated trains. A chart on the inside cover of the report provided an overview (see Figure 10.1). The commission made clear that, up to the recent past, the noise of the machine-using age had been proudly perceived as the sound of progress and prosperity. Now, however, noise had to be considered as a serious health hazard (Brown *et al.* 1930: v–vii, 3, 57, 212).

The clamour of the city, the report said, impaired the hearing of New Yorkers and induced harmful strain upon the nervous system that led to 'neurasthenic and psychasthenic states', to loss of efficiency of workers and thinkers, and to disturbed sleep (Brown *et al.* 1930: 17). The metropolitan newspapers published a questionnaire, so as to map out the roar of the city. Over 11,000 people responded and reported to be annoyed most by the noise of traffic, transportation and radio (Brown *et al.* 1930: 26). Notwithstanding the latter, commission members arranged radio talks so as to 'arouse public consciousness to the evils of noise and the advantages of a quieter city' (Brown *et al.* 1930: 74). Some practical progress in noise abatement was made with respect to the unnecessary whistling in the harbour, the blowing of car horns and the use of open cutouts by mail trucks, as well as to the construction of more silent turnstiles. Moreover, amendments in the Sanitary Code and the Code of Ordinances had been passed so as to control the use of loudspeakers.

According to Dembe, the New York anti-noise campaign, by stimulating research and by raising public consciousness, also indirectly furthered the postwar financial recognition of industrial hearing loss (Dembe 1996). The second New York report, however, published in a limited edition in 1932, stressed the difficulty of really solving the noise problem. Suffering from the economic depression, the commission was dissolved in the same year (Smilor 1971: 35–6; Smilor 1980: 47–148).

The second New York report made clear that the commission could oversee research and propose methods of noise abatement, but had been unable to prompt the city authorities to action (beyond those mentioned above). The report stressed on almost every page, however, that the biggest issue and problem was public consciousness. 'The responsibility for city din rests less on the machine than on public apathy.' In a dramatic tone, the report told a story similar to the ones presented by Leo Marx in *The Machine in the Garden*, except for the last, crucial, turn. Marx describes how, in America in the nineteenth century, the sounds of trains and factories were depicted as aggressive signals that invaded the serene and secure 'peace of an enclosed space', thus symbolizing the disturbance

Source: Brown *et al.* 1930, inside cover.

Figure 10.1 Sources of city noise

of the pastoral ideal (Marx 1964: 29). As the second New York report said:

> One hundred and fifty years ago the world was like a quiet valley . . . One day there was an ominous rumbling on the surrounding hills and a horde of barbarian machines poured down on the quiet valley. With steam whistle war whoops and the horrible clanking of iron jaws they came . . . Resistance was vain, for how could hand power compete with steam? . . . But the swift of mind fled to the further hills where they tried to rebuild the lost world in their dreams . . . Every aspect of the machine being considered marvellous, noise also became a minor god . . . At last, however, the swift of mind returned from the ivory towers they had built in the hills and took over the task of recivilizing the new machine age . . . But though many battles are won, the goal still lies far ahead . . . We cannot expect quiet until the millions realise they have sold their birthright for a radio and an automobile. Therefore, the only permanent contribution the Noise Abatement Commission can make is to assist in educating the people. (*City* 1932: 3–4)

So a quiet city, rather than a pastoral landscape, was sought.[17] And not by throwing out the radio and the automobile, but by changing public opinion. Even law, in the form of a standard noise ordinance, could only be effective if people knew that noise was unhealthy, inefficient and often unsafe. Therefore, the police should act as a educational rather than a punitive body. Moreover, people should behave according to a Noise Etiquette for Automobile Owners. They should not use their horns to summon people within doors, but only blow their horns when necessary to avoid accidents. Furthermore, they should buy a silent car, shift gears silently, investigate unusual noises, have squeaking brakes relined and the car regularly greased, make sure that the muffler functioned properly and have rattles corrected.

In Europe, the noise campaigns likewise focused on traffic and transportation. In the UK, these led to the 1934 amendment of the Road Traffic Act, which prescribed a silencer that reduced the noise of the exhaust, prohibited the sale and use of motor vehicles and trailers that caused excessive noise as a result of defects, lack of repair, faulty adjustment or faulty packing of the load, and banned the sounding of motor horns between 11.30 p.m. and 7 a.m. in built up areas. A few years later the Anti-Noise League made sure that the Highway Code no longer contained 'any positive recommendation to sound the horn' (Strauss 1937: 19).[18] The same League encouraged 'those concerned in the design and the manufacture of noisy machines toward better manners as well as more efficient science', and organized an exhibition so as to make the public familiar with artefacts varying from noiseless typewriters, floating floors and ear plugs to quietly running electric motors, silenced breakers, exhaust silencers and pneumatic railcars (*Noise* 1935: foreword). Revealingly, one of the advertisements in the exhibition catalogue stated that road drills could 'be effectively silenced without loss of power' (*Noise* 1935: 79).

In Paris, the blowing of horns came to be prohibited after the Society for the Suppression of Noise had addressed itself to the Prefect of Police. An educational campaign was also started to reduce 'the jay-walking habits of pedestrians' (Brown *et al*. 1930: 10). Italy banned the use of the horn at night in 1934 and, in Rome from 1935 onwards, even during the day. By 1937 Germany had made silencers obligatory; moreover, engine noise needed to stay below a maximum loudness, 'hooters' had to have an 'approved pattern' and 'sound of unvarying pitch', and the use of horns for other purposes than warning was punishable ('Promoting' 1937: 31). In the same year, Holland renewed its Motor and Bicycle Regulation, and included maxima with respect to the noise volume of motors and horns, as well as a prohibition of the use of the horn at night. In the 1930s, cities such as Wiesbaden, Stuttgart, Zürich, Stockholm, Milan, Rome, Antwerp, Brussels and The Hague all organized 'silence weeks' or 'traffic weeks', to educate the public in reducing the deafening use of car horns ('Breda bindt den strijd' 1935; 'Meer stilte' 1935; *Algemeene* 1936: 5; *Verslag* 1934: 33; *Verslag* 1936: 59–78).

It is clear that symbolism of sound partly modelled the campaigns as well as the response to the campaigns. For instance, the association between silence and social distinction guided the early German campaign, which focused on creating silence for the bourgeois élite. Despite the many practical proposals, advocated during that campaign, promoting the respectability of silence was seen as crucial for noise abatement, whereas industrial noise had no priority. This in turn hampered alliances with labour unions, and inspired opponents to counter the anti-noise campaign with another association: that between noise sensitivity and femininity. Neither the increasing concern with noise as a general health hazard negatively effecting efficiency, nor the introduction of measurement apparatus, however, changed the rhetorical focus of anti-noise societies on public education. Making noise was still seen as a sign of being uncivilized, of having no manners. In a more general sense, noise was thought to have been welcomed because of the positive connotations, such as progress and power, that loud sounds possessed.

As the New York Noise Abatement Commission found out, breaking such symbolic links was very difficult. One of the press responses to its campaign had been the following: 'Isn't it precisely that it is the big noise, the detonation of our national dynamite, that attracts the big crowds which make New York?' (*City* 1932: Chapters 8, 18). In London, a comment on the first annual report of the London Anti-Noise League claimed that the noise of machines would always 'find out a way of returning', because the 'joy of life expresses itself in a crowded chorus' (Y.Y. 1935: 274). The Italian Futurists, indeed, adored city noise as the symbol of the dynamics of modern life, and even introduced city noise into music.[19]

What *did* succeed, however, were exactly those proposed changes in traffic control and city planning that contributed to a new rhythm of city life. As Anthony McElligott made clear in a recent, highly original interpretation of Walter Ruttmann's film *Berlin: Symphony of a City* (1927), the spectacular image of the fast flowing traffic in that film

> might appear chaotic, but it never is. Instead its constituent and apparently anarchic parts are constantly configured into a single pulsating flow of order as a result of an imperceptible traffic plan, and the regulating presence of the traffic police, who together ensure that the underlying structure of urban-based capitalism remains intact. (McElligott 1999: 210)

In the Netherlands, for instance, such a flow of order – a new urban rhythm – came to be reached through the 'silence weeks' mentioned above. According to Adriaan Fokker, president of the Dutch Sound foundation, one had to fight the 'demon' of noise by setting out 'the ideal of the expert professional who silently knew to control his noiseless machine' against the 'noise vulgarian' and 'motor yokel' who tried to impress others by making noise (*Verslag* 1934: 16). Separation of industrial and residential areas, restraint on 'ribbon' development, and the reduction of angles and bends in roads would reduce city and traffic noise, he and other Dutch noise abators stated (*Verslag* 1936: 17). Improvements in the sound levels of technological artefacts themselves, for instance by constructing silencers, new horns and alternative ways of loading, could be of help too. Yet most important, they claimed, were silence campaigns.

In 1935–6 such campaigns were organized in Breda, The Hague, Rotterdam, Groningen and the south of Limburg, often in co-operation with the police and traffic organizations. During 'silence weeks', 'silence months' and 'silence exhibitions', thousands of pamphlets, placards and flags were distributed, and dozens of newspaper articles, radio talks and even newsreels in cinemas covered the campaigns. The basic consideration was to familiarize civilians with the idea that they had to *look out* before they blew their horns or before they forced others to blow their horns. 'Use your eyes in stead of your horn', one pamphlet said. Just as railway stations had replaced the infernal noise of bells and whistles by optical signals, streets should likewise become quiet. Hence people should watch out, stay right, slow down, use silencers, and were summoned to consider their motor as a means of transportation, in stead of a machine for testing other people's eardrums. 'Orderly traffic promotes silence', was one of the slogans of the campaigns ('Promoting' 1937: 32).[20]

The campaigns indeed – at least temporarily and locally – diminished the use of car horns. In the Hague, for instance, the police counted the number of horn blows on several days at three locations between 8 a.m. and 9 a.m., between 12 p.m. and 2 p.m., and again between 4 p.m. and 6 p.m. Before the silence week, they counted over 5,300 passing buses, cars, trucks and motors, and over 5,400 signals. A month after the silence week, over 5,100 vehicles passed and a little over 2,500 horns blowed. No comparable figures were gathered in Rotterdam, but 'progress' was observed and locally the noise was 'notably reduced' (*Verslag* 1936: 24, 30). In 1934, a British industrial psychologist claimed that such a prohibition in the UK had been 'spontaneously followed' by a 'striking reduction in the frequency of the hoot of the motor-car horn during the day'; and in the same year, the Stuttgart police reported 'a general calming of the traffic' as well as a relative 'drop of the number of casualties' (Myers 1934: x; McElligott 1999: 222). Moreover, the behaviour of Dutch bicyclists, motor-cyclists and motorists showed improvement (*Verslag* 1936: 26).

In general, in Holland and elsewhere, traffic control became more visualized by the use of spotlights at night, and by the introduction of optical train signals (Dembe 1996: 172). And as McElligott made clear for Berlin, the city traffic came to be 'collectively directed by traffic signs, regulations, and police hand signals'; commuters were circulated by rail, tram and roads, 'movements forming a grid that contained and controlled the energies of the metropolis' (McElligott 1999: 223). This fostered economic wellbeing and safety, and at the same time created rhythm out of chaos, thus partially reasserting human control over events, in a way comparable to the rituals described by anthropologists for more ancient or remote cultures.

Conclusions: A Sound History

The many manifestations of technology in the late nineteenth and early twentieth centuries drastically changed the sonic environment of Western society. The sounds of factories, trains, trams, automobiles, buses, motorcycles, aircraft, telephones, radio, pneumatic drills, steam-hammers, and of thousands of hooters, brakes, mufflers and gear levers, accompanied those of church bells, whips, street musicians, carpet beating, milk cans and yelling people.

It is this chapter's claim that the sound of technology is an aspect of technological culture highly worth studying, since it has a history of dispute loaded with cultural symbolism. Studying such a symbolism of sound opens up a new entrance into unravelling and understanding modes of response to technological change. The way in which, out of the technological sounds mentioned above, the 'noise problem', the proposed solutions to it, and the responses to such solutions, came to be defined and articulated has been deeply influenced by recurrent patterns in a long-standing symbolism of sound. Such patterns in the cultural meaning of noise and silence became transferred to the sounds of new technologies, and structured the choice of metaphors with help of which people tried to carve out and grasp the noise problem. Moreover, such general lines account for some phenomena in the noise abatement episode of 1900–40 which seem to be incomprehensible at first sight, yet become understandable as manifestations of a recurring symbolism of sound.

The basic pattern of such a symbolism was, as anthropologists and historians have shown, that loud sounds, if positively evaluated, have been attributed with characteristics such as power, strength, progress, prosperity, energy, dynamics, masculinity and control. Yet the very same sounds, in cases they were unwanted and therefore labelled as 'noise', have been continuously thought of as a sign of a deliberate disruption, often by those lower in the hierarchy. The kind of order thought to be threatened varied over time and over the kinds of people complaining. Noise could threaten the pastoral idyll of the nineteenth-century American literary men; society's intellectual strength, cultural maturity and cultivated self-control of which the late nineteenth- and early twentieth-century European intellectuals spoke; and the economical efficiency, health and safety the noise abators of the 1920s and 1930s wanted to protect. Noise referred to conflict and complexity, rudeness, wildness, primitiveness, irrationality, impressive behaviour and revenge. Notwithstanding such variety, noise meant chaos, silence meant order, and rhythm meant control within and over societal life. Consequently, human behaviour and societal organization were seen as the first causes of the dissonance as well as the starting-points for the restoration of harmony.

Solutions were sought for in correspondence with this pattern, as well as with specific contexts. Whereas twentieth-century American literary men could still think of land in which the pastoral ideal could be restored by using technology to create a cultivated garden, the twentieth-century European and American city dwellers had no virgin land or tranquil village left, and sought a quiet city. Such a silence was pursued within a context of individualization of the possession of noise-sources (the automobile, the gramophone, the radio), a de-standardization of nocturnal life, a general discourse on the nervousness of city life, a concern over traffic safety, urban reform and refinement. Therefore, public education through campaigns, traffic control, city planning and new transportation constructions were seen as the most important solutions: thus an attempt was made to create order by civilizing the masses, and by creating a new urban rhythm. Moreover, in line with the basic notion of noise as disruptive behaviour, teaching the public a noise etiquette was, more than anything else, seen as the alpha and omega of noise abatement.

The symbolism of sound described above explains why intellectuals complained about the car and blamed the working classes for making noise at one and the same time, although the automobile started out as the vehicle of the rich. It also explains why education kept its rhetorical predominance among the proposed solutions, even when measurement procedures 'objectified' noise and engineers introduced new means of noise reduction. After all, noise abators made clear, those who did not silently control their machines, displayed vulgarity. Last but not least, the symbolism of sound clarifies the responses to the noise abators' campaigns: the abators' 'refinement' came to be ridiculed as femininity, and they were, not suprisingly, unable to find alliances among the groups they implicitly or explicity blamed, or to the problems of whom (such as problems caused by industrial noise) they paid less attention. On the other hand, abating the positive connotations of loud sounds, such as 'dynamics' and 'strength', turned out to be extremely difficult.

Despite the visible changes in traffic control, transportation constructions and city planning, modern society did not become quiet. According to Smilor, noise abators tragically overlooked the quantitative increase in traffic (Smilor 1971). Finally, every new invention created new sounds, which again and again became the topic of heated controversy.

Acknowledgements

I would like to thank Manuel Stoffers for bringing to my notice several of the German sources, Joke Spruyt and Geert Somsen for correcting the English, and Ernst Homburg, Hans-Joachim Braun, Trevor Pinch, Rein de Wilde and the anonymous referees for their comments on this paper. A slightly different version of this paper has been published in *Social Studies of Science*, 31(1): 37–70. I would like to thank Sage Publications for their permission to re-publish the paper in this reader. All quotes from German and Dutch sources are my translations, unless indicated otherwise.

Notes

1. In 720 BC, the Greek colony Sybaris in Italy prohibited industrial noises in residential areas: see Brown *et al.* (1930: 6, 285–6). With respect to ancient Rome, several complaints about traffic noise are documented: see Schafer (1994: 190); Nieuwenhuizen (1969: 4).

2. Translation quoted from Schafer (1994: 62). See also Bailey (1996: 57); Menninghaus (1996: 475); Brown *et al.* (1930: 286). Schopenhauer was also mentioned by James Sully and Theodor Lessing (see below).

3. For Babbage's campaign, see also Bailey (1996: 61); Sully (1878: 718); Schafer (1994: 66).

4. For other observations concerning the discussion of (street) noise in terms of civilization and barbarism, see Bailey (1996: 60–1).

5. For Lessing's ideas, see also Lessing (1908b); Lessing (1909).

6. For a discussion of the putative 'age of increasing nervousness', see also Saul (1996a: 203).

7. For an interesting review of European law concerning the breach of the peace (the noise of neighbours), see Van Dam (1888).

8. See also Lentz (1994).

9. See also: Hogewind (1926: 11); Baron (1982: 169–70); Marwedel 1987: 104-07. The full title of the German journal was: *Der Anti-Rüpel: Antirowdy: Das Recht auf Stille, Monatsblätter zum Kampf gegen Lärm, Roheit und Unkultur im deutschen Wirtschafts-, Handels- und Verkehrsleben*. From the second issue onwards, its main title was *Das Recht auf Stille*. In *Der Lärm* (1908a: 43), Lessing also mentioned the existence of a 'Society for the Protection from Street Noise' (*Verein zum Schutz*

gegen den Strassenlärm) in Nürnberg. However, I know no additional references to the latter society.

10. The latter source mentions 1927 in stead of 1928 as the start of the French noise abatement society. In 1909, Lessing (1909: 86) also referred to noise abatement societies in Rotterdam and Brussels, but again, no additional references to these societies are known to me.

11. For the successes of Lessing's *Antilärm-Verein*, see Birkefeld and Jung (1994: 51–2).

12. Before the First World War, German noise experts thought that working-class people were so used to industrial noise that city noise did not bother them. See Saul (1996a: 203). In the late 1920s and early 1930s, however, organizations such as the 'German Society of Industrial Hygiene' (*Deutsche Gesellschaft für Gewerbehygiene*) and the 'German Society of Mechanical Engineers' (*Verein Deutscher Ingenieure*) started to abate industrial noise. In 1929, the metal sector acknowledged industrial hearing loss. See Braun (1998); de Bruijn (1984: 5).

13. According to Chester Morrow, one could test the 'state of civilization' attained in a specific country by looking at 'the character of its roads', 'the position of women' and 'the minimizing of noise'. The first two were satisfactory in the US, but 'As to noise we are yet in the depths of degradation'. See Morrow (1913: 121).

14. See: Whiteclay Chambers II (1992: 292); Melosi (1993: 430).

15. Those who used the older definition followed Helmholz. See: Sully (1878: 704–6); Pinkenburg (1903: 7); Lessing (1908a: 37–8); Hogewind (1926: 16–18). For the newer type of definition, see Myers (1934: viii); Davis (1937: 6); Dubois (1937: 3).

16. In Germany, the unit of the *Phon* was used. The loudness of, for instance, 60 Phon concurred with 60 dB, thus – by definition – only for a tone of 1,000 Hz.

17. For this observation, see also Thompson (1999: 266).

18. For information about the Road Traffic Act, see also *Noise* (1935: 7–8).

19. See Birkefeld and Jung (1994); Bijsterveld (2000); also Geilszler (1910), quoted in Hogewind (1926: 15). Likewise, Werner Sombart pointed out to such changes in music: see Lenger (1994: 163).

20. Archives Sound Foundation (*Geluidstichting*) (1933-1942) housed at the Dutch Acoustical Society (*Nederlands Akoestisch Genootschap*), Delft, The Netherlands: Pamphlet 'Anti-Lawaai Comité Groningen' [1936], 'Anti-lawaai-week 23–28 September 1935', 'De anti-lawaaimaand te Breda', unidentified newspaper (probably *Dagblad van Noord-Brabant*) (2 March 1935); '"Meer Stilte". Anti-lawaai-week in de residentie', *De Nieuwsbron* (19 September 1935), letter from Walter Matthies to the Office of the Sound Foundation (5 October 1935), letter from 'Bond van Bedrijfsautohouders in Nederland' to Office of the Sound Foundation (5 February 1936); *Algemeene* 1936.

References

Algemeene inlichtingen over de lawaai-bestrijding (1936), Delft: Geluid-stichting.

Babbage, C. (1989), 'Street Nuisances', in M. Campbell-Kelly (ed.), *The Works of Charles Babbage, Volume 11: Passages from the Life of a Philosopher*, London: William Pickering. Originally published in 1864 as a pamphlet, titled 'A Chapter on Street Nuisances'.

Bailey, P. (1996), 'Breaking the Sound Barrier: A Historian Listens to Noise', *Body and Society*, 2(2): 49–66.

Baron, L. (1982), 'Noise and Degeneration: Theodor Lessing's Crusade for Quiet', *Journal of Contemporary History*, 17: 165–78.

Beyer, R. T. (1999), *Sounds of Our Times: Two Hundred Years of Acoustics*, New York: Springer-Verlag.

Birkefeld, R. and Jung, M. (1994), *Die Stadt, der Lärm und das Licht: Die Veränderung des öffentlichen Raumes durch Motorisierung und Elektrifizierung*, Seelze (Velber): Kallmeyer.

Braun, H.-J. (1998), 'Lärmbelastung und Lärmbekämpfung in der Zwischenkriegszeit', in G. Bayerl and W. Weber (eds), *Sozialgeschichte der Techniek: Ulrich Troitzsch zum 60. Geburtstag*, Münster: Waxmann.

'Breda bindt den strijd tegen het stadlawaai aan' (1935), *De Telegraaf*, March 30.

Brown, E. F., Dennis, E. B. Jr., Henry, J. and Pendray, G. E. (eds) (1930), *City Noise: The Report of the Commission Appointed by Dr. Shirley W. Wynne, Commissioner of Health, to Study Noise in New York City and to Develop Means of Abating It*, New York: Noise Abatement Commission, Department of Health.

Bruijn, A. de (1984), *50 jaar akoestiek in Nederland*, Delft: Nederlands Akoestisch Genootschap.

Bijsterveld, K. (2000), 'A Servile Imitation. Disputes about Machines in Music, 1910–1930', in H.-J. Braun (ed.), *'I Sing the Body Electric'. Music and Technology in the 20th Century*, Hofheim, Germany: Wolke.

City Noise Volume II (1932), New York: Noise Abatement Commission.

Corbin, A. (1999), *Village Bells: Sound and Meaning in the Nineteenth-Century French Countryside*, London: Macmillan. Originally published as (1994), *Les cloches de la terre: Paysage sonore et culture sensible dans les campagnes au XIXe siècle*, Paris: Albin Michel.

Dam, W. J. van (1888), *Burengerucht*, 's-Hertogenbosch: W.C. van Heusden.

Davis, A. H. (1937), *Noise*, London: Watts.

Dembe, A. E. (1996), *Occupation and Disease: How Social Factors Affect the Conception of Work-Related Disorders*, New Haven, CT/London: Yale University Press.

Dubois, A. (1937), *Lawaai en lawaaibestrijding*, Den Haag: Moorman's Periodieke Pers.

—— (1938), 'Voorwoord van den Voorzitter', *Stilte*, 1(1): 3.

Galt, R. H. (1930), 'Results of Noise Surveys, Part I: Noise Out of Doors', *Journal of the Acoustical Society of America*, 2(1): 30–58.

Geilszler, F. A. (1910), 'Die Musik des Lärms', *Der Antirüpel*, No. 3, March.

Haberlandt, M. (1900), 'Vom Lärm', in *Cultur im Alltag: Gesammelte Aufsätze von Michael Haberlandt*, Wien: Wiener Verlag.

Hellpach, W. (1902), *Nervösität und Kultur*, Berlin: Verlag von Johannes Räde.

Hogewind, F. (1926), *Analyse en meting van het dagrumoer*, Utrecht: L. E. Bosch & Zoon.

Horder, L. (1936), 'Foreword', *Quiet*, 1(1): 3.

Lenger, F. (1994), *Werner Sombart, 1863-1941: Eine Biographie*, München: Verlag C.H. Beck.

Lentz, M. (1994), '"Ruhe ist die erste Bürgerpflicht": Lärm, Großstadt und Nervosität im Spiegel Theodor Lessings "Antilärmverein"', *Medizin, Gesellschaft und Geschichte*, 13: 81-105.

Lessing, T. (1908a), *Der Lärm: Eine Kampschrift gegen die Geräusche unseres Lebens*, Wiesbaden: Verlag von J.F. Bergmann.

—— (1908b), 'Die Lärmschutzbewegung', *Dokumente des Fortschritts*, 1, October: 954–61.

—— (1909), 'Ueber Psychologie des Lärms', *Zeitschrift für Psychotherapie und medizinische Psychologie*, 1: 77–87.

Marwedel, R. (1987), *Theodor Lessing: 1872–1933*, Darmstadt/Neuwied: Hermann Luchterhand Verlag.

Marx, L. (1964), *The Machine in the Garden: Technology and the Pastoral Ideal in America*, London/New York: Oxford University Press.

McElligott, A. (1999), 'Walter Ruttmann's *Berlin: Symphony of a City*: Traffic-Mindedness and the City in Interwar Germany', in M. Gee, T. Kirk and J. Steward (eds), *The City in Central Europe. Culture and Society from 1800 to the Present*, Aldershot, Hants: Ashgate Publishing.

McKenzie, D. (1916), *The City of Din: A Tirade against Noise*, London: Adlard & Son, Bartholomew Press.

McShane (1994), *Down the Asphalt Path: The Automobile and the American City*, New York: Columbia University Press.

'Meer stilte. "Anti lawaai"-week in Den Haag' (1935), *Nieuwe Rotterdamsche Courant*, 19 September.

Melosi, M. V. (1993), 'The Urban Environmental Crisis', in L. Fink (ed.), *Major Problems in the Gilded Age and the Progressive Era*, Lexington MA: D. C. Heath.

Menninghaus, W. (1996), 'Lärm und Schweigen. Religion, moderne Kunst und das Zeitalter des Computers', *Merkur*, 50(6): 469–79.

Meyer, O. M. T. and Potman, H. P. (1987), *Voor de bestrijding van het lawaai: Een onderzoek naar de vorming van het geluidhinderbeleid in Nederland*, Nijmegen: n.p.

Morrow, C. F. (1913), 'Anti-noise Legislation now pending in the City Council and under consideration by the Anti-noise Committee', *The Bulletin of the Medical and Chirurgical Faculty of Maryland*, 5(7): 117–21.

Myers, C. S. (1934), 'Preface', in F. C. Bartlett (ed.), *The Problem of Noise*, Cambridge: Cambridge University Press.

Nieuwenhuizen, J. K. (1969), *Stilte Alstublieft*, Eindhoven: Technische Hogeschool.

Noise Abatement Exhibition (1935), London: The Anti-Noise League.

Pinkenburg, G. (1903), *Der Lärm in den Städten und seine Verhinderung*, Jena: Verlag von Gustav Fischer.

'Promoting Quiet Abroad' (1937), *Quiet*, 1(6): 30–3. *Report of The Society for the Suppression of Unnecessary Noise, 1907–1913*, unnamed publisher, no date.

Rowland, S. (1923), 'Noise', *The Nineteenth Century and After*, XCIV(559): 313–23.

Saul, K. (1996a) '"Kein Zeitalter seit Erschaffung der Welt hat so viel und so ungeheuerlichen Lärm gemacht . . ." – Lärmquellen, Lärmbekämpfung und Antilärmbewegung im Deutschen Kaiserreich', in G. Bayerl, N. Fuchsloch and T. Meyer (eds), *Umweltgeschichte – Methoden, Themen*, Münster: Waxmann.

—— (1996b), 'Wider die "Lärmpest". Lärmkritik und Lärmbekämpfung im Deutschen Kaiserreich', in D. Machule, O. Mischer and A. Sywottek (eds), *Macht Stadt krank? Vom Umgang mit Gesundheit und Krankheit*, Hamburg, Dölling und Galitz Verlag.

Schafer, R. M. (1994), *The Soundscape: Our Sonic Environment and the Tuning of the World*, Rochester VT: Destiny Books. Originally published as (1977), *The Tuning of the World*, New York: Knopf.

Schopenhauer, A. (1974), 'Over lawaai en luidruchtigheid', in *Er is geen vrouw die deugt*, Amsterdam: Arbeiderspers. Originally published as 'Über Lärm und Geräusch', in (1851), *Parerga und Paralipomena, kleine philosophische Schriften*, Berlin: A.W. Hahn.

Schwartz, H. (1998), 'Beyond Tone and Decibel: the History of Noise', *The Chronicle of Higher Education*, January 9: B8.

Serle, R. B. (1936), 'The Measurement of Loudness', *Quiet*, 1(1): 19–21.

Smilor, R. W. (1971), 'Cacophony at 34th and 6th: The Noise Problem in America, 1900–1930', *American Studies*, 18(1): 23–8.

—— (1980), 'Toward an Environmental Perspective: The Anti-Noise Campaign, 1893–1932', in M. V. Melosi (ed.), *Pollution and Reform in American Cities, 1870-1930*, Austin TX/London: University of Texas Press.

Strauss, H. G. (1937), 'Noise and Some Legal Remedies', *Quiet*, 1(5): 17–20.

Sully, J. (1878), 'Civilisation and Noise', *The Fortnightly Review*, 24: 704–20.

'The World's Plague of Noise' (1928), *The Literary Digest*, October 6: 18–9.

Thompson, E. (1999), 'Listening to/for Modernity: Architectural Acoustics and the Development of Modern Spaces in America', in P. Galison and E. Thompson (eds), *The Architecture of Science*, Cambridge MA: MIT Press.

Verslag van het "Anti-lawaai Congres", georganiseerd te Delft, op 8 november 1934 door de Koninklijke Nederlandsche Automobiel Club in samenwerking met de Geluidstichting (1934), Delft: KNAC/Geluidstichting.

Verslag van het Tweede Anti-Lawaai-Congres te Delft op 21 april 1936 georganiseerd door de Koninklijke Nederlandsche Automobiel Club en de Geluidstichting (1936), Delft: Geluidstichting.

Whiteclay Chambers II, J. (1992), *The Tyranny of Change: America in the Progressive Era, 1890-1920*, New York: St. Martin's Press.

Wynne, S. W. (1930), 'New York City's Noise Abatement Commission', *Journal of the Acoustical Society of America*, 2(1): 12–7.

Y. Y. (1935), 'Less Noise, Please', *The New Statesman and Nation*, 31 August: 274–5.

11

Medicine's Acoustic Culture

Mediate Auscultation, the Stethoscope and the 'Autopsy of the Living'*

Jonathan Sterne

For some time now, scholars have attended to the problem of the gaze in the history and philosophy of medicine, considering the ways in which the body is imaged and made visible as well as the manners in which protocols of looking shaped and inflected medical practice. Yet one of the most enduring symbols of modern medicine has been a listening technology – the stethoscope. This chapter begins the process of unpacking an aural history of medicine by considering the connection between the stethoscope as a technology and mediate auscultation as a technique of listening. This history of listening is a central component of the genealogy of medical modernity. The diffusion of the stethoscope over the course of the nineteenth century provides a piece of the history of medicine's professionalization.

Moreover, the stethoscope simultaneously marks an important point in the history of listening, and connects it to the history of industrialization and professionalization, marking the articulation of the faculty of hearing to reason through a combination of location, technology, pedagogy, and ideology.

Foucault (1973: xiv) calls clinical medical experience 'that opening up of the concrete individual, for the first time in Western history, to

---

* This chapter first appeared in *Journal of Medical Humanities*, 2001, 21(2). Reproduced with permission.

the language of rationality, that major event in the relationship of man to himself and to the language of things.' Thus, if medicine was one of the first sites where the conceptual tools of rationality and empiricism were combined with techniques of investigation to make the human body an object of knowledge, then the history of the stethoscope is integral to this larger narrative. Foucault, along with Stanley Reiser (1978), offers probably the most developed accounts of the use of the stethoscope as a technique of audition, and my analysis here builds on their work. Both authors argue that modern medicine embodies in its development a movement from the theoretical to the perceptual. The rise of empiricism is key here, but more important than the approach is the construction of a new object. Both chart a new field of medical knowledge, an arrangement of what can be seen and what can be said. Hearing would play a tremendous role in this new medical epistemology.

This history of the stethoscope is not so much about the actual artefact as the technique that it crystallized: mediate auscultation. Auscultation is a noun for the action of listening or hearkening, and the word's use dates from the seventeenth century. It picked up specifically medical connotations in the nineteenth century as the activity of listening to the sound of the movements of organs, air and fluid in the chest (Oxford English Dictionary, s.v. 'auscultation').[1] Listening thus became important to the construction of medical knowledge and its application through the development of a technique and a technology to go with it. Despite early resistance, the doctor's hearing tool became the symbol of a profession (Davis 1981: 88–9). By the end of the nineteenth century, stethoscopy was everywhere in the medical profession. Even by the late 1820s, stethoscopy was becoming so popular that some practitioners who failed to use the instrument 'placed their professional reputations in jeopardy' (Davis 1981: 36).

Like other technological innovations, the stethoscope is an artifact of a technique: it was designed to operate within the parameters of a set of social relationships, and it helped to cement and formalize those relations: the doctor-patient relationship, the structure of clinical research and pedagogy, and the industrialization, rationalization and standardization of medicine (along with the improvement of physicians' social status). It was developed as a technical response to a social and investigative problem in a clinical setting. Its structure and operation were based on a new set of assumptions about the nature of medical knowledge, treatment and patients. The narrative of discovery given by its inventor reflects the importance of these factors to the stethoscope's most basic development. René-Théophile-Hyacinthe Laennec, a young

French doctor, discovered in 1816 that a tube of rolled paper applied
to the chest of a patient could amplify the sound of her heart. Having
failed to obtain a clear sense of her ailment through application of the
hands and percussion of the chest, 'on account of the great degree of
fatness', he moved on to a more innovative approach:

> I rolled a quire of paper into a kind of cylinder and applied one end of it
> to the region of the heart and the other to my ear, and was not a little
> surprised and pleased, to find that I could thereby perceive the action of
> the heart in a manner much more clear and distinct than I had ever been
> able to do by the immediate application of the ear. From this moment I
> imagined that the circumstance might furnish means for enabling us to
> ascertain the character, not only of the action of the heart, but of every
> species of sound produced by the motion of all the thoracic viscera . . .
> With this conviction, I forthwith commenced at the Hospital Necker a
> series of observations, which have been continued to the present time.
> (Laennec 1830: 5)

The 'from this moment I imagined' is key – Laennec's scientific
training and occupational ideology are given the weight of immediacy
in this account; he abstracts a crude acoustic principle behind the act
and proposes a series of investigations. Every movement of the organs
in the human thorax could be tracked by listening to the body with
the aid of an instrument, and those movements could be rendered
meaningful. This was Laennec's innovation, not the physical composition of a simple device to accomplish the task. Laennec claimed that he
had thus invented the technique of mediate auscultation: listening to
the body through a medium at a physical distance. His narrative became
the subject of popular lore throughout the nineteenth century (Davis
1981: 90). This technical approach to hearing, as a highly structured
activity that requires practice to perfect: it was grounded in an emerging
medical epistemology of pathological anatomy and helped reshape the
field. Its effects lay in two distinct areas: in the relational disposition
of bodies and elements in audile medical examination, and in the organization of the knowledge gained through those relationships.

Mediate Auscultation: The Social and Philosophical Basis of a Technique

The technology of the stethoscope was simple enough: Laennec's
original instrument and those descended from it were monaural
('single-eared') instruments. Generally cylindrical in shape, they had

an earpiece at one end and a hole at the other that would be placed on the patient's body. The hole could be plugged with a stopper for specific applications. Later innovations to the monaural stethoscope included making the middle of the instrument flexible (through the use of rubber tubing), and modifying the tube into two halves so that it could be unscrewed for easy transportation (Davis 1981: 97–102).

Physically, the stethoscope was a logical extension of the ear trumpet, which had been in use for centuries. But the use of this trumpet had some important differences. At first, the stethoscope might appear as a kind of reversal of the ear trumpet, where instead of the hearing-impaired person listening out into a functional world, the expert physician listens to the diseased body. But in an important way, the stethoscope was not so much the inversion of the hearing aid as the generalization of its principle. One early model of the monaural stethoscope, called a 'conversation tube', made the equivalence clear: the stethoscope was also usable as a hearing aid. Like sound reproduction technologies that would appear later in the century, the stethoscope was built on a pedagogy of mediate auscultation that rendered the human ear an insufficient conductor of sound (see Sterne (forthcoming) for a discussion of sound reproduction and the supplementation of hearing). In point of fact, the ear *was* insufficient for the purposes of internal medicine, since the stethoscope was designed to render sounds otherwise imperceptible to the human ear as more clearly audible.

While empiricism is usually cited as the operative epistemology of early modern medicine, an epistemology of mediation is equally central to the apprehension of sensory data that would yield up their truth: you had to have the right tools and training to hear it for yourself; the truth might not immediately yield itself up for the untrained listener. Consider Laennec's objections to listening to the patient's body *without* a stethoscope. In a section on immediate auscultation, where physicians would apply their ears directly to the bodies of the sick, Laennec (1830: 25–6) lists five major faults with this technique:

1. Any increased quality of hearing experienced through immediate auscultation as opposed to mediate is a result of the physician's entire face conducting sound when in contact with the patient's body, thus leading to 'serious mistakes in cases where pulmonary obstruction is partial and of small extent.'
2. It is not physically possible to apply the ear to a number of important regions for diagnosis (such as the angle formed by the clavicle and the head of the humerus in lean persons, the lower region of

the sternum when it is depressed, and so forth). Moreover, it is not *socially* possible to apply the physician's ear to the body of respectable women: 'in the case of females, exclusively of reasons of decorum, it is impracticable over the whole space occupied by the mammae.'

3. The application of the naked ear requires applying more pressure to the patient's chest, thereby further fatiguing the patient.

4. This added pressure can lead to extraneous sounds generated by the patients tightening their muscles or the physician's head rubbing against the patient's clothes, which can be mistaken as respiration.

5. 'The uneasy posture which one is frequently forced into, determines the blood to the head and renders the hearing dull. This circumstance, and the repugnance which every one must feel to apply the ear to a patient that is dirty or whose chest is bathed in perspiration, must always prevent the habitual or frequent use of this method.' Since auscultation is most advantageous for the early detection of disease before it presents any visual signs, the physician's presumed reluctance to use it in every single case may prevent effective diagnosis.

6. Finally, the stethoscope adds to the naked ear and the sounds of the patient's body its own acoustic properties, which aid in the detection of certain physical properties in the patient.

Elsewhere, Laennec summarizes his objection to immediate auscultation (auscultation without the aid of an instrument to supplement the faculty of hearing) as follows: 'Independently of its deficiencies, there are other objections to its use: it is always inconvenient both to the physician and patient; in the case of females it is not only indelicate but often impracticable; and in that class of persons found in hospitals it is disgusting' (Laennec 1830: 5). These objections to the use of the naked ear in medicine are instructive because they show the dual basis of an audile/medical procedure – in social differences (in this case, class and gender most explicitly); and in an emergent organization of sensation itself.

Mediate auscultation is a response to the analogy of physical and social distance: Foucault calls the stethoscope 'the measure of a prohibition transformed into disgust, and a material obstacle' (Foucault 1973: 163). Laennec does not mention in these passages the danger of contracting disease; the need for distance between doctor and patient is presented as emphatically social. In the clinical setting at this time, the physician was almost invariably of a higher class status than the patient. Only with the professionalization of medicine and increasing standards of cleanliness – along with urbanization and the gradual specialization of medical knowledge – would the middle classes venture into hospitals more frequently (Cowan 1983: 76–7; Starr 1982: 72–7). Doctors thus occupied a strange position. An aspiring middle-class profession found itself conducting work in one of the culture's most reviled spaces. Laennec (1830: 8), like his contemporaries, thought work in a hospital was essential to learning the methods of mediate auscultation. No doubt this was linked with the aspirations toward the middle-class respect-ability of the medical profession in general. These aspirations also called for the application of middle-class decorum to the bodies of poor women as well, which blended male physicians' self-understanding with their attitudes toward poor women. The physical distance between doctor and patient at the moment of examination was thus a reassertion of social distance even when they inhabited a common space. Even the very language used to describe these procedures renders social difference as spatial: *immediate* auscultation (as opposed to just 'auscultation') was listening to the body *without* distance between physician and patient, whereas mediate auscultation, listening to the body *from a distance* – or literally, with a medium – becomes the default term in medical description.

This condensation of social difference into a logic of mediation thus reveals a shift in practice at a more abstract level. If mediate auscultation provided for a social distance between classes and genders, it also provided the distance between knower and known; it is the physical configuration of a particular form of knowledge. According to Laennec's objections to immediate auscultation, the techniques of stethoscopy not only make up for some of the insufficiencies of the human ear – they isolate the faculty of hearing from the other senses (especially in the binaural stethoscope, which will be discussed further below) and render aberrant any conduction of audible vibration by body parts *other* than the ear. This is the substance of his first objection to immediate auscultation: bones outside of the ear can conduct vibration and therefore sound. The physician's ear, like the physician's eye, thus becomes a separated sense, divided from the others, whose specificity was to be preserved and intensified through the proper use of instru-mentation. The stethoscope provided a means of scientification through technology: rendering audible phenomena otherwise unavailable to the physician's senses, thereby increasing their powers of investigation: 'the prohibition of physical contact makes it possible to fix the virtual [more precisely, an acoustic] image of what is occurring well below the visible area' (Laennec 1830: 164, bracketed material added). Once again, *mediate* auscultation displaces its 'immediate' counterpart as the default status for medical listening in Laennec's account. A simple instrument marks and helps to solidify a whole medical epistemology of mediation.

Moreover, this epistemology of mediation carries with it a variety of contextual demands, a framing of the listening event, a structuring of the doctor-patient relationship according to clear physical and social roles, and a particular preference for instruments. Consider this range of provisions found in textbook instructions for the use of stethoscopes (distilled from Laennec 1830: 27–8; Bennett 1860: 49–50; Flint 1876: 72–4):

1. The role of the stethoscope is to be primarily instrumental; it is to be viewed as a means to an end, an enhancement of medical perception rather than its substance.
2. The stethoscope must be of good quality: it must fit the listener's ears comfortably, the end not exceed a certain diameter (usually of about 1") and its edges be rounded so as not to dig into the patient's skin. (Austin Flint adds that the tubes of the stethoscope should not be obstructed, nor should they be at all stiff or produce any sound of their own).
3. The patient's body should not be covered in heavy or loose coverings. Laennec is more willing to use the stethoscope to listen through clothing than his followers later in the century.
4. The stethoscope must be applied carefully to the surface of the patient's skin, so as to leave no gap between the skin and the end of the instrument; however, excessive pressure should be avoided so as not to cause the patient discomfort.
5. The position of the patient's body varies according to the area being examined. (Physicians should avoid a position that would require too much bending or stooping on their part. Patients may be positioned sitting upright, leaning forward, or in other specified positions depending on the nature of the examination).
6. The examination should cease if the patient is in any way excessively excited or nervous, as this will have an effect on the respiration.
7. Any examination of the patient will only be effective if the physician's ear is already trained and thoroughly practised.

These fundamentals serve as a kind of frame for the examination: establishing a number of constants for the detection of sonic variables. The physical positions of doctor and patient are prescribed, as are the relations among doctor, patient, and instrument. The relation between doctor and instrument is particularly important here. Each author describes listening through the stethoscope as a kind of concentration, an isolation of the sense of hearing from the other senses. Recall that this is one of the advantages of mediate auscultation over immediate auscultation according to Laennec. The proper execution of mediate auscultation depends on the proper separation of hearing from other sensation and also the framing of sound.

The development of the stethoscope and mediate auscultation coincided with the development of new theories of sense perception based on a 'separation of the senses'. While the attribution of different values to different senses is widely shared among different cultures, the separation of the senses in eighteenth- and nineteenth-century philosophy and science took on a distinctive form. From the late eighteenth century onward, theories of perception began to understand each sense as actually, physiologically different from the other senses. This is perhaps most dramatically elaborated in Johannes Müller's theory of perception, where each sense was physiologically distinct; as Jonathan Crary (1990: 89–90) puts it, 'capable of one determinant kind of sensation only, and not of those proper to the other organs of sense'.

Müller's theory rested on three opening premises:

1. The same internal cause excites different sensations in the different senses and in each sense the sensations peculiar to it.
2. the same external cause also gives rise to different sensation in each sense according to the special endowments of the nerve (so that, for example, electricity is perceived as light through the optic nerve but as touch through the skin).
3. The peculiar sensation of each nerve can be excited by several distinct causes, internal and external – so that misperception is a part of perception. Thus, seeing and hearing are to be understood as fundamentally and absolutely different modes of knowing the world, though neither form of knowledge is guaranteed as truth. For Crary, this is the moment when empiricism collides with subjectivism.

It is also the moment where each sense 'gets its due', so to speak, from modern thought. From this point on, it becomes possible – at least conceptually – to think of each of the senses as ideally and totally isolated from one another at a fundamental level. If the sensorium was, before this moment, a kind of complex whole, it becomes an accumulation of parts. Thus, not only vision (as Crary suggests) but hearing becomes its own, specific object of knowledge over the course of the nineteenth century. This new understanding of perception also has significance for the *practice* of perception: as each of the senses is, ideally, autonomous, one of the purposes of the technique is to develop them toward that ideal state. Thus it makes perfect sense for Laennec to suggest that the ear must not be supplemented, in the first instance, with touch through the hands or the combined senses of touch and hearing (via bone conduction) enabled by placing the face directly against a patient's body: in order to get the truest possible sense data, it must be separated from the other senses. If the sense of hearing *is* to be supplemented, then the supplement must come from *outside* the physical body: it can be supplemented through technique and technology. Laennec's stethoscope helped to accomplish this, but later stethoscopes improved upon this principle.

In addition to separating hearing from the other senses, mediate auscultation demanded a particular kind of framing of sound. In other words, only sounds inside the frame were to be analysed or considered. The sounds of the apparatus itself, and the other sounds accompanying auscultation were to be ignored.

The ability to abstract the mind from thoughts and other sounds than those to which the attention is to be directed, is essential to success in auscultation. All persons do not possess this ability equally, and herein is an explanation in part of the fact that all are not alike successful. To develop and cultivate by practice the power of concentration, is an object which the student should keep in view. Generally, at first, complete stillness in the room is indispensable for the study of auscultatory sound; with practice, however, in concentrating the attention, this becomes less and less essential (Flint 1876: 73–4).

This combination of abstraction and framing was soon embodied in a modification of the stethoscope: the binaural stethoscope. Although ideas for binaural instruments go back to at least 1829, the first widely used binaural stethoscope was designed by Arthur Leared in 1851. It consisted of a small chest piece that connected with two gutta percha pipes for the physician's ears (Reiser 1978: 41; Davis 1981: 104). The binaural model quickly found favour for several reasons: by providing sound to both ears, it further helped to isolate physicians from other sounds and concentrate the sound in their auditory fields; it also held itself on the physician's head, thereby freeing both hands for use on the patient; finally, many claimed that it provided a better quality of sound, both in terms of volume and clarity.[2] George Cammann published plans for a binaural stethoscope in 1855, and Cammann's model was the accepted standard of stethoscope design for the rest of the nineteenth century: thirty years later the *Journal of the American Medical Association* would declare that 'Cammann's binaural stethoscope just as he left it, is really the best instrument . . . for auscultatory purposes that we have' (Davis 1981: 104, 259).

While the binaural stethoscope helped to reify in physical form the separation of hearing central to the method of mediate auscultation, it still required proficiency in listening technique: the instrument itself produced sound outside the proper listening frame. Of Cammann's binaural stethoscope, Flint (1876: 71) writes that 'The advantages, however . . . are not appreciated until after some practice. At first, a humming sound is heard which divides the attention and thus obscures the intra-thoracic sounds. After a little practice this humming sound is not heeded, and it ceases to be any obstacle.' As a part of the instrumental reasoning underlying the entire procedure, the character of the instrument itself must be erased from consciousness during mediate auscultation. In classic technological deterministic fashion, the tool stands in for a whole process from which it erases itself. This 'license to forget' (Langdon Winner, quoted in Wise 1997: 187), a kind of mystification, was the social basis of a new medical hermeneutic.

Medicine's Audile Modernity

One of the reasons for the apparent breakthroughs associated with the stethoscope was that, in Laennec's own opinion, it made use of hearing – a 'novel sense' in diagnosis (Davis 1981: 88). The novelty of hearing was not in its presence, however, but in its application: mediate auscultation is not so much a shift to listening in medical practice as a shift *in* listening. Diagnosis shifts from a basis in speech between doctor and patient to the *objectification* of patients – patients' voices now existed in relation to other sounds made by their bodies, rather than in a privileged relationship to them (this is also a result of the clinicization of medicine and the shaping of the doctor-patient relationship through its rationalization and institutionalization). Speaking patients with mute bodies gave way to speaking patients with sounding bodies.

Diagnosis in the seventeenth and eighteenth centuries was based on a combination of the patient's own narrative testimony and the physician's own visual examination of the patient. While the former relies heavily on the patients' subjective account of illness, their person-alities and manners of expression, the latter relies on the physician's own perceptions. Physical examination was usually limited to the taking of the pulse, and occasionally to viewing the body (Reiser 1978: 1–7). The sounds of the body, other than the subject's speaking voice were totally disregarded: one physician was so shocked that he could hear a patient's heartbeat from the bedside he called it 'almost incredible'; another, when asked by his own patient the meaning of a 'blubbering sound' in the patient's chest, could only offer a meagre guess (Reiser 1978: 24). Without a hermeneutic for hearing patients' bodies, the non-verbal sounds they made were meaningless.

The growth of physical examination coincided with a change in orientation toward the body as a whole. Accompanying the changes in diagnostic methods was a change in theories of disease, from an understanding of disease as simply an imbalance of the bodily humours, to the idea that different symptoms might relate to entirely different diseases. As the eighteenth century wore on, efforts to classify diseases based on observation of patients (and less and less by personal narrative) gave way to autopsies to better track the footprints of disease on internal organs. In Reiser's (1978: 19) words, 'the practice of dissecting bodies to find physical evidence of disease began to transform some eighteenth-century physicians from word-oriented, theory-bound scholastics to touch-oriented, observation-bound scientists.' This kind of physical observation brought with it the requirement for new methods. As a result, visual, tactile, and audile techniques of examination increased in importance as medical empiricism gained currency: physicians had to revitalize old techniques of examination and develop new ones.[3]

One can find examples of auscultation and other acoustic methods of examination throughout medical history. Hippocratus is usually cited as the first written example of immediate auscultation, with a long list of followers (such as Laennec 1830: 24). Perhaps the most significant example of acoustic (really audile-tactile) examination prior to Laennec's was Leopold Auenbrugger's monograph entitled *Inventum Novum*, published in 1761. Auenbrugger's treatise is notable because it shifts responsibility for the apprehension of disease from the speech and appearance of the patient to the doctor's senses. Auenbrugger distrusted the accounts of his patients and wanted to make diagnoses by 'the testimony of my own senses' (Auenbrugger 1936: 379) thereby displacing the centrality of patients' own narrative accounts of their illnesses. The technique he advocated was called percussion, the striking of the body to get a sense of its interior composition. But Auenbrugger's treatise was short, vague and incomplete. He neither systematized his observations nor provided a clear explication of his practice. In fact, some physicians confused his procedure with an older practice called succussion, which involved listening for fluid in the chest by physically shaking the patient (Reiser 1978: 21).

Because of this general medical prejudice against engaging in physical activities in diagnosis, Auenbrugger's own unwillingness to promote his findings, and general hostility to medical innovation and experimentation, percussion did not find much favour in the medical profession until Laennec's time (Reiser 1978: 21–2). (Similarly, one of the early objections to instrumentation like the stethoscope was precisely that it would cause physicians to be classed with surgeons as craftsmen. While surgeons used their hands and instruments, physicians had previously shied away from the trappings of physical labour on behalf of their patients.)

Auenbrugger's work also fitted a paradigm that had not yet come into favour within the medical establishment. Percussion required interpretation of auditory symptoms and was based on a theory of disease as a localized phenomenon, which was still not a popular view among doctors in the late eighteenth century. Percussion was essentially meaningless without a system of medical knowledge based on a physiological model of disease (itself made possible through the gathering of anatomical and physiological data through dissection), listening to the interior of the body had no practical informative purpose to physicians of the late eighteenth century. Mediate auscultation expanded on Auenbrugger's work by recontextualizing it as well as adding new techniques. In fact, Laennec saw his work as completing and improving on the work carried out by Auenbrugger (Laennec 1830: 22–3). It was only when the body came to be understood as an assembly of related organs and functions that percussion – and very shortly thereafter mediate auscultation – would take a primary role in medical diagnosis. In the US, this is also for the very good reason that Forbes' was the first English translation of *Inventum Novum* and he coupled it with a digest of Laennec's *Treatise* for general consumption (see Forbes, 1824). Following John Forbes' example, auscultation and percussion were usually grouped together in English-language medical textbooks.

As a mode of empirical verification, autopsy was unsurpassed in popularity in nineteenth-century medicine: it offered a means of checking diagnoses for ailments that weren't cured (a quite frequent event; see Davis 1981: 89; Reiser 1978: 29–30). Developed from the work of Giovanni Battista Morgagni, Matthew Baillie, and Francois-Xavier Bichat, early nineteenth-century anatomy took the autopsy as its primary site of knowledge – the moment when the body would give up its truth.

As medical thought moved from recording patients' accounts of symptoms to the localization of disease, it required a means to transcend the subjectivity of the patient – to verify the condition of interior organs and bodily states. Autopsy served exactly that function: through the organization of hospitals and clinics that provided facilities both for handling the sick and for medical research, it became possible for a patient's death to become a 'spontaneous experimental situation', because autopsy could commence almost immediately after death (Foucault 1973: 137, 141, 143, 144).

Laennec initially demonstrated the effectiveness of his diagnoses through autopsies of his patients. Each of the forty-eight cases discussed in *Treatise on Diseases of the Chest* concludes with Laennec's subsequent findings in an autopsy performed within about a day of the patient's death. In fact, it was those findings that retroactively confirmed the diagnoses of mediate auscultation. It could thus be said in those first few years of diagnosis by stethoscope that patients' bodies were made to speak, but only retroactively: it was the *appearance* of lesions on the organs, the sight of the tissues and fluids that confirmed the auditory diagnosis sometimes made but a day earlier.

As a novel technique of diagnosis through audition, mediate auscultation required visual proof for its legitimation, for its scientificity and its verity; once established, it would take on a life of its own. The autopsy reference, then, is not simply a metaphor: once legitimated, mediate auscultation enabled the movement of the primary site of knowledge in pathological anatomy back from the dead to the living. Hearing surpassed sight in diagnostic precision, and only in the patient's death could the regime of vision again take hold. This primacy of audile diagnosis would continue into the twentieth century.[4]

Laennec's mode of analysis, although grounded in pathological anatomy, was a significant departure from its more orthodox applications. He was less concerned with the status of the organs themselves than their movements and relations. Mediate auscultation is a hydraulic hermeneutics, charting the motions of liquids and gases through the body. Even the patient's own voice becomes subsumed under this hermeneutic.

Like Auenbrugger, Laennec found listening to the patient's body a superior means of diagnosis compared with listening to the patient's narrative account of the illness. The sounds of the patient's body were independent of the patient's free will; patients could not 'conceal, exaggerate or lessen' the sounds their bodies yielded upon examination by mediate auscultation (Barth and Roger 1847: 1). Their speech might deceive, but their bodies would yield up their own truth upon examination. As Reiser argues:

The stethoscope focused the attention of physicians on a new class of disease sign – the sounds produced by defective structures in the body . . . A model of disease, deduced from these sounds and from the assorted lesions in the body found at autopsy, largely replaced the model constructed from the patients' subjective impressions and the physicians' own visual observations of the patient. The physician's withdrawal from such person-centred signs of illness was increased by the fact that the auscultatory process required the physician to isolate himself in a world of sounds, inaudible to the patient. Moreover, the growing success with which disease could be diagnosed through auscultation encouraged the physician to favour techniques that would yield data independent of the opinions and appearance of the patient. (Reiser 1978: 43–4)

The technique of mediate auscultation (and not the stethoscope per se, as might be inferred from Reiser's language) is predicated on a relativization of the human voice; the voice simply becomes one sound among many contending for the physician's attention in the audible world. Listening here moves from a way of apprehending speech to a technique of examination, a mode of constructing knowledge of patients independent of patients' knowledge of themselves or what they might say about themselves. Instead, the truth of their bodies is audible to the man at the other end of the instrument.

As with the shape of sound reproduction technologies themselves (in their divergence from earlier attempts to reproduce sound through automata), the pedagogy of mediate auscultation both marks and actively works toward a general shift from a privileging of the mouth, voice, and speech as the most important sonic location on the body to a diffusion of bodily sounds to be apprehended and sorted out in the ear. The voice becomes one contender among many for the trained auditor's attention. In any case, it is the only sound capable of speaking an untruth in Laennec's hermeneutic. Other sounds could conceivably mislead a physician and lead to misdiagnosis, but they would not deceive in the same way that speech could, since speech was ascribed a level of intentionality that other bodily sounds were not.

This displacement of the voice and the patient's own subjectivity goes even further, since auscultation was the only available method for apprehending the interiority of patients' bodies without physically cutting them up until the discovery of X-rays at the end of the nineteenth century. In fact, Reiser (1978: 36) goes so far as to say that the physician could 'in effect, autopsy the patient while alive', a statement that only makes sense given the privileged status of autopsy in the acquisition

of medical knowledge: while the dead patients lay forever muted, their
bodies could yield up immutable truth through the empiricist's skilful
use of the scalpel.

Thus, patients' speech and voices become relativized in the new
medical hermeneutic. This understanding of the voice as simply one
possible sonic aspect of the body is well illustrated in a small subsection
of Laennec's book dedicated to the auscultation of the voice in the
different regions of the lungs and throat. Here, he postulates a series of
acoustic states of the voice, each connected with a set of interior physical
conditions: broncophonism, aegophonism, and pectoriloquism are each
moments when the voice is conducted in a particular way through an
area of the chest. In this account, the whole thorax becomes a kind of
resonating chamber – the lungs, especially, become like the interior of
a musical instrument:

> the loose texture of the lungs, rendered still more rare by its intermixture
> with air, is a bad conductor of sound; and the softness of the bronchial
> branches, after they cease to be cartilaginous, renders them very unfit
> for its production; while the smallness of the caliber must render whatever
> sound is produced more acute and weaker in them than in the larger trunks.
> But if any one of these conditions is removed, and yet more, if several of
> them are so at the same time, the sound of the voice may become
> perceptible in the smaller bronchial tubes. (Laennec 1830: 38)

So the voice becomes a contender in a whole field of sounds; it may
reveal the truth of the patient's condition, but only if the physician
listens well after extensive practice. The *Treatise* consists of a preliminary
essay on methods of physical diagnosis, and a series of longer essays
on the actual diagnosis of different diseases of the thorax, the bronchia,
the lungs, the pleura (the membrane covering the lung and chest cavity),
the circulation, and the heart.

Thus, the discussion of the voice comes in the middle of a larger
methodological section of the *Treatise*, preceded by a discussion on the
mediate auscultation of respiration and followed by discussions of the
cough, 'rattle,' and 'metallic tinkling'. Laennec's discussion of the different modulations of the cough and respiration are similar to the voice.
However, the rattling and tinkling are only perceptible through the
stethoscope. These are, for Laennec, entirely new sounds – they can only
be described by analogy, although their definition is simple enough.
The rattle consists of 'all the sounds, besides those of health, which the
act of respiration gives rise to, from the passage of air through fluids

in the bronchia or lungs, or by its transmission through any of the air passages partially contracted' (Laennec 1830: 51). The metallic tinkling sounds like the object of its analogy, and is perceived through the stethoscope during speaking, breathing or coughing (Laennec 1830: 58). In addition to these basic divisions, Laennec proposes a whole set of pathological subcategories: the moist crepitous rattle, the mucous, or gurgling rattle, the dry sonorous rattle, the dry sibilous rattle, the dry crepitous rattle with large bubbles or crackling, utricular buzzing, amphoric resonance. In essence, he defines and classifies new sounds; the methodological introduction is a kind of acoustic lexicon of motion in the body. His object is an *animate* body, with each sound charting the space through which it moves. Is there fluid in the lungs? Is there an inflamed membrane? Has an area become hard or more porous? Even the simple directional movement of sound could provide important clues. In a widely cited case from the section on the voice, Laennec listens to the voice through the body of a patient displaying no outward symptoms of tuberculosis:

> [H]er voice seemed to come directly from the chest, and to reach the ear through the central canal of the instrument. This peculiar phenomenon was confined to the space of about an inch square, and was not discoverable in any other part of her chest. Being ignorant of the cause of this singularity, I examined with the view to its elucidation, the greater number of the patients in the hospital, and I found it in about twenty. Almost all these were consumptive cases in an advanced stage of the disease . . . The subsequent death, in the hospital, of the greater number of the individuals who had exhibited this phenomenon, enabled me to ascertain the correctness of my supposition: in every case I found excavations in the lungs, of various sizes, the consequence of the dissolution of tubercles, and all communicating with the bronchia by openings of different diameter. (Laennec 1830: 36–7)

He called this phenomenon *pectoriloquism* and proceeded to chart its perceptibility depending on the location of the lesion in the lung. Laennec's method treats the body as a collection of objects and flows all related to one another; a series of critical co-existences that can be mapped out and verified. His is an innovation of perception.

Here I offer an interpretation differing from Foucault's reading of pectoriloquism. He has sensory innovation in mind with his description of pathological anatomy as a kind of epistemic shift; yet Foucault too quickly attributes an epistemic shift to the genesis of a medical gaze:

in his argument, 'the ear and hand are merely temporary, substitute organs' for the eye; an assertion based on the prior assertion that 'spatial data by right of origin belong to the gaze' (Foucault 1973: 165). 'By right of origin' here is a bare assertion based on belief, rather than an observation on Foucault's part. Yet, even if we were to take Foucault's word for it,[5] and go on believing that sight is inherently a spatial sense and that (by implication) hearing is an inherently temporal sense, his assertion would still not stand up. As Laennec's description shows, it is precisely medical *audition* that renders pathological anatomy a science of the animate. No doubt its practice would continue to require visual verification through autopsy at the experimental level; but at the level of clinical practice, it was the technique of listening that did more than any other single technique to render the medical body as a dynamic field of action. The shift to audile examination opened up the possibility for treatment of the live subject: in many cases, diagnostic knowledge preceded any notion of a cure. Audition was a key modality in perceiving states of patients' bodies.

Positing the hybridization of senses – in this case operating under the sign of vision – is based on the assumption of a prior and particular functional separation of the sensorium, itself left uninterrogated. For Foucault's explanation to work, vision has to be a rational, technical, and spatial sense – and nothing more – whereas hearing has to be a temporal and non-technical sense – and nothing more. Yet, as Laennec's pedagogical language makes abundantly clear, the senses themselves can be trained and shaped to the needs of reason. It is not that hearing becomes more like the gaze in mediate auscultation; it is that both senses become tools of reason in nineteenth-century medical examination.

Extending Foucault's line of thinking, Lisa Cartwright (1995) subsumes medical perception under the sign of vision. She writes that cinema, in conjunction with more familiar nineteenth-century visual technologies, was central to the emergence of a 'distinctly modernist mode of representation in Western scientific and public culture – a mode geared to the temporal and spatial decomposition and reconfiguration of bodies as dynamic fields of action in need of regulation and control' (Cartwright 1995: xi). In her account, cinema was the first visual technology to offer the possibility of directly analysing the body in motion. Yet mediate auscultation was precisely the technique whereby the dead body of pathological anatomy first came back to life. In rendering the interiority of the body available to the physician's ear, it was very much geared toward the spatial decomposition of the body and its surfaces. In providing a means of assessing the motions of the chest – the thoracic cavity – it simultaneously rendered the body as active, and provided an instrument for the identification of actions as *pathological*. If the cinema was a tool of metaphoric vivisection, a tool for seeing inside the living body, of abstracting and cataloguing its functions, naming its orientations and processes; the very logic underlying medical-cinematic technique had grown up with mediate auscultation in the nineteenth century.

Sounds as Signs

The hydraulic hermeneutics of mediate auscultation was itself based on the new logic of signification established by pathological anatomy: as an attempt to systematize the sounds heard through the stethoscope into a codified set of diagnostic signs, Laennec's *Treatise* was one of the first attempts to develop a metalanguage of sound, a set of descriptions for the shape and texture of sounds that was independent of subjective experience (independently verifiable). This is the major thrust of Laennec's *Treatise*; it is also Laennec's most spectacular failure (as judged by physicians later in the century, which I discuss below). Ultimately, the promise of an acoustical lexicon went unfulfilled: as with concert audiences throughout the nineteenth century, the attempt to create a metalanguage of sound quickly became nothing more than a set of metaphors and unverifiable (and therefore unscientific) observations. Laennec's lexical dreams only served to reiterate the primacy of audile-diagnostic technique: method over fixed knowledge.

The transformation of clinical experience into diagnostic knowledge was the purpose of most of Laennec's *Treatise*; 640 of over 700 pages are devoted to detailed discussion of different illnesses in the thoracic region. Throughout, Laennec integrates the use of mediate auscultation into a comprehensive diagnostic method. The result is a sort of lexicon of the body: as it has been established that each sound corresponds with a physical condition, the physician's task is to learn to discern the sounds well enough to be able to diagnose the physical condition. Mediate auscultation, embodied in the stethoscope, becomes the mark of a new age in clinical diagnosis, yet its innovation is not simply in rendering what was previously imperceptible perceptible and thereby relevant. It was precisely the desire for an identifiable order in the resonant world of patients' bodies, an acoustic-thoracic hermeneutic of perceived sounds, which drove the early development of mediate auscultation.

Laennec's *Treatise* is a kind of medical semiotics, a particular under-standing of the relation between signifier and signified. Laennec explains the physical characteristics of each condition in some detail, accompanied by a discussion of symptoms that may be found in the patient, and signs that the physician may discover upon examination. Although Laennec devotes some space to treatment, these are the shortest sections in the *Treatise*. Take, for instance, this excerpt from his discussion of emphysema of the lungs:

'In the case of one lung being principally affected, the augmented sonorousness and increased size of this side, will discriminate the disease from all others, except pneumo-thorax, from which likewise, as will be shown when we come to treat of that disease, it can be readily distinguished' (Laennec 1830: 163). Surrounding that is a description of the different noises yielded up by emphysema of the lungs: in this case he treats the sound as a variation of the crepicious rattle with large bubbles (Laennec 1830: 162–3). Thus, the illness becomes identifiable through sound (as well as other observable phenomena).

If Laennec is assembling a semiotics of the body, he is doing so at multiple levels. The first, to use the language of Charles Sanders Peirce is the *symbolic* level, where the signified is referred to purely by con-vention – through the arbitrary structure of language (Peirce 1955: 112–13). Thus, for instance, pectoriloquism designates a very specific cond-ition of the lungs, as well as the location of that condition. As expected, the inability to find a semantico-referential correspondence between signifier and signified causes a good deal of confusion in Laennec's text. In his exploration of the heart and arteries, Laennec comes upon the bellows-sound, the name of which derives 'from the circumstances of its exactly resembling the noise produced by this instrument when used to blow the fire' (Laennec 1830: 566). Yet he cannot fix the bellows-sound in relation to a lesion in the body. For a few pages, he explores the variety of circumstances in which he encounters it, but each time his hypotheses are led astray; he is forced to a vague conclusion: 'for various reasons I consider this particular sound as owing to a real spasmodic contraction of the heart or arteries' (Laennec 1830: 569). The uncertainty here leads to further experiments and speculations, but no conclusive position is reached. The section ends with a call for further research and a caution against mistaking certain phenomena for the bellows-sound (Laennec 1830: 571–2). The sounds are signs:

The sounds which constitute signs represent certain physical conditions pertaining to the chest. The normal or healthy signs represent physical conditions existing when the organs are not affected by disease; the abnormal or morbid signs represent physical conditions which are deviations from those of health, being incident to the various diseases of the chest. The physical conditions represented by signs may be distinguished as normal or healthy, and abnormal or conditions. (Flint 1876: 14)

The treatise and those works that followed it, and more broadly the method of mediate auscultation itself, can be read as an attempt to set up a system of signs for the purposes of diagnosis. No doubt this is one of the reasons for Laennec's success where others like Auenbrugger before him had failed: in addition to inventing a new technique, he provided a complete guide for its use (Reiser 1978: 28; prior to the innovations of Josef Skoda later in the century, Laennec's teachings did not undergo significant innovation or revision). In fact, the rationalization, codification, and instrumentalization of the sounds produced through mediate auscultation are a key element of its modernity as a technique of listening. Sound operates in the service of science. Yet this attempt to codify is also the least credible aspect of Laennec's method.

By the late nineteenth century, many of Laennec's ideas about the symbolic relationship between sounds and signs came under fire. His typology of sounds was deemed inaccurate, and his notion of the correspondence between diseases and specific sounds was difficult to prove. German physician Josef Skoda attempted to reproduce many of Laennec's findings, and often found that the precision sought by Laennec did not exist. Skoda (1854) argued that each sound heard through auscultation and percussion could be traced to a physical alteration of the texture of the body, but each alternation could have been produced by one of several causes. Rather than diseases producing acoustic pathognomonic signs, each sound indicated nothing more and nothing less than a physical condition of the body. The physician's task was then to interpret the acoustic signs along with others to produce a proper diagnosis. By the late nineteenth century, Skoda's notion of diagnosis had eclipsed Laennec's (Reiser 1978: 28). Similarly, Flint would write that 'very few signs are directly diagnostic of any particular disease. They represents conditions not peculiar to one but common to several diseases' (Austin 1876: 34).

The signification produced by mediate auscultation is both iconic and indexical as well: it is iconic at the level of identifying the sounds themselves, and indexical at the level of the sounds relationship to the state of the body it is supposed to signify. One need only look at Laennec's descriptions of the sounds themselves: they are described by analogy: *like* a metallic rattling, *like* a bellows blowing on the fire, *like* a musical tune containing these notes. It would be for innovators and popularizers like Austin Flint to attempt to better codify the sound itself.

Flint began his textbook by arguing that sounds can be distinguished by pitch, intensity and quality. Using music as the analogy, he defined pitch as musical pitch, intensity as the volume or perceived degree of force, and quality as essentially, the sound's timbre — his analogy is to two different instruments playing the same note. Yet even this apparently more scientific language for the discussion of sound quickly degenerates back into analogy: 'there are some other points of difference; namely, the duration of certain sounds, their continuousness or otherwise, their apparent nearness to or distance from the ear, and their strong resemblance to particular sounds, such as *the bleating of the goat, the chirping of birds*, etc.' (Flint 1876: 32–3, emphasis added).

Although he claims that these additional sounds are of 'lesser importance' in diagnosis, even Flint's more abstract classifying scheme, in the last instance, resorts back to analogy for the most exact description. Having set up an analytical system, Flint retreats somewhat, insisting that sound can *only* be described by analogy. Other medical textbooks offer a more direct analogical approach, for instance suggesting that a most accurate imitation of the heartbeat is accomplished by

> Pronouncing in succession the syllables *lupp, dupp*. The first of these sounds, which is dull, deep and more prolonged than the second, coincides with the shock of the apex of the heart against the thorax, and immediately precedes the radial pulse . . . The second sound, which is sharper, shorter, and more superficial, has its maximum intensity nearly on a level with the third rib . . . These sounds, therefore, in addition to the terms first and second, have also been called inferior and superior, long and short, dull and sharp, systolic and diastolic – which expressions, so far as giving a name is concerned, are synonymous. (Bennett 1860: 55–6)

One could dismiss the author's obvious difficulties in description, arguing that all language is fundamentally metaphoric, so the analogy comes as no surprise. Yet this would conceal a double process in the pedagogy of mediate auscultation and listening to the body in general: the training to recognize the specificity of the sound in the stethoscope, and the training to use the sound in the stethoscope to recognize conditions in the patient's body. The language of analogy is a language of iconicity; the repetition of particular possessed characteristics in each sound. According to Peirce (1955: 102): 'Anything whatever, be it quality, existent individual, or law, is an Icon of anything, in so far as it is like that thing and used as a sign of it.' Of course the physicians are not listening for goats in their patients' bodies; but at the same time, they need some kind of language to describe what it is they *are* hearing. At the level of distinction, then, there initially exists no metalanguage of sound in the body. Laennec's definitions, and the definitions of those who followed, began to move from the iconic to the symbolic, the naming characteristics of sounds – the various rattles, pectoriloquism, bronchiophonism, etc. Yet even these names aren't purely abstract descriptions of the characteristics of the sound; they are simply names designating a set of common experiences. Doctors would have to wait for others to develop a purely analytical language of sound.[6]

The main effect of this absent metalanguage was that mediate auscultation could never be fully abstracted from experience; a full and complete treatise could not be written.[7] Thus, another discourse accompanies the lexicography of mediate auscultation: a discourse of clinical experience and refinement of technique. Throughout, Laennec chides the 'inexperienced observer'; pitfalls in diagnosis can largely be overcome through clinical experience. Forbes, in his introduction to Laennec's *Treatise*, summarizes the position, a common one in medical pedagogy:

> It is only by long and painful trials, (*inter toedia et labores*, as Auenbrugger says of his congenerous discovery) that any useful practical knowledge can be acquired. When, therefore, we hear, as we sometimes do, that certain persons have *tried the stethoscope*, and abandoned it upon finding it useless or deceptive; and when we learn, on inquiry, that *the trial* has extended merely to the hurried examination of a few cases, within the period of a few days or weeks, we can only regret that such students should have been so misdirected, or should have so misunderstood the fundamental principles of the method. (Forbes in Laennec 1830: p. vi, emphasis in original)

Nothing will substitute for the experience of extensive clinical practice and training; nothing will substitute for the sustained experience of hearing through the stethoscope. Later writers would concur: 'I have to suppose that you have made your ears familiar with these sounds' (Bennett 1860: 52; Flint 1876: 69–70 also insists that practice is essential to effective diagnosis). 'Of the peculiar quality of any particular sound, one can form no definite idea otherwise than by experience' (Flint 1876: 31). Clinical experience was institutionalized in medical pedagogy as a way of guaranteeing a kind of common experience, a certain practice of practical knowledge. The goal of clinical experience, then, was to at once render medical knowledge more true and more present through its immediate perception – hearing the rattle, seeing the lesion on the lung – and at the same time transform abstract knowledge into a very specific kind of practical knowledge.

Thus, the sign created by clinical medicine was not simply a *symbol* of an interior state, but aspired to be an index of that state, an absolute accompaniment. Indexical signs accompany their object in experience; an index is a sign which refers to its object not so much because of any similarity or analogy with it, nor because it is associated with the general characteristics which that object happens to possess, but because it is in dynamical (including spatial) connection both with the individual object, on the one hand, and with the senses or memory of the person for whom it serves as a sign on the other (Peirce 1955: 107).

Instrumentalized, the sounds 'discovered' through mediate auscultation are connected with the interior states of the body – in the experience of the well-trained physician, they become indices.

For instance, Flint argues against any kind of abstract formalization beyond the experience of cultivating a clinical technique:

> If we undertake to decide, *a priori*, that certain sounds must be produced by percussion and auscultation when certain conditions are present, we shall be led into error; and so, equally if we undertake to conclude from the nature of the sounds that they represent certain conditions. The only reliable method is to analyse the sounds with differences relating especially to pitch, intensity and quality, and to determine different signs by these differences, the import of each being then established by the constancy of association with physical conditions. *It is by this analytical method only that the distinctive characters of signs can be accurately and clearly ascertained.* (Flint 1876: 33, emphasis added)

Thus, for the sounds produced by mediate auscultation to signify properly – that is to say, indexically – it demands a facility with technique, a certain level of virtuosity. It is not a simple matter of a lexical or formal correspondence, but rather learning the feel of a set of coincidences; learning which events coexist with which other events: 'preconceived notions frequently oppose themselves to the reception of the truth, and have to be got rid of before the real state of matters can be ascertained. Hence the great importance of deriving your first impressions of the sounds to be heard by auscultation, not from books or lectures, but from the living body itself' (Bennett 1860: 31). Indeed, both Skoda and Laennec understood that the sounds perceived through mediate auscultation were themselves produced by the conditions they indexed. The institutionalization of practice also carried with it the construction of normalcy. While Laennec's earlier treatise deals entirely with pathological signs, Flint's innovation was to begin medical education with the healthy body; to construct a set of normal positions from which the diseased body deviated (Davis 1981: 90). Indeed, Flint and others argued that such knowledge of the healthy body was a necessary precursor to diagnosis of disease. Without it, the physician ran a serious risk of misdiagnosis. Once again, this position was based in the privileging of clinical experience over a system of abstracted and therefore objectifiable signs (Flint 1876: 69–70).

One of the early complaints against Laennec and his method was that there were simply too many fine gradations of sound for any single person to master, that Laennec's own claims for the stethoscope were far too grand. As Skoda and others later demonstrated, they were. But the difficulty of learning proper auscultation contributed to its value, made it a mark of initiation, a form of virtuosity: 'No one who has once mastered its difficulties, and who cultivates his profession in that spirit which its high importance and dignity demand, will ever regret the pains taken to overcome them, or willingly forego the great advantages which he has thereby acquired' (Forbes, in Laennec 1830: p. vii).

Certainly, as this passage might suggest, the technique of mediate auscultation should be considered as part of the larger experiential approach to medical education at this time, especially as it relates to the professionalization of medicine; but in addition to rendering virtuosity a proper skill of the virtuous professional, it also depends on the more basic assertion that audition is a skill to be cultivated as well as refined for scientific purposes. A skilled doctor had to have a highly developed sense of hearing.

Over the course of the nineteenth century, the stethoscope became the hallmark of medical modernity. 'Within the nineteenth century the instrument had been applied to every cavity and organ in the body' (Davis 1981: 108). The development of mediate auscultation applied medical and scientific reason to listening, just as a particular practice of hearing the body became integral to everyday functioning of medicine. Part of physicians' elevated cultural status at the end of the century was based in the valuation of the skills specific to their profession. They were, oddly enough, virtuoso listeners; they could hear the body in ways inaccessible to lay people: 'auscultation helped to create the objective physician, who could move away from involvement with the patient's experiences and sensation, to a more detached relation, less with the patient but with the sounds from within the body' (Reiser 1978: 38). Mediate auscultation was an artifact of a new approach to reason and the senses, in which listening moved away from the ideal of spoken exchanges between doctor and patient into the quiet, rhythmic, sonorous clarity of rationality.

Notes

1. Although the entry lists the earliest medical use of the term in English in 1833, it is likely that the term was already in common medical usage when John Forbes first translated Laennec's *Treatise on Mediate Auscultation* into English.

2. For the most part, stethoscope construction in the nineteenth century was not heavily based on the principles of acoustics. Although the instrument embodied a basic principle of acoustics, none of the more advanced thinking concerning acoustics was applied until the turn of the century. Additionally, starting in the 1890s, inventors sought to incorporate new sound reproduction technologies into the stethoscope – most notably, sound recording and electrical amplification (Davis 1981: 109).

3. Of course, the taking of medical history continues down to the present day, but it exists as only one of an array of techniques to be used in medical diagnosis. It is a residual technique.

4. Reiser (1978: 167–8) argues that the emerging predominance of laboratory medicine led to the decline of physical examination, because the latter was seen as less precise and more time consuming; the eclipse of mediate auscultation by other diagnostic methods should be understood in this context. Of course, as with patient histories, the stethoscope remains in current use, but its general importance in accurate diagnosis has greatly diminished.

5. Which is not to say we should believe him. Moreover, as the work of Truax and Feld show, as well as the evidence presented here, audition is very much a spatial sense. Foucault's later work on the confessional in the *History of Sexuality Volume 1* would also rely on an understanding of listening as a spatial sense.

6. The analytical language of sound remains incomplete to this day. While all sorts of aspects of visual phenomena can be described in abstract language (for example, shape, colour, texture, size), apart from the technical language

of engineers and others who work with sound, there exists no commonly used equivalent to describe the texture, shape, density, timbre or rhythm of sound. While there are specialized analytical languages of sound used by musicians, engineers, and others, none has achieved the kind of general currency that abstractions of visual phenomena have in everyday language use.

7. Of course, in order for the linguistic abstraction of vision also requires experience, but that experience is then represented at a more general level in language (for example, through discussion of shape and colour and so forth).

References

Auenbrugger, L. (1936), 'On Percussion of the Chest', translated by J. Forbes, *Bulletin of the History of Medicine*, 4: 373–403.

Barth, J.-B.-P. and Roger, H. (1847), *Practical Treatise on Auscultation*, translated by Patrick Newbigging, Lexington KY: Scrugham & Dunlop.

Bennett, J. H. (1860), *Clinical Lectures on the Principles and Practice of Medicine*, New York: Samuel S. & William Wood.

Cartwright, L. (1995), *Screening the Body: Tracing Medicine's Visual Culture*, Minneapolis: University of Minnesota Press.

Cowan, R. S. (1983), *More Work for Mother: The Ironies of Household Technology from the Open Hearth to the Microwave*, New York: Basic Books.

Crary, J. (1990), *Techniques of the Observer: On Vision and Modernity in the Nineteenth Century*, Cambridge: MIT Press.

Davis, A. B. (1981), *Medicine and Its Technology: An Introduction to the History of Medical Instrumentation*, Westport CT: Greenwood Press.

Feld, S. (1994), 'Aesthetics as Iconicity of Style (uptown title) or (downtown title) "Lift-up-over-sounding": Getting into the Kaluli Groove', in C. Keil and S. Feld, *Music Grooves*, Chicago: University of Chicago Press.

Flint, A. (1876), *A Manual of Percussion and Auscultation; of the Physical Diagnisus of Diseases of the Lungs and Heart, and of Thoracic Aneurism*, Philadelphia: Henry C. Lea.

Forbes, J. (1824), *Original Cases With Descriptions and Observations Illustrating the Use of the Stethoscope and Percussion in the Diagnosis of Diseases of the Chest; Also Commentaries on the Same Subjects Selected and Translated from Auenbrugger, Corvisart, Laennec, and others*, London: Printed for T. and G. Underwood, Fleet Street.

Foucault, M. (1973), *The Birth of the Clinic: An Archaeology of Medical Perception*, translated A.M. Sheridan Smith, New York: Pantheon Books.

—— (1978), *The History of Sexuality, Volume I: An Introduction*, New York: Vintage Books.

Laennec, R. T. H. (1830), *A Treatise on The Diseases of the Chest and on Mediate Auscultation*, 3rd edition, translated J. Forbes, New York: Samuel Wood & Sons, and Collins & Hannay.

Peirce, C. S. (1955), *Philosophical Writings of Peirce. Selected, Edited and with an Introduction by Justus Buchler*, New York: Dover Publications.

Reiser, S. J. (1978), *Medicine and the Reign of Technology*, Cambridge: Cambridge University Press.

Skoda, J. (1854), *Auscultation and Percussion*, translated W. O. Markham, Philadelphia: Lindsay & Blakiston.

Starr, P. (1982), *The Social Transformation of American Medicine*, New York: Basic Books.

Sterne, J. (2001), 'A Machine to Hear for Them: On the Very Possibility of Sound's Reproduction', *Cultural Studies* 15: 259–94.

Truax. B. (1984), *Acoustic Communication*, New York: Ablex Publishing.

Wise, J. M. (1997), *Exploring Technology and Social Space*, Thousand Oaks: Sage Press.

Part III

Anthropologies of Sound

Steven Feld asks in his chapter how might anthropology "help us to imagine auditory cultures as historical formations of distinct sensibilities'. Feld's work enables us to hear the greater symmetry of the Kaluli soundworld and its efforts to adapt to a changing socio-political world within which it finds itself. Feld's hope is that an anthropology of sound might give a voice to the marginalised of the world. Feld's work has a definitive place in the comparative study of soundscapes, a process that Feld terms 'acoustemology' by which he means the investigation into 'the primacy of sound as a modality of knowing and being in the world'.

Cora Bender provides just such an acoustemology through the study of the role of the powwow amongst the Ojibwa Indians of Winscontin. She analyses the role of the powwow in cementing contemporary Native American identity and, paradoxically, their US nationalistic affiliation. In doing so, Bender provides both a cultural history of the powwow and an ethnographic analysis of powwow celebrations. She demonstrates the central role that the powwow plays in the re-appropriation and re-integration of Native American communities, describing its enacting in terms of a renewed source of cultural pride and as an integrator of cultural values that is essentially pan-Indian and cross generational.

Just as the sounds of the powwow act as a unifying force amongst the Ojibwa Indians so Paul Moore describes the divisive sectarian sounds of the drum in Northern Ireland. Moore describes how the sounds of sectarianism structure the year for both Protestants and Catholics in Belfast. The annual activities of marching and drumming evoke cultural memories of presence and colonisation for Protestants in Northern Ireland, sounds which are equally anathema to Catholics in Belfast. Moore analyses how these divisive cultural sounds exist in close proximity to one another, re-inforcing notions of cultural difference and separateness. Moore argues that the sounds of the Protestant community have invariably been associated with industrialism whilst the sounds of Catholicism are associated with the lyricism of pre-industrialisation which is reflected in the rhythms of speech amongst Irish Catholics.

Tacchi's chapter provides an interesting example of the contribution that media anthropology can have in the investigation of contemporary consumer soundworlds. Tacchi investigates the role that radio plays in the daily lives of users in its establishment of 'affective rhythms in the home'. She concentrates upon the routine nature of use (radio as a daily presence) and focuses upon the place of memory and nostalgia that radio plays in the daily lives of her users. Tacchi distinguishes between the visualising memory and the mood or feelings of memory evoked by sound. Radio users often think about their narratives through music or the sounds of the radio that evoke feelings of there past. Tacchi describes radio users as managing their day and moods through radio listening. Tacchi refers to the radio as providing 'the taste of sound' within the daily household of users. The radio thus provides a valuable link, 'a productive engagement with wider society'. In doing so she argues that radio use amongst her sample population demonstrates a desire for coherence and order in the personal narrative of users operationalised through the use of memory, fantasy and nostalgia. She argues that the role of nostalgia need not be verifiable in 'actual' experience but functions equally well in the 'glow' of imaginary states of recollection. The sound nature of the medium of the radio thus offers a more imaginative platform for the self than visually based media such as television.

12

A Rainforest Acoustemology*

Steven Feld

What role can anthropological inquiry have in shaping the discourse of acoustic ecology and soundscape studies? How might it help us imagine auditory culture(s) as historical formations of distinct sensibilities, as sonic geographies of difference? One way to answer is with the simple observation that anthropologists tend toward the Kantian view that all knowledge begins in experience. To jump off that cliff is to study how human experiential patterns and practices construct the habits, systems of belief, knowledge and action we call 'culture'. The pressing issue of concern is with human inventions and sensibilities, with adequately and evocatively representing different experiential worlds. To take up that concern the anthropological project basically must ask, what could it possibly be like to be – to feel, sense, imagine, act, become – a certain kind of person? Deep down the hope is that by giving marginalized voices places to speak and shout and sing from, anthropology can in some measure counter the long-standing arrogance of colonial and imperial authority, of history written in one language, in one voice, as one narrative. This chapter is about giving some voice one kind of alternate reality, one kind of sonic sensibility that I have encountered through anthropological inquiry into a language, music, and acoustic ecology.

* An earlier version of this chapter appeared as part of the article 'Sound Worlds' in Patricia Kruth and Henry Stobart (eds) (2000) *Sound,* Cambridge: Cambridge University Press, pp. 173–200. Reproduced with permission. For more on acoustemology, see also Feld (1996b).

Locating Place as a Global Time-Space

The Kaluli are one of four groups of 2,000 Bosavi people who live in the tropical rainforest of the Great Papuan Plateau in the Southern Highlands Province of Papua New Guinea. On several hundred square miles of lowland and mid-montane forest land, at an altitude of about 2,000 feet, they hunt, fish, gather, and tend land-intensive swidden gardens. Their staple food is sago, processed from wild palms that grow in shallow swamps and creeks branching off of larger river arteries that flow downward from Mt Bosavi, the collapsed cone of an extinct volcano reaching 8,000 feet.

Bosavi was once relatively easy to describe as a classless and small-scale society, inasmuch as no traditionally fixed occupational specializations, stratifications, ranks, professions, ascribed or achieved statuses formed the basis for social differentiation. Life was also generally egalitarian in matters economic and political. With no appointed or elected leaders, speakers, chiefs, bosses, or controllers, the Kaluli people hunted, gathered, gardened, and worked to produce what they needed, taking care of themselves, their neighbours and kin through extensive cooperation in food sharing and labour assistance. The egalitarian dynamics here involved both a lack of centralized social institutions and a lack of deference to persons, roles, categories, or groups based on power, position, or material ownership (E. L. Schieffelin 1976; B. B. Schieffelin 1990).

Hierarchy developed dramatically around the social changes that have more recently refigured Kaluli life, beginning with the advent of colonial government contact, particularly by the late 1950s. But it was evangelical missions that brought sweeping changes to the Bosavi area, beginning in the mid-1960s with the construction of an airstrip. In the early 1970s, the first resident fundamentalist missionaries arrived. A new wave of national government impact followed after Papua New Guinea's independence in 1975. Into the 1980s and 1990s, the presence of a second airstrip, a hospital, schools, aid post stations, mission station, and government development personnel, and particularly local pastors in each village, has introduced increasingly complex forms of deference based on differentiated wealth, particularly with a cash base (B. B. Schieffelin 2000, E. L. Schieffelin 1991).

Currently the Bosavi area is in the throes of a more complex set of changes that implicate cultural and ecological futures. Oil and gas projects are already transforming the surrounding region, and demands and debates about local logging, road access to the area, and large-scale development projects are current. With these have come the chaotic responses that occasional but large infusions of cash and material wealth bring following sporadic patterns of out-migration. The overall effect is the promotion of broader bases of conflict around real, perceived, and possible inequities, and the escalation of unequal access to power and resources along lines of gender, age, multilingualism, and Christian-ization (E. L Schieffelin 1997).

From the Anthropology of Sound to Acoustemology

My own engagement with the Bosavi region over the last 20 years is complexly situated in this history. In 1976 I went to Bosavi because I had heard the first tape recordings from the area, made by Edward L. Schieffelin in 1966–8. I was taken by the musicality of Kaluli expression, but particularly by the relationship of that musicality to the sounds of the rainforest, initially described by Schieffelin in his 1976 book *The Sorrow of the Lonely and the Burning of the Dancers*. It was that relationship that I wanted to investigate.

The general hypothesis that people in some way echo their sound-scape in language and music was first developed by R. Murray Schafer in his 1977 book *The Tuning of the World*, a synthesis of the ideas developed during his time as director of the World Soundscape Project and Simon Fraser University. In that book he develops the concepts of 'soundscape' and 'acoustic ecology', and analyses trends in the trans-formations of sound environments through history. The work of Schafer and his colleagues was broad and stimulating, and invited anthropo-logical and ethnomusicological scrutiny in grounded field studies.

With this in mind, during my first Bosavi research in the 1970s I developed the idea of an ethnography of sound, or study of sound as a symbolic system, an acultural system, in order to relate the importance of acoustic ecology, particularly the avain rainforest soundscape, to the musicality and poetics of Bosavi laments and vocal song. The mediation between this rainforest ecology and Bosavi music turned out to be cosmological, for Kaluli consider birds not just singers but spirits of their dead. Birds appear to one another and speak as people, and to the living their presence is a constant reminder of histories of human loss, an absence made present in sound and motion. The relationship between the construction and evocation of local expressive forms, and the bird world they metaphorized, was a deeply emotional one. From this, I found, came the great aesthetic force of Kaluli lament, poetics and song performance, the subjects of my first research (Feld 1990/1982).

In my subsequent Bosavi research, a growing concern with place, poetic cartography, and everyday meanings of the Bosavi sound world has pushed the idea of sound as a cultural system somewhat farther, toward what I called acoustemology. In one sense this step is a natural development in my concern to understand the place-name maps in Bosavi songs, and how vocal performance articulates their poetic and ecological relationship to the sounds and meanings of the rainforest. But I've also taken this step in critical response to research in acoustic ecology that artificially separates sonic environments from the pervasiveness of human invention. Soundscapes, no less than landscapes, are not just physical exteriors, spatially surrounding or apart from human activity. Soundscapes are perceived and interpreted by human actors who attend to them as a way of making their place in and through the world. Soundscapes are invested with signficance by those whose bodies and lives resonate with them in social time and space. Like landscapes, they are as much psychical as physical phenomena, as much cultural constructs as material ones (Casey 1996).

By acoustemology I wish to suggest a union of acoustics and epistemology, and to investigate the primacy of sound as a modality of knowing and being in the world. Sound both emanates from and penetrates bodies; this reciprocity of reflection and absorption is a creative means of orientation – one that tunes bodies to places and times through their sounding potential. Hearing and producing sound are thus embodied competencies that situate actors and their agency in particular historical worlds. These competencies contribute to their distinct and shared ways of being human; they contribute to possibilities for and realizations of authority, understanding, reflexivity, compassion, and identity.

Following the lead established by Maurice Merleau-Ponty's *Phenomenology of Perception*, then echoed in Don Ihde's *Listening and Voice: A Phenomenology of Sound*, my notion of acoustemology means to explore the reflexive and historical relationships between hearing and speaking, listening and sounding. This reflexivity is embodied doubly: one hears oneself in the act of voicing, and one resonates the physicality of voicing in acts of hearing. Listening and voicing are in a deep reciprocity, an embodied dialogue of inner and outer sounding and resounding built from the historicization of experience. The ongoing dialogue of self and self, self and other, of their interplay in action and reaction, are thus constantly sited at the sense of sound, absorbed and reflected, given and taken in constant exchange. The soundingness of hearing and voicing constitute an embodied sense of presence and of memory. Voice then authorizes identities as identities authorize voice. Voice is evidence, embodied as experiential authority, performed to the exterior or interior as a subjectivity made public, mirrored in hearing as public made subjective.

Sound as a Poetic Cartography

How might an acoustemological perspective on voice and place help reveal the connection between the powerful locality of the Bosavi sound world and its global emplacement? To begin, Bosavi songs are textually constituted as poetic cartographies of rainforest trails. This notion of 'poetic cartographies' is clearly delimited in local compositional and vocal practices around four concepts. These are *tok*, 'paths' of connected localities, whose *sa-salan*, 'inside speaking' or poetic revelation, consists of *bale to*, 'turned over words', metaphors, and *go:no: to*, 'sound words', mimetic phonesthemes. Making song 'paths' is how Kaluli people sing the forest as a poetic fusion of space and time where lives and events are conjoined as vocalized, embodied memories (Feld 1990).

The importance of sound and voice to these memorial and performative practices cannot be overstated. That is because while much of the forest is visually hidden, sound can't be hidden. Acoustic revelatory presence is always in tension with visual hidden presence in everyday experiences of the forest. This sensory tension between the seen and heard, the hidden and revealed, is itself poeticized in two synesthetic metaphors Kaluli use to link forest emplacement to its aesthetic evocation. These are locally known as *dulugu ganalan*, 'lift-up-over sounding', and *a:ba:lan*, 'flowing' (Feld 1994, 1996a, b).

'Lift-up-over-sounding' glosses the seamlessly staggered alternations and overlaps that comprise the sensual experience of the rainforest soundscape. One hears no unision in nature. In the tropical forest height and depth are easily confused, and the lack of visual cues make depth often sensed as the diffuseness of height moving outward. 'Lift-up-over sounding' precisely yet suggestively codes that ambiguous sensation: upward feels like outward. This placing of sound is simultaneously a sounding of place. One knows the time of day, season of year, and placement in relative physical space through the sensual wrap-around of sound in the forest. This way of hearing and sensing the world is mirrored in the production of Kaluli song, where voices overlap and echo with surrounding forest sounds, with instruments, or with other voices to create a dense, multilayered, alternating and interlocking form of expression.

'Lift-up-over sounding' is as potentially omnipresent in the experiences and aesthetics of the Kaluli world as 'harmony' is in the experiences and aesthetics of the West. Like 'harmony', 'lift-up-over sounding' is a grand metaphor modelling sonic relations, the way tones combine together in space and time, as well as social relations, the ways people interact in concert. Whether it is the birds, insects, winds and water-courses of the forest, or the vocalizing of Kaluli, or the overlap and interplay of the two, 'lift-up-over sounding' always comes across as in synchrony but out of phase. By this I mean that however cohesive, 'lift-up-over sounding' always seems to be composed of sound sources at different points of displacement from any momentary or hypothetical sense of unison.

Neither a clear-cut heterophony or polyphony, 'lift-up-over sounding' is more an echophony where one sound may stand out momentarily, then fade into the distance, overlapped or echoed by a new or repeated emergence in the auditory mosaic. The Kaluli concept of 'echo' helps reveal this idea of presence and diffusion. In the Bosavi language 'echo' is represented by the mimetic phonestheme *gugu-go:go:*. *Gu* denotes downward moving sound; reduplicated, *gugu* marks the action as continuous. *Go:* likewise denotes outward moving sound; reduplicated, *go:go:* also marks the action as continuous. So the auditorally ambiguous interplay of continuous downward and continuous outward moving sound is what is heard and felt as echo. In its constant play of immediacy and vagueness, *gugu go:go:* is an ever-present soundmark of the up-is-over forest soundscape.

A similarity of convergences characterizes the metaphorical potency of *a:ba:lan*, 'flowing.' 'Flowing' first glosses the sensuous presence of water moving through and connecting rainforest lands. As it does so, water moves in and out of visual presence and immediacy, yet it always remains audible even when invisible. The local forests are multiply criss-crossed by creeks running off from the high mountain streams of Mt Bosavi. In the mid-montane foothills, one cannot walk for more than a few minutes in any direction without crossing water of some variety. As one walks, these waterways constantly disappear and re-emerge through densities of forest shrubs, hills, and treelines. 'Flowing' is this ever-emerging and receding presence, this constancy of water moving and resounding through and figuring the ground.

'Flowing' equally characterizes the on-and-off, emerging and fading, circulatory motion of a song or songs. Whether within perceptual immediacy or long held in mind, 'flowing' is the lingering grip of a song's images, its progression of sounds and words that stay in mind.

The Western metaphorical counterpart to Kaluli 'flowing' is the 'broken record', the sound that does not turn off but stays with a listener. These are both metaphors for an embodied repeating.

Kaluli notions of 'flow' converge in the vocal performance of songs whose texts are forest 'paths' of named places. Singing a sequence of named places is a way of taking listeners on a journey 'flowing' along local waterways and through contiguous lands. The flow of these poetic song 'paths' signals the connectedness of Bosavi places to people, experiences, and memories. The 'flowing' nature of waters through lands, then, mirrors the 'flowing' nature of songs and places through local biographies and histories.

Song 'paths' derive experientially from everyday life, where people travel through the forest by foot to and from their home longhouse community, going to gardens, to sago places, or to other longhouse communities. Everyday experiences of the forest always involve the intermeshed experience of lands and waters. The most significant kinds of land formations come from the images of *fele*, 'thighs', attached to a *do:m*, 'body'. 'Thighs' are the relatively flatter lands rolling off and downward to either side. These 'thighs' are reached from hilly segments of ascent, descent, and roll-off in the land that are its 'body' sides.

This sense of land as a grounded 'body' of sides and 'thighs' is closely related to the lay and motion of forest waterways. Walking a 'body' implies water below; once crossed there is another 'body' to climb on the other side. Likewise, 'thighs' usually have one or more *eleb*, 'heads' of waters lying off or below to either side. In other words, water reclines, moves along a body lying, typically flowing, downstream along its 'thighs.'

These images construct a world where the body is imagined like the curves of land between, around and over which water flows. Moreover, as these primal landforms are connected like thighs to the body, so the passage of water through them flows like the motion of voice. Voice flows by resounding through the body, feelingfully connecting its contiguous physical segments, sensually resonating throughout. This 'flowing' mirrors that of water through land, with its multiple presences across and along a variety of relatively contiguous but physically distinct forms. The 'flowing' of water and of voice moves through lands and bodies to link their segments and reveal their wholeness.

At their conjunction 'lift-up-over-sounding' and 'flowing' indicate the remarkable creativity with which Kaluli absorb and respond to the sensuousness of the rainforest environment. 'Lift-up-over sounding' naturalizes song form and performance by way of its resonance with the forest world. Likewise, 'flowing' naturalizes poetic cartography as the performance of biographical memory. Together these ideas fuse spatial and temporal experience, link everyday pasts and presents, join the powers of place and of journey. Most importantly, 'lift-up-over sounding' and 'flowing' directly emplace this world not just in texts, but in the reflexive relationship of voicing to hearing. Three case studies follow as illustration.

Singing in and out of Place

First, from a Kaluli ceremonial song genre called *ko:luba*, consider (and hear on Feld 1991, track 10) a song composed by Bifo of the community of Suguniga. This item was one of 90 songs sung at an all night *ko:luba* ceremony when Suguniga visited the community of Sululeb on 5 July 1982.

For *ko:luba*, 12 costumed singer-dancers coupled in various pairs to sing from early evening until dawn; typically about 100 songs were sung in the course of the evening's performance. Each song was repeated in succession five times, first at the rear of the longhouse's main corridor, then in its centre, then in the front, then back again in the centre, and finally back to the rear. In between renditions the dancers moved with a skipping step from one house position to another.

Through each performance the pairs faced one another and moved up and down in place, rhythmically accompanying themselves through both the pulse of their heels bouncing on the longhouse floor, the indexical sounds of costume leaves and feathers in motion, and the up-and-down flapping of a rattle of crayfish claws (*degegado*, named for the clacking sound) arching out of dance belts in the rear of the costume. The costume and dance created a 'lift-up-over-sounding' effect, overlapping the voices. Audience members packed the house and crowded the dance floor. Attendants stood behind and to the side of the dancers to light them with resin torches.

Ko:luba songs consist of a refrain and verses. The refrain repeats a melody and text; this alternates with the verses, which consist of a second melody whose text slightly varies with each repetition. In the Kaluli language the refrain is called the *mo:*, meaning 'trunk' or 'base,' and the verses are called *dun*, 'branches.' *Ko:luba* songs could thus be said to 'branch' out in verses from their 'trunk' or refrain. Here we see how a forest image is poeticized, bringing the sense of locale together with the sensuousness of vocal and dance performance.

Bifo composed his song in the weeks prior to the ceremony at Sululeb; at the ceremony he sang it paired with Wasio, in the 'lift-up-over sounding' fashion where the first voice is echoed and overlapped by the second, singing the exact same melody and text. During the song's very first voicing, while dancing at the rear house position, a man named Hasele loudly burst into tears and continued to cry periodically throughout the song's performance. He cited the names of his brothers as a text to his melodic wept vocalizations. Finally he rushed out to the dance floor with a resin torch, and as the song continued, burned Bifo's back in retaliation for the pain and grieving the song had caused him.

Hasele's intense grief derived from the personal poignancy of Bifo's song. In 1971 Hasele and his two brothers Seligiwo: and Molugu left Bosavi and went to work on a labour contract near Rabaul, a colonial centre far from Bosavi, off the New Guinea mainland on the outlying island of New Britain. Hasele returned to Bosavi the following year, but his brothers stayed near Rabaul. They have never returned to Bosavi, nor have they been heard from again.

mo:	*'trunk'*
uwo:lo	riflebird (*Ptiloris magnificus*) calling
Bolekini uwo:lo:	calling from Bolekini
uwo:lo:	uwo:lo: is calling
wo: wo:	crying out wo: wo:
dun	*'branches'*
Go:go:bo: nabe	could I eat at Go:go:bo:?
ne sago:lomakeya	I have no cousin (there)
ni imolobe	I'm starving
wo: wo:	crying out wo: wo:

With each rendition the song would go through four or five repetitions. Successive 'branches' from the 'trunk' poetically create both a physical map and a social one by the use of alternate placenames and relationship terms. The placenames Mosbi (Pt Moresby), Rabal (Rabaul), and Medi (Mendi) alternate in the first line of successive branches, substituting for Go:go:bo:. These are distant cities known to few Kaluli. In parallel, the relationship terms *no:* (mother), *nao* (brother), and *ada:* (older sister/younger brother) alternate in the second line, substituting for *sago:* (cousin). The poetics of the 'branches' thus play on an ironic parallelism, where successively named places become farther distant and hence more dangerous and lonely, as successively named social relations become closer and hence more familial and secure. Food is the idiom and medium par excellence of Kaluli hospitality, sharing, sociability and relationship, as discussed in Bambi B. Schieffelin's 1990 ethnography, *The Give and Take of Everyday Life*. Food is central to these poetic 'branches' as well; spatial distance and social loss are equated with the pain of starving.

This parallelism of place and social relationship in the song's 'branches' plays off the central 'trunk' image, the longhouse site of Hasele's family, where a lone riflebird (*Ptiloris magnificus*), the spirit bird of the singer, calls in the bird sound words of its onomatopoeic name, *uwo:lo:*. As the 'branches' travel further and further away, the 'trunk' brings the song back, and holds it in a familiar lived-in place. This way the song's form becomes one with its content, producing an image of a lifeworld that is both spatial, with places reaching out and coming back, and temporal, with duration creating a journey of loss.

While Bifo's song was the only one in this particular *ko:luba* that cited placenames from the world beyond Bosavi, the technique was hardly new in 1982. I had heard similar songs in the mid 1970s, songs including names deriving from the first experiences of labour contracts, when Bosavi men left the area in the mid to late 1960s. Nonetheless, Bifo's song was clearly startling and instant in its powers of evocation, and its performance illustrates how singing names of remote places can be as powerfully charged as singing those that are intimately familiar. They also indicate how the Kaluli were quick to extend their song maps to include new worlds both gained and lost.

Listening to a tape playback of this song with me in August of 1992, Hasele nodded his head and smiled gently as he heard himself cry for his brothers. When the song finished, he shrugged his shoulders, swallowed, and said, *sowo: o:ngo: emele mo:mieb ko:lo:*, 'they're like the dead, they won't come back.'

This song's text, performance, and impact speak to local memories of Australian colonial practices of importing rural and remote labourers to coastal plantations in the former territories of Papua and New Guinea. In Bosavi these practices arrived within 30 years of first contact, 15 years of the first colonial census, and almost immediately upon the building of a first local airstrip in 1964. The places whose names locally signify the colony beyond are intensely poeticized, made to evoke the connection between labour and loss, distance and distress. History, region, and remote worlds beyond everyday experience are made local, and take on the sense of being close by, palpably immediate. The sound world of Bosavi becomes the entire space and time of a remote region encapsulated within a colonial territory. As the territory absorbs the Kaluli world, the Kaluli absorb the territory by poetically appropriating its place names into their language, song, and singing. Once voiced, these place names are committed to memory. Local voices know these places; they have heard and felt them resonating through their bodies and through their land. Like water through land and voice through the body, names 'flow,' and in so doing they signal how local knowledge is memorially embodied as vocal knowledge.

What are Your Names?

Bifo's song arose in the male-centred world of Kaluli ceremonies, the part of Kaluli life most strongly associated with male ritual expression. But in laments and in songs for work and leisure Kaluli women voiced similar concerns with place and social memory. In August 1990, Ulahi, the featured composer of the *Voices of the Rainforest* CD, invited me to Wo:lo creek, one of her favourite singing spots, to record some of her new songs. At the conclusion of one of her songs, a *gisalo*, Ulahi spontaneously launched into a fragment that was improvised in the moment (heard on Feld 1991, track six, song two).

wo: wo:	calling out
ni America kalu-o-e	my America men
gi wi o:ba-e	what are your names?
ni Australia gayo-o-e	my Australia women
gi wi o:ba-e	what are your names?
ni America kalu-o-e	my America men
wo: wo:	(calling out)
ni America kalu-o- wo: wo:	my America men (calling out)
gi wi o:ba-e	what are your names?
ni Australia gayo-e	my Australia women
gi wi o:ba-e	what are your names?
ni America kalu-o-wo:	my America men
o wo:— wo: wo:	calling on and on
gi wi o:ba-e	what are your names?
ni Australia gayo-e	my Australia women
ni America kalu-o-e	my America men
a:-ye- wo: wo:	calling out, wondering

I was stunned by this song, but before I could say a word Ulahi continued with a brief reflective apology, here rather literally translated:

well, myself, thinking about it, speaking sadly, I won't see your place but
you see mine, I don't know your names, who are you? I'm wondering,
thinking like that, you people living in far away lands, listening to me, I
haven't heard your land names so who are you? That's what I'm saying.
Steve, having come before you can say 'my name is Steve, American man'
but all the others, what are your names? 'Many people will hear your
Bosavi songs', you said like that to me before, but thinking about it,
singing by myself I'm thinking what are your names? That's what I was
thinking. I don't really know the land names, just America, Australia, so
I'm sadly singing like that so that they can hear it.

The background to this remark was a conversation Ulahi and I had
as we walked together from Bolekini, our village, to the spot on Wo:lu
creek where she sang her songs that day. Ulahi, with whom I'd worked
often since 1976, asked why I wanted to record her songs again. I replied
that many new people would hear her voice because a song man from
my own place (Micky Hart of 'Grateful Dead' rock band fame) was
helping me to make a new recording of Bosavi sounds. I couldn't really
explain how *Voices of the Rainforest* was to be a serious departure from
the academic recordings I'd previously made for scholarly ethnomusicological audiences. And the world of Bosavi had never heard names like
'Grateful Dead'. So I just told Ulahi that, with the help of my friend,
many people in Australia and in America would someday hear her sing.
What stayed in Ulahi's mind, obviously, was the thought of her voice
resonating through America and Australia. But to whom? Who would
be listening in this world beyond? And what would they possibly
understand of her world within? Ulahi's improvised song takes up this
theme, appropriating the place names of the largest of imaginable
worlds beyond, and delicately juxtaposing them with the mystery of
personal names. Imagining her listeners in this way, Ulahi acknowledges
both our presence and absence in her sound world. But placing names
in performance, voicing those names poetically, makes them her own
in the moment and from then on. Here Ulahi both anticipates and
reciprocates the gesture of each distant listener who might hear her
recorded voice, speak her name, or speak the name of her place.

One World or Several?

As a final example I turn to a song I recorded late in 1994. It features a
different kind of sound, one that has penetrated all of the cities as well
as the interior of Papua New Guinea. It is a sound that carries with it

the intertwined histories of missionization and Western choral harmony, the spread of guitars and ukuleles throughout the world. It is the sound of Pan-Pacific acoustic string band popular music. But of course this very urban Papua New Guinea sound, one that developed tremendous momentum and local cassette market appeal around the time of the country's independence in 1975, has a way of sounding incredibly local when taken on by the Kaluli.

Like many other local string band performances, the song 'Papamama' was sung by a group of Kaluli men and women comprising lead and backup vocals, lead guitar, rhythm guitar, bass guitar, and ukulele (heard on Feld 2001, CD 1, track 11). The song is sung first in Tok Pisin, a Papua New Guinea lingua franca of cities and towns, and then in Kaluli. The group's leader, Odo Gaso, also known as Oska, heard the song from a non-Kaluli pastor; he then translated it and set it to the style of string band music he learned as a student at Tari High School.

papamama	father and mother
tanim bel, nau tasol,	change your thoughts, now,
i no tumora	not tomorrow
bratasusa	brother and sister
tanim bel, nau tasol,	change your thoughts, now,
i no tumora	not tomorrow
i no yumi tasol	not only us
olgeta hap Papua Nugini	all places in Papua New Guinea
tanim bel pinis	have already repented
dowo: no:wo:	father, mother
asugo: nodoma o:g wemaka:	turn your thinking, here and now
alibaka:	not tomorrow
nao nado	brother, sister
asugo: nodoma o:g wemaka	turn your thinking, here and now
alibaka:	not tomorrow
ni ko:mbaka:	not only us
Papua Nugini sambo	everyone in Papua New Guinea
asugo: nodolo:	has turned their thoughts

Tok Pisin, although still relatively little heard locally, became part of the linguistic repertory known in Bosavi through the return of labourers, through increasing government presence, and, of course, through missionization, all dating to the early 1970s. Guitars and ukuleles began to appear in the hands of young men returned from labour contracts around the same time. Returnees from provincial high schools, and students at the local mission and government schools also received some encouragement to take up the instrument, although there was little in the way of formal lessons. Throughout the 1970s and well into the 1980s I never heard a guitar or ukulele that was tuned or played as a melody instrument. Young men played them to accompany Tok Pisin songs heard from radio or cassette or pastors. But they were always played like a seed pod rattle and sometimes together with one, the strum always providing more an isometric rhythmic texture, 'lift-up-over sounding' with voices.

The string band sound developed by Odo Gaso and his friends from the late 1980s celebrates some very new skills and practices. First, of course, are the beginnings of some mastery of guitar band styles and the skills in tuning and playing guitar, ukulele and bass.

To this is added some mastery of the harmony introduced by Christian mission hymns and church singing. These musical skills, however, are never completely separate from their articulation in a naturalized Kaluli way. The instrumental part relationships, the vocal part relationships, and the interplay of the two, are given voice as a density of 'lift-up-over sounding'.

In the realm of social organization of musical activities, all indigenous Kaluli vocal practices and musical contexts were formerly gender separate. Only through Christian missionizaton and schooling did Bosavi boys and girls, men and women, begin to sing together and learn to create a 'lift-up-over sounding' blend of vocal registers. The string band format developed by Odo takes this a step farther. Here, as in several other Bosavi bands, the lead voices are a married couple, here Odo and his wife Sibalame, and the 'lift-up-over sounding' is organized by gendered voice registers.

Another interesting dimension to these songs is that the lyrics are typically sung both in Tok Pisin and Bosavi. This is actually quite difficult because of the inevitable prosodic awkwardness of trying to fit the Bosavi word forms into the cadences and number of rhythmic beats of the Western popular song form. Nonetheless, singing the song first in Tok Pisin then in Bosavi works both to demystify, and to appropriate, to make local, language and meaning indexed to places beyond.

Innovations notwithstanding, this new generationally based, gender-mixed, multilingual, and often Christian-inspired or Christian hymn text-based song form consistently indicates tremendous sonic continuities with other kinds of Bosavi song. There is, for example, a densely layered mix of 'lift-up-over sounding' voices and instruments, indicating the Kaluli aesthetic preference for overlapping and echoing layers of sound. At the same time these songs do not typically map a sequence of either forest or distant places. Nonetheless they almost always have a place name, and it is either a regional centre or, as in this case, Papua New Guinea. The imagined province, or the nation, a Christian nation, is a newly placed totality, a stringband sound world that connects remote Kaluli to Papua New Guinea through the idea that the nation is constituted by church, school, and radio.

Sound Worlds as Embodied Histories

All three of these songs – Bifo's ceremonial song, Ulahi's improvised reflection, and Odo's string band innovations – illustrate some of the many intensely local layers of the Kaluli sound world. It is a world where local difference embodies history in sound, where sound is deeply about knowing and being in the world. The world of the Bosavi rainforest, of 'lift-up-over sounding' voices singing 'flowing' song 'paths' articulates the encounter of locality with colonialism, labour contracts, Christian missionization, visiting foreign anthropologists, the nation state, and record companies. This is a sound world where these sensibilities have collided and where they now rebound in circulable cultural representations that embody and express musical histories – that is, histories lived musically. This is a sound world where not only is musical life socially and historically grounded, but social life is itself experienced and made significant musically.

The lived experience of Bosavi song joins the sounds of the forest, the poetics of place, and the voicing of song in a memorial cartography. Acts of making and hearing sounds are cartographically imagined and practised as the making and hearing of a world. Musicking, then, is clearly, for Bosavis as for many other people, a bodily mode of placing oneself in the world, taking the world in and expressing it out as an intimately known and lived world, a world of local knowledge that is articulated as vocal knowledge. Kaluli songs map the sound world as a spacetime of place, of connection, of exchange, of travel, of memory, of fear, of longing and of possibility. It is a sound world whose acoustemology voices an ongoing poetic dialogue, a dialogue where emplacement and displacement embody geographies of local and global difference.

Notes

Most Bosavi words can be pronounced simply by taking the English orthography at phonetic face value. Two additional symbols are used: o: is the phonetic open o, the sound in the English word 'bought;' and a: is the phonetic epsilon, the sound in the English word 'bet'. Bosavi pronunciation and language structure, including phonaesthetics, sound symbolism, and onomatopeia, is detailed in B.B. Schieffelin et al. (1998).

References

Casey, Edward S. (1996), 'How to Get from Space to Place in a Very Short Stretch of Time', in Steven Feld and Keith Basso (eds), *Senses of Place*, Santa Fe: School of American Research Press, pp. 13–52.

Feld, Steven (1990), *Sound and Sentiment: Birds, Weeping, Poetics, and Song in Kaluli Expression*, Philadelphia: University of Pennsylvania Press. (2nd edition; original 1982.)

—— (1991), *Voices of the Rainforest* (CD), Boston: Rykodisc.

—— (1996a), 'A Poetics of Place: Ecological and Aesthetic Co-evolution in a Papua New Guinea Rainforest Community', in Roy F. Ellen and Katsuyoshi Fukui (eds), *Redefining Nature: Ecology, Culture, and Domestication*, Oxford: Berg, pp. 61–87.

—— (1996b), 'Waterfalls of Song: An Acoustemology of Place Resounding in Bosavi, Papua New Guinea', in Steven Feld and Keith Basso (eds), *Senses of Place*, Santa Fé: School of American Research Press, pp. 91–135.

—— (2001), *Bosavi: Rainforest Music from Papua New Guinea* (three CD and booklet), Washington: Smithsonian Folkways Recordings.

Ihde, Don (1976), *Listening and Voice: A Phenomenology of Sound*, Athens: Ohio University Press.

Merleau-Ponty, Maurice (1962), *Phenomenology of Perception*, London: Routledge & Kegan Paul.

Schafer, R. Murray (1977), *The Tuning of the World*, New York: Knopf.

Schieffelin, Bambi B. (1990), *The Give and Take of Everyday Life: Language Socialization of Kaluli Children,* Cambridge: Cambridge University Press.

— (1998), *Bosavi-English-Tok Pisin Dictionary* (with Steven Feld, Ho:ido: Degelo:, Ho:nowo: Degili, Kulu Fuale, Ayasilo Ha:ina, and Da:ina Ha:waba:), Canberra: Pacific Linguistics, C-153, Australian National University.

— (2000) 'Introducing Kaluli Literacy: A Chronology of Influences', in P. Kroskrity (ed.), *Regimes of Language,* Santa Fe NM: School of American Research Press, pp. 293–327.

Schieffelin, Edward L. (1976), *The Sorrow of the Lonely and the Burning of the Dancers,* New York: St. Martin's Press.

— (1991), *Like People You See in a Dream* (with Robert Crittenden), Stanford: Stanford University Press.

— (1997), 'History and the Fate of the Forest', *Anthropological Forum* 7(4): 575–97.

13

Performing Patriotism in Native North America

Ojibwa Powwow-sounds and the Paradoxes of Identity

Cora Bender

The powwow is a category of public dancing and drumming feasts performed by today's Native American communities between northern Canada and the Mexican border, Los Angeles and Connecticut.[1] Ojibwa scholar Robert Desjarlait (1997: 115) explains: '. . . the powwow makes us proud to be Native American.' 'When the powwow ends, we walk away from it with a profound sense of well-being.' 'Powwow is the contemporary Indian's celebration of life and cultural survival', says George P. Horse Capture (1994: 190). 'Everyone is involved: young and old, men and women, all celebrating their Indianness.' The most characteristic feature of the powwow is its strong, pulsating drum sound, which also sells in great numbers on cassette tapes. In addition, the festive performance of its dancers, decked in bright regalia, has also spawned a whole subculture of merchandising and associated sales of arts and crafts. These goods can vary from simple beads and jingles to full-blown costumes and from caps, T-shirts and jewellery to plastic figurines and photo picture calendars. As well as being an important setting for the sale and exchange of these goods, the powwow historically has also been a significant site for intertribal cultural exchange. This exchange today also manifests the added dimension of presenting a strong sense of Native American patriotism. It is to this dimension that the focus of this article is directed.

Powwow History: A Sediment of Layers

The powwow has multiple historical roots in both the indigenous and immigrant cultures of the American Plains area during the nineteenth and early twentieth century.[2] Contrary to 'the limited time depth that has plagued most studies of ritual behaviour' (Guss 2000: 8), the historical dimension of the powwow is comparably well known, not only to cultural historians but also to the organizers of today's powwow, its participants, and to the host of Native cultural experts – although one must always take into account that interpretations of its meaning may differ considerably.

The powwow in its early forms was transmitted along routes of trade and other forms of tribal intercourse from the Pawnee of the Southern Plains to the Omaha and later the more northern Sioux (Wissler 1916) and Ojibwa (Kurath 1957). On this course its social function changed from a Southern Plains healing ritual (Murie 1914) to a Northern Plains warrior society dance (Fletcher and LaFlesche 1911; Howard 1951) and finally a pan-American Indian community festival. In the early twentieth century, the powwow as a forum of intertribal cultural exchange was also extended to the non-Indian immigrant majority. It received inspiration from small town fairs, rodeos, and Wild West shows (Powers 1990: 161) and thus became part of modern-day post-Frontier American popular culture. 'The same form', says David M. Guss about public festivities in general 'may be used to articulate a number of different ideas and over time can easy oscillate between religious devotion, ethnic solidarity, political resistance, national identity, and even commercial spectacle' (Guss 2000: 9). Looking at the powwow, it is possible to see that its social function has indeed altered over time, but nevertheless does not switch or swap in a way of an alternating electric current, but rather it appears to slowly accumulate meaning, very much like the sediment of geological layers. Old functions therefore might not be completely lost in any change over time; in fact – as there is no creation *ex nihilo* – new functions of this festive form only appear to emerge on the basis of an earlier, if unknown or obscure ritualistic function.

The powwow's intriguing character as an early modern cultural hybrid has, over the years, triggered a considerable body of anthropological (Powers 1990; Howard 1983; Hatoum 1999; Toelken 1991), ethnomusicological (Hatton 1986; Browner 2000) and political science (Mattern 1999) research since Howard's seminal article (Howard 1955) first directed broader scholarly notice to the phenomenon among the relocated tribes of Oklahoma. Lately, a few Native American authors have also published on the subject of the powwow (Horse Capture 1994; Desjarlait 1997). The early literature is mostly concerned with what Howard called 'pan-Indianism': an intertribally shared or aimed-at culture of Indian unity that, in Howards perspective, becomes a kind of Indian McDonaldization, eventually wiping out the last remnants of a traditional tribalism (Howard 1983:74; Hertzberg 1971). This view on culture is however slowly being replaced by more recent research about indigenization of Western culture and technology (for example, Valentine 1994). Moreover, historical research and reflective Native American criticism of the term 'pan-Indianism' (Lurie 1965; Desjarlait 1994:123) has made it clear that 'intertribal' culture indeed has a long and respectable history and exists in many forms. Some of these emerged in close connection with European culture contact, such as the religious-political movement led by the famous Tecumseh (c. 1768–1813) and his brother Tenskwatawa, the 'Shawnee Prophet'. Other forms of pan-regional intertribal culture, such as the Plains calumet ritual, flourish independently. Today, pan-Indianism on the one hand and tribal culture on the other should be seen in reality as being closely interrelated. Intertribal or pan-Indian political and expressive culture seem to be especially appealing to younger Native people who find a way back into their local culture a little later in life. Local tribal culture is often a realm dominated by older generations or local reservation 'elites'. Powwows, then, provide an arena to bring people of all ages and at different levels of cultural and tribal involvement together. Also, in many instances, local powwows have come to be regarded as a part of the annual ceremonial calendar of a community and are often juxtaposed with other ritual activities less visible to the non-Native public.[3]

Native American Patriotism

Growing awareness that Native American communities today are not only part of the pluralistic American society but are themselves pluralistic societies (Feest 1996) has led scholars to apply processual and non-essentialist perspectives on the powwow as 'public arena' (Mattern 1999), 'platform for [internal tribal] political debate' (Herle 1994), and as 'social drama' (Goertzen 2001), which mediates contrasts 'between communal and individualistic tendencies' (Gelo 1999) in Indian communities. Seen within a US American context, however, the powwow also acquires a special role as the site for an expression and performance of Native American patriotism. All powwows I visited during my field research in Minnesota and Western Wisconsin in the summer of 2001 were either organized by veterans or in honour of them. Despite this clear connection, patriotism among Native Americans of the US or Canada has only marginally been addressed by anthropological or historical research. Patriotic symbols as such occur most widely in historical Plains Indian art where their use flourished after the lasting confinement of the tribes on reservations during the 1880s. This was also a period of extensive popularization and commercialization of patriotic symbols in mainstream American life, to an extent that a counter organization, the 'Flag Protection Movement' sprang up who tried to prevent the flag from being printed on cigar-boxes, toilet-paper wrappers, even urinals (O'Leary 1999: 232). Only the militarization of the patriotic discourse during World War I brought this folk usage of the flag under criminal jurisdiction (O'Leary 1999: 230). Other than the Plains tribes, the tribes of the Western Great Lakes, among them the Ojibwa, were never renowned for extensive use of American patriotic symbols, says Pohrt (1976: 46). It is important to note, however, that the American eagle together with American colours were used in Ottawa artwork even before 1851 (Graham 1983) and by Ottawa warriors before 1838 (Feest 1984), and that Native groups of the Western Great Lakes participated actively in the Civil War.[4] Today, intertwined with the lives of the Ojibwa as with other American tribes, the absorption of patriotic symbols has become part of daily existence. They occur on TV, on the streets and often in consumer environments such as family restaurants, shopping malls and super-markets. They appear at almost any kind of public political or social activity in the US. As symbols of a 'just cause', patriotic images are used by Native Americans as well as other groups for their own political purposes, like 'America's Walk for Diabetes' shortly after the World Trade Center Bombing in September 2001. As diabetes rates are extremely high among Native Americans, the 'hundreds' that waved flags encompassed a considerable number of Native Americans, too (Kiely 2001). 'Native people are set with a whole myriad of socio-economic problems', says a Native American newspaper from Oklahoma commenting on the World Trade Center bombings:

> Often times, our federal government seems like the source of the problem and less the solution. But like the rest of the world, Indian nations are finding themselves standing in complete support of our federal government against a common threat ... This is no time for public criticism, but rather a time for patience, solidarity, and patriotism ... Today, we are all New Yorkers. (Native American Times 2001)

The conference of the National Congress of American Indians held in
Denver, Colorado in 1994 decided to erect a National Native American
Vietnam Veterans Memorial near Neillsville in west central Wisconsin.
The memorial, a bronze American Indian soldier dedicated to 'The
Forgotten Warrior', holds a rifle in one hand and an eagle feather staff
in the other. Lac Courte Orielles Ojibwa historian Eddie Benton-Banaise,
a veteran himself, explains the practice of Native flag honouring:

> It may be hard to understand but it's the land that we love, it's not the
> government . . . when we honor the flags, and honor the men and women
> who have served this country, it is that person we're honoring. We're not
> war mongers. We don't love war. But we love our uncles and aunties . . .
> It is that act by that person that's being honored. Those flags represent
> those people. (Eddie Benton-Banaise)

The US Flag Code determines that: 'The flag represents a living country
and is itself considered a living thing.' It also specifies the rules of how
to honour the flag properly, a form of practical ceremonial knowledge
which is mediated into Native American communities via two state
institutions: schools and the military.

Changing Public Arenas

With missionaries and government personnel, during the early reservation period, controlling ceremonial activities under conditions believed
by many to indicate cultural surrender, many Native communities chose
at this time to adopt new and more accepted forms of public arena for
their communal performances. For instance, Plains tribes celebrated 4
July (Herbst and Kopp 1993: 22), whereas the Ojibwa and other groups
of Wisconsin were enlisted in large numbers to participate as actors at
the first mass tourist fair at the southern shore of Lake Superior in the
year of 1924. The purpose of employing 'Indians' was to give the event
a special 'savage' flavour – and 'the savages' were grateful for the opportunity to practice then forbidden religious dancing and singing in open
public places (Madeline Island Museum; Alex Gokee, pers. communication). In other areas of the US, especially in the south-west, Native
groups participated in white town fairs and 4 July parades to demonstrate their viability and their double embeddedness in both 'Indian'
and 'white' culture. The Argentine philosopher and anthropologist
García Canclini, writes David Guss, observed that traditional festive
forms in Latin America, although always positioned in opposition to

modernity, do not collapse under the pressure of modernization because they are 'doubly enrolled in two systems of cultural production: historical (a process that gives identity to ethnic groups) and structural (within the present logic of dependent capitalism)' (García Canclini 1988: 486; 1993: 45 in Guss 20001: 5). Among today's Native cultural experts there are different opinions as to the relationship between history and identity. While some stress the timeless antiquity of Native traditions, others, like the Ojibwa councillor and advocate Joe Martineau (Fond du Lac, Minnesota) accept Indian 'pop culture' roots with a smile:

> Powwows, the way we see'em today, are originally from Buffalo Bill [he smiles]. Buffalo Bill had a Wild West Show, and the Indians would come out and do the dances. They'd get in their regalia and put on their feathers and they'd put on a good show for the for the people that were watching. That's where today's powwows came from. During a time when to practice any other type of ceremony could mean imprisonment or even death, these Wild West shows became the only place the drumbeat could be heard. Powwows today are very good for people to get into touch with their culture. (Joe Martineau)

Powwows, however, helped not only to form a specific space in Native communities – the 'powwow ground' that is usually set aside solely for the community powwows – but also a specific Native American audience in the modern sense of the term (Desjarlait 1997), brought about by the forced implementation of the school system into Native Americans' lives. American schools with their multitude of public ceremonies and quasi-religious routines, from flag salutation to football homecoming celebrations, have been an important site of patriotic instruction ever since the tremendous success of George T. Balch's 1890 'Teaching Patriotism in the Public Schools' (O'Leary 1999: 152f.). In this context, schools also taught children the social practice of being proper spectators. After the late nineteenth century boarding school system for Native American children was gradually abandoned, more on-reservation day-schools were subsequently built. Nowadays powwows, the 'celebrations of Indianness', move into the domains once devoted to the mission and the work of civilizing the 'savage'. During the harsh winter season, especially for Veterans' Memorial Day (11 November), powwows take place indoors. At the Lac Courte Oreilles Veterans Powwow, for instance, people celebrate in the tribal gym hall surveyed by a huge American bald eagle mural. Children of the school create neat patriotic pictures and slogans that are hung from the walls for the duration of the powwow.

Native Americans and the US Military

Since the First World War, it has been a tradition for young Native men and women to leave their reservations and either seek work in the big cities or enrol in the services and fight in the 'white man's wars': 17,000 Native American men and women are believed to have participated in the First World War. Because of the different views of who can be identified as a 'Native American' proper, there are different numbers about Native Americans who actually served in the Second World War, between 'over 25,000' (Holm 152) and 'more than 44,000 Native Americans, out of a total population of then 350,000' (Naval Historical Center, Washington DC). Native Americans fought in all branches of the Service in the Second World War and also in Korea, Vietnam, Grenada, Panama, Somalia, the Persian Gulf, and Afghanistan. Some of the explanations given for this seemingly contradictory engagement with the former military enemy do not necessarily sound very convincing to the anthropologist. The alleged Native sense for 'strength, honour, pride, devotion, and wisdom' (Naval Historical Center) could be questioned. Historically, after the turn to the twentieth century, reservation life had not much to offer many young men who often felt stripped of their former adventurous life and also their means of living. There also remained, at that time, a certain social pressure within tribes for men to still conform to a traditional warrior ideal. This might have provided a motive of status for Native youth to enter the services. Other reasons can be found in plain and simple poverty, something that prevails today as it did a hundred years ago. An Ojibwa Vietnam veteran explains:

> I left the reservation when I was very young. There was nothing there, there was no way to make a living. There was a lot of alcoholism and if you wanted to make yourself better and do something with your life you had to leave the reservation. And I chose to go into the military which taught me to grow up, taught me to be a man and gave me some training where I could have a job once I got out. (Pete Christiansen)

The military experience moulded whole generations of Native men who absorbed its ideologies, including the expectation of the equality of the races within the services themselves. This was something, however, in which more often than not they had to find out that ideology and praxis were quite far from each other.

> Whenever you filled out any of your paperwork, you were either 'Caucasian', 'Black', or 'Other', and everybody was always saying that you'd

have to mark out 'Other'. I would always say, 'well I'm not a 'Other', I'm Native American!' and that's what I used to put on all my forms. And of course, they'd come up with the Hollywood things, saying, 'hey, chief, howgh!' but you learn to live with the prejudice and if you're proud in your heart you know who you are. (Pete Christiansen)

The cultural effects of the military service seem contradictory (Camurat 1993). Especially in the aftermath of the First World War, many groups of the Plains Indians underwent a cultural revitalization due to warrior homecoming celebrations (Holm 1985; Powers 1990). On the other hand, many Native soldiers, like work-migrants, experienced a dilution of their own tribal connectedness and a loss of Native language while doing military service 'out there'. Counter to this however, many developed a greater awareness of what it means to be 'Indian' in an environment that only recognized 'Caucasian', 'Black' or 'Other'. In shaping a new consciousness of 'Indianness' beyond tribal boundaries, the military experience therefore can be seen as being crucial for the emergence of notions of a twentieth-century pan-Indian or 'Intertribal' culture. There still seems to be a paradox of identity however in a movement that originates half in the culture of war and half in the culture of protesting against war:

My mom was in the boarding school, my grandma was in the boarding school and they got the language beat outta them. For a long time, it wasn't cool to be Indian. It was illegal to do the things we do today. It was illegal to have a Midewin Grand Medicine Lodge [an Ojibwa curing ceremony, C. B.], they'd put you in jail! But in my generation with activism, with us following in the shirt-tails of the Sixties Revolution . . . and fighting against Vietnam, that's when the Indian Movement took off. (Joe Martineau)

The Powwow Setting

A powwow in itself often generates an overwhelmingly intense sensual experience of sounds, sights, taste, rhythm and flow. It usually lasts four days from Thursday through Sunday, with the largest crowd attending on the weekend. Its proceedings are strictly guarded and kept in proper order by the 'Emcee', the Master of the Ceremonies (Gelo 1999), and the many willing helpers employed by the Powwow Committee. As with other public festivities in America, such as the Saint Patrick's Day Parade in Boston for example, the core group of people organizing the event is often a network of veterans (Guss 2000: 11). Powwow peak season falls during the summer when the attending guests, usually between two and 10,000 in number, often made up from other reservations and cities, camp outside. In the event itself, the drums, of which only one is heard at a time, are situated in the centre of the powwow setting. The spatial arrangement can be seen as a ring of concentric circles of different intensity of involvement (Toelken 1991). The drums are surrounded by the dancing ground, which in turn is framed by both a round of benches reserved for the dancers taking a break, and a sheltered round where people usually bring their lawn-chairs. The outermost of the concentric circles is then the round of vending huts and trucks offering powwow-related merchandise and Indian food ('Indian taco', 'wild rice soup', and so forth). Here, people stroll, walk, shop and sit down to eat during the whole powwow as they like.

A 'drum' consists of a large handcrafted drum surrounded by a varying number of between four and 14 seated 'singers' who beat a rhythm in unison with sticks and sing self-composed songs or songs that they copied from other 'drums' via cassette recordings. The singing, especially in the so-called Northern Style, is high-pitched and vigorous. 'A song is typically begun by the lead singer who is interrupted partway through his phrase by the other members, who complete the phrase. Then a number of musical phrases follow, each pitched slightly lower than the previous one, until a musical cadence is reached in the lower part of the singers' range' (Vennum 1989: 8) 'Most powwow-songs are strophic with an interior repetition, and each strophe is called a 'round' by dancers or 'push-up' by singers in Indian performance terminology' (Browner 2000: 221). The musicians sit under their shelter as if on an island in the midst of the vast empty space of the dancing ground surrounding them. This 'dancing circle' is considered sacred – no dogs, no passers-by and no playing children are allowed to stroll around it or pass. The many visitors who just come to watch and do not care to dance usually take pains to arrive early in order to save a place in the shade for themselves and their families. An interesting feature of a powwow crowd is its mixed generational make-up, something that is also the strongest proof of the powwow's cultural viability. Powwows are fascinating for participants ranging from 'tiny tots' to 'old-timers' and also for teenagers usually more enchanted by Black urban hip-hop culture. In a similar fashion, the powwow offers an opportunity and a stage for different personal and public religious activities. In a given situation, a powwow might be preceded by a public ceremony at the local veterans' memorial site. Here a tribal politician or elder speaks an Ojibwa invocation, and people 'put down tobacco' as a sacred offering.

Anything that will bring all age groups closer to their culture and
traditional teachings is most needed. There are still some ceremonies done
at the dances, such as weddings, name giving, and various honour songs.
These are all important and good ceremonies. Many good prayers are also
done at the powwows. (Joe Martineau)

The dancing ground is opened by a spectacular 'grand entry', usually
twice a day, one during the early afternoon and one by nightfall. At
the indoor winter powwows, the strong back-bouncing of the sound
confined into walls over-tunes all other noise and turns benches and
chairs and people into reverberating media of the drum pulse, the
'heartbeat', as a powwow participant explains

The drum is like a child . . . The drum hide represents the mother's womb,
and the drumbeat is the heartbeat of our nation. If you take care of it in
a good way, it'll work for you. If you do the wrong things, it comes back
to you and to the people around you. (Corky White)

The powwow will start with the dancers lining up at the east entrance.
They're coming in from the east, and when they come in they use the
Grand Entry song. Everywhere [i.e. at all powwows, C.B.] people usually
stand up and their own spiritual advisors will talk for that powwow [i.e.
speak a prayer in the local Native language]. After that they go into the
flag song and the veterans song. The veterans are always the first in any
powwow, the flags and the veterans. (Joe Martineau)

All costumed dancers parade around the dancing ground, presenting
themselves to the audience that has been directed by the emcee to
'stand fast!' The dancers are invariably headed by the military veterans
who have registered before at the powwow entrance and have been
asked there to participate in the grand entry. Conforming to the rhythm
of the song – but not marching! – they step into the arena, carrying
flags and eagle staffs:

For instance, my family might bring an American flag. If I'm too busy
my Mom [will] ask for two veterans to hang that flag. And there's flags
at the powwow that people bring: 'Please could you carry this. It's a
veteran's flag, could you carry it out there?' If Lac du Flambeau [an Ojibwa
reservation in Wisconsin] brings a bunch of flags, when they get here
we ask them to help us out carry our flags also. We have the American,
Canadian, POW-MIA, Army, Navy, Air Force, Coast Guard, Marines, all

those flags! We work it out so all the flags come around the circle. Every
year we end up with way over thirty flags. (Joe Martineau)

Feather staffs decorated with eagle feathers, so-called 'Indian Flags'
or 'Eagle Staffs' are brought to the powwow by the families in whose
possession they are kept. It needs volunteer veterans, however, to carry
the Eagle Staffs into the Grand Entry.

With the veterans and flag carriers, eagle staff carriers come in. Then the
royalty comes in, the kids that have the crowns on, Braves and Princesses.
(Joe Martineau)

The powwow as a feast of communal self-recognition is also the main
stage for the Princess Pageants of the different reservations. In Lac
Courte Oreilles, children from three to eighteen years of age compete
for titles such as 'Tiny Tot', 'Junior Miss Lac Courte Oreilles', 'Miss Lac
Courte Oreilles' or, in the male categories, 'Brave' and 'Warrior'. The
aim of the pageants is not so much to promote beauty as such, as much
as the cultural ideal. The children wear dancing regalia and perform at
the contest dances in the various powwow dancing styles. Older
children are also expected to be able to speak a few phrases in Ojibwa.
As a reward, they receive public acclamation, and small gifts. They act
as communal youth role models and cultural mediators during the
following powwow season when they attend as many powwows as their
families can afford, dance, and shake everybody's hands. No reasons
were given to me for the ceremonial proximity of the veterans' and the
appearance of the 'royalty' in the dancing circle. Possibly, both groups
have the strongest role model ascription and are therefore put together.
It is also possible that the dancing children have an appeasing effect
on the audience in opposing the martial impression left by the soldiers
with their eagle staffs and flags.

Following the royal children, the adult dancers arrive in grand style.
Like the veterans before, they dance singly, some carrying shields or
tomahawk imitations. All dancers, whether young or old, keep up a
quiet, sober and earnest countenance and an expression of dignity,
something that is also reflected by the audience. Onlookers can be seen
quietly moving with the rhythm. There might be occasional eye contact
or a quick smile between dancers and watching family members but
usually there are no shouted acclamations, which might be considered
disrespectful and possibly disruptive of the flow experience. From a
participant's view:

It's not a staged, practiced, rehearsed dance. It's all instant. You hear a good sound, you hear a good song, and the drum beat is just right there . . . You're with the music, with the song! That's very much our spirit, that's the foundation of Indian music. (Eddie Benton-Banaise)

Dancers perform according to an unwritten regulation of six different dance categories – three male and three female, each with their own style of outfit and dance:

After [the royalty] come the Traditional Men, with the bustles [i.e. huge wheel-like bunches of feathers tied to the back]. And then the men with the Grass Dance [regalia] and then the Fancy Dancers. And then the women come, led by the women with the traditional outfits [made of] buckskin and other. Then they're followed by the Jingle Dress Dancers and then the Fancy Shawl Dancers. Then the last ones to come in are the kids, the little ones [children without royal titles, C.B.] . . . Grand Entry is just the dancers. Then the veterans have their veterans dance and then after that we go into the special dances, and each reservation has their own variety of those that go from the Crow Hop to the Sneak-up dance. And then after that they give a talk and then get into the powwow. When everybody else comes in is after Grand Entry. Then they have intertribal [dances], that's when the public is welcome to dance. (Joe Martineau)

Every different style of outfit employed in the powwow has its history (Garcia 1991; Powers 1994). The 'men's and women's traditional' and the 'women's jingle dress' are old; others, like the 'men's fancy dance', are more recent innovations. All styles, however, are somewhat open to interpretation and individual taste. The most recent style is the 'women's fancy shawl dance', which, when it first appeared, created a certain amount of dissent among the powwow community as it employs an athletic and somewhat pantomimic dance image that was hitherto reserved only for male dancing (Mattern 1999: 137). The overall sequence of styles seen in the grand entry, which ranges from the traditional to the modern, reflects ideas of historical succession. At the same time, this sequence is also embedded in the topos of the all embracing 'sacred circle': because of the spiralling nature of the dance, in the course of the celebration, the leading 'traditional' styles after a period begin to catch up with the rear 'modern' styles. They pass them until the whole long parade of dancers appears to be spinning like a spiral, turning around a centre hub, as if revolving endlessly around a central rhythmic heartbeat.

After the flag song and the veterans' song, the flags used are then posted to the left and right of the Emcee's booth, from which they formally retire later in the evening. The surrounding joyous dance feast continues until around 11 p.m. or 12. It is succeeded by a 'forty-nine': a secret drinking party at some place known only to the local Indian youth and an activity frowned upon by the older generation.

The next morning, the powwow resumes with a 'give-away' for the veterans. This event is usually ceremonially performed by the act of 'posting of the colors': each veteran is called out one by one by his or her name to receive some small gifts, such as a T-shirt and a baseball cap with this year's powwow-logo, and to shake hands with all other veterans present. The local veterans post commander – Rusty Barber in the case of the Lac Courte Oreilles Ojibwa reservation – might then 'wanna speak a few words':

Today, at this time for the veterans, it feels good to see that we have quite a few veterans registered. For the sacrifice that they've given to the country. This country right here, the United States, where today, when we look at it, we take democracy pretty lightly. But when we look throughout the world, when we look at some of these countries that are oppressed that does not have freedom of speech, freedom to move about their country as we do. But we have soldiers, airmen, navy, serving, helping people in this peacetime. But sometimes, peacetime doesn't last forever. Sometimes our government ask our troops to go out and to do something to restore democracy to another country. Or just to go out to build new roads, build them villages, schools, with our engineers. (Rusty Barber)

The role of public ceremonies such as these, where the US military is given high honour and tangible tribal recognition, has also been used as an important argument to explain, in cultural terms, the reason for sustained and active Native US military participation. The Naval Historical Center in Washington DC, for example, depicts veterans' ceremonies such as this as patriotic rituals of warrior pride and glory, representative of a particular cultural background and stable male Native soldier identity. In reality, however, many of the veterans honoured are indeed women (see also Women's Memorial n.d.). Observers of recognition ceremonies all too often can see the very human aftermath of military service on those who attend. Combat injuries such as physical scars and poor general health are added to by nervous diseases experienced especially by veterans after contact with agent orange, through more generally to alcoholism and depressive illness. By contrast, the

public recognition itself, as conveyed through the ceremony, is so compelling that, for example, during the 2001 Lac Courte Oreilles 'Honor
the Earth' Powwow, several activists of the Minneapolis-based radical
political American Indian Movement, even lined up alongside the
military veterans to receive their T-shirt and baseball cap. Their celebration in fact was for having seen 'action' at several legendary violent
demonstrations during the 1960s and 1970s.[5] The US military itself has
also been seen to take pleasure in this aspect of powwow celebrations.
In November 1998, as one case in point, the American Forces Press Service
reported 'Marine Creates Native American Powwow to Honor Veterans'
(Williams 1998). Further, the US forces invite Native Americans to hold
powwows at their bases (Vernon Martin, personal communication).

Veterans' Networks

Veterans are not only receivers but also contributors to the organization
of every stage of the powwow. Invariably in the proceedings themselves
though they are considered to be 'shy', with the Emcee often having
to work overtime with his microphone to try and persuade them to
participate fully:

> Seventy-two veterans have registered so far, we're going for a hundred
> here! We have seventy-two veterans. I want to remind you this is for all
> veterans, Native or otherwise! (Powwow MC at the Lac Courte Oreilles
> Powwow Veterans recognition ceremony)[6]

Some veterans also come to powwows as vendors. Veteran Pete
Christiansen sees his trade as a direct work of cultural mediation, which
is in turn guided by a concept of multiculturalism:

> We started out three years ago when we finally got a chance to retire. We
> travel throughout the United States to go to all different types of powwows
> because each different Indian nation has different customs. And we like
> to go there to enjoy their powwows and to meet new friends. It's just
> great! (Pete Christiansen)

Drum groups are also very often organized and maintained by
veterans. One such can be seen in the case of Vernon Martin, a veteran
who teaches drumming and singing at the Lac Courte Oreilles Community College in Reserve, Wisconsin, and who organizes an annual

powwow himself. His biographical details also reveal the existence of
networks of veterans teaching and helping each other as they would
say, to get their lives 'straight':

> My mother went to the Presbyterian Church in the little village we lived
> in. And my Dad was a Catholic, so we were kind of a split family. I never
> felt at home in any religious group. When I went to the military and they
> asked me what religion I was I put 'Presbyterian' on. [My former wife]
> was with the Native American Church, where they use Peyote and I used
> to go with her to a ceremony every once in a while but I didn't feel comf-
> ortable there, either. So, I kept floundering around in Milwaukee, went
> to different churches and finally my wife and I divorced. And I thought,
> gee, I gotta start doing something! So I went back to a friend of mine
> who was in Milwaukee at the time. He was a drummer, he was a drum-
> maker. He said, why don't you come over and practice with us? I sang
> with him for about five or six years and learned all that he could teach
> me, all the songs that he knew. He was a Navy veteran. He passed away
> about five years ago. His name was Joe Ackley. So I give credit to him for
> teaching me. Well, [drumming] keeps my life in order. And I have these
> [sacred, C.B.] things in my home, I have the drum, and I got my feathers,
> and that keeps me straight. (Vernon Martin)

Vernon Martin, in turn, is credited by another Ojibwa veteran, George
Armour, for having re-connected him with drumming and singing
(Thomae 1993).

Having reached a certain degree of spiritual maturity, it is possible
for veterans to acquire the right to carry sacred eagle-bone whistles.
These are sometimes used at powwows, although there is much debate
as to when the use should be considered improper (Desjarlait 1997:123).
An eagle feather that becomes accidentally dropped while dancing in
the powwow, according to Ojibwa belief, represents a fallen warrior. The
dance is subsequently stopped and the feather ceremonially picked up
by four veteran dancers. The unlucky dancer who dropped it is supposed
to pass it on to a respected elder person.

It is also worth stating that even though many Native American men
received ritual recognition as warriors by their families in the aftermath
of the First World War, today this is often not the case. According to
the life history narratives of four Native American veterans from
Wisconsin interviewed by Dawn Scher Thomae for example, two of
them recalled humiliating rites of passage at the time of their army
enlistment, but none was welcomed home by ceremonial activity in

the family at the time of their return (Thomae 1993). Contrary, therefore, to the general view that veterans always receive special recognition in tribal societies, many Native veterans feel that powwows have to be put on in order to provide some means of addressing this lack:

> We had a lot of vets that we knew were vets; we had lots of [vets] that we didn't know were vets and all of them had the same thing in common: nobody really recognized them and said, 'we're proud'a you!' Once we set [the powwow], eight or nine vets died the first year. They were fulfilled. All of these guys went and volunteered to fight, they didn't have to be drafted, they went because they wanted to, and lived and died and gave their life to the country. So, it affected all of them that we finally recognized, 'we're proud'a you!' (Joe Martineau)

Conclusions

The powwow is an important site of indigenous identity-making where progressive political rhetoric of environmentalism and Native self-determination is mingled with a kind of American patriotism that, to a critical view such as that of Lauren Berlant, includes a certain amount of denial of 'racism as national system' (Berlant 1993: 396). However, seen from a Native point of view, the US government and its army might not, in any case, be the main addressees to blame for colonization and cultural loss:

> The overall belief is that it's not everybody that treated us like that. It's not the whole government that did that to us. It was the government, but I have an underlying belief that the Catholic Church also did such bad things. (Joe Martineau)

> There is many different ways. When people look for what is Indian, you could find a different story with every Indian that you talk to. But what I found basically that is 'Indian' is the gift giving. We are really giving people, and this is what we're really well known for. Every year we gift the veterans . . . the biggest part is the spiritual part because - what you need to realize is that in our tribe there's many different ways to believe and the gift that we have [is] to celebrate and to honor the earth, to honor these things that a are a forgotten sometimes like the trees, the earth, the plants and the water. We always think about those things and we talk about those things at the powwow. (Joe Martineau)

As the twentieth century drew to a close, the powwow can be considered to have returned to its older historical meanings. The complex
origin of the powwow and its multiple denotations both as healing
ritual, warrior society performance, and communal feast, is the source
of the present multi-layered function it performs within Native societies.
As a feast that exploits integrative powers to restore healthy self-esteem
in individuals and that can revitalize communities with histories of
disruption and identity struggle, the powwow can very justly be equated
to a healing rite. It is only enabled to take on this meaning because of
its earlier predecessors. The connection between the three, their common meaning, or, to use Rodney Needham's words, the 'connexion
between percussion and transition' (Needham 1967: 613) lies in
providing a stable framework and endowing participants with a feeling
of power in transitory situations. As a festive form that took its shape
in the course of trade and tribal interaction in the vast Plains area, its
nationwide commercialization today still retains that similar function
of building bridges among tribes and between tribes and a culturally
interested white audience.

As a specifically patriotic rite, however, the powwow is a peculiar
phenomenon. According to Anderson (1983), nationalism, of which
this form of patriotism is a part, should be seen as an imaginative
complex linked to the collective experience of simultaneity – a dimension
of social experience which in the case of Europe and of 'the West' in
general, is mediated via particularly narrative literature and newspapers
(see also McLuhan 1998 [1964]; Hobsbawm 1990; Bhabha (ed.) 1990).
In other global cultural settings, where print is not central, there might
be, in contrast, other kinds of media available to take the place of
literature in producing this nationalistic community narrative, such as.
the drum and the dancing circle of the powwow in the present case.
Both these alternative media forms, inherent in the powwow, nevertheless mediate a genuine consciousness of simultaneity of the succession
of generations in time, and of the powwow community as part of a
national perspective. Thus they represent a route to connect Native communities with the wider national American discourse (McElroy 1999).
'Native Americans have shown their willingness to fight and die for this
nation in foreign lands', says Rep. Joe Baca, D-Calif., in a newspaper
article about the proposition of an American Indian holiday. 'They
honour the American flag at every powwow and at many gatherings
and remember all veterans through song, music, and dance. This is about
proud Americans who have given so much to this country' (Melmer
2001). The concept of nationalism as the allegedly most legitimate

political value of our time (Anderson 1983), especially the American variant of it, is nevertheless constructed in tense opposition to the very core assets of American civilization – 'the private [and individualistic, C.B.] rights to life, liberty, and the pursuit of happiness that each defines for himself' (Berns 2001: 130). The transformation of self-interest into common welfare, engendered through US patriotism should, in part, be seen as coming from a particular historical root; a root which has expressed itself in a mainstream Anglo-American narrative, dominant in the US since its conception. Today, it seems that the US patriotic identity is also being threatened by a new conflict – that of established nationalism on the one hand and its dissolution into a conglomerate of diasporic identities (Appadurai 1993: 421) on the other. The historically contextualized notions of united nationhood are held together by the pervasive narrative-driven idioms of patriotism and in addition, by the employment of regular patriotic rites (of which the veterans' inclusion in the powwow is one), mobilized especially in times of crisis (Berlant 1993: 409). In the context of this chapter, Native Americans, with their politics and rhetorics of tribal separateness have always represented a force against this dominant narrative of one-nation nationalism, by posing a threat of dispersion, right in the midst of the melting pot. Growing conflicts however with local white populations about tribal rights to resources and tribally operated casinos since the late 1980s have, on the other hand, heightened the perceived need for the indigenous community to reconnect itself with full American nationhood. Thus the role of the modern powwow, whilst celebrating all that is distinct about Native identity, also seeks through its inclusion of the veterans' performance in the ceremonial, to celebrate a truly patriotic connectedness with mainstream US nationalism. The oppositional nature of these two sentiments can be seen clearly in the playing out of the powwow and particularly in its emphasis on veterans taking part. The sitting of these two aspects of Native life side by side makes sense of why so much Native American discourse appears to take two very different stances on the issue of Native identity and the wider US context. This is no more clearly illustrated than in the dual, seemingly conflicting, statements in this final quotation:

> We need to educate and sensitise our nation to all that Native Americans have done for this nation. We need to take up the cause of Native American sovereignty. (Rep. Joe Baca, D-Calif., in: Melmer 2001)

Notes

1. Field data for this article was obtained during a field trip to Wisconsin and Minnesota in the summer of 2001, and during previous field work periods in the years 1998–2000. My sincerest thanks to all people who had the patience to answer my questions, and who shared thoughts and allowed insights into their lives, especially Eddie Benton-Banaise (La Courte Oreilles), Joe Martineau (Fond du Lac), Pete Christiansen (Lac du Flambeau), and Vernon Martin (Lac Courte Oreilles). Thanks also to Camille LaCapa and Ian Dent for their kind support. Still, all faults and misinterpretations solely rest with the author.

2. Although the powwow as a ceremony is considered to have originated in the Plains area, the term itself is derived from Nantick (an Algonquian language spoken in Massachusetts). 'Pauau' ('medicine man') was adopted as a loanword by the English settlers in the seventeenth century and extended to the gatherings of Native medicine men, later to all kinds of Indian (and still later also non-Indian) gatherings. Around the turn of the twentieth century, it began to appear in newspaper articles and advertising of commercial Indian dance shows in Oklahoma. (Young 1981: 190ff). Powers says it did not become popular nation-wide until the mid-1950s (Powers 1990: xvi).

3. Contemporary Ojibwa in Minnesota for example regard both the annual powwow and the sacred drum dance as part of their year-round ceremonial cycle. Oklahoma tribes used to dance at powwows (crow dances) during the afternoon, and celebrated the ghost dance after nightfall (Herle 1994:61).

4. Prof. Ch. F. Feest, Frankfurt, directed my attention to these facts.

5. Particularly important in this context is the 1971 takeover of the Winter Dam on the Lac Courte Oreilles Ojibwa reservation by Ojibwa protesters. The Lac Courte Oreilles Powwow is said to have originated in the course of these events (Eddie Benton Banaise, recorded interview).

6. It is interesting to note, by the way, how the army practices of racial Othering ('Caucasian, Black or Other') already mentioned are reversed here by the MC into 'Native or Other'.

Interviews, Recordings, Personal Communication

Rusty Barber, speech held at Lac Courte Oreilles 'Honor the Earth Powwow', 21 July 2001.

Eddie Benton Banaise, Lac Courte Oreilles (Wi), recorded interview, 23 July 2001.

Pete Christiansen, Lac du Flambeau (WI), recorded interview, 22 July 2001.

Alex Gokee, Redcliff (WI), personal communication, 7 July 2001.

Vernon Martin, Lac Courte Oreilles (Wi), recorded interview, 24 July 2001.

Joe Martineau, Fond du Lac (MN), recorded interview, 17 July 2001; letter dating 14 January 2002.

Corky White, personal communication, 14 July 2001.

References

Anderson, Benedict (1983), *Imagined Communities. Reflections on the Origin and Spread of Nationalism*, London: Verso.

Appadurai, A. (1993), 'Patriotism and Its Futures', *Public Culture*, 1993(5): 411–29.

Berlant, L. (1993), 'The Theory of Infantile Citizenship', *Public Culture*, 1993(5): 395–410.

Berns, W. (2001), *Making Patriots*, Chicago: University of Chicago Press.

Bhabha, H. (ed.) (1990), *Nation and Narration*, London: Routledge.

Browner, T. (2000), 'Making and Singing Pow-wow Songs. Text, Form, and the Significance of Culture-based Analysis', *Ethnomusicology*, 44(2): 214–33.

Camurat, D. (1993), 'The American Indian in the Great War: Real and Imagined', M.A. thesis, Institut Charles V, Université de Paris VII; http://raven.cc.ukans.edu.

Desjarlait, R. (1997), 'The Contest Powwow versus the Traditional Powwow and the Role of the Native American Community', *Wicazo Sa Review*, 11(2): 115–27.

Feest, Christian F. (1984), 'The 'Arbre Croche Sketchbook'', in *Beadwork and Textiles of the Ottawa*, Harbor Springs: Harbor Springs Historical Commission, pp. 61–83.

—— (1996), 'Old and New Worlds: Discovery, Invention, and Innovation in the Contact of Cultures', in Mario Materassi and Maria Irene Ramalho de Sousa Santos (eds), *The American Columbiad: 'Discovering' America, Inventing the United States*, Amsterdam: VU University Press, pp. 133–48.

Fletcher, A. C. and LaFlesche, F. (1911), *The Omaha Tribe*, 27th Annual Report of the Smithsonian Institution Bureau of American Ethnology, 1905–1906, Washington DC: United States Government Printing Office.

García Canclini, Néstor (1988), 'Culture and Power: The State of Research', *Media, Culture and Society*, 10: 467–97.

Garcia, L. (1991), 'Short History of the Jingle Dress', *Whispering Wind Magazine*, 24(2): 21.

Gelo, D. J. (1999), 'Powwow Patter. Indian emcee discourse on power and identity', *Journal of American Folklore*, 112/443: 40–57.

Goertzen, C. (2001), 'Powwows and Identity on the Piedmont and Coastal Plains of North Carolina', *Ethnomusicology*, 45(1): 58–88.

Graham, S. (1983), *Ottawa Quillwork on Birchbark*, Harbor Springs MI: Harbor Springs Historical Commission, p. 33.

Guss, D. M. (2000), *The Festive State. Race, Ethnicity, and Nationalism as Cultural Performance*, Berkely CA: University of California Press.

Hatoum, R. (1999), 'The "(Intertribal) Powwow" as a "Cultural Phenomenon": A Discussion of the Term "Culture"', *European Review of Native American Studies*, 13(1): 47–51.

Herbst, T. and Kopp, J. (1993), *The Flag in American Indian Art*, New York State Historical Association – University of Washington Press.

Herle, A. (1994), 'Dancing Community. Powwow and Pan-Indianism in North America', *Cambridge Anthropology*, 17(2): 57–83.

Hertzberg, H. W. (1971), *The Search for an American Indian Identity. Modern Pan-Indian Movements*, New York: Syracuse University Press.

Hobsbawm, E. (1990), *Nations and Nationalism Since 1780: Programme, Myth, Reality*, Cambridge: Cambridge University Press.

Holm, T. (1985), 'Fighting a White Man's War: The Extent and Legacy of Indian Participation in World War II', in P. Iverson (ed.), *The Plains Indians of the Twentieth Century*, Norman and London: University of Oklahoma Press, pp. 149—68.

Horse Capture, George (1994), 'Powwow: A Powerful Cultural Revival', in Gšran Burenhult (ed.), *Traditional Peoples Today: Continuity and Change in the Modern World*, St Lucia: University of Queensland Press, pp. 190—1.

Howard, J. (1951), 'Notes on the Dakota Grass Dance', *Journal of Southwest Anthropology*, 7: (n.p.).

— (1955), 'Pan-Indian Culture of Oklahoma'. Scientific Monthly, 81(5): 215–20.

— (1983), 'Pan-Indianism in Native American Music and Dance',. *Ethnomusicology*, 27(1): 71–82.

Kiely, T. (2001), 'Hundreds Show Patriotism at Diabetes Walk', The Clarion-Ledger (Mississippi News), 17 September.

Kurath, G. P. (1957), 'Pan-Indianism in Great Lakes Tribal Festivals', *Journal of American Folklore*, 70: 179–82.

Lurie, N. O. (1965), 'An American Indian Renascence?' *Midcontinent American Studies Journal*, 6(2): 25–50.

Mattern, M. (1999), 'The Powwow as a Public Arena for Negotiating Unity and Diversity in American Indian Life', in D. Champagne (ed.),

Contemporary Native American Cultural Issues, Walnut Creek CA: Altamira Press, pp. 129–43.

Melmer, D. (2001), 'American Indian holiday proposed', *Indian Country Today,* 27 June.

Mc Elroy, J. H. (1999), *American Beliefs. What Keeps a Big Country and a Diverse People United,* Chicago: Ivan R. Dee.

McLuhan, M. (1998), *Understanding Media. The Extensions of Man,* Cambridge MA and London: The MIT Press.

Murie, James R. (1914), 'Pawnee Indian Societies', *American Museum of Natural History, Anthropological Papers,* 11(7): 543–644.

Native American Times (2001), 'Looking for Revenge, Clues, Answers . . . Hope', 12 September.

Naval Historical Center, Department of the Navy, Washington DC; http://www.history. navy.mil.

Needham, R. (1967), 'Percussion and Transition', *Man,* 3(2): 606–14.

O'Leary, C. E. (1999), *To Die For. The Paradox of American Patriotism,* Princeton NJ: Princeton University Press.

Pohrt, R. A. (1976), 'The American Indian and the American Flag', *American Indian Art Magazine,* 1(2): 42–8.

Powers, W. K. (1994), 'Innovation in Lakota Powwow Costume', *American Indian Art Magazine,* 19 (4): 67–73, 103.

—— (1990), *War Dance. Plains Indian Musical Performance,* Tucson: The University of Arizona Press.

Theisz, R. (1989), 'The Bad Speakers and the Long Braids', in Christian F. Feest (ed.), *Indians and Europe: An Interdisciplinary Collection of Essays,* Aachen, Germany: Alano, pp. 427–34.

Thomae, D. S. (1993), 'Wisconsin Warriors: Interviews with Native American Veterans', *Lore Magazine* (Milwaukee Public Museum), 43(3): 9–18.

Toelken, B. (1991), 'Ethnic Selection and Intensification in the Native American Powwow', in Stephen Stern and John A. Cicala (eds), *Creative Ethnicity. Symbols and Strategies of Contemporary Ethnic Life,* Logan UT: Utah State University Press, pp. 137–56.

Valentine, L. P. (1994), *Making It Their Own. Severn Ojibwe Communicative Practices,* Toronto: University of Toronto Press.

Vennum, Thomas (1989), *Ojibway Music from Minnesota: Continuity and Change,* St Paul: Minnesota Historical Society.

Williams, R. (1998), 'Marine Creates Native American Powwow to Honor Veterans', DefenseLink, US Department of Defense; http://www.defenselink.mil/news/Nov1998/ n11191998_9811197.html.

Wissler, C. (1916), 'Societies of the Plains Indians'. *Anthropological Papers of the American Museum of Natural History, New York.*

'Women's Memorial, The' (n.d.), Native American Women Veterans. Women In Military Service For America Memorial, Washington DC, http://www.womensmemorial.org.

Young, Gloria (1981), Powwow Power: Perspectives on Historic and Contemporary Intertribalism. Unpublished Ph.D. thesis, Indiana University.

14

Sectarian Sound and Cultural Identity in Northern Ireland

Paul Moore

Introduction

Free Derry Wall is one of the most immediately recognizable landmarks in Derry. The wall is seen as a central icon in the most recent period of 'Troubles', situated at the mouth of the Bogside in the shadow of the infamous, but now demolished, Rosville Flats. The area has always been famous for Republican murals and the present site is no exception, although now the murals emanate an anodyne tourist sensibility, bereft of the danger and political expectation that filled television screens in the late 1960s and early 1970s. This is a place resonant with visual cultural memory.

Yet Eamon McCann, broadcaster, writer and key figure in the develop-ment of the civil rights movement in Northern Ireland, and most crucially, a resident of the Bogside, points out in his book *War and an Irish Town* that one of his abiding memories of those early revolutionary days was hearing an 'Incredible String Band' album being played by a pirate radio station from the roof of Rosville flats. For McCann cultural memory was prompted by sound.

Protestants have recently realized the importance of the visual in the construction of their own cultural memory. The streets surrounding Harland and Wolff Shipyard, the great symbol of Protestant industrial ascendancy in East Belfast, are now resplendent in Loyalist imagery,

265

some of it even appropriating mythical figures from Irish legend to prove the right of Protestants to inhabit the island. Yet when Protestants speak of their culture they speak of the feelings of pride, honour and aggression – 'the auld blood rising' – when they *hear* the sound of the lambeg drums or the swirl of the pipes in a marching band. Here is another example of cultural memory, once more, evolving and being reinforced through sound.

Sound is therefore a key symbol in the construction of identity in Northern Ireland. Anthony Buckley (1998) has noted that symbols have a dual purpose; on the one hand to illuminate an aspect of the world that would otherwise be neglected or confused and on the other to underline matters of power and the relations between people. It is this latter function that relates to the examination of sound in the Northern Irish context. It is widely accepted that in this region there are numerous visual constructs that act as symbolic information about identity. These include the area where one lives, the place where one works, the sporting colours one wears, and even, for the more extreme, the type of car one drives. The role of sound as a symbolic signifier has not been so readily accepted, however, despite the importance of music, language or the pronunciation of words and letters as benchmarks of cultural identity. Camille O'Reilly (1998: 51) is right to highlight the warning given by Cohen (1987) that symbols are more complex than we imagine because they can be experienced with such diversity and are therefore almost impossible to generalize and translate into words, but it is also the case that symbols have the capacity to turn complex sentiments into what Turner (1967) calls a kind of shorthand. 'The very value and importance of symbols lies in this characteristic ability to convey multiple meanings, varying according to context and the circumstances of the interpreter, and especially in the ability to convey meaning which is difficult or even impossible to express with words' (O'Reilly 1998: 50). Sound, in Northern Ireland, is one such symbol.

Sound and Identity

Balazs (1985: 121) argues that 'we possess such an array of deep associations of the most common everyday sounds. We have learned a language of sound imagery, where we simply seem to know "immediately" what any given sound means.' While Balazs is referring to the way in which we use sound to make meaning of the world around us, it is also the case that we also learn what particular sounds mean culturally. These cultural meanings are identified and learnt as we develop and grow within a society, contributing to the growth of our 'imagined community' (Anderson 1983). Thorn (1996) points out that in some societies hearing, rather than seeing, is believing – citing the work of sound anthropologists such as Bloch (1992), Gell (1995) and Feld (1994). He asserts that 'the soundscape characteristic of any particular set of cultural and geographic circumstances, produces "the foundation of experience" for those whose *whole* [his emphasis] way of life is built on that foundation, not just the narrowly auditory bits' (Thorn 1996: 5). However, if one is growing up in a divided society such as Northern Ireland, the making of meaning through sound attains a duality whereby some sounds connote one's own people and some connote the 'other'. Through this process sounds are believed by those involved in the conflict to make sectarian statements.

This belief is based on the fact that we do not, as some sound psychologists would argue, hear sound as abstract information related to the acoustic properties of given objects. Sound is heard and perceived as events, with particular sound perceptions being used as a means of constructing frameworks of understanding. These frameworks, in turn, do not operate in a vacuum, being subject to the knowledge bases embedded in our cultural repertoire. 'A great deal of our knowledge comes from the available cultural discourses about sounds and their causes. Again, in the same way that visual perception of an event is interdependently linked with labels, names, discourse about that event, so it is for sound' (Forrester 1999).

Having heard sounds as events, this knowledge is then used to construct geographies of cultural memory. Particular sounds are designated as sound marks (Thorn 1998) to construct complex social and physical boundaries. The population of Northern Ireland has been especially adept at this marking off process and ATQ Stewart (1986) writes about the ways in which an accepted sectarian topography dominates the geographical landscape, suggesting that no one teaches where one boundary ends and another starts, the population simply comes to know. It could be the case, however, that we come to know because the sounds of one community end at the point where the sounds of the other community start. Hence the significance of Protestant marching bands walking and playing their tunes right up to the limit of their perceived territory – a symbolic boundary cemented by a sound event.

Many of the sound events heard in the Northern Irish context are constructed and represented as binary opposites. The recognition of these constructions does not entail an acceptance of some crude, one-dimensional understanding of cultural identity. Indeed, it is paradoxical that the success of these binary constructions as symbolic sounds is dependent on what Papastergiadis (2000) so vividly calls the 'elastic metaphor' of cultural identity. The work of Hall (1996) and Bhabba (1994) has shown that it is not enough to see identity as a de-essentialized mosaic, since this metaphor still allows for the notion of separate places where fixed aspects of identity exists. Bhabba, in particular, argues for the notion of a 'third space' within which resides the 'hybrid moment' a space where those involved in conflict about identity have to accept that something else exists that articulates the recognizable power relations while at the same moment undermining and problematizing them. The theoretical problem of expressing this 'third space' is addressed by Papastergiadis (2000) in an essay that offers a means of explaining how the complexities of the Northern Irish conflict can still be represented by symbols (in this case sound) that present themselves as binary opposites. Papastergiadis (2000: 146–50) argues that there are seven contours of cultural identity that need to be traced if a comprehensive analysis of identity is to take place. Starting with the idea of *historical specificity* he asserts the need for a framework for *negotiation across boundaries*, and the addressing of the issue of the *nation state and nation building*. Within this the concepts of *class and gender* need to be confronted in order to develop an 'appreciation of the way cultural identities are contested within certain communities in order to highlight the complex nexus among class, gender and cultural identity' (Papastergiadis 2000: 148). These concepts need in turn to be set within a *context of ambivalence*, recognizing that identity formation is often executed through *unconscious processes*, the sum of these contours encouraging the reader to accept the *heterological character* of cultural identity. These contours are central to the arguments developed in this chapter in relation to sound and identity in Northern Ireland. While the sounds examined express themselves as 'us' and 'them' they are grounded in a sonic environment where specific cultural memories mix with other symbolic iconography to reinforce notions of difference, while at the same moment involving the listeners in shared sound memories/ experiences that complicate identity and act literally as forms of 'oscillation' that Bhabba maintains inhabit the boundary between the self and the other.

Aspects of the Northern Irish Soundscape

The historical representations of the loyalist and nationalist communities resonate with opposing sounds and sound patterns. The Protestant community has always been associated with industrialization (Barton 1998), and Protestant communities in Antrim, Down and parts of Derry are represented as being immersed in the harsh sounds of engineering works, industrial machinery, regulated rhythms and urban volume. Hence O'Dowd, in an analysis of the role of the intellectual in Northern Irish society, suggests that the difference in the Protestant and Catholic education systems has led the Protestant intelligentsia to privilege the technical/industrial. 'The Catholic educational system has been biased historically towards the arts and humanities compared to the more scientific and technical orientation of its Protestant counterpart' (O'Dowd 1991: 159). Nationalist Ireland, on the other hand, is represented as being awash with pastoral sounds; the animals in the field, the soft 'shuck' of farm machinery immortalized by Seamus Heaney, the natural rhythms of the seasonal weather and, at the far reaches of the island, the relaxing coming and going of the tides.

To speak of these sounds is to be reminded that the language used by Protestants is hard and guttural, a linguistic robustness that has come to be known as Ulster-Scots. The Irish language by contrast is soft and lyrical, lilting and musical in its construction. No ritual exemplifies this more clearly than the pronouncing of the letter 'h'. To pronounce the letter with an assertive and clipped 'aitch' is to be Protestant, to sigh the letter with an aspirant 'haitch' is to be Catholic. Donal O'Riagain (1998: 102) argues that these linguistic sounds are more than mere tools for communication. They are instead a vehicle 'for cultural expression, an instrument developed and honed by a people to give voice to their finest and most intimate thoughts, a custom built receptacle in which the collective wisdom of a people can be recorded, stored and passed from one generation to another.' Given the importance of this voice it is no surprise that during the last 10 years the interest in the Irish language and the Ulster-Scots dialects has increased, while institutions such as the Verbal Arts Centre in Derry have been established to archive and promote the voices of all communities.

There is a link in the Northern Irish context between sound events and the construction of the seasons. While time might be measured by the natural evolution of spring, summer and autumn, cultural memory is measured by the start and finish of the 'marching season', a source of pride and cultural reinforcement for one community, a period of fear and perceived triumphalism for the other. A central feature of this season is the insistent vibration of the drum. The most lauded drum in Protestant culture is the lambeg; a percussive heavy-weight designed to instil fear as it headed the march into battle.

Ironically, Schiller (2001:106) argues that while there is a male ethos surrounding the lambeg drum, the drum itself is female and, more importantly in relation to cultural identity, was used by both Protestants and Catholics. However, since as Schiller points out, no sound has an inherent meaning and all meanings are culturally specific and socially constructed, the meaning deriving from a shared consensus between groups of people, the lambeg has come to be representative of the Protestant community.

The stretched goatskin of the lambeg is played using two long, whip-thin rods and the drummer is accompanied by a fife player (who can usually only be heard by the drummer). To the untrained ear the playing of the lambeg appears to be monotone and one-dimensional, but in fact the drum is beaten to particular rhythmic patterns, tunes which are never 'written' but passed from generation to generation in deserted halls across Northern Ireland during the winter months.

Behind the lambeg drums in any parade there will be marching bands. These bands can be split into two types – the formal, usually more mature, bands for whom the music is a key factor and the more informal, younger bands, for whom the politics is more important than the music. For obvious reasons this latter group have come to be known as 'Kick the Pope' or 'Blood and Thunder' bands (Bell 1998). All these bands feature side drums, descended from military bands and in many cases played with a military precision and skill borne from hours of practice and continual testing in formal competition. These accomplished drummers see their role as accompanying the musical prowess of their colleagues, and the sound they make is muted, almost distant, a soft reminder of the pace and pattern that is necessary to make the music sing. For the 'Blood and Thunder' bands, however, the drum is there to indicate a perceived dominance, and in many of these bands the drums adopt an overbearing stance, to the extent that the drums often completely outnumber any other instrument in the band. The central bass drum hammers out the key beat and the other drums pound in unison the message, should it ever be doubted, 'this we will maintain'.

The Catholic population also have their marching bands, parading on St Patrick's Day, to community gatherings, and at the annual Ancient Order of Hiberian parades. Yet the sound they make is culturally different. The dominance and overbearing skirl of the pipes and drums would appear to be once more replaced by the softer, quieter tones as though the bands are apologizing for their existence. A measure of the invisibility of such bands is the fact that people who have grown up in the Protestant tradition have described their surprise when they discovered that the Catholic population also had their tradition of marching and parades. Some of this surprise can be accounted for by geographical and cultural separateness, but the suppressed nature of the nationalist band performance may be an acoustic response to the members' experience of growing up in what they believed to be a repressive society.

By far the most representative drum for the Catholic community, however, is the bodhran. A small hand-held drum, played with a short 'beater' (or indeed by hand), this is the drum most associated with traditional Irish music. The sound it makes is soft, round and full, the role it plays supportive, laying down a rhythmic base onto which layers of fiddle, whistle, flute and ulillean pipe can be laid. A bodhran never dominates, yet always leads, a subtle leadership born out of experience, tradition and a confidence in the importance of the musical statement being produced. Many traditional musicians resent the presence of the bodhran as a musical instrument feeling that it has developed from a Western music tradition that is not 'authentically' Irish. Hence the satirical stories such as that of the man who boarded a train with a case and when asked what was in the case explained it was a gun. His fellow passengers are relieved saying 'Thank God for that – we thought it was a bodhran!' Nevertheless, the sound of the bodhran has become synonomous with nationalist traditional culture and is seen as the mirror of the lambeg in symbolic terms. Schiller (2001: 58) points out, somewhat forlornly, that despite the creation of mixed drumming ensembles such as Different Drums, the probability of the drums being heard simultaneously is not only culturally but musically unlikely:

> Although the stark timbral contrast between the two drums makes them indeed suited for such a combination, the obvious problem results from their extreme difference in volume. A simultaneous performance of both drums will therefore tend to rely on amplification, to level out their differences in volume. This makes it highly unlikely that a community tradition will develop in Ireland which integrates both drums – unless both instruments essentially alter their playing styles and modify their sounds.

It is also significant that in the contemporary context the beating of drums, in this case the electronic drumming associated with rave/ techno music, has been cited as one way in which the cultural divide has been bridged. The importance of the rave scene for young people has been seen as a unifying factor in the community (hence the opposition from paramilitary groups), and there is a great deal of as yet unpublished research evidence that the rave movement may indeed have played a role in forcing young people to question assumed difference. If this is proved to be the case the irony of literally dancing to a different tune will not be lost on those for whom the drums have always signified conflict and tension.

One final drumming of the marching season is, perhaps, worth mentioning since it exists in Bhabba's 'oscillating space'. It is the low drumming drone of the Chinook helicopter as it hovers above contentious parades, violent confrontations and tense standoffs. Different in sound from the buzzing, wasp-like helicopters that ferry military personnel from base to base, the presence of the Chinook means confrontations have taken on a serious dimension. Immortalized sonically in films such as *Apocalypse Now* and *The Deerhunter* the sound of the Chinook may mean different things to each community, but for both communities it signifies a knowledge that 'there's something going on somewhere'.

Religious affiliation is one of the ways in which national identity speaks itself in the Northern Irish context. It is a badge worn to illustrate a belonging to a particular cultural and political tradition. It is natural, therefore, that the sounds of worship should have significance for each community. Ironically, it is unlikely that different religions would understand the sounds produced by the other group at worship because most individuals have not, and never will, attended a religious service of the other faith. The sounds, and the contexts in which they are produced, are therefore imagined. Extreme Protestants will speak of the candles in the Catholic Church, maintaining they can be seen, smelt and *heard*. They describe the whispered prayers as though the whispering was a sign of clandestine conspiracy, and assume the sounds produced by the plastic rattle of rosary beads and the clinking of chalices filled with burning incense. Significantly, Catholics cannot describe the sounds present in Protestant church services because the faiths modelled on the Presbyterian tradition have stripped their worship of all iconic artefacts. What is apparent to Catholics is the extreme nature of the preaching, the long sermons delivered with evangelical zeal by fire-and-brimstone preachers, many of whom hold political office. In reality, most will only have heard such preaching on the streets as they shop, a metallic call to eternity bellowed from a street corner through a battery-driven megaphone by a Bible-driven lay preacher.

When the members of each community leave their work and their worship, their leisure time is still filled with aural reminders of their cultural heritage. The *Riverdance* phenomenon has brought to the world a sanitized ideal of the importance of traditional dance to Ireland, and while many Protestants, particularly in rural areas, have attended Irish dance classes, this activity is seen as a catholic prerogative. Hence the response of Lexie, the Protestant father in the Oscar-nominated short film *Dance Lexie Dance* to the request of his daughter to be allowed to learn Irish dancing – 'We don't dance!' Some would argue, however, that the more 'authentic' form of Irish dance is stepping, a less commercialized form where the feet of the dancers batter a stone or wooden floor with steel-tipped shoes. In either form traditional dancing is seen as a Catholic/nationalist tradition, a complicated assemblage of moves and runes designed to alienate, confuse and intimidate any Protestant other who might wander inadvertently into a ceile literally in full swing. It is perhaps worthy of mention that, in answer to the question 'what is the tradition of Protestant dance in Northern Ireland?' three tongue-in-cheek responses are continually given – rock and roll, ballroom dancing and more recently American line-dancing – two American in origin and one a distant descendent of imperial splendour. Often in humour there lies a kernel of cultural truth.

As Clarke and Critcher (1985) have shown, leisure is a contested site where economic status, gender, social class and technology intersect to transform cultural patterns. It is also a sphere where dominant and subordinate groups struggle for power. This is especially true in the case of sport in Northern Ireland. For the Catholic population, sport is enshrined in the heritage and rules of the Gaelic Association. For this institution sport is a means of cementing cultural identity, hence the emphasis on strictly Irish games (Gaelic football, hurling, camogie), played on a Sunday on an all-Ireland basis and, most crucially, described and communicated with through the Irish language. Essentially it's competitions and teams are classless – a *nation* celebrating its identity through sporting achievement. As Bairner (1997) argues Protestant sport is perceived as class based. The working class plays soccer, the middle class rugby, cricket and, of course, golf. This distinction is reinforced through the grammar school system. Within the Protestant community, for example, selection has meant that the majority of boys from middle-class families attend schools in which rugby, hockey and cricket are the main team sports, whereas football is dominant in secondary schools attended largely by working-class children. It is no surprise, therefore, that a game like rugby retains a solidly middle-class character whereas football can be said to belong to the working class' (Bairner 1997: 98). While these sharp class dichotomies may have become blurred in the contemporary social landscape, the sounds relating to their presentation indicate their persistence. Rugby commentators have a particular

274 ANTHROPOLOGIES OF SOUND

'educated' accent, rugby crowds are dignified and family oriented and the overriding ethos is of an international activity. In contrast the dominant sounds at local football matches are sounds of sectarian bipartisanship, teams aligned with political and religious ideologies and supporters defending not just a team's, but an imagined nation's honour.

The soundscape at a Gaelic Association event is different again. While family oriented, the aural environment speaks of celebration, from the reverent and respectful singing of the national anthem, through the subdued hum of the spectators during the match (Gaelic crowds never sing or chant) to the rapid-fire constancy of the lilted commentary heard on television and radio.

If these are some of the conflicting sectarian sounds that dominate the aural soundscape in Northern Ireland there is still a shared scaffolding that props them up. This scaffolding is the now-clichéd din of shared violence; the staccato bark of gunfire; the quiet before the slamming of a distant bomb; the rush of burning petrol from an in-flight petrol bomb; the clash of broken glass during a riot; the wail of police and army sirens; the silence heard at over 3,000 funerals since 1969.

Representing and Reproducing the Soundscape

Identifying and analysing sectarian sounds in Northern Ireland underlines their importance as purveyors and indicators of cultural memory. The meanings the sounds have appropriated give them a reverence beyond their acoustic structures. They become, in effect, echoes of the sacred, passed without words from generation to generation, underpinning the notion that for communities united against a perceived threat, hearing as well as seeing is believing. It is the shared sanctity of these sounds that makes their re-presentation so difficult.

Two methods of presentation are possible. The first is to record the sounds in context as they happen and to reproduce them as aural snapshots. In this form it could be argued they merely reinforce the sectarian meanings and are difficult (impossible) to present in a way which will engage an audience.

The second method is to compose an artificial soundscape from the recorded sound fragments, juxtaposing them in a way that engages the listener and questions the assumed meanings. This immediately poses the problem of how to engage the listener in a sound event without confusing it with visual props.

One such strategy would involve creating a sound installation and the use of an overused political aphorism to draw the listener to the soundscape. Politicians in Northern Ireland are often accused of 'playing the Orange or Green card'. This seems an appropriate way to frame the soundscape. Having been attracted to the installation the listener would be directed to play an orange or green card as an indication of the cultural background a sound was believed to represent. The soundscape itself would be activated by winding the handle on a wind-up radio positioned in a perspex case. The limited visual stimulus of the coloured cards would in this instance serve to focus attention on the sounds.

One key problem with this strategy is that whereas the sounds in their natural context would be heard as part of the sound immersed nature of everyday life, the collected sounds in the soundscape would be *actively listened to*. Chion (1990) points out that sound in everyday life is omnidirectional, composed of both direct and indirect reflections and many pieces of aural information. Chion (1994) came to call this type of sound 'acousmatic', sound that is heard without its cause being seen. The individual listening to the soundscape, however, has to adopt an active listening position, to move into what Beck (1998) calls the 'aural contract'. It is inevitable that the acceptance of this contract will alter the reaction of the listener because the listening will become predominantly connotative as opposed to denotative.

The second problem in constructing a soundscape is the fact that sound events do have a perspective. Beck describes this perspective in terms of 'in' and 'out' aural spaces, the 'in' space referring to the main frame of the sound picture and the 'out' space referring to the distant peripheral frame. In a soundscape composed of edited, pre-recorded sounds it is difficult to mimic these inner and outer spaces although the work of Van Leeuwen (1999) in relation to the force/field/ground model of sound perspective is a useful starting point.

A soundscape installation also raises the issue of the point of listening. In most sound spaces the hearer does not have a distinct point of hearing but in a contrived physical space the listener is encouraged (forced) to take up a distinct point of listening. Other sound experiences may indeed impose points of listening on the hearer (the Walkman is an obvious example), but in such cases the manufactured nature of the sound source alleviates any notion of sound/meaning corruption. The same is not true if natural, as opposed to manufactured, sounds are being reproduced. In this case the imposition of a listening point may significantly change the sound/listener relationship. Ultimately, as Ferrington (1993) indicates, this is the key problem to be solved – 'the challenge of creating acoustical space in an audio work is difficult . . . The director may use selective focus . . . selective focus begins with prioritizing the sounds to which the listener's attention must be given.'

While the advent of digital editing has made the process of sound composition more sophisticated, it has created two significant problems. Firstly, the sound produced by digital recording/editing is hyper-real and often does not re-present the sounds as heard in the natural context. Secondly, the ability to sample and fuse archived sounds (Sanjek 2001) has led to the growth of new sound forms that resemble constructed soundscapes but that, in reality, are closer to music. To an extent, therefore, this new musical form makes it increasingly difficult for a listener to differentiate between a composition designed for entertainment and a composition designed to evoke meaning. This distinction matters because the listening experience will be dependent on the listener's reading of the purpose of the product.

Finally, there is the perplexing issue of what is known in American acoustical science as 'the cocktail party problem'. In our normal engagement with our spatial environment our aural sense of the world is uncacophonus. When we are confronted with a confused mixture of sounds the ear can identify the differences in the phase of the sound waves received from spatially disparate objects and indicate to the brain which sounds need to be attended to (Cameron 1976). However, in a composed soundscape, listened to from a particular point of listening, all the sound waves are received in the same phase and hence the brain cannot deconstruct the cacophony and know which sound should be listened to. The danger is that a carefully edited soundscape becomes a meaningless jumble of indecipherable noise.

The only way in which these problems can be addressed (rather than solved) is if the composer is aware of them and constantly interrogates the soundscape composition in a self-reflexive manner. It may even be the case that the artificial, manufactured nature of the soundscape will serve the purpose of making the listener confront aural issues that were previously taken for granted.

Conclusion

Forrester (1997) maintains that sound has two qualitative dimensions – one nurturing and the other dissonant. To hear the sounds we were nurtured with, and which we have imbued with cultural meaning, presented in a disruptive context is to give these same sounds dissonance. The two dimensions need not, therefore, be mutually exclusive, just as the two traditions in Northern Ireland have more in common than either side would care to admit. Nevertheless if the analysis of sectarian sounds and their cultural meanings encourages a recognition of the important *differences* between cultural identities then the definition of accepted/acceptable cultural practice may begin to be widened.

> Besides sectarian cultures there are, of course, limitless instances of overlap and inflow: from music, movies, broadcast television, in books and magazines, in the high street and other more or less exotic locations. These are the conditions of (post)modern life. Also, it is vital that we explode the fantasy of total and exclusive identities, which the dichotomous processes of balanced sectarianism inadvertently sustain. (Butler 1994: 55)

References

Anderson B. (1983), *Imagined Communities*, London: Verso.

Bairner, A. (1997) '"Up to their knees?" Football, Sectarianism, Masculinity and Protestant Working-Class Identity', in Shirlow, P. and McGovern, M. (ed.) *Who are the 'People'?: Unionism. Protestantism and Loyalism in Northern Ireland*, London: Pluto Press.

Beck, A. (1998) 'Point of Listening in Radio Plays', *Sound Journal*, No. 1 (http://speke.ukc.ac.uk/sais/souind-journal/beck981.html), pp. 15–25.

Bell, D. (1990) *Acts of Union: Youth Culture and Sectarianism in Northern Ireland*, London: Macmillan.

Bhabba, H. (1994), *The Location of Culture*, London: Routledge.

Bloch, M. (1992), 'What Goes Without Saying: the Conceptualization of Zafimaniry Society', in Kuper, A. (ed.) *Conceptualizing Society*, London: Routledge.

Buckley, A. D. (1998), *Symbols in Northern Ireland*, Belfast: Institute of Irish Studies.

Buckley, A. D. and Kenny, M.C. (1995), *Negotiating Identity: Rhetoric, Metaphor, and Social Drama in Northern Ireland*, London: Smithsonian Institution.

Butler, D. (1994), 'The Study of Culture in Northern Ireland', *Causeway*, 1(3): 50–6.

Cameron, E. W. (1976), *Citizen Kane: The Influence of Radio Drama on Cinematic Design*, in Cameron E. W. (ed.) *Sound and the Cinema*, New York: Redgrave Publishers.

Chion, M. (1994), *Audio-Vision: Sound on Screen*, New York: Columbia University Press.

Clarke, J. and Critcher, C. (1979), *The Devil Makes Work – Leisure in Capitalist Britain*, London: Macmillan.

Cohen, A. P. (1987), *Whalsay: Symbol, Segment and Boundary in a Shetland Island Community*, Manchester: Manchester University Press.

Crozier, M. and Froggatt, R. (eds), *Cultural Traditions in Northern Ireland: Cultural Diversity in Contemporary Europe*, Belfast: Institute of Irish Studies.

Feld, S. (1994), 'From Ethnomusicology to Echo-muse-ecology: Reading R.Murray Schafer in the Papua New Guinea Rainforest', *The Soundscape Newsletter* 8: 4–6.

Ferrington, G. (1998), Audio Design: Creating Multi-sensory Images for the Mind, quoted in Beck A., 'Point of Listening in Radio Plays', *Sound Journal No.* 1 (http://speke.ukc.ac.uk/sais/sound-journal/beck981.html): 15–25.

Forrester M. (1998), 'Auditory Perception and Sound as Event: Theorising Sound Imagery in Psychology', *Sound Journal*, 1, http://www.ukc.ac.uk/sdfva/sound-journal/forrester001.html.

Gell, A. (1995), 'The Language of the Forest: Landscape and Phonological Iconism in Umeda', in Hirsch, E. and O'Hanlon, M. (eds) *The Anthropology of Landscape: Perspectives on Place and Space*, Oxford: Clarendon Press.

Hall, S. and du Gay, P. (eds) (1996), *Questions of Cultural Identity*, London: Sage.

Leeuwen, T. van, (1999), *Speech, Music, Sound*, London: Macmillan.

McCann, E. (1974), *War and an Irish Town*, Harmondsworth: Penguin.

O'Dowd, L. (1991), 'Intellectuals and Political Culture: A Unionist-nationalist Comparison', in Hughes, E. (ed.) *Culture and Politics in Northern Ireland*, Buckingham: Open University Press.

O'Reilly, C. (1998), 'The Irish Language as Symbol: Visual Representations of Irish in Northern Ireland', in Buckley, A.D. (ed.) *Symbols in Northern Ireland*, Belfast: Institute of Irish Studies.

O'Riagain, D. (1998), Language in Everyday Life, in Crozier, M. and Froggatt, R. (eds), *Cultural Traditions in Northern Ireland: Cultural Diversity in Contemporary Europe*, Belfast: Institute of Irish Studies.

Papastergiadis, N. (2000) The Elastic Metaphor: Towards a Theoretical Outline of Cultural Identity, in Fleming, D. (ed.), *Formations: A Twenty-first Century Media Studies Textbook*, Manchester: Manchester Press.

Rowthorn, B. and Wayne, N (1988), *Northern Ireland – The Political Economy of Conflict,* Cambridge: Polity Press.

Sanyek, D. (2001), '"Don't Have No DJ No More": Sampling and the "Autonomous" Creator', in Harrington, C. I. and Bielby, D. (eds), *Popular Culture: Production and Consumption,* Oxford: Blackwell.

Schiller, R. (2001), *The Lambeg and the Bodhran,* Belfast: Institute of Irish Studies.

Stewart, A. T. Q. (1986), *The Narrow Ground: Patterns of Ulster History,* Belfast: Pretani Press.

Thorn, R. (1998), 'Hearing is Believing – The Evidence', *Sound Journal,* 1(1), http://speke.ukc.ac.uk/sais/sound-journal/thorn981.html, 35–45.

Turner, V. W. (1969), *The Ritual Process: Structure and Anti-structure,* London: Routledge & Kegan Paul.

15

Nostalgia and Radio Sound*

Jo Tacchi

Introduction

This chapter is an investigation of the notion of nostalgia and a particular type of radio consumption. The ideas contained herein were generated from a study of the domestic consumption of radio sound in Bristol.[1] Many themes emerged from that research. It showed that radio sound is integrated into daily life in an intimate way and can be understood as forming an important part of domestic environments, or soundscapes, that hold meaning and significance that reaches beyond the immediate context and physical confines of the home.

Sound can create a texture within which one can move around and live. Radio sound can be seen to mediate between individuals in the home and the wider world (Tacchi 1998). On a sensory level, radio sound is particularly open to sensory creativity – a quality that itself makes the experience, activity, and meaning of listening to the radio difficult to describe in words. Households and domestic relationships are embedded in a larger social and meaningful world. Through examining the use of radio sound in the home we can see how meanings and relationships are negotiated and made, both within the household and beyond.

* This paper was published in a slightly different form as 'Nostalgia, Radio Listening and Everyday Life', in *Media@LSE Electronic Working Paper*, no. 1, December 2000. Reproduced with permission.

Radio sound possesses certain 'mood'-generating qualities. As a medium that moves through time, radio sound helps to establish affective rhythms in the home. This is to begin to understand the way in which listening to the radio can help with domestic routines, but at the same time recognizing that radio sound provides a sort of affective momentum. Examination of the affective qualities of radio sound can help us to understand its mood generating capacity; why it seems so easily to be able to put us in certain moods, make us feel better, and so on, even though we may not actually be paying very much attention to the radio.

In this chapter I discuss just one of these themes – the way in which radio consumption appears to hold the power to connect across time and memories. Radio sound can be seen to play a connecting role for individuals and for groups of people. A sense of community can be gained from radio listening and, at the same time, on another level, radio sound, with its particular qualities, is seen to make connections that draw on memories and nostalgia. Such connections do not require rationalization, or linguistic expression. They are experienced as one aspect of everyday life that is ongoing and is more than just one memory or one connection. I use the term 'nostalgia' to describe how this works in certain instances and hope to demonstrate that whereas 'nostalgia' as a concept holds somewhat negative social values, it can be seen to consist, in experience, of positive social practices.

This chapter has a simple structure. The first half consists mainly of examples from my research of what I consider to be nostalgic practices associated with the consumption of radio sound. The second half goes on to explore nostalgia as a concept and looks for ways of theoretically contextualizing and thus understanding these practices. It draws upon the work of other anthropologists, who explore the practice of nostalgia in very different contexts.

As such this chapter attempts to present material that establishes the consumption of radio sound as very much more complex and embedded in everyday life and emotions than it might at first appear.[2] It seeks to illustrate the particular properties of radio sound that make it a medium for nostalgic practices. Of the respondents used in this paper to illustrate these points, I met Jenny and Paul at a local listener panel for a commercial radio station that plays popular music from the past forty years (Classic Gold), Kerri through an introduction from another respondent and Lynne at a single-parent social club. All of these respondents live in Bristol and their names have been changed to protect their privacy.

The Power to Connect

When Jenny attended her first Classic Gold listener panel she was asked about her interest in Classic Gold. She told the panel that she had begun to listen after the death of her mother. She said that the station brought back memories of the past, and helped her with her grieving process. I later interviewed Jenny at her home, a three-bedroom semi-detached house in a suburban area of Bristol. She lives there with her husband, who is a skilled factory worker, and her two sons aged seven and ten. Jenny was born in Bristol and has lived here all her life. Before she had children, she worked in the same factory as her husband. Now she works part time as a dinner lady. Jenny's mother died two years ago:

> [S]ince my mum died I found that I needed something here . . . she lived about five, ten minutes away, I used to see her quite a lot. She was a widow . . . I used to go round and see her, and I did miss her, especially coming back from school, in the mornings. When you get up, everything's going on, getting ready to go out, but the bit was when I came back – my husband works shifts, so if he was like working mornings, when I came back from school about quarter past nine I found this was the most loneliest part of the day, very quiet . . . When I came back I used to feel terrible and rather than just go out and find something to do I thought 'no, I have to stick this out, but I need something', so, I just put the radio on one day and it just happened to be Classic Gold and I just, it was very funny because a lot of my childhood was that type of record. I can remember things, certain records make me remember things . . . there was a certain record I remember seeing my dad standing at the sink shaving, and it reminds me of this *every* time it comes on . . .

Jenny's use of Classic Gold could be seen as nostalgic. Interestingly, she appears to be reaching back across time and across memories, bringing something into the present, to take her into the future. The memories evoked by the radio are, she says, all good, and although she recognizes that there may be an aspect of selectivity in her remembering, it is not usually particularly visual images, or actual specific events that are evoked, rather it is a feeling, a mood, a kind of experience, which does not interfere with the present, but enhances it.

Kerri is forty-seven years old. She works part time as a community safety officer, working with the Asian community in Bristol. She also works part time for the BBC as a link person with the Asian community. Kerri was born in Delhi and has lived in Bristol for the past twenty-six years. She is married and has a son of twenty-three and a daughter of twenty-five. Her early memories of radio from 'back home' are of the BBC's World Service, and various Asian stations. When she is carrying out household tasks that she finds boring, listening to music that she first heard in her youth, creates nostalgic memories of her life in India and her move to England, a time of great excitement for her;

> . . . what I do, I still love the old music, because it brings me closer to home I think, when I was eighteen or nineteen, because I got married when I was nineteen, the type of music I listened to then, now if it suddenly comes on air I know certain times they're going to play the old things, like Brunel does, I still love Brunel [Classic Gold], that's another one I like, because they play the music that I used to listen to back home . . . It just brings back my good old days. I remember, oh!, when I first came to this country twenty-six years ago, Mary Hopkin was singing *Those Were the Days*, you know! [laughter]

But nostalgia and memories do not have to relate to specific and easily explained, or rationalizable, connections. Connections, as they are lived and managed, do not have to be rationalizable, linguistically or otherwise. They are experienced as just one element, or aspect, of everyday life and ongoing identity creation. Here we can look at the notion of the creation of dynamic 'new ethnicities' (Gillespie 1995), using the example of Lynne, a white woman, who draws heavily on Jamaican culture and music to live her life, as a white woman in a white culture. I met Lynne at the single parent social group. She is thirty years old, with a son aged four years, whose father is Jamaican. Lynne grew up in a rural area close to Bristol and lived in Bath before moving to Bristol nine years ago. She used to work in insurance, but since Dan's birth has lived on income support. Recently, she has begun an art course, and plans to go on to take a degree in fine art. Art has always been a hobby of hers, and she feels lucky to be spending a lot of her time drawing and painting. She lives in a small flat, with only one bed/sitting room, a kitchen and a bathroom. She lives in a street with a Jamaican name.

When Lynne was a child, she remembers her mother listening to Radio 2:

> that was the soft music wasn't it, that was particularly aimed at housewives, and they had recipes and they had 'what's the recipe today Jim?' and who else, oh yea, Terry Wogan, then it switched to David Hamilton . . .

Researcher: so did she listen to it a lot?

Lynne: Yea, all the time, then later on, my Dad, he listened to Radio Bristol, and they ... but my mum would have the radio on all day that she was in the house ... you know I can remember the radio quite vividly

As a teenager, Lynne remembers it being 'compulsory' to listen to the chart show on the radio on Sundays, and to write down and remember the chart positions. When the charts were announced in the week, someone would always smuggle a radio into school, so that at break times they could find out what was happening. Up until the age of fourteen, Lynne liked more or less the same music as her friends, but then, at fourteen, her tastes changed:

Lynne: They played Bob Marley's *I Don't Want to Wait in Vain* and I really liked that. Everyone said 'Oh, that's a thoughtless song' but I really liked that, and ever since then, I've really liked reggae, and Stevie Wonder, *Sir Duke*, so from listening then I started to move into soul and reggae, before I knew anything you know, because I lived in the countryside, there were no black people, no black, they didn't know anything about it.

Researcher: Was this just you, or your friends as well?

Lynne: Just me, just my personal taste. I mean they liked Pink Floyd, Emerson Lake and Palmer, Queen, and Abba ...

Nowadays, the TV dominates the media consumption in Lynne's flat, with her son being the 'telly addict', while Lynne prefers to get on with her art, or listen to music. Her son does not like the radio, and as there is only one radio in the flat, in the same room as the TV (bed/sitting room) the radio is not used as often as Lynne would like. She tends to listen mainly when Dan is asleep, or staying with friends. Whenever she gets the chance, the radio will be turned on, and it is tuned to a local pirate station, 'I stumbled across pirate radio stations and they just happened to play the music that I like ... they don't just stick to one type of it, they also will play, I've heard them playing Shirley Bassey, gospel, very traditional ... reggae, right up to ragga, to the more commercial soul, they play a lot of soul.' She will listen to the radio at least a couple of times a week, to relax after a busy day, or to help her to get through boring housework:

I often do my ironing to the radio, especially if its reggae because I dance to it while I'm doing the ironing, and housework, you know, boring chores like that . . . well I enjoy doing boring tasks like ironing if I can listen to the radio . . . you can enjoy dancing to the music while you're doing something boring like chopping up the onions . . . it gives you sort of energy you know, do the job faster, you can actually enjoy cooking along to the music . . . it just makes mundane jobs more bearable.

When Lynne gets the chance, if her son is away with friends, she will switch the radio on and turn up the volume:

I think, 'Oh yea, turn the radio up' and I'm actually dancing around the living room . . . I'm dancing away in front of the mirror and all sorts . . .

I think it's a sort of moment that you've got to yourself, you know, like Dan's gone and turn the volume up and you're dancing about. And a couple of times I've done it with friends you know, they've come in and put the music on really loud, dancing around. My friend came over from the countryside and walked in here and said 'wow, what's this music Lynne?' and it was funk music, which I'm not so much, I like it but it doesn't appeal to me as much as reggae, but she really liked it, and it was up and she was dancing around my living room. I was making the tea or something, she was dancing around.

Mostly though, Lynne will listen to the radio when she is alone, as many of her friends have a different taste in music. She will listen to blues music on tape if she is very tired but can't sleep: 'they're very relaxing, and they're very moody and depressed so if I'm in that sort of mood I listen to them, their problems are always worse. Whereas reggae's a more happier mood music.' She has reggae music on tape, but her collection is limited, and the radio will play more variety. She explains that she likes the pirate stations, not simply because of the music they play, but also because it is a way for her to maintain a connection with a world of which she is not fully a part:

well it's a way of keeping in touch with what's going on, especially, I mean, I've got a child and I can't go out to the clubs very much. And another thing is some of the reggae clubs in Bristol are so rough that you don't wanna go out to them, the environment isn't very nice you know, they're filthy places, some of the people are on drugs. Whereas, on the other hand, some of my friends are really nice, but they wouldn't listen

to reggae, or they wouldn't mix in that culture, that scene, they don't
know about it. So I find it keeps me in touch with what's on, I'm aware,
but I'm not having to go out to it . . .

Radio sound for Lynne, makes a connection with the world of
Jamaican reggae culture of which she is physically unable to be a part.
Her paintings and drawings around the flat, of a Jamaican mother and
child (which she drew when pregnant), of Bob Marley, and other
Caribbean images, help to maintain the link that is central to her sense
of self. Radio, as a sound medium, has a quality that allows for fluid
creation and (re)creation of connections. Lynne's use of radio sound
makes connections with the culture and music of Jamaica, as expressed
and experienced by her, here in Bristol. The connections are tangible,
incorporating memories, imagination, and what we could define as
'nostalgia'. Her affective link with Jamaican music and culture pre-dates
her relationship with Dan's father but is continued through her child's
cultural heritage which in some ways legitimates her own fascination
and claim for a connection.

Nostalgia

Seremetakis (1994) tells the story of the disappearance of a fruit in
Greece. The fruit was like a peach and was referred to as 'the breast of
Aphrodite' because of its texture, appearance, taste and smell. This fruit
was gradually replaced by imported and hybrid peaches, conforming
to EEC standards. Seremetakis, on visits to Greece, would enquire if
anyone had come across Aphrodite's peach. The reaction of friends and
relatives at first, was that it was still around, they just hadn't come across
it recently. Gradually the realization dawned that it had gone – it now
only existed in memory. The memory of the peach, Seremetakis says,
is nostalgic. There is a difference between the American and the Greek
uses of nostalgia, which points to 'different cultural experiences of the
senses and memory' (Seremetakis 1994). She sees the American definition of nostalgia as implying 'trivializing romantic sentimentality',
whereas the Greek definition of *nostalghía* 'is the desire or longing with
burning pain to journey. It evokes the sensory dimension of memory
in exile and estrangement; it mixes bodily and emotional pain and ties
painful experiences of spiritual and somatic exile to the notion of
maturation and ripening' (Seremetakis 1994).

Seremetakis chooses Greece as a site to examine senses and memory,
because she sees it as on the margins of modernity. And it is from the

margins, that one can get a better view of the centre. Modernity threatens the viability and standing of sensory memory;

> The particular effacement of sensory memory in modernity, is mainly a consequence of an extreme division of labor, perceptual specialization and rationalization. The senses, in modernity, are detached from each other, re-functioned and externalized as utilitarian instruments, and as media and objects of commodification. The carving out and partitioning of separate domains of perceptual acquisition also authorizes the sheer literality of sensory experience. The literal is a symbolic logic produced by the scientific rationalization of the senses and/or by a culture of specialized consumption. (Seremetakis 1994: 9–10)

Classen (1993) looks at the Western historical construction of the five senses and their values, demonstrating how they are culturally constructed. She shows how sight, as '*the* sense of science' provides us with 'most of our models of the universe, from maps and charts to diagrams' (Classen 1993: 6). The quality of sight that gives it its 'objective' character and separates the viewer from the viewed makes the scientific rationale possible. At the same time 'This 'objectivity', nonetheless, by its very visual basis, is grounded in a very peculiar 'view' of the world, and, bird's eye view though it may be, this view is still limited and conditioned by the characteristics of vision' (Classen 1993: 6). This is just one of the ways in which we know and make sense of the world.

Classen demonstrates how one could equate vision with surface perception, scientific understanding and linearity, whilst sound might be more easily equated with depth perception, interior understanding and dynamism. We could say that an emphasis on visual, objective reality, threatens the creativity of sound, so that elements of culture that reside in this mode have been devalued. However, given the emphasis on the visual, sound may also have freedom to work in creative ways and through the consumption of radio sound the power of nostalgia may have real affective depth.

For a term such as nostalgia, reducing it to 'trivializing romantic sentimentality' serves to confine the past and remove it 'from any transactional and material relation to the present', isolating, and making the past consumable, as a 'unit of time' (Seremetakis 1994: 4). In the American sense, nostalgia 'freezes the past in such a manner as to preclude it from any capacity for social transformation in the present, preventing the present from establishing a dynamic perceptual relationship to its history. Whereas the Greek etymology evokes the transformative impact

of the past as unreconciled historical experience' (Seremetakis 1994: 4).
In Greek, the etymology of the senses is closely associated with the
etymology of emotion and feeling. There are no 'clear cut boundaries
between the senses and emotions, the mind and body, pleasure and
pain, the voluntary and the involuntary, and affective and aesthetic
experience' (Seremetakis 1994: 5). The memory of Aphrodite's peach,
produces a memory of the peach that evokes a taste, felt in the body,
with both pleasure in remembering, and pain in its loss, so that every
other peach which tries to take its place is tasteless in comparison.
More than just this fruit, Seremetakis argues that a whole epoch can
become 'tasteless' when a sensorial culture, made up of a 'dynamic
interaction between perception, memory and a landscape of artefacts',
is dissolved into disconnected pieces. In Greece, the 'characterisation
anosto (tasteless) . . . deals with the cultural incapacity to codify past,
present, and anticipatory experiences at the level of sensory existence'
(Seremetakis 1994: 8). Tastelessness is brought about by modernity and
its 'scientific rationalization of the senses'. The consumption and use
of radio sound demonstrates that sound as a sense is still used to great
effect, in everyday life. It does appear to be entwined with everyday life
and emotions, perhaps counteracting our experience of the 'tasteless'
public sphere by providing us with personal and private flavours.

Nostalgia is seen here as both a mode of consumption and a mode
of production – it is consumed through radio and music and at the same
time it is practised, it is a mode of production. In Britain, things like
records and films, from the past, or evocative of the past, are said to be
nostalgic. Often there is a romantic sentimentality attached, and there
is a sense of the past as a separate unit of time. Nevertheless, when we
consider how this nostalgia is experienced – it is bodily, through the
senses, emotions and memories. To say that one 'sensed' something in
Britain, is to say that, through intuition, or some other, non-rationalizable
means, one 'knows' something. This, then, constitutes a way of knowing
that is not privileged, but nevertheless is experienced bodily. Nostalgia
and memories can thus be experienced, or 'tasted', in a way that is non-
linear and does not lend itself easily to linguistic translation. And in
practice, the use of radio sound as nostalgia can be much more than
romantic sentimentality. Paul demonstrates this.

Paul is twenty-nine years old, works as a teacher, and lives alone in
Bristol in a rented flat. He listens to Classic Gold which 'reminds' him
of the 1960s, which his parents tell him he would have loved. The
sociality of the 1960s is experienced by Paul, imaginatively, through
the tales of his parents, and materially through his listening to Classic

Gold radio. Just as the memory of the taste of the peach is remembered both by those who tasted it, and by those who heard the memories of those who tasted it, memories of a past can be materially evoked and lived by Paul, whose memories are based on those of his parents, in their stories of a 'lovely time'.

Paul's nostalgic memories are more than romantic sentimentality. They are a way of life for him. Remembering in the way that he does adds to his sense of himself as a social person – it is a social activity in that it contributes to his sociality (Tacchi 1998). The close knit family, the 'cheery get togethers', that he sees as resonant of the 1960s, are a part of his life, which are in some ways emphasized by the way in which he lives. For example, Paul 'lives' at his parents home, in Wales. He works in Bristol, and has rented a flat, where he stays from Monday until Friday. But at weekends and holidays, he is to be found 'back home'. His tiresome train journeys to and from Bristol, emphasize his inclusion in, and his temporary separation from, his family, who, for him, epitomize the ideal family of the past. His belonging to his family, and their ideal characteristics, are thus clarified and felt by him. If his life were different and he lived at 'home' all of the time, this aspect of his family life, which he prizes so highly, might not be so apparent.

In his Bristol flat, he uses Classic Gold as an almost constant accompaniment, because it 'generates a nice atmosphere';

Paul: Its nice to hear that music again, you know, I sort of grew up
             with that music when I was younger.
Researcher: Some of them are from before you were born
Paul: Exactly yes, um, because my mother and father says, they said
             to me a few years back, its a shame you weren't around in the
             sixties because it would have suited you down to the ground,
             you really are, you like that era, I said yes, I probably would
             have, you know, the spirit of togetherness, because I love the
             family holidays, the Butlins and my mother and father, we
             used to love Butlins, we used to go there every year with my
             elder brother and sister who are a bit older than I am, and
             you know I used to join in all the games . . .

Paul demonstrates that Anderson's 'imagined community' (1983) can be thought of in a temporal as well as a spatial sense. He makes sense of the present, through nostalgic practices, experienced positively.

Battaglia (1995) challenges the definition, by some scholars, of nostalgia as a negative notion. Rather, it should be considered in different contexts, *contingently*. She questions the 'assumption that nostalgia has a *categorically* negative social value for indigenous actors' (Battaglia 1995: 77). On the contrary, Battaglia finds that nostalgia 'may in fact be a vehicle for knowledge, rather than only a yearning for something lost' (Battaglia 1995: 77). Her study looks at migrant urban Trobrianders in Port Moresby, Papua New Guinea, and the first yam festival to be held there in 1985. These festivals are linked nostalgically with the yam competitions of their former Trobriand Islands home. Battaglia suggests that these nostalgic practices give the Trobriand Islanders now living in an urban context an 'attachment of appropriate feelings toward their own histories, products, and capabilities' (Battaglia 1995: 77). That is to say that, for urban Trobrianders, participation in the yam festival is a nostalgic act that connects them with 'Home'. At the same time it allows a form of resistance to their 'postcolonial' detachment from that Home and its culture.

In Bristol, radio sound, and the nostalgic practices that it enables could be viewed as creating both a link to past or distant memories and places, and a resistance to conditions of modernity that fragment such connections, often experienced in terms of isolation or loneliness. (Conversely, it could be understood as highly selective forgetting or denial.) Emphasizing a view of nostalgia as embodied, Battaglia detaches 'the notion of nostalgia from the merely sentimental attitude with which we may too easily associate it' (Battaglia 1995: 77). Nostalgia, in her observation of it, is 'embodied; it is the practice of yam growing for urban Trobrianders who talk about the gardens of 'Home' . . . as distinct from their 'house' to which they have returned each day for twenty years after working 'for cash' in Port Moresby' (Battaglia 1995: 77). Battaglia thinks of this as a 'practical or active nostalgia' that is 'transformative action with a connective purpose' (Battaglia 1995: 78). Thus it is that practical nostalgia may involve connections with a past object, which nevertheless contribute to future relationships:

Indeed, nostalgia for a sense of future – for an experience, however imaginary, of possessing the means of controlling the future – may function as a powerful force for social reconnection. In permitting creative lapses from dominant realities, it is such a nostalgia that enables or recalls to practice more meaningful patterns of relationship and self-action. The capacity of nostalgia to engender its own ironies is hence a central consideration here, and bears directly on how local and national cultural identities are argued and contested. (Battaglia 1995: 78)

The nostalgia that Battaglia observed, in the urban Trobriand case, does not replace authentic engagement with culture, 'it is not for Trobriand subjects merely a yearning for some real or authentic thing. Rather, it generates a sense of productive engagement which is at once more personal and larger than any product it might find as its object' (Battaglia 1995: 93). The textured soundscapes that are created with the help of radio sound, in the homes of listeners, is, similarly, personal, and it extends beyond the sound that their radio sets emit, it is a 'productive engagement' with wider society, yet it can be contained in the domestic sphere. That is not to suggest that 'nostalgic listening' is confined to the domestic sphere which the research discussed here concentrates upon – it surely happens also in cars and workplaces.

Conclusion

Nostalgic practice, as cultural practice, 'abides in a convergence of mimesis and poesis – in acts of replicating the social conditions of and for feeling', and through such actions the 'experience of social life is supplemented and qualitatively altered' (Battaglia 1995: 93). The key notion here is that nostalgic practices supplement social life, and qualitatively alter it. For example, Jenny was able, through the use of radio sound, to enhance her life and self, add to her domestic experience, and *feel* better about her everyday life and her self within it. She could make connections with memories evoked by the sound, and with imaginary others, who make and consume the same sound, although her case is particular and specific to her own life and experiences. It helped her, she feels, in her grieving process – it may be that it *altered* it, by substituting another activity, or she may have been distracted from her grief. In any case, it gave her a sense of not being alone and isolated with the grief caused by the loss of her mother. As Battaglia suggests, this nostalgic practice, as social action, enabled her to break from the situation she found herself in and to connect with other sources of meaning and feeling; it 'opens subjects to creative reconfiguration: nostalgic practice invites self-problematization' (Battaglia 1995: 93). For Jenny and others, they can work on self and sociality in a safe environment, created in and via a soundscape that is not, and need not be, as fixed or recognized officially, or even expressible linguistically, as other aspects of their social and personal lives. It operates alongside the more visible aspects of life, having its own depths, being bodily felt through affect, yet always working in conjunction with, rather than at odds with, everyday domestic and public social selves. It may be that the affective aspects of nostalgic practices, connected and managed by, amongst other things, radio sound, constitutes the very core of the thing we call 'everyday life'.

Battaglia further suggests that 'it follows that any notion of an integral, coherent self – any vehicle universally applied to such – must be seriously reconsidered, together with any notion that an aesthetic of self-wholeness or completeness extends in practice across cultures and times' (Battaglia 1995: 93).

My research suggests that everyday domestic life in Bristol is often geared towards the creation and recreation of the idea of a coherent self, and that this is an ongoing enterprise, and sometimes a struggle. It is variously undertaken and is experienced in different sensory modalities. It is not just a question of establishing a role, or a role in a relationship, but is an ongoing attempt to maintain a sense of self in that and other roles and that and other relationships. The fact that one is a wife and mother, or a single parent on income support, is not, in itself enough. This is not the end of the enterprise. Such roles establish a 'state', but not a 'state of mind'. As a state, they may provide a fixed point from which, and with which, one may develop links, relationships, feelings and meanings, but in practice it is an ongoing journey, which changes, sometimes subtly, sometimes more dramatically.

Nostalgia suggests looking back. It can be demonstrated that through nostalgic practices, the past, imagined or real, as Battaglia and Seremetakis remind us, can be brought into the present, as a feeling that alters the present, and can further be projected into the future. For urban Trobrianders, nostalgic practices 'reinvented the present'. It was not simply representing a tradition, it was creating a 'gap', 'in which alternative, cohabiting identities could become apparent' (Battaglia 1995: 93). Much of my data would support Battaglia's claim that for practitioners of nostalgia, '"lapsing" into it', they may 'come to realize a productive capacity' (Battaglia 1995: 93). In the Bristol case, this productive capacity could be described in terms of producing a sense of self, relationships and everyday worlds that they can live with; a creative potential, drawing on memories, fantasy and feelings, in a creative and fluid reality that does not need to be fixed in terms of verbal, or even conscious, explanation; that does not challenge in any direct way, official or dominant views of society and life within it, and yet can maintain stability over time. Thus, nostalgia can be, as Battaglia asserts, a 'vehicle for knowledge and experience with a culturally specific historicity and a wholly *contingent* aesthetic efficacy' (Battaglia 1995: 93).

Nostalgia is experienced personally, it is embodied, it is contingent, and potentially both positive and negative. Because of this, in order to understand nostalgic practices a researcher must engage in the lives of people on a more than superficial level. Whilst the study of radio consumption reported upon here is not ethnography in the traditional anthropological sense, engagement in the lives of respondents beyond a single in-depth interview has allowed me to develop with some confidence the ideas about nostalgia and radio listening contained in this paper. Without such engagement the experiential nature of radio listening, nostalgia and their role in everyday life would have been hard to uncover.

Such a research approach allows me to state that nostalgia has a link with the past, with memories, experienced first hand, or in tales told by others. The verification of memories is not what nostalgia, as discussed in this paper, is about. It is an embodied feeling that can, I suggest, be evoked through the use of radio sound, or created by it, as it does not have to pre-exist the experience. As such, radio sound can be seen to have a connecting power with (actual or imagined) pasts. Radio sound and nostalgia also hold this connecting power in terms of the present, and the future.

By looking in detail at a medium that is as unassuming and 'natural-ized' as radio in the home, we are able to catch a glimpse of everyday living that can be obscured by more visual and prominent media. Not all that has been discussed about radio sound is transferable to other media; it is the quality of radio sound in domestic life that has been the focus of this investigation. However, it could be concluded that everyday life has many hidden depths, crevices, corners, threads and strands, that go beyond the surface structures, and observable behaviours, which are amenable to quantifying scientific examination. The potential meanings of words such as 'intimate', 'friend' and 'company' when used in relation to radio, have more significance than a linguistic analysis can uncover. This paper has demonstrated how radio sound facilitates connections across time in sensory and affective realms. In order to understand the consumption of radio sound in the home, one must incorporate the experiential and affective aspects of everyday living.

Notes

1. Bristol is a city in the South West of England with a population of around 400,000 people. The data were obtained through in-depth interviews which formed the major part of an anthropological study of the role of radio in everyday life carried out between 1992 and 1996 (Tacchi 1997) and funded by

the Economic and Social Research Council. The study took an ethnographic approach using in-depth interviews, participant observation, observation at two local commercial radio listener panels, and focus groups. Some respondents completed diaries of their listening practices. A major problem facing an anthropologist interested in carrying out ethnographic research on radio listening is how to carry out participant observation. I sought ways of getting to know my respondents beyond the in-depth interviews which are now widely used by 'reception ethnographers' in the fields of media and cultural studies (Moores 1993). To this end I attended a single parent social club for one year. There I got to know people in a social setting and establish a relationship with them that, whilst always clearly one of 'researcher and researched', often came closer to friends and confidantes. In addition I attended two local radio listener panels over a two-year period enabling a more extended and holistic relationship to develop with those that I went on to interview.

2. It also serves to continue an argument presented elsewhere (Tacchi 2000) that urges radio studies, or the study of radio, to embrace a variety of disciplinary approaches.

References

Anderson, B. (1983), *Imagined Communities: Reflections on the Origin and Spread of Nationalism*, London: Verso.

Battaglia, D. (1995), 'On Practical Nostalgia: Self-Prospecting Among Urban Trobrianders', in D. Battaglia (ed.) *Rhetorics of Self-Making*, London: University of California Press.

Classen, C. (1993), *Worlds of Sense: Exploring the Senses in History and Across Cultures*, London: Routledge.

Gillespie, M. (1995), *Television, Ethnicity and Cultural Change*, London: Comedia.

Moores, S. (1993), *Interpreting Audiences: The Ethnography of Media Consumption*, London: Sage.

Seremetakis, C. N. (1994), 'The Memory of the Senses, Part I: Marks of the Transitory' In C. N. Seremetakis (ed.), *The Senses Still: Perception and Memory as Material Culture in Modernity*, London: University of Chicago Press.

Tacchi, J. (2000), 'The Need for Radio Theory in the Digital Age', *International Journal of Cultural Studies*, 3(2): 289–98.

—— (1998), 'Radio Texture: Between Self and Others', in D. Miller (ed.), *Material Cultures: Why Some Things Matter*, London: UCL Press/ University of Chicago Press.

—— (1997), 'Radio Sound as Material Culture in the Home', unpublished PhD Thesis, University College London.

Part IV

Sounds in the City

The city is a noisy aural landscape as well as an edifice built of steel and concrete. The essays in this section attempt to re-think the relationship between time and place in urban contexts through thinking about streets and neighbourhoods as acoustic environments or soundscapes. We foregrounded this in our introductory essay and cited the work of Murray Shafer and Bruce Smith who have both argued that an attention to sound helps us orientate the physical landscape in time. In this sense, an attention to sound helps put the city in motion and alerts us to how places change as they are animated by sound. Sound and movement are closely related in the navigation of urban experience. The use of personal stereo or car hi fi are good examples of the ways in which people try to control their experience of moving to and through cities.

Fran Tonkiss, in her beautiful essay 'Aural Postcards', points to the importance of the sonic in understanding the aesthetic quality of city life. She argues that while the visual spectacle of the city might be the 'the action', the atmosphere of urban experience is affected through sound. She argues that the modern city is ultimately a sonic phenomenon. She suggests that, today, the signature tune of modern cities is the rattle of mass transit reminding all who hear it that 'the city is a sort of machine'. Her essay also foregrounds the ways in which memories are kept in 'sound souvenirs' that are collected as we pass through the urban landscape at particular moments in time. This is not just a matter of the unique quality of one city as opposed to another but it is also a reminder of the interconnection that exists between this and another place. She cites a friend who is reminded of Italy when he hears church bells ring in the early morning in London's Soho district. She comments on how difficult it is to find silence in the city. Even in 'muted hours' there is a background murmur. As the lights go out on the cityscape the sound goes down but it is never completely still.

The relationship between urban landscape, memory and community is foregrounded in Les Back's essay on football stadiums and fan plainsong. He argues that football stadiums operate like altars of memory. The grounds become the place in which identities and histories are brought to life through group singing. He begins his essay by asking why blind football fans attend matches when they cannot see the action? His answer is that the meaning of the game for football fans is to be found as much in the sonic as the visual dimensions of 'spectatorship'. Back also looks at the ways in which notions of identity and belonging are coded racially within the performance of songs and collective rituals that are brought to life on matchdays. Here boundaries are drawn within sound and communities are composed within these seemingly simple and banal forms of collective singing.

The role of sound in the composition of the city picked up in Jean-Paul Thibaud's contribution. He argues that urbanites use of their personal stereos transforms their experience of place. This does not mean that the Walkman-listener is entirely cut off from the urban environment. Rather, a precarious balance is created between what s/he hears and travels through. Thibaud argues that this leads to a 'derealization' of urban space achieved through the technical mediation of the sound equipment. Unsettling the relationship between sound and vision produces new ways of experiencing the city. This is not just a matter of protecting the walking listener from the noise of the city or to distract attention away from the boredom of commuting. Rather, it enables the citizen to filter or enhance the events and places that give meaning to living in a city. Thibaud argues that through such forms of 'musical nomadism' new forms of public behaviour have emerged that have transformed the shape and appearance of city life.

Caroline Bassett draws attention to the relationship between space and time and public and private life in her discussion of mobile phones. She argues that mobile phones have changed the experience of the urban landscape and the way people navigate the city. She suggests that at the heart of the 'spatial economy' of mobile phone use is a dialectic between presence/absence. The person one is speaking to on the phone is simultaneously absent and present, whereas the people standing next to the user only hears half the story. More than this, Bassett points to the ways in which mobile phones enable city dwellers to make connections with people in an increasingly fragmented lifestyle. Here she suggests that the mobile phone functions as a 'mnemonic operator' enabling the users to have an inventory of the places and people s/he is connected to. The mobile becomes the means through which its users manage the overlapping spaces of work, home and leisure.

Michael Bull concludes the section by examining automobiles and their interiors as a kind of soundscape. In this sense the car function as a 'homely place' that travels through urban space from residence to work and all places in-between. By combining theoretical and empirical reflections he shows how drivers rewrite what he calls their 'daily scripts' through music and sound. So, the 'script' associated with driving (empty and mundane time) is reclaimed and transformed through the construction of a privatized sound world in which the radio or CD player offers a meaningful refuge. Bull concludes that there is an ambivalent relationship to public space embedded in the everyday use of the automobile. It is a privatized space in which citizens construct their 'own protective bubble' to guard against the experiential ravages of urban life. Yet, at the same time drivers actively reconstruct their experience precisely through the commercial sounds of popular music.

16

Aural Postcards
Sound, Memory and the City

Fran Tonkiss

Below is shadow where any blasé thing takes place: clarinets and love-
making, fists and the voices of sorrowful women. A city like this makes
me dream tall and feel in on things. Hep.

(Morrison 2001: 7)

Sound gives us the city as matter and as memory. In this register, the
double life of cities – the way they slide between the material and the
perceptual, the hard and the soft – is spoken out loud, made audible.
The clamour, the density, the sheer weight of the modern city is heard
as a machinic, constant and 'general assault on the senses' (Mumford
1961: 539). And then – listen – there is the way a city comes to us in
memory and reverie, its cadences, whispers and sighs like the voices of
sorrowful women. The Babel of the crowd and the wordless solitude of
the individual in a noisy city capture in sound a larger urban tension
between collective and subjective life. Sometimes it can be hard to hear
anything, hard even to listen to one's own thoughts, amongst all the
noise.

Listening and not Listening in the City

More than one social theorist has been dazzled by the *spectacle* of the
modern city. For Georg Simmel, urban experience was essentially and
frenetically visual. And Walter Benjamin, who was shortsighted but
finely tuned to sound, nevertheless remarked that urban sociality was

more a question of looking at than of listening to: 'Interpersonal relationships in big cities', he wrote, 'are distinguished by a marked preponderance of the activity of the eye over the activity of the ear' (Benjamin 1983: 38). The primacy these moderns give to the visual over the aural says something about the aesthetic quality of city life. As in the cinema when the sound tape doesn't come in and the reel unwinds silently, there is a thinness, a lightness, a kind of estrangement about seeing without sound. It offers surface without depth, appearance without resonance. Where the visual is action and spectacle, sound is atmosphere. But the modern city, for all that there is to see, is not only spectacular: it is sonic.

Cities provided a soundstage for the drama of modern life. As a heightened visual scene engaged the urban subject in new kinds of attention and distraction (Crary 2001), so logics of listening in the city came to be divided between the engineered and the accidental, between sound and noise (see Barry 2000). Modern auditory technologies – in architecture and design as well as in recording and broadcasting – served to marshal and discipline sound in space, from the muted interior of the office building to the total acoustics of the concert hall (Thompson 2002). These ways of attending to sound, whether in order to pacify, to purify or to amplify it, carved out acoustic order from the discordant rhythms of the city. Cities, after all, insist on the senses at the level of sound. It is easier and more effective to shut your eyes than it is to cover your ears. Ears cannot discriminate in the way eyes can – as with smell, hearing puts us in a submissive sensuous relation to the city. And yet still we glance at sounds in the city, we don't gaze. Individuals' relation to sound in the everyday spaces of the city tends to be one of distraction rather than attention. The exemplary urban attitude Simmel describes as 'blasé in this sense implies as much a dulling of sound as a dimming of vision. As a blank reaction to overstimulation, a narrowing or 'peculiar adjustment' of the senses (Simmel 1903: 179), the blasé posture inures the metropolitan to the hectic ambience of city life. It enacts at the subjective level a larger modern will to calm, to filter, to rationalize sound.

Acquired indifference is both the side-effect of and the best defence against 'too much indulgence in the nervous, metallic pleasure of cities' (Sontag 1982: 373). It is an attitude that flattens perception in the aural as in the visual realm; it gives us the fiction that people who speak to you on the street cannot be heard. Social deafness offers one kind of urban freedom – the lonely liberty of knowing that nobody is listening, no one likely to speak. In rendering technical what otherwise is simply learned, the mobile technologies of the personal stereo or telephone realize this logic of separation and of indifference perfectly. They reverse the modern intent of the concert hall or public address system as means of organizing a collective 'culture of listening' (Thompson 2002). Immersed in a private soundscape, engaged in another interactive scene, you do not have to be in the city as a shared perceptual or social space. No one else can really know where you are. Yet such acute individualization also finds its expression in the renegade desire to stand out, to announce your presence, somehow to make yourself heard. For when nobody is listening, it can be hard for a person to stay within earshot of anyone, to 'remain audible even to himself' (Simmel 1903: 184).

Not listening in the city makes spaces smaller, tamer, more predictable. The pretence that you do not hear – a common conspiracy of silence – in this way is a response, passing as lack of response, to the modern city as a place of strangers. Some people, though, sound stranger than others; certain voices jar to certain other ears. The immigrant, it has been said, is *audible*, and indeed those forms of race thinking that cannot bring themselves to speak of skin often are happy to talk of language. Speaking the same language is always a first requirement of 'assimilation', but the city as polyglot soundscape is a space in which differences remain audible and translations incomplete. The modern city, in its confusion of tongues, bespeaks otherness. In its many accents we hear a more literal version of what Roland Barthes meant when he wrote of the city as that 'place where the other is and where we ourselves are other, as the place where we play the other' (Barthes 1997: 171).

Barthes had an ear for the city. Although semiotics might seem a stringently visual form of cultural analysis, Barthes' semiology of the urban unfolded space using a metaphor of language as sound, not simply as noiseless sign. For all his insistence that it should be seen as a kind of 'writing' or 'text', Barthes' city kept bursting into speech in ways that go beyond the mute language of architectural symbols. 'The city', he claimed, 'speaks to its inhabitants, we speak our city, the city where we are, simply by living in it, by wandering through it' (Barthes 1997: 168). Walking the city, people invent their own urban idioms, a local language written in the streets and read as if out loud. A strange city, too, can seem like a language you don't know. Gradually you pick up a few words, recognize certain expressions, try out some turns of phrase. Walking, we compose spatial sentences that begin to make sense, come to master the intricate grammar of the streets; slowly, we learn to make the spaces of the city speak. Even laid out as a system of signs, cities won't rest quiet on the page – finally and vividly, the city for Barthes is a kind of poem that he wants 'to grasp and make sing' (Barthes 1997: 172).

Sound Souvenirs: Memory and the City

Walter Benjamin had that knack for making cities speak and sing. He souvenired sounds from different places, composed urban vignettes as if they were aural postcards. In Marseilles Benjamin tried to catch noises like butterflies in the empty streets up above the harbour – 'in these deserted corners', he wrote, 'all sounds and things still have their silences' (Benjamin 1928: 132). Amongst the travel souvenirs of other journeys, Benjamin brought back the 'soundless tumult' of the Alcazar in Seville and the bells of Freiburg Minster, still ringing in his ears in the echo of memory. It was this latter that led him to consider how

> The special sense of a town is formed in part for its inhabitants – and perhaps even in the memory of the traveller who has stayed there – by the timbre and intervals with which its tower-clocks begin to chime. (Benjamin 1925–6: 82)
>
> The special sense of a city maybe no longer is given by tower-clocks and church-bells – by sounds, that is, which tell time – but rather by those that tell of motion. The peculiar sounds of transit are the signature tunes of modern cities. These are sounds that remind us the city is a sort of machine. The diesel stammer of London taxis, the wheeze of its buses. The clatter of the Melbourne tram. The two-stroke sputter of Rome. The note that sounds as the doors shut on the Paris metro, and the flick, flick, flick of the handles. The many sirens of different cities.

Such sounds are kept as souvenirs. In Paris one summer, in an apartment near the Gare de Lyon, I would go to sleep to the scrapes and the slides of the rollerbladers on the concourse outside the station, and to the low noise of late trains coming in, going out, heading south. In Sydney, another summer and living under the flightpath, I was woken each morning by the first plane of the day down from Singapore (sound telling time again, more reliable than a cheap alarm clock and louder than Freiburg Minster). Sounds can deceive and displace, too – or at least can open out spaces to imaginative translations. A friend in London tells me that when he cycles through Soho in the early morning and hears the sound of church bells, it makes him think he is in Italy.

In these ways, sound threads itself through the memory of place. When, in the summer of 1949, E.B. White returned to New York as if to an old love affair, the sounds of the city were as evocative as somebody's remembered smell. As he orients himself again to familiar streets, it is sound that gives up the feel of the city. The heat of July is there in the murmur of electric fans, the passage of a politician in the scream of a siren. And there are silences that mark what has gone: the elevated railway has just about disappeared and he 'misses the sound . . . the tremor of the thing' (White 1999: 48). Sound here works through metonym, aural fragments that speak of something larger. White knows that New York is a great port city, for example, even if the only boat he sees during his stay is a little sloop on the East River. He hears 'the *Queen Mary* blow one midnight, though, and the sound carried the whole history of departure and longing and loss' (White 1999: 23).

This relation of sound to memory is audibly present in the moment of 'recall', the melding of space, sound and memory there in the concept of 'resonance'; a movement in the air like sound you can touch. Benjamin – still myopic, still highly tuned – writes in his *Berlin Chronicle* that

> The *deja vu* effect has often been described. But I wonder whether the term is actually well chosen, and whether the appropriate metaphor to the process would not be far better taken from the realm of acoustics. One ought to speak of events that reach us like an echo awakened by a call, a sound that seems to have been heard somewhere in the darkness of past life. (Benjamin 1932: 59)

Such sound memories make us what Elias Canetti has called an 'ear-witness' to the scene. Canetti would have agreed with Benjamin's proposition – said of Kafka, whom both men admired – that 'He who listens hard doesn't see.' Hearing has its own relation to truth: to testimony, to spoken evidence, to placing trust in words rather than in images, to accepting things that are promised, even if they cannot be shown. Hearing likewise involves a special relationship to remembering. It might, as Benjamin says, *be* the sense of memory. The past comes to us in its most unbidden, immediate and sensuous forms not in the artifice of the travel photograph, but in the accident of sounds half-remembered. This is something like the difference between record and memory. There is a quality in those sounds not quite recalled that has the texture and the delicacy of memory itself. What music was playing, on that day, in that place? Do you remember where you were, when you heard the news? What words did she say, exactly, the last time I saw her? It might be less affecting if we had telescopes and cameras for the ears, if we could amplify and capture the echo and shudder of memory, if we took and kept our passing snapshots of sound.

The Silences of Cities

In the deserted corners of a city like Marseilles, Benjamin had said, 'all sounds and things still have their silences.' But how do we hear silence in the city, how is it that silence sounds *different* when we listen for it in cities? Somehow it is not the same as the deep 'soundlessness of the suburbs' (Self 1999: 118), but more provisional, chancier, kind of illicit. Stumbling across silence in the city – a quiet quarter, a lull in the traffic – can be like uncovering a secret. If music, as Adorno had it, is 'an art of time', so silence has the art of keeping time still. A minute's silence, after all, reminds you how slowly even the shortest time can pass. But while some forms of silence contain their sense of the timeless, the silences of cities seem precarious, as if only for the time being. It is a silence that is always about to be broken, or left behind. Think of the peculiar quiet of Sunday morning in the heart of a city like London. The place is stilled, gathered together, holding its breath.

Peter Ackroyd has written of the 'teeming' silence of London, a silence that shivers with the absence of all the people somewhere else, all the noise just out of earshot. And in these fragile spaces there invariably remains the incidental music of urban life: the low grumble of traffic, the drip of water somewhere, 'all the little noises that live inside the silences of the city' (Auster 1998: 279). If every sound and everything in the city has its silence, so silence gains its quality from a larger geography of sound. Empty space that doesn't talk back is as evocative as the hush that falls over the crowd, the telephone that doesn't ring, the dog that doesn't bark. A blasé manner of being in the city may lead you to not listen, but soundlessness – those moments in those places when the city stops speaking – can be strangely arresting. Quiet spaces are the weird negative of others making noise, where silence has stolen away and enclosed itself in place. Mostly, though, even in muted hours, there is the background murmur of the city talking to itself. Sometimes singing, perhaps, under its breath. Night comes to the city not only with the lights going out, but with the sound going down. It never turns off, it is just that some things – the cadence of night voices, distant traffic – grow louder in the mix. Still, late at night the quiet creeps in and it is as though you hear the city sleep. It can make you dream tall.

References

Ackroyd, P. (2000), *London: A Biography*, London: Chatto & Windus.
Auster, P. (1998), 'Appendix 3: *Squeeze Play*, by "Paul Benjamin" , in *Hand to Mouth: A Chronicle of Early Failure*, New York: Henry Holt & Co.

Barry, A. (2000), 'Noise', in S. Pile and N. Thrift (eds), *City A–Z*, London: Routledge.

Barthes, R. (1997) 'Semiology and the Urban', in N. Leach (ed.), *Rethinking Architecture*, London: Routledge.

Benjamin, W. (1925–6) 'One Way Street', in (1985), *One Way Street and Other Writings*, London: Verso, pp. 45–104.

—— (1928), 'Marseilles', in P. Demetz (ed.) (1986), *Reflections: Essays, Aphorisms, Autobiographical Writings*, New York: Schocken, pp. 131–6.

—— (1932), 'A Berlin Chronicle' in P. Demetz (ed.) (1986), *Reflections: Essays, Aphorisms, Autobiographical Writings*, New York: Schocken, pp. 3–60.

—— (1983), *Charles Baudelaire: A Lyric Poet in the Era of High Capitalism*, Harry Zohn (trans.), London: Verso.

Crary, J. (2001), *Suspensions of Perception: Attention, Spectacle, and Modern Culture*, Cambridge: MIT Press.

Morrison, T. (2001), *Jazz*, London: Vintage.

Mumford, L. (1961), *The City in History: Its Origins, its Transformations and its Prospects*, London: Penguin.

Self, W. (1999), 'Big Dome', in *London: The Lives of the City*. Granta 65 (Spring): 116–25.

Simmel, G. (1903), 'The Metropolis and Mental Life', in D. Frisby and M. Featherstone (eds) (1997), *Simmel on Culture*, London: Sage, pp. 174–85.

Sontag, S. (1978), 'Unguided Tour', in (1982) *A Susan Sontag Reader*, Harmondsworth: Penguin.

Thompson, E. (2002), *The Soundscape of Modernity: Architectural Acoustics and the Culture of Listening in America, 1900–1933*, Cambridge: MIT Press.

White, E.B. (1999), *Here is New York*, New York: The Little Bookroom.

17

Sounds in the Crowd

Les Back

I have always been perplexed by the devotion of blind football fans. At the club where I go to watch the football there is a small but committed group of such fans. Like everyone else they make their pilgrimage to the New Den, the home of Millwall Football club, on alternate Saturdays to support their beloved team. Football fans always speak of 'watching the game' but the presence of the blind supporters at the live spectacle also foregrounds the fact that a football ground is a sensory landscape that involves much more than the narrowly visual. I have sat next to one young boy who goes to Millwall on a number of times. The club provides him with headphones so that he can hear the local commentator describe the action on the pitch. Recently, I asked him why he loved coming to the games so much when he could listen to the same commentary at home. He explained, between sips of his half-time Coke, 'I love the atmosphere, that's why . . . and my Dad always gets me a Coke and a Hamburger. I hear things that you probably don't – the sounds in the crowd, I can tell by the way people react what they are seeing.'

Experiencing football as a fan was always as much about the sounds of the stadium as the visual exhibition of the game itself. Danny Blanchflower, former Spurs captain, once said that 'The noise of the crowd, the singing and chanting, is the oxygen we players breathe' (quoted in Thrills 1998). The corporeal nature of the fan culture needs to be represented in all its sensory dimensions. Particularly important here is the culture of sound, the songs that are sung and the acoustic quality of the noises in the crowd. It is primarily through songs and banter that a structure of feeling is produced in football stadiums. John Bale has argued that the 'sound of sport is a major medium for the enhancement of the sport landscape experience' (Bale 1994: 141). It is this auditory aspect, the formless noise and the spontaneous plainsong of football that I want to focus on in the remaining parts of this chapter.

Football stadiums can operate as sacred ground for their devotees. Much is often made of the parallels between the liturgy of football and religion. There are many examples of the distress and controversy caused when teams are forced to move grounds either temporarily or permanently. John Bale has described this issue through his discussion of Charlton Athletic's temporary move from the Valley (Bale 1994) and Garry Robson has discussed similar issues in relation to Millwall's move from their Coldblow Lane ground to the New Den (Robson 2000). As Bale has pointed out the ground itself can serve as the key site that holds the history of the club, and all it stands for, *in place*. In his book he referred to correspondence he had with a Manchester City fan:

> I have been a supporter since birth, well, since my parents first took me when I was around two years old. Since that time my interest has revolved more around the stadium than the team. Of course, I support the team through and through, but to me the club is Maine Road as that is the only part that rarely changes. Managers, players, directors, and even supporters come and go but the stadium never disappears. (cited in Bale 1994: 133)

This sense of football ground as sustaining historical continuity is underscored by the request often made by fans to have their ashes scattered on the pitch itself after their death. The playing surface provides a connection to past and future heroes who perform on it but it also serves literally and metaphorically as an altar of memory and commemoration. The physical structure of the ground is associated with a sense of geopiety (Tuan 1976) because it is a home that 'incarnates the past' (Tuan 1974: 247). It is a place to both play and be at home.

It is through this play that identities are animated and felt and taking these rituals seriously can provide insight into the inclusions and exclusions that operate. For example, one can only fully understand the degree to which particular football clubs are open to black and ethnic minority fans and players by understanding the often implicit and embodied normative structures at the heart of particular local football cultures. A key question is 'how do football clubs provide a means to ritualize community and represent locality and how do these issues connect with questions of ethnicity and race?' I want to suggest that part of the answer can be found by listening to football culture, listening to the sounds in the crowd and in the way that the young boy from Millwall suggests.

'South London is Wonderful': Locality, Football Culture and 'Symbolic Homes'

In line with other recent work (Robson 1999, 2000; Giulianotti 1993, 1999; Armstrong 1998, Armstrong and Giulianotti 1997), I want to begin with the idea that the triumph and despair of the club's fortunes encode the broader traces of social identity and cultural history. In this sense, football can offer a context in which urban cultural change and uncertainty are diluted through the renewal of the sense of place and belonging that is captured as fans move towards and through the turnstiles on matchdays.

In a sense the stadium provides one sphere in which the theatre of locality, to use Christian Bromberger's (1993) terms, is produced, made and renewed. The key here is to see how locality is produced through patterns of ritual and cultural life, rather than constituting an underlying ethological essence (Appadurai 1995). In cultural theory 'the local' is invariably coded as the parochial antithesis of our current globalizing world. Bruce Robbins has appealed recently that 'we cannot be content to set against [globalization] the childish reassurance of belonging to "a" place' (Robbins 1998: 3). The churlishness about localism on the part of left intellectuals has a long history. Garry Robson in his excellent recent study of football culture suggests that this ambivalence to the embodied culture of football and it's attendant rhetoric of locality amounts to a 'leftist-intellectualist opprobrium' (Robson 2000: 6). In the case of clubs like Millwall, he argues, urban myths ultimately reduce the club and its supporters to the breeding ground of proto-fascism. Taken together these positions mean that football fans that construct themselves as 'local patriots' are viewed as either 'infantile' or 'fascistic'. In order to avoid these shortcomings, local identity should be viewed as a product that is achieved through the practice of culture and commemorative rituals. This is not to suggest that the *symbolic home* that a stadium provides to its fans are a phantasm or a mirage. Rather, it is the arena for the embodiment of particular forms of social life, that have their own routines and cultural modes of expression. In short the football stadium provides one context in which local identity can be ritually defined, regardless of the changes taking place in its immediate environment and patterns of migration. For example, a Millwall fan coming to the New Den may be returning to an ancestral home, place of former residence or family association. The process of attending the match is a communion with the affective community that is embodied in supporting Millwall football club.

The fan cultures of particular clubs often share common ritual elements. For example, football songs are largely drawn from a relatively limited repertoire of melodies. With slight modifications the tunes for Rod Stewart's 'Sailin', or 'When the Saint's Go Marching in' or versions of Brit pop hits by Blur or Oasis can be heard in most of England's stadia. At the same time each fan culture exhibits distinct forms of prescribed formal ritual behaviour and symbolism. In order to understand the range of racist activity one needs to examine the relationship between processes of racialization and the collective ritual and symbolic practices that give any particular fan culture meaning. In this sense differences with regard to the level and intensity of racism need to be understood in terms of the way racist practices are nested within the ritual and collective symbolism of each fan culture. This is a very different type of argument from that which suggests that the fan cultures of particular clubs are wholly racist. Rather, we would suggest it is a matter of identifying the points where racialization takes place and equally those aspects of fan cultures that are more open to cultural difference and diversity.

It was exactly these issues that The Culture of Racism in Football Project conducted with my friends and colleagues John Solomos and Tim Crabbe attempted to understand. As part of a larger study of racism in football culture we looked at the histories of two football clubs in south London: Crystal Palace Football Club and Millwall Football Club. We immediately found a stark contrast between the high frequency of racism observed amongst some sections of Millwall's support, when compared to neighbouring Crystal Palace where racial abuse from fans was almost non-existent. There are some common features within the ritual forms of expression used at these clubs. For example, both clubs sing a song entitled 'South London is Wonderful.' Here is the Crystal Palace version:

Oh South Lon-don is won-der-ful,_____ oh South Lon-don is won-der-ful, it's full of tits, fan-ny and Pal-ace,__ oh South Lon-don is won-der-ful.

Interestingly, in Millwall's rendition of the song there is a second verse, which contrasts south London with a racist image of east London where Millwall's main rivals West Ham play:

Oh South Lon - don   is won - der - ful,____   oh South Lon - don   is won - der -
Oh East Lon - don   is like Ben - gal,____   oh East Lon - don   is like Ben -

ful,   it's full of tits,   fan - ny and Mill - wall,____   oh South Lon - don   is won - der - ful.
gal,   it's like the back   streets of Bom - bay,____   oh East Lon - don   is like Ben - gal.

The song evokes notions of Asianness by way of stigmatizing and vilifying east London. It is primarily directed at white East London racists – those who would be alarmed about the fact that their beloved area was like a foreign, alien country.

What is offered in the song is a series of stark contrasts between Self and Other. The first part of the song is a celebration of the self, which is expressed through the region. South London is also desired because of it's women folk – or more correctly particular sexualized anatomical objects – and the Club's home location. Thus, South London is a place full of sex and football! The absent racial presence here is the implicit understanding that South London is white or at best a place where black and white cockneys stand proudly side by side within a culture normalized by 'whiteness'.

East London is coded through a contrasting language of racial and Oriental Otherness. Race is transcoded through all of these references from the 'foreign back street' to the 'oriental city' so that the racialized subject of 'the Paki' can be invoked without actually being referred to directly. These images are all the product of a particular racialized imagination. Bombay is neither in Bengal nor Pakistan! The inconsistency and inaccuracies here show the notion of the 'Paki' provides a cipher to denote all aspects of a foreign subcontinent Otherness.

While the two fan cultures are in many ways contrasting, they also share the same melodies in their football songs. For example, the Eagles' collective song 'We are Palace' and Millwall's hymn 'No-one Likes Us' are both sung to the melody of Rod Stewart's 'Sailin''.

Despite these shared elements the difference between the two clubs with regard to the frequency of racism can to some degree be explained through an understanding of the contrasting nature of these fan cultures. As Garry Robson has pointed out, Millwall's collective imagery and symbolism is tightly bound up with the reproduction of a local, class-inflected masculine culture that bears the traces of the white working-class communities that worked in the docks and that have in large part disappeared (Robson 2000). Traditionally, the club's support is drawn from the areas of Bermondsey and inner south-east London. The irony of this situation is that today the club's support is drawn from the outer London suburbs from where fans migrate every Saturday to New Cross, reversing – albeit temporarily – the patterns of residential 'white flight'. According to the 1991 census 40 per cent of the population in the Marlowe ward in which the New Den is located is drawn from the ethnic minority communities. However, the culturally heterogeneous nature of South London life is not evident in the collective symbolism of Millwall. Rather, as Robson suggests, Millwall's collective imaginary is embodied and sustained through ritual and recursive means.

This concern with the pageantry and symbolism of the working-class past is enshrined in the club's theme song 'Let 'Em Come' performed by Roy Green and played before every home game. The tune has also been taken up amongst the fans as one of the collective rallying cries. The lyrics of the verses represents a pre-war Cockney idyll, complete with jellied eels, beer and reference to Millwall's ancestral home, The Old Den in Coldblow Lane:

It's Saturday a Coldblow Lane and we've all come down to cheer
We've got our jellied eels and our glass of beer
Come rain or shine all the time our families we'll bring
And as the Lions run on the pitch everyone will sing
Let em come, Let 'em come, Let 'em come . . .

The version sung in the ground also culminates with an altering of the melody like a pub singer giving a rendition of a popular song on the Old Kent Road. The sung version sounds like this:

At the core of Millwall culture is a form of 'neighbourhood nationalism' that is defined through local and class specific terms of inclusion and exclusion. Black participation is determined by the degree of shared experience of region, class and masculinity. In this sense Millwall represents a largely white enclave in an increasingly multi-racial environment.

In contrast Crystal Palace, located just five miles away, is less intensely connected with a white working-class past and the forms of localism that follow from this in the case of Millwall. Palace fandom is more mixed in terms of its class composition. It reflects the diverse quality of the south London suburbs of Croydon, Bromley and Merton. This to some extent comes through in the symbolism and ritual of Palace fandom. The Club's nickname was changed in the 1970s from 'The Glaziers' to 'The Eagles.' The main rallying cry for fans is a two note melodic dirge that intones the word 'Eagles':

For Palace, the Dave Clark Five's 1960s hit 'Glad All Over' is the equivalent of Millwall's 'Let 'em Come'. The melody of this tune is altered slightly in the fan's rendition. The song resounds with the enduring traces of post-war social change in this part of suburban London. In this sense 'Glad All Over' resonates with the experience of class mobility, improvements in council housing and 1960s affluence that affected this district and the families from which Palace fans are drawn.

'Glad All Over' – fan version

Alongside Palace's middle-class fans the club draws support from white working-class enclaves like New Addington and other suburban council estates and the contemporary forms of multiculture evident in districts like Thornton Heath, Norbury, Streatham and Forest Hill. Selhurst Park is located at the boundary of three wards, namely South Norwood, Thornton Heath and Whitehorse Manor and at the 1991 census the ethnic minority proportion of the total population was 20 per cent, 31 per cent and 30 per cent respectively. The association between Palace and black London was amplified during the 1980s by the string of black Londoners who played for the team including Vince Hillaire, Andy Gray, Ian Wright, John Salako and Dean Gordon.

I want to stress the importance of understanding the relationship between the two different contexts and the frequency and propensity for racist action. Put simply, we want to suggest that the different experience of these two clubs can only be understood by appreciating the ways in which the various fan cultures either inhibit or facilitate the expression of particular styles of racism. This, as we will argue, does not necessarily mean that one club is simply more racist than another. Rather, we suggest that there are different styles of expression in each case, be it the crude explicit racism of Millwall fans or the rather mute forms of racial stereotyping exhibited by Palace fans.

There is an overwhelming tendency for people involved in both the recreational and professional cultures of the game to play down the significance of racism in football and to speak, in very general terms, about the 'improvements' witnessed since the 1970s and 1980s (Back, Crabbe and Solomos 2001). This approach, at once, ignores the uneven development of racism within the game and the complex means by which racialized notions can be expressed in contemporary fan culture as illustrated in Millwall's version of 'South London is Wonderful'. It is more accurate to view cultures of racism in football as subject to the twin processes of continuity and change and a close attention to fan song provides exactly such a place to make sense of such complex combinations.

'Humour and Menace': The Melodies of Racism

The mass crowds of the years immediately after the Second World War must have garnered an awesome sound. These voices were not disciplined in song – rather they were a mass of the sharp-witted work-place wind-ups. Keith, a Millwall fan remembers what it was like to go to the Old Den in those days:

> My first memories I suppose have got to be the atmosphere. Obviously at that time which was – when I first started to go on a regular basis was the early sixties and I mean obviously all the docks was thriving then and we all had an average gate of 17 18 to 22 thousand. And obviously that's where Millwall I think got their reputation for their noise and for their crowd getting behind them and everything else. And Yeah I suppose it was the atmosphere down there and that's what I fell in love with the Club was the atmosphere and of course with the dockland wit I suppose. It used to be four bob to get in then and I always used to say two bob for the football and two bob for the wit. (Interview, 8 November 1995)

As the boom of British pop music emerged in the 1960s, so too a culture of singing – what we want to refer to as football plainsong – emerged in the grounds themselves.

Merseyside played a central role in the development of football fan song in England. Keith reflected: 'I think basically I suppose the Beatles came from Liverpool and I think they all thought they were a bit of songwriters themselves and a lot of them came from them' (interview, 8 November 1995). Catherine Long has pointed out there was little direct connection between local pop musicians and the city's football culture (see Williams, Long and Hopkins 2000). Nevertheless, the noise generated by the mass terrace of the Kop became the standard against which fans measured their vocal power. The Liverpool home end, named after a bloody battle during the South African Boer war, was at one time the largest single span structure in English football. Connections between empire and slavery are written into the cityscape of Merseyside through street names and monuments like the Kop. Similarly, Everton F.C. was founded by Will Charles Cuff, who lived in the then affluent suburb of Everton. Cuff attended the Congressional Church of St Domingo that was named after two Merseyside Streets that derived their names from slave trade connections with St Domingo (Hodgson 1985). In 1878 St Domingo F.C. was founded and later renamed Everton.

However, these imperial traces were overshadowed as Anfield and Goodison Park emerged as two of the iconic grounds in football culture. Adrian Thrills wrote of the unique quality of the Kop:

> Inspired partly by the pugnacious humour that is part of the city's character and partly by the strains of the beat boom that was sweeping the port's nightclubs, the 28,000 souls who stood on the Kop started to express themselves with passionate versions of pop hits such as 'She Loves You' by the Beatles, 'I Like It' by Freddie and The Dreamers' and 'Anyone Who Had a Heart' by Cilla Black. 'You'll Never Walk Alone,' the song that was to become their anthem was written by Rodgers and Hammerstein for the musical Carousel, but adopted by the Kop after Gerry and the Pacemakers charted with the track in 1963. (Thrills 1998: 31)

Mass singing of club anthems possessed a phatic quality, it revealed shared feelings and established an atmosphere of sociability rather than communication. The songs were always addressed to an audience but they were not about conversation – rather they were about being affective i.e. raising the home team's game, or stifling the opposition. Nowhere was this more evident than at Liverpool.

While the crowd noises are the player's oxygen, as Danny Blanchflower said, football songs are also about suffocation and intimidation. Vince Hillaire, one of the first black players to play for Crystal Palace, remembers visiting Anfield:

> Terry Venables liked players to go out for a warm-up before the games. I'm putting the boots on and that and I'm thinking: 'Well, Anfield, first time I've ever played here'. Anyway I was putting the boots on and it

must be about quarter-past/half-past two, the ground's filling up, I mean it was a full house so it must be 20,000 people in the ground already, and I've run out and I can hear the buzz out there, and I've run out the tunnel and all of a sudden – well, it seemed all of a sudden I think – it just, the ground was silent, completely silent, kicking balls around, and all of a sudden I heard this lone voice in the Kop go: 'Dayo – we say dayo, we say dayo, we say dayo', and then the rest of the Kop started. Looking back on it was quite funny, very humorous – it wasn't nasty, but it did intimidate me for a bit, until the game started and we got, we got into the game. The stick – well, it makes me laugh, you know, when I hear about if you – it's a public order offence now to do something like that. If that was the case in the mid-70s and up to the mid-80s there'd probably be no-one left watching football, they'd all be in like prison or banned from the grounds for life and that. It was a bit, it was unmerciful and a lot of the, the black players that played then, that's the only debt of gratitude I think that the players playing now owe them a bit because they did take some merciless stick and that and it was malicious and nasty and, you know, no need for it, but yet – and you had to turn a deaf'un, you know, you cut the deaf'un and – but, you know, it'd be a lie if you said it didn't get to you a bit, you know, it worried you. (interview, 27 January 1997)

The 'Dayo' chant is sung in the form of a Calypso parody. It has no explicit racist content but its associations are clear – minstrelsy blackness of a primitive lazy bones.

Da - yo,   d - d - da - yo,__   day –light come and we wan-na go home.

Another staple form of racist abuse is the making of 'Monkey noises.' This crude form of mistreatment and aping attempted to reduce black players to subhumans.

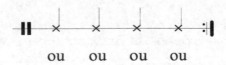

ou   ou   ou   ou

The primary purpose of the forms of abuse, most common during the 1970s and 1980s, was to suffocate black players on the field of play. The paradox in the performance of this chant is that it is the white abuser who 'apes' the monkey while no doubt is left over the intention as to who is the target.

The transfer of black footballer John Barnes to Liverpool brought the issue of race, locality and team loyalties into sharp focus on Merseyside particularly in the 1987 Merseyside derbies (see Back, Crabbe and Solomos 2001: 50–5). Garth Crooks summed up the fans effusive singing and Anfield's reputation as one of the most difficult places to play. The humour of the Liverpool fans was a 'satirical sword . . . Before you even get the generals of Anfield, you had to deal with the infantry [of the Kop]. (quoted in Nawrat and Hutchings 1995)

It is within sound that the unique registers of each fan culture can be found. A good example of this can be found at Millwall. There is a song that has no words and melody. It is immediately recognizable but it doesn't have a name. For the sake of description I will call it here the Lions Roar. The roar is one of the truly unique aspects of Millwall fan culture. It possess a drone like quality that is impossible to represent in words. I have attempted to notate it here musically in an attempt to describe its tonal quality. It begins with the first syllable of Millwall but the word is never fully formed in the song, unlike the Crystal Palace's dirge 'Eagles' discussed previously. It is sung through staggered breathing so that as one fan starts to sing the song another catches a breath so the sound produced is like a huge single voice that appears ceaseless needing neither inhalation or pause. It is curiously both the most musical of all the examples of football plainsong discussed here, but at the same time it has no words and no melody.

The Lion's Road

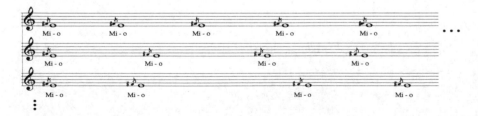

Garry Robson's description of the Lion's Roar is worth quoting at length:

Being effectively wordless, and lacking any harmonic resolution, this merging of the resonating individual voice with sustained collective performance produces an atmosphere of extraordinary intensity, a kind of sonic field in which time stands still and being itself hangs, static unelaborated in the air. As the roar of one singer dies another begins, crashing into and rolling over another against the sustained aural backdrop of thousands of open throats and resonating chests . . . This is collective minemonic immersion of the most extraordinary kind, and represents – despite being seen from without as savage, inchoate and moronic – an exemplary ritualising practice which draws upon a deeply rooted and anthropologically widespread musical technique: the sonic constitution and activation of a group's implicit sense of the world. (Robson 2000: 183)

The song is about the expression of a collective presence within the stadium. It is addressed to the opposition fans but also has an autophonic quality in that it is about the fans building an internal highly symbolic sense of themselves. Here, being and voice are fused as the sound of fan identity resonates in terms of both its identity and its collective quality.

Conclusions

The sounds of football are not only those heard in the stadium. In fact, for those who live close to football grounds match days are first announced through the clatter of horses' hooves as the police arrive hours before kick off. The key argument I want to emphasize is that listening to football culture enables us to think differently about it. It is within these sonic landscapes and the melodies of plainsong that the traces of history and identity are registered. Finally, I want to return to the question of how football culture defines the contours of inclusion and exclusion. One of the paradoxes of the Millwall fans who sing with pride that 'South London is Wonderful' is that many of them no longer live in South London but reside in the white hinterlands of the region in Kent, Sussex and Surrey.

John Berger has pointed out in his wonderful little book *And our Faces, My Heart, Brief as Photos* that the term 'home' has been taken over by two kinds of moralists. He writes that it 'became the keystone for a code of domestic morality, safeguarding the property (which included women) of the family'. Simultaneously, the notion of homeland supplied the first article of faith for patriotism, 'persuading men to die in wars which often served no interest except that of a minority of their ruling class' (Berger 1984: 55). This second form of moralism can be connected to the racially exclusive notions of local patriotism that we suggest are manifest in the rituals of football support.

A key mechanism through which racism is manifest within the rituals of football culture is through racializing the normative structure of collective identities. As a result it is necessary to establish a distinction between the expression of *denotative racism* which is explicit (the Dayo chants, monkey chanting, racist epithets) and *connotative racism* (racialized collective identities – 'South London is wonderful East London is Like Bengal') which maintain the hegemony of the 'white norm'. An examination of football plainsong is particularly revealing. Like the work songs of the early industrial period they represent social life 'connotatively rather than denotatively, figuratively rather than functionally' (Porter 1992: 152). Put another way, the songs and rituals of football support provide a means to represent locality and social life in the realm of metaphor and symbolism.

These songs can also combine explicit or denotative elements while at the same time implicitly invoking connotations about identity, regionalism and belonging. This particular example is important because it focuses on these processes of racial normalization within football culture. The fact that a song like 'South London is Wonderful/ East London is Like Bengal' relies on the assumption that both the perpetrators and the audience is white – albeit with a few assimilated black peers – show, how and to what extent football fan culture continues to be defined as a white preserve. There is, however, a tension here because two kinds of conclusion can follow from the discussion of chants like this. It can be read as the tip of a prodigious iceberg like whiteness that lies at the heart of English football culture. Or, it can be viewed as a specific moment in the racialization of particular patterns of culture and embodied social identities. The best course is to pursue the latter strategy.

It is important here to stress that these processes of white normalization are necessarily stable or functional in the sense that they are based on some autochthonic social foundation. The anthropologist Maurice Bloch has suggested that a ritual type of authority works precisely because it inhibits communication. Here, ritual speech acts – like songs – provide a mechanism to formalize or standardize social life. As a result, dissent, dialogue or even conversation is impossible: 'in a song, therefore, no argument or reasoning can be communicated, no adaption to the reality of the situation is possible. *You cannot argue with a song'* (Bloch 1974: 71). This may be so. As I have shown fans certainly trade insults through singing but the form of the songs and the collective identities expressed within them remain. However, while one cannot argue with a song, *one can stop singing it*. In recent years, the numbers of fans who are willing to give full voice to 'South London is Wonderful, East London is like Bengal' has ebbed at Millwall. It is noticeable that voices simply fall away when the 'East London is like Bengal' second verse is called. This may well be a sign of the lack of willingness to participate in the revelry of racism. Might this also be a sign of a greater sense of openness to black and ethnic minority fans within the culture of football support itself?

I want to end by stressing that the notion of home need not necessarily always involve exclusions. John Berger has argued that beneath the patriarchal and nationalistic conceptions of 'home' that are current today there is another meaning. Here, the notion of 'home' means simply the centre of one's world, not in a geographical but an ontological sense, a place to be found, a place of Being. Bob, a Millwall fan in his 1970s, articulated precisely this sense of 'home'. He lives in Croydon in a neighbouring borough to his beloved team. Each Saturday of every home game Bob makes the short train ride from East Croydon to New Cross Gate. As he passed through New Cross in August 1995 to see the Lions play Southend he mentioned with sadness the recent death of his friend and companion 'Black George'. He looked out of the train window into the streets where he spent his youth: 'Of course the area has really gone down hill since then, it used to be that people could leave their doors open and everything but that's all changed now. All that's left of me from that time is my family and Millwall.' The rituals of football culture provide a context to summon notions of self and being that cannot necessarily be articulated in any other way.

In this sense, 'home' is produced not simply through a particular address or residence but through the interconnection of habitation, memory and ritual. The centre of Bob's world, the places where he feels at home, is in his family and Millwall. As Berger concludes 'without a home at the centre of the real, one was not only shelterless, but also lost in non-being, in unreality. Without home everything was fragmentation' (Berger 1984: 56). Playing at 'home' in the context of the rituals of football support provides such a sensory centre.

References

Armstrong, G. (1999), 'Kicking Off with the Wannabe Warriors' in Perryman, M. (ed.) (1999), *The Ingerland Factor: Home Truths from Football*, Edinburgh: Mainstream.

—— (1998), *Football Hooligans: Knowing the Score*, Berg: Oxford.

Armstrong, G. and Giulianotti, R. (eds) (1997), *Entering the Field: New Perspectives on World Football*, Oxford and New York: Berg.

Appadurai, A. (1995), 'The Production of Locality', in Fardon, R. (ed) *Counterworks: Managing the Diversity of Knowledge*, London: Routledge.

Back, L., Crabbe, T., and Solomos, J. (2001), *The Changing Face of Football: Racism, Identity and Multiculture in the English game*, Oxford: Berg.

Bale, J. (1994), *Landscapes of Modern Sport*, Leicester: Leicester University Press.

Berger, J. (1995), *Face To Face with Jeremy Isaacs*, London: British Broadcasting Association.

Bloch, M. (1974), 'Symbols, Song, Dance and Features of Articulation, or is Religion an Extreme Form of Traditional Authority', *Archives Europennes de Sociologie*, XV(1): 55–81.

Bromberger, C. (1993), '"Allez L' O. M., Forza Juve": The Passion for Football in Marseille and Turin' in Redhead, S. (ed.), *Passion and the Fashion: Football Fandom in the New Europe*, Altershot: Avebury.

Giulianotti, R. (1999), *Football: A Sociology of the Global Game*, Cambridge: Polity.

—— (1993) 'Soccer Casuals as Cultural Intermediaries' in Redhead, S. (ed.), *The Passion and the Fashion: Football Fandom in the New Europe*, Aldershot: Avebury.

Hodgson, D. (1985), *The Everton Story*, London: Arthur Baker Limited.

Nawrat, C. and Hutchings, S. (1995), *The Sunday Times Illustrated History of Football*, London: Reed International Books.

Porter, G. (1992), *The English Occupational Song*, Uppsala: Swedish Science Press.

Robbins, B. (1998), 'Introduction Part 1: Actually Existing Cosmopolitanism', in P. Cheah and B. Robbins (eds), *Cosmopolitics: Thinking and Feeling Beyond the Nation*, Minneapolis and London: University of Minnesota Press.

Robson, G. (1999), 'Millwall Football Club: Masculinity, Race and Belonging' in S. Mundt (ed.) *Cultural Studies and the Working Class*, New York: Cassell.

—— (2000), *'No One Likes Us, We Don't Care': The Myth and Reality of Millwall Fandom*, Oxford: Berg.

Thrill, A. (1998), *You're Not Singing Anymore: A Riotous Celebration of Football Chants and the Culture that Spawned Them*, London: Ebury Press.

Tuan, Yi-Fu (1974), *Topophilia,* Englewood Cliffs NJ: Prentice-Hall.
—— (1976), 'Geopiety' in Lowenthall, D. and Bowden, M. J. *Geographies of the Mind: Essays in Historical Geography,* New York: Oxford University Press
Williams, J. Long, C. and Hopkins, S. (2000), *Passing Rhythms: Football, Music and Popular Culture in Liverpool,* Oxford: Berg Publishers.

18

The Sonic Composition of the City

Jean-Paul Thibaud

A common phenomenon now marks the ordinary experience of city dwellers: walking through the city to music. Equipped with headphones, the Walkman listener strolls along and takes in the musical scenery on his/her way. A kind of tuning in is created between his ear and his step. New sonic territories are composed in the course of this mobile listening experience. As the body moves in synch with the music, the listener transforms the public scene and provides a new tonality to the city street. His footsteps seem to say what his ears may be trying to hide. How does music with headphones mobilize the walker's gait? What does this contemporary form of urban mobility stand for? How should we consider this micro-ecology of musical navigation?

Using a Walkman in public places is part of an urban tactic that consists of decomposing the territorial structure of the city and recomposing it through spatio-phonic behaviours. Double movement of deterritorialization and reterritorialization. This new urban nomad is here and there at the same time, transported by the secret rhythm of his Walkman and in direct contact with the place he's walking through. The bounce in his step, the variations in his stride and the unexpected change of his daily route explain at times his imaginary drift but always brings him back to where he started. 'All music of the body is music of the body of the earth' affirms Daniel Charles (1979). Musicalization of the step and sonic rhythms go together.

We see him fully absorbed, lost in his sonic universe, whereas just one more step, a scream, or a glance is all it takes to bring him back into contact with his surroundings. We mustn't be mistaken – the Walkman listener is not entirely cut off from the urban environment. His being rooted in the urban space leans more towards an instability of perceived forms. The precarious balance it creates between what he hears and what he travels through, between what he sees and what he listens to, between what he perceives and what he expresses, reveals a delinquent practice consisting of 'living not in the margins but rather in the thresholds of social codes that are foiled and displaced' (De Certeau 1984).

Using a Walkman is part of a process of derealization of urban space that depends on the technical mediation of spatio-phonic behaviours. As a transposable object, the Walkman offers itself as one of the most advanced stages of *musica mobilis*. It involves *mobile listening*. As an involvement shield, the Walkman 'momentarily allows us to position ourselves outside the social theatre' (Kouloumdjian 1985). It is part of *secret listening*. As a schizophonic object, the Walkman develops 'the separation between an original sound and its electro-acoustic reproduction' (Schafer 1979). It participates in *listening of elsewhere*. Thus, as a manager of sensorial channels, it questions the relationship between the dweller and his environment and enables new modes of experiencing the city.

The Hidden Sides of the City

The walking listener reveals the hidden sides of the city according to three movements. The first movement is *from visible to audible*. By affirming the importance of sound as an essential feature of his urban experience, the Walkman user brings us to reconsider the visual paradigm that predominates in the social sciences (Bull 2000). It is less a question of adopting a new point of view but rather a question of listening to the voices of the city. The city is also to be heard and not only to be seen. In this respect, listening with headphones on is like a wonderful decoding instrument of the urban sonic environment. The walking listener uses it not only to protect himself from the sonic aggressions of the city but also to filter and enhance the events that give the place its meaning. Depending upon the places and what is happening in them, the sound volume of the Walkman is used in order to be able to listen to or to mask conversations, bells ringing, children's screams, traffic noise, and so forth. What come out of the urban noise are the sounds that signify the place, those that qualify the space with a singular voice. Thus, this selective listening enables a hierachization of everyday sounds and a decomposition of the urban soundscape. A new figure of the city dweller may be in the process of being born. Instead of the eye-oriented *flâneur* dear to Walter Benjamin, mustn't we substitute the discriminating listening of the musicalized passer-by?

The second movement is *from perception to action.* Using a Walkman is not limited to reintroducing the audible in our experience of urban space. It also reveals everyday sounds as closely related to social practices. There is no such thing as pure perception, free from the course of action and practical activities in which the perceiving subject is involved. If the Walkman voices are superimposed on those of the city, the steps of the city dweller also interfere with what he hears: 'the Walkman brings with him a mixture of music and body and the Walkman user invents the art of coordination on a daily level in order to settle into the space he occupies, a "short" circuit' (Hosokawa 1984). A few more feet are sometimes enough to pick up the reception of a radio station, a sudden swaying may affect the music of the Walkman starting to lack energy, arriving at a noisy crossroad makes the long-awaited favourite song suddenly inaudible. Walking is also a sonic action that mobilizes the step as much as the ear. The passer-by with headphones navigates through several worlds at once, the one in which he hears and the one in which he walks. Passer-by *par excellence*, he orchestrates 'a synthesis and a coordination between two heterogeneous series' (Deleuze 1969): entanglement between the ear and the step.

The third movement is *from private listening to public secret.* The Walkman phenomenon presents a particular heuristic interest in the sense that it also reveals the taken for granted of everyday life. 'Breaching experiment' Harold Garfinkel (1967) would say. Making observable what usually goes unnoticed, the walking listener provides partial access to the mystery of appearance. By establishing a disjunction between the visible and the audible, a disturbance of the human sensorium and a form of strangeness in everyday life, it questions the evidence of the 'perceptive faith' (Merleau-Ponty 1991). Thus, between the fully explicit and overt behaviour and the complete secret, the Walkman user provides a whole range of intermediary operations: dancing pace that escapes the understanding of others, incongruous movements and gestures that only make sense to the listener, speech with strange voices while listening to the music, and so forth. What are the minimal conditions for a space to be public? The problematic nature of these phenomena can be explained by the fact that they render public – by not following them – the social codes from which the expressive order of the body constitutes a shared signifying system. In other words, these kinds of intersubjective discordance uncover the unsuspected background of social life (Thibaud, 1994).

These preliminary remarks bring us to consider the way public places are experienced. It requires thinking in terms of thresholds, knots, and configurations. A constant reminder of in-between practices. Thresholds when the Walkman user leaves his house: interpenetration of private and public. Knots when he makes use of his senses: interferences between the ear, the step and the built environment. Configurations when he moves around the city to music: interstice of lived itineraries.

Doors, Bridges and Interchanges

The transition from one's home into the public realm represents a special moment in Walkman use. Many Walkman users have specific daily habits in the street. They carry out a series of operations in a very precise and regular order. Public places are marked by an access ritual characterized by a repeated ordering of thresholds enabling the Walkman user to fit into the rhythm of the street.

Doors

The door of the house may also function as a sonic door. On one hand, the door serves as a transition between two places of distinct status; on the other hand, as an intermediary between two kinds of listening experience. Leaving one's home is often synonymous with turning on the Walkman and coming home is equated with turning it off. It is paradoxical that access to public space is associated with the beginning of private listening whereas entering the private realm is associated with openness towards the surroundings. What is the relationship between coming through the door and turning on the Walkman? Where specifically is the threshold that marks the change in listening? The exit door serves as a transitional space between getting the Walkman ready and turning it on: 'I usually put my headphones on when I walk out the door or they are already positioned on my head and all I have to do is press a button.' Listening to headphones begins outside the home. The distinction established between putting on the headphones and starting to actually listen leads to a differentiation between leaving one's home and entering a public space. Closing the door to one's home is still considered a private act even if one is physically outside. 'Turning on' the Walkman can be understood in two ways: as the moment one begins to listen to the Walkman and also as the beginning of the

Walkman-user's voyage. Hearing the music marks the moment that the individual admits that he has entered into a public space. The threshold between public and private is defined less in terms of physical access (stepping out the door) and more in terms of a change of perceptual orientation. We are dealing here with a *paradoxical territorialization* in the sense that this approach to the public realm implies restricted sonic accessibility combined with an increased visual exposure. This exiting ritual reveals the differentiated status that we give to speech according to the type of space we find ourselves in. The contact that joins the city dweller to his domestic space must be maintained up until the last moment, in other words, up until the door is closed: 'When I'm outside, I lock the door, turn on my Walkman, ensure that all is working well, that everything is hooked up. Sometimes I turn it on before but it is difficult to say goodbye to the person I live with.' This description validates the hypothesis according to which the walking listener changes his perceptual orientation once he left his house. Whereas it seems appropriate to remain sonically accessible in domestic places, being available in public places seems less necessary. A first type of threshold can be revealed: we call this border point a 'sonic door' where the contact with family life has still to be maintained or can be interrupted. In other words, the sonic door deals with the phatic function of communication. It involves the possibility to shift our modes of attention towards others.

Bridges

Spatial transitions of the walking listener are not always expressed by such radical changes of perceptive attitude. Sonic continuity can be sought in the passage from one place to another. Listening with headphones establishes a 'sonic bridge' between domestic and public spaces: 'I close the door before listening to the music unless there's a good song on the radio, but then I locate it on my Walkman as soon as I turn it on to be able to continue listening to the song.' This is what may be referred to as a *phonic deterritorialization* of the urban environment in the sense that the walking listener neutralizes the sonic delimitations between domestic and public spaces by establishing a continual listening between the two spaces. This musical link tends to neutralize the sonic identity of the places. The spatial decontextualization of listening with headphones creates a sonic bridge between the interior and exterior. A sonic bridge is the listening device that encourages the reaching of a material limit without requalifying the sonic space of the listener. In contrast with the sonic door, which marks the reaching of a threshold by modifying the sound context, the sonic bridge establishes an auditory continuity independent of the places travelled through. It is part of a double movement of retrospection (the past listening affects the sonic programme to come) and anticipation (turning on the Walkman occurs before the Walkman listener's stroll outside). Sometimes even a momentary overlap is produced between the radiophonic domestic diffusion and diffusion of the same programme by the walking listener: 'Sometimes I listen to King FM at home. If the radio is always on and I put King FM on my Walkman, it amplifies the music. It is almost like when you are in a cave.' Creating a resonance between different sonic emissions makes the listener incapable of developing a sonic place marker. Acoustic characteristics of these sonic productions being practically identical, no clue makes it possible to differentiate one from another. This confusion of diverse sonic sources constitutes an interesting example of neutralization of the territorial power of sound.

Interchanges

A third type of threshold consists in adjusting the sound volume of the Walkman in terms of movement, modulating the listening conditions according to the sonic context of the street: 'When I go out, I adjust the volume of my Walkman so it is neither too loud nor too low, because there could be noises from a car or something like that. So I need to adjust the volume in harmony with the situation.' Becoming attuned to the situation consists in stabilizing the level of intensity between the sounds of the Walkman and the one of the urban environment. Regulating the volume of the Walkman makes it possible to maintain the preponderance of electro-acoustic productions without necessarily masking urban noises. The listener is looking for the minimal intensity gap between these two sonic sources: 'neither too strong nor too weak' we were told. We are referring in this case to 'sonic interchange' in the sense that a reversal of the foreground-background relationship could occur at any given moment: outside voices, perceived as sonic background, can suddenly mask the musical emission and show up in the foreground. This is what happens in particular when the walking listener enters a public space. Adjusting the volume consists in stabilizing the foreground-background relationship and attempting to maintain the same balance of intensity throughout the walking route. We witness a *sonic reterritorialization* of the urban space in the sense that sonic urban occurrences are recomposed in terms of musical dynamics.

While researching audible thresholds, the walking listener creates a new
sonic organization of the street based on a relative mastering of sonic
urban masks.

As soon as we no longer limit accessibility of free circulation of the
body in space, we may pose a question about public sensorial instrumentation. By upholding the existence of a plurality of transitions to
public places, the walking listener makes the 'in-between' an essential
category of structuring urban territory. We must then 'start in the middle,
from the middle, enter and exit, neither begin nor finish' (Deleuze 1980).

The Knots of the Urban Environment

Listening to headphones creates powerful and complex links with the
characteristics of the urban milieu. The walking listener enters into a
relationship with the urban environment – sonic, built and visual – by
experiencing situations of interference, in other words, situations in
which different types of space-time connect.

Intense urban noises – road noise, sirens, warning signals – punctuate
the flow of the musical audition and conditions the degree of autonomy
of listening with headphones. Acoustic permeability of headphones
doesn't fully prevent the total intrusion of voices of the city in the
listener's perceptive field. When this happens, several solutions are
imaginable. It is possible to rewind the tape and play the piece again
to the point where listening was momentarily interrupted: 'If there is
an intense noise in the street and I can't hear the music, I put the song
on again.' The other possibility is to turn up the volume: 'When there's
a great deal of noise around, I make the Walkman louder.' Or the listener
can wait for calm to occur: 'If I turn up the volume and I still can't hear,
I just have to wait.' In any case, people are not always annoyed this
situation of sonic interference. It may be sought after by the user or
may be somewhat beneficial. Certain sonic occurrences are not just a
nuisance; they provide informational value that may be momentarily
significant in terms of hearing the music. The listener voluntarily goes
from listening to headphones to listening to the city by intentionally
increasing the permeability of his earphones: 'The other day, I lowered
the volume because I wanted to hear the bells, I wanted to know the
exact time, so I lowered the volume to hear the chimes.' Whatever the
tactic applied, the Walkman user is situated within two simultaneous
sonic worlds. We are referring in this case to an *interphonic knot* – in
other words, the point of convergence between two sonic spaces of a
different nature – that of the walking listener and that of the street.

The built environment also interferes with listening to the radio. Buildings are sometimes an obstacle to the propagation of radio waves and limit the reception of radio programmes. The architecture of spaces and the height and form of edifices become audible through the use of headphones: 'It's hard to pick up a radio station in the city because of all those huge and tall buildings. Buildings are a sort of screen.' A transduction occurs between the material urban forms and the perceived sonic forms, the visible becomes audible. Depending on the particular case, the listener momentarily loses the station that he's in the midst of listening to or picks up two at a time. It is remarkable that walking listeners are capable of localizing zones of radio-wave disturbance so precisely. On their walking route, they identify radio territories in the city and acquire their own knowledge. Different individuals, unknown from each other, make us aware of the same urban phonography. The town centre is often evoked in similar terms: 'When you are in the centre, reception is not very good so you have to find a radio station which gets better reception.' 'It depends on the radio station I want to listen to, it's really bad in the city centre.' Regarding the lake in the city centre, 'Reception of the radio station Bellevue is better on this side of the lake, you lose the station when you are on the other side.' 'On one side of the lake, I listened to two stations at once, but I moved the tuner and I lost one of them.' The position of the listener in regards to the built environment is significant in terms of the conditions of radiophonic reception. We are referring in this case to a *topophonic knot*, in other words, the interference point between media listening and architectural space. This invisible urban side brings us closer to the experience of Fernand Deligny (1980), who when retracing the daily walking patterns of autistic children, revealed the existence of 'chevêtres', common areas to all children without previous disclosure of these places. A 'communal' relationship occurs when the walking listeners are linked to each other by a community of behaviour and territory that has not been outwardly expressed.

Finally, listening to headphones establishes strange connections between the visual and the musical landscapes. Depending upon the music listened to, the city takes on varying tones and moods. The attention paid to the elements of the visual landscape seems to depend in particular upon the musical style: 'Sometimes when I listen to classical music while I'm walking, I notice the trees and nature surrounding me, much more than I normally would. Listening to rock and roll makes me notice the cars that pass by.' These cultural associations between sound and image are undoubtedly largely influenced by stereotypes found in film and television productions. This extract illustrates a phenomenon of aesthetization of the visual environment through music. Many authors have studied this significant trait of urban visual culture and have insisted on the particular role that the Walkman plays in this evolution. Ian Chambers (1986) considers the Walkman an aesthetic device of the city, Paolo Prato (1984) calls it a 'spectacul-arization process' and Claus-Dieter Rath (1986) affirms the birth of the city-screen by referring to the role that the Walkman plays in this regard. The objects seen are not apprehended in an equivalent and neutral manner. They are subjected to choices and visual reconfigurations in terms of headphone listening: 'There is often a coincidence between what I listen to and what I see, so I can see things that are a bit more elementary, occasionally a bit clearer, and something reaches me.' The walking listener is particularly sensitive to the connection established between the eye and the ear, to the ' rhythmic harmony between the music, the listener's body, and the exterior environment' (Cave and Cotton 1984). We refer to the *visiophonic knot* to designate this con-vergence point between the audible and the visible, a discovery of synchronized intersensorial sequences.

The Walkman should not be reduced to the status of a simple object of the environment among many: it is interposed between users and his milieux rather than situated at a distance from the relationship. This analysis is close to the definition of 'quasi-objects' provided by Michel Serres: 'This quasi-object is not an object, but it is one nevertheless, since it is not a subject, since it is in the world, it is also a quasi-object, since it marks or designates a subject which without it wouldn't be' (Serres 1980). The Walkman is a third term to be situated at the level of the man-milieu relationship, it is on one hand inseparable from the perceived subject (of the user) and nonetheless distinct from him. The knots to which we have just referred must not be confused with the 'centre' of the 'city centre' where city dwellers would come to be together but rather as a 'pluralist aesthetics of the situation' (Serres 1972) that connects the diverse socioecological components of passing places.

The Interstice of Lived Itineraries

Rather than uncover urban territories based on the spatial and visual order of the city, the walking listener makes it possible to identify several navigational practices. The musical walking patterns of the walking listener could be synthesized through a typology of strolls. Each stroll can be regarded in two ways – first as an art to master the act of getting around, and secondly, as a means to reveal the complex relationship between listening and moving. If both listening to music and walking involves time, the typology that we are offering underlines various kinds of spatio-phonic procedures. We may distinguish six types of walking practices that often overlap.

The 'route' consists in choosing a musical itinerary that goes from one place to another. This itinerary proposes two variants. On one hand, when a route is taken regularly, daily – like, for example, the path to work – the walking listener rediscovers it each day by changing the music he listens to. The same route may be heard in different ways. On the other hand, an occasional or exceptional itinerary could be listened to with the same sonic programme as that of another route. The walking listener appropriates the space he walks through in terms of his familiarity with the musical pieces. Thus, the route *superposes* a double temporality – one of which is walking around and the other is the music. This diversifies or homogenizes the perception of the urban environment.

The 'stride' consists in minimizing occasions for stopping and in encouraging continuity of the walk. Not saying 'hello' to an acquaintance on the street, limiting the possibility of speaking to others, neutralizing visual stimulation in the street and synchronizing one's steps to musical rhythms are just some of the tactics allowed when listening to headphones. The stride gives priority to musical rhythms, provides partial autonomy to the urban temporality and restricts occasions for diversion offered by the street. The Walkman user's step remains regular in the sense that certain 'exterior' sonic events are still out the user's perceptive realm. The stride *substitutes* the musical listening temporality over the one of the public environment.

The 'gait' consists in establishing variations of walking speeds, and modulating the step according to the music. These variations are set off either by particularly intense sonic occurrences coming from the street (acceleration of the walk to escape acoustic interruptions and re-establish quality headphone listening) or changes in musical tempos. In the second case, the variation is expressed by an acceleration or slowing down of the walk and can be voluntarily sought by the walking listener (programming the gait in particular of joggers). The act of listening may concern the urban soundscape or the musical programs on the Walkman, but in both cases the gait *transposes* the rhythmic qualities of sonic time at the level of the walking expression of the listener.

The 'style' consists of composing figures through the help of gestures, putting movements into form in a way that makes them aesthetic. The walking listener breaks down the music he listens to in rhythmic sequences and in sonic flows and makes up for it through gestures. By reacting in this way, he provides an original form of getting around – sort of an in-between walking and dancing – and thus metamorphoses the place travelled through just as a result of his presence. The street becomes an urban scene in which an improvised choreographic scene takes place more or less exhibited and remarked. The style *configures* the urban space by partially defunctionalizing the act of getting around and by establishing an intertwining of the bodily rhythms of the passer-by and the musical rhythms he hears.

The 'detour' consists in increasing the travel distance in regards to the most direct route going from one place to another. It can be revealed through various practices: avoiding noisy areas that prevent headphone listening, choice of a route with the least amount of social visibility, which enables the dance-walk, backtracking when the Walkman user becomes lost in his music. Whether freely chosen or not, the detour traces a winding itinerary in terms of the expressive and perceptive behaviour of the Walkman user or in terms of his awareness of his surrounding social environment. By indirectly or directly taking paths linked to headphone listening, the walking listener *retraces* his own urban cartography, he demonstrates it as he maps it out.

The 'short cut' consists in shortening effectively or subjectively the time of the walk, in taking the shortest route to get from one point to the next. While it may be opposite to the detour, it does not necessarily involve contrary elements. The walking listener may, of course, decide to go home by the most direct route when the battery of his Walkman is low, but he can also be so absorbed in listening that he doesn't notice the time spent for his stroll. Forgetting part of the trip subjectively reduces the duration of the trip and offers a time-saving element in regards to commuting time. By concentrating on the experience of the Walkman listener's sonic time, the shortcut *miscounts* the clocklike time in favour of musical dynamics.

This typology makes it possible to specify the resources available to the Walkman listener to show others how he appropriates and redefines urban territory in terms of headphone listening. Through his body expressions and through his organization of itineraries, the passer-by renders public and accessible to others these ways of navigating through the city. He recounts his musical perception of the urban space in his walks like Stillman, in the *City of Glass* by Paul Auster, and draws the letters from a coded message through the movement of his steps.

The Sensibilization of Urban Life

The Walkman functions like a technological device that introduces the senses within the urban territory. The thresholds, knots, and arrangements it creates need to be apprehended phenomenologically, according to the variable combinations of visibility and audibility. To conclude, we wish to show – based on musical nomadism – how new modes of appearance and behaviour in public are constituted.

A Spacing-regulating Device

The use of the Walkman in urban environments is linked to the art of behaviour that sets up intervals and regulates spacing. Headphones are what we could call a 'primary earshell', in other words, an envelope which becomes part of the listening condition of the passer-by, but can be also taken off anytime. The walking listener filters the information delivered by the urban environment and plays with the perceptual orientation possibilities offered to him. He can adopt diverse points of view and listening not entirely based on the position of his body in space but also on the modalities of headphone listening. This technical mediation guarantees a diversity of perspectives, a moving off centre of the self. It orchestrates diverse types of distancing by operating a separation of the eye and the ear. This active reconfiguration of perspectives by the Walkman listener contributes to the possible creation of a common public space: 'the common world is over once we view it from only one point of view, when it is only allowed to present itself from a single perspective' (Arendt 1961).

A Mobile Operator of Configurations

Through his meanderings, his stride and his gait, the walking listener shapes the urban space without necessarily providing a reason for his actions. By keeping the content of his headphone listening a secret, he hides elements of a pragmatic context that would enable the observer to give meaning to the Walkman listener's behaviour. But again, by demonstrating diverse types of instability of perceived forms, the walking listener questions the expressive power of appearance. It is not really a question of revealing perceptible forms but rather of showing how these forms are made and then unmade: morphogenesis when gestures and steps adjust to musical rhythms, anamorphosis when sonic emissions are filtered by headphones . . . The difficult problem of the relationship between sensoriality and intelligibility is introduced. The walking listener instantly invites us to respond to Karl Mannheim's already ancient request: 'the most obvious task that we must accomplish is to be able to think at the very base of frames of mobile reference'.

References

Arendt, H. (1961), *Condition de l'homme moderne,* Paris: Calmann-Lévy.

Bull, M. (2000), *Sounding Out the City,* Oxford: Berg.

Cave, F. and Cotten, C. (1984), *Investigation préliminaire d'une modification volontaire de l'environnement sonore et social. L'exemple du «Walkman»,* Paris: Ministère de l'Environnement.

Chambers, I. (1986), *Popular Culture. The Metropolitan Experience,* London and New York: Methuen & Co.

Charles, D. (1979), Flux de marche avec piétinement, *Traverses,* (14–15): 81–92.

De Certeau, M. (1984), *The Practice of Everyday Life,* Berkeley, University of California Press.

Deleuze, G. (1969), *Logique du sens,* Paris: Editions de Minuit.

Deleuze, G. and Guattari, F. (1980), *Mille Plateaux,* Paris: Edition de Minuit.

Deligny, F. (1980), *Les enfants du silence,* Paris: Galilée et Spirali.

Garfinfel, H. (1967), *Studies in Ethnomethodology,* Englewood Cliffs: Prentice Hall.

Hosokawa, S. (1984), 'The Walkman Effect', *Popular Music,* 4: 165–80.

Kouloumdjian, M.F. (1985), *Le Walkman et ses pratiques,* Ecully: IRPEACS/CNRS.

Merleau-Ponty, M. (1991), *Le visible et l'invisible,* Paris: Editions Gallimard.

Prato, P. (1984), 'Music in the Streets: the Example of Washington Square Park in New York City', *Popular Music,* (4): 151–63.

Rath, C. D. (1986), 'La "Sociologie des sens" de Simmel revue à l'époque de la télévision', *Georges Simmel, la sociologie et l'expérience du monde moderne,* Paris : Méridiens Klincksieck, pp. 189–203.

Schafer, R. M. (1979), *Le Paysage Sonore,* Paris: J. C. Lattès.

Serres, M. (1972), *L'interférence,* Paris: Minuit.

—— (1980), *Le parasite,* Paris: Edition Grasset.

Thibaud, J. P. (1994), Les mobilisations de l'auditeur-baladeur: une sociabilité publicative, *Réseaux. Communication, Technologie, Société,* 65: 71–83.

19

How Many Movements?[1]

Caroline Bassett

[T]here are two texts which simply alternate: you might almost believe they had nothing in common, but they are in fact inextricably bound up with each other, as though neither could exist on its own ... but ... only in their fragile over-lapping ...

(Perec, 1996)

Th Ground Wher u Walk

I left my pictur on th ground wher u walk ...

(A text message poem, *Guardian, OnLine*, 5 December 2002)

In the city where I live, advertising flyers are often taped to the ground by those who post them. In rain-soaked England, the images dissolve very quickly; but the taped outlines remain far longer. These empty squares produce *ad hoc* grids; hop-scotch pathways through the city. I often find myself falling into step with these grids when I use my mobile; not entirely absent-mindedly but not entirely intentionally either. This is how I walk when I am talking into another space, when I am walking *here* but listening *there*, receiving or sending text messages, making or taking calls.

This way of walking is something like the pavement game children play, the game where stepping on the cracks between stones is prohibited because the ground is full of monsters only held at bay by this

343

ritual. Children engaged in these games operate with extra care: every step matters. For me the inverse is true, I am operating in a distracted way: each step matters *less*. This outside city space engages my vision but I am not necessarily attending closely to what I see in this space and I am certainly not seeking to control it. Rather, I am focused on a second space, the auditory space opened up through the phone. It is there, into that space, that I direct my emotions and my intellectual attention – and it is into that space that I seek to be *heard*.

The spatial economy of mobile telephony is complex. To explore it demands consideration of the dynamics not only of virtual space (the bubble into which we speak when we make a connection), but also of physical space as it comes to be penetrated by virtual space. In this sense, whenever a mobile is used it connects not two spaces but four or more. Mobiles play a part in the production of contemporary space. They also play a part in the production of contemporary subjectivity because to ask how the connections mobiles make are produced, maintained, re-produced, and understood is also to ask how this kind of technology might allow the negotiation of new forms of subjectivity. It is this negotiation that I look at here. And I begin by looking at what has ended.

The 'Incarceration Vacation'

The more you see, the less you hold . . . [this is] a dis-possession of the hand in favour of a greater trajectory for the eye.

(De Certeau 1984: 113).

You Extend From What You Walk On

(Gretchen Hofner, from *Crow in Heels*)

Back in the 1970s, in the *Practice of Everyday Life*, the French theorist Michael de Certeau contrasted the embedded perspective produced by walking in the city at ground level with the strategic viewpoint from on high, a view usually enabled by technology (De Certeau, 1984). For De Certeau walking was a spatializing, *narrativizing* practice. Those who felt their way through the streets, tracing out their own trajectories, produced a second, ghostly mapping of the city; one that confounded the official city of the planners and architects – at least for a time.

Today I still walk in the city. But I am no longer a pedestrian in the old sense because I am no longer embedded in my immediate locality or environment, even when I walk rather than go by car. The penetration of the old spaces of the everyday by mobile phone users now largely goes unnoticed; routine and habituation mask what is an extra-ordinary shift. Today the city streets are full of virtual doorways, opening into other places. Countless ways through, ways out, and ways in to the city space, are constructed and de-constructed by a myriad of mobile-phone owners, who transform as they use. This change in space means that today I can walk here in the streets and simultaneously connect with other people in far away spaces. I find new perspectives, and not only because I can be *reached* on my mobile phone but also because I can use it to *reach out*. (The difference between the mobile phone and the Walkman inheres in this distinction: the mobile, unlike the Walkman offers the possibility of remote intervention). One way to describe this is simply to say that my perspective has shifted. Another way would be to say that I have more than one perspective available to me. Perhaps it is already clear that the (negative) place accorded to information technology in De Certeau's consideration of the dialectics of power, control and freedom is challenged by the case of the mobile.[2]

Let me turn from walking to riding. Elsewhere in the *Practice of Everyday Life*, De Certeau explores a train journey as an 'incarceration vacation' – a space in which passengers submit to the discipline of the rails but where they paradoxically find some freedom from other responsibilities; where they are *made* unaccountable. For De Certeau there is some pleasure to be found in this unexpected freedom – and some allure in the expanded if prosthetic expansion of perspective it offers the traveller. Perhaps De Certeau himself could sometimes find compensations in technology. Here, at any rate De Certeau brings the human into a close relation with the technology in question, which in a sense becomes the grounds from which his vision extends: what she 'walks' on.

The mobile phone changes this dynamic. For the mobile phone user, travel no longer presumes a broken connection. There is no dislocation between the world of the train and the world beyond: not even the temporary dislocation the journey used to produce. Each world is shot through with the other. De Certeau (1984: 113) called the train a mobile symbol. Today, mobile phones are at once a new symbol of a particular kind of contemporary freedom to move and act in multiple spaces, and a symbol of 'always on' accountability/surveillance. Now that we have this new symbol it is evident that the priority the visual is accorded in De Certeau's economy of spatial power and his sense of the automatic connection between the strategic and the scopic needs thinking about.

That is, an older sense of the distinction between the landscape and the journey, and of the spatial dynamics under-pinning this distinction, no longer pertains. These days, as mobile-equipped travellers, we operate in that speed-blurred band that used to demarcate the division between landscape beyond the rails and the fast-moving space of the train. Or rather, there is no longer a boundary but only an *interface*. You are advised to 'take your world with you' when you go because this is the end of the incarceration vacation with its unexpected freedom and its constraint. The question is what comes next.

How Many Movements?

In what follows, I address this question from two directions. First, I explore mobile telephony in relation to questions of attention, drawing partly on Jonathan Crary's account of the suspension of perception in modern culture (Crary 2000). To me it is clear that a dialectic of presence/absence is at the heart of the spatial economy enabled by the mobile phone: the interesting questions cohere around *how* this dialectic operates. Considering presence/absence by way of attention is useful because it allows some rather abstract formulations concerning ICTs in general and virtual space in particular to be thought through in more nuanced ways – and in ways that relate more specifically to the mobile phone.

The second approach I make is centred on the inventory and here I begin with the concept of the inventory as developed by Georges Perec, another French theorist of the everyday. Perec combined a sense of the importance of the jumbled, half-forgotten, objects and processes in the production of everyday life, with a sense that this form of everyday life – the infra-ordinary as he describes it – might be investigated through various experiments with numerological systems. The mode of inventory, as he develops it, is essentially one of these experiments. For Perec the inventory offers a means by which to codify experience and thereby to recall and record various aspects of everyday life. In his hands, however, the inventory is not ultimately a reductive codification but rather an expansive *narrative* process. Perec does not seek to explore the reduction of experience to the bullet point, the reduction of life to code, or the reduction of an 'organic' space to one technologically produced and therefore 'artificial'. Rather he unfolds worlds from their barest essentials. In his hands the inventory functions as a catalyst for a particular kind of distention or decompression – for a *return* to an experience in all its complexity. As Perec (1997: 13) sees it 'space as inventory' is also 'space as invention'. What he produces is a numerological system (a form of artificial memory, as I explore below) that is also a poetics: a way of re-making space that involves technical production and imagination. The concept of the inventory as thus described is suggestive. It helps develop forms of thinking about ways in which technologies such as the mobile phone operate – and for thinking about ways in which compression and decompression, encoding and decoding, can be understood as *more* than technical processes (although they are also always technical processes). At the very least, Perec's sense of the possible re-production of a complex space from the thinnest of possible cues – from bald lists, single items, the bare technical description of a process – *from the single act of calling up a number perhaps* – seems to me to open up ways of thinking about the translations between spaces performed by mobile phone users that go beyond the presumption that today we are simply in thrall to the pure logic of the database. Now, having 'inventorized' my two terms, I will continue, in the fine tradition of Perec, by *using* this inventory to open things up a little further.

Attention and Imagination

Exploring the connections between attention and perception Crary suggests that in contemporary life '[I]ndividuals define and shape themselves in terms of a capacity for 'paying attention', that is, for a *disengagement* with the broader field of attraction, whether visual or auditory, for the sake of isolating or focusing on a reduced number of stimuli' (Crary, 2000:1, my italics). Following Crary, I understand that the category of attention is important both in the contemporary (highly technologized) production of the subject and in the contemporary production of space. The capacity to switch attention from one space to another is very evident in mobile phone use, because this has honed considerably our ability to engage/dis-engage from particular stimuli, and from particular kinds of spaces – and has expanded the times and places when we can perform these rapid switches.

So what is going on here? To begin to answer this I return momentarily to my own distracted walking in the city on the one hand, and to the children's pavement game on the other. I think that both can be used to say something about the kind of role that attention plays in everyday spatial practices. In both of these cases it is clear that paying attention (or failing to pay attention) is not only about looking and nor is it about where precisely the gaze is directed (about the angle of the gaze). That is, attention is not purely a matter of geometry. Rather, attention is *invested*. It is, as Crary puts it 'continuous with states of distraction, reverie, dissociation, and trance' (Crary 2000: 46).

Because it involves investment, attention clearly also involves a form of selection. Equally clearly, selection is not necessarily a free act on the part of the individual (either I am selected – which is to say my attention is 'caught' by a particular event, or I select something – which is to say I choose to direct my attention to a particular place). Free or not, as an individual's capacity to pay attention is limited, any selection is made at the expense of other objects/spaces. To pay attention is therefore to prioritize: to invest and to disinvest. Below I ask how and why mobile space tends to be prioritized over the physical space, in the sense that we tend to give it more attention, looking at this in relation to modes of perception, and in relation to sensation and affect. Finally, it is interesting to consider how forms of attention might organize the relationship between what is and what is not attended to. I think one reason that I follow the taped grids, empty of content, when I walk in these streets using my phone is that they echo my own state. In my absent-minded meandering I too am often there, but there 'in outline only'.

Modes of Perception?

When you're expatriated, you're a little deaf, you can hear things but you can't get the full experience . . .

(Radio 4, found voice)

There exists a gulf between the world according to sound and the world according to sight.

(Bull 2001: 241)

How far does the mode of perception within which the mobile operates relate to the way we prioritize mobile space over physical space? In the case of the mobile it is evident that use does involve prioritising one *mode* of perception at the expense of another. That is, when I turn my attention away from the streets and towards the thin thread of talk I prioritize the auditory at the expense of the embodied and visual world. (I could put this differently: my attention may be *directed* away from my embodied engagement with my immediate physical environment: most obviously when my phone rings.) *Pace* De Certeau, this might be understood as a dispossession of the hand in favour of a greater trajectory for the heard (see above). In his account of Walkman use

Michael Bull explores how sense perception is engaged differently in relation to the aural than the visual. Bull suggests the personal stereo can re-organize urban space because it overlays it with a new and overwhelming aesthetic. Sound, as he says, 'engulfs the spatial'. In Bull's account of the Walkman, the prioritization of the auditory space is above all a means by which users re-aestheticize their everyday experience of urban space as a whole. This is often achieved through a process of negation – as Bull puts it, in the case of the Walkman the present becomes consumed by the 'far away' (Bull 2001: 241). Bull's account is compelling and clearly speaks to other kinds of mobile media. However it is also clear that something slightly different is also going on in the case of mobile phones – not least because most mobile interactions do not pack a powerful aesthetic punch. As I want to go on to suggest, the satisfactions mobile space offers are located elsewhere.

Connective Force

> We're forever meeting people who have watches, very seldom people who have compasses.
>
> (Perec 1997: 83)

Many of interactions hosted by mobiles comprise humdrum, banal, often apparently unnecessary conversations. On the other hand they are clearly *compelling*: phone space is often prioritized over local space, and phone use has very quickly become an integral part of everyday life. Anybody who has looked at phone use amongst other people, who has considered their own use of the phone, or who has witnessed the irritation phones cause in certain public spaces, will be aware of this conundrum. How can it be explained? First, I stress that in making a distinction between the kind of spatial economy afforded by the mobile and that offered by the personal stereo, I am not looking at the question of aesthetics. The relationship between the priority afforded to one space and the neglect this attention affords another, might be considered in relation to the affective priority one kind of space claims over another without specific reference to the question of the aesthetic qualities of that space. In fact it seems not just useful but necessary to look at affect since, without considering the affective or invested, the conundrum I have set out above cannot be addressed at all. The point perhaps, is to set aside the content of mobile phone calls and consider instead but the forms of connections mobile telephony allows, the *processes* it enables. The key here is to consider not the content of the phone call, but the process of making or receiving the call. What makes this kind of space compelling, is not what it contains, but what communicational experience it offers the user. Considered this way the mobile's attractions become more evident – and some use characteristics that are otherwise baffling, for instance the tendency of much phone talk to remain at the level of the phatic or the gestural also become more explicable.

Crary, citing Binet and Fere, suggests that 'attention increases the force of certain sensations while it weakens others' (Crary 2000: 39). I think this is suggestive. It points to ways in which particular elements of 'phone use might be felt more intensely than others; and might indeed become excessive, breaking out into spaces beyond the 'phone. Following this line of thought it is tempting to suggest that mobile spaces compel attention because they produce an accelerated, intensified, sense of freedom of movement and of speed-up – a sense that might spill over from the phone space into others spheres of life. Connecting to a mobile space is often experienced as going 'live'. That is, with a mobile the user can move at (communicational) speeds that neither walking, riding nor even flying, can accommodate, even though they have come to seem natural. In these spaces the user is also produced as a highly mobilized subject, as somebody able to keep up with contemporary life. Perhaps this explains why I pay more attention to the live mediated transactions on offer through my mobile than to the 'live' live events of the street.

The Selfish Phone

> If you don't have a mobile, people don't care about you . . .
>
> (Sussex University Student)

Finally, I want to suggest that the mobile commands attention by *offering* a form of attention. Within the newly created and individualized bubble of the call or the return call, the user is always needed and wanted: flattered by attention on the one hand, able to control the demand for a response on the other. There is a form of compensation going on here: the space of the city is often indifferent – I am lost in the crowd, I am anonymous. On my phone, in my space, I matter. On the phone I have a certain form of presence and this may well compensate for any limitations in bandwidth, any constraints on the range, scope and scale of the reality in which I matter. Here then, is another way in which these spaces are interdependent. Attention on one stems from neglect *in* (as well as *to*) another space, and relates to it. At least as I read it, a form of narcissism is integral to the dynamics of mobile phone use – something that doesn't seem to operate in the same way in relation to the personal stereo (although it quite clearly does pertain to some kinds of Web-based interaction). Overall, what is being fetishized here (rather than aestheticized, in fact) is not a particular form of content, (a particular kind of sound, for instance) but rather a particular form of life: a life operating at a particular speed and intensity, but one that can also be controlled. Mobiles give their users an enhanced and risk free sense of 'being live/being alive', even though (because) this 'liveness' is maintained in an artificially controlled bubble.

The Collective Imaginary

It should by now be clear that the spaces into which we shift our attention (and those from which we shift our attention) by way of mobiles, are not purely technological spaces. To some extent they are imagined. This simple proposition is important. It means that the city streets and the auditory spaces within which we connect are technically achieved spaces, *and* also, as a part of this, spaces of the collective and individual imaginary. It means that these spaces are, in their technical iterations *and* in their imaginary formations, *and* in their political economy, social productions. It also means they are *connected* social productions. This is not to say that they are not 'real'. Indeed, these connected productions (amongst others) help *comprise* everyday life: Henri Lefebvre understood everyday life itself in spatial terms: partly as that which is projected into space, and partly as that which takes place *as space* (Lefebvre 1991). To understand that everyday life is space, and that this space is partly produced through a collective imagination, is not to deny the force of technological change or innovation: to deny the extra-ordinary shift that the mobile has produced. On the contrary it is to seek to account for that force in all its specificity.

Reconciling Oneself

As we increasingly switch our attention from one place to another, each time at the expense of the last (perhaps because we increasingly seek sensation itself, over any sustained engagement with discrete content) our lives become fragmented. To some extent we become a 'patchwork of dis-connected states' (Crary 2000: 1). Something that is useful about attention is precisely that it is never presumes absolute presence – and cannot therefore presume absolute disconnection. When I switch my attention into my phone, I leave some part of myself behind. As a consequence I have some part of myself to return to: to reconcile with. Perhaps, indeed, I need to think harder not only about and *what* and *who* I am *between and across* these states, *between and across* these spaces, but also about how I operate to make these moves in the first place. It is at this point that I return to consider Perec and his concept of inventory.

Space as Inventory, Self as Experience

Space as inventory, space as invention.

(Perec 1997: 13)

As a cultural form, database represents the world as a list of items and it refuses to order this list. In contrast, a narrative creates a cause-and-effect trajectory of seemingly unordered items (events). Therefore, database and narrative are natural enemies. Competing for the same territory of human culture, each claims an exclusive right to make meaning out of the world.

(Manovich: 1998)

Lev Manovich has written brilliantly on the tension between narrative and database, arguing that a database logic has overwhelmed narrative and is now the dominant cultural form (Manovich 1998). Manovich argues that the database represents the world as an un-ordered list of items, whereas narrative produces trajectories of what seemed unordered. Seen this way around narrative becomes a subset of what is done with a database, with the latter as the central, defining, logic of a computerized society. I want to suggest here that the concept of the inventory can be used to challenge the claim that the logic of the database is always dominant. To make this argument I want first to briefly set out the logic of the inventory stressing its function as a mnemonic.

Mnemonic Operators

In *Species of Spaces,* his examination of spatial practices and narrative identity, Perec attributes extreme importance to the everyday. He argues that to recall the trivial, insignificant, ordinary details about a life, through the process of drawing up an inventory of that life, is to open up the space of that life; to recall what is important about it. Our hoard of detritus is also our life's treasure *because* it is key to our identity over time, the key to who we are. The inventory, in other words, is the hook upon which is hung experience over time. Perec's inventories thus function as mnemonics, examples of the art of memory, or *artificial memory* (see Yates 1966): they are reminders of who we are. The process of inventory turns Perec's past life into a memory palace, which is, in the manner of the oldest such palaces, both a system, and the memory of a system: both the means to remember a life and a life story. (In a sense, remembered objects narrate Perec's life story back to him.) I note here that, like all forms of artificial memory, the mode of inventory is a mode of encoding and decoding, of compression and decompression. Today, the mobile phone functions as a mnemonic operator. In this case, however, the mnemonic operation is not performed in order to recall a past life. Rather the mnemonic operation, the mode of inventory, *describes* some of the ways in which users operate in a world that demands that they operate in many places at once. The inventory thus describes the means by which individuals achieve a series of negotiations between and across the multiple overlapping *spaces* they inhabit simultaneously – to different degrees, in different *states* – when they use mobiles and other similar technologies.

The mode of inventory begins with the list itself. With lists of friends perhaps. With the numbers ascribed to them, with the number ascribed to the caller. The inventory includes a certain degree of codification – in this aspect it reflects Perec's ongoing engagement with numerology. But, like other experiments with numerology and even automatic writing, inventory-making is also always a *poetic* process, albeit a peculiarly automated one. The inventory allows for the systematic collection and ordering of objects, but it also guarantees that the list so collected, will itself be productive, will have new implications. The space produced through the inventory is in this way also 'space as invention'. As Perec put it: space is a doubt.

Let me now return to re-consider my claim that the database might well be re-thought through the concept of inventory. This claim may sound as though it overstretches what is in a sense a literary conceit. However, one reason why Perec's sense of the inventory is useful here is because it underscores a real difference between two ways of thinking about the database operations. The first would be to understand the database as a technical architecture (this essentially is what Manovich does). The second approach looks at the database as it is used. This second way of thinking insists that the user be brought into the loop. Why does this matter? All databases involve codification – and therefore a process of compression and randomization (the compression of the non-absolute into the reductive mode of the pre-programmed experience). However all database *use* also involves a process of decompression or translation – and this is a process in which the user is *implicated*, a process that does not end with a technical operation. *Many kinds of databases tend to become inventories when they are accessed.* For this reason the inventory offers an alternative to the database as a way of accounting for movements in and out of databases, for movements in and out of virtual spaces in general, and perhaps for movements 'across and between' mobile bubbles and city streets. More specifically, consideration of the mode of inventory can suggest something specific about the processes of translation that go on in relation to the mobile phone use, and in relation to forms of mobile subjectivity. In short, the inventory makes it more feasible to consider narrative processes even in the fractured conditions within which we operate.

Consideration of attention/inattention rather than presence/absence on the one hand, and of the inventory that distends, rather than the database that compresses, on the other, come together to suggest an approach to thinking about (telephonic) mobility and everyday life that does not focus on disconnection and fragmentation as an assumed starting point. Rather, it produces a focus on how connection and continuity get made across and between different spaces. Finally, perhaps it is possible to use the mode of inventory to say something about the nature of this space/these spaces and the nature of this practice of space/ spaces as a *social* practice. The mobile phone is an(other) example of the dialectic characteristically operating around information technology – which offers us more freedom and simultaneously exerts over us more control. This dialectic might be opened up precisely by exploring the numerological production of a space – not as a technological space only (one operating according to the rules of logic) but rather by reading this technological space as a material *social* construction. Regarded as a practice of space, and as a practice that makes space, the mobile phone draws up the cultural conditions under which it itself is made – all the species of space – into itself: like a map, a dream, or even like a prayer might do. Paradoxically then, these private bubbles into which we speak, these bubbles that demand our attention, in which we find a particular form of self validation, in which we tend to speak one-to-one – these spaces that seem so intimate, so personal, and perhaps so free, are actually neither individual nor private spaces. Rather, they can be viewed as collective constructions. They are *socially* symbolic.

Notes

1. In *Approaches to What*, Georges Perec asks his readers 'how many movements does it takes to dial a phone number? Why?' (Perec 1997: 211).

2. Frederic Jameson (1981: 81) has suggested that the narrative text 'draw[s] the Real into its own texture' and might thus work to map the world as dream or prayer.

References

Bull, M. (2001), 'Personal Stereos and the Aural Reconfiguration of Representational Space', in S. Munt (ed.), *TechnoSpaces, Inside the New Media*, London: Continuum.

Crary, J. (2000), *Suspensions of Perception*, London: MIT.

De Certeau, M. (1984), *The Practice of Everyday Life*, London: University of California Press.

Hills, M. (2001), 'Virtually Out There', in Munt, S. (ed.), *TechnoSpaces, Inside the New Media*, London: Continuum.

Jameson, F. (1981), *The Political Unconscious: Narrative as a Socially Symbolic Act*, London: Methuen.

Lefebvre, H. (1991), *The Production of Space*, Oxford: Blackwell.

Manovich, Lev, 'The Database as a Symbolic Form', http://transcriptions.english.ucsb.edu/courses/warner/english235/Schedule_files/Manovich/Database_as_symbolic_form.html, or www.manovich.net/

Perec, G. (1997), *Species of Spaces*, London: Penguin.

—— (1996), *W, or the Memory of Childhood*, London: Harvill.

Yates, F. (1966), *The Art of Memory*, London: Routledge.

20

Soundscapes of the Car
A Critical Study of Automobile Habitation

Michael Bull

> When I get in my car I turn on my radio. I haven't got a journey to make before I get home. I'm already home. I shut my door, turn on my radio and I'm home. I wind the windows down so I can hear what's going on and sometimes as the sun's setting and I'm in town and I think. Wow. What a beautiful city that I'm living in, but it's always at the same time when that certain track comes on. It's a boost.
>
> (Automobile user)

> Today the highway might well be the site of the radio's most captive audiences, its most attentive audience. The car is likely to be your most intensive radio experience, perhaps even your most intensive media experience altogether. Usually radio is a background medium, but in the car it becomes all-pervasive, all consuming . . . the car radio envelops you in its own space, providing an infinite soundtrack for the external landscape that scrapes the windshield. The sound of the radio fills up the car encapsulates you in walls made of words.
>
> (Loktev 1993)

> For twenty-five centuries Western knowledge has tried to look upon the world. It has failed to understand that the world is nor for beholding. It is for hearing . . . Now we must learn to judge a society by its noise.
>
> (Attali 1985)

To each his own bubble, that is the law today.

(Baudrillard 1993)

This chapter discusses the manner in which we lay claim to the spaces we inhabit through the automobile. While it is commonplace to comment upon the automobile as a technological extension of the driver, in this chapter I focus specifically upon the auditory nature of that technological form of habitation. I do so in order to discuss the specific relational qualities attached to driving to mediated sound in the form of radio or cassette sound. The nature of this aural technological habitation will be discussed through the use of qualitative interview material filtered through an eclectic mix of critical theory.

The metaphor of the car as a home has a long anecdotal history in cultural theory. The root of this is discerned in the automobile as metaphor for the dominant Western values of individualism and private property, which is coupled to the romantic imagery embodied in travel as signifying individual freedom. The cultural meaning of the automobile as a privatized entity is inscribed into its very origin. From the move away from travelling collectively in trains at the beginning of the twentieth century (Sachs 1992), to the discomfort of inhabiting restricted spaces with strangers (Simmel 1997) to the desire for smooth, unbroken journeys unfettered by timetables (Urry 1999); these concerns have become embodied in everyday attitudes towards automobile use.[1] The image of mobile and free dwelling on the road denotes the representation of the heroic period of the automobile made mass and democratic. Yet this very democratization of autonomy and control is mediated by the power of the car, hence is dependent. This observation prompted Adorno to remark in 1942: 'And which driver is not tempted, merely by the power of the engine, to wipe out the vermin of the street, pedestrians, children and cyclists?' (Adorno 1974: 40). This description of 'road rage' also signifies the contradictory nature of the automobile embodied in everyday use whereby the driver is simultaneously all-powerful and controlled, not just by technology of the automobile, but by other drivers and the road system itself. The values embodied in the car also rest uneasily with a growing antipathy to the mundane nature of many aspects of urban everyday life for car users (Sennett 1990; Bauman 1993). Jacobson, catches the ambivalence of control while at the driving wheel:

In the car you are physically cocooned . . . It is the last private space in an overwhelmingly public world, the nearest we get to a lavatory at the bottom of the garden, where people once went to have a little time to them. Thus does the motor car perpetuate it. The worse it gets on the roads, the more we seek the solace of our vehicle. This is the way the world will end – trillions of us fleeing Armageddon, one per car. (Jacobson 2000)

The contradiction appears to be resolved by the nature of automobile habitation itself. Jacobson's metaphor of the garden lavatory is instructive: the car as a private, traditional immobile space of habitation. Yet traditionally Jacobson's escapees retreated into spaces of silence, to be alone with their thoughts. Car habitation, in contrast to this, is infused with multiple sounds. The aural privacy of the automobile is gained precisely through the exorcizing of the random sounds of the environment by the mediated sounds of the cassette or radio.

> You have to get it above the noise of the car . . . You switch off to the noise of the car because it's the same noise you get all the time. (Sharon)

The automobile as sound environment has been commented upon by Stockfeld:

> The car is one of the most powerful listening environments today, as one of the few places where you can listen to whatever you like, as loud as you like, without being concerned about disturbing others, and even singing along a the top of your voice – the car is the most ubiquitous concert hall and the 'bathroom' of our time. (Stockfeld 1994: 33)

We can see from this that descriptions of automobile habitation are awash with domestic metaphors of habitation. More recently the car as 'home' is described as becoming increasingly filled with gadgets to make the driver feel even more at 'home'. Automobiles are increasingly represented as safe technological zones protecting the drivers from the road and, paradoxically, from themselves.

> I want to suggest that the nature of this 'dwellingness' has changed from 'dwelling on the road' to 'dwelling in the car' . . . car drivers control the social mix in their car just like homeowner control those visiting their home. The car has become a 'home from home', a place to perform business, romance, family, friendship, crime and so on . . . The car driver is surrounded by control systems that allow a simulation of the domestic environment, a home from home moving flexibly and riskily through strange environments. (Urry 1999: 16–17)

There has indeed been a shift in the nature and meaning of auto-mobile habitation, which I locate in the development of the automobile as a creator of a mediated soundscape (Schafer 1977). I suggest that the historical turning point between 'dwelling on the road' and 'dwelling in the car' can be located in a very specific technological development: the placing of a radio within the automobile. This has radically trans-formed the nature of driving and the driver's experience of space, time and place. Thus, an understanding of automobile habitation should focus upon the mediated aural nature of that experience. The custom fitting of radios into cars began in the early 1960s, and by the 1970s they were standard equipment in most cars. This was followed by the development of portable tape decks installed in automobiles:

Tape decks made music consumers mobile, indeed automobile . . . Thus the American mass market was opened up by the car playback system. The mediated sound of the radio and later the cassette deck produce their own specific aural relational qualities. (Kittler 1999: 108)

Automobile habitation is usefully understood as representing wider social transformations in which the intimate nature of an industrialized soundworld in the form of radio sounds, recorded music, and television increasingly represent large parts of a privatized everyday lifeworld of urban citizens. This affects habitual everyday notions of what it might mean to 'inhabit' certain spaces such as, the automobile, the street, the shopping arcade or indeed the living room.

Music was no longer a necessarily public, communal experience, but could be heard at home, divorced from the settings in which it was originally produced. Sound recording, then, gave a powerful boost to the 'privatization' of experience, which may have held to be a fund-amental aspect of twentieth-century culture (Crissell 1986: 26).

The nature of these everyday aural privatized experiences has, how-ever, remained unexplored, or rather 'invisible' in accounts of everyday life that rather prioritize the visual nature of that experience. Cultural and urban accounts of everyday experience tend to locate experience in a form of visual silence thereby ignoring the specific relational qualities attached to aural experience. These relational qualities will be sketched out in the following section before I describe the everyday nature of auditized automobile habitation.

Sounding out Experience

If the world is for hearing, as Attali suggests, then there exists an unexplored gulf between the world according to sound and the world
according to sight. Sound has its own distinctive relational qualities;
as Berkeley observed, 'sounds are as close to us as our thoughts' (quoted
in Ree 1999: 36). Sound is essentially non-spatial in character, or rather
sound engulfs the spatial, thus making the relation between subject and
object problematic. Sound inhabits the subject just as the subject might
be said to inhabit sound, whereas vision, in contrast to sound, represents
distance, the singular, the objectifying (Jay 1993). Therefore aural
relational experience might well differ from a more visually orientated
one. This is not to suggest that they are mutually exclusive but merely
to suggest that the relational nature of a technologized auditory experience differs epistemologically from an explanation that prioritizes the
visual. In the following pages I argue that technologies of sound affect
automobile drivers' relation to the spaces they inhabit in very specific
ways. In doing so I draw upon Lefebvre's understanding of social space
together with the early work of Adorno, whose work on technology and
the historical construction of the senses has been largely neglected or
misunderstood.

What then are the relational qualities of sound in the car and what
do forms of aural habitation consist of? In the following pages I draw
upon empirical accounts of automobile habitation and reflect on the
specifically aural qualities of that experience. The inhabiting of automobile space has cognitive, aesthetic and moral significance that are
all relational in so much as they inform us of the ways in which car users
relate to their surroundings, others and themselves.[2] By focusing upon
the auditory and the technologized nature of everyday experience of
automobile users, I explain their attempts at creating manageable sites
of habitation.

Sounding out Automobile Habitation

The proximity of the aural defines car habitation for many drivers.
Drivers often describe the discomfort of spending time in their cars with
only the sound of the engine to accompany them. Driving without the
mediation of music or the voice qualitatively changes the experience
of driving. Many drivers habitually switch on their radio as they enter
their automobile describing the space of the car as becoming energized
as soon as the radio or music system is switched on:

In the mornings I feel relaxed when I get into my car. After rushing around getting ready, it's nice to unwind, put on my music and the heater and get myself ready for the day. (Jonathan)

I suppose I feel at ease. I put the radio on, put the keys in the ignition and I'm away. I've had new furry covers put on the car seats, so they are really comfortable and snug. In a way too, I suppose after getting out of the house, getting into Ruby (the car) is a way for me to relax and unwind. (Alexandra)

It comes on automatically when I switch the ignition on. Like I never switch the power off, so it automatically comes on as soon as I start the car. (Alicia)

Well it's on anyway. When the car starts it switches on. So it comes on automatically. (Gale)

I can't even start my car without music being on. It's automatic. Straight away, amplifiers turned on. Boom boom! (Kerry)

Mediated sound becomes a component part of what it is to drive. The sound of music competes with the sound of the engine and the spaces outside the automobile. Adorno in his early work describes this aural proximity in terms of states of 'we-ness', which refers to the substitution of 'direct' experience by a mediated, technologized form of aural experience. Music or recorded sound is both colonizing and utopian, according to Adorno, as it increasingly fills the spaces of 'habitation' in everyday Western culture. Recorded sound, according to Adorno

Takes the place of the utopia it promises. By circling people, by enveloping them – as inherent in the acoustical phenomenon – and turning them as listeners into participants, it contributes ideologically to the integration which modern society never tires of achieving in reality. It leaves no room for conceptual reflection between itself and the subject, and so it creates an illusion of immediacy in a totally mediated world, a proximity between strangers, of warmth for those who come to feel the chill of the unmitigated struggle of all against all. Most important among the functions of consumed music – which keeps evoking memories of a language of immediacy – may be that it eases men's suffering under the universal mediations, as if one were still living face to face in spite of it all. (Adorno 1976: 46)

Without necessarily endorsing the implied totalitarian nature of technology in the above quotation, Adorno's insight is significant in its heightening of the auratic quality of music together with its integrative and utopian function. The subjective desire to transcend the everyday through music becomes a focal point of his analysis, as is the desire to remain 'connected' to specific cultural products. The nature of this 'connection' constitutes the state of 'we-ness'. The 'social' thus undergoes a transformation through the colonization of representational space by forms of communication technology, and the 'site' of experience is subsequently transformed.[3] Increasingly, for critical theorists, the technologically produced products of the culture industry, in all its forms, becomes a substitute for the subject's sense of the social, community or sense of place. This, for Adorno, produces consumers who become increasingly 'addicted' to using those products as a substitute for the above. Central to this is a transformed notion of relational experience:

Addicted conduct generally has a social component: it is one possible reaction too the atomisation which, as sociologists have noticed, parallels the compression of the social network. The addict manages to cope with the situation of social pressure, as well as his loneliness, by dressing it up, so to speak, as a reality of his own being; he turns the formula 'Leave me alone!' into something like an illusory private realm, where he thinks he can be himself. (Adorno 1976: 15)

Music, for Adorno, increasingly fills the gap left by the absence of any meaningful sense of the experienced social. Technology is perceived as paradoxically enhancing and increasingly constituting that impoverishment that, for Adorno, contributes to the dependency of the user/listener. Music, as such, becomes a substitute for community, warmth and social contact. In this isolated world of the listener a need arises to substitute or replace one's sense of insecurity with the products of the culture industry, leading to new forms of dependency. However, it is specifically from Adorno's recognition of an 'unfulfilled' articulated through the auditory that a potentially active formation of agency and intentionality might be developed. The aural nature of 'we-ness' can be charted in the behaviour of automobile users in their everyday experience. For many users the radio/sound are integral components of automobile habitation:

Well, the stereo's the most important thing in my car. I don't like driving especially if I'm doing long distances on the motorway. I have to have music. (Alicia)

It's lonely in the car. I like to have music. (Joan)

I don't like the dark anyway. But when it's really late at night and the streets are really deserted, I think that does help. You know. You turn it up or whatever and at night when I have the radio on, they have like 'Late Night Love' and it's just hearing other people's voices, and it's actually quite funny listening to stuff they say. I think if I didn't have that I would be a bit more freaked out about driving late at night. (Alice)

I put it on Radio 4, because I knew I had a long drive. So it depends what kind of drive, Radio 4, I wanted someone talking to me, yes, I need someone talking to me, so I put it on Radio 4. I want to be listening to a voice telling me about various bits of news, etc. (Sharon)

The talking stations are very much to key yourself into the world – to engage. (John)

It connects me to the world because you've got someone talking to you, to connect you. (Ben)

Automobile users thus appear to prefer inhabiting an accompanied soundscape. However, many drivers prefer this auditized space to be occupied solely by themselves. Drivers often mention that the space of the car is preferably a privatized space.

As a private sphere the car is first and foremost a transportation environment, different in kind from the living, leisure and working spheres. For many drivers the time spent in the car may well be the only regular opportunity for reflection, voluntary solitude and concentrated listening to the radio or to record music, the only chance to do nothing without having to appear to be doing something else. In the car you can be at peace, you are whoever you like (Stockfelt 1994: 30).

It's a totally different environment. I like driving, I love driving on the road and you like driving on your own because it's a totally separate environment. It's a total indulgence, it's your environment. You control it. You can do whatever you like in it. It's like time off. You're travelling from A to B, but it's the ultimate idleness, really. You're not really doing anything but listening. It's great . . . So when there's someone else in the car with you, you don't have so much control over the environment. You can't let go so much. (Sharon)

The privatized aural space of the car becomes a space whereby drivers reclaim time, away from the restrictions of the day. The mundane activity of the day is transformed into a personally possessed time. Listening to music/radio enhances the drivers' sense of time control/occupancy.

I always have the radio on when I'm driving on my own and I'm always really annoyed when people in the car with me don't want the radio on. I just enjoy really, especially if I'm doing a drive I do regularly, that, I can sort of switch off and also if I'm doing it at a similar time. I can key into the Radio 4 schedule, and I know where I am in reference to whatever's on the radio. (Susan)

It's my time. I'm at home. I feel that I'm in my own space. More so than I would be in a tube listening with a Walkman. I feel totally at home. I could stop the car in the middle of a lane and eat in my car . . . A lot of people used to say: Joyce doesn't have a room. She has a car. (Jo)

It's much more convenient to use my own car. I can relax, I listen to the Breakfast Show on Radio 1 and get into my own time. (Alexandra)

The sound of the radio voice or music fills up or overlays the contingency of driving, transforming the potential frustration associated with powerlessness into pleasurable, possessed time:

It's good if you're in a traffic jam 'cos you can just forget where you are and just listen to it. It's more background though. I usually sing along. (Gale)

I couldn't drive without music. Driving without music is too boring. (John)

Sometimes you can just lose an hour, I can completely forget say between Swindon and Cheltenham. It will be like, did I do that? Because I've been so involved in my music. It's like I'm on autopilot. (Lizzy)

It's really boring in a car without sound. I don't want to go on a journey in a car without a radio. (Mark)

Not only does time pass more pleasurably, it is also potentially more predictable:

> I always go at a certain time, so I always listen to the same programme, a dance programme. I look forward to it. The relax programme! (Sharon)

> It's important that the same programme comes on at the same time. I feel I start the day when I listen to the day's Story at 9.45. (Susan)

> I have a few favourite sings along tapes. These are for long journeys. I will have them on the side, on the passenger seat, a selection of tapes because you can't rely on the radio for such a long journey. (Lizzie)

The structure, duration and meaning of the journey are increasingly mediated by sound. While automobile drivers speak of the car in terms of 'home' the aural space of the car differs from that of the living room. Radio programmes or music listened to in the car do not repeat patterns of domestic consumption.

> I think there's something specific about the car. There's a certain kind of sound you can achieve in the car that you can't at home. I think it's the smaller space. I just don't get the same feeling at home as I do in the car. I don't have the music on as loud at home. (In the car) I feel freer. (James)

> I play it louder if I'm on my own and I let myself go a bit more if I'm on my own. (Gale)

Music or sound is chosen to suit the time of day or the mood of the driver.

> I have to have it on loud [Radio 1]. Each track identity free, repetitious, high energy, that makes me drive very carelessly! (Susan)

> I'm more likely to listen after work on the way home or when I'm doing something else because its much more relaxing and it's a different type of music as well. I'll listen to a dance station, such as Kiss or Radio 1 if they've got some good dance music on and that will make me feel good. And then there's the tapes. Tapes are reserved for those times when there's nothing on the radio. Then I've got my selection of tapes, and for long journeys - tapes are a way of recording how far you've got. So you change every 45 minutes. When you're on your own – so you say that journey will take four tapes. (Sharon)

Many drivers take a selection of tapes so as to be able to match their mood to the music. The music both enhances the time of the journey – the experience of driving itself – and enables drivers to control their thoughts:

It's about switching off, there's also the pleasure if I know I'm going out. Music is a way of shaking things off. (Susan)

The pleasure is definitely in the listening. I sometimes go and slap it on and get away from reality. (James)

The success of music/sound in transforming the experience of driving is largely dependent upon the intensity of sound. This means that all other sounds have to be masked by the aural sounds of the car:

If I'm on my own then I do have it on pretty loud. (Jo)

Especially along a motorway, I'll have it on really loud, cos there's nothing to do, I'm usually on a motorway when its dark anyway so I like to. It's really nice if I'm on my own – it's nice company, so I have it up loud. (Kate)

The aural space of the automobile thus becomes a safe and intimate environment inhabited by the mediated presence of consumer culture. Making the mobile, contingent nature of the journey into one that has the appearance of precisely the opposite of this. However this aural form of habitation often includes interaction with the drivers themselves contributing to the soundscape of the automobile.

Singing in the Car

The car is a space of performance and communication where drivers report being in dialogue with the radio or singing in their auditized/ privatized space. Baudrillard's bubble (Baudrillard 1993) is however a fragile one, in which even aural absorption doesn't fully protect the aural bubble of habitation. The space of a car is both one to look out from and to be looked into. It is simultaneously private and public. Drivers both lose themselves in the pleasure of habitation and become increasingly aware of the 'look' of others. Many drivers sing or talk to their radio while driving:

Actually that's one thing I love about my car – she's all mine. I don't have to share her with anyone. I can do what I like in my car – with reason – I can turn the radio up full blast and have a good sing song without anyone looking at me. Actually, sometimes I suddenly realize that I'm merrily singing along, and the person in the next car is having a good laugh at me, but I forgot that people can see in and I get really embarrassed. (Alexandria)

I'll sing along at the top of my voice and I always worry what people in other cars think when they see me. They think I'm talking to myself or something . . . I just sing along all the time. I don't stop, like every song that comes on. Cos I watch a lot of music channels at home, so I know the words to a lot of songs. If I'm listening to the radio, I'll sing along to practically every song that comes on. (Alicia)

It's the embarrassment factor. When you're in your car and you get caught talking to the radio, dancing or smiling – it happens so regularly. When you're on the motorway, there's no one there, but in town, it's different. In town you switch to the fact that you're visible. (John)

I'm sitting there mouthing off to it. You talk, as you would any time when you're on your own. If the TV's on and there were some news programmes, I'd talk, like that's a load of rubbish, etc., I'd chatter away to it. (Sharon)

The space of the car becomes a free space in which the driver feels free to indulge his or her aural whims with no inhibitions. Houses have other occupants or neighbours to inhibit any such desire:

The louder the better. In fact, I use my car, I use it more than in the house, because I don't want to annoy the neighbours. But in the car, traffic is very noisy, so nobody can hear you. I sing incredibly loudly, especially on the motorway. In fact I have certain cassettes that I put on to sing incredibly loudly to. (Susan)

The sound of music together with the sound of their own voice acts so as to provide a greater sense of presence as well as transforming the time of driving. Drivers, even in the act of singing, are not, of course, hermetically sealed from the outside world. The very act of driving requires a steady focus on the road. Outside space becomes the space of the road before the driver. Drivers may well 'look' to music but more often report the intimacy of sound in their space. Sometimes this auditory home encompasses the aestheticization of the world outside of the automobile:

> When I'm sat in a traffic jam or at traffic lights, in town especially, to ease the boredom, I quite enjoy watching what's going on around me. I look in other people's cars, and watch people walking down the street. I like to see what they're doing and where they're going. As I am in my car a lot, I do need something to take away the boredom. The radio is good for that too. Actually I find music in the car changes how I look at the outside. It entertains me to watch other people with my music on. It is as if they are walking along to the music. (Richard)

Sound thus acts to transform the representational space of habitation, both within and outside of the automobile.

> You and the car are one thing and that's it and that's your space. Outside it's different. You're in your own time capsule, it's like your living room, your mobile living room. (Sharon)

> It's an extension of my space when I'm on the road. (Susan)

Drivers do experience their space as one that is hermetically sealed:

> When you're in your car you don't notice the pollution even though you're in your car which is polluting the atmosphere. Somehow you don't notice it. And I do find when I'm in London and I'm on foot and I'm having to walk and get a tube I'm much more tired at the end of the day and actually have a headache. It does get to me a bit more. The chaos of the city. Whereas in my car I can be stuck in a traffic jam for three hours and it doesn't affect me. I stay calm. (Jo)

> I think you're in your own little bubble. You're in your own little world and you have a certain amount of control and you don't have so much interruption. (John)

> When I'm in my car with the radio on, nothing outside seems to matter. It's like I'm the only one who is really there, and everyone else, the drivers, the people walking by are not king of real. I suppose it seems like that because I'm shut off from other drivers. They don't seem real. (Alex)

This hermetically and aurally sealed form of living in a privatized public space also affects the driver's relation to the act of driving. Driving is invariably described as more pleasurable when accompanied by music or radio sound. Some drivers report avoiding certain kinds of music as they feel they might drive too quickly or get 'carried away' by the sweeping or emotional force of the music, but this is by no means universal. Equally drivers sometimes report moving or manoeuvring through traffic in a dance-like manner, as if the relation between the driver and the act of driving were essentially aesthetic. Descriptions of driving often take on a romantic or filmic resonance in the literature:

> Who can resist keeping the station tuned to 'Born to be Wild' whilst racing down the interstate? Crankin' it up. Firin' up a cigarette. Rollin' down the windows. Exceedin' the speed limit . . . Dreamin of automotive decadence. (Locktev 1993: 206)

While this is of course one structural possibility of the aural experience of driving, it is incorrect to stereotype the aural experience of driving under this heroic banner. More interestingly, the following driver describes the simultaneous nature of listening and driving in which the private experience of listening is seen as paralleling the public occupancy of the road:

> It's very strange, what happens. You're driving on a very low level in terms of your awareness of you're driving and you drive on this low level . . . This whole conversation is going on in your head with the radio which is on a totally separate level and you're absolutely, you feel 100 per cent aware of both. You're quite capable of taking in information from both, but they're both separate. (Sharon)

The Aural Management of Space and Time in the Car

Drivers spend an increasing amount of their daily lives in automobiles, often involved in mundane and repetitive journeys. The above analysis demonstrates a variety of practices in which the daily scripts of experience are continually rewritten. These areas of everyday life, undertaken in public spaces, have often been assumed to be 'unscripted' and void of interest. Automobile habitation rather sees inhabitants rewriting their daily scripts through the mediation of sound. The aural script of 'driving time' is imposed upon those mundane and routine periods of empty time, thereby reclaiming and transforming them. Alternatively, the 'script' is extended into linear time in order to delay involvement in the 'bad' script of the unpleasurable and inevitable everyday. The need to reappropriate time and script it in as many activities as possible is indicated in the above analysis of automobile use. Automobile habitation permits an analysis of the ways in which drivers redraw the meaning of journey times thus confounding traditional dichotomous definitions of the partitioning of the everyday into meaningful/meaningless time:

> We can happily become lost in the anonymous ritualised journeys to and from work, for we know that this surrenders nothing that is important to ourselves. We do not live or do identity work in these places. Real life is elsewhere. (Cohen and Taylor 1976: 50)

Automobile habitation, with its privatized sound world, rather represents a form of 'compensatory metaphysics' in which time is transformed and experience heightened. The aural habitation of place and time becomes a way of re-inscribing the ritual of everyday practices with the driver's own chosen, more meaningful set of 'rituals'. What becomes clear is that the notion that 'real life is elsewhere' is experienced negatively by many automobile users who use the radio or the cassette as a means to reclaiming significance in the present.

Automobiles appear to operate as symbolic 'sanctuaries' in which drivers operationalize strategies of 'centredness' (Sennett 1990). This sanctuary represents a physical zone of 'immunity' between the river and the world or space beyond. Historically this zone was thought to be imbued with qualities not attributable to the world beyond, as in the spaces of a church. Sennett attributes this withdrawal to recognition that the urban world is one of confusion and instability, lacking in any clear definition. The attempt to create order, stability and control within some 'inner' realm is understood in terms of a progressive 'privatization of experience' in the work of Sennett. Following Sennett, the automobile might constitute one of the last, albeit problematic, refuges of a retreating public subjectivity. The 'automobile sanctuary' is conceptually enhanced through privatized listening, which erects a convincing and intimate barrier between the subject and the exterior world. Automobile users consistently refer to the car through the metaphor of 'home'. Yet a home in which they are preferably the sole occupant accompanied by the sounds of the radio or CD. Adorno frequently dwells on the historical process in terms of the auditory 'colonization' of the 'site' of experience by the social network:

We might conceive a series leading from the man who cannot work without the blare of the radio to the one that kills time and paralyses loneliness by filling his ears with the illusion of 'being with' no matter what. (Adorno 1991: 16)

Adorno points to the problematic nature of the 'site' of experience whereby the subject dresses up this 'site' which is actually an 'illusory realm' filled out by society. However, the above analysis indicates that automobile habitation is not merely 'passive' in its constitution. While Adorno's analysis of auditory experience, like Lefebvre's understanding of representational space, drifts towards notions of the colonization of experience, an empirical understanding of automobile use suggests a more dialectical process in which drivers actively reconstruct their experience precisely through the mediated sounds of the culture industry. Such an analysis sheds light on the ambivalent relation to public spaces embedded in the everyday use of the automobile.

Notes

1. Sachs notes that: 'Far from being a mere means of transport, automobiles crystallise life plans and world images, needs and hopes, which in turn stamp the technological contrivance with a cultural meaning. In this interchange, culture and technology prove mutually reinforcing. Technology does not fall from the sky; rather, the aspirations of a society combine with technical possibility to inject a bit of culture into the design like a genetic code. Yet neither do lifestyle and desire emerge from the thin air of culture; instead they coalesce around a given technology' (Sachs 1992: 92).

2. 'Social space ought to be seen as a complex interaction of three interwoven, yet distinct processes – those of cognitive, aesthetic and moral "spacings" and their respective products' (Bauman 1993: 145).

3. If car use transforms the relationship between the driver and urban space then this relationship can be located conceptually within Lefebvre's understanding of representational space, by which he means: 'Space as directly lived through its associated images and symbols, and hence the space of "inhabiters" and "users" . . . This is the dominated – and hence passively experienced – space, which the imagination seeks to change and appropriate. It overlays physical space, making symbolic use of its object . . . Representational space is alive: it

speaks. It has an effective kernel or centre: Ego, bed, bedroom, dwelling house; or square, church, graveyard. It embraces the loci or passion, of action and lived situations . . . It may be directional, situational or relational, because it is essentially qualitative, fluid and dynamic' (Lefebvre 1991: 39–42). The 'site' of experience exists for Lefebvre with representational space. This can be described phenomenologically in terms of the direction, situation and relation of the experiencing subject. Lefebvre's analysis is able to accommodate a qualitative, multi-layered and dynamic evaluation of experience in relation to its surroundings. However, in doing so Lefebvre appears to create an either/or dichotomy that sits uneasily with h is otherwise fluid analysis of experience.

References

An Investigation of the Safety Implications of Wireless Communication in Vehicles (1997), http:/www.nhtsa.dot.gov/people/injury/research/wireless.

Adorno, T. (1974), *Minima Moralia: Reflections on a Damaged Life*, London: New Left Books.

—— (1991), *The Culture Industry: Selected Essays on Mass Culture*, London: Routledge.

Arato, A. and Gebhardt, E. (eds) (1992), *The Essential Frankfurt School Reader*, New York: Continuum.

Auge, M. (1995), *Non-places: Introduction to Anthropology of Supermodernity*, London: Verso.

Bachelard, G. (1994), *The Poetics of Space: The Classical Look at how we Experience Intimate Places*, Boston: Beacon Press.

Baudrillard, J. (1993), *Symbolic Exchange and Death*, London: Sage.

Bauman, Z. (1993), *Postmodern Ethics*, Oxford: Blackwell.

Bose, A. MIT Archives, MC 261, *Hifi for GM Cars*, lecture 3/19/84 to EECS Seminar, 2 audiocassettes.

Brodsky, W. (2002), 'The Effects of Music Tempo on Simulated driving Performance and Vehicular Control', in *Transportational Research Part F*, Oxford: Pergamon Press, pp. 219–41.

Brown, B., Green, N. and Harper, R. (eds) (2002), *Wireless World. Social and Interactional Aspects of the Mobile Age*, London. Springer.

Cohen, S. and Taylor, L. (1976), *Escape Attempts*, London: Routledge.

Crissel, A. (1986), *Understanding Radio*, London: Routledge.

Frisby, D. and Featherstone. M. (eds) (1997), *Simmel on Culture*, London: Sage.

Horkheimer, M. and Adorno, T. (1973), *The Dialectic of Enlightenment*, London: Penguin.

Jarviluoma, H. (ed.) (1994), *Soundscapes. Essays on Vroom and Moo*, Tampere: Tampere University Press.

Kay, K. (1997), *Asphalt Nation. How the Automobile Took Over America and How We Can Take it Back*, Berkeley CA: University of California Press.

Lefebvre, H. (1991), *The Production of Space*, Oxford: Blackwell.

Loktev, J. (1993), 'Static Motion, or the Confessions of a Compulsive Radio Driver', *Semiotexte* VI (1): 37–53.

Miller, D. (ed.) (2001), *Car Cultures*, Oxford: Berg.

O'Connell, S. (1998), *The Car in British Society*, Manchester: Manchester University Press.

Robinson, J and R. Putnam (1999), *Time For Life. The Surprising Ways Americans Use Their Time*, Philadelphia: Pennsylvania State University Press.

Sachs, W. (1992), *For Love of the Automobile. Looking Back into the History of our Desires*. Berkeley CA: University of California Press.

Schafer, R. (1977), *The Tuning of the World*, New York: Knopf.

Schivelbusch, W. (1986), *The Railway Journey. The Industrialisation of Time and Space in the 19th Century*. Berkeley CA: University of California Press.

Sennett, R. (1990), *The Conscience of the Eye*, London: Faber & Faber.

—— (1994), *Flesh and Stone. The Body and the City in Western Civilization*, New York: Norton.

Simmel, G. (1997), 'The Metropolis and Mental Life', in Frisby, D. and Featherstone, M., *Simmel on Culture*, London: Sage.

Sloboda, J. A. (1999), 'Everyday Use of Music Listening: A Preliminary Study', in Suk Won Yi (ed.), *Mind, Music and Science*, Seoul: Western Music Institute, pp. 354–69.

Stockfeld, O. (1994), *Cars, Buildings, Soundscapes* in Jarviluoma, H., *Soundscapes. Essays on Vroom and Moo*, Tampere: Tampere University Press.

Urry, J. (1999), *Automobility, Car Culture and Weightless Travel*, draft, Lancaster University at http:/www.lancaster.ac.uk/soc030ju.html.

—— (2000), *Sociology Beyond Societies: Mobilities for the Twenty-first Century*, London: Routledge.

Part V

Living and Thinking
with Music

Theodor W. Adorno wrote that 'to interpret music means: to make music' (Adorno 1992: 3). By this he meant that music needed to be understood in the context of performance and practice. The translation of music into words is partial and always incomplete by the very nature of the form. The writers in this section have all attempted to grapple with these issues: How can we write about music? What does music have to teach us about issues of identity, belonging and memory? We began this book by citing Ralph Ellison's invitation to 'live with music.' Many of the authors in this section are themselves musicians and one thing they all share a commitment to both live and think with music.

The section opens with Paul's Gilroy's essay *Between the Blues and the Blues Dance*. Himself an accomplished guitarist, Gilroy reflects on his own beginnings as a musician and examines the interplay between past and present in musical performance. He takes guitarist Jimi Hendrix as a seminal figure in thinking about the relationship between individuality and modernism within the history of the African diaspora. Calling on Hendrix's notion of the 'electric church', Gilroy foregrounds the ways in which music can produce and nourish a community of listeners in which collective and individual sensibilities are fashioned through 'active listening'. He identifies the moral, artistic and political continuities, as well as breaks, between the 'blues and the blues dance' in the music of the African diaspora.

This is followed by Vic Seidler's personal contemplation on sound in the experience of the Jewish diaspora. He asks where do sounds belong? He examines the ways in which the sonic traces of memory intersect with silence and erasure. Here parental 'sound proofing', which muted Jewish resonances was an attempt to protect the children from the painful reminders of the Holocaust as well as a fear that 'sounding Jewish' would provoke anti-Semitism. He points to the ways in which migrant communities are shaped by their sound worlds and the historical and cultural contexts in which this takes place. Seidler shows that disapora traces remain in sound and music regardless of the listeners' ability to hear them. This can change over time and missing these registers at one moment does not mean they are lost forever. Seidler suggests that sounds call us through time. For him this mean that the music that passed him by in his twenties are now key ways for him to explore his sense of Jewishness.

From a different angle, Sanjay Sharma interrogates the ways in which alterity is both present and constructed in sound. Here he questions the ways in which the 'sounds of the other' are signalled within contemporary debates about cultural mixing and fusion. He cautions against the celebration of an assimilatory form of cultural hybridity that skims the aesthetic surfaces of diasporic cultures. He argues that this produces a situation where multicultural practices and hybrid identities enter into what he calls the 'smorgasbord of contemporary urban culture.' Sharma equally points to the untranslatability of Asian sounds where something remains in the sounds themselves that is inaccessible to the regimes of hegemonic representation. This means that music can form a place through which 'minitorian becomings' are possible in particular places and times. He concludes that 'untranslatable Asian sounds' evade appropriation yet their 'alterity is at work all around us'.

Stuart Hall's article documents the ways in which calypso travelled to Britain with post-war colonial citizen migrants from the West Indies. The article was a response to the release of in 2002 of a collection of classic calypso recordings entitled *London is the Place for Me: Trinidadian Calypso in London, 1950–1956* (Honest Jons Records HJRLP2) featuring artists like Lord Kitchener. Calypso is closely associated with carnival. Much of the power of the music is its capacity to turn the world upside down and document the world from the vantage point of the singer. Here we hear the world narrated through the voices of post-war migrants from the Caribbean many of whom, like Lord Kitchener himself, sailed to Britain on the Empire Windrush. As Hall puts it, political commentary to licentious stories of everyday life are 'all grist to the Calypsonian's mill'. What is significant about calypso is that it was, in a sense, the first Caribbean musical form to take on this role in the context of the UK. The music provides witness to the presence of black people at key events like the Queen's coronation in 1953 as a well as documenting the life these colonial citizens made in Britain.

The role of music in providing a means to give voice to the marginalized is also discussed in Susan McClary's essay on blues singer Bessie Smith. The prominence of female blues singers in the 'classic' period of blues is what McClary takes as her key focus. She shows that what is interesting about this music are the ways in which desire and pleasure are articulated from a woman's point of view. McClary argues that throughout the span of Western culture women have been 'spoken for rather than being permitted to speak'. She suggests the emergence of

'Blues Queens' and the music they made offer an 'unparalleled moment in the history of cultural representation'. She also examines the ways in which the collective sensibilities that are produced between the audience and the performers. This combination of individual and collective experiences is a common motif in the discussion of black music. The call-and-response or antiphonic quality of these forms blur the relationship between audience and performer. This is picked up in the interview with William (Lez) Henry, a reggae dancehall DJ and sociologist. He talks about the ways in which the microphone provides an instrument to document the hidden voice of black expression for the children of the Windrush generation. In a parallel way to the calypso performers, the DJs who were born and bred in London used and innovated musical idioms that had their origin in Jamaica and applied them to their experience in Britain. The sounds systems through which reggae is performed and created became a vehicle for the creation of unique forms of DJ vocal performance.

Julian Henriques' contribution 'Sonic Dominance' develops the discussion of the reggae sound system dance and examines the ways in which the sound system produces a particular acoustic environment. Here his notion of sonic dominance describes the times and places where the sonic medium displaces the usual dominance of the visual medium. He characterizes the sound system session as a 'living laboratory for the investigation of sound'. Henriques uses the sound system to re-think the relationship between the body and sound in this soundscape. He argues that the transformative effects achieved in the dance hall are evidence of a different kind of rationality in which time, place and memory are recombined. As a result it becomes a key site for the experience of cultural, historic and political connections within the African diaspora where it is possible to be in different places at the same time and at different times at the same place.

The last chapter in this section is by the renowned urban sociologist Richard Sennett. Sennett himself is a highly trained musician and cellist. In his recent book *Respect* (Sennett 2003) he reflects movingly on his life as a performing musician and the damage that afflicted the tendons on his left hand and ended his career at the age of 21. It was in part as a result of his damaged hand that he became a writer. In many of his books there are traces of this musical training even if they are not always evident on first reading. In the essay reproduced here he examines the relationship between touch and sound in musical performance and the centrality of resistance between fingers and the instrument itself. Sennett foregrounds the relationship between the material and acoustic in the production of a *geistlich* or soulful sound. It is for this reason that, when musicians talk about performers who have nuance and feel in their music, that they describe this as 'touch'. But as Sennett points out 'touch' is always sonic and manifest in the auditory realm because as he puts it 'only sounds sound'.

References

Adorno, T. W. (1992), *Quasi Una Fantatsia: Essays on Modern Music,* London and New York: Verso.

Sennett, R. (2003), *Respect: The Formation of Character in an Age of Inequality,* London: Allen Lane.

21

Between the Blues and the Blues Dance

Some Soundscapes of the Black Atlantic

Paul Gilroy

A note of music comes with us and is 'we'; unlike the visual arts, which seemed previously to point so far above us, out into the realm of the rigorous, objective and cosmic, but which in fact stop at our graves, it emulates good works by accompanying us beyond the grave.

(Ernst Bloch)

. . . the single factor that drove me to practice was that sound I had heard from the Hawaiian or country-and-western steel peddle guitar. That cry sounded human to me. I wanted to sustain a note like a singer. I wanted to phrase a note, like a sax player. By bending the strings by trilling my hand-and I have big fat hands – I could achieve something that approximated a vocal vibrato; I could sustain a note. I wanted to connect my guitar to human emotions: by fooling with the feedback between amplifier and instrument, I started experimenting with sounds that expressed my feelings, whether happy or sad, bouncy or bluesy. I was looking for ways to let my guitar sing.

(B. B. King)

My obsessions with music and sound predated the happy day in early 1969 when my father gave me an electric guitar. A cheap white, sub-Fender Vox, impossible to intonate accurately, I played it through a succession of borrowed amplifiers until, after four years, I had eventually saved enough to buy a real instrument made in London in the long-forgotten workshop of Emile Grimshaw and Sons, sometime banjo-manufacturers of Golden Square.

Initially inspired by Tim Renwick and Curtis Mayfield, Steve Stills, and the three Kings, but above all, by Hendrix, I have always had to work at my playing. The awe-inspiring ease with which the much more gifted players around me could spontaneously pluck out perfectly accurate versions of 'Littlewing', 'End of A Holiday' or 'Rollin' and Tumblin' after hearing them once or twice on French radio or American Forces Broadcasting late at night was never my style. I had neither the patience nor the ears to reproduce the wah wah solo from 'White Room' just like the record or master the intricacies of Michael Bloomfield's hippified transcodings of Hubert Sumlin and the futuristic speculations of Pete Cosey (heard with Muddy Waters long before we discovered him again with Miles).

At school I was laughed at for playing what was not yet named 'air guitar'. The rhythmic signature of Stovall's Plantation and the sublime ruminations of Son House and Lightnin' Hopkins would be approximated but never duplicated. Aspiring to possess the blues from the leafy edges of North London was in any case, riddled with contradictions. But Hendrix's anglophile afro-modernism resolved many of them. It certainly freed me prematurely from any mimetic obligations and pointed our generation of players and thinkers, via 'Red House' back in the direction of Albert King and the ur text of black self-making, with a voice and an electric guitar. That characteristic double address bespoke a public dialogue that drew upon different elements of self-hood. I thought I recognized it from Du Bois' helpful, pointed observations on the slaves' articulate message to the world but these were not only songs of sorrow, they were songs of triumph, obscene repudiation and transcendent dissent from the sour world that racism made.

My friend and bandmate Ed Vulliamy and I stood side by side and open mouthed as Jimi's set fell apart at the 1970 Isle of Wight Festival with his words about skinheads still ringing in our ears. There was real disappointment at Mitch Mitchell's inability to lock in with Billy Cox and I felt nostalgic for the Sly-quoting angularity of the Band of Gypsies but that down-home version 'Midnight Lightning' for ever sealed my fate. There could be no turning back and the struggle to make meaningful musical noise would dominate my life from that point on. Music would be woven into my other passions and productions and, once I had glimpsed it for myself, I was determined to show its special place in black metaculture to others.

I got into a fight at a party with somebody who took the 'Clapton is God' line then beloved of all the racist little Englanders and terrified suburbanites. Once I found more productive outlets for my evangelical fervour, I discovered that Hendrix helped yet again, not only by being the best but by being prepared creatively to damage the superficial integrity of the traditions in which he positioned himself. The modernist desire to transgress creatively was pivotal. After all, gypsy that he was, he had also wanted to be buried in England, his adopted homeland. His greatest moment as a live performer was that systematic assault upon the patriotic musical heart of the imperial nation in whose paratroops he had served with pride. It was then hell-bent upon destroying the Vietcong with the same fervour that currently guides its impossible and interminable war on terror.

In explaining artistic choices that felt eccentric then but no longer do so, Hendrix spoke from time to time about what he called 'the electric church'. It was a collective social body of musical celebrants that gathered periodically to engage the amplified modernist offshoots of the Mississippi delta and harness them in the causes of human creativity and liberation. Its ritual events had become loud, he told Dick Cavett in July 1969, not only because the appalling state of the world meant that many people were in need of being woken up by the shock that elevated volume could supply, but also because, if the wake-up-call could only be delivered on the correct frequency it could, in turn, promote a direct encounter with the souls of the people involved. Here, too, Du Bois' sense of where music augmented the power of words and writing supplied an active presence, although Hendrix's comment suggests a departure from his more conventional, and by then rather outdated, understanding of the workings of the black public sphere. Music would now produce its own public world: a social corona that could nourish or host an alternative sensibility a structure of feeling that might function to make wrongs and injustices more bearable in the short term but could also promote a sense of different possibilities, providing healing glimpses of an alternative moral, artistic and political order.

The electric church was all around us then; it was inseparable from the revolutionary upsurge of that moment. The traditional celebrations of Afro-Baptism had been profaned and adapted to the task of community defence. Under the banners of black power and anti-colonial solidarity its irregular services began to alter the political mentality of black Britons and to transform understanding of our emergent place in the post-colonial world. This could be done without a recognizably political word being spoken aloud. The church's fundamentally oppositional character

was disguised by its intimate relationship with the innocent and playful music and dance with which 'negroes' re-affirmed their infra-human nature.

I argued with my Brixtonian cousins about Jimi. He had been frustratingly far from the centre of their south London world, but he and his talk about the electric church as a source of meaning in a world from which meaning had been drained by the politicians' 'ego scene' came to mind while looking at this striking photograph of the crowd taken at a community reggae festival in south London's Brockwell Park during the summer of 1974. Taken by Chris Steele-Perkins, it has been brought back to life by Steve Barrow and Mark Ainley who have used it as the cover art for their worthwhile anthology of African American Rhythm and Blues tunes adapted into the Jamaican idiom. The idea that we could be slipping into darkness was something that then made sense at every point on the rim of the north Atlantic.

The faces of a large section of the assembled multitude have been captured as they listen raptly. They are not dancing. Movement appears to have been minimal even though the way that people danced to reggae in those days is a complex question that deserves detailed discussion beyond the scope of this brief piece. The power of this image derives largely from the way that their active listening has been en-framed. They seem to have become a community of listeners. We cannot, of course, know exactly what they were listening to. It is certainly tempting to imagine that the camera has caught them transfixed by the dread message of hope and resilience in the face of suffering that was so common to the insurgent musical culture of that moment long ago.

The image registers what must have been a routine occurrence at that time. This was a period in which, thanks to the reach and trans-local potency of phonographic technology, remote listening had acquired both social and political significance in the black Atlantic world animated by the chance to connect liberation struggles in the West with movements in what we now call the global South. Communication and analysis were conducted through the subaltern channels of a distinctive sonic and musical culture, transmitted unwittingly through the inhospitable infrastructure of greedy industries that had been colonized and had their dismal commodities bent to unorthodox purposes. It is abundantly clear from the musical forms and styles that were then popular right across this black world that hearing together had become connected to the possibility of thinking and acting together as well as to the larger processes of solidarity that were in the process of networking different black communities from Johannesburg to South Carolina via London and Kingston.

To a twenty-first century eye, this striking image shows something of what happened when the ethical and political language of human rights was articulated in the distinctive forms of the black Atlantic vernacular and transmitted into the everyday rhythm of post-colonial life in the metropole.

The mostly youthful faces caught by the camera are both male and female. They convey a mixture of deep concentration with what looks like a profound, ineffable sadness. That sorrowful mood defies being interpreted over-simply as either resignation or resistance and has seldom been captured as powerfully. Something like it can be glimpsed on page 137 of *Twelve Million Black Voices*, Richard Wright's famous exploration of the accelerated urban modernity of inter-war black life on Chicago's south side where a similarly disturbing photograph was given the caption: 'strange moods fill our children'. In Brixton forty years later, this concentrated sorrow was not the blues of the north Atlantic or the saudade of its southern counterpart though a comparable trans-coding of the history of racial terror means that it was kin to both. During that moment, with black Britain's emergent self-understanding still infused in the political language of Ethiopianist desires for flight and healing liberation, the image reveals an apprehension of the existential peril and ontological jeopardy in which racial hierarchy placed its victims. Marley, who had fled the US when his call-up papers for Vietnam had arrived in his mother's mailbox, had already delivered that message straight to black Britain's head, as the idiom of the time had it.

This portrait of community in the form of a crowd bound together by its collective mood of shock and stress as well as its shared emotion is all the more disturbing because, although the picture suggests that audience members were connected by a unanimity of feeling, they cannot actually see each others' faces. They are not in a circle and this is not a ring shout. Instead this crowd is confronted only by the backs of the heads of the people in front of them. They look forward, without staring in a strange unison, directing their synchronized rhythm of being in the world past the point where the photographer stood – between the audience and the stage that commands their attention.

They are a young and in many cases a stylish group. Today they provide us with a frozen example of what UK Blak's first poet laureate, Linton Kwesi Johnson, had identified at that very moment as 'a bran new breed of blacks'. We might add that this new formation had been, of necessity, developing a novel culture tempered by life in Britain with its distinctive mixture of feelings: promises combined with racist exclusion, violence and thwarted opportunity. Those routine post-colonial injuries were being compounded by the condescension dished out by too many supposed allies, helpers and friends. That view of black British life still bears upon interpretation of this photograph and the sonics that it silently captures. An empty benevolence mired in the assumption that the lives of black settlers could be defined by their cultural pathology, still echoes through historical reflections on the plight and destiny of this transitional generation composed mostly of young people who had not migrated as their parents had done but acceded to the dubious entitlements of British subjecthood conferred by birth alone. That view shaped almost all attempts to interpret their predicament, and its residue survives even today in a common sense view which makes the generation between the citizen migrants of the 1950s and the more assertively British-born group that succeeded them, into the custodians of a special crisis of identity, deeper and more disturbing than anything experienced by others before or since. Against that mistaken supposition, I submit this photographic evidence that suggests other more affirmative possibilities that derive from a sense of what that culture of sound and music brought into the lives of the transitional group to which I belong. We were not so much lost as lucky. An unusually eloquent, militant and musically rich culture oriented us and gave us the welcome right to employ it in order to defend ourselves, identify our interests and change our circumstances. We were buoyed up by a worldwide movement for democratic change and energized by the intensity of a very special period in the cultural life of our diaspora. Artistic innovations like Dub had, for example, taught us the value of what, in Adorno's words, could be 'communicated in the shock of the unintelligible'. The history of Punk without which post-war British life makes no sense, cannot be grasped without appreciating the force of the insights transmitted into what Dick Hebdige called its 'white ethnicity' from these dread sources.

More significant than the crowd's hip headgear, unstraightened 'Afro' hair and palpably soulful stance is that intense concentration common to their sorrowful, resilient expression. Many of them seem, understandably, to be trying to evade the camera's intrusion and surveillance. More practical issues aside, it is as though they do not want to be caught in a moment that reveals them to be as vulnerable as they are unified. They are united in the vulnerability they share as a racialized and marginalized group, in the wound they seem to carry as a collective cultural burden on their journeys towards and also away from Englishness and against the exclusionary force of its downpressive political and cultural codes. They seem to be and to belong together but that imperilled togetherness, that apparently elemental collectivity, is an untidy and asymmetrical affair marked by the way that racism intervened to block and to channel individuality into the patterns demanded by functional race hierarchy.

The photograph is also haunting because its subjects have been caught in what is wrongly understood as the inert or passive act of listening. The limitations of that view are repudiated by the common mood etched on their faces. Their concentration suggests not pleasure but a demanding variety of work. Whenever it was visible in daylight, that kind of cultural work proceeded deceptively, masquerading under the banner of play. It was mostly an orphic, underground phenomenon that did not seek overground recognition largely because it feared for its own survival in the cold light of colder northern days. The hidden public spaces in which it made its new metropolitan home and through which it found its own way hosted a complex process of intercultural and transcultural syncretism that is still poorly understood and only partially mapped. This was cultural work that incorporated defensive and affirmative elements: working over and working through the memories of slavery and colonialism, past sufferings and contemporary resistances so that they could provide resources for interpreting the present and imagining a better future for blacks and for the whole world.

The most enduring, although not perhaps its most significant result of this elaborate exercise, was the ability of many to assert their belonging to Britain with an authority and legitimacy that could not be denied and, in the process, to have changed what Britain was, largely by forcing acceptance of the fact that they were here to stay. These possibilities were celebrated and enacted in the musical cultures to which the photograph alludes. They were evident from distinctively local styles of toasting and dubbing, in the category of 'Lovers' Rock' and in the very different relationship to African American cultural and political traditions that was the conceptual premise of so much black British musicking. Dennis Matumbi was the high priest of our electric church. Shaka and Neil Fraser would eventually be its missionaries.

The late-night cultural work involved was not, of course, Labour, though in some circumstances it became Labour's active, desperate negation. Claimed back from the harsh, split world that immigrant labour made and held in place, the super-exploited social body composed of immigrants and their persecuted children required spaces of healing and autonomy. Musical culture and the elaborate social relations that eddied around it, at least until the digital revolution changed the game, created that locus and invested it with a precious democratic energy in which audiences and performers could interact and collaborate. The soundscape of that struggle and transition interests me again now as a historian. The representation of that interpretative community as an audience is especially apposite given that the ability to listen in this intense, collective way seems lately to have dropped out of black popular culture. Here were community and solidarity, momentarily constituted in the very process, in the act of interpretation itself. First pirate radio then the anti-social cultures of mobile privatization replaced the ancient authority of the electric church with something shallower and more consumer-friendly.

The Steele-Perkins photograph has another useful attribute. It directs attention towards the independent power of a world of sound that was never reducible to the potency and oppositional lyricism of even the best and most compelling songs from that special period: revolutionary or compensatory. That world of sound celebrated here was specified hesitantly but repeatedly in the same vernacular code as something like a 'bass culture'. It was shaped by a fundamental awareness that as far as understanding the predicament of these sufferers was concerned, vision was not the master sense and words alone could not be a stable or trustworthy medium of expression and communication. This difficult lesson had been administered by a cumulative training in tactical communication conveyed to us by the dub cuts that had begun to damage the semiotic integrity of even the most forgettable version sides.

It is worth recalling that, at this precise historical point, the black community in that part of South London found itself at the forefront of a deep and bitter conflict between its young people and the police and media, which had articulated the problem of Britain's black settlement through the diabolical figure of the mugger–deviant, predator and vanguard of black urban insurgency. A few months earlier, a public display of fireworks for 5 November in the same park had been transformed into a large-scale disturbance. The young men roughly arrested at that event had been tried and received lengthy sentences for offences deriving from their refusal to accept the authority of what they saw as unjust and partial law; its universal aspirations compromised by perverse attachments to the ideas of racial difference and black inferiority.

In finely-detailed black-and-white tones, the photograph offers an striking image of black Britain emerging from the confluence of its Caribbean antecedents with novel north American aspirations buoyed up by the transnational vision of Black Power. The dissenters' goal of equal rights and justice had already been specified explicitly as alternative to peace by a whole host of artists. Again, it is impossible to know whether the crowd has been caught up in the music of a live band or, as is far more likely, just transfixed by music and/or toasting coming from one of the sound systems whose speaker boxes we can see piled up in the background. The preference for recorded rather than live performance was an interesting and disturbing feature of the soundscape of the period, which did not reveal an absolute enthusiasm for music made and heard in real time. The aesthetic and anti-aesthetic codes that governed this economy of pleasure, escape, transcendence and desire specified instead that the highest value was to be placed on and invested in art that spoke to the immediate circumstances in which it appeared but relied upon processes of intermixture and combination that made elsewhere audible. Remote black communities became present to each other by these means. When local DJs rode a Jamaican rhythm or sung over the radically unfinished version sides that had been dispatched northwards in anticipation of precisely that additional input, Britain or more accurately London and other metropolitan nodes of cosmopolitan settlement could be experienced as continuous with the increasingly distant but more easily accessible Caribbean. The sonic coming together of these divergent elements, expressions of geographically separated but genealogically related cultures, contributed to the appealing manifestation of a third, utopian space, sometimes labelled Africa, in which the wrongs and hurt of babylonian existence could be systematically undone and white supremacy overthrown in the name of higher human freedoms.

About the time the picture was being taken in Brixton, I misspent a couple of youthful hours peering at the startling geometric patterns being made in finely textured powder as, in a Frisbee placed over a speaker, that unlikely medium responded to the sound waves of my favourite music. After that accidental discovery, I wondered how my own body might be affected by the sonic pounding to which I have regularly exposed it. The physical impact of the sound on the cornflour in my improvized dish was disturbing because of its precision and its apparent predictability. I had seen those magical patterns once before, in an old UNESCO Courier article about the mathematical rules governing natural forms, but encountering the sound with a new sense of its physical power in mind, was another matter altogether. A few weeks later I can recall wondering how Sir Lee's 'Whip Them No Skip Them' earthquaking from the wardrobe-sized speaker boxes of a south London sound system, was reshaping my cells, blood and sinews.

The physical transformation of the body in its encounters with musical sound has not been much discussed by critics and historians of the black Atlantic soundscape. It may not matter in the grand scheme of things, but that impact or rather interaction between body and sound provides a second stimulus for this argument, which is directed now against the limited idea that we encounter sound only, or even mainly through our capacity to hear and to make interpretative sense of it. For me, remembering the physical inscription of sound in matter provides a useful warning against the over-aestheticization of music and all mistaken if well intentioned attempts to approach organized sound as an exclusively cognitive problem. In the services of the electric church, the body is present as an object as well as an agent and it is not clear at all how musical sounds act upon it at various volumes particularly when drugs also become part of the experience in which music becomes organized and meaningful sound.

The idea of a bass culture raised by Ralph Ellison at the end of his epic *Invisible Man* is helpful here. At the end of the novel, so concerned with the relationship of human senses to the perception of racial difference, Ellison's character aspires to speak on the lower frequencies in the name of a new and emphatically disembodied humanity. Somewhere towards the other end of the chain of cold-war humanism that encompassed black British life, Linton Kwesi Johnson articulated what we can now read as an urgent and notable response to Ellison's tentative, questioning call in his second book of poems, *Dread, Beat and Blood.*

Repeated references to the cultural world that the phonograph created, tie both texts together more tightly than the disarming actions of their 'mugger' protagonists. For Johnson, 'bass history is a moving is a hurting black story' while Ellison's picaresque hero, as is well known, falls inside the recording of Louis Armstrong singing 'What did I do to be so black and so blue?' while under the influence of a reefer. Once inside that holy space – not yet the province of the *electric* church because this is, after all, a wind-up gramophone – he discovers not only a different sense of time but 'a new analytical way of listening to music . . . that night I found myself not only hearing in time but hearing in space as well. I not only entered the music but descended, like Dante, into its depths'.[1] Johnson's complex poem 'Bass Culture' constructs a similar journey and can be read as an echoed reply. His activist choices diverge sharply from the 'cowardly' pathway taken by Ellison's retreating invisible man. His is another rebel music. This time it is heard socially in the collective communal setting of the blues dance that presents most of the same existential and political choices that bounded Ellison's Harlem but, perhaps, because Jah herb is stronger than Ellison's refer they are embraced rather than refused:

> hotta dan de hites of fire
> livin heat doun volcano core!
> is de cultural wave a dread people deal[2]

This passionate popular rage, 'bitta cause a blues, cause a maggot suffering, cause a blood klaat pressure' is a revolutionary and utopian spirit that identifies emancipation with a change of rhythm. Shaped by the sonic innovations of dub and their novel acoustic architecture in the vernacular setting of a different underground than the over-illuminated urban cave Ellison had in mind, Johnson invests the power to act politically in the experience of hearing that damaged, beautiful beat. His words counterpoint it and associate the resulting tides of feeling with a cultural rupture that is also a musical event for which the power of the horns of Jericho provide the most appropriate Ethiopianist motif. This a musical cue that ties Rico Rodriguez's eventful contribution to the apocalyptic dub of 'Ghost Town' to the more recent offering by The Streets. While this sonic happening cannot itself abolish oppression, it can certainly powerful enough to disperse and fragment it, winning important time for healing and recovery in the process and making an eventual triumph more likely:

> an the beat jus lash
> when the wall mus smash,
> an the beat will shiff
> as the culture allta
> when oppression scatta[3]

Something like that awareness of the power of sound would flow from these invigorating, disreputable sources into the mainstream of British culture through the conduits of Punk and its political adjunct, Rock Against Racism. Yet another version of it was forced upon me more recently. Last summer my ears rang for a week after standing too close to Robben Ford, soaking up his Californian Buddhist mutations of the blues. The high point of that smoky north-London encounter was his brave, delicate reading of Willie Dixon's Vietnam era tune 'It Don't Make Sense (You Can't Make Peace)'. It was heard this time in the context of an emergent global movement against American imperial power. Ford, whose elegant blues-be-bop playing I had first enjoyed twenty-seven years ago when he was a youthful member of the LA Express, had revived Dixon's wise lament during the summer of 2002. Originally directed at Nixon, Westmoreland, Kissinger and company, the song's observation that American might was sufficient to 'crush any country in a matter of weeks' had seemed apposite once more as the reinvigorated US war machine re-organized itself in Kuwait and Qatar under the direction of Bush II. The song makes no explicit mention of the war in Indo-China but, galvanized by its intertexts: the more casual references in Freddie King's 'Yonder Wall' or the more explicit fare served up by J. B. Lenoir and one or two other brave souls, it loses nothing by its calculated indirectness.

Listening to Robben raise the spirits of Albert Collins, Otis Rush and, of course, Albert King, while taking in the surprisingly large number of black people in the room, I felt obliged to ask how we should articulate the evident connections between the sculpted soundscape of tone, volume, voice and rhythm and the emotional and psychological effects that it both solicits and creates. There should be nothing automatic or overly mystical in this of course, but we do need to leave room for it in analyses of the way music is heard and made useful as an image of the will: individual and collective.

These questions point firstly to more than a refined understanding of the technological capacities of sound reproduction. And secondly to what might be called a phenomenology of sonic pleasures. On another occasion, after rushing over to Hammersmith to enjoy Anita Baker's first British appearance, I remember being disappointed by her live shows because I had only shivered once during the entire performance. It had seemed antiseptic and overly rehearsed. The physical effects on the body are not the same where pre-recorded music is played and modified even in the odd acoustic space of the sound-system environment that nurtured Linton Kwesi Johnson's radical phenomenology of liberation. The frequencies of address are different and the patterns of sociality vary where a different balance is being struck between hearing and move-ment and there is a bigger space for theatricality, grace and dance. I got that telltale shiver when Robben tore into his solo on 'It don't Make Sense'. There were swirling torrents of sound: cascading mutant be-bop pentatonics, Milesified probings, angry sounds in sheets of smouldering melancholy. Chorus after swelling chorus, wave after wave of crisp wailing notes breaking on the beach of our wounded subjectivity. There was the electric church all right and Willie Dixon was absolutely right, none of the absurd world against which that musical attack was directed made any sort of sense.

Here, I begin to run out of words and must face the fact that sound becomes an esoteric subject very quickly when we shift away from thinking about its reception and reproduction and consider, instead, the immediate intricacies of its musical production. Historically and analytically, there are difficulties involved in integrating or braiding together the resulting strands of thought into a single overarching dia-sporic soundscape that reveals the localization as well as the globalization of the world. The shared obligation to convene the public space of the electric church helps but it does not solve these difficulties. It is telling and perplexing that the 'auratic' properties of real time music were never the favoured vehicle for the patterns of play and memory that grew up around music in the Caribbean and subsequently set the template for black Britain's musical cultures.

Tonight that enigma bothers me while I peer into the grille of my amplifier assessing the subtle sonic properties of different types of EL34 and the infinitely variable characteristics of the various custom pick ups and string gauges I employ with the different instruments I play obsessively. Making that music, that sound, in real time has gone out of style. If it meets at all, the electric church has to operate under the disabling weight of computerized dance music that is easily commodified and privatized so that it can afford the simplest of routes into to the simulated ecstasy of togetherness.

Searching in vain for a response, I am struck by the peculiar poetics with which the tonal attributes of electrified instruments – especially guitars – are now conventionally described. Contending vocabularies taken from the play of colour, light and other sources are becoming progressively more elaborate but remain equally adrift from making sense of the sonic work involved in moving a crowd towards the revival tents of the electric church. Tonight, rather than convene that collective subject, I am invited by a selection of articles in the latest issue of one of the glossy guitar porn magazines I have been reading to worry whether the front pickup on my superstrat is sounding too 'glassy' and to think about the way that my amp's gain settings transform the sonic properties of various pick-up types. Oddly enough, rebel Robben is featured here in one ad extolling the properties of the 'Tone Pros'® bridge system, which makes tuning stable at last.

I still play every day but, until now, I have not wanted to be anything like open about the place it occupies in my life as a form of discipline and a means to organize and shape the rest of what I do as a teacher and writer. So, here, instead of a conclusion, is a photograph of the newest instrument that has fallen into my welcoming hands. I hope to use its unusual resonance in future congregations of our local electric church. Needless to say, it too employs the post-modern tuning possibilities of the Tone Pros® system.

Notes

1. Ellison, R., *Invisible Man*, Penguin, p. 11.
2. Kwesi Johnson, L., *Dread, Beat and Blood*, p. 58.
3. Ibid., p. 59.

22

Diasporic Sounds
Dis/Located Sounds

Vic Seidler

Where do sounds belong? Do they have particular places of origin or can they cross boundaries with ease? Can people take their sounds with them as they migrate from one culture to another? Do these sounds serve to remind people of where they have come from, as if they have never left, or do these sounds express a yearning for what has been left behind so that they sometimes become difficult to hear again?

When my mother was forced to leave Vienna, when Hitler's troops marched in, she was shocked to have to leave the city she loved. There was no longer a place for her and she was warned to leave as soon as she could. She felt a sense of rejection that could make it difficult for her to bring the music she loved with her. But whenever she heard a waltz she smiled and she would claim it as a 'Vienna waltz' as if the music and dances were connected for her with the place. She was always too restless to sit down and listen to the music but when it entered her world she would dream with it. She would remind us that she had danced to these melodies when she was young. She could recognize this as her music and she could recognize herself, even for a moment, through this music.

One of her early boyfriends in Vienna played the piano and would play in particular clubs in the city. My mother would go and listen. He wanted to marry her but her family did not really approve and she seemed to take him for granted. But it was important for her that he played piano, created the music that she loved. When she came to London she seemed to lose contact with Walter. She was lucky enough to bring some of her furniture with her from Vienna that came soon after her mother arrived in London. I do not know whether she brought music with her but we soon acquired some old 78s of waltz music. There was also some Yiddish music that my mother knew from her mother but she did not really identify with it closely for herself. She identified herself with the modernity which city life in Vienna promised. Even though her parents were orthodox, she craved the freedom of urban life. She wanted to go out to dances at night and her mother sometimes arranged her bed so her father who was strict would not realize that she was still out.

My mother claimed this music as her own and she did not easily share it with her children. For her it was connected with a painful past from which she wanted to protect her children. She did not want the sounds to leak through to connect us, as children, to a history that carried too many painful reminders. Rather we were to be protected from the past so that we could be free to create 'English' identities in the present. She feared that the traumatic histories that she carried would hurt her children and make it more difficult for us to grow up to be 'like everyone else'. This was the dream of modernity that offered us a safety that she had learnt you could never take for granted. For her safety was somehow linked to invisibility and she feared representations of Jewish life that might provoke anti-Semitism. In some way this resonated with the idea of being 'seen and not heard'.

As children, when our mother remarried Leo who had grown up near Leipzig before fleeing quite late to London having been rescued by a young medical student from Trinidad who was studying at Cambridge, the atmosphere in the family was to change. He had married my mother who had four young boys though we were largely hidden from view during their courting. In those early years he was keen to speak English with as little an accent as possible and to pay the price of assimilation. He rarely talked about his prewar life in Germany but readily reminded us at the dinner table that children should be 'seen and not heard' and that the motto of Winchester school was that 'silence was golden and that speech was silver'.

Somehow Englishness was identified in Leo's mind with the value of silence. This resonated with his background in Germany, which was more controlled and ordered than the waltz that was more spontaneous. As you learned the value of silence, so as children you learnt to control your sounds. Growing up in a largely refugee Jewish community in north-west London you knew that your parents had come from somewhere else but you were not supposed to ask too many questions because they had 'suffered more than enough'. So you learned to listen even if it was to Yiddish and German that you were not supposed to understand. You got used to the sound of different languages and making out what was intended, even if you could not engage in the conversation yourself. These languages did not seem 'out of place' for us, but were part of the atmosphere in which we grew up. We assumed that families always worked with the sound of different languages. We recognized these language as part of an adult world that we were to be excluded from. We also knew that difference could be dangerous.

Soundings

The first sounds that you hear as a baby find a deep resonance. It is through hearing the sound of the mother's voice that you know where you are in the world. It is through this voice that you feel comfort and security. We think about a mother tongue as the language in which your mother first spoke or sang to you. Often it is these sounds that we yearn for. We were looked after by nurses as well as by our mother – that was the fashion in middle-class life at the time. This meant that there were different sounds that we heard and possibly different songs. I am not sure what language my mother felt easy enough to sing to us in or what rhymes came easily to her lips. There was the tune *Henchen Klein* in German but there was also ambivalence since she always wanted her children to grow up to be English, and so as different from herself. She did not want to 'pass on' what she knew herself because she felt this could damage the future we could grow into ourselves.

Often, years later, it was through the ways I saw my mother handle my own children as a grandmother that I found some clues of what it was like for her as a mother. I think she liked the physical activity and closeness that breastfeeding brings but felt uneasy with voice, possibly because there was ambivalence about what tunes could be sung. It was as if there had been a double break between herself and her mother's generation that would have sung most naturally in Yiddish and what she learnt as a girl as Viennese German. There was then the break with Vienna and with a traumatized history that she had wanted to leave behind. It was as if part of her wanted the past not to exist for her. She wanted her children to grow up as if they did not have a past. It was too painful to re/member the tunes.

Sometimes there are fewer breaks and there are ancestral voices that are passed from generation to generation. Mothers sing the same songs to their babies that their mothers sang to them. Often new mothers feel a need to connect back to their own mothers, as if there is a need to touch base in this new transition. It can be as if women need to hear the voices of their own mothers as they learn to become mothers themselves. Even if the relationship has been difficult and remains unresolved this can be a transitional time in which emotions begin to surface. My mother-in-law who came from a Polish background but who had migrated to Brazil in the 1950s was much easier with babies. She was much more spontaneous in her contact and was able to enter the sound world of babies. She would appreciate and respond to the sounds they make rather than dismiss them as somehow irrational. She would be able to communicate through sound, recognizing the meaning that sounds carried before they had transformed into words.

Even though she carried her own traumatic history, having been taken off to a labour camp when she was still a teenager in the hope that it might save her older sister who was already married, she seemed able to leave this history behind for a moment as she linked to the energy and sound of a baby. She entered into the sound world and could meet the baby through recognizing the sounds. This was a gift that was very different from a middle-class British tradition that often says that children are only interesting when they come into language, as if it is through language that they enter culture and so become human. This is part of a literary tradition that often values text over voice. It is as if meaning only comes through the structure of the sentence. This is a vision that Wittgenstein questions in his later writings when he appreciates that language is often built upon the natural expression of sound and gesture.

Sound is linked to gesture and so to bodily movement. Often sounds are not disembodied and we appreciate this when we connect sound to movement and so to dance. When the young child makes a sound reaching towards an apple that is beyond its reach on the table, this is a way of saying that it wants the apple. Later the child may learn to say this so that it does not have to reach out any longer, hoping that someone might reach the apple. This is a simple example but it questions the relationship of meaning to language and so the Lacanian vision that it is through language that the child somehow enters culture. This is to link the imaginary to language as if language exists as an autonomous structure of words.

When we talk about a child coming into its own voice we are recognizing the individuality of voice. This is a process that takes time and moves through stages of transformation as Freud was attempting to interpret. This is connected to a sense of whether children feel that they are being listened to. There seems to be a connection here between 'being listened to' and the notion that you are 'being seen' as a person in your own right. When we talk about giving voice to our experience, we are hoping that what we say will be understood and that we will find some kind of resonance. This is not simply a matter of whether the language we use is being understood.

Resonance

When a child comes home saying that she has been bullied at school and that her friends have been picking on her, she wants her experience to be validated by someone. When we say that 'it was nothing' and she is going to have to go back into school the next day 'as if it were nothing' so that she does not let her friends know that they have hurt her because otherwise they would have won and she would give them some kind of victory, we are giving advice but not necessarily listening. Sometimes it is too painful for parents to listen because they do not want to be reminded of their own experiences at school. But often it can be more helpful to acknowledge how hurtful it can be and so to allow children to have tears that they might not allow themselves to have in school. Children might have to sound off and even express the rage they did not feel safe enough to express in the setting of the school.

It is through breaking the silence in this way and creating a space in which children can actually give voice to their emotions and feelings that they might come into a place where they can think about appropriate strategies that they might need to follow in school. This is not a question of interpretation, as psychoanalysis might present it, but of actively giving voice to a range of emotions that can help to move the child on. This is a matter of giving voice to experience, not simply offering an interpretation of what has been going on in the relationships. Often this opens up a path of exploration in which hurt might give way to anger. Sometimes young women feel that they cannot express anger because they have learnt to evaluate it as a threat to their femininity. In this way we are challenging cultural norms as we recognize a tension between the girl 'working through' her experience and the cultural expectations of femininity.

Often there is a subversive character of voice as children explore through sound what they are feeling. Often it is through sound that they might come to a recognition of anger that they would not have wanted to intellectually acknowledge to themselves. Often boys learn to discount what they have experienced covering over a sense of hurt with the protective notion 'that it was nothing really'. They learn that they cannot acknowledge their hurt without threatening their male identities. Often they will resist giving voice to their hurt, though parents might detect that something is amiss when they take out their anger on their younger siblings. This can mark a dislocation where the hurt is transformed into anger, which can only be expressed indirectly through 'taking it out' on others. It is as if the hurt cannot be sounded and finds no resonance in others. Rather, as it is transmuted into anger so it is projected onto others, often those less powerful than yourself who are forced to take it on themselves.

Often young men learn to keep their silence so that they will not express the hurts they carry to others, and will do their best to hide it from themselves. This can be intensified with migrant communities where particular masculinities can be feminized, as has traditionally happened to Asian masculinities in Britain. Through music they can often recognize tensions that they cannot name for themselves. Within diverse diasporic spaces they can explore emotions and feelings they might otherwise be unable to name, because they are deemed threatening to sustaining prevailing dominant masculinities. Often young people are growing up into a world that their parents cannot understand.

Growing up in the 1950s it was through the early days of rock and roll that we found a music that we could call our own and that helped to name some of the fears and anxieties we lived with in our everyday lives. There was an emotional intensity in the sounds, when Elvis for instance, sang that 'only the lonely know the way I feel tonight' that we could identify with and that helped to connect us into a new world of adolescence. It was in the sound spaces that were created in the Jewish youth clubs in north-west London that we found a freedom to explore our own diasporic identities. When we listened to Buddy Holly sing about Peggy Sue we entered a different world that was also a world that did not separate us off but somehow included us within an adolescent identity. Somehow this music came to express future hopes and a life that could be lived on our own terms.

Recently I heard the social psychologist Michael Billig talk about his book *Rock and Roll Jews*. He played the same songs from the late 1950s that we knew by heart. It was the rhythms that brought body and sound together that allowed for its own forms of forgetfulness. For even if we were dancing within the diasporic space of a local synagogue youth club there was a taste of freedom and ecstasy of movement. It struck me how a generation is marked by the particular sound world that you grow into as a teenager. Often this music seems to touch in ways that later music somehow cannot reach. At the time we did not realize the resonances that allowed so many of these soul songs to have been written by Jewish songwriters who often shared similar urban spaces in the Bronx. They were writing these songs out of their own experiences of poverty and exclusion. This marked a particular historical moment in the musical relationship between blacks and Jews.

Somehow these sounds could move across spaces and they could speak to the anxieties and insecurities of the adolescent lives we were living in north-west London. In some ways we felt ourselves to be outsiders who were trying to enter a culture that was not our own. It was through this music that we could make ourselves at home, find a sound world that could connect us with the wider adolescent community. In these years we did not want to know what our parents had lived through in the past. There were rare moments, like when my mother lit the Friday night candles and would cover her face with her hand and cry from the depths of her being. This sound always surprised us, because again we did not know where it was coming from. It seemed to come from nowhere but it had an intensity all of its own. When the moment was over she would remove the cloth from her head and she would return to the present, as if nothing had happened. But those sounds told a story that interrupted the present. At some level we knew that through those sounds she was expressing the pain that she otherwise carried silently through the week. It was ritual moment when a different reality somehow broke through and disturbed the peace of our everyday lives, echoing a traumatic history we were not ready to hear about.

Where did these sounds come from? They were part of the Sabbath ritual but they also sounded a different reality. Somehow these ritual moments that lasted only a few seconds broke the silence that otherwise surrounded by my mother's traumatic history. The sound echoed from a past that she otherwise did not want to allow to resonate in the present. She would return to the family, wiping away her momentary tears and you knew not to ask about the depth of loss that seemed to well up in those few moments. It was as if she had to sound from the depths of her loss for those moments each week, to be able to retain her silence through the rest of the week. It was as if these were the moments in which she could allow herself to weep for those she had lost and the life she had lost. But there was something in the intensity of her sound that still lives with me as I reflect back on her life. In some way it was the reverse of the sounds of the waltz that would take her back to Vienna. Through these sounds she would be able to cross the boundaries of space and time. It was the waltz that echoed and allowed her to recall.

Transcultural Sounds

The ways that particular migrant communities are shaped by their own sound worlds needs to be specified historically and culturally. Within the postwar Jewish refugee community I was growing up in we very much wanted to belong to the national culture. We could not feel that we lived between different spaces because our parents wanted to settle here and make their lives here. They did not have countries that they could return to because they had been expelled and made to feel unwelcome. Often they felt a sense of bitterness and did not know what music they could claim as their own. Often there was a silence and a blankness where there could have been a sound culture that could otherwise be 'passed on'. My mother could identify with particular popular songs like Sophie Tucker but there was little tradition of Jewish music because the break had already been made when her parents had moved to Vienna. It was the ambivalence about the sounds of an assimilated Viennese culture that we unconsciously picked up. It felt easier for my mother to insist that as children born in England, this could have nothing to do with us.

A later migration of Gujarati Indians into Britain involved people with very different aspirations. They did not feel the same need to assimilate into the dominant culture, though they wanted to make their lives here and consider that England is their home. Rather the older generation, who were born in India or East Africa, were concerned that their children should not become too 'Westernized'. Talking to a friend about what it was like for her to grow up in an immigrant community, I was struck by the fact that she did not feel the same urge 'to belong'. Rather she knew who she was as a Gujarati Asian and she was firm in her own sense of identity. She was happy living in England because this was where her family and those people she loved lived. But she did not think of herself as 'British Asian', although she knew other people who did. Somehow it had become clear for her that she was a Gujarati Indian women living in England. This was enough for her. She knew what her citizenship was and she had been brought to England soon after she had been born.

Reflecting upon growing up in a northern town where there were very few other Asian families, she very much wanted to be white. She would eat at her friend's house and eat English food. She did not like the Indian food that her mother cooked. She listened to the groups of the time and would have wanted to be Madonna. She identified with this music as her own. It was only later when the family moved and she was given the option of going to a school with Asian children that she was introduced to Indian music. For the first time she began to mix with Asian girls and it was very strange at the beginning because she did not feel that she belonged. It was through the sounds that a transformation began to take place and she began to identify herself with Indian music and culture. Gradually she found herself listening to more and more of this music. Somehow it had come to resonate with her.

She knows that many people do not feel the same way as her. An old friend from the early days feels very little connection with Indian culture. She does not know the language and would never be seen wearing a sari or a suit. As she explains it, the difference seems to rely upon what community you grew up in and whether it was mainly white. If you have been to a school with mainly whites and now work in an industry with few Asians then you might find it difficult to relate to Indian music and culture. You might find it difficult to understand Hindi enough to watch Indian movies and you might feel no urge to return to India because you know that if you belong anywhere it is here where you have made your life. You might feel little real connection with India other than the notion that this is where your family had come from. Once you had visited you might feel little urge to return, preferring to visit other places when you can take holidays.

It might be that you can move between sound worlds, having grown up with Indian music in the family but if you have grown up mainly with white people you might identify yourself with Western sound cultures. Sometimes these sound cultures are global having reached across borders, as did pop music in the early 1960s. My partner grew up in Brazil but we share a whole range of musical references. Growing up as a teenager in Sao Paulo she danced to Neil Sedaka and Elvis as I did in London. There was a hybrid music culture because she also identified with Brazilian music, with the sounds of Gil and Milton Nascimento. She moved easily between these different sound cultures, knowing that these Brazilian sounds would resonate forever with her.

At the same time her father, a survivor of Buchenwald who had lived for awhile in New York after the war before migrating to be with his brothers who had made it to Brazil, used to listen to Yiddish music that would sound the prewar Jewish world in Poland. He would spend time listening to his records as the family spoke Yiddish, English and Portuguese. They had moved from Poland to a postwar settlement camp in Germany before moving to New York and eventually to Brazil. These different spaces were remembered through different sound worlds. Through music the 'old country' could be invoked and feelings brought to mind.

But the younger generation wanted to put this Yiddish world behind them in their desire to assimilate into a dominant Brazilian culture. Even if they spoke Yiddish at home they would not speak it in their own youth community. Rather, it was a language that was identified with poverty and immigration. They often did not register Yiddish as a source of meanings and values that could be translated into the modern lives they aspired to themselves. It was through the embodied music of Afro-Brazilian culture that they wanted to identify themselves. As you learnt to move to these rhythms as well as to the globalized pop music that defined the experience of a global generation, you looked towards future identities. The concern was with 'who' you wanted to become, which was often defined in opposition to what your parent's identified with.

As Anna moved to England and we got together it was through music that she maintained her connection with Brazil. She felt *saudades* – yearning – for Brazil and for her friends that she had left behind to make a new life in England. She had moved between different spaces before, but it was her connection with Brazil that gave her a sense of freedom and heartfelt connection to herself. She never really wanted to become English and always knew herself as Brazilian though she lived in London. She wanted the children to feel a connection with Brazil through the music, even if they never learnt the language. She brought a different cultural experience with her that had to be negotiated within a different setting. It was partly through sharing sound worlds that we negotiated diverse diasporic spaces.

Often when you migrate into a different culture there is always a question of what you are prepared to give up in order to be accepted within the dominant culture. Within a postmodern culture where there is a greater tolerance of difference, there is often more space to create diasporic identities. Sometimes this involves fusions between different musical styles while at other times we recognize identities as shifting through time and age. A weakness of thinking of identifications in positional terms is that we can find it difficult to appreciate how certain sounds might call us at different moments in our lives. In my twenties I never thought that a time might come when I would need to explore my Jewish identities and that music and sound might be an important part of these explorations. It was partly through music that I could return to some of the sounds of my childhood, but there were also

echoes of cultural memories that had been disavowed in my families
conviction that safety lay in leaving traumatic histories behind so that
children could grow up into the sound worlds of the present and so
assimilate and become 'like everyone else'.

Within more multicultural Britain there are different pressures and
the diverse migrant groups feel less need to assimilate into a dominant
culture. Often diasporic spaces, in which fusion sound cultures can be
created, help people to work through the pressures, anxieties and hopes
of everyday life that they might not otherwise be able to express. Often
it is through lyrics and sound that young people can recognize the
pressures they live in their everyday lives. Often they feel estranged from
the expectations of their parents as they learn to cope with schooling
in Britain. Sometimes they cannot speak to their parents because
communication has broken down and they feel that their parents just
cannot grasp what they are living through. Often the welcome sound
spaces in which for a time at least they feel they can escape from the
pressures of a racist society. They can take pride in their own music forms
as they find ways of expressing the pains and uncertainties of growing
up into a very different world from the one that their parents knew.

Different generations of migrations have had to deal with different
issues as they learn to translate between different cultural spaces. Often
the younger generation feels that its parents have little to teach them
and they can feel very much on their own. This is what we felt growing
up in the 1950s and it means something quite different for young Asian
and Afro-Caribbean people growing up in the new millennium. We
might have felt that, when we grew up and became parents ourselves,
our children would not feel that we were quite so out of it, especially
because they also listen to the Beatles. But we were wrong and a different
generation has to find its own way through its own sounds as it explores
ways of feeling more 'at ease' with itself as well as with the larger world
that is changing so quickly with new technologies and globalized media
cultures.

23

The Sounds of Alterity

Sanjay Sharma

> Missy Elliot's track, 'Get Ur Freak On' uses a sample from an Asian Bhangra
> sound . . . That sound represents 'roots' – you know, the tradition of Asian
> culture. Well, the hip hop beats in the track are about 'routes' – spelt
> r-o-u-t-e-s – that's about where the identity and music is going and
> fusing . . .

An undergraduate confidently made the above assertion in a seminar
presentation for a youth cultures class. The student appears to juxtapose
a South Asian sound rooted in musical tradition and stasis against the
inherent syncretism and dynamism of black hip-hop music. This characterization of Asian music could be explained away by the continuing
force of neo-orientalist discourses of Asianness, and a concomitant
failure to correctly apply the *de rigueur* non-essentialist theory of musical
syncretism to Asian culture. But like the incessant musical refrain of
the sitar-sample in 'Get ur Freak On', this reductive (predictable?) invocation of an Asian musical authenticity demands attention. Does Missy
Elliot's inventive hip hop sampling of an 'Asian sound' represent a
(belated) creative musical fusion? Or is it merely a shrewd Madonna-
esque act of neo-orientalizing cultural appropriation? Or is there something more going on here?

The complex processes and politics of mixing, fusion, syncretism of
contemporary youth culture have been seized by the master concept
of hybridity, something that seems to get cultural commentators and
theorists alike all worked up. The zeal of journalists from fashion style
bibles such as i-D and The Face for all things hybrid has been faithful
in celebrating a new-found British multicultural cool in which the rise

of a vibrant syncretic Asian youth culture plays a pivotal role. In sharp contrast, Ali Nobil (2001) in the respectable *Third Text* wants to be rid of hybridity for 'its reductive racialized premises'. He bizarrely castigates Homi Bhabha and Stuart Hall for banally venerating hybridity and committing the holy academic sin of popularizing it for the media fashion police. Nobil does present a pointed critique of how Asian youth music culture has been represented and taken up by a highly commodi-fied commercial culture that voraciously feeds on ethnic difference. But his critique fails to interrogate or move beyond the contested politics of hybridity itself (see Sharma et al. 1996; Banerjea 2000; Hutnyk 2001). This failing is not only an academic one in relation to a gross misreading of Bhabha and Hall; Nobil's anti-hybridity stance (read anti-cultural studies) disables the creative role of critical analysis for inventing new ways of thinking (Guattari and Deleuze 1994). In fact, his analysis is remarkable for saying little about the workings and (political) possib-ilities of Asian musical cultural productions themselves.

It is worthwhile to dwell on how far hybridity takes us when consider-ing the sounds of contemporary Asian dance music, even if its limits soon become clear when trying to unravel the politics of Missy Elliot's *Get Ur Freak On*. The issue doesn't simply lie with this talented performer's authorial intent or the music's politico-cultural effects (fusional hybridity as cultural innovation and progressive identities). Conversely, neither is it only a question of the heterophillic appetite of contemp-orary multicultural capitalism (ethnic hybridity sells). This hybridity problematic of cultural creativity versus appropriation already assumes what's at stake – obfuscating other modalities of how Asian sounds operate in Western popular culture. The articulation of the multiplicity of Asianness shouldn't be reduced to some pre-figured identity-difference, meaning, consumption practice or politico-musical effect.

What is at stake, however, is activating the radical alterity of these sounds: the possibility that the earthy kick of the dhol, the transcend-ental heartbeat of the tabla, the esoteric twang of the sitar, the ecstatic devotional grain of the quawal's voice, or even the amatory 'shun shun' of anklets worn by Bollywood dancing women escape contemporary discourses of neo-orientalism. This kind of musical activation does not attempt to privilege aesthetics or ethics over politics. Likewise, it has become too tempting to read off a radical politics from various black/ Asian youth dance music subcultures. The politics of the alterity of Asian sounds is connected to (though still not determined by) a 'politics of transfiguration' (Gilroy 1993), which seeks to pursue the sublime and struggles to present the unrepresentable, articulate the ineffable in a racialized dominant culture.

Impossible Asians

In recent times there has been a greater visibility and positivity attached to the sign 'Asian'. Compared to an earlier period of relative obscurity, 'invisibility' and denigration, it has become difficult to ignore the rise of a range of differentiated Asian cultural practices in the realms of art, film, fashion, comedy, literature and especially music. Conceived in terms of their hybrid British-Asianness, these cultural productions not only appear to challenge the racial exclusivity of national identity, but apparently contest notions of an essentialist Asian identity burdened by a primordial ethnicity. Is it surprising that the recent visibility of 'new hybrid' Asian culture has occurred during the moment of an acknowledgement and approval of a liberal multicultural diversity in Britain? But the celebratory constituents of multiculturalism such as the impact of popular Asian dance music or the declaration that the 'Indian Curry' is Britain's national dish (*Guardian*, 31 October 1999) hardly designate that Asian culture has been finally liberated from its orientalized status. On the contrary, the recognition of multiculture cannot be divorced from the concurrent intensification of the fetishization of ethnic otherness in the West. The charged arena of global popular media culture has proved to be a pivotal site for advancing this process. The ubiquitous Madonna's conceited appropriation and vacuous aggrandisement of 'Eastern culture' (Kalra and Hutnyk 1998) exemplifies a contemporary multicultural moment of neo-orientalism that inaugurates a new-found fascination and idealization of what can be labelled as a 'postmodern hybrid' ethnic authenticity. Mercer (1999/2000: 56) identifies this process as 'a new and wholly unanticipated predicament of "hypervisibility".'

The new-found hypervisibility and popularity of 'hybrid' Asian fashion, film and music, summed up by the specious label 'Asian Kool' (created by the style media) signifies a splitting of Asian cultural representation in terms of a 'postmodern hybrid' against a traditional, ossified culture. However much they may resist, talented musicians such as Asian Dub Foundation (ADF), Nitin Sawhney and Fun-Da-Mental are caught up in this popular discourse of multicultural hybridity. They have received popular critical recognition primarily because of their syncretic ability to draw upon 'Eastern' and 'Western' cultural elements. These supposedly new hybrid forms of Asianness are seen to represent a kind of elite avant-garde in commercial culture: fashionably and effortlessly fusing translatable elements from the 'East' with a 'modern' Western way of being. The music of these artists has been considered at the cutting edge of cultural innovation (while leaving behind the discordant untranslatable elements of their traditional and unassimil-atable parental culture). Such type of assimilatory hybridity is celebrated because it represents a 'postmodern future' of mixing and fusion, different cultural elements coming together and creating something novel in Western culture. Ossified cultures are abandoned, boundaries are fractured as new multicultural practices and hybrid identities enter into the smorgasbord of contemporary urban culture. Such an idealized assimilatory Asian hybridity fails to address the grounds on which the political antagonism and dissonance of cultural difference are played out in a racialized dominant culture. It still remains regulated by a neo-orientalist discourse of 'postmodern' ethnic authenticity that effectively proscribes the articulation of the alterity of the Asian-Other.

Rey Chow (1998) takes issue with the current hypervisibility and idealization of otherness when she argues that it is anchored in pro-cesses of (epistemological) violence, domination and appropriation, which is present in contemporary academic discourses, as well as the embattled terrain of popular culture. She compares the discourse of ethnicity to that of sexuality, which, prolifically circulated in Western societies, was however considered to be something repressed and in need of liberation. Ethnicity is now also a 'repressed truth' that needs to be revealed through processes of representation. A panopticist inter-rogating gaze of a 'multicultural ethnicity apparatus' demands that the other be represented – in our case, vis-à-vis the binarism of a 'pre-modern traditional' or 'postmodern hybrid' Asian identity – which is invariably framed by the question: 'How authentic are you?' (Chow 1998: 103). In a racialized culture, the representation, or more precisely, the alterity of Asian-Otherness is an 'impossibility' (cf. Kawash 1998).

Untranslatable Asians

If we read hybridity as the *de facto* state of all cultures, in itself it tells us nothing of the relations of power between different cultural encounters, configurations and practices. However, Bhabha's (1994) often misunder-stood take on hybridity does not locate the problematic of cultural difference at the boundaries of existing social differences (race, gender, nation and so forth), and nor is his idea of a nascent 'third space' a border site in which differences are to be crossed over. Rather, Bhabha is inter-ested in the conditions of emergence and address of a culture, which is always marked by an 'undecidability' in the advent of its arrival (Bennett and Bhabha 1998). It means that there are no anterior unambivalent grounds of cultural authority that determine which identity-differences or political representations are to matter. Bhabha's identification of the immanent process of the hybridity of culture is not dependent on the accretion of difference or predicated on cultural interaction of unmediated exchange but more on the grating against each other of different, sometimes incommensurable knowledge systems and cultural practices – the things that don't necessarily fit together. It is these 'untranslatable' differences that most accounts (and critiques) of hybridity either ignore or just don't know what to do with.

Contemporary Asian dance music characterized as a hybrid youth culture does not seem to say much about the actual sounds of the music. While the pounding Bhangra beat of Malkit Singh may be now effortlessly played alongside the tabla drum 'n bass of Talvin Singh, the different kinds and degrees of musical syncretisms and affects operating become obscured. The critical and commercial success of Talvin's hyperfusion sound of postmodern multicultural Britain in comparison to the relatively limited appeal of Malkit's 'traditional' bass-driven diasporic dhol is suggestive that some types of ethnic hybridity are preferable over others in popular culture (usually the more hybrid the better, although this doesn't equate to being any less ethnically 'authentic').

We can all agree that the diasporic Asian sounds of Malkit, Talvin, Nitin Sawhney, Badmarsh and Shri, Fun-Da-Mental, B21, and Sister India are uniquely 'made in Britain'. If Asian dance music is one of the pulsing soundtracks of multicultural urban Britain, what is the actual status of the Asianness of the music? For all the complex and intricate sampling, mixing and fusion of ADF's dub with rock guitar or Fun-Da-Mental's quawali with hip-hop or Sawhney's tabla with flemenco, what makes this music British-Asian? Turning to the ethnicity of the artists is an essentialist move that is wholly wanting. However, the Asianness of this music does have something to do with specific musical arrangement, structure, performativity and modalities of sound (qualities of tone, timbre and rhythm, vocalization) which have become signified as 'sounding Asian'.

If 'Asian' is a discursive identity formation operating in the West, any anti-essentialist reading needs to resist dissolving its diasporic cultural specificity and everyday lived experience as just a simple construct or effect of racialization (cf. Gilroy 1993). Gilroy's project of wanting to hold on to a black identity and music equally rejects the transmission of fixed essences. He draws on LeRoi Jones concept of the 'changing same' in order to highlight how 'hybrid' cultural traditions are continually remade and created anew. There is much to credit Gilroy for reviving Jones formulation as it enables black cultural practices to be

connected with the histories of racial terror as well as the temporality
of their cultural transformations.

The breaks and flows of the 'changing same', nevertheless, would
function in specific ways across space and time. For an Asian identity
and culture, its relationship to, and routes into, European modernity
have not been identical with the 'Black Atlantic'. While blackness has
been subject to intense somatic racial categorization, Asianness has also
been specifically 'othered' in terms of being imbued with an excess of
'culture' (the trope of ethnicity), and its particular mode of racialization
has been played out through a neo-orientalizing discourse which as we
have seen demands its authenticity. Even if we accept the cultural
transformations and translations of both British and Asian identity in
syncretic musical productions, there is an impossibility of the multiplicity of this music's Asianness from being represented (and consumed)
in popular culture. However, it is precisely the alterity of this Asianness
– through the incommensurable untranslatable sounds – which give
rise to the cultural dissonances able to withstand and eschew neo-
orientalist regimes of power-knowledge. But how do these 'untranslatable'
Asian sounds work?

In a conversation between Stuart Hall and Sarat Maharaj (2001) the
issue of cultural (un)translatability is raised. Hall in effect works from
a linguistic-representational model in dealing with the ontology of
difference. He states:

> The difference which is untranslatable is not a fixed and essential thing;
> it is itself a product of translation and is itself, always in motion . . . I think
> the only way in which people who are different can come to constitute
> a common conversation is by recognising the inadequacy of each of our
> positions as well as what is not translatable. (Hall and Maharj 2001: 51)

Maharaj acknowledges this well-known poststructuralist understanding of untranslatability, but questions the utility of a representational
model that ostensibly doesn't contest the notion that all meaning is
discursive. As Maharaj inquires:

> How do we deal with difference without fixing it as a version of ourselves?
> How do we deal with difference without entirely reducing it to the terms
> and categories of our own language? . . . It is not able to face the fact that
> it has demolished the other in some way . . . This act of violation at the
> heart of language [representation], at the heart of conceiving the other
> leads me to look for para-linguistic ways of engaging the other . . . (Hall
> and Maharaj 2001: 54)

What Maharaj reiterates is that the untranslatable – the alterity of the other – can't be articulated in regimes of hegemonic representation. He urges that an ethical encounter with the other (resistant to the epistemic violence of making the other the same) needs to be engendered – a 'modality which goes with, around, through and beyond the linguistic' (Hall and Maharaj 2001: 56).

It is no coincidence that Maharaj is interested in exploring the field of the sonic, as the analysis of sound and music has been pushing at the limits of representational meaning based approaches. Jeremy Gilbert and Ewan Pearson (1999) attempt to capture the complex debates over how music is supposed to work. The effects of music have been often understood as possessing and producing meanings. But music has also been considered to have effects that work in 'ways that are not dependent on us understanding something . . . or being able to represent accurately those experiences through language' (Gilbert and Pearson 1999: 39). Musical effects immediately invoke the production of bodily pleasure that cannot be simply reduced to musical meanings. In this respect, these writers emphasize the 'materiality of sound' that operates on an alternative register to linguistic (or visual) communication. Nevertheless, in highlighting 'music's corporeality' and its ability to 'hail the body directly', they want to avoid continuing (or simply inverting) the mind/body, physical/mental metaphysical dualism of Western thought. It requires breaking down these binaristic distinctions by theorizing materiality as an effect of power and function of discourse. Their understanding of materiality and discourse (*vis-à-vis* Butler and Laclau) conceives it as more than a linguistic practice, though they maintain that 'there can be no pure "activity", no merely physical "experience" which is not also discursive' (Gilbert and Pearson 1999: 51). Because there isn't a stable differentiation between the discursive and non-discursive, it implies 'that the difference of meaning and affect more or less disappears. Rather than being a clear distinction between the two, "meaning" can be seen as merely one part of a broad continuum of effects which discourse can have' (Gilbert and Pearson 1999: 51).

How the sounds of 'hybrid' Asian music works can be now considered beyond the kinds of (orientalizable) meanings and effects it may produce in the circuits of multicultural capitalist consumption. This music's 'Asianness' is more than what its identitarian ethnic marker allows for; its alterity operates in the realm of untranslatable musical affects that are not reducible to the logic of representation and identity. To obtain a better grasp of this, it is interesting to explore how Ajay Naidu and Ekow Eshun invoke the alterity of Asian sounds:

There are many allegories about what tabla is 'supposed' to sound like (i.e. the dialogue between a man and a woman, or the . . . heartbeat). One of the most profound effects its sound has created has been to shine the spotlight on modern music for South Asian youth worldwide. Hindustani musical science follows a 16-beat cycle coupled with the ambient and ever-present drone; this combination in its essence is jungle music . . . The new sound reminds young people who they are (culturally) in a way that is dextrous, facile, strong and complex . . . [W]ithin the 16-beat cycle . . . lie four open notes. This is the space that is a tabla player's place to reveal . . . true artistry . . . This space is also a place in the music where the listener is open to the 'space between' worlds, consciousness and cultures. (Naidu 2000, sleeve notes)

I say that John Coltrane is the first hippie. I look at John Coltrane's last records, records like Cosmic Music, Insterstellar Space, Om. Coltrane famously tripped in '65, then did this record Om . . . He starts using 'Om', the Indian chant, and he's trying to assemble a universal music, and the whole thing about the Om is that it turns the human into this huge, giant, vibrating powerstation really. Om is this operation to turn yourself into an energy field . . . I look at that whole strain of music from Coltrane through to Sun Ra, through to Alice Coltrane. A whole kind of holiness through volume, a holy amplification. (Eshun 1999: 183)

Both these writers seemingly draw on notions of a 'transcendental' Asian sound, but they need to be approached through the register of the affective. Moreover, they simply aren't concerned with explaining or interpreting the meaning of these sounds, but rather inciting how they work – the rhizomatic connections these sounds make outside of aborescent structures of meaning, knowledge and representation (Deleuze and Guattari 1987). Naidu writing the sleevenotes of *Tabla Beat Science* identifies the 'changing same' of an Asian sound and echoes Bhabha's interstitial third space of cultural articulation and emergence when trying to capture the untranslatable performative sonic force of the tabla. Eshun is more self-consciously Deleuzian in mechanically conceptualizing 'Om' as an active affective sound that has the potential to deterritorialize normatized subjectivity. However, there is a danger that his 'postblack', posthuman project may too readily aestheticize music. As Jeffrey Nealon notes:

There is no liberatory deterritorializing – no freedom or transformation – per se; only site-specific, more or less forceful imbrications of form and content that can respond to – disrupt and reinscribe – existing norms. Deterritorialization, if it happens, always happens in a specific context, in response to a specific content. (Nealon 1998: 136)

It would be foolish to discuss the sounds of the new Asian music without highlighting that its popular consumption has taken place 'in a kind of licentious cultural playground where voyeuristic clubbers not only get to taste the other but eradicate his/her presence altogether' (Banerjea 2000: 76). But it is important to stress that the range of effects of Asian sounds can't be known or determined in advance. Rather, their singularity has been invested by an affective multicultural gaze that has come to signify these sounds as authentically 'Asian' (as exotic, primordial, ethnic . . .). The untranslatability of these sounds marks the possibilities that they are invested in otherwise, that they can deterritorialize existing racialized norms. These sounds also create the space for a 'becoming-Asian', a minoritarian Asianness that not only disrupts its own hegemonic formation but also lies outside of a neo-orientalist production and demand of authenticity. Deleuze has elaborated a minor politics in the following way:

When a minority creates models for itself, it's because it wants to become a majority, and probably has to, to survive . . . But its power comes from what it's managed to create, which to some extent goes into the model, but doesn't depend on it. A people is always a creative minority, and remains one even when it acquires a majority: it can be both at once because the two things aren't lived out on the same plane. (Deleuze 1995: 173–4)

A subaltern musical politics of transfiguration is not an unrealizable utopia, but a register for concrete, site-specific minoritarian-becomings. Untranslatable Asian sounds operate on a sonic plane that evades capture and yet their alterity is at work all around us. Just take a listen to the visceral intensity of Fun-Da-Mental's 'Ja sha taan' or Nitin Sawhney's sublime 'Homelands' . . . the problem is that we just don't hear it.

References

Banerjea, K. (2000), 'Sounds of Whose Underground? The Fine Tuning of Diaspora in an Age of Mechanical Reproduction', *Theory, Culture and Society*, 17(3): 64–79.

Bennett, D. and Bhabha, H. (1998), 'Liberalism and Minority Culture: Reflections on "Culture's in between"', in D. Bennett (ed.) *Multicultural States: Rethinking Identity and Difference*, London: Routledge.

Bhabha, H. (1994), *The Location of Culture*, London: Routledge.

Chow, R. (1998), *Ethics after Idealism*, Bloomington and Indianapolis: Indiana University Press.

Deleuze, G. (1995), *Dialogues*, New York: Columbia.

Deleuze, G. and Guattari, F. (1987), *A Thousand Plateaus: Capitalism and Schizophrenia*, London: Athlone Press.

Eshun, K. (1999), *More Brilliant than the Sun: Adventures in Sonicfiction*, London: Quartet Books.

Gilbert, J. and Peason, E. (1999), *Discographies: Dance Music, Culture and the Politics of Sound*, London: Routledge.

Gilroy, P. (1993), *The Black Atlantic: Modernity and Double Consciousness*, Cambridge MA: Harvard University Press.

Guardian (1999), 'What Kind of England do we Really Stand For?' 31 October.

Guattari, F. and Deleuze, G. (1994), *What is Philosophy?* New York: Columbia University Press.

Hall, S. and Maharaj, S. (2001), 'Modernity and Difference: a Conversation' in S. Campbel and G. Tawadros (eds) *inIVAnnovations 6*, London: inIVA.

Hutnyk, J. (2001), *Critique of Exotica: Music, Politics, and the Culture Industry*, London: Pluto Press.

Kalra, V. and Hutnyk, J. (1998), 'Brimful of Agitation, Authenticity and Appropriation: Madonna's Asian Kool', *Postcolonial Studies*, 1(3): 339–56.

Kawash, S. (1998), 'Men: moving bodies, or, the cinematic politics of deportation' in E. Kaufman and K. Heller (eds) *Deleuze and Guattari: New Mappings in Politics, Philosophy, and Culture*, London: University of Minnesota Press.

Mercer, K. (1999/2000), 'Ethnicity and Internationality: New British Art and Diaspora-based Blackness', *Third Text*, 49: 51–62.

Naidu, A. (2000), Sleevenotes. *Tabla Beat Science*, Axiom Records.

Nealon, J. (1998), *Alterity Politics: Ethics and Performative Subjectivity*, London: Duke University Press.

Nobil, A. (2001), 'Whose Underground? Asian Cool and the Poverty of Hybridity', *Third Text*, 54: 71–84.

Sharma, S., Hutnyk, J. and Sharma, A. (eds) (1996), *Dis-orienting Rhythms: the Politics of the New Asian Dance Music*, London: Zed Books.

24

Calypso Kings

Stuart Hall

Since West Indians first began to settle in Britain in large numbers after the Second World War, a succession of black musics have transformed the British music scene. Ska, bluebeat and, of course reggae were followed by rap, dance hall, 'jungle', techno and house.

But the oldest of these musical forms is the calypso – the music and lyrics associated with the Trinidad Carnival – which, according to Lloyd Bradley, became 'the official sound-track of black Britain' in the1950s and early 1960s. Calypso was the first popular music transported directly from the West Indies and, in the early days, migrants from the southern Caribbean would meet to listen nostalgically to the recording of that year's winning calypso or their favourite calypsonian, and relive memories of the street marching, the costume floats and steel pan music that dominate Port of Spain in the four-day saturnalia leading up to the beginning of Lent.

However, shortly after the arrival of the first postwar contingent, calypso music about the migration experience also started to be composed and performed in Britain, about Britain. Now this neatly forgotten moment in the story of Britain's black diaspora can be recaptured in word and sound.

The start of the postwar Caribbean diaspora is usually associated with the arrival of the rather dilapidated troop-ship, the SS Empire Windrush, which docked at Tilbury in June 1948. The ship had been sent to scour the Caribbean and bring back Second World War volunteers who had been given temporary home leave to visit their families before returning to Britain to be demobbed. Three hundred servicemen and women from throughout the islands gathered in Jamaica for the return trip, and as the ship's capacity was 600, the extra berths were offered to anyone who wanted to emigrate and could stump up the fare of £28. No papers or visas were required because these were the innocent days when all West Indians had right of entry as legitimate British passport holders. Among those who took up the option were two of the Caribbean's most famous and best-loved calypsonians, Lord Beginner and Lord Kitchener.

Aldwyn 'Lord Kitchener' Roberts, a Trinidadian and former nightclub vocalist, had worked on several of the other islands before deciding – as he told Mike and Trevor Phillips, the authors of *Windrush: The Irresistible Rise of Multi-Racial Britain* – that he had always wanted to visit England. Kitchener, a colourful presence on the voyage, helped to organize a concert to raise funds to pay the passage of a stowaway woman who had been discovered (there were many stowaways, some of whom dived overboard and swam to safety when the boat finally docked). As the ship neared land, Kitchener was overcome by 'the wonderful feeling that I'm going to land on the mother country . . . touch the soil of the mother country' and was moved to compose the song 'London Is the Place for Me'.

A week later, he visited a London dance club called the Paramount where, to his surprise, he discovered many of his fellow passengers already well in place, jiving and dancing. A month later, a band led by a twenty-two-year-old Guyanese trumpeter Rannie Hart started to play regularly in the saloon bar of the Queens Hotel in Brixton and with them, hoping to extend the popularity of calypso, was their star, Lord Kitchener. He went on to a highly successful career, playing at pubs, dance clubs, cellar bars and the semi-legal 'bottle parties' of the London and Manchester underground scenes until he returned permanently to Trinidad in 1962.

Confined for some small time to clubs and dancehalls, calypso really made its breakthrough in 1950, with the triumph of the West Indies cricket team at Lords. This was a symbolic victory, and a major reversal of fortunes. The great Trinidadian historian C. L. R. James, who wrote the best book ever written about cricket, *Beyond a Boundary*, has long argued that true West Indian independence and the national consciousness it required would be impossible until the West Indies had taken on the colonizers at their sacred game and mastered it sufficiently to defeat them at home in open play: 1950 was that moment. The West Indian team included three of the world's finest batmen, but the true heroes of the game and architects of victory were the spinners, Ramadhin and Valentine.

It is difficult to believe reports that there were only 30 or 40 West Indians present at the ground, but however many there were, they made their presence felt by exuberant shouting, singing and the rattling of tin cans throughout the game, in ways that astonished the natives and transformed for ever the ethos of test cricket. 'Unnecessary' was the snotty opinion of the MCC diarist.

But the victory moved the calypsonian Lord Beginner, another Windrush survivor, to compose on the spot the calypso that became the anthem of the moment – *Cricket, Lovely Cricket*, with its telling refrain, 'With those little pals of mine/Ramadhin and Valentine' while Kitchener himself led the march round the field and down into Piccadilly. People stared at this extraordinary sight out of windows – 'I think it was the first time they'd ever seen such a thing in England', Kitchener observed. 'And we're dancing Trinidad-style, like mas, ad dance right down Piccadilly and . . . around Eros.' The Caribbean ethos and style of celebration was the most commented upon aspect of the game and marks the moment when a distinctively new Caribbean spirit and rhythm first announced itself as an emergent element in the rapidly changing national culture.

In fact, calypso in Britain has an interesting prehistory. The oldest living calypsonian on a recent Honest John CD celebrating calypso music written in Britain in the 1950s is Young Tiger, now 82, who was born in Trinidad, became a seaman on oil tankers, sailing the seven seas and finally disembarking in Glasgow in 1942. Although not musically trained, he played and sang a little and when he and a friend landed a job in the famous *Minstrel Show*, they were bitten by the showbiz bug. Singing and playing all sorts of music in the small London drinking clubs, he composed a Christmas Calypso in 1943, which became a seasonal favourite. Playing and singing with a rumba band at the swanky Orchid Room, Young Tiger adopted the calypsonian's practice of instant commentary on the rich and famous and composed a few verses on the spot when Prince Philip and his party paid the club a visit. Reprimanded by management, Young Tiger was surprised when, the following night, royalty returned in force to hear the composition – which he had since thrown away. This royal connection may have prompted the composition of his 'Coronation Calypso' in 1953.

After playing and touring with a number of successful groups, he recorded with Melodisc, the first British company to produce calypso records, a cover version of 'Single Man' by the calypsonian Tiger – and thus inherited the title Young Tiger.

Though he had never had the ambition to be a professional musician, George 'Young Tiger' Brown was 'steeped in calypso' and greatly admired the calypsonian's gift as poet, raconteur and reporter. He left Trinidad before the steel bands that are now so closely associated with calypso music really took hold, though he remembers as a child hearing the pans being played in the backyards of Charlotte Street, Port of Spain, and the shango and 'tambo-bambo' music (played on various lengths of bamboo) that were their precursors and the preferred instruments of popular music at the time.

It is difficult to separate the spirit of calypso from its context in the Trinidad Carnival. Preparing for Carnival is an all-year-round activity. As the Carnival season approaches, the clubs enter a period of feverish activity, designing and completing the construction of the elaborate costumes and astonishing head-dresses that the bands will wear for the parade. Richly coloured fabrics, sequinned plumes and feathers are suspended across wire, steel and fibreglass frames according to the year's theme. In the period leading up to the opening day – Jour Ouvert – the calypsonians compete in their respective tents, hoping their own compositions will win favour as the favourite for the Road March, and so lead the 'jump-up', or joovay – the dancing and rhythmic shuffling through the streets to the accompaniment of drums, bottles and whistles with which the days of revelling climax. For a few days, the whole town gives itself up to pure bacchanal, known as 'playing Ole Mas'. The word 'mas' has multiple derivations: 'Masking', the Christian 'mass' (with which the days of revelling conclude on Ash Wednesday) and 'masquerade'.

Trinidad Carnival is a syncretic popular form, drawing on Christian tradition and pagan ritual, fused in the vortex of plantation society. It is now more than 200 years old. The French settlers (in Trinidad, and places of largely Catholic settlement, like Martinique and Haiti, which also have carnivals) brought their custom of grand pre-Easter balls in the plantation houses and parading masked through the streets. The slaves were also allowed a few days of revelling, often marching in the streets in rough costumes and crude disguises, in both imitation and ironic mimicry of their masters, to the accompaniment of much drumming, prancing and threatening stick play. The authorities were constantly trying to ban this practice of ritualized popular resistance, without success.

The calypso, a topical song associated with Carnival, especially composed for the occasion, was much influenced by this carnivalesque tradition – a period of licensed expression, when for a time, the normal rules of everyday life are suspended, the world is turned upside down, and the people of 'the below' are granted the freedom both to revel in public and to comment on and satirize the actions and behaviour of those in authority. The calypsonian is free to comment ironically on any aspect or event of everyday life, to expose the sexual and political scandals of the politicians and the rich, to recount gossip and to scandalize the powerful without fear of redress. Political commentary, the quirks, foibles, the petty dramas and the licentious stories of everyday street life are grist to the calypsonian's mill. The calypso is the repository of that year's distilled popular knowledge and wisdom – the informal 'court' before which every powerful figure fears being judged.

The essence of the successful calypso lies in capturing the event or occasion in a vivid, piquant, creole idiom. The music has a driving, springy, forward-impelled, rolling two beat, adaptable to the rhythmic movement of the road march. The lyrics, which are strung across and accented so as to insinuate themselves between the bass rhythm, are driven by the sinuous lilt of Trinidanian creole speech patterns. Unlike later black British music, which has been dominated by the prevalence of almost unintelligible deep Jamaican patois, the calypso's rhymes depend on the Trinidadian accent, but the language is otherwise well enunciated in Caribbean standard English. Kitchener reported that, when he first began to sing in a Brixton pub, the manager fired him because he said his customers couldn't understand what 'Kitch' was saying. But before the mixed audience of the Sunset Club, when Kitchener began to sing, 'Kitch come go to bed/I have a small comb to scratch your head', the punters understood the sexual references well enough, and those who didn't get it had its meaning explained to them by the Caribbean customers.

This carnivalesque tradition was finely adapted and retuned to the migrant experience in Britain. There are calypsos composed about specific events, like the Coronation, the Test match victory at Lords, the Jamaican hurricane, the birth of Ghana, the West Indian Federation. Many more offer satirical but largely good-humoured commentary on bizarre aspects of daily life as the migrants first experience them: nosy English landladies; putting money in the geezer for hot water for a bath; English housewives; dogs; riding the underground; Lyons Corner Houses; the weather. Others range more broadly – mixed marriages (Beginner's Mix Up Matrimony), race and those who vainly try to pass as European (Kitchener's 'You can't get away from the fact/If you ain't white you considered black') and, of course, sex (Kitch's scandalous 'Saxophone No 2', with the complaint that his new girlfriend won't stop 'blowing me saxophone').

These compositions represent a vibrant, piquantly observed and often hilarious running commentary on life for the newly arrived immigrant in the London of the 1950s. They crystallize the migrants' first response to the encounter with the strange object, 'the English at home'. They have to be seen as part and parcel of the experience that produced the West Indian novel, which emerged in London at about the same moment, with writers like V. S. Naipaul, George Lamming and Sam Selvon. Lamming has said that his generation (and, incidentally, mine) came as members of the individual islands and only in London discovered that they were 'West Indian'. C. L. R. James, writing about another famous Trinidadian calypsonian, Sparrow, observed that, 'He is in every way a genuinely West Indian artist . . . a living proof that there is a West Indian nation.'

Much the same is true of the black British calypso, which began as a Trinidadian music and, in London, became the first signature music of the whole West Indian community. The calypsos of the 1950s therefore must be 'read' and heard alongside books like *Lonely Londoners* by Sam Selvon (also a Trinidadian) as offering the most telling insights into the early days of the migrant experience. They are still overwhelmingly jaunty and positive in attitude – this is the music of a minority who have travelled to a strange or strangely familiar place in search of a better life and are determined to survive and prosper. The same confidence, grit and determination are evident in the press and magazine images of immigrant families arriving during the 1950s at London railway stations.

As I have written elsewhere:

Men, women and children already battened down against the freezing weather by the ubiquitous wearing of hats. People dressed up to the nines, for 'travelling' and even more for 'arrival'. Wearing that expectant look – facing the camera, open and outward, into something they cannot yet see . . . a new life . . . 'Face the music, darling, and let's make a move.'

But the darker shadows are also already evident. Kitchener's 'Sweet Jamaica' invites Jamaicans to reflect on their decision to leave home and family behind only to find themselves 'Crying with regret/No sort of employment can they get' and to think fondly of the ackee and saltfish they have left behind in the islands where the sun shines every day. As 'The Mighty Terror' accurately observed, 'No Carnival in Britain' – but, of course, there was to be one; and the Notting Hill Carnival, which survives despite the best-engineered efforts to close it down or dampen its insurgent spirit, remains one of the few homes for indigenous calypso left in Britain.

'London Is the Place for Me' is a witty and joyous testament to the creative power of popular culture and a document of more innocent times. It constitutes one of the best starting points for that rich, unfinished history of the black British diaspora and its intricate interweaving with British life that remains to be written.

25

Bessie Smith
'Thinking Blues'*

Susan McClary

Bessie Smith was known during her illustrious career as the Empress of the Blues. Like many of the black women who became stars during the first decade of mass-mediated recording, Smith regarded blues as one of several marketable genres. For although born and raised in Tennessee, she learned about blues not from oral tradition but from her mentor and rival, Ma Rainey. Rainey in turn had learned this mode of expression – at least according to her testimony – from a young girl whom she overheard singing to herself after one of Rainey's tent shows, sometime during the first decade of the twentieth century. Rainey incorporated blues into her act (Ma and Pa Rainey, 'Assassinators of the Blues', with the Rabbit Foot minstrels) and found that her audiences responded enthusiastically when she offered them what they perceived as their own music. Smith absorbed both style and format, then, from a context devoted to public entertainment, and when she moved into more urban environments, she continued fusing blues with the popular songs of vaudeville and with a newly emerging idiom known as jazz.

As I have already mentioned, by the time blues started showing up in written and recorded form, it already had merged with commercial enterprises. Yet there exists a cultural mythology (stemming largely from the 1960s) that wants to trace a pure lineage of blues from a cluster of rural, male blues singers recorded in the 1930s. And that mythology tends either to erase the women who first brought the blues to broad

* First published in McClary, S. (2000), *Conventional Wisdom. The Content of Musical Form.* Berkeley CA: University of California Press, pp. 42–9. Reproduced with permission.

attention or else to condemn them for having compromised that pure lineage with commercial popular culture.

But Simon Frith and Howard Horne have suggested that the reason for this marginalization might involve even more complex cultural tensions. If the blues came to represent an unassailable virile form of masculinity to British rockers (the musicians largely responsible for the mythologizing of Delta blues), then women could not be acknowledged at all in the canon – let alone as its progenitors. Frith and Horne go on to explain that this association in England of blues/rock with manliness may help account for why so few women art-students in the 1960s turned to music for self-expression; they became, instead, the vanguard of feminist visual and performance artists (Frith and Horne 1987: 92). Although these are the concerns of a later and very different group of listeners/practitioners, they have, in effect, shaped the ways we now usually understand the historical role and contributions of women blues singers.

Purity and authenticity were rarely urgent maters for working black musicians who had to negotiate with real conditions – the securing of gigs, audiences, and recording deals – or else face destitution. And prevailing conditions differed considerably according to gender. Male bluesmen often took the option of roaming through the region, playing on the streets, in juke joints, or at festivities as opportunities arose. As a result, many of them remained closely tied to and sustained by the traditional community. Women did not have access to the same kind of mobility, and few became itinerant musicians. Yet with the increasing instability of the southern black population at the turn of the century – the massive migrations to northern cities motivated by poverty, Jim Crow laws, and lynchings – women, too, were often compelled to leave home. By and large, however, they sought the security of steady employment. As Daphne Harrison has shown, many of the performers who came to be celebrated as the blues queens were displaced young women who found they could patch together a living performing in travelling minstrel shows, vaudeville, urban clubs, and (after the industry reluctantly agreed to try black women singers) the new medium of recording.

What resulted was an explosion of female creativity that animated the 1920s – one of the few such moments in Western music history. These women and the market they helped produce exerted significant cultural and economic power for about a decade. As *The Metronome* reported in January 1922 (a scant two years after Mamie Smith recorded the first blues number), 'One of the phonograph companies made over four million dollars on the Blues. Now every phonograph company has a colored girl recording. Blues are here to stay' (quoted in Harrison 1988: 44).

If the blues produced under these conditions bear traces of its social contexts, that makes it no different from any other kind of music. Rather than hearing women's jazz-and-pop flavoured blues as corrupt, writers such as Hazel Carby, Daphne Harrison, and Toni Morrison have treated it as a genre that registered with keen accuracy the shocks and jolts of early black urban life, including the first direct encounters of the black population with the pressures of capitalist economies (see Carby 1990: 139; Harrison 1988; for a remarkable fictional exploration of this world see Morrison 1992). If some of us prefer to turn to the rural bluesmen in an imagined pastoral setting, it is partly because we can thereby pretend to retreat from the harsh realities of industrialized modernity.

One of the extraordinary contributions of so-called Classic Blues is its articulation of desire and pleasure from the woman's point of view. Throughout the span of Western culture, women have been spoken for more than they have been permitted to speak. And given the tendency for women to be reduced to sexuality and the body, many female artists have tried to avoid this terrain altogether.[1] As a result, vocabularies of the body and of erotic feelings have been constructed principally by men, even when they are projected onto women, as in opera and much popular music. Thus the blues queens offer an unparalleled moment in the history of cultural representation. As Carby puts it:

> What has been called the 'Classic Blues' . . . is a discourse that articulates a cultural and political struggle over sexual relations: a struggle that is directed against the objectification of female sexuality within a patriarchal order but which also tries to reclaim women's bodies as the sexual and sensual subjects of women's song . . . The women blues singers occupied a privileged space; they had broken out of the boundaries of the home and taken their sensuality and sexuality out of the private and into the public sphere. (Carby 1990: 241, 247)[2]

Accounting for how and why this happened is very complex. On the one hand, African-based cultures tend to treat the body and eroticism as crucial elements of human life: the shame or prurience that attends sexuality in so many European cultures is often absent. But on the other hand, the bodily components of African American culture have repeatedly been misconstrued within the dominant society.[3] Because black women were often defined as oversexed by whites, (see 'The Hottentot and the Prostitute: Toward an Iconography of Female Sexuality,' and 'Black Sexuality and Modern Consciousness' in Gilman 1985) it was risky for them to sing explicitly about desire: entrepreneurs in the culture industry cheerfully exploited the stereotype of the libidinal black female in posters, sheet music, and staging (recall, for instance, the salacious marketing of so brilliant a performer as Josephine Baker); and singers who lacked clout sometimes were pressured into prostitution, as Billie Holiday's painful memories make clear. They also encountered severe castigation from the black middle class, which often adopted the mores and attitudes of white bourgeois culture.

This was yet another set of issues that had to be negotiated with great care by each female performer, within each song. Despite the personal dangers and social controversies, these women left us an invaluable legacy revealing how female pleasure, sexual independence, and woman-to-woman address could sound – a legacy Angela Davis (1998) does not hesitate to identify as feminist. Several of them, including Rainey and Smith, even celebrated their bisexuality in their lyrics.

I want now to focus on 'Thinking Blues', one of Bessie Smith's own blues numbers, which was recorded in New York in 1928.[4] Smith's lyrics in 'Thinking Blues' deal with some of the central themes of women's blues: broken relationships, remorse, and pleading. Yet in contrast to some of the male-composed lyrics that she also performed superbly, 'Thinking Blues' articulates a vision of female subjectivity that balances self-possessed dignity with flashes of humour and a powerfully embodied sense of the erotic; simply the stress on the verb 'to think' in the opening and final lines presents a different kind of experience from the passive suffering often ascribed to women in general and Smith in particular.[5]

Bessie Smith: 'Thinking Blues'

Did you ever sit thinking with a thousand things on your mind?
Did you ever sit thinking with a thousand things on your mind?
Thinkin' about someone who has treated you so nice and kind.

Then you get an old letter and you begin to read,
You get an old letter and you begin to read,
Got the blues so bad, 'til that man of mine I wanna see.

Don't you hear me, baby, knockin' on your door?
Don't you hear me, baby, knockin' on your door?
Have you got the nerve to drive me from your door?

Have you got the nerve to say that you don't want me any more?
Have you got the nerve to say that you don't want me any more?
The Good Book says you got to reap what you sow.

Take me back, baby, and try me one more time.
Take me back, baby, and try me one more time.
That's the only way I can get these thinking blues off my mind.

Bessie Smith, 'Thinking Blues.' Used by permission of
Hal Leonard Corporation.

As is the case in many blues numbers, 'Thinking Blues' suggests a possible narrative framework but moves freely among many forms of implied address from verse to verse. Sometimes she hails the listener as though in conversation ('Did you ever sit thinking?'); at other times, she seems to retreat into soliloquy ('Then you get an old letter'); and finally, she speaks as though directly to the man whom she has evidently left and whom she wants back. As she approaches him, she moves from tentative questioning ('Do you have the nerve to say?'), to demands ('Take me back baby').

Thus while there is a clear rhetorical shape to the sequence of five choruses - a move from public address to internalized reflection to simulated encounter, a steady increase in intensity – the blues convention that underlies the piece minimalizes the narrative component of the music itself. What we get instead is a series of meditations on a single situation, as Smith returns to the problem nagging her with a new approach in each verse. The repetition suggests personal obsession, but at the same time, her use of the blues invites the listener to identify with her predicament. What she sings sounds utterly familiar: we can relate. As John Coltrane once said, the audience heard 'we' even if the singer said 'I' (quoted in Carby 1990: 242). She invokes and brings into being a temporary community that bears witness to and empathizes with her subjective expression; made intersubjective by her use of shared codes.

Yet as transparent as it may seem, her performance refuses to offer a single easily identified affect – even within any particular verse. The structure of the blues, in which the first line of each chorus occurs twice, permits her to shift implications radically from moment to moment. She couches each statement within an apparently limitless range of ambiguities and ambivalences – she lives a grey area, never truly giving anything away even while suggesting a whole range of possibilities.

At times her moans seem to spell grief, but in the next moment a similar glissando will suddenly turn into a sly, insinuating grind. On 'Have you got the nerve to say that you don't want me no more?' is she seducing? Grovelling? Taunting? And taunting her lover or herself? This sentence is a central event in the song, and she turns it every which way but loose. Yet what is she is saying underneath all those layers of irony? The final line, 'Take me back, try me one more time', clarifies a great deal – this is what she wants; no more indirection. But while her words may plead, the power of her delivery and her nuances destabilize the potential abjection of her appeal. This lady is in charge, even if she 'ain't too proud to beg'.

In 'Thinking Blues', the musicians elect the option of remaining on V for 9 and 10 rather than moving down through IV. We may never know who chose to do it that way, but the rhetorical effect is to maintain a single, steady affect through the last line until the moment of cadence in bar 11. Smith's delivery of each verse's final line takes advantage of this detail by driving all the way through rather than releasing the energy in stages, and it becomes especially insistent in verse 3 ('have you got the nerve to drive me from your door?') and 4 ('the Good Book says you got to reap what you sow').

In this recording, Smith is accompanied by some of her favourite sidemen: Demas Dean on cornet, Fred Longshaw on piano, the incomparable Charlie Green on trombone. All three were jazz musicians – Green played regularly with Fletcher Henderson - and the performance presents a fusion between the demands of jazz ensemble- playing and the more intimate qualities of the blues. One of the most obvious jazz elements is standardization: in order to facilitate group improvization, the blues pattern here (and elsewhere in Classic Blues) has been regularized, so that each chorus follows the twelve-bar progression.

Consistent with the blues, however, is their style of bending pitches, rhythms, timbres, and rhetorical conventions to signify on the standard pattern. The song is structured according to call and response, with Dean and Green answering Smith in turn on alternate lines, thus playing up the asymmetries already inherent in the pattern. Each instrumentalist carefully links his contributions with Smith's words and expressive decisions: in other words, all elements of the song – whether sung or played – are vocal in conception and execution. Green and Dean never tire of intensifying or ironicizing Smith's inflections. Green tends to get down with her growls and innuendoes, while Dean contributes astringent, strutting counter-motives that keep Smith and her trombonist from spiralling too deeply into the funky zone. Even Langshaw – whose principal task is to maintain the harmonies and the groove at the piano – throws in subtle melodic comments and echoes here and there.

Smith's three instrumentalists amplify the various shadings of her delivery (they act as extensions of her utterances), but they also serve as an exemplary cluster of listeners who react audibly to her calls, thus granting her the social legitimation of community. If technology had permitted a live performance, we would also hear actual listeners lending their support through sympathetic moans, appreciative hoots for the double entendres, and responses such as 'Sing it, Bessie!' or (as we would put it today) 'You go, girl!'

Notes

1. Carby argues that the black women responsible for literary works tended to minimalize sexuality, which is why women's blues become such important documents. Women composers and musicians in the European art tradition too have often tried to minimize references to sexuality: in fact, many feminist musicologists were disconcerted by my discussions in *Feminine Endings*. I owe my serious concern with this repertory to Barbara Christian. When I was first beginning to work on issues involving women and music, I explained to Christian that women had only recently begun to deal explicitly with gender and sexuality in their music. To which she responded: 'Ever hear of Bessie Smith?' I have never forgotten that lesson.

2. For the importance of joy and pleasure in black culture in general, see Dent (1992: 1–20).

3. See bell hooks (1992), for a critique of several music videos featuring black women. For a discussion of this problem in music studies, see Walser and McLary (1994).

4. Bessie Smith, 'Thinking Blues,' Demas Dean, cornet; Charlie Green, trombone; Fred Longshaw, piano (9 February 1928, Columbia 14292-D).

5. See, for instance, Schuller (1968: 241): 'Her tragic early death was perhaps a less painful exit than a long decline into oblivion. For Bessie Smith was one of the great tragic figures, not only of jazz, but of her period.' He then adds, 'But Bessie Smith was a supreme artist, and as such her art transcends the particulars of life that informed that art.'

References

Carby, H. (1990), '"It Jus Be's Dat Way Sometime": The Sexual Politics of Women's Blues', in Ellen Carol DuBois and Vicki L. Ruiz (eds), *Unequal Sisters: A Multi-Cultural Reader in U.S. Women's History*, New York: Routledge.

Davis, A. (1998), *Blues Legacies and Black Feminism: Gertrude 'Ma' Rainey, Bessie Smith, and Billie Holliday*, New York: Pantheon.

Dent, G. (1992), 'Black Pleasure, Black Joy: An Introduction', in Dent, G. (ed.), *Black Popular Culture*, Seattle: Bay Press.

Frith, S. and Horne, H. (1987), *Art into Pop*, London: Methuen.

Gilman, S. L. (1985), *Difference and Pathology: Stereotypes of Sexuality, Race, and Madness*, Ithaca: Cornell University Press.

Harrison, D. (1988), *Black Pearls: Blues Queens of the 1920s*, Brunswick: Rutgers University Press.

bell hooks (1992), 'Selling Hot Pussy: Representations of Black Female Sexuality in the Cultural Marketplace', *Black Looks: Race and Representation*, Boston: South End Press.

Morrison, T. (1992), *Jazz*, New York: Alfred A. Knopf.

Schuller, G. (1968), 'Early Jazz: Its Roots and Musical Development', Oxford: Oxford University Press.

Walser, R. and McLary, S. (1994), 'Theorizing the Body in African-American Music', *Black Music Research Journal*, 14: 75–84.

26

'Chatting' for Change!
Interview with William (Lez) Henry

LB: I wonder if we could just start by you just telling me about how you got involved in music, at the beginning as a performer.

LH: I've always been surrounded by music, one of the things I say to people is that what made me strong was music, you know, as well as my family and Rastafari and stuff like that, but music, I've always been surrounded by music. My mother, she often frames things in music. So if you speak to her about when she first came to England she will say things like that's when Kitchener did this, or Kitchener sang about that. So things have always kinda been framed around that. But as a performer I always wanted to chat[1] but I never had the courage to perform. But I knew that I could write because I was always into poetry and stuff, and from school, from schooldays I used to articulate things in verse . . . In 1977 I was always into reggae music especially deejaying, because . . . I've always loved the Jamaican language and how people use the language, and I've always loved the sound of it. So we were always into toasting, you know, and we would toast, make up our own lyrics and chat, me and my twin brother especially. But in 1978–9, yard tapes, Jamaican tapes started coming over, and what they did was they gave us an alternative, and I would say political perspective on what was going on in Jamaica. It was completely different from what you would get on recorded releases, it was completely different from what you would get in the so-called Gleaner, you know, sanitized mediums like that, you got a different perspective. Around 1978, 1979 we started to get these yard tapes, especially General Echo, Nicodemus, Sassafras; Burru Banton came a bit later, but Lone Ranger, people like that, you got them, but you've got them in the raw, like unexpurgated form, on the sound system saying everything. Mutabaruka was coming through as well, they were sampling Mutabaruka a lot into things like the M16 or Scandal rhythm. It was about 1980, 1981, when I started to write lyrics. I didn't have a sophisticated system; I had a cassette. You just pressed record and it would record through the mic. I'd have my music playing through the speakers and I would chat. I didn't know anything about Jamaica as I hadn't reached there yet, so everything I spoke about was London, whether it was me driving my Stag and us wearing Burberry coats, or, you know, people mugging people and grabbing an fleeing and whatever. Then, as I said, 1981, 31 December the first time I'd chatted, and I'm a bit Red[2] and went on Saxon, chatted some of my lyrics, just blew the place apart completely 'cause they just was not used to anyone talking about London. One of the first lyrics I chatted was called 'Parasite and Hypocrite', and some of it went; 'see dem in the mornin', dem ah preach over fence, watch dem in the night, dem ah bun I-shense (marijuana) dem ah parasite and hypocrite, Jah Jah ah guh trow dem in the bottomless pit. Mi nah goah church an guh bow to no priest, priests ah mek dem money outah lies and deceit, worsah dan de muggers who ah roam Britain street, tek people money in di name of di lord, buy fast car an posh-up dem yard.' Crowd 'kick up' because that's the kind of things I was talking about. So, from then I suppose I never really looked back.

LB: It's interesting what you were saying just a minute ago about how through the yard tapes you got a different sense of a kind of political analysis of what was going on in Jamaica too.

LH: Yeah, definitely. Definitely. Because what you have to understand is one of my sisters is Jamaican middle class, that's what she is. Owns a shop, lives in a very nice area, whatever. And in some ways this was the representation that was in the Gleaner, anyone who wasn't Jamaican middle class was ignorant. They were uneducated, unintelligent, unable to articulate their own oppression, so you never ever got their side of the story. Yeah, you got things couched in Rastafari sensibilities about sufferation and the mystical Babylon that didn't have a face. But when you got yard tapes you started to get names, so those unidentified so-called Babylon, Babylonians got a face, and not only that you actually got the personal stories like, for instance, this little thing called the Ten Cent Bulla being discussed. A Bulla is like a, you know, the Jamaican Bulla cake, it's like a kind of bun thing, but most of the sufferers couldn't afford them, because say it might be a dollar. So they made little ones and they called it the Ten Cent Bulla. And so the Ten Cent Bulla was the life saver, and those were the things you would get on cassettes, and not on records. And then you would also get things about area leaders, so you would find out, you know, who runs this area, which political party supports him and I'll tell you one of the best things that I learned from Jamaican tapes was about the influx of guns into Jamaica, and how they swapped them for marijuana, and in some ways if you look at what's going on now, everything is on Jamaica as the coke centre of the world, but no-one speaks about how it gets there. And this was the same thing what happened with the guns. So, for instance, in 1979, 1980 you had a load of lyrics talking about guns, the different kinds of – like what the enforcer sounds like, booyakka, braggadap, kinda thing. These are things they were saying in Jamaica because they imitate the sounds of the gun, it's almost like an onomatopoeia thing. So you add the M16 wadat wadat wadat wadat or whatever. And this was what you were getting in the lyrics. But . . .

LB: Yeah, but in the actual sound of the voice, not in words.

LH: In the sound of the voice then what they would do is, so for instance, Hugh Brown did this lyric. Hugh Brown chatted this lyric the gist of it was they don't make guns in Jamaica so where do you get it from, 'tell dem seh we get it from the Chiney man, mi seh di one from over Hong Kong', and that's what he was doing. But it was like the lyrics were like 'some ah swap it fi money, some ah swap it fi gun, the plane make ah circle den di plane touch dun'. Ganja fi gun, plane gone with the ganja, we left with the gun, then them wonder why we're the ones being shot? So you had these kinds of commentaries that were missing in the recognized media, because you would never hear that. All you heard was, you know, the sufferers are, they're all this, they're all killing themselves, because they're all ignorant, they're uneducated and blah blah blah. Yet to me some of the most articulate social commentary was coming from them. And I suppose once I sat down and I really thought about some of what they were saying I had to say to myself, well they could be exactly the same as me, because I left school with no O levels or any qualifications, but I could articulate myself well. So how was I educated, not necessarily in school, I was astute and aware enough to form this kind of critique that wasn't recognized or represented anywhere. And to me this is what they were doing in Jamaica. So basically what they were doing was they were giving you their side of the story, and you could use their side of the story to make sense out of the general story you were getting. Especially from Jamaican middle-class people, because for instance, Bob Marley, my sister dismissed him. In 1976 she came to England and I was playing my Bob Marley stuff, and she was saying like what you doing playing this little illiterate Rasta guy, because as far as they were concerned there was no worth in anything they did. Why? One reason was because they didn't supposedly articulate themselves in the English language, you know, they used Patwah, so therefore whatever you say in Patwah, because it's not really a language you use for communication on a serious level, could be dismissed. So they never ever looked at reggae music to listen to the stories that people were telling, because for instance – in fact I'll give you an example. Frankie Paul did a tune called 'Fire Deh ah Muss Muss Tail him Tink ah Cool Breeze'. What it is, is someone set the mouse's tail on fire, and the mouse is running so fast he doesn't realize his tail is on fire – he's in trouble, running cause his tail's on fire but he's forgotten why. So in other words it's like watch your arse because someone's burning it, that's the Jamaican thing. Frankie Paul did this tune 1984, 1985. Barry Gee who used to be on the radio played it and dedicated it to Edward Seaga and they banned him from the radio. And to me this captures it, so there can be this type of commentary, even like political, social, cultural commentary going on, and the people who the voice represents know what is being said and who it's being said about, but the point is as soon as Barry Gee did that people directly assoc- iate that critique with the government. To me in a lot of ways that's exactly how it works.

LB: So, just in terms of making the connection then between – I mean that's a tremendously insightful characterization of how the, you know, the explicit implicit basis . . . communication with, but I suppose in the context of then the kind of music that you were making in the early 1980s is a very different kind of context, but it's using some of the same kinds of resources and strategies really.

LH: Definitely, because one of the things is, as far as I'm concerned, I articulate myself in Patwah, the only difference was that from

1 January 1982, people heard on a wider scale what Lez Henry thought. Or what Papa Levi or Macka B, thought. Or what anybody thought. Whereas before it would be like if you're reasoning with your bredrin . . . and then they'll say well this is this and that is that and then someone will come up with something, and say something and you'll think yeah, that really makes a lot of sense, you know. The difference is you weren't on the sound system articulating that. Once you actually look at the world you live in, and you start to articulate your tales, not just of oppression but also of transcendence and whatever, every day, everyday living, all aspects of being, once you start to do that and people recognize what you're doing, whether they agree or necessarily disagree in some ways it takes on its own dynamic, because it will be discussed. It starts to be discussed in alternative spaces, alternative public arenas . . . But once you go out there and you air that to an audience, that takes on a different type of political dimension. It may not be political in the sense that, you know, it doesn't necessarily affect governance directly, but it does affect the political sensibilities of the people you're exposing to those knowledges. And that's why I believe everything is political.

LB: And I suppose in a sense the power of what you're talking about too is that those people almost by definition are excluded or debarred from the mainstreams discussions.

LH: From the regular, yeah, regular political space, because you see the difference is it's, for me it's the difference between overstanding, do people have something of value to say about governance, the way we're governed as political subjects in say Britain? If they do, why don't we hear these stories? One of the reasons why we don't hear these stories is because sometimes the stories that people are ready to tell, their personal narratives are quite uncomfortable for the people who rule. But more importantly for me is they are excluded from the public arena through various mechanisms . . . If you articulate this type of politics in a dancehall the parameters for discussion are widened. They have to be, because you can say anything you please. You can say anything you please about anyone you please. I mean a good way to think about it was Papa Levi and that Maggie Baggie thing with Margaret Thatcher. Now, when I spoke to David Rodigan about it, what he said to me was that Levi should have known better, that he couldn't chat that live to London, because the programme was being broadcast live to London.

LB: Yeah, is this on his programme?

LH: Yeah, this was on Rodigan's Live to London at the Academy in Brixton, and Levi started chatting about . . .

LB: Yeah, just to sort of contextualize, tell us a little bit about who David Rodigan is.

LH: Right, David Rodigan is one of the top 'legal' radio Deejays in the UK. Although Chris Goldfinger, on Radio 1, is probably bigger than Rodigan now. But, what happened was during the 1980s . . .

LB: And also obviously Rodigan is, he's a white Deejay too, so he's positioned in a . . .

LH: Yeah, in some ways, but what you have to understand, one of the things what I respect Rodigan for is – and in some ways maybe it's not such a good thing but if he doesn't like your tune he'll tell you and he won't play it. He won't pretend that he likes it and say oh yeah, I'll play it and then he won't. He'll tell you that he won't, I don't like it, I won't play it. Now a lot of people resented that, but personal choices, that's up to them. One of the reasons why that became a problem for a lot of producers in Britain was because they thought he didn't like it because it was British music, and then there was the thing with whether he's supposed to be involved with Fashion Records, so everything that comes out of Fashion all of a sudden is good, he plays it, blah blah blah. But Rodigan is respected, and during the heyday of British Deejaying there were loads of live performances on the radio, especially Radio London's Rockers FM with Tony Williams and stuff like that. Now, Rodigan ran this Live to London thing, I think he did a couple of them, and on one of them he decided to get Papa Levi who was the hottest Deejay at the time, just been signed to Island Records, got a massive deal or whatever, featured on Bob Marley's compilation thing where they did this video, some posthumous thing for Bob Marley, and Levi was the only British performer who was on that video. So that's the scale of what was expected of him. Levi went on the Live to London on Rodigan's thing, and got carried away and did this lyric called Maggie Baggie[3] and it was all about Margaret Thatcher who was the then Prime Minister. Now, some of what he said, like he spoke about Denis putting his fingers in Maggie's Baggie and had all shit on his finger, and whatever, some of it – but what the problem was, was Levi did it Live to London. It was probably about eight on a Saturday evening, on Capital Radio. And obviously Rodigan tried to stop him, but couldn't stop him. Levi must have finished the lyrics, bury Margaret Thatcher, the crowd was going crazy, Levi's career was finished after that. And that's a political decision, because of that his career was finished. Rodigan apparently nearly lost his job over it as well. Now, one of the things I said was Levi chatted that lyric every week in dancehalls and no one really didn't care. That's why he chatted it there. Now, this is what happens when the alternative public sphere encroaches on the recognized public sphere, or arena. This is exactly what happens, because for us the lyric wasn't no big deal, it was nothing in fact, it was just a disrespect lyric to Thatcher. It wasn't as politically profound as some of Levi's other lyrics, that perhaps he could have chatted on air and got away with. But because he was directly disrespecting Thatcher. Rodigan nearly lost his job through it, and I don't know if he did another Live to London after that. Or if he did it was a long time after that. But, you know, I try and get my head round why Levi did it, but then I don't have to think too hard about it in some ways. Because he's just like that. And he was young. Well when I say young, he was probably about 21 when he did that, or something like that, or 22. But my problem has always been why couldn't he say that when you had Spitting Image who used to roast Thatcher mercilessly after nine o'clock or whatever it was, Kenny Everett used to lambaste her every week on his shows and whatever.

LB: I think this thing you said about the spectrum of what can be said is really telling, for Lez, on the one hand in the mainstream public sphere of politics the spectrum's actually very narrow.

LH: We have these so-called radio stations, like Choice FM or whatever, who are designated as black music stations, yet they – what's the word, what's it called, censor. They censor what can be said. So, for instance, you know, I did a tune a few years ago called Time to Make a Change, in 1998, and in the tune I said 'dem don't waan listen to Lezlee, dem wouldah much prefer listen to Presley, who pirate di rock an roll, teef weh di blues, den said ah nigger's only fit to shine his shoes'. Because of that they would not play my tune on Choice FM. They wouldn't play it. So I actually did an interview for Channel 5 with Daddy Ernie from Choice FM, we were talking about it on that, and the woman was saying to him 'But why couldn't you play Lezlee's tune, if you're a black music programme and you're supposed to be going across the spectrum of black representation and what can be said, why couldn't you play Lezlee's tune'? And he was just saying well, you know, because blah blah, but at the end of the day they sanction and control us just as much as so-called narrow political spheres outside as well, they do the same thing. And a lot of the times it's not down to the politics of the radio station, sometimes it's down to the politics of the individual on what can and cannot be aired or discussed on this programme. Because at the same time, he can play Jamaican Deejays talking about 'the Pope is a battyman', 'Queen Elizabeth fi dead'. But it can't be that close to home.

LB: It's interesting what you're saying because in some ways it seems to be almost a story about what, the boundaries over what can be said are almost, it's almost like the kind of harping back to a sort of simulation story. There are some things that can't be assimilated within even a debate of people who can disagree.

LH: Yeah, yeah definitely.

LB: So there's like a, there is a fence around saying . . .

LH: Because you can't be a prophet in your own town. That's what it is.

LB: But the other thing you said which I thought was really interesting and true and profound was the way in which in the dance the spectrum is so broad.

LH: Yeah.

LB: And the only thing that determines or can affect the story as it's being told at the centre as it's being aired is whether the crowd like it or not.

LH: Exactly. Because ultimately, it's what I've always said, they are your judge, jury and executioners. So if you chat something that they directly don't like they will boo you off or drown you out. That's what they'll do, they'll drown you out. And unless the sound system owner is a complete fool he will take you off, otherwise the next thing will be his set, especially if there's more than one set, won't be allowed to play any more. And this is what happens. So, like I could give you an example, down the road there in Deptford Crypt I was chatting on our sound one night, Ghetto-tone and I chatted this lyric about not rating any boy who will grab and flee, grabs women's purses, you know, grab and flee . . . And like some guys that I actually went to school with, who make their living that way, came up and it was 'oy Lezlee don't disrespek' because you know that's how we make our money. Cause that's what they do. So even in there I would say – for me it didn't bother me because I just chat anyway. I'm not saying

I'm any kind of bad man, but I know them and I doubt if they was going to bring me anything because of that. Someone else they might have just turned them over in there. But those kind of things happen and I know that. I say you're free to say what you want, but sometimes you have to be able to back it. Because yeah, people will agree with you, 99.9 per cent of the people may agree with you, but that 1 per cent element that disagrees with you may be the roughest element in there, and that can bring you problems. Because I had the same thing in Birmingham, these guys threatened to cut me up in Birmingham once when I performed up there, and it was 'cause I went out there on the stage and said 'yeah, mi name Lezlee Lyrix, I come from London and yuh caan test mi wid lyrics. Mi have more lyrics than the whole of dem deejay bout yah', and they came and they waited for me backstage, . . . you know, waited there. Seriously.

LB: What was it that they disagreed . . .

LH: I'll tell you what, and this is what me and even my bredrin,4 because me and my bredrin went up there and we said was if I was backstage and another deejay said 'mi have di most lyrics' or whatever, I would have went out there and said 'you wanna go lyrics for lyrics bwoy?' in front of the crowd, because that's what you should do. But because they knew they couldn't test mi wid lyrics the violence is the option backstage. That's happened to me a lot of times.

LB: Could I just ask you a little bit about, thinking of dancehall as a place of, as a democratic space in that way, because I suppose what you're saying there are limits . . .

LH: Yeah, it's very much like no-one couldn't go out there and say I'm a batty man and I'm proud, or I'm a lesbian and I'm proud, yet they know that there are – I don't personally know any homosexual Deejays but there must be out there. But I do know a couple of women who are lesbians openly, but not on the mic they won't say that, but if you ask them off the mic they will tell you they are. But, you know, when I say democratic . . .

LB: Yeah, so there's, there is democracy but there's limits on it as well.

LH: Definitely. Because for instance, people have an idea of what can be articulated in that space. So even though I say it's free, it's free in the way that you can critique anyone or anything, you're getting that spilling over in the work, not even spilling over, it's probably been going on forever in the music that's been coming

from Jamaica, where they just slate the Government, slate everybody, like Capleton, who's one of my favourite Deejays had this
lyric that – and in fact if you want to know about political, and
political awareness and stuff, to me this lyric more than any other
sums up how this space works as an alternative site of a different
type of representation, be it political, cultural, or whatever. Capelton
had this lyric, didn't have a name because he never did it as a
release, it was just a lyric that he chatted in dancehalls, and the
lyric goes like this, 'dis yah one yah nah fi play, Saul an Goliath
get slew any way, any day some way, bout dis yuh nuh haffi
write'. You don't have to write about it because he hasn't released
it as a record but who is meant to hear it will hear, that's what
he's really saying, so he would say 'bout dis yuh nuh haffi write,
Emperor Selassie I ah im shine di light, yuh nuh si di height, dis
yuh nah fi telivise, cah di ghetto yout dem still ah guh get wise,
outah di slum yuh watch di youth dem ah rise, caan stop di
ghetto yout dem fram survive'. That's what he said. 'So when dem
come bow yah, ah keep up fuckry wi dust dem out like powder'
so this could be like the Police, the soldiers, the press, anybody.
When they come here keeping up their fuckry, 'wi dust dem out
like powder', yeah, 'Emperor Sielassie 1 is di Emperor, man ah
real lion man ah nuh rentah', so you're not a rentah, rentah
dread, Rastitute, you're ah real lion, Rasta lion haffi stand up.
'Man ah real lion, man ah nuh rentah, nuh Alice innah wonder-
land fi come yah come wonder' . . . don't come here to wander
or wonder, right, and then he goes . . . 'tink seh August Town',
this is the place he was deejaying in Jamaica, 'come yah tuh
pamper', because you know you pamper babies, you don't
pamper your enemies, right, so we ain't here to pamper. Then
he goes on 'bun dem cartoon, mek wi bun dem Santa, woman
wi lotion, woman wi pamper, our nature make one not a divider'
that's obviously anti-homosexuality, right, then he goes 'watch
it mek mi put on ah fire pan Busta' so this is Bustamante,
Alexander Bustamante, one of the famous historical figures,
'watch it mek mi put on ah fire pan Busta, put another fire pan
Edward Seaga, put another fire pan di one weh name Shearer,
watch it mek mi bun dung dem world order. Bun dung Michael
Manley an im fardah, bun PJ because im don't waan Lana',
because they say that P. J. Patterson is a queer in Jamaica. And
that, to me just sums it up. Everybody gets it. All the political
parties get it. But what is really significant about what he's saying

is you don't have to play it, you don't have to write about it, you don't have to put it on the TV, the youths are still going to hear the words and rise up. Because they know that what they're saying, you know, it's like one of the things that I could teach from my PhD what I disagreed with in some of what Paul Gilroy wrote was they underestimated the power of this type of commentary, because who, the people who these words are being articulated for, and in some ways the sounds as well, will always hear those sounds, and they will always hear those words. Always. It doesn't matter what you do to try and suppress it, they will hear them. So, for instance, you can ban, loads of the tunes in Jamaica get banned, and in some ways it's stupid when they ban them because the youths will still hear them, because as soon as that cassette is made – and nowadays it's even easier because it's CD, they just whack them on CDs. You know, I've told you this before, but if me and you went to New York and there was a clash in Japan the night before, I guarantee the CD would be on the street the next morning. That's how quick they move. Because they use the 'net and everything, they use everything.

LB: So this is a kind of globalization from below.

LH: Yeah, because one of the things what this guy says, Stolzoff, he called them limited circulation tapes, but limited according to whom? Yeah they're not going to sell or circulate 1.3 million copies, but you can bet your bottom dollar that the communities who need or who desire to hear those voices and those sounds and those rhythms or whatever will be exposed to them, they always are.

LB: Let me just ask you to say a little bit more about sound, not just the words but the sound, and why the sound.

LH: Let me tell you something Les, when I went to Jamaica, 1987, I was Deejaying with a yout called Leslie Thunder, and another one called Chicken Chest, and that was the first thing they said to me, they said to me 'nah man, you haffi draw it fram down here suh people know dat you mean it'. That's what they used to say. You have to draw it from here soh, right down here, as deep as you can, and then people will know that you mean what you're saying.

LB: From just the same words where you're saying it's coming from . . .

LH: Yeah, from right here, round your stomach, wherever, you draw it out, that's what they say. That's what they say. That's why, in fact, a lot of people do not understand why people love Shabba, you know, they love Shabba because of the voice. Not just because of what he says, because the thing is Shabba has some of the most profound political commentary that has been said about Jamaican society, but people don't want to hear that, because they love Shabba with the slackness and blah blah, but what people love about Shabba is the sound of his voice. It's the sounds, that's why sometimes he doesn't have to say anything, he doesn't have to say anything substantial . . . For Shabba it's like you see what I was talking about bringing it from here, if you listen to Shabba and you listen to – because Shabba's voice is deep but it's not gruff deep. His voice is just deep, it's almost like he – it comes from like some kind of, it's hard to explain but he is one of the few Deejays who have ever had that tone in his voice. Capleton has it in a different way, because Capleton, the sound of Capleton's voice is it's gruff but Capleton just generates so much excitement with his voice, he doesn't even have to really Deejay, Capleton can just go out there and say some of the things he says, like – I can't do it, I'll be honest with you, what Capleton became renowned for was he would be chatting and then he would say something really rapid like, emotive, whatever, but the way he does it was completely unique, and if you listen to him talk it comes out of his natural speech anyway. And Shabba is like the other end, because Shabba has so much melody in his voice.

LB: Because your position as both a performer and a creator of the music, and a writer and interpreter of performing is a unique one could I ask you about, because in some ways what we're trying to get to or to talk about is this stuff that is impossible to translate into words. Or even to find ways of thinking about where it comes from. Not just physically in the body but its cultural kind of history and legacy. And I just wonder if I could ask you a little bit about that problem of translation when you start to want to interpret this, these kind of cultural forms within another sort of language really, a language that's both inside and outside.

LH: Oh, I don't know where to start Les. Because even . . .

LB: Well just in a – if I could say on the problem of translating Shabba's voice or Capleton's idioms, what does that . . .

LH: Yeah, because you see what it is, one of the reasons why, I suppose, one of the reasons why it would be difficult is because it's almost like they are of the culture that I know. So I can appreciate on a level that maybe I can't articulate why they are so significant, especially for not just the words but like what you said, but maybe the idioms or the tones or whatever. But to try and translate it, oh I don't know, it's problematic Les.

LB: Is it that these kinds of . . .

LH: Because, all right, I'll give you a example, you know what I said before about my sister saying Bob Marley, whatever, it's the same kind of thing they would say about Capleton or Shabba or any of them so-called ghetto youths . . . what I'm saying is like for instance middle-class Jamaicans wouldn't appreciate the cultural sensibilities that are being rendered, and the cultural sensibilities that are being represented, and therefore articulated just in the nuances of those voices and those sounds. They wouldn't appreciate them.

LB: The sounds.

LH: Now, for instance, it's like if I hear – the other day my daughter said to me what's your favourite Bob Marley tune, so I got out my Natty Dread album, all scratched up, and played 'So Jah Seh' it's my favourite Bob Marley tune, and it's not, it's partly for the words but for me in fact that tune, in some ways for me it's like a song of my ancestors when they were suffering. That's the only way I can think about it. And I think this is what is captured in a lot of the voices and the sounds, it's like a wailing from the past, but it's not just a lamentation, it's something else, and it's really hard for me to put it into words. Like Keith Hudson did a tune called 'Flesh of my Skin', which is probably my all-time favourite reggae record, it just moves me every time I hear it even now, and again it's not necessarily the words, it's just the sound of it. It's something that he captures in the way that he, something that is captured in the way that he sounds. And it just makes me think about the kind of society that gave birth to those sounds and those voices, so people can try and separate what we do from the past, but what we do is born of that past. But it doesn't just necessarily have to be, you know, songs of sufferation or whatever, it's something else. But the essence of it is captured in those echoes of the past, if that makes sense. That's where the sound comes from, that's where Shabba gets his sound from, that's where Capleton, that's where Bob Marley got his from. That's why one of the things what I argue a lot of times when I talk to people is I'll say to them you talk about Bob Marley as if you can separate what he did from where he came from, what he was exposed to, what he knew growing up as a yout in Trench Town or whatever, one of the roughest, you know, most deprived areas in Kingston, and you cannot separate that from what he did. It's impossible. So then you can take a step back, and how can you separate that from that history of that particular island, their position in this so-called New World, and those voices. Because one of the things you have to understand, Les – and this is how I try to get my head around it – people were singing and expressing themselves like that, just like I was in my front room in my cassette. But then something happened and there was a wider exposure to those voices. To those voices, those sounds, those tones, those narratives that are echoing from the past. But they were always there, so we just maintain that, that's what, for me is what happens. You know, this is what is being represented in these spaces, which is why whenever I try to think about it, I try to put it in this context, that we're just doing what we've always done. Maybe if when we were in West Africa having our little communal cathartic sessions at the end of the month purging ourselves of whatever, openly, in these places, we're doing the same thing but in a different way. So it's not just about victimhood, which is what a lot of people try to reduce it to; there's also a celebration of self, there's a celebration of a self that we've transcended these things. There's also a celebration of a self that we can be articulate and intelligent but sometimes it's for people on the outside to understand those articulations. And not try to measure them by other cultural values or sensibilities or whatever, and say well, you know, 'dem ignorant because blah blah blah'.

LB: So Lez, in terms of the power of both the music and the culture which surrounds it, creation and performance, where does that power come from do you think? The power that it has to, for people to be committed, be interested, for it to resonate?

LH: Well to me Les, when you say the power, the power comes from yourself. It comes from yourself. It's like in the 1970s when they used to say for God's sake we've got to get more power to the people; the people already have the power but sometimes they don't recognize that. The power is already there, the power comes from, that woman did that book – *Tapping the Power Within* – we all have it. The power's there but, you know, if we believe that we are powerless then we will be powerless because, for instance the way the political system works for me is it teaches you that there is a correct procedure to air your grievances. So if you have a problem you go here, then this person will take it to this one and that one will take it to that one, and blah blah, and by the time it gets to wherever it's got they've probably forgotten the face behind whatever the problem was. But if you sit down or you mobilize yourself within your own community then the problem is always immediate so the solutions have to be immediate, they have to be. And the only way you're going to find an immediate solution to your problem is by empowering yourself. It's the only way to do it. Because I know for instance, when I went to Greensleeves Records in 1985 with a track and oh yeah, Lezlee, this is great, blah blah blah blah blah blah, the difference between me and those other Deejays was I already had a trade, so I wasn't beholden to anybody. Emma was accusing me of being a hero when we were in Norway. But what I said to her is what I know, don't tell me I don't know, and what I know that I can do for myself, don't tell me I cannot do it, because I know that I can, I'm already doing it. So, when I went to Greensleeves and Chris Cracknell who was the manager said to me you have to do this, and you have to do that, I said I don't have to do none of that. Why do I have to do that? I'm not beholden to you for anything so you can get fucked, you know, I'm quite happy to be a plumber. I had the same argument with Smiley Culture once, he said to me oh if you do this or I can get you a job doing that or do you want to do this for me, and I was you fuck off, who are you talking to. I'm used to doing for myself, so at the end of the day, you know, one of the things that empowered me was my music.

Notes

1. In DJ culture we 'chat' mike. This is not to be confused with idle 'chit chat' as 'chatting' generally denotes profound social commentary, hence 'chatting for change'.

2. Red is a term that in some ways describes being 'charged' or 'high on marijuana', but it must not be confused with 'stoned', for when you are 'Red' you reason as Rastafari teaches us, but when you are 'stoned' you cut off your capacity to 'reason'.

3. 'Baggie' is a Jamaican term for knickers.

4. 'Bredrin' is 'brethren' but can be used as plural or singular.

27

Sonic Dominance and the Reggae Sound System Session

Julian Henriques

Sound connects people; it draws us together.[1] It was Count Basie who drew me towards one of the editors of this volume. He was playing *Lester Leaps In*. And it was the sound of the music that pulled me in through a half-open door. There in front of an empty classroom an old 78 wind-up gramophone was spinning. Lez Back was preparing a lecture on jazz in pre-war Germany. We hadn't met before, but we quickly got to talking about mutual research interests . . .

This piece suggests how it might be possible to understand some effects and affects of sound and the nature and qualities of the sonic.[2] To do this I identify a particular phenomenon that I am calling sonic dominance. Football crowds, raves,[3] political demonstrations and certain religious rituals are other contexts that produce this phenomenon of sonic dominance. But my personal favourite site for the experience of sonic dominance is the Reggae sound system session. For me this is the epistemic example.[4]

The first thing that strikes you in a Reggae sound system session is the sound itself. The sheer physical force, volume, weight and mass of it. Sonic dominance is hard, extreme and excessive. At the same time the sound is also soft and embracing and it makes for an enveloping, immersive and intense experience. The sound pervades, or even invades the body, like smell. Sonic dominance is both a near over-load of sound and a super saturation of sound. You're lost inside it, submerged under it. This volume of sound crashes down on you like an ocean wave, you feel the pressure of the weight of the air like diving deep underwater. There's no escape, no cut off, no choice but to be there. Even more than music heard normally at this level, sound allows us to block out rational processes, making the experience imminent, immediate and unmediated. But the more powerful and unrepeatable experience, the more it's impossible to ever be fully described – and paradoxically the more it demands to be pointed out, gestured towards, discussed and endlessly elaborated in all its effects and affects. Sonic dominance is visceral, stuff and guts. Sound at this level cannot but touch you and connect you to your body. Its not just heard in the ears, but felt over the entire surface of the skin. The bass line beats on your chest, vibrating the flesh, playing on the bone and resonating the genitals.

Sonic dominance occurs when and where the sonic medium displaces the usual or normal dominance of the visual medium. With sonic dominance sound has the near monopoly of attention. The aural sensory modality becomes *the* sensory modality rather than one among the others of seeing, smelling, touching and tasting. This dominance of the sonic can of course always be interrupted for example by smelling fire, or seeing a gun or a knife. It's only with deep religious trance states that, for example, the sense of pain can be blocked out completely.

This relationship between the different senses and how the senses are organized hierarchically and non-hierarchically is one central theme of this piece.[5] With the sonic, as I will discuss, environment, context and the *combination* of the senses are all particularly vital. A further complication is that with respect to the relative importance of the senses, people's everyday practice is often different from their own understanding of what they are doing. This is a point Pierre Bourdieu makes: 'It is because subjects do not, strictly speaking, know what they are doing that what they do has more meaning than they know.'[6] And in turn a person's own understanding may be different again from how social and philosophical theory considers the relative importance of the senses.

Generally speaking the aural and the sonic world is probably more useful and important for the understanding of life and the negotiation of the everyday world than people might think it is. In practice it is the cooperation between the senses that's usually more important than any rigid hierarchy. By contrast the thrust of much of the Western philosophical and social science tradition has been to privilege the visual sense as the source of knowledge above all others. One of the ambitions for the present piece and the project of which it is a part, is for theory to recognize what is already embodied in practice with respect to the sonic – notwithstanding W. B Yates' reminder: 'Man can embody the truth, but he cannot know it.'[7]

I choose the word 'dominance' deliberately to suggest both the power and the pleasure of the sonic. This requires a distinction between two different aspects of power. Normally power is considered as being *owned and used over others*, as with oppression or subjugation. As distinct from this, power can also be considered as being *shared with others*, as with peaceful collective endeavours. It's this creative capacity and productive power of the multitude – as Hardt and Negri theorize it – that Empire feeds off.[8] Sonic dominance is important in this second sense, as a life force. Another of the themes to be developed here is how the sonic suggests an understanding that is based on connection, combination and synthesis, rather than division, separation or analysis alone. In the sound system session sound is dominant. But it's also irresistible. Bob Marley was obviously thinking about sound system when he sang: 'The one good thing about music/When it hits you feel no pain.' What you do feel is pleasure, or something that even defies commodification – joy.[9]

The Dancehall crowd attends the session, as do those taking part in the Carnival parade in Port of Spain or Notting Hill in London, for the pleasures of the experience. They enjoy the feeling they're 'taking charge', 'owning the street' and assuming their own value, importance and identity on 'the road mek to walk on Carnival Day'.[10] And sound plays a big part in this. It's as if the sound itself becomes both a source and expression of this power. But, as would be expected from the contextual and relational understanding being developed, the effects and affects of sonic dominance are not necessarily and predictably any one thing. This is a kind of power that can be used for good or ill. How sound is used depends on the particular social, political and cultural conventions and traditions. And also the leadership of the crowd is a critical issue. The crowds in Coliseum in Ancient Rome, or some football crowds, or a Nazi rally demonstrate how sonic dominance can be used negatively and destructively. Sonic dominance does carry this edge of risk, even abandon. As my local pirate radio station DJ Charlie B on Vibes FM has it: 'Tune in, pump up the volume and rip off the knob. We just don't care.'

The Reggae Sound System

The Reggae sound system is considered here as an already occurring socially and culturally constituted living laboratory.[11] This technical model or apparatus will be used for the demonstration and investigation of the phenomenon of sonic dominance.[12] The Reggae sound system has its place in an aural, oral, acoustic, auditory and musical landscape that is extremely rich and varied. And in Jamaica there are other social institutions where the sonic is used in similar way as in the sound system, namely the numerous local Baptist churches and the Jamaican African-inspired religions forms such as Kumina, Myal and Pocomania.[13, 14]

Of all sound systems the best known, longest established and most renowned all over the world is Stone Love. Founded by Mr Winston 'Wee Pow' Powell, Stone Love has several sets of equipment that with their crews are continuously working. One is based locally in Kingston, another caters for the rest of Jamaica and the third one is more-or-less permanently on world tour. Stone Love has been instrumental in promoting Reggae music worldwide in North America, Europe and Japan. At home Mr Powell has even used the appeal of their music to help bridge some of the political and class divisions of the island. Travelling from gig to gig as a circus does, the sound system can be described as a peripatetic, highly mobile, circulating nomadic institution.[15] The sound system is inseparable from movement not only through time, but also through space.

For their followers and fans, Stone Love has successfully defended its position at the top of the sound system league table for the last 30 years. At special competitive sound system 'clashes' they have consistently beaten off the rival systems for the support of the crowd. This is earned on the power and quality of their sound, the Selector's choice of music and the one-off 'dub plate specials' they have been exclusively commissioned from the leading recording artists of the moment.

Technologically a Reggae sound system is a mobile apparatus for the production and mixing of large volumes of sound. It consists of the 'set', this is the amplification equipment capable of producing some 19,000 watts of well-mixed sound (as I was told by the Stone Love Chief Speaker Builder and Engineer, Horace McNeal). The other major components of the set are the banks of loud speakers. Usually three speaker stacks are used in a triangular configuration to point *inwards into* the 'Dancehall crowd' or audience, rather than directed *outwards onto* an audience as they would be either side of a stage. The sound system session creates a special bowl, or receptacle, or amphitheatre that is entirely filled with the sound and the crowd, but open to the sky above.

Sound systems are microcosms of the social, cultural and economic sonic relationships in which they partake. They are a form of expression that comes out of the downtown areas of West Kingston. In the 1960s

Prince Buster called his most popular sound system Voice of the People.
They also constitute a form of entertainment that's part of the creativity
of Reggae and Dancehall culture. Only recently have there been sound
systems under middle-class ownership. Only in the last 10 years or so
has Stone Love been playing in the uptown clubs to a new middle-class
audience. Like the Reggae music genre itself absorbing other musical
influences, the apparatus of the sound system is sufficiently robust to
take on all-comers – mixing and blending to strengthen rather than
weaken itself.

Over the last 40 years, Reggae sound systems in Jamaica have become
institutions on a par with the local churches and football teams. Sound
systems also inspire loyalty and fervour in a similar manner. They employ
large numbers of people and directly influence the lives of many others
from the peanut vendors to the politicians who employ them to draw
the crowds to their meetings. They have also had a very considerable
influence on the development of the Reggae music. The current Dancehall Reggae is so named because, as it was banned from the radio, it
could only be heard on the sound systems at the open-air dancehalls.

This takes us into the political arena to the battleline, in which sound
and particularly sonic dominance, is invariably involved. With a Jamaican
society that is both highly polarized and an immensely complex mix
of colour, class and caste,[16] Dancehall culture often serves as the borderline between the poor and working classes and the Jamaican middle
classes. Despite Reggae music being acknowledged as giving Jamaica its
global profile, amongst the middle classes none but the youth can hear
anything of merit in the current music. Significantly this opposition
to the sound system and its culture is expressed as criticism of the
pleasures of the body and the female body in particular.

The older generation of the Jamaican middle classes consider Dancehall – the style and attitude, lewd dances, immodest fashions, extrava-
gant hair and makeup – entirely and absolutely excessive. For them the
lyrics promote only violence and 'slackness' as it is called in Jamaica.
(If the Bad Body hangs loose, relaxed and slack, then presumably the
Good Body must be tight-lipped, upright and uptight.) Calls for
censorship and the banning of Dancehall are common in the newspaper
opinion columns. Curbs and regulation are discussed on the numerous
radio talk shows that are a particular feature of the Jamaican media
landscape (in resonance with Jamaica's strong oral culture). To the
outraged middle classes Dancehall is simply out of control. Indeed it
thrives on a particular creativity and imagination grounded in extrava-
gance, free flows, excess, surplus and an economy of pleasure.[17] This

runs counter to conventional middle-class mores of an ex-colonial island that from the standpoint of the metropolis appear particularly prim and distinctly old-fashioned. To this extent attitudes tend to conform to conventional psychodynamic models of desire. Broadly these can be characterized as being motivated by fear, insufficiency and lack – the very opposite of surplus.

The sound system's playing of the music is also considered to be excessive – too loud. This is, of course, the kind of evaluation that places the sound system in the midst of controversies over regulation. This dynamic of expression and repression, pleasure and restraint, amplification and filter is often a critical feature of the sonic.[18] The Noise Abatement Act, 1996 attempted to restrict the volume and times sound systems are allowed to play. It states: 'the level of noise in Jamaica both day and night has become truly appalling and it is affecting the health and welfare of the nation.'[19] As a consequence of the debate over this alleged noise pollution, the Sound System Association of Jamaica was formed. Its purpose, the Association's co-founder and Press Officer Ms Louise Frazer-Bennett told me, was to fight what it saw as the restrictions to their freedom and to defend the music as the key form of cultural expression for Jamaica's poor and working-class communities.

To the Jamaican middle-class body politic the apparently uncontrollable excesses and social nature of the sonic have caused it to be considered as dangerous to the status quo. In social theory only the Marxist tradition values solidarity, sociality and social relationships, in any case. Otherwise the social nature of being has most often been theorized as inferior, without rationality and threatening to the individual. The crowd in particular is to be feared, as was detailed in Gustav Le Bon's *The Crowd: A study of the Popular Mind* published in 1900. And Jacques Attali in *Noise: the Political Economy of Music* identifies one of the reasons why this association of the sonic and the social is considered dangerous.[20] He claims musical forms can *anticipate* social forms. Certainly contemporary youth sub-cultures invariably use musical sound, possibly more than visual image, as their point of self-identification, if not rebellion. In fact, one important feature of the sound system culture is that it provides a tradition prescribing limits of time and place for such sociality to prevent it becoming 'too' excessive. Bakhtin's description of European carnival 'turning the world upside down' or Durkheim's 'collective effervescence' are precisely the exceptions to prove the rule. The continuance of carnival and Reggae sound systems evidences the political value of such safety valves as temporary licences for transgression.

These fears of the body as a threat to rationality are deeply felt and go back a long way in the Western philosophical tradition. And in as much as sound is connected to the body it only fuels them. In *The Birth of Tragedy* Nietzsche locates the moment of origin for this in Western culture in the conflict between Apollo and Dionysus in ancient Greek mythology. Apollo's victory for the rational control over Dionysus' bacchic emotional excess was reprieved in Titian's Renaissance masterpiece *The Flaying of Marsyas*. Here the poor Satyr's punishment of having his skin torn off from his body – literally disembodiment – was for daring to compete with Apollo in a musical competition. This is a lesson in rational discipline. The body out of rational control is thought to be subject to all types of dangerous excesses associated with intoxication, reverie and the sublime.

Sonic dominance takes us to the sound barrier – that is the edge of sound. Electronic amplification pushes the sonic to the limits. On one side is music, on the other noise. On one side is regulation, modulations and moderation, on the other is irregularity, unpredictability and excess. Noise disrupts, dislocates and interrupts the so-called harmony of the status quo.[21] Noise is not signal, not music, not organized, not normal, not under control. It breaks the socially prescribes rules. Noise is 'rude and uncouth', 'strange' and 'wild' – the words use used by a ship's surgeon to describe the slaves made to sing and dance on their crossing.[22] Noise takes sound *out of order*. It's chaos. And this, of course, is its creativity, and this is equally obviously necessary for the continued growth of the social and political body as a whole. With sonic dominance the Reggae sound system is exploring a similar borderline of sound's threshold with noise that, at the beginning of the century proved so productive for the Western tradition of Modernism. The Futurist Luigi Russolo made 'noise machines' and published *The Art of Noise* in 1913.[23] Noise comes from outside the theoretical system from the bits in between, intervals, gaps, folds and interstices. [24] Sonic dominance comes *from outside* the official uptown social system from the abandoned margins of society, that is the ghettos of downtown West Kingston.

The Intensity and Materiality of Sound

The sound just hits you. You can't ignore it. You have to feel it. Describing the Reggae sound system session the word 'dominance' is intended to suggest the material substance and the imminence of the sound. The effects and affects of the intensity or overload of sound may be compared to the extreme 'underload' that is produced both in the absolute silence of anaechoic chambers, in meditation techniques using an image or repeated sound 'mantra' and in experimental conditions of sensory deprivation.[25] Such extreme low threshold states break the norm of modest amounts of sensory stimulation. With sensory deprivation hallucinations are commonplace and instructively these tend to be floating out of body experiences. With sensory overload the opposite is the case, as they tend to be grounding 'into body' experiences as expressed in movement and dance. Overload and underload both tend to circumvent normal rational process.[26]

When the Reggae sound system is considered as an experimental apparatus for producing the conditions for sonic dominance we're lead back to the nineteenth-century foundation of scientific psychology. In 1860 Gustav Fechner published *Elements of Psychophysics* in which he described his experimental measurement of sensation and the physiology of the senses.[27] Fechner's concern was to establish a quantitative relationship between mind and body, which is mental sensation and material stimulus.[28] He investigated the minimum sensitivity of the sensory system at the lowest possibly thresholds of audibility, visibility and tactile sensation. To do this he developed the methodology of the just noticeable difference (JND) as the basic unit of the measurement of the intensity of sensation. By contrast sonic dominance occurs at the upper threshold of the sensitivity of the auditory sensory system. It could be described in terms of the just bearable difference (JBD) as an obverse reflection of the foundation of the science of psychology.

This idea of excess as pain, ordeal and even abuse – as well as pleasure – is also very much part of the world that has produced the Reggae sound system and Dancehall culture. In Jamaican parlance one of the terms used express this is 'sufferation'.[29] And this attitude also extends to technical equipment. Discussing his speaker designs, Stone Love's Chief Equipment Builder and Engineer put it thus: 'we abuse things in Jamaica, we abuse musical equipment, what the man makes the things to do, we ahead of it.'[30]

The sonic dominance generated in the Reggae sound system session draws attention to our intimate and multiple connections not only with our body, but also with our spatial and temporal environments. One way this has been described is in Merleau-Ponty's phenomenology. Referring to our relationship with the world Merleau-Ponty deploys the term 'chiasm', which in physiology means the intertwining or criss-crossing of nerves.[31] This contrasts with the normal visual assumption of the chasm between observer and observed. The sonic operates with the qualities of mood, colour, texture, timbre and affect, rather than the quantities of measured calculation. The particular spatiality attaching to the sonic has been described as 'acoustic space.'[32] This is a kind of space you are inside as well as outside and it is inside you as well as you being inside it.[33] In fact with sound it simply does not make sense to think of having an inside and an outside in the way that the visual sensory modality, with its preoccupation with surfaces, restricts us. Sound is both surface and depth at once. As emphasized by sonic dominance, sound is everywhere, hardly even making the dualistic division between here and there.

In fact, sonic dominance helps to generate a specific particular sense of *place* rather than a general abstract idea of space.[34] It's unique, immediate and the place of tradition and ritual performance. Indeed the Reggae sound system session draws inspiration from a rich array of creolized West African religious ceremonies that continue to be practised in Jamaica today. Acoustic space and sonic place are the antithesis to the typically post-modern 'non-places' of airports, shopping malls, high streets and ATM aprons that Marc Auge discusses.[35] Those are generic, abstract and empty spaces. Sonic spaces are by contrast specific, particular and fully impregnated with the living tradition of the moment. Each has a certain definite haeccity or 'thisness' about it.[36]

Considering time, sonic dominance contributes to the generation of a particular specific sense of event. This is the cyclical yet unrepeatable place of recurring ritual, rather than the abstract notion of continuous time or the idea of progress. Sonic time, like sonic space, is not travelled in straight lines. It's too heterogeneous for that. If written it would be in layers and with the depths of a palimpsest. In contrast, the writing of visual space is in Euclidean straight lines and flat planes on the uniform blank expanse of a *tabula rasa*.

These qualities of space and time associated with the sonic dominance makes it a multi-dimensional and multi-temporal experience, like filmic time and space.[37] By contrast, the visual modality tends to be seen as separating and isolating, most notably in the idea of the single point of view. This idea of linear perspective is quite a modern one.[38] Before the Renaissance invention of perspective, space was pictured in what appears to our modern eye as a more 'jumbled' fashion in for example in Brugal's work and most medieval painting. Another way of putting this might be to consider such canvases as an acoustic type of visual representation.[39] Often considered as drawing on more ancient 'primitive' forms, the rebirth of Modernism at the beginning of last century certainly exploded the single point of view and the linear time line with the complexities of multiple perspective and space/time. We can identify this in the 'volumes' of Picasso's African inspired sculptures; Braque's fractured

Cubist canvasses; Dziga Vertov's all seeing from everywhere *Man with a Movie Camera*; the Symbolist poets obsession with the idea of 'simultaneity'; and even Einstein's Theory of Relativity.

The Ethereal and Material Combined

But there is, of course, the other side to sound besides its material reality. The crowds attend the sound system Dancehall sessions not only for the quality of the sound, but also for the music they play: the latest rhythms, the 'revival' of old-school classics from the past and the 'specials' by the most popular recording artists of the day. Indeed the musical richness and rhythmic complexity within the current Dancehall incarnation of the Reggae music genre is probably greater than at any period up to now.[40] With a top class sound system like Stone Love there's a softness, roundness and fullness to the mix. A Jamaican sound man would call this 'bare' sound that has a 'bounce' to it.

So while sonic dominance pumps up materiality of sound, it does not deny its ethereal qualities. These are the form, structure or pattern by which sound has been analysed and understood in the Western musical tradition. Pythagoras was possibly the first to consider this aspect of sound when he said he was listening to the music of the spheres. In fact to approach the sonic from its material aspect allows the inclusion of its ethereal aspect to a greater extent than when it is approached in the opposite direction. (In the same manner we shall see in the next section that sonic dominance is more inclusive of the visual than the visual dominance is of the sonic.)

In the Reggae sound system session the aural is both a medium for oral or musical codes of communication, as well as a material thing in and of itself. You feel *both* the air as the gaseous liquid medium that 'carries' the sound *and* hear the waveform of the shape of the sound. This is sound as both content and form, acoustic energy and sign wave information, both substance and code, particle and pattern. This illustrates how the conjunction *both/and* rather than the separation *either/or* appears to be particularly appropriate for thinking with and about sound. As already noted, sound can often be characterized as making connections, combinations and being inclusive in the way that the visual sensory modality tends to do the opposite and separate things. Musician and theorist Anthony Moore has coined the phrase 'either and both' for this.[41]

This combination and relationship of either and both the material and ethereal is of vital importance, as is the distinction between them. Each is necessary for the other in what could be described as an archetypal

manner of female and male, or earth and sky, or yin and yang. Both need
to be strong. Indeed Jamaican society, and Dancehall culture in particular, value both macho male aggression and female beauty and fertility.
The Reggae sound system session provides the arena for this highly
charged sexuality.

This 'either and both' relationship of the two side of sound at the
normal macro scale of human listening can also be considered as
analogous to the behaviour of light at the subatomic scale of quantum
mechanics. According to Hiesenberg's Uncertainty Principle quanta of
light behave both as a wave, or energy, and as a particle, or matter –
both at the same time. This double-sided character of sound being two
things at the same time may not conform to Western notions of rationality – but it is a common characteristic of Reggae sound system sessions
in several further respects to be discussed.

The materiality of sound is like the sense of touch that connects us
with our bodies and the world with the 'thisness' of experience mentioned above. At the same moment, again like touch, sound has this
other opposite aspect that separates us from ourselves, each other and
the world. *The sonic is as disembodying as it is embodying.* Just as the
tactile sense is pre-eminent in determining the organisms simultaneous
connection with and separation from its environment[42] the sonic sense
plays a similar combining and separating role.

Historically it has been the disembodying rather than embodying
aspect of sound that technology first captured with Thomas Edison's
invention of the phonograph in 1877 and with it the public imagination.
In his *Gramophone, Film, Typewriter,* Frederick Kittler gives a fascinating
account of how the first use for phonographic voice recording was to
listen to the literally disembodied voices of the dead.[43] This same theme
was also taken up in Jean Cocteau's film *Orpheus* where the hero listens
for his instructions from the dead in radio broadcasts. So once it became
technically possible to record and transmit sound, why was sound
thought capable of making this connection to bridge the chasm between
life and death? It might be again because of the haeccity it evokes. The
sonic helps to give us our own particular individuality. People's voices,
like their bodily gestures, posture or gait, are as unique to them as their
fingerprints, or iris patterns, or indeed a tiger's stripes or a leopard's
spots. This is an aspect of the materiality of sound Roland Barthes refers
to in *The Grain of the Voice.*[44] The amazing magic of the first phono-
graphs is the same type of effect that anthropologists describe as being
experienced by members of non-literate societies when they first listen
to the reading of a book.

The critical point to note here is this: *it is only because the voice has once been embodied that it can subsequently be disembodied.* Thus Little Nipper when he listens so attentively in the famous HMV brand logo is hearing not just the ethereal sound to his master's voice but also remembering the authority embodied in it.

Communications theory, along with the technology and the scientific understanding of the acoustic, has also tended to pursue the sonic exclusively in its ethereal disembodied aspect. It tends to forget the other aspect of the material embodiment of sound, just as written culture tends to disregard – and disrespect – the qualities of the oral culture it supersedes. The breakthrough of information theory, as inaugurated by Claude Shannon in 1937 was to consider communication mathematically, that is as pure digital signal message without the noise, interference, dirt and other marginal matter belonging to the analogue body of the medium that usually surrounds it. When sampled and converted into purely digital information the computer can then store, manipulate, reproduce and transmit it ad infinitum – without the decay and delay that burdens analogue modulations. Only at the end point of consumption does this pure transparent digital code need converting back into analogue amplitudes – the only ones human animal senses can appreciate.

But while digital audio and video technologies are efficient and convenient, often it feels there is something missing. Invariably this 'something' is difficult to describe.[45] Extrapolating from the Reggae sound system's production of sonic dominance it can be suggested that this hard-to-define quality missing from the digital is to do with the particular sensual bodily pleasures of the materiality of the sonic. There are three of them. One is the pleasure of remembering – nostalgia. Certainly the crackle and surface noise of a vinyl LP has its own enchantment – this term recalling the ancient power of music that caused Odysseus to wax his ears against the sirens singing. The grain in film and its judder through the gate of the projector has these associations too. This is perhaps the rekindling the old flame of a past pleasure, a bodily remembering. Maybe, as compared with its cold clinical digital counterpart, the warmth and texture of analogue reproduction is to be enjoyed sympathetically as the trace of the medium's *own* bodily ache, a nostalgia – for its own source.

A second kind of pleasure of the materiality of the medium is to do with the kind of ambiguity associated with the either and both of medium and message, or noise and signal. One example of this is the stroke of the skilled water colourist's brush. The clumps of hair of an only half-wet brush can, for example, easily be used to depict clumps of grass, that is exploit the material nature of the medium in its message. Lucien Freud's brushwork in oils provides another example. From close up, at the micro scale his self-portraits are confused and meaningless daubs of paint.[46] But from the appropriate viewing distance an image with depth and rich detail miraculously emerges. It is as if as sensory beings we like to complete the picture ourselves, to make our own Gestalt forms out of the material, to achieve the pleasure of closure for ourselves. This is the pleasure of participation apparent to every good storyteller. A further point is that medium and message are always intimately connected. One example of this, described by David Rodowick, is how the new cinema digital projection technology that is set to replace film projection 'favours' or 'seems to feel right for' digitally originated 'films' like *Shrek*, rather than ones shot on celluloid.[47]

The third type of pleasure is pure sensation. This is untranslatable, irreducible and an end in itself. Especially when sound is the dominant sensory modality it becomes pure sensory experience. The study of affect has long been a neglected area of psychology until the current growing interest in the body, especially in Feminist theory. The work of Eve Sedgwick and Adam Frank has lead to a revival of interest in bodily sensation and affect. The key figure here is the psychologist Silvan Tomkins: 'It is enjoyable to enjoy. It is exciting to be excited. It is terrorising to be terrorized and angering to be angered. Affect is self-validating with or without any further referent.'[48]

This is what sonic dominance brings to the fore. Such pleasure can never be made to disappear entirely, because it is literally embodied in each of us. But at the same time they can be undervalued and impoverished and made inaccessible – for reasons that might well have to do with their bodily associations. This is what happens as and when a new level of mediation or encoding is introduced.[49] Digital recording has rendered analogue recording deficient in exactly this manner. The historic example of this process is of course the manner in which written culture engineered its suppression of oral culture.[50] In this instance, the intrinsic qualities of oral communication, that is bodily performance, were in principle impossible for the new visual written code to capture. As a result or because of this lack or inadequacy, the new visual code introduces a new set of yardsticks – like storage, reproduction and individual ownership – by which the old oral code is condemned as irredeemably inferior.[51]

Sonic and Visual Sensory Regimes

With sonic dominance sound displaces vision as the dominant sensory modality. The polemical value of the idea of dominance is to draw attention to the fact of how often visual dominance is assumed as the taken for granted norm. In the Reggae sound system session the sound becomes a thing in and of itself. This is unlike with a concert or stage show, as its called in Jamaica, where the crowd can usually see the artist performing live in front of them. In the session there is hardly any visual source, reference, location or origin to the sound. The artist who made the recording is present only via his or her disembodied voice. Even the Selector playing the record is often shrouded in darkness. This allows the sound to have its own autonomy. Sound in the session is a specific yet pervasive thing. And this allows the individuals in the crowd to have a relationship not *with* the sound as something separate from them, but *in* the sound as something which is a part of them. Breaking the normal synchronization between sound and image allows the crowd surrounded by the speaker stacks, or the guys right up next to a box, to be literally inside the sound and the sound to be inside them.

The sonic dominance produced in the context of the Reggae sound system session can be considered as an experiment in what it would be like if the world were ruled by sound, or at least understood in terms of a sonic metaphor. One of the critical differences between the regime of the ear established moment by moment by sonic dominance and the regime of the eye is that the sonic tends to be much more accommodating to the visual than the visual is to the sonic. Where the visual modality excludes others, the sonic includes them. There is ample evidence for this in the sound system session itself. Here the sonic environment is considered to provide the ideal setting for what is called 'modelling' – being seen to be there, in what, with whom, and so forth. Further the live video camera link to television monitors and sometimes video projection screens illustrates the value for the visual of its integration with the sonic experience. The sound system session is very much a multi-media, multi-sensory environment.

In general terms it can be said that the Western philosophical tradition tends to organize the senses hierarchically clearly privileging the visual sensory modality as the best foundation for knowledge. Vision and sight has been the over-arching troupe at least since Descartes and the Enlightenment.[52] A founding metaphor for this tradition is Plato's cave – where the shadow images of the real world play on the wall. Indeed the visual imperative is so strong few stop to remark that by far the most striking sensory feature of any cave is not visual at all but sonic – the echo.[53] The philosophical assertion of the visual hierarchy of the senses is quite counter-intuitive. But this has not prevented its reflection being seen in everyday common sense assumptions. Blinded by images and our exposure to screens we see ourselves living in a visual rather than a sonic culture.

Tending to ignore experience, everyday practice, or the actual operation of the sensory modalities, social, literary, psychoanalytic, anthropological and cultural theory over recent decades has done nothing but follow this visual suit. With a few exceptions such as Louis Althusser's idea of the 'hailing up' or interpolation of subjects, there has been an obsession with the Gaze and the interminable 'reading' of everything as 'text'. Consequently sonic culture, listening, and energetic approaches have been ignored, as with, for example, Lacan's conversion of Freud's psychodynamic model to his own linguistic one. As was mentioned in the opening section there has been a long association between the visual, the rational and the mind. This has been distinguished from – and indeed opposed to – the sonic, the irrational and the body.[54]

Against this it has to be pointed out that the visually dominated hierarchy of the senses, besides not being practically accurate, is by no means universal across cultures. The Western model of the five senses, which are primarily orientated around vision to favour instrumental reason, has been handed down to us from Aristotle. But this is certainly not the only possible system. In 1883 Lord Kelvin, in his *The Six Gateways to Knowledge,* divided the sense of touch into the sense of heat and the sense of force.[55] The educationalist and philosopher Rudolph Steiner developed a twelvefold sensory system: touch; life sense; self-movement; balance; smell; taste; sight; temperature sense; hearing; speech sense; concept sense; and ego sense.[56]

In her *Culture and the Senses,* anthropologist Kathryn Linn Geurts studied a society in which the dominant sense was not even one of the five normally considered definitive.[57] For the Anlo-Ewe speaking people of South Eastern Ghana the most important sense is balance. The sense of balancing – physically, psychologically, spiritually and metaphorically – orientates all the other bodily senses in the way the visual sense does in the Western philosophical tradition.[58] Geurts discusses the senses as: 'ways of embodying cultural categories, or making into body certain cultural values or aspects of *being* that the particular cultural community has historically deemed precious and dear' (italics in original). It would be expected from the Sapir-Whorf hypothesis on use and language that the importance of a sensory modality would be manifest in the sheer amount of vocabulary, which is indeed what Geurts found. Certainly I found the Stone Love engineers and many of those involved in the sound system way of life had a huge vocabulary for describing the all the nuances, fine grain detail, variety of types, effects and affects of the sound to which they are sensitive and sensible.

But why does it matter which is the dominant sense or even how many senses there are? I suggest this becomes increasingly important as Feminist and other research takes up the theoretical issues at stake in mind/body dualism. This is often to develop an understanding of the intelligence of the body that displaces the traditional privilege of the mind.[59] The processes of embodiment can only take place through the sensory perception. As long at the focus was on the abstract mental processes then the uniformity of the sense data originating from the different senses was easy to assume. Investigating embodiment requires more careful consideration of specific and unique qualities of the sensory modalities themselves. The Reggae sound system and its production of sonic dominance can be used to explore precisely this question with respect to sound. The senses are very context specific. Perhaps the only context-free distinction between sound and vision is with respect to the passage of time. Sound is time-based in a way that image is not (though of course cinema relies on the optical illusion of the movement of the image through time at a rate of 25 still frames per second). Music cannot be played backwards, images can. The written – in space – tends to maintain the status quo, whereas the spoken – in time – often questions it.

Maybe because of the congruities between hearing and touch, the sonic sensory modality often evokes emotional associations in the way that mere images fail to do. Sounds evoke images more than images evoke sounds. The advertising executives who partner their products with our musically intimate memories have consistently exploited this sensory tendency, as has Nick Hornby in his successful books *High Fidelity* and *31 Songs*. Music and ritual are close cousins as has been described in numerous anthropological studies and more recently in sociology by Michel Maffesoli.[60] Seeing and hearing work in different ways. As Marcel DuChamps put it: 'One can look at seeing; one can't hear hearing.'

Certainly, in practice, the other sensory modalities are often considered as having specific and unique qualities. Taste, for example, has been considered as the most all embracing of the senses. For more than 500 years people's 'good' or 'bad' taste has been considered to define them comprehensively. Etymologically the word derives from the Old French *taster* with the more embodied meaning of to 'feel, handle, or touch.'[61] Congruent with these origins, taste is understood physiologically as the most 'primitive' of the senses with the nerves from the taste sensors running directly to the hippocampus, which is philogenically the oldest part of the brain. In his monumental *Rememberance of Things Past*, Marcel Proust exploits this fact when he uses the taste of a Madalena biscuit to trigger feelings and associations long forgotten by the more advanced conscious, rational brain.

Also the various capabilities and sensitivities of the different sensory modes are increasingly being recognized in the new sciences where 'audification' or 'sonification' is proving to be a much more revealing way of understanding complex data than the more conventional visualization. One example of this is the work of Florian Dombois on earthquakes.[62] His audio seismology allows much more accurate understanding of these phenomena than any visual representation. Indeed hearing is often considered capable of recognising proportional relationships much better than vision can. Indeed, the recognition of the musical octave has been identified across the broadest range of cultures.[63]

Again, if we turn to actual practice, any idea of the philosophical hierarchy or competition between sensory modalities dissolves into combination, cooperation and augmentation. Rather than the dominance of any one sense, or any hierarchy of senses, in practice it is more like a matrix of senses, or flux, or web of the senses whose priorities vary according to the relevant context. At any one moment it is a multi-sensory impression of the world, on which a full understanding depends.[64] So my emphasis on sound in sonic dominance does not imply any ambition to replace or displace one visual hierarchy with another sonic one. While such a separation might be expected from the either/or binary logic of the visual domination, it is simply not the case with the 'either and both' 'reasoning' – as Jamaican Rastafarian philosophy calls it – of the sonic. Unlike the hierarchy of visual domination that tends to take the credit for the information received via the other senses; the sonic tends to respect each particular sense as such.

Transduction and Sonic Embodiment

In the Reggae sound system session sonic dominance amplifies the pleasures of sound. These pleasures have so far been described in terms of how sound makes 'either and both' connections: with ourselves through the sensation itself; with other people in the dance; with the visual and other sensory modalities of the event; and with the multiple times, spaces and traditions of the dancehall. And based on these, sonic dominance also produces one further type of connection, not horizontally, but vertically to 'the higher level' as would be said in Jamaica. If sonic dominance is the imminence of sound, this is the transcendence.

To suggest that a Dancehall crowd is drawn there for some kind of quasi-spiritual experience implies that the sound system session has certain common features with Jamaican Baptist Church services and African-inspired spiritual rituals. While this is true, I would like to try to go further in understanding the processes and mechanisms by which this kind of transformation takes place. To do so I will describe the sonic dominance of the sound system session as producing what can be called 'transduction'. It might be that this process of transduction is what generates the pleasure, joy and the excess for which Dancehall is famous.

The Reggae sound system session offers several ready examples of transduction. The OED definition of transduction is 'the action of leading or bringing across.'[65] One example of a transducer, without which no sound system could function, is the loudspeaker. Engineers readily describe the speaker as a transducer, that is the device that converts energy from one form to another. With a speaker this is the transfiguration of electromagnetic waves on which the amplifier operates, into the sound waves we can hear. As Mr Horace McNeal, Stone Love's Chief Builder and Engineer, explained to me, this is done via the electromagnetic coil moving the speaker diaphragm. Another example of a transducer is a microphone – simply a speaker in reverse. Here sound waves are converted into electromagnetic waves for amplification etc. In the context of the Reggae sound system session, as would be expected, the DJ uses a mike to address the crowd and 'build the vibes'.

The third example of transduction is concerned not with electromagnetic flows but with bodily currents. The human body can be considered as a sensory transducer – in dance. At its simplest a musical bass line provokes the kinetic movement of tapping your foot to the rhythm. This occurs automatically and without thinking about it, as a bodily rather than a rational response. It's a transformation sonic energy into kinetic energy. The Reggae sound system session as a highly elaborated social and cultural apparatus that informs and forms this movement into the shape of the current dance craze. The two sides of the sonic, the ethereal and the material, are amplified by tradition and technology respectively. This rich and exciting dance world of the sound system session deserves full investigation and analysis in its own right.[66] I shall just give a hint of what the dance is like here:

... most dramatic is the Drive By dance, where the men lean back as in a car and have their hands in the air in front of them mimicking hands on the steering wheel, driving, windscreen wipers on the cue bellowed by DJ Skyjuice. A formation of five or six dancers then sweep across the length of the arena, proceeded by the video camera and its spotlight and surrounded by the moving circle of the crowd . . .[67]

Due to its unavoidable bodily associations and the fact that a sense of movement is not one of the privileged five, it should not be surprising that dance, particular African dance, is so often reduced and biologized as 'natural rhythm'. As a helpful counter to this Merleau-Ponty's phenomenology emphasizes that without motility, this potential for movement, the world would not make sense or have depth.[68] My use of the term transduction, as a connection or homology between physical and social circuits, flows and fields, is not intended as any kind of reductionism. Rather it is intended to open up the imaginative and scientific possibilities – taking its inspiration from, for example, Norbert Wiener's application of the principles of mechanical feedback processes to human behaviour. This gave birth to the new science of cybernetics.[69]

This concept of transduction again exemplifies how the condition of sonic dominance can reveal the often hidden functioning of the senses. At each point of transduction, electromagnetic, sonic or cultural, one thing changes into another. This creates a surplus. Transduction describes a process of transcending the dualities of form/content, pattern/substance, body/mind and matter/spirit. A transducer is a device for achieving the escape velocity to leave the world of either/or and enter the world of either and both. It increases speed and energy, in the same way as the Reggae sound system set amplifies sound.

Sonic dominance transduces the crowd across several thresholds over the passage of the session through until dawn. It generates a very special type of environment and experience – a place between places and a time out of time. Anthropologist Victor Turner[70] describes these as 'liminal' states or places. Outside normal society, these are thresholds where transition, transfigurations and rites of passage occur.[71] In such liminal states communication often takes place at a sublime or heightened level, communicating in an unworldly language, like the Pentecostal speaking in tongues so common in the Jamaican churches.[72] Maybe music provides a similar ethereal language. As noted with sensory deprivation, liminal states of overload have similar affects and effects. Periods of isolation, suffering and ordeal are invariably the prerequisites for the leader's rebirth into their new role, according to most religious creeds.

With the extremes of excess or deprivation it would seem a process of either and both desensitization and sensitization takes place.

As a liminal state the sound system session provides ample evidence many of the roles, figures and practices common to both Western and African mythologies. Thresholds traditionally require Guardians. In the world of the Reggae sound system, this role falls on the Gateman who controls not only entry into the session but is also in charge of security inside the venue. Like Cerberus the three-headed serpent-tailed dog at the entrance to the Greek mythological underworld of Hades, the Gateman's role is to challenge and test those who would wish to cross over the threshold.

And any such crossing requires a Guide to offer the hope of a safe return journey. In the Reggae sound system session this role is taken by the Selector who chooses the records to fit the mood and vibe of the crowd and the DJ who gives them verbal feedback and encouragement. The sound system session shares certain features with ancient African traditions. The Call and Response feedback between DJ and audience for instance, which has also been taken up in the Jamaican Baptist churches, links the roles of DJ and priest for many of the Dancehall crowd. Here the DJ guides their transformative journey through the night and ensures a safe and peaceful re-entry into the normal world at dawn. The DJ, feeling the vibe of the crowd and the music, is often said to be 'riding the riddem', matching his words and their content perfectly to the beat. In the Reggae sound system session it is the DJ who's in control, he or she rides the spirit on the currents of the music. This, in fact, transposes the usual idea of spirit possession, as in Voodoo, where it is the gods who ride the possessed.

Another example of a Guardian god is Legba, the West African god/goddess of crossroads.[73] Caribbean folklore renames this Trickster god as Anancy, who takes the form of a spider, sitting in the middle of its web. For the Greeks the god of transformation and communication is Hermes, for the Romans, Mercury. Invariably, crossroads are the places for these strange transformations: where Oedipus killed his father; where *Macbeth's* witches meet; and where Robert Johnson tells us he sold his soul for the devil's gift of the Blues. Such currents run deep under the normal consciousness of rational thought.

The sonic dominance of the Reggae sound system session generates its own particular state of being and its own particular logic and distinct and different form of rationality. Traditional Aristotelian logic, which is considered as the rational norm, eschews contradiction.[74] It states that A and not A cannot both be true at the same time. But Dancehall

sessions are replete with instances of 'either and both' logic. Dancehall
culture readily embraces such apparent contradictions. Often negative
'gangster' lyrics appear on one side and the uplifting positive 'cultural'
lyrics on the other side of the same 7" 45 rpm single (which is still the
common currency of the Jamaican music market). A sound system
engineer I spoke to, as well as being happy to explain to me how trans-
ducers worked on the basis of a college degree in electronic engineering,
was also comfortable using the word 'science' in the colloquial Jamaican
meaning of magic, Obeah or Voodoo. Indeed at one Stone Love dance,
once all the equipment was set up and tested, the Engineer dusted off
all the control knobs with a dry paint brush and had the inside of the
each of the speaker boxes in each of the stacks washed out with soap
and water. Further research is required but this might be considered a
ritual or spiritual cleansing – to complement the purity of the sound.[75]

This leads us into a substantial research area concerning the relationship between technology and tradition and indeed technology and
magic.[76] Particularly relevant here is the central thesis of Bruno Latour's
We Have Never Been Modern, that is the modern and ancient have always
co-existed in the way that the average city street mixes buildings of
different historical styles and periods.[77] Latour goes further than Walter
Benjamin's idea of Modernism involving a return of the repressed of
'the primitive'.[78] Extending Latour's anti-developmental approach, I
would suggest: *we have always been modern*, either and both ancient and
modern. The Reggae sound system session is evidence of this. Just as
it's a diasporic apparatus – different places at the same time, it is also a
syncretic apparatus – different times at the same place. Observing a
Jamaican Kumina 'duty' or ceremony, what literally struck me most
powerfully was the thud of the air from the playing of the drums. It
made me realize that if the electromechanical coil against the loudspeaker diaphragm makes it a transducer, so equally does the mechanical
hand against the animal skin.[79]

Both the material and ethereal aspects of sound evidently and intimately connect us to our body. Sensation, sensitivity and sensuality are
all bodily experiences. The exposed flesh, minimal thongs and 'pussy
printers' of the Dancehall dress style that so scandalize the Jamaican
middle classes, do nothing if not celebrate the female body. Sonic dominance engenders this body – creating it and sexing it. As Freud described
dreams for the Unconscious, I'd like to call the sonic 'the royal road'
to the body, the *sonic* body, the body touched by sound. This is a whole
resonating, specific, shared, social, immediate and fleshy body. The term
'sonic body' implies either and both the body of the sound and the

sound of the body. The corporeality of the sonic body expresses itself in sound and performs through sound. We can listen to the sonic body both symptomatically, as with a doctor's stethoscope to the chest, and sympathetically with our hearts open to its song. Listening puts us both inside ourselves and outside ourselves. Listening to the Reggae sound system it might be possible to understand its sonic rationality. And this could be a model for our thinking in other places. As David Levin put it: 'By virtue of developing our listening, we may find ourselves granted the sense of a different norm, a different measure, a different principle for thinking the 'ratio' of rationality.' [80]

Notes

1. Ideas are conversational beings, dialogic is the only logic in this sense. The impetus for my current research sprang from a conversation with Stuart Hall. I would also like to thank my Goldsmiths College colleges John Hutnyk, Dave Morley and Keith Negus for their helpful comments on earlier drafts. My thanks also to Bibi Bakare-Yusuf for her generous suggestions.

2. The landmark work on acoustic soundscapes is Schafer (1977). For a pioneering approach to thinking in and with sound see Eshun(1998).

3. See for example Gaillot (circa 2000).

4. My most recent research has been with Stone Love but for other films I've worked with other sound systems in the UK: Saxon Sound in *We the Ragamuffin* and JB International in the feature *Babymother*.

5. For an accessible account of the importance of the senses that is both phenomenological and Shamanistic see Abram (1996).

6. Bourdieu (1977).

7. Quoted in Levin (1985: 30).

8. Hardt and Negri (2000: 103).

9. I must thank Bibi Bakare-Yusuf for emphasizing this last point to me and in her own dancehall research.

10. See Howe (1977).

11. Investigating the sensory extremes of sonic dominance one benefit of taking an already socially and culturally constituted apparatus is that custom and practice offer a better guarantee of safety than artifically created laboratory conditions might be able to do.

12. There have been several other approaches to Reggae and Dancehall culture such as Carolyn Cooper's (1993) pioneering study of dancehall culture. Other

approaches have concentrated on anthropological and sociological investigation: Stolzoff (2000) and Bradley (2000). Another focus of research has been the lyrics, see for example: Cooper (1994). One of the few to investigate the sonic aspect of the sound system is Chude-Sokei (1997). The image and music of reggae is well covered in Salewicz and Boot (2001). For a unique phenomenologically informed approach to Dancehall see Bakare-Yusuf (2001). Hebdige (1979) was the first to consider the sonic aspects of the sound system as such.

13. For the most comprehensive anthropological account of Kumina and other Jamaican ceremonies see Ryman (1984) and, for their influence on reggae music, White (1984).

14. In other contexts, as with the sound system session, the visual sensory modality is also used to provide sensory orientation, focus and amplification. Examples of such apparatus from further afield would include Bentham's panopticon prison design and the 1609 Leiden anatomy theatre. As I will suggest below, one of the critical functions that sonic dominance facilitates is a particular kind of transformation. In this respect the Reggae sound system session can be considered as an apparatus akin to an alchemical laboratory.

15. See Braidotti (1994) and Deleuze and Gauttari (1988).

16. See for example my father's early study of these issues: Henriques (1953).

17. See Hardt and Negri (1994) and Bataille (1988).

18. As I will be exploring in further research how sonic dominance is achieved through certain technological operations. Principal of these is the separation of different sound frequencies through gates and filters and then their combination in the configuration of the speaker stacks and the 'mix' set by the pre amp controls.

19. Section 7, Memorandum of Objects and Reasons.

20. Attali (1985).

21. For a evocative and provocative discussion of this idea of interruption see Serres (1982).

22. See especially chapter 2, *Sound Barrier and Sound Management*, in Cruz, Jon (1999: 45).

23. See Kahn (1999).

24. Deleuze (1986, 1993) and chapter 14 in Deleuze and Gauttari (1988).

25. The most detailed experiments were conducted by D. O. Hebb at McGill University, Montreal, Canada in 1958.

26. This 'super liminal' state may be contrasted with subliminal states first identified by Vance Packard (1957), who described how product advertising messages are suggested to potential buyers below the level of conscious awareness.

27. Fechner (1966).

28. And a hundred years later this interest was transfigured into on in the quantitative measurement of the difference between the psychological and the

social in the European Social Psychology and Social Categorization theory. See my critique of this in Henriques et al. (1984, 1998).

29. For the most stimulating discussion of the relationship between pain and the creativity of the imagination see Scarry (1985).

30. Interview with Horace McNeal, Stone Love Chief Speaker Builder and Engineer, Jones Town, Kingston, 26 July 2002.

31. See Merleau-Ponty (1962) and Weate (2003).

32. Williams (1955). D. C. Williams was one of Marshall McLuhan's collaborators in the 1950s.

33. I am reminded of one of my inspirations for this piece in Ralph Ellison's prologue to *Invisible Man*. He describes the Invisible Man living underground: 'Now I have one radio-phonograph; I plan to have five. There is a certain acoustic deadness in my hole, and when I have music I want to feel its vibration, not only with my ears but with my whole body. I'd like to hear five recordings of Louis Armstrong playing and singing "What Did I Do to Be so Black and Blue" – all at the same time' (emphasis in original).

34. The distinction space and place is important, see Casey (1993).

35. Auge and Howe (1995).

36. Deleuze and Gauttari discuss haeccity in relation to their distinction between rationalized and non-rationalized spaces in Chapter 14 of Deleuze and Gauttari (1988).

37. I explored this idea of filmic space/time which is in fact the dream space into which every cinema audience enters in my dance drama *Exit No Exit*, using repeated action, speed changes and reverse motion. My inspiration was Maya Deren's film *Choreography for the Camera*. See also Henriques (2002).

38. See Ivins (1938, 1975) and Latour (1990).

39. Romanyshyn (1989).

40. Some of the artists currently recording on these rhythms that I particularly like are Elephant Man and the group T.O.K.

41. Anthony Moore talk *Membranes in Space and the Transmitting Ear*, Goldsmiths College, 20 March 2003. See also Moore (2003).

42. Soesman (1990).

43. See Kittler (1999) and Taussig (1993) and also, for the importance of the materiality of the medium of communication, Crary (1993, 2001). This relationship between speaker and listener is also explored with regard to hearing voices that are not there in Blackman (2001). See also Ree (1999).

44. Barthes (1977).

45. See Henriques (2002).

46. Lucien Freud *Self Portrait* XXX in his 2002 Tate exhibition was the one that struck me in this way particularly.

47. David Rodowick presentation, University of London, School of Advanced Studies, Symposia for Screen Studies, 14 February 2003.

48. See Sedgwick and Frank (1995).

49. Wilden (1972).

50. I have benefited from discussions with Brian Rotman on these matters for many years. See Rotman (1993, 2002).

51. In the 1950s investigating the sung origins of Homer's *Iliad* and *Odyssey* Alfred Lord recorded and analysed the contemporary Slavic epic sung tradition in Yugoslavia. He wrote: 'The truth of the matter is that our concept of "the original" of "the song," simply makes no sense in oral traditions. To us it seems so basic, so logical, since we are brought up in a society in which writing has fixed the norm of a stable first creation in art, that we feel there must be an "original" for everything. The first singing in an oral tradition does not coincide with this concept of the "original." We might as well be prepared to face the fact that we are in a different world of thought, the pattern of which does not always fit our cherished terms. In oral tradition the idea of an original is illogical . . . Our greatest error is to attempt to make 'scientifically' rigid a phenomenon that is fluid . . .' (Lord 1960, 2000).

52. See Jay (1993), Rorty (1979), Jacobs (2001). For a phenomenological explorations of the visual sense see Levin (1985, 1988).

53. My thanks to Nigel Helyer (also known as Dr Sonique) for making this point is his talk to the School of Sound Conference, London 23 April 2003.

54. Levin (1985).

55. See Kahn (1999: 77).

56. See Soesman (1990).

57. Geurts (2003). Another very interesting account of the senses is to be found in Stoller (1989).

58. The importance of this sense of balance continues across the African diaspora into the Americas with the sense of the special significance of dance, movement and more generally style in Jamaican Dancehall culture and are perhaps also being expressed by the phrase 'walk the walk.' See also Hurtston (1934).

59. See for example Grosz (1994), Falk (1994), Wilson (1998).

60. Maffesoli (1996).

61. Stoller, Paul (1989: 23–24).

62. Domblais, Florian (2001).

63. Frederick Kittler made this point in his talk at Goldsmiths College on 6 March 2003. See also Lawlor (1982: 13).

64. Further, each sensory modality is not as discrete and separate from the others as is often assumed. In practice synesthesia is a commonplace occurrence, certainly in the everyday language of the senses. This is full of mixed metaphors of 'warm' or 'loud' colours and 'bright' or 'brittle' sounds. Qualities of one sense are readily transposed onto another, see Abram (1996) for a revealing account

of this. Also the senses are themselves not singular, rather they are bifurcated. We have stereo hearing and binocular vision to give the additional dimension of 'depth' to these sensory fields.

65. In this respect transduction may be related to other types of qualitative change such as phase change (between solid, liquid and gas); transduction as used in cellular biology to describe the passage of chemicals across the semi-permeable membrane of the cell wall; and Malcolm Gladwell's idea of the 'tipping point' whereat continuous increments (for example, in product sales) suddenly produces the breakthrough or discontinuous result of 'it's everywhere'. For a philosophical account of transduction drawing on Simondon's work see MacKenzie (2002).

66. L'Atoinette Osunide Stines the choreographer for my film *Babymother*, has been consistently helpful and informative for my interest is Dancehall dance. There has been very little published on Jamaican dance to date, but see Chapter 5 in Bakare-Yusuf (2001). Of the literature on African dance, one most revealing account is Chernoff (1979).

67. Taken from my field notes of Stone Love, Metro Media, Venus Love and Young Fresh sound systems dance, Stakeland, Half Way Tree, Kingston, Saturday 17 August 2002, 4.30 am.

68. Merleau-Ponty (1962).

69. Wiener (1950).

70. Turner (1974).

71. For one of the most vivid accounts of such initiation rites see Somé (1994).

72. Michel Serres gives an interesting account from a communication theory point of view in Serres (1982).

73. See Brown (1947, 1969) and Bakare-Yusuf and Weate (forthcoming 2004).

74. Alfred Korzybski e development of a non-Aristotelian logic in the 1930's. His famous slogan was: 'The map is not the territory.' This idea of a logic that embraces contradiction is also gestured towards in Freud's idea of the Unconscious operating prior to the conscious evaluative markings of good and bad.

75. This would be supported by the observation I have also made of Jamaican market traders ritually cleaning their pitch with limes and herbs before setting out their wares. They told me it was to bring a good day's trade.

76. For a very readily account of this read Davis 1998). See also Bausinger (1961, 1990), and Zimmerman (1990).

77. Latour (1993).

78. Taussig (1993).

79. I would also like thank L'Antionette Stines and Kumina King Oliver for taking me to witness this Kumina 'duty' on a recent research trip in Jamaica.

80. See Levin (1989: 33).

References

Abram, D. (1996), *The Spell of the Sensuous*, London: Random House.

Attali, J. (1985), *Noise: The Political Economy of Music*, Manchester: Manchester University Press.

Auge, M. and Howe, J. (1995), *Non-Places: Introduction to and Anthropology of Super Modernity*, London: Verso.

Bakare-Yusuf, B. (2001), 'The Sea of Memory: Embodiment and Agency', in The Black Diaspora, Ph.D. dissertation, Faculty of Social Sciences, University of Warwick

Bakare-Yusuf, B. and Weate, J. (forthcoming 2004), *Ojuelegba: The Sacred Profanities of a West African Crossroad* in Salm, S. and Falola, T. (eds) *African Urban Cultures*, Carolina: Academic Press.

Barthes, R. (1977), 'The Grain of the Voice', in *Music, Image, Text*, London: Fontana

Bataille, G. (1988), *The Accursed Share: An Essay on General Economy*, vol. 1, Consumption, New York: Zone Books.

Bausinger, H. (1961, 1990), *Folk Culture in a World of Technology*, Bloomington IN: University Press.

Blackman, L. (2001), *Hearing Voices: Embodiment and Experience*, London: Free Association.

Bourdieu, P. (1977), *Outline of a Theory of Practice*, Cambridge: Cambridge University Press.

Bradley, L. (2000), *Bass Culture: When Reggae Was King*, London Viking.

Braidotti, R. (1994), *Nomadic Subjects*, New York: Columbia University Press.

Brown, N. O. (1947, 1969), *Hermes the Thief: The Evolution of a Myth*, New York: Vantage Books.

Casey, E. S. (1993), *Getting Back into Place: Toward a Renewed Understanding of the Place-World*, Indiana University Press.

Chernoff, J. M. (1979), *African Rhythm and African Sensibility: Aesthetics and Social Action in African Musical Idioms*, Chicago: Chicago University Press.

Chude-Sokei, L. (1997), 'Dr Satan's Echo Chamber': Reggae, Technology and the Diaspora Process', Bob Marley Lecture, Institute of Caribbean Studies, Reggae Studies Unit, University of the West Indies.

Cooper, C. (1993), *Noises in the Blood: Orality, Gender and the 'Vulgar' Body of Jamaican Popular Culture*, London: Macmillan.

Cooper, C. (1994), '"Lyrical Gun": Metaphor and Role Play in Jamaican Dancehall Culture', in *The Massachusetts Review*, Autumn–Winter.

Crary, J. (1993), *The Techniques of the Observer*, Cambridge MA: MIT Press.

—— (2001), *The Suspension of Perception: Attention, Spectacle and Modern Culture*, Cambridge: MIT Press.

Cruz, J. (1999), *Culture on the Margins: The Black Spiritual and the Rise of American Cultural Interpretation*, Princeton: Princeton University Press.

Davis, E. (1998), *TechGnosis: Myth, magic and Mysticism in the Age of Information*, London: Serpents Tail.

Deleuze, G. (1986a), *Cinema 1. The Movement Image,* London: Athlone Press.

—— (1986b), *Cinema 2. The Time Image*, London: Athlone Press.

—— (1993), *The Fold: Leibniz and the Baroque,* London: Athlone Press.

Deleuze, G. and Gauttari, F. (1988), *A Thousand Plateaux: Capitalism and Schizophrenia*, London: Athlone Press.

Domblais, F. (2001), 'Using Audification in Planetary Seismology', in Proceedings of the 2001 International Conference on Auditory Display, Espoo, Finland, 29 July–1 August 2001 (see also http://www.gmd.de/ projects/auditory-seismology/).

Eshun, Kodwo (1998), *More Brilliant Than the Sun: Adventures in Sonic Fiction*, London: Quartet.

Falk, P. (1994), *The Consuming Body*, London: Sage.

Fechner, G. T. (1966), *Elements of Psychophysics,* vol. 1, New York: Holt, Rinehart & Winston.

Gaillot, M. (undated, circa 2000), *Multiple Meaning: Techno - an artistic and political laboratory of the present*, Paris: Editions Dis Voir.

Geurts, K. L. (2003), *Culture of the Senses: Bodily Ways of Knowing in an African Community*, Berkeley CA: California University Press.

Grosz, E. (1994), *Volatile Bodies: Towards Corporeal Feminism*, Bloomington: Indian University Press.

Hardt, M. and Negri, A. (1994), *Labour of Dionysus: A Critique of the State-Form*, Minneapolis: University of Minnesota Press.

Hardt, M. and Negri, A. (2000), *Empire*, Cambridge MA: Harvard University Press.

Hebdige, D. (1979), *Subculture: The Meaning of Style*, London: Methuen.

Henriques, F. (1953), *Family and Colour in Jamaica*, London: Eyre & Spottiswoode.

Henriques, J. (2002a), '"Sonic" Scriptwriting: writing memorable movies', in *Scriptwriter*, Issue 3, March.

—— (2002b), 'Thinking without Trace', *Journal of Visual Culture*, 1(3): 355–8.

Henriques, J., Hollway, W., Urwin, C., Venn, C. and Walkerdine, V. (1984, 1998), *Changing the Subject: Psychology, Social Regulation and Subjectivity*, London: Routledge.

Howe, D. (ed.) (1977), *The Road Mek to Walk on Carnival Day: the Battle for the West Indian Carnival in Britain*, London: Race Today Publications.

Hurtston, Z. N. (1934), 'Characteristics of Negro Expression' in Cunard, N. (ed.) *Negro*, London: Lawrence & Wishart.

Ivins, W. M. Jr (1938, 1975), *On the Rationalization of Sight*, New York: Da Capo.

Jacobs, K. (2001), *The Eye's Mind: Literary Modernism and Visual Culture*, Ithaca: Cornell University Press.

Jay, Martin (1993), *Downcast Eyes*, Berkeley: University of California Press.

Kahn, D. (1999), *Noise Water Meat: A history of Sound in the Arts*, Cambridge MA: MIT Press.

Kittler, F. A. (1999), *Gramophone, Film, Typewriter*, Stanford: Stanford University Press.

Latour, B. (1990), *Drawing Things Together*, Lynch. M. and Woolgar, S. *Representation in Scientific Practice*, Cambridge MA: MIT Press, pp. 19–68.

—— (1993), *We Have Never Been Modern*, Harlow: Pearson.

Lawlor, R. (1982), *Sacred Geometry*, London: Thames & Hudson.

Levin, D. M. (1985), *The Body's Recollection of Being: Phenomenological Psychology and the Deconstruction of Nihilism*, London: Routledge & Kegan Paul.

—— (1988), *The Opening of Vision*, London: Routledge.

—— (1989), *The Listening Self: Personal Growth, Social Change and the Closure of Metaphysics*, London: Routledge.

Lord, A. B. (1960, 2000), *The Singer of Tales*, Cambridge MA: Cambridge University Press.

MacKenzie, A. (2002), *Transduction: Bodies and Machines at Speed*, London: Continuum.

Maffesoli, M. (1996), *The Time of the Tribes: The Decline of Individualism in Mass Society*, London: Sage.

Merleau-Ponty, M. (1962), *The Phenomenology of Perception*, London: Routledge & Kegan Paul.

Mona and Davis, Erik (1999), *Roots and Wires: Polyrhythmic Cyberspace and the Black Electronic* http://www.levity.com/figment/cybercont.html.

Moore, A. (2003), 'Membranes in Space and the Transmitting Ear', *Cybersonica '03*, London: Cybersalon, pp. 5–9.

Ree, J. (1999), *I see a Voice: A Philosophical History of Language, Deafness and the Senses*, London: HarperCollins.

Romanyshyn, R. D. (1989), *Technology as Symptom and Dream*, London: Routledge.

Rorty, R. (1979), *Philosophy and the Mirror of Nature*, New Jersey: Princeton University Press.

Rotman, B. (1993), *Ad Infinitum: the Ghost in Turing's Machine – Taking God Out of Mathematics and Putting the Body Back In*, Standford: Stanford University Press.

—— (2002), 'The Alphabetic Body', *Parallax*, 8(1): 92–104.

Ryman, Cheryl (1984), 'Kumina – Stability and Change', *The African Caribbean Institute of Jamaica Research Review*, 1, 81–128.

Salewicz, C. and Boot, A. (2001), *Reggae Explosion: The Story of Jamaican Music*, London Virgin Publishing.

Scarry, E. (1985), *The Body in Pain: the Making and Unmaking of the World*, Oxford: Oxford University Press.

Schafer, R. M. (1977), *The Tuning of the World*, New York Alfred A. Knopf.

Sedgwick, E. K. and Frank, A. (1995), *Shame and its Sisters: a Silvan Tomkins Reader*, Durham: Duke University Press.

Serres, Michel (1982), *The Parasite*, Baltimore: John Hopkins University Press.

Soesman, Albert (1990), *Our Twelve Senses*, Stroud: Hawthorne Press.

Somé, M. P. (1994), *Of Water and the Spirit: Ritual, Magic and initiation in the life of an African Shaman*, New York: Penguin Arkana.

Stoller, P. (1989), *The Taste of Ethnographic Things: the Senses in Anthropology*, Philadelphia PA: University of Pennsylvania Press.

Stolzoff, N. C. (2000), *Wake the Town and Tell the People*, Durham: Duke University Press.

Taussig, M. (1993), *Mimesis and Alterity: A Particular History of the Senses*, London: Routledge.

Turner, V. (1974), *Dramas, Fields and Metaphors*, Ithaca: Cornell University Press.

White, G. (1984), 'The Development of Jamaican Popular Music pt 2', *The African Caribbean Institute of Jamaica Research Review* 1, 47–80.

Wiener, N. (1950), *The Human Use of Human Beings*, New York: Anchor.

Wilden, A. (1972), *System and Structure: Essays in Communication and Exchange*, London: Tavistock Anthony.

Williams D.C . (1955), 'Acoustic Space', *Explorations*, (February): 15–20.

Wilson, E. A. (1998), *Neural Geographies: Feminism and the Microstructure of Cognition*, London: Routledge.

Zimmerman, M. E. (1990), *Heidegger's Confrontation with Modernity: Technology, Politics, Art*, Bloomington: Indian University Press.

28

Resistance

Richard Sennett

The Garden of Eden in which a child prodigy dwells is indeed the sheer
ease of making sound. Exit from that musical Garden began for me when
I began to perform in public. (Richard Sennett on losing his nerve – (and
finding it again – with the help of Agatha Christie)

For musicians, the sense of touch defines our physical experience of
art: lips applied to reed, fingers pushing down keys or strings. It might
seem that the more easily we touch, the better we play, but facility is
only half the story. A pianist or a violinist must constantly explore
resistance, either in the instrument or in the musician's own body.

Like every cellist, I learned about touch through mastering movements like vibrato. Vibrato is the rocking motion of the left hand on a
string that colours a note around its precise pitch; waves of sound spread
out in vibrato like ripples from a pool into which one has thrown a
stone. Vibrato does not start with the contact of the fingertip and the
string; it begins further back at the elbow, the impulse to rock starting
from that anchor, passing through the forearm into the palm of the
hand and then through the finger.

There are many kinds of vibratos, some slow and liquid that colour
long notes, some that last no more than an instant. These rocking
movements of the left hand are also like fingerprints, giving every cellist
his or her own distinctive sound. Janos Starker's vibrato is focused, the
colouring of his notes is light, whereas Jacqueline du Pre often has a
wide, wild vibrato. But even for her, vibrato is the result of discipline.

Freedom to rock requires that a cellist first master the capacity to play
perfectly in tune. If a young cellist fails in that mastery, every time he

or she vibrates the note will sound sour, accentuating the inaccuracy of pitch. At an advanced stage of our training, we use vibrato to gain entry to the contemporary world of semitones, the notes that lie between the normal divisions of the chromatic scale. But even playing the works of Boulez or Elliott Carter, we must still aim at a precise tonal centre. There are acoustical reasons for this distinction between the sour and the vibrant, related to the overtones set going by a string. Still, the need for mastery of pitch in order to vibrate well tells a elementary truth: freedom depends on control, whereas purely impulsive expression produces just mess – a piece of folk wisdom as true of the hand as of the heart.

When I began studying the cello at the age of eight, vibrato came easily to me, in part because I was blessed with a sense of perfect pitch. The Garden of Eden in which a child prodigy dwells is indeed the sheer ease of making sound. Exit from that musical Garden began for me when I began to perform in public.

I have yet to meet the musician who walks on stage with the same insouciance he or she might feel in walking to the bank or in practising in private – although it has been said of the violinist Fritz Kreisler that he barely noticed that he played in front of thousands of people. Usually stage fright follows the outlines of a simple story.

Chapter one begins at the moment of anticipation: faced with performing, adrenaline flows, and the stomach tightens, which is why few musicians dare eat before performing. Chapter two is the withdrawal (before the event) into a concentrated silence – again, a 'natural' like Arthur Rubinstein often entertained in his dressing room before a performance, but most musicians can barely manage to cope with the presence of their partners. Chapter three opens when we walk on stage, and is hard to describe; it's like a trance in which we become hyper-alert.

In this trance our bodies can betray us, and no more so than in the work of vibrato. The vibrating forearm suddenly promises to release the tensions built up in chapters one and two, but it can be a false promise. Energy can flow away from the elbow; often the wrist begins to flex, further cutting off the secure transmission of energy from elbow to finger. The result of the short circuit is that the weakened hand may then begin pushing too hard on the string in order to recover strength; the fingers may lock on to the fingerboard beneath the string; movement then will become jerky rather than fluid. These concrete events are what may make a musician sound 'nervous' to an audience, even when the cellist is in the midst of performing technical feats.

Nerves have cost us the loss of coherent vibrating touch, and so the problem may seem simply a matter of learning to relax. At least it seemed so to me, aged thirteen and fourteen, when I suddenly lost control of my vibrato in concerts. By fifteen, I had discovered one simple way to trick my nerves: reading non-stop during the hours before concerts; the murder mysteries of Agatha Christie were particularly calming, and usually, but not always, took me out of myself. Once I'd found a way to deal with my own stage fright, I became more attuned to other dimensions of resistance, as part of the expressive process.

From its origins, the cello was not a perfect machine. For reasons we still don't fully understand, the cellos made by late seventeenth-century makers have remained the greatest examples of the luthier's art, but even these are physically imperfect in sounding the E and F notes on the G string; though powerful instruments, they have a tendency to fracture these two tones into a kind of bleating noise like a sheep singing. To vibrate under these conditions risks an even worse sound. Yet when the cellist faces the instrument's limitations on the G-string, carrying on despite the bleating sound, the result can be an immense physical release and feeling of freedom.

When I once performed the Schubert Cello Quintet with Jacqueline du Pre – she was barely adolescent at the time – she was gripped by a crisis of nerves until the famous moment in the first movement when the second cello becomes mired in this danger zone. Her F bleated for a fraction of a second, but then she conquered it; she began making a richly vibrant, generous sound; her body relaxed.

In the performing trance, physical resistance often heightens the musician's awareness of the music itself. For instance, in the Adagio of Beethoven's Cello Sonata Op. 102, No. 1, the cellist is called to play octaves closest to the pegbox; it's a perilous procedure because the cut of the fingerboard does not easily accommodate the stretched hand pushing down two strings at once. To vibrate the strings under these conditions is a challenge, but rising to that challenge often gives the octaves the urgency the score requires, while simultaneously calming down the nervous player.

What I'm describing is not a Romantic struggle with wood and gut impeding the soul – rather an experience of which musicians themselves are mostly unconscious. At best, we use the word 'focus' to describe it: loss of focus equals loss of touch. The sense of control we have on stage is nothing like the freedom of the rehearsal studio, no return to the garden where we play unselfconsciously without worrying about mistakes. Now hundreds of thousands of people are listening. Indeed, making a mistake on stage can be a signal to us to pay more bodily attention. There is a kind of dialogue between courting danger and feeling physically free which, on stage, keeps us focused.

By the time I'd entered the conservatory, I'd learned one further and larger thing about what happens when resistance is not faced squarely. If the whole arm ceases to serve the cellist – breaking secure contact between flesh, string and wood – the cellist's perceptions of her or himself performing can split in two. In one domain there is the ideal of what the music should sound like; in the other, awareness of the music as it actually sounds, sounds which are insufficient, and from which the musician withdraws. This is just what Du Pre remarked to me a few years after our performance of the Schubert quintet – she had heard two musics that evening, one in her head where everything is beautiful and just right, the other in her ears, neither right nor beautiful. For her, the divide did not last long; in fact it can only be a matter of a few moments in which the artist is aware the music doesn't sound as it should; then this divide disappears as the body takes over, the artist's feeling that it should sound differently fades away, and he or she again converts to the immediate sound.

Romanticism provided a misleading vocabulary for this divide; musical notations like 'innerlich' or 'geistlich' ('inwardly' or 'with soulful feeling') suggest the musician's soul will at a particularly expressive moment withdraw to higher realm than the physical. The musician's fingers remain, unfortunately, on strings. It's not intentions, desires and longings that matter on stage; only the concrete and objective counts, because only sound sounds. I don't know if there's a German word like *outerlichkeit* – 'outwardness' but there should be. Paradoxically, it's just the physical fusion between wood, strings and body which courts danger, which is alive to resistance in performing, that rouses listeners to feel a musician to be 'in' the music, in contrast to the performer who seems disconnected, although he may have beautiful dreams.

When we are 'in touch', as American slang puts it, we do not dwell in the garden, conflict and danger-free. But no more is the performing stage a scene of exile; in the heightened trance-like state in which performing occurs, danger and being in touch become expressively inseparable. The resistance of physical objects and their sounds can challenge the body yet, in the paradox I've described, relax it as well, as in a successful vibrato. When performing well, every musician feels the poet Wallace Stevens' famous declaration, 'no truth but in things'.

Afterword

The Indefensible Ear
A History

Hillel Schwartz

Underlying the litany of twentieth-century anti-noise polemics is the claim that human hearing is constant, involuntary, and nearly impossible to shut off. That is, the ordinary unassisted ear takes in all sounds within its individual range, whether we are awake, drowsing, or 'sound' asleep, and whether we want to hear them, are indifferent to them, or make every effort to ignore them.

In consequence (so runs the underlying claim), the ear is a particularly vulnerable organ of perception: always in operation, unreflectively accumulative, and naively open to even the most harmful of loud, high, or concussive sounds. What's worse, as anti-noise polemicists repeat and repeat and repeat, the ear lacks the most rudimentary of defences: it has no equivalent to the eyelids that protect vision; the lips and tongue that protect taste; the nasal hairs and sneezes that protect smell; and the general mobility that protects touch and proprioception.

If this were all, the polemic would hardly be modern. Most of this claim could have been, and was, made centuries earlier, with the possible exception of early twentieth-century studies showing the immediate and residual impact of night noises upon those apparently asleep. There was, however, another, new, and seemingly contradictory element to the underlying claim of the litany: that the human ear is an active agent in its own right, not simply a well-tempered receiver. For human hearing to be constant, involuntary, *and* active, in a twenty-four-hour-day world devoted at once to excess and to streamlining, this was the special jeopardy of the modern ear.

Manic and obsessive, the ear bravely, persistently, foolishly exposes itself and its cilia to fatigue, danger, discomfort, and destruction. From such a perspective, the ear is our true bodily *avant garde*, in all senses of the term – military, psychological, cultural. Militarily, the ear is our sentinel, armed only with wax, doing what it must to warn us of incoming fire and looming disaster, and doing this often better and always more continually than the eye. Psychologically, in pairs, the ears help us determine and change direction while maintaining our balance, doing what it must to keep us focused in the midst of flux. Culturally, the ear is what Cubists might have called a *collagiste*, what Dadaists might have called a collector of fragments, doing what it must to welcome simultaneous caterwauling universes of sound. And like every *avant garde*, the ear must suffer for its causes. Taken altogether, this modern understanding of human hearing derives from a complex convergence of sources and forces. It derives from a late nineteenth-century neurophysiological reassessment of the ear itself as no mere passive receptacle but as a transducer and amplifier, so that the ear comes to situate itself within a crowd of assertive verbs rather than among a series of architectonic nouns. Earlier, it was the aural labyrinth that had most intrigued and drawn to itself metaphor and myth, culminating in the labyrinthine analogies of Nietzsche, but by the twentieth century it was the energetic, transitive aspect of the ear, rather than the sheerly spatial, that would attract such physio-philosophical analogies as 'accommodation,' 'recruitment,' and 'threshold shift'.

Hearing, which had previously been considered a reactive physiological function, was thus shifted much closer to, and increasingly conflated with, the mental faculty of listening. Once neurologists had found the ear to be an electrochemical transducer and an electrical amplifier, the ear had even more in common with the brain, itself newly discovered to be a hotbed of electrochemical interactions. Listening, which had been supposed to be selective and wilful, had long been contrasted with hearing, which was supposed to be indiscriminate and automatic; but turn-of-the-century studies of hypnotism, catatonia, coma, and hysterical deafness in psychiatric clinics, along with other studies of forms of attention and advertising, weakened the polarity of these traditional opposites. Listening itself might well be indiscriminate and automatic, as for example with telegraph and telephone operators, and hearing might well be specific and voluntary, as with hypnotic commands, only some of which would be 'heard' and acted upon (the best hypnotist cannot command a person to commit suicide).

So the ear, in its relentless hearing, was also a listener, therefore complicit in such dubious acts as 'overhearing', which amidst crowded streets and apartment buildings was perhaps as involuntary as it was inevitable.

The model of the telephone contributed substantially, at least in the early days, to the conflation of hearing and listening, overhearing and 'listening in'. Imputing an extraordinary and dramatic effectiveness to telephone conversations, people equated being heard with being listened to; the one followed from the other more regularly and 'naturally' over the telephone than in ordinary face-to-face conversation. I suspect that this was due as much to the social fact of overhearing as to any technological mystique. On early telephones, and to this day among generations born before 1930, people tended to raise their voices when they spoke, and to shout if a connection was 'long-distance'. For at least fifty years, the telephone was a far more insistent medium of social discourse than it is now (or maybe not, given the loud and nearly Pavlovian responsiveness of people carrying cell phones). Since one was likely to be overheard by neighbours, family, and (at public phone booths, or on cell phones) by strangers, you had to mean what you said and you presumed that what the other party heard was what you, loudly, meant.

Our modern understanding of human hearing derives concomitantly from a popular technological reassessment of the ear itself as a sensitive instrument, by analogy less with the horns of gramophones or radio antennae than with recording devices that register sounds in the first place – the ear as analogous not with the stationary horn or wire but with the moving needle, the microphone/telephone pick-up, the actively straining medium.

I use that word 'medium' intentionally, because the modern understanding of human hearing also derives from the mid-to-late nineteenth-century rush to hear voices from Beyond, which began first in upper New York State as a rapping and tapping and soon was transported by mentalist magicians, fudging photographers, and spiritualist mediums into a symphony of knockings, whispers, ethereal voices, and distant echoes overheard in parlours and theatres in North and South America, Europe and Australia. The ear was such a 'sensitive', another word for medium, that it could reach where legs might tremble and eyes fail, to the Other Side, across death and into the world of the timeless. Listening, in this melodramatic and spiritual scenario, was to be intent, intimate, and intrepid, as it was surely also for the builders of the first crystal radio sets who strained to hear signals through the crackling ether and the constant, almost impermeable static. Some of these amateur radio operators admitted to enjoying the static, as if the end result of listening were hearing.

So there also appeared a practical medical reassessment of the ear, with campaigns mounted of a sudden at the century's end against ear-pulling and ear-tugging, traditional practices of irate grammar-school teachers, exasperated nannies, bored children, and doting aunts and uncles. As the first city-wide and nation-wide hearing tests were instituted, with admittedly subjective testing devices such as the ticking of pocket watches, public health advocates began to insist that even the outer ears, the auricles, of children not be treated as inert pieces of flesh conveniently exposed to a pinch or the rap of a pointer, lest deafness result.

In fashion, too, the ear was reassessed and given a more active, exuberant role, at first in sustaining longer heavier ear-rings. During the 1920s, with the bobbed haircuts and smaller hats for women and a steep decline in numbers of fully bearded men, the adult ear was exposed in public, pricked up for the excitements of jazz and the wind from auto rallies. 'Big ears', so-called by certain cosmetic companies and that new species of sculptor, the cosmetic surgeon, became a public embarrassment now that they were so visible, but they also became an icon for the involuntary rudeness of overhearing, which was increasingly a problem in a world of small cheap apartments built without the insulation customary a century or more before – apartments gradually being filled with modern equipment whose sounds readily penetrated the thinner floors and walls: pianos, flush toilets, radios, vacuum cleaners. The more the ear became physically exposed, the more it seemed to intrude upon, and violate, intimacies.

In tandem, an anatomical reassessment of the ear was made as the inner ear began to reveal its secrets. Of all organs considered the most inaccessible, the inner ear was so tightly woven into the brain and skull, and so acutely sensitive to pain, that to explore it while in lively process was all but impossible, and would remain so, really, until improvements in imaging techniques during the 1970s. Nonetheless, a series of risky oto-surgical techniques had been developed in Europe at the end of the previous century, which revealed some of the extraordinary qualities of the cilia and the cochlea. The ecology of the inner ear was not only electrically dynamic but fluidly dynamic, at just the time when physicists and mathematicians were resuming their interest in the complex motion of fluids in general and waves in particular.

The modern understanding of human hearing derives, hence and in addition, from Rayleigh's codification of the science of acoustics and the subsequent popular scientific lectures on acoustics, which made sound waves appear at once very elusive and very penetrating in that they were found to travel easily around corners and through crevices, most swiftly along the metal and liquid conduits increasingly employed in modern construction. *And* their vibrations could produce intriguing patterns, shift flames. Acoustics in popular demonstration showed itself to be not merely a science of reception but of inception and deception; the ear, by direct association, was far more than a troublesome receptacle.

Troublesome, I say, because the incidence of earaches in the nineteenth century was high. According to my reading in private diaries, letters, household health manuals, and outpatient clinic treatment records, I would guess that very few children and few adults escaped from a series of earaches. If we count illnesses called 'catarrh', which usually involved earache, I would guess that earache was as common in the eighteenth and nineteenth centuries as what we today call the common cold, and it was catered to by just as many concoctions to make it go away.

So a medical reassessment of the ear, of hearing and of deafness, was in order: the earache was re-centred upon the ear. Instead of being seen as a symptom of a larger constitutional illness, or as a side-effect of other medication or disease, it was seen as a problem related to the health of the ear itself. It would, however, take some time for the medical reassessment to lead to significantly better aural health or ear care, since one of the primary drugs used to treat a whole spasm of illnesses in the eighteenth and nineteenth centuries, quinine, was ototoxic – that is, the pharmaceutical most prescribed by physicians or sold by medicine men for a wide variety of aches and pains was responsible, in large or frequent doses, for severe organic injury to the ear and to hearing.

The centrality of hearing itself was being reassessed at the turn of the twentieth century. We are told by cultural critics and historians (except Martin Jay) that modernity has been marked by a supreme victory of the visual over the aural in the hierarchy of the senses, but to people between 1870 and the First World War, the most amazing new elements in modern society were keenly aural in their impact and influence: the player piano, the gramophone, the telephone, the radio, the subway train, the elevated train, and, during the Great War, the loudspeaker and high-powered, extremely loud artillery. Nor should I neglect the drill press and electrical lathes that made possible all the other clacking, clicking, and crackling noises from mass-produced machines rather suddenly pervading the home, the office, and the public thoroughfare: washing machines and vacuum cleaners, typewriters and office printing machines, automobiles and motorcycles. In this 'Age of Noise', as people began to call it, hearing was crucial in order to make one's way in the world and to keep from being run over when crossing the street or the train tracks. Or, politically, to keep clear of tyranny. 'We live now in the noisiest age ever known', wrote a contributor to the *London Times* in 1938. 'This isle, like Caliban's, is full of noises . . . There are voices, too . . . bull-like voices that roar coarse insults and brutal hatred; and there are rasping voices that creak our showy defiance and grandiose half-truths . . . noises that tell of huge and hideous material destruction.'

Hearing had to be active and almost preternaturally attentive; and yet, simultaneously, it was all the more in jeopardy from the higher, louder, more ubiquitous, and more continuously abrasive sounds of the urban and sometimes the suburban environment (with lawn mowers, for example, and young people winding ragtime pieces through their pianolas). Addressing the Musicians' Club of London in 1937, a church organist observed that 'Life in a big city has become one long pandemonium . . . nowadays, no one can be sure of quiet at any hour of the day or night.' Furthermore, 'No greater disservice was ever done to music than by allowing it to be tapped like electricity, gas, and water.'

In this context, the modern understanding of human hearing also derives from at least a century of agreement in the industrial West that noise is an inescapable element of modernity, linked not only to energetic industry, large-scale manufacturing, aggressive commerce and marketing but also and inevitably linked to the expansion of urban complexes, *horizontally* out to suburbs and the countryside via highway, railroads, flight paths, radio, television, and power lines, *vertically* below ground in the form of subways, above ground in the form of increasingly layered streets and overpasses, larger and taller apartment and business buildings, more resonant plumbing, and the louder, more piercing, more collectively perpetual warning signals requisite to horizontal expansion and vertical living: firemen's bells and trumpets, sirens, whistles, automobile horns, alarm clocks, buzzers, and electric bells. So, wrote the arch-conservative English music critic Constant Lambert in a 1930s book on modern music, 'The modern composer who uses in his score 16 pianos, an electric buzzer, an aeroplane propeller, and a pneumatic drill' excites no wonderment, for 'he is providing little more than an average background to a telephone conversation in a public call-office.'

Inversely related were new social scientific postulates connecting loud sounds, constant sound, and designated 'noise' directly to mental, emotional, and physical fatigue, all of which seemed to be growing toward an epidemic of neurasthenia or nervous exhaustion, beginning among 'brain-workers,' housewives, artists, and other sensitive souls, but spreading at length to young working men and women. A large literature arose during the *fin de siècle* condemning fatigue as an economic expense, indicating inefficiency or lost hours of work; explaining fatigue as a cultural expense, indicating psychological or intellectual handicap; and looking to levels of fatigue as an index to social or cultural or racial health, assessed via rates of insanity, child abandonment, divorce, and suicide.

Given the *fin de siècle* fears of exhaustion, of the human motor running down and the environment itself being depleted of sources of energy, our modern understanding of human hearing derives finally from a fear of being overwhelmed and a deep anxiety about being once again frustrated. Being overwhelmed – by so many, so loud, and such nerve-wracking noises that the physical system would break down, with the ear as the very epitome of this breakdown, since it was least protected and was charged with being most constantly attentive to ever-more signals, advertisements, warnings, news, and rumours. Being frustrated: at every attempt to reduce the 'din', in parallel (sometimes explicitly drawn) with a century of public action and recurrent frustration with attempts to reduce the smoke and dust in the air of large cities and industrial towns, attempts at first successful but always eventually undone by the growth of population, encouragement of heavy industry, increasing volumes and speed of traffic. It was with this sense of frustration that Eldon Moore, author of *Heredity – Mainly Human*, suggested in 1937 an active telephone campaign against noisemakers – a campaign of calling and then hanging up, day and night, to give noisemakers a bit of their own medicine.

In sum, the world seemed to be more encumbered with sound than ever before, so that the ear had to do active duty as bodyguard, herald, explorer, and confidant. But because it was on constant guard duty, because it was charged with announcing the arrival of the most unpleasant along with the most welcome sounds, because it had to be attentive to new sounds while cognisant of the old, and because it had to be as alert to a whisper or an infant's whimper as to an incoming shell or a speeding motorcycle, the modern ear was perpetually in danger of being overtaxed.

Tinnitus was taken as one sign of this overtaxing. It is significant that, although we still have found no reliable general remedy for noise-in-the-ear, the twentieth century has posed the question of tinnitus in terms of an overactive or overtaxed ear, while earlier approaches had mostly to do with structural defects, impacted cerumen or wax, and catarrh. Although ancient, noise-in-the-ear was a malady newly and closely associated with a modern world in which each personal engagement was a sonic engagement and in which noise itself, however idiosyncratically defined, was privately as well as publicly inescapable.

Tinnitus was just one among many evidences that the ear was in jeopardy from its own mission, because its mission was, in the modern world, just about impossible. Relentless and indiscriminate, without natural defences against natural or unnatural enemies, in a modern world that shrieked each stage of progress, the ear was almost an atavism – evolutionarily older than the eye and designed to be effective in prediluvian soundscapes where few sounds were invasive and only one (a nearby crack of thunder) physically destructive of cilia. To compensate for the dangers of the industrial soundscape, the ear had become increasingly active, but it was active *and* innocent, outgoing *and* naive.

This, of course, rendered the ear in desperate need of protection, especially since there was – and so far, still is – no reliable corrective to severe deafness.

The more common and constant the claim that the ear is, of all organs of perception, the most indefensible, the more strident should be the demand for means of protection, yes? Especially after the First World War, with the social consciousness of something called 'shell-shock', and with major refinements in radio and public address systems. These phenomena all underscored the physical, psychic, and emotional power of amplified sound. Yet, although the same technology that perpetually assaulted, overwhelmed, and injured ears seemed also to promise a new type of hearing aid that would more adequately amplify sounds for ears already injured, hearing aids, like ear plugs, were rather last resorts than first lines of defence.

True, Science had stepped in:

- to reduce electrical interference and 'static';
- to redesign auditoriums and, soon, movie theatres for 'talkies';
- to reconfigure automobile mufflers;
- to retool microphones and telephones for better reception/broadcast;
- to rethink and revamp the measurement of the loudness of individual sounds and the acuity of individual ears.

Paradoxically, such scientific ventures only further emphasized the vulnerability of the ear itself. If so much expertise was needed to re-engineer the modern world to protect the ancient ear, then just think how essentially indefensible must be that lonely, exposed ear itself.

As twentieth-century physiology showed the ear to harbour cilia thinner and more sensitive than the most delicate of electrical wires, so audiometry would show the normal human ear to have markedly different sensitivities at different frequencies and therefore to be especially susceptible to harm according not only to volume or loudness but to the wave quality of the sound itself.

Scientists also inadvertently put ears into new jeopardy, in part because the devices designed to reduce noise so improved clarity that sounds appeared subjectively to be louder than ever; in part because the same devices could be adapted to make more powerful sounds; and in part because the devices were installed in more places and situations than ever before, expanding the horizon or increasing the density of the soundscape with, for example, loudspeaker trucks and radio advertising on the street; broadcasts from low-flying commercial airplanes; recorded music in factories and shops, and stronger sirens on more kinds of emergency vehicles.

Always on the alert and therefore always feeding sounds to the brain, the indefensible ear was at once subject and vehicle for modern advertising and political propaganda, which – with radio and talkies – were as much and as effectively aural as visual. The indefensible ear was at once subject and vehicle for opinion polls, whose subjects were interviewed aurally and most often over the telephone. The indefensible ear was at once subject and vehicle for new forms of warfare, especially where silence was of great moment, as with submarines, or where noise was a countermeasure, as with radio communications, or where noise itself was a weapon, as with Stuka divebombing.

In all of this, the ear plug or ear defender had the most minor of roles. To this day neither ear plugs nor hearing aids are used regularly enough to satisfy any specialist in occupational and industrial injuries or aging (85 per cent of older Americans who could benefit from a hearing aid don't use one, according to the most recent statistics.). One would think that, given a widely and deeply evolved sense of the ear as indefensible, people would instantly reach for ear plugs (like T. Hawksley's 1937 Antiphones or Sound Killers, made of clay and fibre, which promised to make life in a flat bearable, 'piano practice, wireless, barking dogs and thunderstorms' all 'unheard') as soon as they approached a high-volume or noisy environment, and they would work furiously to make the environment itself quieter.

Why don't they? What? Why don't they? What did you say? I said, why don't they? Wide open, say? No: Why don't they? Why don't people everywhere work relentlessly and successfully to defend the defenceless ear?

I shall suggest ten answers to this question, starting back around 1900 and working my way up to the present.

1. The Problem of the Ear in Space

Unlike the liver and spleen in France, kidneys and throat in England, colon and skin in Germany, or blood and stomach in the United States, the ear has not been at the centre of popular physiology in the modern West. It has been perceived instead as a relatively isolated and specialist organ, a distant appendage whose debilities do not immediately or intrinsically affect the rest of the psycho-physical system, except perhaps for those curiously misapprehended Eustachian tubes. Although earache ranks high in terms of pain both acute and chronic, rarely is it associated with external acoustic aggravation and indeed is rarely treated with reference to external noise or loud sound. Whatever protection the ear merits, either from internal or external assault or blockage, remains near the bottom of the list of priorities.

2. The Problem of the Ear in Relative Time

Hearing loss is usually gradual and has not been easily attributable to a single punctual event or causal situation, other than gunshot, sequelae to ototoxic diseases such as scarlet fever, and side-effects of such ototoxic drugs as quinine or, later, streptomycin. The need to defend the ear has therefore been vitiated, other than near artillery during warfare and in certain industries such as boilermaking, by the slowness with which deafness appears.

3. The Problem of the Ear in Absolute Time

Given that the loss of hearing has also been accepted as a natural consequence of growing old, which consequence has been statistically demonstrated for almost all societies regardless of their state of economic development or urbanization, the defencelessness of the ear loses its individual emotional edge when confounded with the panhuman remorselessness of gradual hearing loss through to old age.

It would seem pointless, wouldn't it, to defend an ear against the inevitable?

4. The Problem of the Ear in Economic Time

Given that hearing loss is gradual, natural, and not often attributable to a specific site or event, compensation for hearing loss has been blocked not only by thorny problems of assigning blame but by equally thorny problems of determining the value of hearing to the accomplishment of all jobs other than those requiring headsets or rapid group conversation. Generally, hearing loss and total deafness have been undervalued in workmen's compensation schemes as compared to partial or total blindness or loss of a limb. And at the lower end of the economic spectrum, where we find the workers in some of the dirtiest and noisiest trades and industries, the workforce is often so multilingual that visual cues are used far more than aural cues, hence the value of good hearing is never as high as good sight, muscular strength, kinaesthetic agility. So the inclination to defend the ear is weak, and pressure to defend the ear comes least from those most affected by aural assault.

5. The Problem of the Ear in Generational Time

Each generation believes that the sounds beloved of the next generation are too loud, raucous, dissonant or disuptive to qualify as music. This pattern of generational argument goes back to at least the 1580s in the West, but has been aggravated since the nineteenth century with the proliferation of new, larger or louder instruments, played in larger and louder contexts, and with the twentieth century electrical amplification of these sounds through radio and gramophone loudspeakers and public address systems. The generational argument is conducted on several fronts: the younger generation is disordering settled society with its so-called music; the younger generation is giving way to barbarous impulses that make all future civilization unlikely; the younger generation is destroying the hearing of those in their presence; the younger generation is destroying its own hearing. And this argument is made not only vis-à-vis music but vis-à-vis the volume, tone, and pitch of daily speech, of public oratory, of assemblies, of advertisement. One would think that amidst this argument, the old would come to the defence of the ear against the onslaughts of the young, and so they do, but it turns out that they refuse to put the music or speech patterns of the young in the context of the noisy urban, industrial, or well-trafficked society they themselves created for the young, and instead they make the question of noise and the defence of the ear a question of the public sphere and the defence of their own right to be there, so that to don ear plugs or 'ear defenders', as they were called in the Second World War, would be a sign that they had been forced to retreat into a private realm of quiet and had given over the public sphere to the 'noisemakers'.

6. The Problem of the Ear in the Mind

Since hearing loss is usually gradual, and since in this century we have increasingly conflated hearing with listening, much of the early symptomology of hearing loss has typically been disregarded as simple fatigue, inattentiveness, environmental interruption, or it has been welcomed as an inobtrusive way to escape the incessant volume, variety, and vastness of sounds in modern life. Why defend the ear when a little bit of deafness goes a long way?

7. The Problem of the Ear in the World

At the tail end of industrial revolution, in the throes of late capitalism, and now with multinational corporate takeovers and mergers, defenselessness evokes neither compassion nor compensation. Hearing loss is a minor event, hard to configure into a major social or political dilemma of the same order as massive dislocations of populations due to war, genocide, famine, climate change, and enormous pressures to migrate out of poverty toward power. Nor does hearing loss, even at its most general and acute, disturb the polity in the same way, say, as AIDS, tuberculosis, alcoholism, or cancer. Those four entities, by the by, can be attacked aggressively because we have identified at least some of their causal agents, whereas the agents of hearing loss are either distressingly diffuse or interwoven with processes of industrial development and demographic mobility.

8. The Problem of the Ear out of this World

Perhaps, facing cybernetic transformation, it doesn't really matter if the ear suffers. Soon we will have prostheses for everything, jacks that screw directly into the brain, bypassing the awkward mechanics of a merely electrochemical system of hearing bound to an atavistic organ called the ear. The ear may be defenceless precisely because it is scheduled by Darwinian steps to vanish, as it certainly does in popular depictions of aliens and super-humans in books, comic strips, and movies.

9. The Problem of the Ear Unwritten

The new universal written language being generated by Internet Web site addresses and instructions is a language whose punctuation refers neither to the taking of breaths nor to the reestablishment of an aural pattern of emphasis. It is rather a language with a syntax and punctuation entirely visual. True, the audio side of computers is being perfected so that music can travel as easily as images over digital pathways, but most of the audio itself is filled with spoken language or lyrics that rely rather on repetition and refrain than on acute hearing to be understood, and most of what is ostensibly meant to be understood is, as this sentence is, a run-on, a mad-dashing-hatter of words often in a potpourri of languages or dialects. The ear that is trained to hear pauses and silence is being written and driven out of this new language, which is at once highly syllabified and highly meshed. Ears already encumbered with some degrees of hearing loss, in fact may hear the world in that foggy way that the new universally fogged language is making popular. Defend the ear from what?

10. The Problem of the Ear Refuted

Deaf communities, resurgent, have staked a claim to gestural languages as integral to a true and admirable culture of the deaf. Their gestural languages are rich, expressive, internally coherent, inventive, and flexible. I applaud them, and I deplore the imperial move in the 1880s by teachers of the deaf to stop the teaching of 'sign language'. But today, in connection with the visual orientation of semiotics and a postmodern literature nearly impossible to read aloud but often a delight to the eye, the exaltation of gestural languages further contributes to a profound disregard for the defenceless ear. After all, we can communicate quite successfully with each other and with chimpanzees through gesture.

What to Do, What to Do?

I have two serious proposals.

My first proposal: if, as I have been suggesting, the indefensible ear has drawn to it neither the general sympathy nor the genuine political and cultural activism it deserves, we might reconsider our strategies in terms of what does drive people to sympathize and act.

Earthquakes. Earthquakes do drive people to act, not because of what people hear, which can be enormously loud, but because of what we feel. It is the vibrations that move us.

Well, then, in order to succeed at the anti-noise business in defence of the indefensible ear, we should focus on 'bad vibrations'. Anti-noise advocates, as well as advocates for a rich but benign soundscape, should call attention to the threats of acoustic vibration rather than the threats of particular volumes or pitches of sound. The most successful anti-noise campaigns of this century were campaigns that drew upon 'bad vibrations' – the campaign at the turn of the last century in Europe, North America, and eventually South America and the Middle East, against the ringing of church bells every day at all hours day and night, and the campaign in the United States and Canada in 1969–71 against overland flights by Supersonic Transport planes (like the Concorde). In the first instance, church bells were attacked not only as audible interruptions of the sleep of hospital patients and home-bound invalids, but also as threats to the architectural integrity of neighbouring houses and businesses, because many of them rang at low, rumbling registers. Most church bells have now been restricted in most parts of the world to some Sabbath ringing or, at most, to daytime peals. In the second case, it was the likelihood of sonic booms across the land rattling windows and bones and minds and shaking loose plaster and load-bearing beams that led not only to regulations barring Corcorde overflights but also to the abandonment of a Boeing Supersonic Transport project, which had already, by 1971, used up several billion dollars of government financing. In both cases, the success of the anti-noise campaign was due to the fact that it invoked danger to property and property values. In a cynical vein, I might say that the ear remained defenceless and without powerful spokespersons, but that property certainly had its defenders, and since sound AS vibration is in fact what seems to do most of the damage to the cilia in our ears, a near side-effect of a popular and bourgeois concern with property damage from vibrations would be the protection of those cilia.

My second proposal: stop talking about the ear as defenceless. This only involves us in technical disputes about the degree to which the ear accommodates or becomes safely accustomed to certain levels or qualities of sound, and these technical disputes will continue as we learn more about the neurobiology of the ear, which so far does seem to be a bit more resilient than anti-noise activists would acknowledge, and a bit less resilient than lawyers for industrial noise-polluters would argue. Instead, talk about the ear as an organ that fights back. Talk about the ear as an organ that, in response to threats either acoustic or vibratory, makes its complaints known. We have discovered recently, for example, that the ear, in addition to being a receiver and an amplifier, actually does broadcast sounds that, on occasion, others can hear. Waxing poetic, we might even say that the ear sings, but that its song can become shrill with earache, tinnitus, or buzzing confusion if mistreated. 'The Ear Strikes Back' might be the new motto of anti-noise groups, for if the ear does not audibly protest with the characteristic ringing of temporary threshold shift, it acts more ingeniously to isolate us from the world, to make us appear shy, slow, stupid, or unfeeling.

Slow gradual deafness may be at once the ear's remorse and the ear's revenge.

DID YOU HEAR ME?

Index

acoustemology, 226–7
acoustic, 49–50, 491
  ecology, 223
  engineering, 130
  see also music, sound, technology
Adorno, T., 6, 9–10, 358, 361–3, 372, 376, 387
Anderson, B., 267, 290
Annales School, 44
Aristotle, 35, 43, 465
Armstrong, G., 313
Armstrong, L., 391
Attali, J., 1, 29, 357, 456
audiotape, 85–6
auditory
  and aesthetic experience, 7–9
  imagination, 61–6
  scripts, 370–1
  space, 117–23 passim, 364–7
  vibrations, 196, 491
  see also music, senses, sound
Auge, M., 459
Auster, P., 339
automobiles, 183, 357–73 passim
  and noise, 178–9, 181
  and the city, 169, 178
  as acoustic chambers, 9
  singing in, 367–70
  traffic, 166–7

Babbage, C., 166
Back, L., 451
Bacon, F., 44, 48
Bale, J., 312
Barrie, J.M., 75
Barry, A., 304
Barthes, R., 11, 98–9, 305, 462
  see also music, performance
bass culture, 391
Battaglia, D., 291–3
Baudrillard, J., 89, 358
Beatles, The 407
bells, 38, 45, 128–9, 142, 145, 330
  church bells, 26–8, 167
  railroad bells, 142, 181
  village bells, 117–23
  see also sound
Bentham, J., 38, 53
Benjamin, W., 9, 103, 303, 306, 331, 471
Berendt, J.E., 2, 15
Bhabba, H., 268, 410, 412
Bijsterveld, K., 8
Billig, M., 402
black Atlantic, 385
black public sphere, 383
blindness, 311
Bloch, E., 381
Bloch, M., 324–5

Boulez, P., 85, 482
Bourdieu, P., 4
Braque, G., 459
Buchenwald, 405
Bull, M., 330, 348–9

Cage, J., 10, 72, 78, 81, 85–9
Canetti, E., 307
carnival, 422–4, 453
Carter, E., 482
Cartwright, L., 207
Chambers, I., 337
Chan, S., 12
Chanan, M., 95, 101–104
cinema, 8, 207
cities, 304–308
    centres, 337
    cosmopolitan, 390
    everyday rhythm of, 385
    football stadiums, 312–25 passim
    locality, 313
    Marseilles, 306
    musical itineraries, 338–9
    New York, 306–307
    Paris, 306
    pathways, 343–4
    sonic universe, 329–30
    walking, 305, 329–41, 344, 491–2
    see also noise
Classen, C., 42, 288
community, 312
    black, 383–8 passim
Collins, A., 392
colonization, 385
Coltrane, J., 416, 431
Corbin, A., 5, 45, 48, 117–23, 128
Crary, J., 198, 304, 346–58
cybernetics, 469

dance, 13, 249–52, 400, 469
database, 353–4

Davis, A., 430
De Certeau, M., 344–5, 348
deafness, 65–6, 491
    social, 304
deep listening, 3, 12
Deleuze, G., 331, 335
Dialectic of Enlightenment, 7
digital audio, 462
Dionysius of Syracuse, 28–9
drumming
    amongst the Ojibwa Native
        Americans, 249–50, 254
    bodhran drumming, 271–2
    electronic drumming, 271
    lambeg drumming in Belfast, 266,
        270
    see also sound, music
Durkheim, E., 456

Edison, T., 461
electronic broadcast media, 104
Elias, N., 91–2
Elliot, J., 51
Elliot, T.S., 45
Ellison, R., 10–11, 391
Ellul, J., 43
empiricism, 194
Enlightenment, 42–54 passim
evangelical missions, 224

fan cultures, 313–19
Febvre, L., 44
Feld, S., 3, 127, 267
film, 411
    Apocalypse Now, 10
    Being There, 42
    Orpheus, 461
    sound, 77
    time, 459
Finnigan, R., 107
football, 311–25
    The Lion's Roar, 322–3

Foucault, M., 5, 31, 191, 195, 206–207
Free Derry Wall, 265
Freud, S., 31–2
Frith, S., 428

Galileo, G., 51
Garfinkle, H., 3311
Geertz, C., 2
Geurts, K.L., 465
Gilman, S., 429
Gilroy, P., 12–13, 410, 413
Globe Theatre, 130–1
Gould, G., 10, 35
gramophone, 183, 391, 428, 489, 491
Grass, G., 25
Guattari, F., 81, 410
guitar, 381–2, 394

Hall, S., 410
Hardy, T., 105
Hebdige, D., 387
Hendrix, J., 382–3
home
    symbolic, 313, 325
    see also city, football, music, sound
Hornby, N., 466
Hosokawa, S., 331

identities
    Asian, 414–17
    Asian-British, 411
    black diaspora, 419
    Englishness, 398–9
    hybridity, 409–11
    Jewish, 406
Ihde, D., 226
Incredible String Band, 265
individualization, 183

industrialization
    sounds of, 143, 152
Isle of Wight Festival, 382

Jacobson, H., 358–9
James, C.L.R., 420, 424
Jay, M., 43, 361, 491
Jayes, J., 34
Joan of Ark, 34
Johnson, B., 130
Joyce, J., 138
jukebox, 14
Jung, C., 32

Kafka, F., 307
Kaluli, 224–38
    poetic cartographies, 227
Kandinsky, W., 80
Kant, I., 223
King, A., 382, 392
King, B. B., 381
Kittler, F., 461
Kundera, M., 29
Kwesi Johnson, L., 391

Laennec, R., 192–215 passim
Lamming, G., 424
Latour, B., 471
Le Bon, G., 456
Lefebvre, H., 361
Lessing, T., 167
Lévi-Strauss, C., 83–4
listening, 28–30, 460
    active, 385–90
    and body, 193, 390, 393
    and distance, 63–4, 193–9 passim, 195–6
    and hearing, 488–90
    compulsory, 285
    confessionals, 30–3
    cultures of, 305, 385–90

epistemology of, 127–30, 137–8
history of, 191–215 passim
mobile, 329–41
movement, 393
phonic deterritoralization, 333
rationalization of, 192–200 passim
solitary, 286, 304, 329–41
sonic deterritoralization, 334
see also music
Locke, J., 44
Loktev, J., 357
looking, 347

Maffesoli, M., 466
Mahler, G., 10
Mann, T., 33
Manovich, L., 352
Marley, B., 287, 438, 447, 453
Marsh, N., 49
McLuhan, M., 42, 46–47
McNeill, WW., 93
mediate auscultation, 192–200
medicine, 192
    doctors, 196
Merleau-Ponty, M., 226, 331, 458, 469
microphone, 38
Millwall Football Club, 312–319 passim
mind
    as machine, 168
mobile phones, 344–55 passim, 489
Modernism, 78–79
Mondrian, P., 80
Moore, P., 5
Mozart, A.W., 63
music
    and aura, 103
    and body, 94, 229–30, 452, 456, 462, 471–2, 481–4
    and dependency, 363

and de-territoralization, 81, 234
and education and training, 106, 108
and emotion, 393
and gender, 427–33 passim
and identity, 284–5, 378, 398, 406, 456
and marginalization, 427–8
and mathematics, 84
and memory, 35, 232–3, 398–400
and nostalgia, 281–94 passim
and psychoanalysis, 32
and racism, 428
and rhythm, 94–8 passim, 393, 423, 460
and slavery, 145
and society, 29–30
as lived experience, 237–8
Asian dance, 410, 413
avant garde, 77–89 passim
Brazilian, 404
calypso, 419–25 passim
calypso parody, 321
choral tradition, 106–108
Dancehall, 470
driving to, 361–72 passim
extra-musical sounds, 82
folk-traditions, 79
football chants/songs, 314–20
globalization, 110, 234–6, 407
Hip-Hop, 409
Indian, 404–405
Jamaican, 389, 435–49 passim, 451–72 passim
jazz, 427
multicultural, 109–10
musica practica, 98–101
oppositional, 392
performance, 95–6, 98–102, 229–34, 393, 431–3, 435–49 passim, 481–4

performance and electronic
    technology, 10
popular music, 109–10, 131
privatized, 360
Punk, 387, 392
Reggae, 435, 451–72 passim
Rock and Roll, 402
songs, 229, 389
the Blues, 382, 427–33
'the electric church', 383–4,
    395
Thinking Blues 430–1
to aestheticize, 416
traditional art music, 108
vaudeville, 79, 428
waltz, 398
Yiddish, 398

Nagel, T., 4
Naipaul, V.S., 424
Nietzsche, F., 33, 457, 488
noise, 462
    abatement campaigns, 172–82,
        456, 487
    and automobiles, 169
    and culture, 140, 166–7, 457
    and disruption, 167–8
    and education, 170
    and football, 311–12
    and health, 176, 491–501 passim
    and inefficiency, 173–4
    and social class, 141–2
    control, 330
    musical, 382, 457
    traffic, 174–5
    trains, 167, 170
    urban, 166–72 passim, 491
    urban versus rural, 138, 151–9
        passim, 158–62, 169–70, 177–8,
        269–70
Novalis, 33

ocularcentrism, 43, 127
Ong, W., 42, 45, 53

Paine, T., 49
Panopticon, 5, 3
Peirce, C. S., 221
Perec, G., 343, 346, 353
Picasso, P., 459
Plato, 42, 96, 13
powwow, 241–59 passim
Pride, C., 15
privatization of experience, 8
Proust, M., 467
Putnam, R., 106
Pythagoras, 34

racism, 386, 389, 428
    connotive, 324
    denotive, 324
    dominant culture, 412
    see also football, music, sound
radio, 47, 178, 181, 183, 237, 336,
        370, 441–2, 489, 591, 595
    and the everyday, 294
    BBC World Service, 284
    Classic Gold, 289
    consumption, 281–94 passim
    in automobiles, 360–1
    pirate, 453
Rainey, Ma, 427
rationalism, 34
reading
    print revolution, 42, 49
    see also Ong, W., Paine, T.
Reggae, 286–7
Reid, T., 44, 52
Robson, G., 313
Rock against Racism, 392
Romanticism, 483–4
Roth, J., 9
Rush, B., 52
Rush, O., 392

Sachs, W., 358
Schaeffer, P., 82–4
Schafer, M., 6, 128, 159, 225, 330,
    360
Schieffelin, E.L., 225
Schmidt, L., 6
Schopenhauer, A., 35
    and urban noise,166
Schutz, A., 96–98
Schwartz, H., 7
Scruton, R., 82
Seidler, V., 16
Sennett, R., 3, 358, 371
senses, 2–3, 452–3, 458, 487–96
    hierarchy of, 41–54, 92, 288,
        464–7
    separation of, 198–9, 304, 325
    touch, 481–4
    see also Aristotle, Benjamin, W.,
        Simmel, G.
September 11th, 2, 244
Seremetakis, C. N., 287–9
Serres, M., 337
Shakespeare, W., 129
Shostakovich, D., 85
silence, 10, 31, 35
    and slavery, 147–8
    and the city, 171–2, 179, 183, 308
    exhibitions, 181
    religious, 150–1
    weeks, 180
    zones of, 174
Simmel, G., 303, 305, 358
Smith, B., 1
Smith, Bessie, 427–33 passim
Smith, M., 128
Socrates, 34
Sontag, S., 304
sound
    acoustic landscapes, 16
    alterity, 409–17 passim

amplification of, 193, 393, 451–72
    passim, 490
and the Bible, 34
and liminal states, 469–70
and localism, 118–19, 402
and memory, 303–307, 397–403
    passim
and modernization, 139
and music, 77–89 passim
and nationalism, 257–58
and nationality, 138–43 passim
and Native Americans, 141,
    241–59 passim
and nature, 36–8, 139, 143
and noise, 140, 142
and order, 139
and 'otherness', 140
and resistance, 146–48, 389
and sensuality, 248–9
and social class, 133–4, 137,
    138–43 passim
and speed, 118
and technology, 49, 127–8, 361,
    393, 452–5, 490
as cultural memory, 267
as signs, 208–15 passim
Asian, 415–16
auratic qualities of, 393
clapping, 67–75
contested, 8, 121–2, 141–2, 144–5,
    151–8 passim, 182–4, 389
diasporic, 16, 397–407 passim
difference, 413–15
dominance of, 7–8
dreams, 32–3
electronic, 84–5, 381–94 passim
everyday, 266, 282
exoticism, 7–8, 47
fragmented, 119
harmonic order, 33, 118, 142
identity, 14, 118, 241–5, 266–8

ideologies of, 158–9
imagination, 36–9, 61–6
immanence of, 37
inner, 33–4
industrialized, 165–89 passim,
    360–1
intensity of, 457–8
intimate, 9
keynote, 159
materiality of, 460
measurement of, 175–6, 183
nature of, 361, 451–2, 460–1
non verbal, 134
of London, 127–35 passim
of the crowd, 311–25, 456, 460
orientalism, 7–8, 15, 140–1,
    415
physical inscription of, 390
place, 14, 117–23 passim, 402
plantation, 143–51
power, 29, 272, 392
privatized, 371–2
progress, 138–43 passim, 170
racism, 14–15, 314–321 passim
religious, 272
scapes, 381
seasonal, 269–70
sectarian, 5, 265–77 passim
security, 122–3
slavery, 143–59 passim
sonic bridges, 9
    innovations, 391–2
    knots, 335
    see also city, listening, sound,
        Walkman
South Asian, 409
surveillance, 29–30
symbolism of, 179, 182–4, 266
to smack, 68
transcultural, 404–407
transient nature of, 128

urban, 149–51, 269, 303–308,
    491–2
    see also auditory, McLuhan, music
soundscapes, 21, 132, 138
    diasporic, 393, 397
    non-Western, 226–38 passim
Soupault, P., 81
space, 346
    and clapping, 73
    and mobile phones, 344, 349
    and place, 312
    auditory, 15, 458–9
    imagined, 351–2
    inflection and musical language,
        101
    inhabitable, 358–61
    inner speech, 64–5
    mobile, 349–50
    private, 9, 365, 370
    public, 393
    representational, 369
    third space, 268, 412
    transformation of, 12, 339
SS Empire Windrush, 419
Starker, J., 481
Steele-Perkins, C., 384
stethoscope, 192, 192–215 passim
Stockfeld, O., 359
Storr, A., 96

Tagg, P., 95
Takemitsu, T., 38
technology, 38, 407, 462
    and de-auraticization, 104
    and dislocated sounds, 127
    and railroads, 152
    and the avant garde, 80
    and the everyday, 361–7 passim
    musical performance, 102, 454–5
    sounds of, 165, 182–3, 491–2
Thompson, E., 304

time
  and memory, 282–8
  and rhythm, 91, 282
  clocks, 153
  empty, 370–1
  inner and outer, 97
  interactional, 96–98
  social time, 91–4
  sonic, 459–60
Truax, B., 138
Turner, V., 469

Urry, J., 358–9

Varese, E., 80, 87–8
vibrato, 481–2
vision
  and memory, 41, 265
  and objectivity, 206
  and sound, 336–7
  and the city, 303–304
  and urban design, 171
  Cartesian perspectivalism, 43
  hypervisibility, 411
  nobility of, 43
  see also McLuhan

voice, 462
  ancestral, 399
  and culture, 92–109 passim, 223,
    227–30
  and social action, 92–3
  and technology, 54
  bodies, 70, 204–205, 400
  displacement of, 204–205
  individuality of, 400–401
  mother's, 399–400
  Sirens, 7, 71
  speaking in tongues, 470
  subversive, 401
  see also sound, music

Walkmans, 6, 9, 102, 329–41 passim,
    348–49
Western Philosophy, 35
Wittgenstein, L., 400
World Soundscape Project, 225
Wright, R., 385

Yates, F., 353
Yates, W.B., 453
youth cultures, 409, 456

Zaroastrianism, 34